THE MEDIATORS

THE
MEDIATORS

Henry David Gray

American Congregational Center
298 Fairfax Avenue, Ventura, California 93003
1515 Garfield Avenue, South Pasadena, California 91030

Library of Congress Catalogue Card No. 84-71687

To
E. Cary Hoge Mead

compassionate matriarch
to the many within her immediate and world-wide
Christian Family

woman of insight and action in
Christian Mission

fearless and steadfast advocate of
Christian Liberty

winsome and devout prayer partner in
Christian Ministry

whose commanding presence inspires
Christian Conduct

whose delight in beauty of music, art, architecture
and garden has created
An Enduring Heritage

and through whom
God's Amazing Grace
has wrought miracles of love

TABLE OF CONTENTS

PREFACE

This is an account of the proceedings leading up to the merger of approximately 4000 Congregational Christian Churches with the Evangelical and Reformed Church in 1957.

Scrupulous scholarship, re-study of the Congregational classics, and constant reference to reports, speeches, letters and detailed notes is made. The author was chairman of the Committee on Congregational Polity (1950-1954), a member of the General Council's 9-person Constitutional Commission (1954-1956), and served continuously since 1936 as a national or international officer or editor (or both) in the Congregational fellowship. This included one or more terms on the General Council's, Commissions on Evangelism and Devotional Life, The Theological Commission, The Stewardship Commission, and the Committee on Free Church Polity and Unity. As national Secretary for Young People's Work and Student Life, the author chaired, organized or served on the College Embassy Week, Student Workers Seminars, University Christian Missions, the Curriculum Committee, the Work Camp Committee, the Associates in Reading and Thinking, and 26 other committees. He was one of the nine voting delegates of the General Council to the Constitutional Convention which created the National Council of Churches, and served as Moderator of the Hampshire Association in Massachusetts and the Los Angeles Association in California. Conference services include Boards of Directors, Education, College Work, Camp and Constitutional Committees. He was chairman of the Constitutional Committee of the Southern California/Southwest Conference and the Pasadena Council of Churches Constitutional Committee.

In these and many other capacities the author was intimately associated with persons who became vigorous proponents of the CC/ER merger. They were his friends and co-workers.

Both proponents and opponents of the CC/ER merger have presented their stories in print in Gunneman's account of the United Church of Christ and Burton's account of the opposition. There is a third book, Keiling's "Die Enstehung der...United Church of Christ" in German, which is not available in English.

It was the conviction of "The Mediators" that neither the ardent advocates of merger nor the equally ardent opponents of merger represented the vast majority of the Congregational Churches and their members. We were dismayed by the clash; for to us the Congregational Christian Way was preeminently a *thinking, gracious, tolerant* and reasonable Way. We believed at least 80% of the fellowship supported neither extreme.

The Rev. William Keith, D.D., minister of the First Congregational Church of Kalamazoo and the author are the only two leaders of "the middle way" still alive. At his urging and with his constant comment on each chapter, this record has been produced in order that the majority position of our people and Churches may be understood.

In particular, this book reprints the "Congregationalism as Seen in its Fundamental Documents" and "Congregationalism as Practiced in the United States" from the Polity and Unity Report because these reports "disappeared" (although 40,000 were printed). The Polity and Unity Report (1954) is the ONLY complete report on Congregationalism in Documents and Practice EVER MADE in any country at any time. In this, it is unique and ought to be in the library of every Church minister, theological school and historical collection of every congregationally organized church-body. No Church Historian of any Christian denomination can claim to know the Congregational Way AD 1954 USA without study of the *Documents* and *Practice* documents reproduced herein.

"The Mediators" presents the entire CC/ER controversy from a kindly viewpoint which depends upon the truth to set minds free. It is a work for thinking Christians.

Henry David Gray

CHAPTER ONE

A Hot Day and a Cool Idea

It was hot in Cleveland on Friday, June 23, 1950. The central plaza was amazingly deserted. Shade from the pitiless noon day sun was afforded by a sapling canopy over a stone bench. I sat down, laid my jacket beside me, then dropped my head in my hands. The session of the General Council of the Congregational Christian Churches had been divisive. More important than lunch was some bridge across the chasm which divided our Churches and prisoned our fellowship.

The pause created by the appeal of Judge Steinbrink's decision on the Basis of Union with the Evangelical and Reformed Churches might be a time for prayerful reconciliation. But how? My General Council motion authorizing *joint* financing of the appeal, in search of a finding of "fact" was alive, temporarily tabled to give time for formulation, but every wording I tried faced a seven-to-one negative vote. Nor did prayer and scripture yield a ready answer.

An hour or more passed. Delegates started to return from lunch. One of them saw me and stopped. It was Rev. L. Wendell Fifield. "May I join you, Henry?"

"Of course. Do sit down."

"I'll stand awhile. We sat all morning in the auditorium and I've been sitting at a luncheon meeting in the Hotel. Henry, the 600-to-100 vote split bothers me, and it bothers three-fourths of the delegates. Your motion requesting added time hasn't a chance to pass, (he paused) but the higher-ups are afraid of it and men like Meek and Houser and Walton and Keith[1] are looking for some kind of positive action that all can agree on. Everybody's saying the two sides aren't talking about the same thing; they can't even agree on what Congregationalism really is. . ."

"Say that last part again, Wendell, slowly."

He repeated.

We both sat quietly for a few moments.

"Wendell, I wonder if you haven't singled out the one positive action which just might be acceptable to all. Suppose this period of waiting for final court action were to be used to study what Congregationalism *is,* not what John, Jane, or Joe *think* it is?"

"Say that over again, Henry."

I did.

Wendell took out a pencil and began to write. Half an hour later the rough draft of a resolution was framed.

"If you'll move it, Wendell, I'll second it and ask that my pending motion be withdrawn. But you'll have to meet with the strategists at the Cleveland[2] and at the Hollenden[3] to smooth out the language and win the prior approval of both pro-merger and pro-Congregational. Otherwise there will be a debate. Amendments will be made and the resolution may lose all its strength, sanity, and balance."

"That means talking to a lot of people."

"Yes it does. Don't meet with either group 'till you first have the support of folks like Horton, Douglass, Penner, Archibald, Waser and Burton."[4]

"Any others?"

"They will suggest others."

"So they will. Will you do something for me?"

"Anything I can."

"Pray for me."

"Count on it."

"Thanks, Henry," and he was gone, NOT towards the auditorium but back to the Hotel Cleveland.

The Search for Study

In 1983 it seems strange that it was necessary *to search for study* in 1950. Among the reasons for this situation four were explosive. The special General Council meeting in Cleveland,[5] February 1949, to vote on the Basis of Union for the Congregational Christian Churches and the Evangelical and Reformed Church left a residue of hurt persons. Zealots for union felt thwarted, obstructed by the courts. Certain prominent Continuation Committee[6] members persistently attributed the worst motives to each move by

2

merger protagonists. At the opening session of the 1950 General Council, the Secretary's address posited Classic Congregationalism ("A")[7] and Congregationalism ("B")[8] as equally valid interpretations of Congregational polity; the "B" came in the guise of totally autonomous bodies at every level from local, state, national, to international and was a radically new concept of our fellowship.

With these four—and additional views—asserted with fervor it was clear that prior support had to be enlisted if any positive steps were to be taken. While Wendell buttonholed key people at the Hotel Cleveland I did the same at the Music Hall in the Civic Auditorium complex. After Rev. Howard Conn's[9] "Council Lecture" I sought his support. Howard's word was "I'm for anything that puts wrangling behind. But I'm not ready to commit myself 'till I see the wording." Bill Keith's comment was, "It sounds good, Henry, but I'm not sure any resolution saying the findings of *another* committee are to be considered can be passed. In fact, I'd omit that sentence." I returned to the Hotel Cleveland to eat at the coffee shop.

About 8:30 or 9:00 p.m. a very weary Wendell met me in the lobby. "I want you to look at the revised wording, Henry. The phrase 'study and report' may make study a waste of time."

"I don't think so, Wendell. Facts carry their own weight."

"There's more, too. A whole sentence says nothing in the study will affect any past decisions of the General Council."

"That's protection. . ."

"Yes, yes, Henry. But how will Malcolm Burton see it?"

"Wendell, you've succeeded by taking the mergerites one at a time. Why not go right now to the Hollenden with me. Meet with the whole roomful at once."

"I don't think that would work."

"A meeting with eight or twelve might. At least you would get a fair hearing."

"Do you really think this could happen, Henry? Or are we flailing our arms?"

"Our churches are entitled to know what Congregational polity is. That's important no matter what the General Council does with the report. Besides, once a committee is appointed its study takes on a life of its own. Who's to limit its report?"

"Let's go to the Hollenden."

It was past midnight before I returned to the Hotel Cleveland.

The Next Day

The Saturday morning Council meeting faced a potentially explosive credentials request, one that involved the whole question of the right of a group of Churches to organize an association "on their own." Fortunately this request was referred to the Business Committee. Numerous actions were taken without debate such as the call for a special study of the responsibility of the fellowship for older people.

The General Council Executive Committee functioned as the Business Committee of Council meetings. Rev. L. Wendell Fifield was an Executive Committee member. Before the meeting he had secured consent to place our resolution before the assembly. I seconded the resolution and requested that my previous motion scheduled as "the order of the day" be withdrawn. "The Moderator declared Mr. Gray's motion withdrawn."[10] To our great joy the following motion was voted, unanimously so far as I could hear.

> "Resolved: that the Executive Committee appoint a special committee representing all points of view, to make a careful study of the principles and polity of Congregationalism. This study is to have particular reference to the spiritual and legal methods for the participation of the free autonomous fellowships in the ecumenical movement.
>
> "The constituting of this committee is not to be interpreted as affecting any past action of the General Council. The Committee has no powers other than those of study and report to the General Council."[11]

Sunday evening Rev. Frederick M. Meek's Council sermon voiced the spirit of all "The Mediators":

> "Our present peril will not be resolved and our spiritual sickness will not be healed until we become again a people who are not comparative strangers through neglect of our covenants and of the promises of God in Christ... There is nothing in the world more binding that a promise, a covenant spoken or unspoken; but few things are less enforceable by compulsion... How easy it is for us to become immersed in organization rather than in the cause... so that we forsake God for men."[12]

Nothing undermined the sense of hope germinated by the Fifield resolution. Though a handful said, "How can you trust them (the Executive Committee) to appoint people representing all points of view?" the vast majority voiced confidence. As Rev. Wallace W. Anderson put it, "Now that court action is in abeyance this gives

4

us a chance to be reasonable. We need more facts and less fireworks." Points of real difference existed. These surfaced in the vote to pay the bills of one side in the courts, in the split-vote re-election of the Secretary and in refusal to seat the elected delegate of an Association because the Association had not been "recognized" by a Conference. Overshadowing all differences was the evident determination of the great majority to find a way forward with goodwill through study, research, analysis and prayer. The change of atmosphere was electric. Differences were real. So was the will to deal with them fairly.

What were the roots of our differences? There were persons of integrity and goodwill who adhered to each one of the three chief positions.

FOR The Merger

Varied reasons were given for advocacy of the merger of the Evangelical Reformed Church and the Congregational Christian Churches. Idealistic supporters quoted "That they all may be one" from the gospel of John.[13] They spoke of "the sundered body of Christ," of "the sin of division," of "one Lord, one faith, one baptism." Nothing dissuaded the idealists from an almost mystic belief that the merger was "the will of God," and an inevitable step toward "the reunion of Christendom."

A sizeable number of the merger proponents were impressed with the practical advantages of the CC/ER merger. Geographically Evangelical and Reformed Churches outnumbered Congregational Churches in Pennsylvania and certain other states while Congregational Church strength was greatest in the Northeast and certain other states. "We'll become a 'national church'" it was said. A single central office, publishing, communication, and service center was to effect large monetary savings and improve the quality of services like that of the monthly magazine. In cities like Chicago, Milwaukee, Pittsburgh, Philadelphia, and Los Angeles it was anticipated that great gain would come by merger of local Churches and concentration of new church monies in "high potential areas."

A sizeable number favored the merger as a pioneer venture in uniting a Continental-derived Church with Anglo-Saxon-rooted Churches. The same people usually thought of the merging of the Congregational and Presbyterial polities as pioneering the way into wider church union. There were not a few who regarded the E & R as more theological and liturgical and the Congregational

5

Churches as more liberal and spontaneous, hoping by merger to attain the best of both traditions. Advantage was claimed for two languages, German and English, and even for diversity of social customs.

An important body of people looked to the merger as a pathway to greater health and strength. Definition of "health and strength" varied, but a common view was that the Congregational denomination was "too loosely organized to be effective," "too lax in ministerial 'standards'," too casual in ministerial "placement," and "out of touch with the common man."

The major gain by merger appeared to be a large number to be a powerful activist role in public life. Rev. Truman B. Douglass put it this way: "strength must speak to strength in our time. Big government and big business will listen to a big church." Rev. Albert J. Penner once said, "We need a new church for a new age." It will not do to attribute to men like Douglass and Penner some sinister, hidden, dark motives. I found them deeply devoted to the righting of obvious wrongs and sincerely persuaded that a larger, more centralized church body was essential if real progress was to be accomplished.

These were by no means all the reasons stated by proponents of the ER/CC merger. This brief sketch may suffice to indicate a few important facets of a many-sided body of people.

FOR Classic Congregationalism

Revs. Malcolm K. Burton, James E. Fifield, Marion Bradshaw, Warren S. Archibald and Raymond A. Waser were a few of the champions of Classic Congregationalism. Each of these men and many other people opposed the ER/CC merger, but there was variety among them just as there was among the merger proponents. Here are some concerns of those who were FOR Classic Congregationalism.

Concern for freedom was pivotal. Each Church must be free to govern itself, call its minister, control its properties and funds, and state its own opinions. Each member must be free to covenant with the Church of his choice and to give or not to give money or service. Each minister must be free to choose his own educational program, answer a Church's call as God directed: in short be responsible to God and to the Church Meeting, period!

Frequently voiced by protagonists of Classic Congregationalism was dismay at the statements on public issues made by the Council for Social Action and other wider-church bodies. These statements

6

appeared to claim to represent over a million Congregationalists, whereas actually they were voted by a few. Even if voted by a General Council or state Conference they represented no more than the views of those who had voted for them.

Independence was precious to defenders of classic Congregationalism, not just in terms of specific freedoms, but also as a general principle of church polity, and largely in public polity. These were the idealists of old New England's "rugged individual," and of the self-reliance of the frontier. As Gibran put it in one of his books "let there be room between us for our growing."

The Congregational heritage was infinitely precious to its proponents. Martyrs had been needed to rid the Churches of state control, bishops, "set" prayers, ancient creeds, liturgical dress, non-New-Testament sacramentalism; the Jesus of history seemed lost in the confines of clergy who didn't bother to preach.

The name "Congregational" had high value for all who defended the way of the Pilgrims. They expected their children to cherish the Mayflower, Plymouth Colony, John Robinson, Governor Bradford and Thomas Hooker. Among the cherished names was "the American Board," the American Board of Commissioners for Foreign Missions, America's first foreign missionary enterprise, linked by living souls with heroes and martyrs in Bulgaria, Greece, Turkey, India, Syria, Iran, Thailand, Burma, Singapore, China, Japan, the Islands of the Pacific and throughout Africa and Latin America.

Stewardship of the monies given or bequeathed for Congregational causes was a sacred trust to virtually all the classic-Congregationalism people. A surprising number were direct descendents of those who had given funds, properties, or bequests; these trusts should hold true to the intent of the donors.

The Mediators

Far-sighted people like Presidents Donald Cowling of Carleton College, James A. Blaisdell of Claremont Colleges and Arthur C. McGiffert of Chicago Theological School shared the vision of Protestant unity without uniformity. Dr. McGiffert signed the "findings" of the Evanston Meeting (Nov. 4, 5, 1947). The final section of the Findings read:

"We call for strong leadership on the part of the Congregational Christian Churches, in which we hope the Evangelical and Reformed Church will share, to explore and vigorously promote ways and

7

means of bringing about a federative union of Protestantism. Congregationalists can appropriately take the lead here for our Congregational Christian fellowship is in itself a federation of churches.

"We heartily approve the revolutionary move the General Council has already made along this line by inviting other denominations which accord one another mutual recognition of ministries and sacraments to participate in a plenary conference to consider the possibilities of closer unity.

"We call upon our churches to put their strength behind this movement, in even greater force and vigor than has been devoted to the merger. We urge that our leaders in this enterprise be instructed to accept as their task the achievement of unity according to the federative rather than the organic principle.

"We call upon our churches to lift their eyes away from secondary matters and see this wide and hopeful horizon: a federative union in which many denominations will have a part. Its federative structure will express the fellowship and catholic unity of Protestantism and conserve the rich and diverse treasures of the bodies constituting it. Such unity can become a more adequate instrument in the Hand of God for the bringing in of His Kingdom."[14]

Because no history of the mediators has been written there is need to identify some of them. Because it has been claimed that the mediators were "last minute advocates" who "just needed time to get used to a radical merger," there is need to quote at length from documents prior to the 1950 Cleveland meeting of the General Council.

Who Were the Mediators?

I pass by reluctantly Rev. David McKeith who had worked hard at the Grand Rapids Council in 1944, and Rev. William Frazier who told me at Grinnell in 1946, "This is a nightmare. The ox and the ass unequally yoked together!" Will delighted in biblical allusions.

Strangely, the initial impetus for the mediators was a request of E & R leader Rev. George W. Richards, D.D. In August, 1939, on behalf of the World Conference on Faith and Order held at Clarens, Switzerland, Dr. Richards requested a group of Congregationalists from several countries then meeting at Yale University to produce a document on the nature of the Church as understood by Congregationalists.

8

They did. The Commission on Interchurch Relations and Christian Unity published their statement. Herein are stated with remarkable clarity an ardent desire for "union (which) permits a maximum of freedom in Christ." The Statement repays review, even in summary form. Here it is.[15]

"It is a happy day which brings the people of the various branches of Christ's Church to enquire sympathetically into the truth about each other. This in itself is an earnest of a better future.

"It is the mystery of the Church as Congregationalists know it that though no central authority appears to the eye, every true member recognizes that it has an authoritative center. The authoritative center is God—as He reveals Himself in Jesus Christ and speaks through His Holy Spirit. 'Where two or three are gathered together in my name, there am I in the midst of them.' There is a certain completeness about the smallest group gathered to celebrate God's presence, for the reason that He is there, and that He is all-sufficient. It is because He may also be present, however, to others besides the two or three, because indeed He may be the center of a fellowship extending from generation to generation and destined to cover the whole earth, that no local congregation or single communion can be regarded as independent of the greater Church throughout the world. The invisible center of the visible Church— and of the invisible *Una Sancta,* too, though that is not here under consideration—is God.

"The Spirit and the Church

"All Christian communions recognize the Holy Spirit in doctrine and in worship: it is a decisive characteristic of the Congregational Churches that the Spirit is acknowledged in their polity and general ecclesiastical practice as well. It is probably at this point that Congregationalism differs most widely from the other orders of the Church. If God, that living and present God who speaks in the Spirit, is really to rule the Church, Congregationalists believe that His freedom to communicate Himself to whom He will and as He will must be humanly unqualified; and to confine His grace to any single channel must condition that freedom. Congregationalists never waver from the felt necessity of trusting the free guidance of God.

"No person or persons in Congregationalism ever need, against their will, to allow others to make decisions for them; and on the other hand they do not need to hesitate to reach decisions concerning themselves, since their action will not necessarily serve as precedent for other people. No scholar has to suffer because the teaching of the Church seems to conflict with the truth that he has

9

discovered. The whole system is designed to protect integrity of conscience. Because the system leaves the Holy Spirit free, it is attractive to those who love freedom.

"Wider Church-Body Recommendations

"One of the secrets of the peculiar sense of vitality felt within Congregationalism is due to the dynamic conception of unity in which the parts influence each other. The plenary or national council, to choose one instance to illustrate a universal principle, may and does pass resolutions affecting provinces, dioceses, associations, churches, but these are passed down to the smaller bodies invariably in the form of recommendations, nothing more; and similarly the smaller make their recommendations to the greater as they will. Congregationalism by its inner character easily resists any tendency to stale down into traditionalism.

"All Members Share Ministry

"Since a church is constituted on the human side by the covenant the members make, it is clear that the members as well as the ministry are of the essence of it. It flourishes or declines in proportion as all the members live up or fail to live up to their covenant obligations. In Congregationalism the treasure of the Gospel is not guarded by a hierarchy but by minister *and people.*

"There are many Congregationalists who are reluctant to use the words 'sacrament' or 'sacramental', so many overtones of primitive paganism do they carry. They see in the Lord's Supper a symbol (a) of the constant bestowal of spiritual refreshment and strength through the grace of God in the Gospel of Jesus, and (b) of the cleansing and renewal continuously desired and expected by the believer as a result of his fulfillment of the tri-partite covenant into which, upon his confession of faith, he entered with God and with the Church.

"The Role of Love

"The genius of Congregationalism is seen when the parts do not harmonize, when, for instance, the local church interprets the will of God differently from the conference, or diocese. In such a case there is no thought that the latter must have its way, since it is the larger or the superior, as in the strongly centralized system. The rule is the rule of Christian love: to cooperate at every point possible, and where this is impossible, to hold the differences in abeyance till the spirit of Christ operating upon both parties brings about the synthesis on the higher level to which at first they could not attain.

"Meaningful Union

"Congregationalism is Catholicism liberated from the authoritarian idea; and Congregationalists seek union with all others who would allow them to retain their Congregational principles. Congregationalists believe that they hold a key to the ecumenical future, in that the wide variety of Christian witness in the world calls not for a polity or practice which would require the abandonment or compromising of many of the forms developed in the several communions and consecrated by age, but rather for one which, while constantly drawing the parts to ever closer union, permits a maximum of freedom in Christ."

The Mediators of the Yale conference had religious convictions. This continued to be the central concern for the mediators. In 1940 at Mills College I addressed 200 delegates to the Pilgrim Fellowship national assembly. These young people came from forty states, the District of Columbia and the then-territory of Hawaii. These two emphases of unity and spiritual freedom may be seen in that address, published in *Pilgrim Highroad* May 1941. There were *young* mediators!

Among the mediators, persons of notable sincerity, thoughtfulness, and fine temper, was Rev. William A. Keith of Kalamazoo, member for years of the Executive Committee of the General Council. Rev. Frederick M. Meek of Old South Church in Boston made an eloquent statement of the mediator's faith in his installation sermon as minister of the Old South Church in Boston. The Rev. Charles M. Houser of Ft. Wayne and then of Plymouth, Des Moines, in his inimitably gracious way bore testimony in the numerous General Council committees on which he served.

Rev. Wallace W. Anderson of Portland, Maine and later United Church, Bridgeport, bore kindly (if sometimes exasperated) witness on the Executive Committee; his letters and conversations with me bore the marks of heartache and hope. Rev. Raymond McConnell of Lincoln's great central Church preached and pled for "a basis in the spiritual nature of God's people." President James A. Blaisdell of Claremont Colleges wrote with lucidity and insight; for he saw the ER/CC merger as a major hindrance to the federative union which could embrace virtually all Protestant Christians. President Donald Cowling of Carleton College bemoaned, "The grasp for power which is the gasp of the religiously dying." What shall we say of the vast body of great hearts like Chidley of Winchester, Thompson of Grand Rapids, Phillips of Omaha, McQueen of Deluth, Brown of Evanston, the Krumbine

11

brothers of Shaker Heights, Ohio and Fresno, California, state conference Superintendents Johnson of the Rockies, Minton of Pennsylvania and the immediate past editor of *The Congregationalist,* Rev. William E. Gilroy!

There have been few more prevalent oversights in Congregational history than the omission of the mediators from the record. Their deep devotion merits its due.

It is time to ask, For what did the mediators stand? I quote from the address I prepared for the February 1949 special meeting of the General Council. It was written prior to that assembly. It breathes the spirit of the mediators:

"Above All Selfish Fears and Cares[16]

"As we meet here we are not in a condition of spirit to act under the sure guidance of God's Spirit. Yet it is only as we are able to follow that Spirit that we shall rise from the level of expediency to the level of Christian action. Too often power has gone out of our church councils because we have sought to settle matters with our own judgement in terms of what seems to us to be the best policy at the moment, rather than to probe the apparent issues to their proper depth and submit them to Christ's judgement. We talk about 'pushing a motion through' rather than about finding and following the guidance of God's Spirit.

"Over the months and years of our difference, debate has seemed to center on the issues of procedures which are the expression of principles, rather than on the principles themselves. Some of us have longed for and pleaded for some word which would rise above our selfish fears and cares. There is yet time to face the fundamental issues with wisdom, understanding, and charity. Nothing is ever lost when honest men face their differences and take the time to find God's answer to their needs. Conclusions are too often only the point at which we grow weary of thinking. Surely our unhappy divisions are to be healed, not by a search for a lowest common denominator, or by any device of expediency, but rather by a universal penitence, by a common understanding of the things we most surely believe and by a more faithful obedience to the Word and Will of God, as the Holy Spirit taketh the things of Christ and revealeth them to us. This leads us to that for which we stand.

"What are the principles which distinguish the churches of our Congregational order? How are these principles related to the issues of this hour?

"Foremost stands our interpretation of the place of the Holy Spirit in the life of our churches. From the beginning our churches have believed that the guidance of the Spirit was the church's source of common life, love, and spiritual power. It has been our witness that we must obey God rather than man, and to maintain that witness, over 200 men and women have given their lives. To Congregationalists the Holy Spirit has been the voice of God, the living Christ, the authoritative Word, the inspiring Guide. That Holy Spirit has been the personal Word of God to men.

"Our Congregational concept of the church rests on our doctrine of the Spirit. Hence, the church has been to us the gathered company of believers who recognized the headship of Christ, and of Him alone. The witness of the Spirit with our spirits that we are the children of God is the foundation of our churchmanship. Indeed, with us, churchmanship and discipleship are identical. We stand for the principle that what constitutes a Christian Church is the gathered fellowship of believers committed to Christ and to Him alone. The polity founded on this principle has recently been described as 'the most courageous and most scriptural venture of faith possible to Christian communities, for it takes the promises of God seriously and, depriving believers of all external support or control, casts them wholly upon the Spirit. The depth to which it can fall corresponds to the heights to which it aspires. It gives full, practical expression to the undeniably scriptural view that the Church is the people, and holds it better to run all risks than to sacrifice the principle which makes the congregation of believers responsible for the quality of their own spiritual life.'

"This Congregational view of the Church well accords with scripture. There are but two meanings of 'ecclesia' in the New Testament. The word is used 105 times of the church; 86 clearly refer to the local church, and 18 to the great universal church. None refer to any geographically or otherwise bounded denomination.

"The Local Church

"It is our Congregational belief that the ordering of the life of the church must be rooted in the nature of the gospel she proclaims. That is to say it must be a theological and not merely a sociological ordering. The order which seemed to us best to accord with the gospel holds that the local gathering of believers is not a church, but the church. I once held a bar of gold in my hand. It was refined to 99+% purity. It was only a small part of all the gold in the world, but it was pure gold. Other bars might be added to it, but the addition of them would not change its essence. It was gold, not because of its bulk, but because of what it was in itself. The local church is the church because of what it is in itself, the fellowship of which Christ alone is Lord. It is no contrivance of man. It is the creation of Christ.

"According to our gospel, Christ must reign in the local church, and His word alone must be finally authoritative. This means that the local church cannot enter into any hierarchy of churches, or church courts, but must preserve in herself the undisputed and sovereign sway of Christ.

"Much of our weakness today stems from the fact that we have too often fallen from our own principles of churchmanship. Too often we act locally on the basis of the best compromise we can secure. We accept the standard of the secular world as the standard of the church. This is a major tragedy of our hour. The channel of God's Word to men is blocked at the point of Spirit-with-spirit guidance in the local church, and the revival of the whole world waits for the Word which we Christians ought to speak of, but cannot speak. The Word is not stopped because there are Presbyterian, Congregational, Baptist, or other denominations. It is stopped because the principle of the kingship of Christ has been replaced by reliance on expedient action, based on the wisdom or unwisdom of man. The world's revival awaits the awakened church, and that means first and foremost the local company of believers.

"Church Councils

"The doctrine of the Holy Spirit as the energizing power of the church local has meaning for the association of churches one with another. Congregational Church councils have prayed and debated for 24 days on end seeking guidance, but at every point what was sought was guidance, and the Council was above all a Council of Churches. It was not itself a church. Its functions were derivative. In its own right it had no power whatever. This General Council, by its own constitution, makes no claim to legislative or judicial power. Advice, counsel, and the performance of such functions as may, from time to time, be requested by the churches—these are the historic purposes of Church Councils among Congregationalists. This is no denial of the presence of spiritual guidance 'where two or three are gathered together in (Christ's) name.' Wherever men wait patiently on God, He will surely lead them. But any and every temporary delegated council has been felt among us to be at best the source of recommendations to the churches, where those suggestions are tested in the on-going life of the living body of Christ. The Council is not A church or THE church.

"The powers of a Congregational Church Council are moral and declarative. If Christ, and Christ alone is to rule in each one of our churches, then no association, conference, or council must 'lord it' over the churches. The crucial point for Congregationalists is that the Church Universal is not made up of many churches in union or in federation, or any thing of the kind. It is created by God and made evident in the spiritual life which conditions the very being of particular churches.

"Congregational Churches, says a 1938 General Council publication, 'depend upon the essential spirit of fellowship to unify them that they may become in truth, the body of Christ.'[17]

"Our Contribution

"The unity of a fellowship held together by common love and loyalty to the Kingship of Christ is our Congregational contribution to the churches of all the world. Here is the vital and distinctive way in which the work of the Holy Spirit in informing and transforming the life of the world may be aided by Church Councils. Dr. James A. Blaisdell, former president of Pomona College wrote on January 28, of this year:[18]

"'... today we stand at the open door of a new world of spiritual thinking. It is a world of new global contracts and of deep intellectual confusion but it is also a world of profound spiritual ponderings. We shall not prosper by demanding commitment to ancient formulas or by increasing a distant over-all officialdom in the name of unity. For the future lies with those who will find their fellowship and spread their quiet contagion in the simpler company of those who, first of all, are spiritual seekers. This is our permanent "bond of union".'

"Dr. Albert Peel of England, phrased it this way:[19]

"'If Congregationalists will show confidence and trust in their basic principles, there is no doubt at all but that the organization of the church of the future will be Congregational. But if, instead of trusting entirely to the leading of the Spirit of God, they begin to fear, to rely on organization and machinery, on creeds and customs, on central institutions and officials and funds, the day will certainly not be theirs. If they continue to show to the world that in regard to both thought and practice—development of doctrine, acceptance of new truth, adaption of organization and worship—they are following the gleam, they have a greater service to render to the Kingdom of God than ever.'

"On such grounds it is clear that just as no church meeting can rob the individual Christian of his responsibility to follow Christ according to his conscience, so no council may rob the local church of its responsibility to seek and follow the will of Christ. The council has moral and declarative, but no legislative or judicial weight.

"Shortly after I became a national officer of our fellowship, I asked Dr. Douglas Horton the question, 'What authority has a Congregational national officer?' His epic reply has stayed with me over the years. 'All the authority that anyone will give him.' This is all the authority any council or officer ought to have or needs to have, according to our gospel. '"Flight to authority" is widespread in every age of social and intellectual unrest. It is a symptom of loss of nerve, and that is why it is prevalent in our own day.' Over against this flight to authority, we believe that, 'Any conception of the authority of church councils which weakens the particular church's sense of direct reponsibility to its Lord is totally foreign to a church order, and is an infection from the order of the world which always tends to concentrate authority at the center.'

"What Do We Want Union For?

"Much of the discussion of the issue before us, on all sides, has seemed to move on the plane of expediency, and has been related to overhead costs, size, publication ventures, and lobby influence, on government on the one side; and institutional responsibilities and safe-guarding of funds, on the other. These issues are important, but they are not as important as the ends they are designed to serve. What Do We Want Union For?

"Surely there could be only one answer, to help men and women to become Christians, or to become better Christians. All else is subsidiary to this end. Our associations, conferences, boards and this Council exist to serve a religious purpose.

"Church order is finally important not in order to provide an efficient organization, or dignified assemblies, or even adequate sustentation and church extension funds, but to bear witness to the gospel. The criterion by which it is judged should always be the Gospel.

"The question then is, 'Can the Spirit and power of God be expected to reach men more immediately and effectively through the Church or the Churches (conceived as fellowships of believers)?'

"The one central question before us really is, 'How can we best serve the gracious and winning purposes of the God and Father of our Lord Jesus Christ?' The answer to this question must be a spiritual answer.

"Is Ecumenicity the Spiritual Answer?

"Is ecumenicity that spiritual answer? What kind of ecumenical contribution should flower from the root and stem of Congregationalism?

" 'Christian union, taken on its own merits, is a question which has not much interested Congregationalists until recently because it has seemed to them irrelevant to the real issue of unity. In 1931 Dr. Selbie described (our) position. (We) are quite clear that among all true Christians, . . . there is a unity of the Spirit which nothing can disturb and which would not in any way be enhanced by the inclusion of all in one vast organization.'

"In early New England 'the first Church of Christ' did not regard itself as denominational. All who accepted its mutual covenent were free to use their 39 Articles of Religion, Westminister Confession, or Lutheran Creed. I venture to say that most of the churches here represented are composed of members who cherish many traditions. Among my churches's 1450 members there are 47 former Roman Catholics, and representatives of 36 other traditions. I venture to say further that those here present have been among the foremost leaders in interchurch activities of every sort. Innumerable Congregationalists like myself have founded local Councils of Churches, Councils of Christian Education, and Y.M.C.A. or student services. I venture to say yet further that many of us have contributed time, talent, and money to the great common Christian work of the Friends' Service Committee, the Unitarian Service Committee, Church World Service and other agencies too numerous to mention. My own church has shipped overseas at least a quarter of a ton of food and clothing every month for over three years. These are inevitable expressions of free churchmanship. They grow out of the awakening of conscience by Christ. They are modern fruits of the Spirit. They are expresssions of the ecumenicity of love. We fervently pray and work for greater

17

love and understanding and common Christian worship and work across all denominational lines. And we are making progress in extending this ecumenicity of love. 'Assimilation . . . is something altogether different from unity in Christ; that unity has to be found at a very much deeper level, and when found, it will be a power and a flame that will kindle throughout the world the spirit of love and reconciliation. Sincere though our efforts are to find the grounds of agreement between Christians, we are not even within the Kingdom of Heaven where the hidden treasure lies. We are like children who, playing with a paint-box, decide to try the effect of mixing all the colors together, in the hope that some dazzling super-color will result. They are dissappointed when they find themselves with a dirty mixture between gray and brown.'

"The Key to REAL Union

"To the common life of Christ's Churches, each of us brings our special contribution. Many of us believe the Congregational principle of Christ's Kingship, and the free assocation of churches under it, holds the key to the widest possible fellowship and common intercourse of the churches of Christendom. We feel no need to apologize for the beneficient influence of the Congregational Churches on this and on other people. We rather believe that the kind of a fellowship in which men and churches are free to think and act according to the dictates of conscience under Christ, holds the best hope for the Church Universal and the world as well. 'We hold with deep conviction that the winning of the world waits for the re-birth of free and spontaneous spiritual fellowships and contagious example far more than for the magnitude, mechanisms and potencies of great formal organization. The Church's contribution to a truly "one world" is a unity of spirit which is in no wise dependent on unity of organization.'

"And there is a yet more important point, which springs from our theological and scriptural foundations. Any ecumenicity must begin with oneness of spirit. Political or ecclesiastical union may or may not be ecumenical, in the Christian meaning of that word.

"Unity of spirit is very rarely achieved in a few years, especially when it involves close to two million persons scattered throughout a wide country. The churches of India negotiated for 20 years before union, and allowed a 30-year post union period for adjustment. We have expected to do in eight years with inadequate means of fellowship between the Evangelical-Reformed Church and the

Congregational Christian Churches a far-reaching task of dealing with the life of the soul and spirit of man.

"The Basis of Union

"It has been said, of course, that the Basis of Union provides an adequate foundation for spiritual union. Some of us feel that this is to begin at the wrong place. Churches and Church Councils have to be organized with polity and corporate structures, but this structure is only a vehicle for realizing their true, primary and only ultimate task—the spiritual task! An experience of fellowship, prayer, worship, and common work with the Evangelical Reformed Church all over the nation is the proper starting point for a union of churches.

"Taking the Basis of Union as it stands, unfounded on a widespread common Christian experience of fellowship, is it even true that the churchmanship we hold dear is safe-guarded in that document? 'To begin with, the enabling instrument itself is now in such complicated condition as to render it both unworthy and indefinite. It would seem to be axiomatic that a covenant which aims to bind together nearly two million people in the deepest areas of their lives should be characterized, as the most primary necessity, by absolute simplicity and an indisputably transparent clarity. The fact that a very large number of intelligent persons, even if they are mistaken, see it as distinctly contradictory in its provisions cannot but indicate the lack of these qualities which are of such elemental importance.'

"To be specific, let us apply the doctrine we have been proclaiming to just three of the many points at issue among us.

"The Nature of the Church

"First as to the nature of the Church, and here my words are largely those of Dr. James A. Blaisdell, one of our noblest elder statesmen and fathers of the churches.[20] It is obvious that the E & R churches are not just becoming Congregational churches, therefore to say that our Congregational churches are making no changes in this new relationship is absurd. The E & R churches have a different attitude in the matter of creed from the Congregationalists. Our very identity is in our freedom of thought and interpretation. According to the Basis of Union in the form issued in 1943, the doctrinal standards of the Evangelical and Reformed Church are the Heidelburg Catechism, Luther's Catechism, and the Augsburg

19

Confession. They are accepted as authoritative interpretations . . . of scripture. Where there are differences, ministers,
members and congregations are allowed to adhere to the interpretation of one of these. Now it would be presumptuous to say that
these are not good attitudes and forms of church life. But it is certainly true that they are not the Congregationalism in which we
have believed and in which we have been participants. Very significantly the practice of over-all authority in E & R churches is
expressed in the ecclesiastical control of all its educational institutions, the Boards of Trustees of all such institutions being
appointed by ecclesiastical authorities. So far as yet indicated any
Union will buy us into this form of responsibility for these institutions and into this form of ecclesiastical oversight.

"Stewardship of our Heritage

"Can we say Congregationalism is safe-guarded in the proposed
structure of the Board of Home Mission of the United Church? In
Congregationalism, wider bodies are created by the direct representatives of the churches. In Presbyterianism, according to Dr.
James Moffat, one of the true basic characteristics is a series of
graded representations, the higher being in each instance, dependent upon the lower. The Basis of Union decrees for the Board of
Home Missions a powerful executive committee, elected by Board
Members, who are elected by corporate members who are elected
by General Synod members, who are elected by State Conference
members, who are elected by local church members. Is this Congregationalism? It may be objected that Congregationalism is
impractical for our time. If so, then let us debate that issue on its
merits. But let us not claim to husband the heritage unless we can
make good the claim. The Board of Home Missions controls grants
to aided conferences, money for buildings, our work in evangelism,
institutional support, education, publication, ministerial relief,
and the farflung work of the American Missionary Association.

"What's In A Name?

"Can it be truly said that the change in name from a free voluntary Council of Congregational Churches to a United Church is
meaningless, when centuries of church life bear testimony to the
striking contrast for which these words, church and churches,
stand, both in theology and in polity? If we desire to trade in our
traditional belief for a 1949 model, let us be candid about what we

20

are doing, and why we are doing it. No lasting good can come from failure to recognize and face the nature of the choice before us.

"It would seem to be clear that the Basis of Union fails to face many basic issues. Beyond that we return to the far more fundamental point—no basis of Christian experience and fellowship across the nation exists between the people of the Evangelical and Reformed Church and the Congregational Christian Churches. Such a religious basis is the only true foundation for a union of churches.

"Spiritual Unions

"Church unions must be spiritual unions. That we all have failed to find the guidance of the Spirit is painfully clear. On every side the fruit of our controversy has been bickering, misunderstanding, impatience, strife, bitterness, and broken personal relationships. But 'the fruit of the Spirit is love, joy, peace, good temper, kindliness, generosity, fidelity, gentleness, self-control. Those who belong to Christ have crucified the flesh with its emotions and passions. As we live by the Spirit let us be guided by the Spirit.'[21] So reads the Book we all profess to follow.

"The only victory to be won here is the victory of love. Our hearts are well nigh broken. We feel more like crying than singing. At least once before this has happened in the history of our Churches. Williston Walker reports the National Council of 1865 in these words:[22]

"'It was a Council well worthy of the churches, both in the distinguished character of its membership and the thoroughness with which the topics presented to its consideration were discussed . . . One of the tasks was the adoption of a statement of faith . . . The proposed paragraph . . . was earnestly debated, until it became evident that, if pushed to a vote it would be adopted by a decided majority of the Council, and as evident that this affirmation . . . would seem unduly devisive . . . to a respectable minority. Such was the state of affairs in the Council when the day came which had been set apart for an excursion to the historic scenes of Plymouth. To a few of the body it seemed that a reunion on a spot so fragrant with the memory of the struggles and sufferings by which Congregationalism was planted on American soil would furnish a fitting occasion for the presentation of (a new) declaration . . . Such a form was prepared. Presented to the Council assembled on Burial Hill at Plymouth, it was accepted, subject to slight verbal revision, and after the return of the Council to Boston

21

was adopted by a rising vote without opposition, on June 23, 1865.'

"May it not come to pass that this Council of 1949 will heal the hurts and renew the hearts of all of us by finding a Basis of Union whose ecumenicity is wide enough to take us all in? As Edwin Markham wrote:

"'He drew a circle that shut me out,
Heretic, rebel, a thing to flout,
But love and I had the will to wit,
We drew a circle that took him in.'

"God grant that the circle drawn may take us in."

The Hope Behind the Cleveland Resolution

Behind the Cleveland Resolution was the hope that a truly inclusive Polity and Unity Committee would be appointed. The mediators were fully persuaded that goodwill would prevail if a mood of research, study, prayer, and expectation could prevail.

I returned to California from Cleveland in 1950 to plunge into the final ten weeks needed to create the 1950 Church-of-the-Year, the Church Campus, sanctuary, Button Hall, and offices of Oneonta Congregational Church.

A telegram arrived in the latter part of August. It read:

"Executive Committee unanimously elected you member of special committee authorized by Fifield resolution. This appointment offers great opportunity and challenge. Please wire or phone acceptance to me at 287 Fourth Avenue, New York City if possible before noon, September 27th.

"Arthur Gray Chairman Executive
Committee of the General Council"

The following handwritten letter from L. Wendell Fifield, dated July 17, 1950, refers to the genesis of the Free Church Polity and Unity Committee at Cleveland:

"Dear Henry:

"Mrs. Fifield went to the hospital very soon after my return from Cleveland for a successful operation. My time was pretty well consumed with hospital visits and domestic duties. There was little time for letter writing. Hence I have not been able sooner to write and tell you how much I appreciated your fine, friendly, and instructive attitude at Cleveland. It was a great help to the conciliatory spirit of the Council and an inspiration to us all.

22

"I especially was grateful for the opportunity to come to know you so much better through our common sharing of vital matters. In such fashion are abiding friendships built.

"All indications are that the 'special committee' idea is catching and producing a common interest for us all. I shall spend much time thinking through its personnel and program during the summer. A letter to all delegates asking for names and suggestions goes out this week.

"I cannot close without thanking you again for the kind and generous words you spoke on my behalf in relating to the moderator. As things turned out, however, I have the feeling that, as chairman of the Special Committee, I can be of greater service to our fellowship than had I been elected moderator.

"We go to Maine next week for the month of August. Then back to work again. What a privilege to be a minister in days such as these!

"My best wishes always,

"Wendell"

At the meeting at Wellesley College in June-July, 1949, the Sixth Assembly of the International Congregational Council received a statement on Congregationalism in the classic tradition:[23]

"*First*: a Congregational church is a covenant fellowship, binding the members to God and to one another through Christ, the Head of the Church—a fellowship in faith, in worship, in mutual service and in the service of mankind. Its duty to the world is to spread the Gospel and to work for such political and economic conditions as are implied in the Gospel.

"*Second*: The principle of spiritual authority exemplified in church meeting, where the whole fellowship is brought to a common mind by the Holy Spirit, is of universal application. Congregational churches have gone into unions with one another and with other churches on the basis that Christ rules in His Church only by the Spirit, and that He has not delegated coercive authority to individual officers or synods. We believe this to be the one principle of unity and authority for the universal Church. This principle is applicable not less in the political life of world, involving government by persuasion, by discussion and by consent. Thus Christ rules in His Church and thus He must also in the world."

23

CHAPTER 1 NOTES

1. Revs. Frederick M. Meek, Charles M. Houser, Alfred G. Walton, William A. Keith.
2. Hotel Cleveland.
3. Hollenden Hotel NOTE: The dialogues in this chapter are reconstructed from the author's extensive notes, from writings and correspondence of those quoted, and occasionally, from memory.
4. Revs. Douglas Horton, Truman B. Douglass, Albert J. Penner (merger proponents) and Revs. Warren S. Archibald, Raymond A. Waser, Malcolm K. Burton (merger opponents).
5. *Minutes*, 1949 General Council, Congregational Christian Churches, Feb. 4-5, 1949, Cleveland, pub. N.Y.
6. See Continuation Committee, 1947 ff.
7. *Minutes*, 1950 General Council, p. 65 f. N.Y.
8. Ibid, 66 f.
9. Rev. Howard J. Conn, Minneapolis
10. *Minutes*, 1950, op.cit. 19
11. Ibid.
12. Ibid, 60, 61, 62
13. John 17:21
14. *The Evanston Meeting*, (Nov. 4, 5, 1947) 190 ministers and members from 27 states unanimously adopted these and additional "Findings" prepared by a committee of 11 which included Revs. H. E. Brown, H. E. Hansen, C. F. Jacobs, W. A. Keith, A. C. McGiffert, G. W. Shepherd, M. Strang.
15. *Congregational Beliefs*, Comm. Interchurch Relations & Christian Unity, NY, 1940, prepared for the use of the World Conference of Faith and Order.
16. *Above All Selfish Fears and Cares*, Oneonta Congregational Church, South Pasadena, California 1949
17. Peel, Albert, *Christian Freedom Passim* 1938, Independent Press, London
18. James A. Blaisdell, January 28, 1949
19. Albert Peel, *Christian Freedom*, Independent Press, London, 1938, see also *Passim*
20. *The Unfolding Story, Passim*, privately pub. So. Pasadena, CA 1949
21. Gal. 5:22-25
22. Williston Walker, *History of the Congregational Churches*.
23. Frederick L. Fagley (ed), *Proceedings, Sixth International Congregational Council*, Pilgrim Press, Boston, 1949, p. 39.

CHAPTER TWO

The Selection and the Start

How do you select a committee to do something that many consider impossible? At Cleveland it was plain that neither proponents nor opponents of the Congregational Christian Churches merger with the Evangelical and Reformed Church were confident that "another committee" could be either inclusively representative, or, perceptive enough to fulfill the hopes of the mediators.

A Wide-Armed Action

The first notable breakthrough was a July 1950 letter to all Cleveland Council delegates soliciting nominations for committee membership. The letter suggested several standards. These standards and the story of the selection process were reported by Dr. L. Wendell Fifield. His account follows:

"Members of the Special Committee should be chosen, not on the basis of recognition or reward, but because of their ability to make real contribution to this study. Members should be chosen because of their capacity to submerge present opinions in the interests of a fair and unprejudiced study. The purpose of the Special Committee is neither to confirm nor disprove any present ideas, but rather through open-minded study to discover the fundamental truths about matters within the scope of the resolution.

"The special purposes of this method were, first to make the selection of the committee the undertaking of the entire General Council and second to discover potential members who had a real contribution to make and who would bring a fresh attitude and approach to the study.

"Over three hundred names were received by the committee for their consideration. This large and representative response indicated a very great interest in and hope for this committee. It should be noted in passing that no employed official of our General Council suggested any names for the consideration of the committee. Nor did they participate in the deliberations of the committee. They very properly felt that there should be no 'officialdom' involved in the selection.

"This large response to the request of the nominating committee revealed a very great wealth of leadership and wisdom available for the proposed study. The committee felt that so far as possible it should be utilized. However, the special committee, which was officially named the Committee on Free Church Polity and Unity by vote of the Executive Committee must be relatively small in size. This was necessary both for reasons of economy and of efficiency."[1]

Advisory Panels

In an effort to provide all possible data and opinions four Advisory Panels enlisted as members forty-five outstanding educators, lawyers, superintendents and national executives, plus a Youth Panel nominated by the national Pilgrim Fellowship.

"In order that many ministers and laymen who could not be included on the committee might share in this work, six advisory panels determined by geographical location were also set up. These panels have been asked by the Executive Committee to organize study groups in their Conferences, Associations and churches. Study material for the use of these groups will soon be prepared by the committee.

"This committee and panel organization insures that this study will be carried forward in congregational fashion. The various panels will hold meetings at times and places yet to be determined. The chairman of each panel will be invited to meet at least once each year with the committee thus relating the work of the panels closely to the committee itself."[2]

The Selections Are Made

After creating the panel organization the General Council's Nominating Committee turned its attention to the selection of committee members.

"Several principles guided it in its selection.

"1. The size of the committee should not be arbitrarily determined. The number of those essential to the committee's purposes should determine its size.

"2. The first criterion for selection should be the ability of those selected to make a real contribution to the purposes of the committee. This meant that there must be on the committee members of authority in the field of Congregational history, those competent and informed in the legal profession, those who understood the problem from the view-point of the pulpit and also the pew and those who represent the point of view of youth and the various activities of our fellowship—the women's work for example. It was also thought wise to include outstanding educators in other fields than that of church history.

"3. In accordance with the instructions of the General Council that the committee was 'to represent all points of view', there should be placed upon the committee members who were widely known to be 'pro-merger' and 'anti-merger' in order that both of these viewpoints should be properly represented on the committee.

"4. In the event that a choice was necessary between two possible members of equal competence on the basis of the above criteria, the prevailing consideration should be wide-spread geographical representation. Thus at no sacrifice to the committee's competence, it was possible to have its membership nation-wide and thus representative of our total fellowship geographically as well as in every other way.

"As a result, while all the members of the committee were not equally well known in any one section of the country, every member of the committee was well known and recognized as competent and able in some section of the country.

"It is an interesting commentary upon the importance of the committee that with the exception of two members who were out of the country, and one member who was traveling and could not be reached at once, all members telegraphed or telephoned acceptance of membership on the committee within a day of the time they were notified."[3]

Chairman Restates Objective

Wendell had been appointed chairman by the Executive Committee. After reporting on the selection of the commitee members he reiterated the hope for impartial study.

"1. I was entirely responsible for the resolution which I presented at Cleveland. No one asked me to do it. I wrote the resolution before I consulted with anyone. After writing it I consulted with a considerable number of people of every point of view and received valuable suggestions as to phraseology. But no changes were suggested as to content and purpose. I make this statement to make it crystal-clear that this resolution and the resultant study is not in any way a new move by any group in the merger controversy. It was prompted by no purpose other than that stated in the resolution itself.

"2. I shall do everything within my power to see that the study is kept entirely out of the merger controversy. The study deals with fundamental principles rather than their application to specific situations. Its purpose is to try objectively and honestly to find the answer to the as yet unanswered question raised by the resolution. I shall ask the members of the committee and the panels to maintain an objective, judicial, and studious attitude at all times. I ask all of our fellowship to consider as authentic only such statements as are officially released by the committee. After the final report is presented it will be the responsibility of the General Council to determine its uses and applications.

"3. Since this enterprise is one on the part of our entire fellowship to discover the ways in which congregational polity makes possible the relating of 'free autonomous churches to the ecumenical movement', the committee will seek to keep our fellowship accurately informed of the progress of the work of the committee and the panels. Furthermore, all members of our fellowship are invited to send in suggestions or ideas for the committee's consideration at any time."[4]

The Committee Members

The Executive Committee elected twenty-one members of the Committee on Free Church Polity and Unity. Eight regular meetings were held. Attendance at these meetings was: 19, 16, 17, 18, 20, 20, 18, 20. The importance of the meetings to all was evident, for the 21 were busy people scattered from Maine to California and from Florida to Washington.

Geographically New England predominated, as it did in the number of Congregational Churches and members; about one third of the denomination was in New England and 8 of the 21 committee members were from New England. Mid-Atlantic had 3 members, the Southeast 1, the Midwest 4, the Northwest 1 and the Southwest 4.

Strong proponents of the CC/ER merger were Charles Merrill, Ronald Bainton, Ross Cannon, Lucy Eldredge and William

Halfaker. Ardent opponents were Malcolm Burton, Eghbert Briggs, Edwin Williams and Norman Whitehouse.

Active mediators were Frederick Meek, Frederick Whittaker and Henry David Gray. Wendell Fifield insisted on acting as impartial chairman until the final vote. In favor of the merger but with sagacious concern were Arthur Bradford, Alfred Hurst, Robert Kleinschmidt, William Pratt, Veo Small, Arthur Swartz, Ken Stokes (Pilgrim Fellowship President) and Mrs. Robert Williams.

Some denominations might consider church polity a ministerial specialty. There were ten ministers of churches, two theological seminary church historians, two educators, three church-body executives, one lawyer, a leading churchwoman, a leading churchman and a youth representative.

The Christian Churches which had united with the Congregational Churches in 1931 were represented by Lucy Eldredge, William Halfaker, and Alfred Hurst. A direct descendent of the famed Pilgrim governor was Arthur Bradford. Others had Congregational roots of many generations. And there were those who had chosen to become Congregational.

When announcement of the membership of the committee was made it was greeted with almost unanimous approval, though many still maintained, "All they can do is study. It won't make any difference."

A Strenuous Interlude

I was appointed in August and the first meeting was called for December 12 and 13 at 287 Fourth Ave., New York City.

The dedication of the church campus, sanctuary, Button Hall, office wing, chapel, Founder's House and "cottage" took place October 10th. I was absolutely determined that this be a debt-free dedication because payment of principal and interest would cripple program expansion. On Oneonta's fortieth birthday I prayed for 40 new members, and enlisted 44.

My mediator position was emphasized at Cleveland when the Council elected me one of the nine ministerial principals to the founding, constitutional convention of the National Council of the Churches of Christ in the United States. Prior to that assembly in Cleveland just after Thanksgiving the intricacies of melding a dozen bodies into one had to be mastered.

There was no summer vacation in 1950! But Oneonta graciously freed me for the week between the National Council in Cleveland and the Polity Committee in New York.

29

Cleveland in a blizzard! Baggage misplaced at Chicago. American Airlines provided "the essentials" with a smile. To return to California for my week's vacation proved more costly than a holiday in Bermuda!

What a holiday! An inexpensive $10 room in a Hamilton "guest house", lunch self-made via grocery shop, local bus rides—and miles and miles of walking. I was totally free to swim in the coves, roam the beaches, sleep, read, and plan sermons, talks and New Testament bases of polity. All "at ease". This unexpected delight began what became a long series of visits to Bermuda.

In 1950 the return to New York permitted attendance at Riverside Church Sunday morning and at Fifth Ave. Presbyterian Sunday night. Both Dr. Fosdick and Dr. Buttrick welcomed me, which was as gracious as it was unexpected.

Setting the Sails

The initial meeting of the Polity and Unity Committee opened with a chaplain, a custom followed thereafter. Following introductions, the Chairman requested each of us, in turn, to voice our concept of the committee's task. In glancing at the minutes I see my name is not listed! I arrived just as the chaplain was finishing. In front of me are four pages of notes and quotes of what was said by each member.

Dr. Ronald H. Bainton led off, as was fitting, since he was the distinguished Professor of Ecclesiastical History at Yale, and author of a 1950 best seller *Here I Stand*, the story of Luther. Ronald had three concerns. "Neither the Congregationalism A nor the Congregationalism B of Dr. Douglas Horton's Cleveland address *is* Congregationalism. This committee's task is to describe *real* Congregationalism. The nature of the relation of the C.C. Churches to the E. & R. should be made clear. And we should inquire into 'What forms of interdenominational cooperation are possible, in addition to organic union'."[5]

Veo Small and Fred Whittaker made no preliminary remarks. Others in attendance expressed five chief concerns. Bradford phrased the first, "what is the meaning of participation in ecumenism?"[6] to which Burton added, "What *is* the ecumenical movement? We had better differentiate between federation and organic union."[7]

Cannon voiced a second aim: "find ways in which free churches CAN move foreward into the ecumenical church. We must not be stalled by study. We need to define the points of sharpest division in the CC/ER merger, then ask 'are these problems of philosophy or problems of administration'?"[8] Stokes echoed this view, adding, "Can a church be presbyterial outwardly and congregational in practice?"[9] Mrs. Williams put the position even more clearly, "*We* are to discover ways to go ahead. If we need to alter our polity we must do so to better serve. Maybe that is the unique contribution of our churches to our day."[10]

A third emphasis was pragmatic. Merrill suggested that the committee "be divided into three seven-person sub-committees on ecumenism, congregationalism, and the interplay between the two."[11] Pratt stressed the practical need to get a "simple answer" and to keep the "constituency informed".[12] Ed Williams commented, "Get clear what you want your lawyers to do."[13]

Halfaker led off on a fourth aim. "Our need is to clarify our confusion, to find the basis upon which we can discuss and solve the problems of union without a rupture of the fellowship."[14] Hurst approached this point using as an illustration the 1931 Union of the Christian Churches with the Congregational Churches. "At Seattle (1931) we of the Christian Churches were uniting with the whole of Congregationalism, not with congeries of churches or with a self-centered Council. Our confusion will be cleared up if we analyze the name 'Christian *Church*', NOT Churches."[15] Whitehouse thrust this point into its theological context. "What IS the nature of the Church?"[16]

Fundamentals of Philosophy

Several fundamentals of philosophy were introduced as a fifth major view of the polity and unity committee's work.

Kleinschmidt posed the proposition that the essence of New England Congregationalism was not organization but an approach to religion in which "the essence of Christianity is its direct appeal to the heart and mind." "External union might be disastrous for intellectual independence. There is great strength in diversity. When we gain unity of spirit we will not need to discuss questions of merger."[17]

A prophetic incident occurred at this point. Someone suggested (I did not write down the name) that all views had been heard, why not go to lunch. Chairman Fifield firmly but graciously responded, "This is one committee where everyone will be heard. No one will be cut off. No one will be shut out. Each of the panel chairmen here is as free to speak as any member of the committee. That's a ruling from the chair."[18] It was a wise statement which did much to relax a certain tension in the room.

It was Fred Meek who articulated the basic philosophic and theological questions. "Polity," he said, "is a technique for the securing and conserving of Christian experience. The inherent strength of Congregationalism is reliance on the Spirit. What is the nature of the Spirit? Can a Council of free Churches have authority, or, is such a Council only for advice? How do Congregationalists give the testimony of free churches to Christianity—and to the whole world's religious life? Is it not an illustration of our neglect of our basic beliefs that, in this year 1950, the 400th anniversary of the birth of Robert Browne, our denomination has borne no witness to 'reformation without tarrying for any'? Have we nothing to say as to the meaning of the Church Universal?"[19]

Partisans

The afternoon started off quietly. The eight panel chairmen spoke briefly, adding emphasis to one or more of the points presented above. Hugh Vernon White remarked that "organic, functional, and federated unions (were) in existence" and that "Organic union is not now possible *except* as we alter our polity."[20]

Bainton demurred. Burton exhulted, "That's exactly what I've been saying. We've got to face it."[21] Cannon's voice rose a bit. "Then it's our duty to change our polity. The kingdom of God can't wait."[22] Whitehouse chuckled, "It will *have* to wait on the courts."[23]

It was all the chairman could do to keep only one person speaking at a time. Few bothered to address the chair as one person interrupted another. Voices rose. The whole merger controversy was debouching upon us. I took notes, scribbled possible resolutions, definitions and descriptions, acutely aware that Wendell's great dream hatched on a hot Cleveland square was crumbling.

About 3:30 Wendell held up his hand. "I need a cup of coffee. We'll take a break 'till 4:10."[24] The room emptied quickly. I gathered my papers together then started for the door. Wendell took my arm. "Wait a moment, Henry. I want to talk to you alone." He closed the door. "Henry, you haven't said a thing. You've been writing . . . and I hope thinking. This committee's getting nowhere. Now I'm pretty sick—but that's confidential—I've got to lie down for a while. When we re-assemble I'm going to call on you first thing."[25] And he was gone.

A glass of water substituted for a cup of coffee. The quietest place available was the vacant conference room. Pacing the room for exercise I mulled over the statements made and the stalemated meeting. Clearly, a positive focus had to enlist all members. But how? And precisely what?

It was nearly four fifteen when Wendell took his place, called the meeting to order, and announced, "I've asked Dr. Gray to analyze our situation and make some positive proposals."[26]

A Proposal for Study

As I began to speak, actually I *had* NO "proposals" in mind. "Each of us has put into words a 'first concept' of the Polity and Unity Committee. Perhaps this is a suitable time to focus on the enabling resolution. The operative words appear to be 'study and report'. Obviously there can be no useful 'report' unless it is based on solid 'study'. How can we find out what Congregational polity is today? So far as I know there has never been a study of Congregational polity based directly, solely and objectively on our national-level charters and by-laws, our state constitution, our association articles and our local Church basic documents. I propose we collect these and write a summary of them."[27]

"A waste of time," said Merrill.

"It can't be done short of a decade," added Cannon.

"I'm not quite finished."

"Go on," directed the chairman.

"Documents become out-dated. What's actually done may differ from what is supposed to be done. It would appear that we need to ask officers on all levels of organization to describe their *practice*. The state superintendents and geographic panels might provide facts and direct us to knowledgeable sources."[28]

Cannon spoke up, "*That's* not impossible." Burton claimed, "It's not as easy as you think, Ross."[29] Then Fred Meek spoke at some length, beginning, "I see merit in the idea before us. We've talked all day on the basis of personal opinion. At the very least the study Dr. Gray proposes would direct us to facts, especially the analysis of fundamental written documents."[30] The gist of his remarks was "Let us at least *begin* with an agreed-upon basis; that means *what we say we are* in our basic charters."

Bill Halfaker concurred with this caveat. "What we *say* we are isn't always what we *really* are!"[31]

Ed Williams remarked, "As a lawyer I like to start with whatever facts are available. I'm not familiar with how scholars search for facts. Lawyers begin with written law and prefer the written testimony of authorities."[32]

33

Alfred Hurst volunteered, "I could secure the 'handbook' of the Southern Convention of the Christian Churches and other written foundations of our polity."[33]

Arthur Bradford recounted a bit of history of the 1913 "Committee of Nineteen" which sought to state a dynamic polity for the Congregational Churches in order to relate the "Boards" directly to the Churches through the General Council. "No effort was made to do what is presently proposed. The report was an exercise in thinking and compromising. I'm not sure but that it might have been wiser to begin in the manner now under discussion."[34]

Wendell had his watch on the table beside him. "The hour is late. Since I am resolved that all actions of this commitee *be committee actions* I would appreciate discussion of the printed letter I sent to the General Council delegates and the Churches dated October 17, 1950 with regard to this committee, the merger, membership selection, and panels. We can take Dr. Gray's proposals under advisement, discuss them tonight, and act on them tomorrow if that is your will."[35]

Heads nodded assent.

After discussion it was voted, "That the Committee declares it will address itself to the basic principles and polity of Congregationalism and will not take sides in the merger controversy."[36] Members of the Committee were not to be members of the panels, though they might be invited to attend in their geograhic area as advisors.

The Evening and the Morning

A pleasant dinner at Calvary Episcopal Church was the setting for informal discussion during the evening. At Wendell's request I framed a statement on ecumenism inclusive enough to embrace the ideas expressed by all members of the Committee during the evening. It was voted. The record in the minutes is identical to my hand-written version. "The ecumenical movement is the outward expression of the inward unity of Christ's followers throughout the world which shows itself in many attitudes, in diverse patterns, including organic, federative, and co-operative movements."[37] We adjourned at nine o'clock. My head ached. A couple of us got a cup of chocolate apiece and then I returned to the noisy George Washington Hotel to wrestle with some reasonable framework for study of documents and practice.

Wednesday, December 13th the Committee met at 9:30. After prayer by Fred Meek a thorough discussion of committee voting, records, publicity and responsibility for nurture of Christian spirit in Congregationalism was held. It was not more than a half hour but goodwill reigned and objective study triumphed.

At ten panel chairmen joined us. A series of motions was made, discussed briefly and voted unanimously. The seventeen votes activated the panels, provided for a discussion "syllabus" and bibliography, authorized budget request, set up publicity procedure, and authorized the chairman to appoint a "special subcommittee on Congregational Christian polity . . . to study this matter through correspondence and to present a report at our next meeting on present Congregational Christian polity."[38]

The Congregational Polity Committee consisted of Revs. Arthur H. Bradford, Malcolm K. Burton, Alfred W. Hurst, Frederick W. Whittaker with Henry David Gray, Chairman.

One of the gracious aspects of all votes, beginning with my initial wording of our very first vote, was the openness by which the wording was changed until it said what the whole Committee wanted to say. There are seven changes in my hand-written copy of the first motion. This fortunate process encouraged by Chairman Fifield made possible the unaniminity of all votes. It was one of his many wise and fruitful procedures. I posed four separate statements on "the ecumenical movement" and there were eight improvements made by the Commitee on the final draft. Votes like this were true Committee actions and became a hallmark of unusually perceptive decisions.

Delightful Dividend

The Committee adjourned about four p.m. Wendell impressed upon me the central importance of the Polity Committee, in a brief after-session. He was exhausted.

New York means Broadway. I bought a newspaper, discovered John Gielgut was playing the lead in "The Lady's Not For Burning", bought a ticket, ate a bite, and revelled in Christopher Fry's marvelous poetic play rendered to perfection.

This "third night extra" yielded rich dividends over the four years of the Committee's study! It also meant an early plane to Los Angeles, and time aboard to write my Sunday sermon, catch up on Committee notes—and think.

In What Form?

Initially it was supposed that the national, state, association and local basic documents could be gathered by Bradford, Burton,

Hurst, Whittaker and Gray. My "first try" at a form to encapsulate our findings was a series of "propositions". Neither of these procedures was effective, and confusion resulted when Polity Committee members and Panel Chairmen requested documents from the same sources.

Adding to the confusion was the apparent absence of readily available basic documents for many church-bodies. Those assembled from some state conferences and from many area associations of Churches were often illegible.

Hurst and Whittaker's December, 1950, letters reported some of these facts. Bradford had not understood that he was to secure the Massachusetts documents. In the end the national church-body documents were secured by my personal visits to the denominational offices in New York and Boston. Those of the state conferences necessitated personal letters, telegrams and phone calls to state superintendents and/or registrars. I asked each superintendent to supply the contact names for a "representative" one-third of the associations within the conference area, then pursued those contacts individually. We had assumed the assembling of representative documents from about 5,700. Churches would be our most difficult task. In fact, it proved to be the easiest!

There had also been confusion as to the collection of documents or reports of actual practice. This was understandable. No determination of the form of our report had yet been made. As far as our Committee was concerned the confusion was resolved by my letter of April 4, 1951 (Gray to Burton):

> "I am not concerned with the fact that there is some overlapping in the sub-committees. Dr. Minton (chairman, state superintendents panel) and I discussed that at some length in New York in January. He had the feeling that his investigation was to cover the fundamental documents—that is, constitutions and by-laws of state conferences, associations, and local churches. Our group was to attempt to get a cross-section grass-roots reaction concerning the *actual practices* being followed.
>
> "All of us, as a matter of fact, are working at the same problem, namely, how can the free churches take their places properly and effectively in the ecumenical movement? I see no reason for concern if all of us approach the same major problem from different angles.
>
> "When we meet on Tuesday, April 17th, at 10:00 a.m. at 287 Fourth Avenue, there will be ample opportunity to draw together the varying threads. Our sub-committee's work is described in most general terms in the minutes of the December 12-13 meeting as covering 'Congregational Christian Polity'. Nothing that I, or any

of the members, have done to date has deviated from that instruction. And the paper on which I am now working on 'Foundation Principles on Church Polity in New Testament Theology' will be directly applicable to our job.

"I am not concerned that we shall, severally and separately, do too much work on these themes. I am concerned lest we do too little!"[39]

When the Polity Committee met all day April 16th, Hurst, Burton, Whittaker and Gray were present. Our report to the General Committee, prepared by three writers, "with the assistance of approximately fifty correspondents", "is quite obviously only a report of progress. We of the Committee rejoice to find more unanimity than we had expected to find, and we are now ready to proceed further as you direct."

Here is the gist of our typed report:

"Pursuant to December arrangements we completed by correspondence a series of questions on Congregationalism as it is in practice. The country was divided into areas, and replies were sought by individual committeemen from representative persons in all areas. Many returns have been received; more will yet be obtained. Meantime, Mr. Hurst prepared a paper concerning the Christian Church practice, and the Chairman prepared (1) a tentative statement concerning the theological basis of Congregationalism and (2) 33 provocative propositions concerning contemporary Congregationalism. Mr. Hurst's paper and those of the Chairman are in your hands. To these we now add the results of our April 16th meeting at which the questionnaire and replies thereto were the basis of our discussion.

"We expected to find such wide diversity within Congregationalism as to make description difficult, if not impossible. And at some points this proved to be true. But more often the situation is better described as basic agreement in principle, with minor variations in practice. It should be borne in mind, however, that our wide sampling is in no way to be construed as covering every association, let alone every Church. Here then, are the headings used in our 'Compiled Questions':

"1. *The Nature of the Local Church.*
"2. *Church Membership.*
"3. *Ministerial Recognition.*
"4. *How Churches Secure Ministers.*
"5. *Ministerial Relationships.*
"6. *The Sacraments.*"[40]

The form of my "33 propositions" did not commend itself to anybody! It sounded too stiff and formidable and most of the Polity and Unity Committee members sensed in the word "proposition", an "authority" we neither claimed nor desired. My attempts to put into numbered sentences that which was in the documents, and so far as possible in actual words and phrases from the documents, were simply "statements". This was the designation and form agreed upon at the second general meeting April 18, 19, 1951.

An account of the details of each meeting is best left to the secretary's minutes. These did not record discussion or single out the significance of the recorded votes. It is the change from argument to search for facts, and, from defense of viewpoint to quest for theological foundation which was impressive.

From the Educators' Panel, for example, came a question posed by Professor Walter M. Horton of Oberlin School of Theology: "In what sense is an associational meeting of various churches—local, state, national, world—a true church meeting in the Congregational sense and qualified to invoke the guidance of the Holy Spirit".[41] This goes to the heart of the nature of the Church as a gathered company of Christ-followers who have voluntarily covenanted to live, work, worship and serve as a continuing people of the God and Father of our Lord Jesus Christ.

From the Superintendents' Panel came a tabulated report on the constitutions of 32 of the 39 state conferences submitted "to place these facts before the Committee on Free Church Polity and Unity without further interpretation",[42] thus underscoring the search for *what is* rather than *what we think is* Congregational Polity.

The Youth Panel's report, dated February 22, 1951, accepted the "basically theological" root of our denominational travial but stressed a "study on a theological level, must (be done) in such a way that it will have meaning for the many 'nontheological' minds of our fellowship."[43]

At this second general meeting there were three additional important actions.

The study Syllabus for use by the geographic Panels was reviewed item by item—almost word by word—and was referred to a central committee for final editing. As released September 11, 1951, it contained five sections as follows:

I   Church Union.
II   Forms of Church Union.
III   Churches of the Congregational order.

IV   What is the position of the Congregational Churches as
      to polity?
V   The Congregational Christian Churches in their relation to
      church union.
A copy of the Syllabus is printed herein as Appendix 3.
A brief bibliography was printed with the Syllabus. This was
considered a "minimum adequate" background for study, NOT an
exhaustive list of the literature on either ecumenicity or Congregationalism.

The Syllabus, Bibliography and Panel Report had chief emphasis
at the second general meeting, along with the Polity Committee
report. The latter included my straightforward approach to theology and polity.

*Tentative Thoughts Concerning the Theological Basis
for Congregational Polity*

What is printed here is precisely what was presented on April
18, 1951. It emphasizes "the mediators'" concern for religion, for
Christian theology and Christian faith as the essential ground of
any polity deserving the name *Church* polity.

"The polity of a Church must be rooted in the nature of the Gospel
she proclaims. That is to say, its foundation and raison d'etre is
theological rather than sociological or psychological or political.
The Elizabethan Independents were keenly aware of this necessity,
and therefore it was from their understanding of the Gospel that they
derived their interpretation of Church Polity. We may not fully
agree with their understanding of every detail of the scriptures, but it
is surely true for us as for them that our polity is an outward expression of our Christian experience and convictions. Any thorough
going attempt to understand, evaluate, or alter Congregational
Church practices must go much deeper than adjustments and altera-
tions in ecclesiastical organization, must reach, indeed, to the very
heart of our Christian faith.

"All books of the New Testament bear witness to the undeniably
Christian conviction that God's living Word in Christ must authenticate itself to conscience by shining in its own light. For us, truth is
true because it is truth and not because it is in a Book, given in a
creed, or proclaimed by a pope or council. We belong to the Church
because we belong to Christ and not vice-versa. Our final loyalty is
to Him, and to Him alone. It is that loyalty which has led us to
recognize our brotherhood, and has caused us to associate together
under a voluntary covenant of allegiance to Him.

39

"The Church, in *any* valid use of the term, must ever be the creation of God and not of ourselves. He may and does use men to do His work, but it is His work to the extent that it shares the Divine Spirit. This is true whether we use 'Church' to mean (as it does in 86 out of the 105 times it is used in the New Testament) the local church, or to mean (as it does in all other instances but one in the New Testament) the invisible Church universal. To the degree that Christ's Spirit is present in the local church it is the 'outcrop of the whole great Church' in all generations, everywhere. To the degree that Christ's Spirit is present in whatever visible forms the invisible Church universal may take, to that degree, and only to that degree, do such visible forms show the true character of the whole great Church which is the Body of Christ.

"The theological implications of biblical teaching reach into every facet of free Church polity and unity.

"If the Church is primarily a spiritual unity then it is only incidentally possessed of any polity at all! Ideally it would seem to follow that fellow Christians should so deal with each other in love as to need the barest minimum of orderly procedures, either locally or universally. And the chief purpose of Associations, Conferences, General Councils, Mid-Winter Meetings ad infinitum would appear to be to wait before God in sincere and humble prayer that His voice may be heard and His will done. Indeed, is it not plain that our chief weaknesses as Congregational Christians arise from our failure to put into practice in Church Meetings and Councils of Churches those principles which thrust themselves into the very center of our polity because of our belief in 'the crown rights of the Redeemer' which compels us to say with the prophets 'Though He slay me, yet will I trust Him'.

"According to the principles of the New Testament church unity is not of law but of love, and it can never be achieved by means of an overall Constitution and By-Laws. Forced union is neither union nor unity, but dissention and division, as we have learned to our sorrow and shame.

"According to the New Testament 'authority' is not of office but of insight; our faith in the divine initiative and in the power of grace to elicit faith is such that we are ready to follow the way of freedom. It was Forsyth who said, 'The fundamental difference between a Church and a democracy lies in the principle that no numbers can create a real authority such as the Church confesses, whereas democracy as such will listen to no authority but what its numbers and majorities do create.' In our day and time it is open to question whether or not the obvious 'flight to authority' in every aspect of life is not simply a loss of nerve, a symptom of degeneracy, and a substitute for vital Christian experience. It would seem to be inescapably true that acceptance of the sole lordship of Christ must mean that the individual Christian conscience and the convenanted Church can acknowledge no authority except God, and Him only.

"According to the principles of the New Testament, the Church's fellowship is not made real in Church Meeting or in wider gatherings representative of the Churches, except as the Master inspires the heart of the meeting. According to the principles of the New Testament the basis of our fellowship is not at all the mechanical 'recognition' of a Church, Minister, Association, Conference, etc. by successively wider bodies. Far other foundations for fellowship are required by our Gospel, since a humble heart sincerely lifted anywhere in the name of Christ meets God, and therefore enjoys that fellowship from which all Christian fellowship derives.

"This is the basis of our fellowship. Upon this broad basis the free Church is gathered together by God, *as a new kind of community,* a community of Christ, in which the assembly of even two or three, provided it be truly gathered in His name, constitutes the Church. The Church so formed unites the largest possible freedom with the closest possible fellowship. Organization is quite incidental to fellowship, and may even be destructive of it. Fellowship is fellow-feeling, fellow recognition of one Lord, fellow-sharing; all of which is killed if it is compelled by others or by organization. Fellowship does not demand compromise of convictions and interests, but is confident that all opinions can be drawn together by God if those who hold differing views come together and stay together in His presence.

"Our hardest task may be not to maintain an outward appearance of Congregational Christian unity in our denomination, but rather to maintain a Christ-like discontent with all attitudes, acts, policies, procedures, and relationships which fall short of true fellowship in Christ. Only when that is accomplished are we fit for either fellowship or union with any other Christians whatsoever. To have fellowship is to meet in Christ's name, trusting to the Holy Spirit to lead us into the truth, and determined never to impose anything on anybody apart from personal insight and conviction.

"According to the principles of the New Testament the Church's organization is not of force but of freedom. Every human organization is a political structure, and can therefore be no more than the best available compromise of interests and convictions. How then can unity of organization possibly be *the* important manifestation of the one, holy, catholic, and apostolic Church? Must it not inevitably be true that the more the Church conforms to the idea of a State (even a world state) the more it will demand (in the name of Christ!) the surrender of distinctive convictions and cherished concerns? If it be true that God calls some to be teachers, preachers, etc. may it not also be true that, in the manifold richness of the Gospel, he calls some to be Episcopalians, Methodists, and even Congregational

Christians? If the Church is a new community of Christ may it not need to lay aside organizational patterns whose ancestry is more surely traced to the Roman Empire than to the Gospels? A Church polity whose organizational structure sought inspiration in the New Testament would appear to require faith, freedom, and fellowship rather than creeds, synods, and disciplines.

"According to the New Testament, the Church's convictions are not of creed but of experience, and whatever statements of faith are made are but testimonies to what we believe and never tests of our fitness for membership. This is not to say that we thereby lack convictions; for the demands of a clean conscience before God and a right relation to Him are far higher, harder, and holier than the acceptance of any creed.

"According to the New Testament, the Church's influence is not of power but of persons. Loss of influence often goes with gain in power. And by the nature of our Gospel we are committed to trust in God rather than confidence in ourselves. Some time past Oman laid his finger on the pulse that beats beneath the wrist of power when he said, 'Magnitude of result is undoubtedly with the Church which has bulk and skillful leadership and temporal advantages, but the promise of the future is for the Church which approximates more closely to the ideal of the many or the few who are truly met in the name of One who unites men, not by enslaving them to His will, but by setting them free with the liberty of God's children.' The influence of Jesus was exercised by contagion, persuasion, example, and inspiration, and He seems to have thought rather less of the power of a highly organized religion than did His followers of the Middle Ages, or perhaps even than do His followers in the twentieth century. *Is* the most effective instrument of Christian influence a powerful organization where lobbies are headed in the halls of government, or can we learn something from the decadence of faith at the Church's height of power? Surely the Church's mission is not to achieve sufficient power to make men or governments obey its will. Is it not rather to *be* a new order of community bearing a prophetic witness to society, dedicated to self-effacing service, nurturing the souls of its members severally, and acknowledging as its strength nothing but goodness, wisdom, love, mercy, understanding, and holiness.

"According to the New Testament, the Church's quest for union is therefore first and foremost a determination to find unity at the Master's feet. If Union involves the suppression or the loss of the peculiar witness or experience embodied in any Church, then, to that extent it impoverishes truth and robs the Gospel of some element of its worth.

"We must find our unity in Christ by the way of grace and faith, the way of insight and acceptace, but it would appear to be equally true that all who truly and deeply share such Christian unity must perforce yearn to give outward and visible evidence to the world of their inward and invisible one-ness in Christ. Union would then be unity making itself visible in Church order. The manifold, rich, and free unity of believers evident in 'The Acts of the Apostles' might well indicate a direction in which similar unity might now be realized. Must not we of the Reformed tradition remember that Protestant denominations came to break up a hollow, outgrown organizational unity, in order that we may prepare for a unity which is flexible and free, and founded on faith in Christ alone, a union which, therefore, will be more likely to be permanent among free men.

"According to the New Testament, there is but one hope of either unity or union, and that is to be made one in Christ. This is a very different thing than the search for quick ways toward uniformity, lest we be 'too late' to save the world. The high goal of being made one in Christ would not be brought nearer, nor would the world be saved by any kind of unity or union which sets organizational conformity above freedom of conscience, or which puts the united strength of men in place of utter reliance on God. Neither would a least common denominator 'Church' compounded of the doctrines and procedures of all ecclesiastical organizations bring in the Kingdom of God, since it could not be more than the symbol of how little we could agree on, instead of being the emblem of how God had drawn us together. The ideal of Hildebrand, under every cloak of beneficence, is a too easy solution for a deep difficulty, the difficulty of being instruments of God for the winning of free acceptance of the Gospel by individuals and by the Church. 'Church order is finally important not in order to provide an efficient organization, or dignified assemblies, or even adequate sustentation and church extension funds, but to bear witness to the Gospel. The criterion by which it is judged should always be the Gospel.'[44]

"If we follow the principles of the New Testament, the Churches meeting in council must refuse to allow the secular practices of contemporary political, educational, and business life to govern their proceedings. The expedient and politic answer may not be the Christian answer. The election of picked candidates may not be those whom the Spirit would call. There have been very few (and all abortive) attempts to make Congregational church councils into super-bodies which hold rule over the Churches. Councils historically and presently are chiefly called for definite purposes and then dissolved. The district Conferences, the Boards, and the General Council have continuing bodies chiefly of an admnistrative nature. There could be no New Testament basis on which to claim that any or all of these are a 'Church' or are 'Churches'. Neither is there theological foundation for such a claim in Gospel, though, of course, the immediate pragmatic results obtained by an organiza-

43

tion erected on such a basis would undoubtedly be substantial. Yet, if we believe in the free Church interpretation of the Gospel (and I would be willing to say in the New Testament Gospel) then we must find the Church in the common life in an ongoing community, or in the universal fellowship of believers.

"K.L.C. Smith, who is not Congregationalist as far as I have been able to discover, well describes our free church polity in these words: 'When men fail most greviously, the *practice* of a gathered church may . . . degenerate . . . (but) the polity is the most courageous and most scriptural venture of faith possible to Christian communities, for it takes the promises of God seriously, and, depriving believers of all external support or control, casts them wholly upon the Spirit. The depth to which it can fall corresponds to the height to which it aspires. It gives full, practical expession to the undeniably scriptural view that the church is the people, and holds it better to run all risks than to sacrifice the principle which makes the congregation of believers responsible for the quality of their own Spiritual life.'[45] Churches insist upon the autonomy of the local church because only so can they safeguard the essential principles of the immediate contact between the local group and the Divine Head of the Church, and of immediate responsibility to Him.

"Any theological introduction to Congregational polity must look toward unity with others; for it is of the essence of our theology to be inclusive rather than exclusive, provided only that there be sincere desire to be included. There has yet to be made any sold contribution to the creation of a *church* order, not patterned after secular society, but born of the Spirit. I believe such a church order is possible, but I believe it will be found by way of the Gospel rather than by way of sociology."

In summary, the second general meeting was an earnest effort by all to "study" Congregational polity from its New Testament roots to its contemporary fruits.

Content of the General Meetings

Each general meeting of the Polity and Unity Committee had dual emphases. One emphasis was on the detailed, phrase-by-phrase, and word-by-word discussion, alteration and approval of what became sections of the final report. The second was extended consideration of one or more facets of the report being created.

As early as the December 1951 meeting disputation regarding the Congregational Polity Committee's first draft of "Congregational Polity as seen in its Basic Documents" was challenged. The southeast panel chairman asserted, "This statement on ordination won't do. It just isn't correct."[46] He referred to provisions for ordination in association documents, and a few state conference documents. The only answer was to produce the documents. One area association in Oxford County, Maine, recognized as Congregational ministers only those ordained by a Church. Across the nation in the majority of associations, the practice was for a Church to invite seven or more sister Churches to constitute "a vicinage council" which joined with the Church in the ordination proceedings. In most other cases a Church requested all the Churches of its area association (often a county) to act with it in ordination procedures. In Northern California and two other state conferences, the area associations and Churches, annually, requested the Conference to act with the Church in ordination proceedings. Hawaii, the Christian Churches Southern Convention, and Puerto Rico were mild exceptions to these usages. There WAS an extremely large degree of nearly identical provisions in the documents. Therefore I responded to the questioner, "Our objective is to be inclusive. Let's get wording which correctly describes the exact degree of variety."[47] This "editing by committee" procedure became characteristic of our work. No wording was accepted until unanimously agreed.

Before me are handwritten changes made in the local Church, association, and conference statements describing Congregationalism—in its Documents. Burton often exclaimed, "That's what the constitution says!" Again and again Halfaker or Cannon asserted, "That can't be right." Whittaker read many of the documents; his suggestion usually was a substitute wording, "Why not put it this way?" It cannot be reiterated too often that THIS committee made every sentence its own. I wrote numerous drafts, most of which are before me. There are crossed out words, recast sentences, subtractions and additions, not just in the first draft, but in every draft right up to the final accepted statements.

I write at length on this point to emphasize both the extraordinary persistence of the committee members, and, to underscore the fact that the final product states accurately what Congregationalism said it was in its Documents, A.D. 1954, when the final vote was taken.

The Mood of the Meetings

When twenty of our twenty-one assembled in New York for the second general meeting April 18, 19, 1951 there was a mood of common quest. Regardless of the view of each member, all dealt with reports and discussions in an atmosphere of goodwill and conciliation. All votes taken at the meeting were unanimous because the matter under consideration was explored thoroughly and the expression of our finding was worded and reworded until we could agree.

I do not imply that there were no divisions of opinion. Proponents of the CC/ER merger like Bainton, Mrs. Williams, Cannon and Halfaker questioned as vigorously as opponents like Burton, Briggs and Whitehouse. Yet all agreed to hold in abeyance their personal opinions in favor of as fair and accurate a determination as was possible of the matter under review.

The primary accomplishment of the second meeting was completion of all but editorial work on the Syllabus to spark discussion in the Panels—both professional and geographic.

A brief bibliography was attached to the Syllabus. Oddly, the inclusion or exclusion of books on this list evoked more debate than did the Syllabus questions and topics. I insisted on inclusion of excellent British works like *"Congregationalism Today"*. Meek was the only other member who had read most of the British literature. He vigorously supported listing it. Bainton had included several history books heavily weighted in favor of connectionalism in Connecticut, both the "Saybrook" version (1709) and the Presbycongregational version of 1801. The denouement was inclusion of the historical documents sans prolemics.

Perhaps as many as half the Committee members expected the Syllabus and Bibliography to promote vigorous discussion in panels, ministers' meetings, and among Church members. By April, 1951, all of us were aware that no study of Congregationalism had ever been made, anywhere, on the triple foundation of history, contemorary documents and contemporary practice. This gave zest to the undertaking. It was also the reason many of us doubted the value of a list of questions and books as the basis for study, analysis and investigation. To do a thorough piece of work required actual examination of what we said we were in our documents, and our actual usage in practice.

By April 1951 more than 180 persons had been elected to the Committee or panels by the Executive Committee of the General Council. The importance attached to the effort is indicated by the fact that only one person found it impossible to serve. Obviously there was a reservoir of hope that our study, research and accurate report might become the basis of fruitful ecumenical relationship of free Churches. To the mediators this confirmed our belief that Congregationalists overwhelmingly supported neither extreme position on the CC/ER merger, or, on free church polity and unity.

Toward Kennebunkport

Immediately after the initial meeting I wrote to the members of the Congregational Polity Committee as follows:

"Dear Friends: The Committee on Free Church Polity and Unity has given us a very large and difficult and important assignment as members of the subcommittee on Congregational Polity.

"When we met for lunch in New York the following procedure was arranged as a preliminary guide in our work:

"1. All of you are to send to me suggested questions concerning Congregational Polity, which questions are then to be combined by me for return to you.

"2. Each one of you is to select one or more persons in our state conferences, as indicated in the division of states below, *to whom you are to address personal letters of inquiry covering the material assembled in our collated questions. The object of this is to secure from a thoughtful and balanced observer on the field accurate information both as to the 'paper relationships' and the actual practice of Congregational Polity in each of the states. I have already conferred with Dr. Minton, and he will get to me as quickly as posible the data which is to be assembled by the superintendents so that it may also be on hand for our consideration.

"Professor Whittaker:	New England, Middle Atlantic, New York, Pennsylvania
"Mr. Hurst:	Southeast up to and including Louisiana and Missouri; also Ohio, Illinois, Indiana
"Dr. Bradford:	Michigan, Wisconsin, Minnesota, North Dakota, South Dakota, Iowa, Nebraska
"Dr. Burton:	Colorado, Wyoming, Utah, Idaho, Germany, Kansas, Afro-Christian
"Dr. Gray:	Northern California, Oregon, Southern California-Southwest, Hawaii, Washington

"3. By February first I should like to receive from you the replies to your inquiries.

47

"4. I am to prepare the preliminary paper on Congregational Polity which is to be circulated to you by no later than March first, which paper will take account of the material we have gathered to date.

"5. At the same time Mr. Hurst will write a similar paper on the practices of the Christian Churches for circulation among us.

"6. On Tuesday April 17, we will plan to spend the day together in New York in order to whip into shape our report of progress for the General Committee.

"You will note that I used the term 'report of progress'. I hardly think it can be more than that since there is involved at least the following:

"1. The relationship of theology and polity in Congregationalism.

"2. The theory of polity as represented by our written documents now in force.

"3. The practices currently being followed.

"4. What is the peculiar contribution of Congregational Polity?

"5. By what means can free churches take their proper place in the ecumenical movement. The latter is obviously the question which we need an answer to, but I think our progress toward it may well require a large measure of consideration to the preliminary questions."

Replies came with surprising promptness, so that by March 12, 1951 I could write to the committee:[48]

"Dear Friends:

"A heavy and prolonged siege of flu prevented me from meeting the March 1st deadline for getting the enclosed material to you. Sorry.

"Herewith are:

"1. A compiled list of questions, being the sum of those which you sent to me. It is my understanding that you are now to complete writing to those in your several areas of the country, as per our New York meeting assignments and to bring these results with you to your April meeting.

"2. A tentative series of 'Propositions' based on replies already received from some of you, and on examination of constitutions (local, assoc., state and national). These may (or may not) form a framework for our report to the general committee, as we may decide at the April meeting.

"As we move more deeply into our subject it becomes obvious that there *are* certain well recognized characteristics of a Congregational Church and it becomes equally clear that these are often more honored in the breach than in the observance of them. Furthermore, there are areas in which no definition seems likely to adequately cover all our diverse theories and practices. My hope for our April meeting is that we shall be able to designate areas of clear fact as to what a Congregational Church is and areas of doubt in such workmanlike fashion as to provide the general committee with a foundation for general agreement on the one hand, and for further study on the other hand.

"The '33 Propositions' deal presently with Numbers 2 and 3 of the five points listed in my December letter. I expect to prepare a statement on each of the other points in time for our meeting, and would suggest that all of you do likewise."

The April 1951 general meeting reviewed what had been prepared, with much questioning and not a few changes of wording. Nevertheless it was apparent that the polity of our individual Churches *was* describable. In fact, aside from the New England pattern of dual (spiritual and financial/legal) organization, there was a reasonable similarity of constitutions, charters and by-laws.

Aside from Hawaii, Puerto Rico and the Southern Convention of the Christian Churches, both the area associations and the state conferences were describable, so far as documents on hand indicated. I was instructed to collect additional associational documents and wrote to the state superintendents on June 21, 1951:[49]

"The material handed us by the General Council office lacks an association constitution from your state. I should like to be able to count on you to send copies of these documents to me by July 3.

"Every member of the Committee on Congregational polity will study *all* the documents independently. Then a joint report will be prepared. We have already done a huge research job, and we intend to leave nothing undone which will help to analyze our polity, understand its implications, and lead Churches of our order into fruitful ecumenical relations. Your help will be greatly appreciated."

I compressed all available material in "33 Propositions concerning Contemporary Congregationalism". Here is the introduction to those Propositions:

"Any collection of data concerning contemporary Congregationalism produces a plethora of facts and opinions. The number and variety of them suggests, at first glance, that the Congregational Christian Churches of the United States are a conglomeration of all possible polity practices. More careful scrutiny discovers definitive characteristics which are both positive and negative. Since this present paper is nothing more than a point of beginning, these characteristics may perhaps be best stated in the form of thirty-three propositions. Thus set forth, they may properly be made the subject of study, debate, and re-statement."

Perhaps even more important as an indication of the viewpoint and aspiration of the mediators is my closing "Comment":

"The foregoing '33 Propositions' are not offered as either a finished statement of contemporary Congregationalism, or as a statement of which Congregationalism idealy ought to be. The omission of the basic issues of theology is deliberate; for the attempt has been to describe as crisply as possible the existent relationships rather than to discuss the foundation of Congregational polity in theology; in the Crown rights of the Redeemer, the competence of the Spirit-led Church meeting, or the meaning of the Spirit as the common spirit of the Church.

"The existent relationship, as set forth in our basic constitutional documents, and as modified in practice, may not be ideal. But before we can fruitfully discuss the ideal, it seemed well to try to find a measure of agreement on the actual.

"If I might try a bow at a venture I should say that what is needed for true unit of Christ's Churches in not a new admixture of existent polities, but some as-yet-undiscovered form of structure which shall rightly express spiritual purposes and divine motivation rather than parallel the political or legal structures of the secular world. A Christian Church polity must of necessity be of God, and it must, therefore, be a polity of grace and not of law. I believe there is guidance toward such a polity in the New Testament, in the experience of the saints, and in the present-day leadings of the Spirit. The Committee on Polity and Unity will perform a great creative service if it can be so led of God as to discover His will for His Churches in this present age."

July 9, 1951 Wendell called a joint meeting of the Central Committee and the Congregational Polity Committee at Kennebunkport, Maine, August 21, 22, and 23. The surroundings at this beauty spot encouraged informal discussion. Of special delight to me was the opportunity to share before breakfast walks with Ronald Bainton. History and Anthropology were my academic first love. Nature in all its wonders kept pace thanks to my biologist brother Billy. Bainton combined history, joy in nature and very considerable artistic skill. His sketches of flowers or of people were strong and clear. They had character. It was fun to compare notes on trees, flowers and birds, and his uncompromising approach to art provided an insight of great value about six months later.

The Kennebunkport meeting was one of the determinative gatherings of the Committee on Free Church Polity and Unity. Here, undivided attention was given to Congregational Polity as seen in its contemporary documents. All 39 state conference documents were on hand.

Our first surprise was the virtually unanimous agreement on the polity of the Churches individually. My handwritten original has 13 Propositions. Of the 18 corrections made at Kennebunkport all but two were clarifications of language. Considerable debate centered on the "meaning" or "authority" of a vicinage or associational Council in the ordination, recognition or installation of a minister. Whittaker and Hurst contended that the Council had "authority" in matters of ministerial standing. Bradford phrased his comment as a question, "Does not the minister hold his standing in the association? Isn't that where his credentials are lodged?"[50]

Burton insisted that nobody whatsoever outside the Church could, or should "presume to tell the Church what to do."[51] Bainton held to the connectional view dominant in the "Plan of Union" (1801-1852) of Connecticut Congregationalists and the Presbyterian Church.

In the end I modified the Proposition to read[52] that a "council *may withhold 'recognition' or may give counsel,* but it exercises no authority over the Church . . . *The minister may exercise his full duties whether or not he is 'recognized' by a Council.*"

The second material change also related to the ministry, as to the acceptance by others of ordination by one Church. Here the word "will" was deleted and the word "may" substituted. Action by a Church "*may* be or *may* not be accepted as valid by other Congregational Churches."[53]

In my own experience there had been two instances when action by a Church *and* by an association (!) had NOT been considered valid by other Congregational Churches to which the minister was commended. Both were extreme. They had no hint of ecclesiasticism whatever; the grounds of non-acceptance were moral and legal. I could find both historical and contemporary examples of individual Church action which HAD BEEN ACCEPTED, such as that of the distinguished Edwin Pond Parker in 1860 at Hartford.

Besides "editorial changes" and the two instances mentioned above, the great gain at Kennebunkport was a re-numbering of the paragraphs so that they followed one another more suitably.

Of the five Propositions regarding area association four gained approval with minute changes. The fifth was a long section concerning the association's credentials committee and Church or ministerial "standing". There was general accord for the position that more associational documents must be studied before we could make a definitive statement.

The four Propositions concerning conferences were approved with two slight changes in wording which merely clarified.

The national-level-body "statements" (for that was the term we now began to use instead of "propositions") were only tentative because of extreme difficulty in securing the documents. I do note, however, that the handwritten first draft of August 1951 is substantially close to the final approved version of February 1954.

The importance of Kennebunkport lay in the acceptance by all of the fundamental idea that IT WAS POSSIBLE to state what Congregationalism believed itself to be in its documents. From this meeting onward no one took seriously the canard, "We Congregationalists don't know what our polity is."

Questions continued. But by the November 28, 29, 1951 general meeting in New York there was acceptance of a document (with revisions, of course) presenting "Congregational Polity as described in contemporary documents."[54] Furthermore the Congregational Polity Committee was requested to add "a fourth section on the General Council and Boards".[55] We were directed to send to the geographic panels the documents, as revised, asking for "information with regard to actual practices . . . this information to be returned to the chairman" of the Congregational Polity Committee "for further discussion." This was the inception of a second, separate report which eventually was titled, "Congregationalism as It Is Practiced in the United States."[56]

The only storm clouds at the November 1951 meeting arose because of an historical report "proporting to show that Congregationalism has been a changing denomination throughout its history."[57] Patently, to live is to change, but to elevate "change" as THE normative characteristic of Congregationalism is to misread history, as the discussion made plain.

It may be that the change in the climate of the general Committee can be indicated by an event for which I have written sources.

At the "Central Committee" meeting of June 8, 1951, ardent merger opponent Malcolm Burton and outspoken proponent Charles Merrill became emotionally involved. Burton's letter to Merrill dated May 21st and the disagreement on June 8 led Merrill to write a more-than-two-page, single-space letter to Burton, dated June 15, which letter Merrill sent to me in the hope that some mellowing might be encouraged all around. The letter says rather bluntly what many thought, and accents the extraordinary achievement of Burton, Merrill and the whole general Committee. Persons who disagreed almost violently eventually voted to adopt the Polity and Unity Report with no dissenting voice.

Here is the letter:[58] (Merrill to Burton, 6/15/51)

"Dear Malcolm:

"It has seemed to me that perhaps I ought to write you somewhat fully with regard to what you spoke of as my being 'agitated' in the Central Committee meeting not long ago.

"I will frankly confess that it had a personal element in it. I can't remember when I have been accused of being 'fuzzy and indefinite' in my writing. Whatever other mistakes I have made, people generally seemed to think that what I wrote was clear and plain. It made me wonder whether age was beginning to tell on me more than I realized.

"Moreover, it seemed to me that the whole tenor of your letter was that somebody was being underhanded and crooked and you started with me as a text.

"But I was, I hope, 'agitated' for another reason. The question that people have asked me most often of our Polity Committee has been: How is Malcolm Burton behaving? I have been glad to say that you were behaving very well. Your letter made it impossible for me to say that anymore, at least for a time.

"Again, when I seconded Dr. Fifield's resolution at the Cleveland Council, I expressed the hope that this Committee might be able to extract from the merger controversy the distrust and suspicion that seemed to be too prevalent. I still feel that this is incomparably more important than what we are able to find out with regard to denominational polity and its relation to the ecumenical movement. Your letter seemed to go exactly contrary to this purpose of the Committee, partly because of the letter itself and partly because of the people to whom you sent it.

"I was sorry that you felt obliged to take a fall out of Miss Eldredge. I don't suppose your leaving out 'Miss' before her name was intentional. However, it added to the disagreeable impression one got from your reference to her 'slanting'. I have never before heard her honesty called in question; on the contrary, I have always heard her spoken of in high terms.

"I was also 'agitated' because it seemed to me that you were returning to what I had hoped was being given up; namely, the 'vendetta' against Douglas Horton. Perhaps you feel that vendetta is a strong term; however, I believe that one of the most regrettable things in the merger controversy of the past years has been what has been said about him by way of innuendo as well as direct charges. Now Dr. Horton is a man with whom I frequently do not agree. I do not think that he and I have exactly the same ideas of Congregational Polity. He was, of course, very influential in framing the Basis of Union. I would have framed it differently, in definite respects; however, that he has been dishonorable or crooked or that in any deliberate way he has altered Minutes or intentionally taken unfair advantage, I do not believe. I understand that Henry Gray agrees with this.

"Now this vendetta has done a great deal of harm. I did not attend all of the pro-merger meetings that were held at Oberlin. I did, however, attend enough of them to realize how strong was the feeling of resentment on the part of a large number of very decent people against the way in which the anti-merger people had attacked Dr. Horton, and had otherwise engaged in disseminating suspicion and distrust.

"There have been, of course, regrettable things said and regrettable things done on both sides. However, I don't believe that if one went through the pro-merger literature, as during the fall of 1948, he would have felt that he was going through 'muck', as Dr. Calkins and I felt when we went through it in order to prepare an answer.

"May I make a comment on the close of your letter. You refer to someone who said that some day the report of our Committee would be handed to us for signature on the dotted line. Don't you really think that that was a bit of cheap cynicism which, on reflection, was hardly worth quoting?

"I am writing all this quite plainly and frankly in part because I have come to the conclusion that you have not quite understood what you were doing and perhaps that is true of some of your friends. The readiness with which you agreed, around the table in your home in New London, to write a letter which would exonerate me from any intentional slanting of the Minutes leads me to this conclusion. I don't think you realize how sharp your harpoons are. You are intent

54

upon an accurate statement of things in which you are particularly interested and so intent are you that you forget that people of equal honesty with yourself don't understand them in the same way . . .

"In view of my having known you since those days when you and your brother used to come down with your father to Burlington and since the day when very early in your ministry I met you at Massena Springs, and in view of my great respect for and real friendship with your father, may I say another frank word. Perhaps you are at a parting of the ways. You can go on and write other letters and take other action after the manner of the one you wrote May 21st. As I have suggested above, you will do this honestly, thinking that you are accomplishing the Lord's work. On the other hand, perhaps there is a lesson for you in this present episode. You have very seriously hurt the feelings of a good friend of yours and a good friend of your father's. You did it unintentionally. Why do it again?"

I must emphasize that this letter was NOT sent to Burton. Merrill had let out his feelings, as he said to me later. Here is unvarnished testimony to our personal and committee traumas.

Progress Nevertheless!

With the knowledge of the strong emotions associated with the enterprise, I wrote to the members of the Congregational Polity Committee on November 2, 1951:[59]

"I urgently need from you (all except Hurst, who has already sent in his) the material outlined at Kennebunkport as follows:

"1. Study the 'Propositions' and the State and Association constitutions in relation to each other and send me your suggestions for further revision.
"2. Study the 'Theological statement' read at the April meeting in New York with a view to writing your own or suggesting revision in the one presented.
"3. Put in writing your best thought on the question 'How can the Congregational Churches move into more fruitful ecumenical relationships' in the light of your study of our own polity.

"I should like to have your material re: all three points as soon as possible, since it is to be collated and sent to all members of the General Committee.

"Also, I am calling a meeting of our committee for ten o'clock, Tuesday morning, November 27th, at 287 Fourth Avenue. Miss Debus will indicate which room we are to use. As you know, it is my earnest hope that we can bring to the November meeting of the General Committee a substantial report as the basis of its deliberation.

"It is going to be exceedingly hard to draw together the material, which you send me, in time to get it to all the members of the General Committee for their study but I shall do my best to get it to them if you can get it to me soon. I am looking forward to a most important meeting when we get together again."

This letter to Burton, Hurst, Whittaker with a copy to Fifield was a deliberate attempt to spotlight the objective research. I had conferred with Fred Meek and with Bill Keith about the Burton-Merrill situation. All three of us felt that concentration on the task in hand held the only promise of overleaping the emotional charge twixt pro and anti-merger. It was our position that we must resolutely lay aside our feelings and submit ourselves whole-heartedly to whatever discipline the facts in the documents required.

The November meeting of the General Committee was a first fruit of the common quest for objectivity. On February 8, 1952, I was able to write to the general chairman:[60]

"Here are three copies of the report on Contemporary Congregational Polity. I have carefully checked them against the constitutions and other basic documents, and I believe that the Association, Conference, and National sections are accurate, except for the material included in the appendix on Hawaii and the Southern Convention, which of course differs so much from the general rule as to be non-describable in the same sentences . . .

"After the Central Committee has gone over it, if there are any significant changes I would appreciate the opportunity to check them with the documents in my possession, for I do not want anything to go out with my name attached to it unless it can be supported in the full light of discussion at the General Council, or thereafter. I am sorry that this is late but I think you will see that the National Section proved a much bigger job than had been anticipated.

"With every good wish, and with much appreciation of your magnificent leadership of this committee."

On the National Level

The national section had indeed proved to be exceptionally difficult.

First, the charters, powers-of-attorney, by-laws, and procedures of nearly all the national church-bodies had never been collected, or, if they had been, they were not made available. It was necessary to visit in turn offices of the General Council, the Home Board, the American Board (foreign), the Council for Social

Action, the Missions Council, and even a number of the organizations whose affairs had been conducted since 1936 by the device of powers of attorney.

Second, once assembled the national level church-body documents followed no discernable pattern. Each had to be described. Most perplexing was the interdependence of national church-bodies . . . for which there might or might not be provision in the documents. Likewise the relation of the national church-bodies to the state conferences and the area associations was sometimes described and sometimes omitted. The relation of the Churches to the national church-bodies was often stated in far more general terms than those used, for example, in the conference documents.

On March 14 Wendell sent me the detailed suggestions of the Central Committee. Miss Debus added a note on the manner of electing delegates to the General Council—which was amended at the 1952 Claremont meeting of the General Council.

With all these corrections, and the addition of six definitions, the "Report on Congregational Polity as Described in Its Constitutional Documents" was mimeographed at Oneonta Congregational Church and distributed to all present at the Claremont meeting of the General Council. In the form of a printed leaflet it became grist for the discussions of the geographic Panels and supplied an outline for the collection of corresponding data on "Congregational Polity as Practiced."

The June 16, 17, 1952
Meeting of the Committee on Free Church Polity and Unity

The meetings were held in South Pasadena at the Oneonta Congregational Church of which I was minister. The Church graciously supplied housing, meals, meeting rooms and secretarial services.

Of immediate concern was a review of our Report, which now included an introduction to committee selection and procedure, the Syllabus, an introductory statement on Congregational Polity, then Congregational Polity as Described in its Constitutional Documents with these closing paragraphs by Wendell Fifield:

"The study deals with the spiritual considerations involved in the problem presented by the resolution. The committee is dealing, not just with organizations, their documents, their property and the like, but with spiritual fellowships and their relationships to each other. Whatever may be the other conclusions reached regarding 'free church polity and unity'—and these are being earnestly sought by the committee—both freedom and unity, when applied to Christian institutions, must find their ultimate harmony in spiritual experience and spiritual fellowship.

"In closing this tentative report I should like to express deep appreciation on the part of the Committee for the many expressions of confidence and hope which we have received. We are also deeply grateful for the fact that the work of this Committee and its panels has served as a uniting factor in our fellowship as we have shared the effort to discover the way in which freedom and unity relate to each other in Protestantism.

"As for myself, my two years as chairman of this committee have strengthened the conviction which I voiced at Cleveland in presenting my resolution that this whole problem is a fundamental one for the future of Protestantism. It involves the eighteen million constituents of the churches with free church polity in our country. The answer to it cannot be quickly discovered for it does not lie in any superficial nor opportunist judgment. Nor is it to be established on the basis of wishful thinking, personal preferences, nor desires. The *right* and *true* answer must be found.

"To me it is a great source of satisfaction that our Congregational fellowship has undertaken this search for a solution. Such a search is devoid of the satisfactions of immediate achievements. But it is my very deep conviction that we are involved in an even greater adventure in this search. We have, profiting by our experiences, undertaken the search for those fundamental considerations which must underlie all relationships between the free, autonomous churches and ecumenicity if these relationships are to be enduringly successful.

"No one can tell what the final results of this study will be. But if it is pursued in a spirit of objectivity, in a spirit of prayer, in the spirit of the Christ in whose service we all seek to share, it will bring to us the knowledge of God's will for our fellowship's future. And whatever may be the relationship of His Will to our own ideas and wishes, this is what we most need to know."[61]

Next the Committee discussed at length the rumor that the Committee was to be discharged at Claremont and the deluge of resolutions and letters this provoked, leading to a unanimous vote of the Executive Committee to recommend that the Committee be continued to 1954.

Our concern was to retain the momentum which had been achieved, to plan ahead in the expectation of continuance, and to collect, organize and analyze data on Congregational Polity as Practiced. To this end I was instructed to request all geographic

Panels to report on *Practice* using the outline provided by the Documentary Statement.

By mid-1953 a careful comparison of history, documents and practice was hoped for. This then could be the basis for recommendations as to how Congregational Churches could participate effectively in the Church Universal.

August 15th, Wendell wrote:[62]

"The meeting of the General Council at Claremont was a significant one for our organization. The Council indicated its confidence in us and our work by voting unanimously to continue it during this biennium. Dr. Douglas Horton made the motion. In a statement made before the Council the 'Continuing Committee' expressed their confidence in our committee. Hundreds of delegates spoke to me personally of their belief in and hope for the work of our group.

"The resolution adopted by the Council relative to the procedure concerning the proposed union with the E. and R. Church during the coming two years provided that the Executive Committee establish a consulting relationship with the Committee on Free Church Polity and Unity during the drafting of the proposed constitution. This action constitutes our committee, it seems to me, as an advisory board of review though it in no way involves us in the controversy itself.

"The Executive Committee gave unanimous approval to our committee in various resolutions passed by them.

"These widespread commendations of the first two years of our work should be a source of deep satisfaction to us all. At the same time, it should bring to us a very deep sense of responsibility. Our fellowship is looking to us to produce very definite answers to the questions involved in our study. We reported progress this year. Two years hence we must report accomplishments.

"Our fellowship expects us to produce a report that will resolve the issues of the relationship between the polity of the free churches and the movement toward unity. These issues are basic to the whole future of Protestantism. . .

"I trust that all committee and panel members will feel a deep and consecrated desire to help in every possible way in the work which lies before us."

In a penned note to me he said, "The report is an excellent one and, regardless of what happens in this merger business, is a permanent contribution to our fellowship."[63]

In part, overlapping sessions of the Committee on Free Church Polity and Unity were pre-Council gatherings in Claremont for prayer, meditation, Bible study and discussion. These were an attempt of the mediators to lift the CC/ER merger out of the realm of law and advocacy into the realm of spiritual life, work and unity.

I do not remember who first proposed a resolution affirming our desire to unite with others, and, specifically, with the Evangelical and Reformed Church on *that* level. Many hands and minds were at work in framing what came to be known as "the Claremont Resolution."

Friday night, June 20, 1952, ninety-five per cent of the delegates to the General Council of the Congregational Christian Churches meeting at Claremont, California, voted in favor of a resolution concerning the proposed union with the Evangelical and Reformed Church.

This is the only nearly unanimous action ever taken, either by our churches or by a General Council meeting.

In 1948 the churches initially voted for the union by less than sixty-five per cent. When these churches voted in 1948 more than one in three voted "No." In 1949 efforts made during the extension-of-voting period had raised that to 72.8 per cent of the churches voting. Over 1,100 churches voted against "the Basis of Union!" At Omaha in 1956 one in eight of the General Council delegates voted against union.

At Claremont in 1952 only one in nineteen voted against union!

In June 1952 we were virtually a united fellowship and the General Council vote expressed "the substantial unity" of the churches, as it is required to do by its constitution.

"The Claremont Resolution" looked forward to a united fellowship with the Evangelical and Reformed Church and asked the joint executive committees to draft a proposed constitution for the General Synod of the united fellowship. It provided for "representatives of the different points of view among us"[64] on all important committees dealing with the union, and required that "every effort be made to preserve all the spiritual and temporal freedoms and rights now possessed by the Churches"[65] & other bodies. This was sound churchmanship, representative of the great spirit of the Claremont meeting under the gracious, firm, and fair leadership of Moderator Vere Loper. When fairness prevailed and the Spirit of the Master was given sway, the result was a resolution upon which 95 per cent could agree. Here is a real basis upon which our churches can unite with the Evangelical and Reformed Church.

Here is a basis for union rather than a basis for division.

Here is a bridge between the opposing viewpoints in our fellowship by which those who regard church union as a modern mandate and those who regard free churchmanship as a sacred trust can be brought together.

The Motive for Union

Many of us are eager for spiritual union. We are also eager to avoid the extremes of authoritarianism and libertarianism. To us, the fundamental motive for church union is to increase devotion and service to God according to the kindly, righteous, judicious, free spirit of Jesus Christ. To us, the Church is Christ's Church and its task is to bear witness to God's grace made known to us in Him. Church union is of worth insofar as it serves spiritual purposes. Unity of the spirit is an aim devoutly to be sought, but that goal *may* or *may not* be brought closer by organizational unification. We find it strange to read about organizational "re-union" of a Church of Christ which has never been organizationally united! In today's world those lands in which one Church dominates are examples of what we do not want to become (e.g., Spain, Eire, Italy, Greece, etc.) We believe free churchmanship offers the best way into spiritual oneness, into union without unification, into the largest possible usefulness for Christ! We believe the great present need of the ecumenical movement is a new, broad, creative free polity. We believe it is tragic that no attempt is being made to find and follow divine guidance toward such a polity. We believe the outmoded notions of centralization now being urged upon us will make necessary a new reformation in days to come. We believe the Church of Christ Universal is best served by vigorous, dedicated, free churches in the closest possible voluntary fellowship.

The Claremont Resolution was an open door to fresh vistas of hope for the Church Universal. Here it is in full:

"BE IT RESOLVED that this General Council of Congregational Christian Churches continues to look forward to a united fellowship of the Evangelical and Reformed and the Congregational Christian communions; and

"BE IT FURTHER RESOLVED that the Executive Committee be instructed to seek joint meetings with the General Council of the Evangelical and Reformed Church; that the resolutions submitted

61

by the Massachussets Congregational Conference and the New York Congregational Christian Conference be referred to those two bodies meeting jointly; and that all other resolutions and suggestions originating in our fellowship which are of common interest to the two communions be likewise referred to them; and

"BE IT FURTHER RESOLVED that those two bodies meeting jointly be requested, *if both approve*, to be responsible for *the preparation of a draft of a proposed constitution for the General Synod* of the united fellowship to be made available to the membership of both communions for discussion and suggestions.

"BE IT RESOLVED that on all the Congregational Christian bodies responsible for the implementing of the resolution above there be *representatives of the different points of view among us*; and that the process of cooption be employed whenever desirable; and

"BE IT FURTHER RESOLVED that the Executive Committee is requested to establish a consulting relationship with the Committee on Free Church Polity and Unity during the drafting of the proposed constitution; and

"BE IT FURTHER RESOLVED that in the preparation of such a draft every effort be made to preserve all the spiritual and temporal freedoms and rights now possessed by the individuals, churches, associations, conferences, and boards of this communion.

"(and) BE IT FURTHER RESOLVED that pending the final judgment of the New York Court of Appeals concerning the present appeal of the Cadman Church to that court no action should be taken which would in any way conflict with the due process of law or jeopardize the rights and standing of the General Council in the eyes of the law."[66]

The Claremont Resolution gave the mediators hope. As news of it spread across the country, Fred Meek said, "Something positive may yet be reached." The seventeen-to-one vote re-affirmed our conviction that Congregationalists wanted union with liberty, one Church Universal on the basis of New Testament polity.

This was the ONE resolution concerning "the merger" to which I gave a "yes" vote—and plunged into the tough task of gathering data to compile "Congregational Polity as Practiced in the United States" with renewed vigor and hope.

From M. Russell Boynton and Harry R. Butman of the New England Geographic Panel came a letter dated September 23, 1952, which expressed the widespread feeling about the increased value of our work.

"The work of the Committee on Free Church Polity and Unity is of first importance, as it is dealing with the matters which cannot be settled in the courts. The decisions of this Committee will bear significantly on our denominational future. As Massachusetts is the oldest and largest of the Congregational states, we have a very large share of responsibility for the successful prosecution of this task."[67]

Many who studied "Congregational Polity in the Documents" wrote as did Rev. James B. Yee of East Hampton, Connecticut (Oct. 12, '52):

"I have gone over it a couple of times carefully and for all the looking for the unacceptable, I really have to admit that I find nothing in the statement but what I agree with."[68]

The optimistic note was sounded by ardent proponents of the "merger" (which word I felt to be rather misleading). Charles Merrill wrote (Nov. 10, '52):

"Thank you very much for your good letter of October 14.

"You're quite right about 'merger'; however, I suppose it sprang up as a popular word and I am afraid that first and last we sometimes waste effort in opposing a popular word even if it is not technically accurate and may be even undesirable.

"I am quite with you in feeling the need for a stronger spiritual foundation. Wendell has asked me to act as chaplain at the December meeting of the Polity Committee. I have been studying anew the 17th Chapter of John and hope that I can comment on it in my chaplain's remarks in a non-controversial way. Certainly the union for which Jesus prayed was nothing if not spiritual. It does seem as if we ought to agree upon this and then in a perfectly friendly way go on to ask how a visible expression can best be given to the spiritual unity.

"Meanwhile, I am taking with me on a trip to New York your little book on 'The Upward Call'. I like what I have read of it already.

"I hope your work is developing most interestingly and fruitfully this fall and that you are keeping well."[69]

CHAPTER 2 NOTES

1. Leaflet *The Committee on Free Church Polity and Unity*, Oct. 17, 1950
2. Ibid
3. Leaflet Fifield, Oct. 17, 1950
4. Leaflet Fifield, Oct. 17, 1950
5. hdg notes written at the meeting. Hereafter referred to as "Notes."
6. Notes

7. Ibid
8. Notes
9. Ibid
10. Ibid
11. Ibid
12. Ibid
13. Ibid
14. Ibid
15. Ibid
16. Ibid
17. Ibid
18. Notes
19. Ibid
20. Ibid
21. Ibid
22. Ibid
23. Ibid
24. Notes
25. Ibid
26. Ibid
27. Ibid
28. Notes
29. Ibid
30. Ibid
31. Ibid
32. Ibid
33. Ibid
34. Ibid
35. PU Minutes, Dec. 12, 1950
36. Notes
37. PU Minutes, Dec. 13, 1950
38. PU Minutes, Dec. 12, 1950
39. Written Memo
40. Polity Committee Report, Apr. 17, 1951
41. Educators' Panel Report, 4/18/51
42. Superintendents' Panel Report, 4/18/51
43. Youth Panel Report, 4/18/51
44. Orchard, Ronald K., *Congregationalism To-day,* 1943, Independent Press, London, p. 74
45. Smith, K.L.C., *The Church and the Churches,* 1945, SCM Press, London, p. 29
46. Notes
47. Ibid
48. Gray to PU Committee members, Mar. 12, 1951
49. Gray to State Conference Superintendents, June 21, 1951
50. Notes
51. Ibid
52. Ibid
53. Kennebunkport Notes, Gray, op.cit.
54. PU Minutes 11/29/51
55. Ibid

56. Ibid
57. Educators' Panel Report 11/28/51
58. Merrill to Burton, 6-15-51
59. Gray to PU Committee Members, Nov. 2, 1951
60. Gray to Fifield, 2-8-52
61. Document circulated at 1952 General Council
62. Fifield to PU Committee members, August 15, 1952
63. Grey PU file, 1952 General Council meeting
64. Minutes, 1952 General Conference, 20, NY
65. Ibid, 20
66. Minutes, 1952 General Council, op.cit. 20
67. New England Panel to Gray, Sept. 23, 1952
68. Yee to Gray, Oct. 12, 1952
69. Merrill to Gray, Nov. 10, 1952

CHAPTER THREE

The Girding

Summer 1952, after the Claremont Council, was a time to gird for the yet harder task concerning Congregational Polity in practice,and the exploration of the possibilities of church unity expressed in organizational form for congregationally ordered Churches.

The evening before the last day of the General Council's meetings I left Southern California with 22 teenagers on a 77-day study/ mission "Odyssey" to Ireland, England, Scotland, France, Switzerland, Italy, Egypt, Lebanon, Jordan, Israel, Cyprus, Turkey, Greece . . . New York and Hartford. Face to face with Church leaders in each land we studied the polity of Congregationalists, Scots Presbyterians, French Evangelical Protestants, Swiss Reformed, Waldensians, Baptists and Copts in Egypt, Episcopalians in Lebanon and Jordan, Baptists in Israel, Eastern Orthodox at the patriarchate in Istanbul, Greek Orthodox and Greek Evangelical in Greece, and Roman Catholic in Italy including an audience with the pope. All 22 of us learned that polity makes a difference. The persecution of free church members in France (social and economic), in Italy, Egypt, the lands of the Bible, Turkey and Greece bore simple but eloquent testimony to the practical and spiritual fruits grown on authoritarian polity roots. The open-armed Waldensians and Greek Evangelicals showed us love triumphant over legal, social, educational, and even physical abuse and harassment. The Ecumenical Patriarch exemplified an Orthodox outreach to all Christian brothers, even under the restraints of Turkish law and custom.

If I had not been a free churchman on New Testament and theological grounds, the experiences of summer '52 would have made me one by the evident results of centralized creed, code and cult, in contrast to the transparent beauty of lives lived in free Churches, especially in Greece and Italy.

Home again on September 7th I was bone weary—as the toll of twenty-four hours a day for 77 successive days with 22 teenagers as guide, lecturer, travel escort, chaplain, physician, coach and confidant. They were a choice family of God, all part of our One-onta Pilgrim Fellowship. From them I learned anew that God can do great works if we are open to His Spirit. It is the Spirit that gives life and strength, and makes one family out of 22 very individual persons.

The task ahead in Congregational Polity was first to find the facts concering *practice*, and then, if possible, to discover how the Spirit could be given free course to unite peoples and churches in the only way that counts . . . in spirit and in truth.

Congregational Polity as Practiced

Just a few days after homecoming there arrived three letters from Dr. L. Wendell Fifield, general chairman. He fully realized the expectancy engendered by the Claremont General Council and sought to enlist the panels, superintendents, and committee members in an all-out effort to complete the mandate of our enlarged "study and report" in the 1952-1954 biennium.

The letter to the committee members read in part.[1] (9/5/52)

"I have given considerable thought to the effective functioning of our Committee on Free Church Polity and Unity during the next two years. The widespread confidence evidenced toward us by our fellowship places great responsibility upon us. I am sending you at this time some suggestions that I hope will be helpful to you as a committee member.

"Special emphasis should be put this fall upon the functioning of the Geographical Panels. *You can help*. While you cannot, by vote of the committee, serve as a member of one of these panels, you can establish a useful liaison with them. I suggest that you get in touch with the chairman of the panel in your area. Have a visit with him. Give him your impression of the importance of our work. Offer your help and cooperation. Give him any suggestions you think may be helpful. Keep advised as to the progress of the panel this fall. . . .

"I personally would greatly appreciate it if you would check on the personnel of each panel to be sure that both 'pro's' and 'anti's' are adequately represented. And then send me your opinion. It is very difficult at a distance to be sure that each panel is so composed as to merit the confidence of every Congregationalist in the area. I should like to supplement the judgment of the Panel Chairman with your opinion. Beyond these suggestions you will doubtless think of others which, in your advisory capacity, you can suggest to help make our Geographical Panels 100% effective in their work. . . .

"Now that we have virtually concluded the exploratory stage and entered the accomplishment stage of our work, we must function increasingly through committee groups. In order to do this, I am appointing the committees for this biennium with consideration for geographical proximity. This is done in the anticipation that committtees will work not alone through letters but also will hold meetings as their effective service may indicate. . . .

"The Committee on Congregational Polity for the biennium was: Henry David Gray, chairman; Burton, Pratt, Small, Swartz.

"Meantime, let us all be thinking and praying concerning our work. It certainly has been put squarely up to us, as I indicated in my letter to the entire organization, and we must not fail our fellowship.

"My anticipation of a splendid year of work together with my best wishes accompany this letter."

The letter to the state Conference Superintendents asked for close co-operation concluding:[2]

"Will you feel a responsibility to transmit either to your panel or directly to me any ideas that you may have at any time that will be helpful to our committee?

"May I also ask that in the event that any activities of your Geographical Panel seem to you to be ill-advised, you take up the matter promptly and frankly with its chairman.

"Our organization will very soon involve over a thousand Congregationalists in its work. It is very important that there be no overlapping, misunderstanding, duplication or cross purposes at any time. You can greatly help me, as chairman of the committee, by advising me at this point.

"The Committee on Free Church Polity and Unity has a very great sense of humility and of responsibility in the face of its vital task. I am sure that every one of its members wish me, in this letter, to express to you best wishes in your important work and join with me in requesting your prayers and your frank and fullest cooperation."

In the letter to the Geographic Panels stress was laid on the key importance of Congregational Polity as Practiced.[3]

"Plan to make report to Dr. Henry David Gray as requested in the printed report of his committee. This was the request to ascertain the actual practices of Congregationalism in your area and compare them with the report on Congregational Polity as found in the Documents. Prompt report to Dr. Gray will be very helpful as we need a report from his committee dealing with this matter at our meeting in November. . . . I suggest the quickest way to proceed is to send a copy directly to each association, conference and typical churches and ask them to report to you promptly. We must press for this information. Our fellowship expects results from us now, and we cannot proceed much further until we know what Congregationalism is in actual practice at present. There is no way to find out except to go to the source. This suggestion is of the utmost importance, therefore. . . .

"The effective functioning of the Geographical Panels will determine to no small degree whether our committee will have a report in 1954 which will measure up to the hopes and anticipations of our fellowship."

October 21, 1952, I wrote to the 1952-1954 members of the Congregational Polity Committee:[4]

"We have a rather difficult assignment this biennium which will require careful planning if it is to be accomplished. The problem is how to assemble authoritative data on present Congregational practice, and then to compile this in a useable form comparable to our report presented at the last Central Council on the basis of the documents. I wish that each one of you would give some thought to this matter and would send to me a one-page digest of your thinking on the matter of procedure. I am terribly anxious that our job shall be done thoroughly for it may prove to be the 'missing link' needed to enable us to move forward into unity with freedom."

I must not mislead; not everyone was optimistic. Malcolm Burton's letter to me of October 30 well expresses a view held by some:[5]

"Again I'm the skeptic, but having seen the good job you did on the documents perhaps I shouldn't be.

"On practice, however, it is more than ever one man's word against another. With such partisan attitudes in our fellowship as we have today, and with various leaders hauling and tugging at us to conform to their ideas, I fear that an objective study is next to impossible.

"Our committee ought to take a courageous stand. But we're more likely to wind up as mealy-mouthed as Brother Crawford of the lawyer's panel.

"My own thoughts are expressed in the manuscript for my book which I now consider finished. You saw only about half or two-thirds of it, and it's all been revised since Claremont (only slightly in most places, simply for smoother reading).

"My position in my book is that nothing is fixed or reliable at present and that different concepts are battling for supremacy within our fellowship. I give the advice that observers should wait another ten years or more before attempting an appraisal."

New York, N.Y., December 3-4, 1952

An entire briefcase was needed to carry the polity letters to New York for a special Congregational Polity meeting on December 2nd. My first draft was sketchy but it was obvious that a rather high degree of similarity prevailed concerning Congregational polity in the New England Churches. The main thrust of our meeting was analytical and procedural, in the expectation that each of us would seek out information from certain geographic panels, state superintendents, area association scribes, and Church ministers or clerks. Once compiled, I would send drafts for revision as quickly as possible.

Thus the Congregational Polity Commitee was able to report a plan for progress to the General Committee on December 3-4. Indicative of the dedication of the Polity and Unity Committee members is the fact that only one person, Miss Lucy Eldredge, did not choose to continue for the second two years. Another woman merger proponent was appointed by the Executive Committee as her replacement, Mrs. Rees T. Williams of New York. By happenchance three of our twenty-one were now named Williams. We had Ed Williams of Ohio, Mrs. R. T. Williams of New York and Mrs. R. Williams of Florida! Fred Whittaker was now secretary.

Two useful aspects of the December 1952 meeting were a prolonged general discussion and two long conversations with Wendell Fifield, for whom I had developed admiration, respect and affection.

The general discussion began when the Congregational Polity Committee submitted its report on December 3 and expanded the next day to include the meaning of ecumenicity for Congregationalists, the form of the final report towards which we were working, and, in particular, the Educators' Panel view of Congregational Polity as seen in our history in America.

By mid-afternoon of December 4 the Educators' Panel was requested to delve into "historic Congregational precedents in the field of ecumenicity,"[6] the "whole matter of the content and form of the report to the General Council (was) referred to the Central Committee without power"[7] to decide thereon, and the Congregational Polity Committee was encouraged to proceed with the Practice section with all deliberate speed and due caution.

It was the need for both speed and caution which concerned Wendell. Apparently off-the-record objections to the Documents section were made by denominational officials. The complaints did not challenge the report so much as object that what was said did not represent actual practice. For this reason Wendell accented the need for exactness in Congregational Polity as Practiced. "Some way must be found to write what will be immediately recognized as fair and accurate."[8] He told me he faced constant challenge: "Two very influential executives think this whole business is an exercise in futility."[9] I was sorry that there was pressure on Wendell, who was not really well, but not entirely suprised. He ended our after-session conversation with the admonition, "Do the best you can. The only hope of objectivity lies in your report. I may even have to call a special meeting to deal with what Bainton has written."[10]

History as Witness or Wish Fulfillment

The "special meeting" was held in Boston on February 11 and 12, 1953. Present were Bainton, Bradford, Burton, Meek, Merrill, Whittaker, Chairman Fifield and myself as chairman of the Congregational Polity Committe.

Three happenings hastened the meeting. In January the Rev. Harry R. Butman published in *The Free Lance* a long review of Malcolm Burton's book *Destiny for Congregationalism*. The review opened with these words:

"Malcolm K. Burton's forthcoming book, 'Destiny for Congregationalism', is a work no serious student of contemporary Congregationalism can afford to ignore. The book is a sword, and the razor edge of its logic is backed by a massive weight of fact. And Mr. Burton swings his weapon well.

"For weapon this book is, make no mistake. Never in modern times has such a critical appraisal of our denominaton appeared, nor such a merciless analysis of the details of our flight from freedom . . . . The biting quality of his arguments, so pronounced in his pamphleteering days, has not been lessened by the lag in merger action, but has rather been made more lethal by the backing of sober thought and close study."[11]

Second, I mailed 83 letters to superintendents and panel members and received 36 replies within two weeks. These letters indicated high expectation of action by our committee.

Third, by word of mouth and letter there was spreading a vague idea that Congregational history showed a polity almost "presbyterial" and certainly "connectional" in character.

Faced with pre-judgment on the central issue, yet possessed of the first fruits of our collection and systemization work on Congregational Polity as Practiced, an early meeting was essential. Hence, the Boston gathering.

I packed two large briefcases, one with letters, drafts, and panel reports regarding "Practice," and one with historical documents from Church history, from England, Holland, New England and the "Plan of Union," 1852, 1865, 1871, 1913, 1931 and 1936 national meetings—all marked and tabbed for ready reference.

The meeting ranged over the accuracy possible in the "Practice" section, which was answered by the 37 replies and panel reports, to the section on "organic union" which I was asked to write based on Merrill's draft, to the outline of our final report which Wendell undertook to piece together, to Professor Ronald Bainton's paper on "Congregational Polity in our History."

In front of me are both my notes and Wendell Fifield's notes on the Boston meeting, together with 5½-page single-spaced comments by Ronald Bainton dated February 13, 1953.

Consideration of the form of the Polity and Unity Report led to general agreement on an introduction, spiritual and theological basis of ecumenicity, the syllabus, Congregational Polity in Documents, Practice and History, types of church union, and recommendations. The most exciting development was the emergence of covenant church union. Informal discussion on the first evening centered on the inherent hurdles which free churchmanship presented to union or unification movements. I listened most of the evening. Then I commented, "The major failure of the approaches discussed is that they are based on expediency. The search seems to be for an innocuous way to do what some want to do, namely merge. Where is religious conviction in all this?" Bainton replied, "Religion isn't limited to statements of belief. It also embraces action." Burton felt, "The point is just how to do what New York wants to do." Then Bradford spoke in his slow, soft voice, "Let us not prejudge the issue. Henry, can you suggest what action a Congregational Church COULD take which would be religiously sound and yet permit union? Surely we are not condemned to isolation just because we hold religious convictions."

There was silence. Wendell was first to speak. "We seem to have come to the heart of the question of how Congregationalists can participate in the ecumenical movement. That's what our whole study is all about. Perhaps I might phrase the question this way: What is unique in Congregationalism that we can contribute to the ecumenical movement?"[12] To that I replied rather slowly and hesitantly, "Just thinking aloud I'd say the religious foundation of a Congregational Church is a covenant between persons who voluntarily accept the God and Father of our Lord Jesus Christ as their God, and who agree to live and work together as God's Spirit leads them. There just isn't any authority except conscience under Christ, and, even there, differences are fully accepted. There is no demand for conformity. None at all. I think what I've said is true of substantially all the Church constitutions or Articles of Association I've ever read."[13]

Wendell leaned forward, "Is what you have just said applicable *beyond* the local Church?"[14]

"What do you mean?"

"Is an association based on a covenant?"

"Not in the sense that its members are pledged to live and work together in a single worshipping Church."

"But isn't there an agreement between those present to seek the mind of Christ?"

"Of course."

Burton commented, "The agreement of certain elected representatives who function for several hours and then go home to bed isn't the same as a Church covenant." Meek sharpened the discussion. "Malcolm's correct. No church-body outside the Church is a truly 'gathered people of God'. Nevertheless I'm not prepared to say that such bodies have no convenantal basis whatsoever. They exist only because of agreements between Churches. Now the word 'agreement' is not exactly the same as the word 'covenant' but both words imply a basis for common action."[15]

Again there was silence. The hour was late. Wendell summed up, "This may be an approach to the ecumenical opportunity. It comes rather tardily into our discussions, and none of us are quite sure what it means. It is an idea that must be studied, developed, and given form and substance between now and the June meeting of the general committee. Decision as to its value and what should be done about it rests with the entire committee. May I suggest that evaluation of the idea be withheld until it is presented in completed form by the Central Committee in June."[16]

With a benediction, the meeting adjourned.

Under date of March 16, 1953, a general memo from Wendell Fifield stated the substance of the covenant idea.

An historical paper by Professor Bainton presented on the morning of February 12 traced CHANGES in Congregational Churches across the centuries. As reiterated in his lengthy memo of February 18, the main points were:

> "Our historians should address themselves to the question of what is essential to Congregationalism. Plainly our original pattern has been modified in a great many respects. The early Congregational settlements in this country were theocratic rather than democratic. There was a union of church and state, and in several notable instances, a restrictive franchise. The arm of the magistrate was invoked to enforce ecclesiastical penalties, Witches and Quakers were hanged. Ministers were ordained not for life, but only for the duration of service in a particular parish. The Christian year was utterly rejected, and the festival of Thanksgiving instituted in its stead. The observance of Christmas did not return to New England until the 1850's. Church architecture was severely anti-Catholic. The center of the church was the pulpit before which were ranged in rows the banks of pews. Singing was without even the giving of pitch. Windows were plain glass. The taking of the covenant carried with it subscription to a statement of faith, in the beginning the Westminster Confession for substance of Doctrine.
>
> "Today church and state are separate; religious liberty is endorsed; ministers are ordained for life; the Christian year has come back even to Lent and Good Friday; many churches center on the alter with pulpit and lectern on the sides; church music is planned and elaborate; and storied windows have become almost the rule. Since 1931 there has been no written statement of faith.
>
> "In the face of so much change some claim that the essence of Congregationalism consists in its polity, and that this has remained unchanged. To which the reply is that Congregationalism for well nigh a century was Presbyterian in structure in the state of Connecticut.
>
> "What then is distinctive and abiding in our witness? I should be tempted to look for the permanent element in the concept of the holy commonwealth, a society organized under God, directed by the elect, conducted by persuasion. . . .
>
> "Another point profoundly affecting the attitude of Congregationalists to other bodies has been the distinction between the fundamentals and the non-essentials. On the latter we have been willing to allow great diversity of practice to those who did not make absolutes out of the non-essentials. That is why we are ready to

75

permit either sprinkling or immersion, only to those, however, who will respect and work in fellowship with those of another persuasion. In this area our spirit has been widely latitudinarian, but on points which we consider fundamental, we have been quite rigid.

"Our Theological Committee is commissioned to draft a statement of the bearing of theology upon the possibilities of church union. We are all agreed, of course, that as the disciples of a common Lord, we should be one, but precisely in what sense we should be one, is under discussion. For some, a spiritual sense suffices, whereas others see an organizational unity as implied. For myself I would side with those who find in this text of John's Gospel nothing going beyond a spiritual unity. I would emphatically dissent from those who insist that any division in organization is scandal and sin. I would roundly affirm that the sects have performed a very useful function in the life of the Church. Sometimes schism has been necessary in order to correct moral and doctrinal abuses, and the rivalry of the sects has been a mutual stimulus. The Church of Rome, in fact, is never so fine as when confronted by a strong Protestantism. The sects have revived and conserved variant elements in the common tradition which otherwise might have lapsed. The formation of smaller entities has also produced stronger loyalties and more intimate fellowships. There is, of course, no point in preserving divisions after their purpose has been served, but we are not to brand all divisions as scandal and sin, whether in the past or in the present. Only is there scandal and sin if the division is marked by rancor and a lack of mutual respect and brotherly love. . . .

"I would hold that the individualism of Protestantism applies only to the direct relationship of the individual to God and does not require one form and one form only of polity, and when it comes to the sense of the meeting, this can be felt and acted on even in a Presbyterial or an Episcopal system, though I concede that Congregational church government is more conducive to the application of this principle.

"Another point of which we have heard much is that the Holy Spirit is constricted by organization. The fewer rules and the less centralization, the freer is the scope of the Spirit. But here let us recall the early practice with regard to music. The supposition was that the giving of pitch for singing impeded the Spirit. Experience, however, has certainly demonstrated that the Spirit can obtain greater heights under a framework of rules and even under the direction of a conductor.

"Some adduce the authority of Scripture and remind us that early Congregationalists thought to find their polity in the New Testament and believed that the New Testament pattern should be binding for all times and circumstances. I would submit that subsequent scholarship has rendered dubious the assumption that only one form of polity is discoverable in the New Testament itself. Even in the very early periods some diversity was manifest. . . . .

"As for the merger with the E and R, I think we should do something more positive than simply to say that we will not forsake the autonomy of the local church. Neither do I think we should be bound by the advice of the Council at Claremont to proceed only on a national level. I cannot see that there is any particular reason for union at the national level. To make our national bodies larger or to make larger the blocks of sending up a delegate would only be to make our structure more unwieldy. The point at which the union has merit is in the local churches and associations because in some areas Congregationalists are weak and in others the E and R are scattered. These isolated churches would be strengthened by the larger fellowship. . . . .

"Finally I would say that although a majority should be tender of a minority and not try to ram a program down the throat of the unwilling, at the same time a minority should have respect for the wishes of a majority and not seek to frustrate it by a long succession of legal suits. Even the Quakers have sometimes disowned members simply for rambunctiousness. The Holy Spirit is a Spirit of mutual regard and brotherly respect."[17]

There is a temporateness in the memo which was not in the meeting, chiefly because of a heated argument between Bainton and Burton. Burton flatly asserted, "It won't do to pick and choose what bits of history you want to. That's not Congregationalism."[18] The gentle spirit of my companion at Kennebunkport vanished. His face flushed. His voice rose. He addressed the chairman. "Do I have to put up with this impertinence? Here I am Professor of Ecclesiastical History at Yale, the oldest and most respected divinity school in the country, and this man who hasn't even a B.D. has the affrontery to tell me I'm misreading Congregational history. This is preposterous."[19] Burton cut in, "Is it? Then prove me wrong!"[20]

Wendell tapped the table, a rare gesture for him. "Gentlemen," he said, "Gentlemen. Let's be reasonable. Does anyone else wish to comment on Dr. Bainton's paper?"[21]

I inquired, "Is the paper proposed for inclusion in our report, or is it for information only?"[22]

The author answered, "It's the official report of the Educators' Panel of which I am chairman, with regard to Congregational polity in our history."[23]

"In that case, Mr. Chairman, I would respectfully present, from the sources themselves, the precise history of our polity . . . but

NOT of the customs followed by particular Churches with reference to statements of faith, forms of work, baptismal procedures, festivals, architecture or the Christian Year."[24]

"I think we understand what 'polity' means, Henry," was Wendell's dry remark. "Proceed."[25]

"This will take some time."

"Is it necessary?"

"Only if the question before us is to include Professor Bainton's statement in the Committee Report as our finding about Congregational polity in our history."

Dr. Bainton answered, "That's exactly what my paper is."[26]

I pulled over my second briefcase and took out ten volumes with tabs for place marks. "In that case, Mr. Chairman, I propose to trace Congregational polity through the actual statements of our Churches, especially as recorded in councils, or at the request of councils."[27]

"Proceed," Wendell said, almost grimly.

The same volumes are piled before me as I write. A great many of the tabs are still in place. There has never been any question as to the "Congregational Principles" of Robert Browne (1582). As Williston Walker wrote, "The model for their organization Browne found in the New Testament. The believers should be united to God and to one another by a covenant, entered into, not by compulsion, but willingly."[28] Of such a church "Christ is the head."[29] Browne maintained the "meeting of sundrie churches are when the weaker churches seeke helpe of the stronger, for deciding or redressing of matters or else the stronger looke to them for redresse."[30]

"These twin emphases in polity have remained constant in Congregational polity, that is the self-completeness of each Church under Christ as head, and, the duty and privilege of each Church to seek or to give advice or counsel, *willingly*. Our cardinal historic documents never retreat from these twin propositions. Whenever any body of Churches or ministers strayed from loyalty to these principles, as in the Connecticut/Presbyterian 1801 'Plan of Union' the immediate result was schism; the denouement was reaffirmation (1852, 1865, 1871) of both principles.

"Dr. Bainton referred to unions in Canada and India. Both resulted in division of Congregationalism. Neither has existed long enough to establish a pattern. In both countries the Congregational Churches were off-shoots of missionary bodies which retained un-congregational control over them. In both lands free congregational churches are being gathered at the present time.

"The more salient fact for Congregationalists in the United States is the *direct, unvarying* witness of all our major synods and councils except Saybrook. The testimony of the 'London Confession of 1589' proves that the Barrowism presented by some contemporary historians as 'connectional' is presbyterially organized *within* the local Church; as Walker says, 'the administration of the church is the concern of all the brethern,' and there is NO authoritative over-body. None.[31]

"The sharp distinction between congregational and presbyterial polities is stated explicitly in 'The Points of Difference' of 1603,[32] in the 'Army Debates' under Cromwell,[33] in the Savoy Declaration of 1658,[34] in the Heads of Agreement of 1691,[35] in the Massachusetts Proposals of 1705,[36] in the Saybrook Platform of 1708,[37] the Synod of 1680,[38] and in the Boston declaration of 1865.[39]

"We are not limited to councils which compared, contrasted or sought to combine congregational and presbyterial polities.

"Our unbroken line in America exhibits positive proclamation of the Congregational Way from the first general meeting, the Cambridge Synod of 1646, to the Constitution of the newly uniting Congregational and Christian Churches in 1931 in Seattle."

I then quoted from each of the above documents, from the Synods of 1657, 1662, and 1669, from the 1871 Constitution of the National Council of the Congregational Churches and from the 1931 Constitution of the General Council of the Congregational Christian Churches.

The books of John Wise of Ipswich (1710-1717) set the tone for all New England except Connecticut, and Nathaniel Emmons in 1860 put our polity plainly: "One church has as much power as another. All churches are sisters, and stand upon a level . . . Since every Christian Church is a free, voluntary society, it is in its own nature absolutely independent."[40]

"The 1865 Declaration acknowledged 'no rule of faith but the word of God' and declared 'adherence to the faith and order of the primitive churches held by our fathers' in the following:

"'*Resolved*, That this Council recognizes as distinctive of the Congregational polity—

"'First, The principle that the local or Congregational Church derives its power and authority directly from Christ, and is not subject to any ecclesiastical government exterior or superior to itself.

79

"'Second, That every local or Congregational Church is bound to observe the duties of mutual respect and charity which are inlcuded in the communion of Churches one with another; and that every Church which refuses to give an account of its proceedings, when kindly and orderly desired to do so by neighboring churches, violates the law of Christ.

"'Third, That the ministry of the gospel by members of the Churches who have been duly called and set apart to that work implies in itself no power of government, and that ministers of the gospel not elected to office in any Church are not a hierarchy, nor are they invested with any official power in or over the Churches.'[41]

"When the National Council was organized at Oberlin in 1871 Congregational polity was re-stated as distictively as it was by Robert Browne!

"'The right of government resides in local Churches, . . . which are responsible directly to the Lord Jesus Christ, the One Head of the Church universal and of all particular Churches; but that all Churches, being in communion one with another as parts of Christ's catholic Church, have mutual duties subsisting in the obligations of fellowship.

"'The Churches, therefore, while establishing this National Council for the furtherance of the common interests and work of all the churches, do maintain the Scriptural and inalienable right of each Church to self-government and administration; and this National Council shall never exercise legislative or judicial authority, nor consent to act as a council of reference.'[42]

"In point of fact the General Council which created the Committee on Free Church Polity and Unity re-affirmed the essence of Congregational polity.

"'We hold sacred the freedom of the individual soul and the right of private judgment. We stand for the autonomy of the local church and its independence of ecclesiastic control. We cherish the fellowship of churches, united in district, state and national bodies for counsel and co-operation.'[43]

"The witness of Congregational history is clear. The twin principles of freedom and fellowship for counsel and advice have NOT been changed.

"Possibly confusion comes because of slipshod usage of the word 'church' to mean everything from a building, to a denomination, to the universal company of Christ's followers, to a particular people of God. Let us reject this confusion. To claim the presence of God's Spirit 'where two or three are gathered together in Christ's Name' has nothing whatever to do with whether those who are gathered shall compel others to believe or act as they feel led to believe or act. *If* the Spirit is present what emerges will be convincing *for those to whom the Spirit spoke.*

"When the General Council assembles it is about a thousand persons, present by virtue of office or by election, serving for two years under a constitution and By-laws. NO WAY is the General Council A CHURCH OF BELIEVERS who have covenanted with God and with one another, VOLUNTARILY AND ON THEIR OWN BEHALF (*not* by the election of others) TO LIVE TOGETHER AND WORK TOGETHER, *NOT* for two years but forever, or until covenantal bonds are mutually released.

"There really isn't the slightest doubt as to what our history says Congregational polity IS."

My long presentation was listened to with concentrated attention. No sooner was it over than Malcolm leaned forward with index finger pointed and said, "There, Rollie, *that's* what history says."[44] I think all were as shocked as I was by this outburst, especially the use of the familiar diminutive for the noted professor's name. The chairman looked his disapproval, then addressed the meeting. "Are there questions?"

Whittaker, himself an historian, volunteered, "Dr. Gray and Dr. Bainton are discussing two different streams of history. Does Dr. Gray contend what he has presented is THE ONLY possible reading of Congregational polity in our history?"[45]

"Not at all," I replied. "Obviously all history is subject to interpretation, and selection too. What IS clear is that our declarations of polity are unusually consistent. The eddies of difference never became determinative. Congregational polity in the main stream of our history is undisputably reflected in the historic documents from which I have quoted AND THERE ARE NO OTHER DOCUMENTS OF EQUAL STANDING."[46]

Professor Bainton started to say something, caught himself, folded up his manuscript, and concluded, "I'm not going to argue about whether or not I know Congregational history."[47]

The Chairman asked the committee, "Does anyone wish to vote against Dr. Gray's presentation." No one spoke. "Then," he continued, "we will proceed to our discussion of organic union after lunch."

It must be one of the oddest quirks of history that Charles Merrill's paper on organic union was remanded to me with the request to include all forms of union which had been mentioned in the meeting. I agreed to do this, if permitted to do so in the autumn and relay the revision to Dr. Merrill. This was agreed upon.

When we adjourned in Boston the testimony of history was established. And I was weary.

Steady Progress at Seabury House

Seabury House in Greenwich, Connecticut, was the site of the June 15 through 19, 1953 meeting of the general committee.

In preparation I wrote to Congregational Polity Committee members on May 7:[48]

"We will need to be ready to present our findings in regards to Congregational practice. At the present moment I have received from our correspondents in the various areas about 75% of all the expected returns. I suppose this is a sufficiently representative group for us to use as a sampling. It represents all different states and all different shades of opinion. I may say though, that there is a remarkable similarity through the larger portion of the returns.

"1. Shall I make a digest of these returns and circulate it to you?

"2. Could you get to me by the last day of May your reactions and comments on such an abstract if you received it by May 15th?

"3. Is there any addition you wish to make on our already published document dealing with the polity of the denomination as it appears in its printed documents? The comments which I have had in writing have all been of a minor revisionary character. Not any have suggested that we were in error in any important point. Mostly, it has been the addition of details or the approbation of what we have already done.

"4. It turns out, from my advance information now received, that the International Council meeting to be held in St. Andrews this summer is to deal very largely with some of the same issues with which we are wrestling. It is therefore important that our work should be in such shape as to be able to be quoted as representative of the American Congregational scene.

"5. I would like very much to be able to feel that our polity subcommittee had some special contribution of a positive character to make. Would you be willing to send to me whatever concrete suggestions you have as to the precise steps we might take toward larger co-operative endeavor within the framework of the free churches. I am especially interested in the *concrete*. Moreover, I wish that you might be able, in our polity committee, to bring to the Seabury House meeting the set of 'Articles' which presented the 'Congregational' view of a national Congregational pattern. If you would be willing to write such, and send it to me, I should be more than pleased.

"Our committee has not done as much work this year as perhaps it ought to have, and I feel that we should do as much as we can in this next period ahead, since the Seabury House meeting will prove to be the most important we have yet held in the history of our committee. It is bound to. We now have at hand the material from our documentary study, and we are in the process of having in hand, all the material from our pragmatic comments on the documents and on present-day Congregationalism. Therefore, it sould be possible for us to go ahead and do something very worthwhile as grist of the mill at Seabury. I hope very much that we may be able to do this, and look forward to receiving from you, your early comments on this letter."

Concerning my letter Wendell wrote to me on May 14, 1953:[49]

"Thanks for the copy of the letter. It is fine. I share with you the hope that we can produce something that can be quoted. I contemplate the coming meeting with a mixture of eagerness, enthusiasm, awe, and concern."

The Seabury sessions were marked by serious, detailed discussion and editing of the printed "Report of Congregational Polity as Described in its Constitutional Documents." Of the twenty changes recorded on my working copy fifteen were improvements in word choice or minor additions or subtractions.

The five additional changes were:

1. A change in the association/church section to remove the word "recognition" which had acquired technical meaning in the courts. "Received into the fellowship" replaced it.
2. A new paragraph was framed to describe the Laymen's Fellowship.
3. A replacement paragraph described the voting membership of the General Council as required by action of the Claremont amendment to its constitution.
4. Under "National Societies" we inserted an important qualifying phrase, "accepted by the General Council as the agency of the Congregational Christian Churches for . . ."
5. Council for Social Action substitute wording to reflect decisions made at Claremont was inserted.

With these changes the Documents report was given tentative approval;[50] since we had decided that final approval of all sections would be voted upon at our final meeting only.

Congregational Practice and Union of Churches

Each person had studied my preliminary collation of replies on "Congregational Christian Polity as it is Practiced in the U.S." On Monday (6/15/53) the chairman asked each to comment on that report and to relate the Churches to the ecumenical movement in the light of all we have learned since 1950.

My hand-written notes made as members spoke are before me. Bainton began, "The system we have is one of responsibility without authority." That implies "diversity within the same structure ... (and) ... union without sacrifice of Congregational essentials." He espoused the position that the Apostle Paul acted as "an overseer" of the Churches using "persuasion"; he might even be called "Bishop Paul." (*That* was said half in jest.) Then the professor raised a key issue, "Why are we interested in union with the Evangelical and Reformed Church when we are closer to the Disciples?"[51]

Whittaker was troubled by my spiritual and theological basis for polity. "Any polity which recognizes no loyalty beyond the local church excludes (others) from fellowship." We may need to "set up a new denomination to include several others called simply 'The Church of Christ', or, 'United Protestant Church'."[52]

Small remarked that "Congregationalism is more like a living organism than a legal order." "Freedom and responsibility need definition, especially with reference to the relationships of church, association, conference, and general council." Above all "be sure the committee report is NOT either *for* or *against* the merger."[53]

Kleinschmidt injected a critical note, "I have a feeling that we, in this committee, take it for granted that we *want* church union without asking what are the real results other than an emotional feeling of unity." "The practical values of unity need to be explored."[54]

Bradford addressed a central issue much overlooked. "The preservation of our fellowship is my chief concern. To try to advance church union by uniting a piece of a denomination with another doesn't make sense to me. One of the precious values of our denomination is our fellowship with many differing points of view."[55]

Briggs was blunt. "Make the report understandable."[56]

84

Louise Williams added, "Few people in our churches know anything about polity or unity." She implied that our committee report should be disseminated and studied widely, then concluded, "We have to think about possible fellowship with others perhaps beyond the proposed E & R merger."[57]

Ed Williams remarked, "You can't mix presbyterial and congregational government. The United Church of Canada did NOT succeed in doing this. There is a large Presbyterian Church growing much faster than the United Church. What made the United Church in Canada possible was the handling of property rights through a special Act of Parliament. There is no legal way to take such action in the United States."[58]

Swartz voiced the aim of many, "I hope we can chart a course *in principle* applicable to any future ecumenical movements. I'd be glad to go along if we can move forward apart from the E & R."[59]

Cannon did not like the tone of those who had spoken. "Are we only to unite with like-groups, or is there a need to carry a diminished Congregational witness into a wider union?"[60]

Mary Ann Williams spoke at considerable length outlining a fresh position as the result of much thought. In brief she asked the question, "Is organic union the goal which expresses Christian unity?" then answered it by saying, "Organizational unity is the outgrowth of witnessing together." It is a mistake to refer to the Church of South India procedures as applicable to the U.S. "The younger churches take actions which are valid for them, but they do not necessarily give a pattern for us." Perhaps we need *local ecumenicity* most, and "wider co-operation with visitors . . . even joint financial objectives," by means of which "a sure foundation would be given to whatever type of union resulted therefrom." Our emphasis should be on "doing what can be done now." She concluded her eloquent statement: "Discover truth together. Make voluntary local unions by initiative."[61]

Hurst maintained that the committee report should (1) "re-affirm the ecumenical ideal," (2) "re-affirm Congregational principles," (3) "state the spiritual situation," (4) depict "a united form in which Congregational Christians can share," (5) "cultivate fellowship relations on levels beyond the local church," (6) seek to portray "an actual visible and comprehensible embodiment of a united church."[62]

Fifield spoke in detail of the work yet to be done by the committee under three points: (1) "Is organic union possible? under

85

what circumstances? (2) Are there ways to *alter* Congregational Polity "such as a constitutional convention by instructed delegates from the Churches?" (3) "The constructive thing is to find out what CAN be done, and then chart its course. I still believe there is a way . . . and we are moving in the direction of finding it."[63]

Bradford terminated our discussion, "My plea is to keep the unity of our Congregational Christian fellowship."[64]

COMPARISON of the Seabury, 1953, statements with those made in New York in 1950 reveals a remarkable degree of coming together. Wrestling with the written documents had compelled us to see the characteristics of Congregational Polity. Virtually all of us now asked, "What CAN be done which will both enlarge liberty and effect some kind of united action?" On Tuesday we tackled Polity in Practice!

Congregational Polity as Practiced

My handwritten first draft of "Congregational Polity as it is currently Practiced in the United States"[65] is before me. Changes made in the paragraphs about the Churches are of two types: rearrangement of paragraphs, or clarification of language. There are no substantial changes. This was one of our pleasant surprises; for nobody knew what would be uncovered by the 140 persons who, by now, were contributing to our study.

The only keen discussion concerned the Church/association/conference/national bodies relationship. All agreed as to what the relationship was. The difficulty was how to put it into words. In June 1953 we saw both the "voluntary" and the "responsible" character of the relationships. I did not frame my definition of "responsible freedom" until aboard the plane.

There were varying opinions about the paragraphs on the associations. This was obviously a weak link in Congregational Polity. Wording the paragraph on "credentials" required inclusion of the custom prevailing in Northern California, Vermont and those areas like Wyoming where association and conference are identical. This was accomplished as follows: "In several conferences one or more of the associations has designated the conference, or a conference committee, to perform (credential) functions on behalf of the association."[66]

Standards for membership of Churches in an association pitted Burton against Cannon; one claiming "the Church is the sole judge of its own membership" and the other asserting "every parliamen-

86

tary body has the elementary right to determine its own membership." Final wording was not achieved at this meeting.[67]

The state Conference paragraphs show mostly editorial changes in this version. But neither the conferences nor the national church-bodies had been thoroughly canvassed with regard to Practice in June 1953. Requests had been sent but pursuit of replies was yet to come.

By Thursday I was instructed (1) to "revise the section on doctrine," (2) "digest the introduction to practice section," (3) "to prepare a section on distinctive features of Congregational Polity needed as a prelude to union," (4) to complete the "Congregational Polity as Practiced" statements, (5) to send "the revised section on organic union to Alfred Swartz" and (6) to organize suggestions as to how to set up a commission or convention on Covenant Union."[68]

Covenant Union

The Seabury 1953 meetings explored the idea of "Covenant Union" at length.

Wendell Fifield presented a slightly more-than-three-page statement consisting of seven sections.[69] In the course of detailed discussion the statement was reduced to five paragraphs on one page.

The issues under debate were: How do free Churches enter ANY wider church-body with ANY authority? What happens to Churches which vote against union? What are the powers of the General Council? Can the General Council act without approval of the Churches?

None of these issues was resolved at this meeting; they became a main facet of our study in 1953-1954. My task included preparation of "Principles and Procedures as a Basis for Union" and a try at phrasing "A Summary of Polity Principles on Ecumenicity as Determined by our History, Polity and Practice."

CHAPTER 3 NOTES

1. W. Fifield to H. D. Gray, Sept. 5, 1952.
2. Fifield to Conference Superintendents, Sept. 5, 1952.
3. Fifield to Geographic Panels, Sept. 5, 1952
4. Gray to members Congregational Polity Committee (CPC)
5. M. K. Burton to Gray, Oct. 30, 1952
6. PU Minutes 12/3-4/52
7. Ibid

8. Notes
9. Notes
10. Notes
11. *Free Lance,* ed. & pub. Joseph J. Russell, Holbrook, MA, January, 1953
12. Notes
13. Ibid
14. Notes
15. Ibid
16. Ibid
17. Ronald Bainton, Boston, Feb. 12, 1953.
18. Notes
19. Ibid
20. Ibid
21. Ibid
22. Ibid
23. Ibid
24. Ibid
25. Ibid
26. Ibid
27. Ibid
28. Quotation indicates my reconstruction from notes and pencil-marked books. Direct quotations from others are indicated separately.
29. Walker, Williston, *Creeds, Platforms of Congregationalism,* 1893, Scribners, N.Y., p. 13
30. Ibid, p. 14
31. Ibid, p. 31
32. Walker, op. cit., pp. 78 ff.
33. Woodhouse, A.S.P. (ed), *Puritanism and Liberty,* (1647-9), J. M. Dent, London 1938/51 *passion*
34. Peel, Albert, *The Savoy Declaration,* Independent Press, London, 1939, pp. 70ff.
35. Walker, op. cit, pp. 455-462
36. Dexter, Henry M., *Congregationalism,* etc., 1880, Harper, N.Y., pp. 488-494
37. Walker, op. cit., pp. 503-506
38. Ibid, pp. 409-439
39. Ibid, pp. 553-569
40. Dexter, op. cit., p. 508, note
41. Walker, op. cit., pp. 567-568
42. Ibid, p. 573
43. 1954 Minutes, General Council, N.Y., p. 112
44. Notes
45. Ibid
46. Ibid
47. Ibid
48. Gray to CPC members, May 7, 1953
49. Fifield to Gray, May 14, 1953
50. Minutes, PU June 15-19, 1953
51. Notes
52. Ibid
53. Ibid

54. Ibid
55. Notes
56. Ibid
57. Ibid
58. Ibid
59. Ibid
60. Ibid
61. Notes
62. Ibid
63. Ibid
64. Ibid
65. hdg file
66. Gray PU file, some handwritten some typed versions, all dated.
67. Notes
68. PU Minutes, 6/53
69. Gray, PU Committee file

CHAPTER FOUR

Congregational Churchmanship at St. Andrews World Council

I travelled directly from Greenwich, Connecticut to St. Andrews, Scotland, where the Seventh International Congregational Council met 20 June to 29 June, 1953. The grey stone walls of the ancient University were swathed in the light rain called "Scottish mist." Of the sixty-eight U.S. delegates, only one, Rev. Max Strang of Iowa, was a C.C./E.R. merger opponent. Five were mild mediators. I was the sole active mediator. Sixty-one were proponents of the merger. Ordinarily, this would not have been noticeable. But the theme of St. Andrews was "Congregational Churchmanship."

Saturday evening was given over to ceremonial welcome. Then Sunday morning the Rev. Douglas Horton, M.A., D.D., moderator of the ICC, immediately set the scene for a re-definition of Congregational Polity:

> "If the constituting fact of the Church is the presence of Christ, then polity must be made to conform to the expectedness of His presence, providing authority at the point where He is most likely to make His will known. To us Congregationalists this means that the local Church must be left free, for we know that Christ is accustomed to make his will known there. That fact alone gives the local Church its authority. . . .

> "Our task . . . will not be finished until the Congregational Churches of the world remind one of the unity of heaven. . . .

> "In order to assist us all in the development of our oneness, I trust that this body will authorize a continuing committee to publish a

book on the theme of this meeting itself. One could wish that the thoughts, . . . laid . . . on our hearts by our speakers, might be gathered together in logical unity, . . . and . . . be made . . . a volume on *Congregational Churchmanship* which by its very excellence might *become normative for our Congregational world.* The working together to produce such a book would be unitive: the book itself would become a symbol of our oneness in Christ. . . .

"It is all very well to realize that Christ, being at the heart of every Church makes it to the inwardly prepared a vestibule of heaven. But it is very terrible to realize that Christ is also our judge. Said John Owen, 'It is Christ who . . . will come Himself . . . to take vengeance on them that obey not the gospel.' (*An Exposition on Psalm CXXX,* page 266, 1690)

"Christ will be present at these meetings at St. Andrews. He will be watching us. His vengeance is not usually violent. It can sometimes be wished that it were: it would then be more evident and resistible. The vengeance He takes upon those who turn away from Him is the desiccation of motive, the growth of a sense of meaninglessness in life. In a communion it takes the form of a loss of the sense of mission. Let us determine that this shall not happen here. . . .

"There can be no lessening of the sense of mission among those who wait upon the Lord. His arm is not shortened, and those who yield themselves to be His instruments do not rust and grow dull. . . .

"Let us here be prepared to fight a good fight. Let us be ready to receive new insights and new powers; God through us *can* clothe our Churches in strength and through them *can* come His will to be done on earth as it is—in heaven."[1]

At the first plenary session a "Message to the Churches" was introduced which cannonized the moderator's novel interpretations of Congregational Polity. Not having had time to read the document I moved that action be postponed until all had both read it and shared in the Council's discussions. The delay may have been granted as a courtesy since I had been the speaker on theology in 1949, the convenor of the first International Congregational Youth Assembly, one of six members of the 1945 War Damage Survey team, leader of youth Odysseys to the British Churches in 1948 and 1952, and was the author of two widely read books published in London. I feel sure that action was NOT postponed because I was chairman of the Congregational Polity Committee!!

The ICC program at St. Andrews hammered at the following novel ideas: occasional council = church; the presence of the Holy Spirit = authority for council actions; the mission of the Churches = service directed by councils, and Congregational superintendent = classic bishop. All the American speakers had received from me copies of reports of the Committee on Polity and Unity, and must, therefore, have been aware that though no final votes had been taken we already KNEW the testimony of our Documents and our History, and, we were in the process of a thorough, painstaking study of our practice.

President R. H. Stafford forthrightly declared, "I must confess . . . that . . . no value save of expediency attaches to any item in Church polity."[2] Yet he continued:

"Now our question is: The local Church being by definition independent, on what terms is it related to these representative bodies? What powers, if any, have Councils over Churches?

"That question involves obviously some inquiry as to the nature of a Council as such. Here I find myself under the irksome compulsion to dissent from the thesis expounded by Dr. Douglas Horton in his book, *Congregationalism*. . . . Dr. Horton maintains that a Council of Churches is itself in effect a Church. 'My thesis,' he says, 'is that a *council is a kind of congregation*, is the same kind that John Robinson described.' (p. 18). The difference from a local Church lies only in the material of which the two are made: ' . . . The material of a local Church is Christian believers, and that of a Council is Christian believers directly or indirectly appointed to it by their Churches . . . It is . . . a congregation of members, elected by the Churches . . . or by other councils.'

"But that difference may well be decisive. That Dr. Horton does not so see it is due doubtless to an unusual situation confronting our American Churches as he wrote. His novel thesis bears the marks of an ingenious device *ad hoc*. The issue had arisen whether our General Council were free to unite for itself with the General Synod of the Evangelical and Reformed Church. It appeared that the projected union of the two denominations as a whole was not as yet feasible or expedient. To unite their top representative bodies would, however, be a step in that direction. Dr. Horton desired that step to be taken. On the prevailing view, however, the General Council could hardly take it, and invite its far-reaching consequences, without a clear specific mandate from at least a majority of its members' constituencies. Naturally, on the other hand, it is free to take this step or any other at its pleasure, for itself only, without binding the Churches legally, that is to say without binding them

93

save by inevitable implication, if, as Dr. Horton alleges, the General Council be a Church in and by itself, with all the rights and privileges thereunto appertaining.

"If I had been in Dr. Horton's position, and had been as bright as he is, I am bound to say that I would probably have come up with just this ingenious device."[3]

"One can hardly fail to agree with how Dr. Horton feels, as a competent progressive leader confronting a reactionary minority in stiff-necked opposition. Yet I must dissent soberly from his thesis that a Council of Churches is itself a Church of any sort. I return to the 1865 definition, not from reverence for precedent, for I should feel free to disagree here also if in fact I did, but because it runs along with what I would call a theological definition of Congregationalism, to which I find myself deeply committed. You recall that at Boston the organized Church was defined as 'a congregation of faithful or believing men, dwelling together in one city, town, or convenient neighbourhood.' . . . The concluding participle is the crux of the statement: 'dwelling together.' That word has weight."[4]

"The Church . . . is wholly present wherever faithful men dwell together in unity of worship and service. The Church then is a way of living together. It is that quality of habitual mutuality in good will which makes the Churches households of faith."[5]

"And every local Church is a family. It is the fact that it is a society of brothers living together under God as their Father that makes it a Church. It is this gracious intimacy of familiar relationship which is the principle of regular Christian association. That principle is the Church, an essence existing without remainder in every local concretion of such fellowship, and nowhere else.

"But a Council is not a family. Its members do not dwell together. To live for a few days as guests in the same community for a special purpose does not constitute a familial relationship. Hence a Council is not a Church. It has not a Church's freedom to act for itself."[6]

"A self-governing household is what every local unit of the Christian Movement is by nature and right, whether it know that it is so or not. Congregational Churches in the special sense are local Churches which recognize and stress this truth, and join in alliance for counsel and co-operation with other churches equally of a mind to heed and practice it. The only direct measure of discipline which these Churches can take against one of themselves is collectively to dismiss it from association with them, though of course with no thought of depriving it of whatever standing it may have intrinsically as a Church of Christ."[7]

"If . . . no statute can be deemed properly a law unless it reflect with reasonable accuracy the predominant judgment and will of the society to which it is to apply; if law be the mirror of consensus, as it were, then a Congregational Council is a law-making body."[8]

"To my mind our Superintendency is clearly episcopacy without benefit of apostolic succession, yet, as we trust, under immediate guidance of the Holy Spirit. As long as none but moral authority is permitted to these *de facto* bishops; as long as they are never permitted to say officially, 'Do this, or else,' they are in practice good and profitable servants of our Congregational economy, whether in theory there be a place for them in this system or not."[9]

"Most of the business of the denomination is in fact transacted at the joint midwinter meeting of the Boards, with no others officially present. Yet the Boards are only very indirectly representative of the Churches. A critic might not unreasonably label the members of the Midwinter Meetings an oligarchy, bypassing the democratic process which is surely basic to Congregational ways of thought and action; though they bypass it innocently, and under sheer force of necessity. The result of the present haphazard arrangement, however, is inevitably that for people who value conservation of time and efficiency of performance the Midwinter Meetings are interesting; while, not to put too fine a point on it, the General Council, ostensibly the supreme organ of the national fellowship, is a bore."[10]

The Rev. Henry Smith Leiper, M.A., D.D., listed twelve propositions the essence of which was: It is the will of God that we all be one, the world needs ONE Church; a multi-denominational Church "makes sense only to a madman." Organic unity is what "the world understands." "The circumstances prevailing today call for stress on the fellowship," and we must heed "the oecumenical imperative."[11]

The only clear note of warning appeared in the Rev. Boynton Merrill, D.D.'s Council Sermon.

"Is it not possible that just as the early Church ceased being the lengthened shadow of the penniless Teacher of the crucified risen Christ and was slowly changed into 'the Holy Roman Empire wearing mitre and chasuble' so the Church of our day, being very much in and of the world, has also been infiltrated and even subtly captured by a world which permits to the Church her dreams but rejects her demand for deeds?"[12]

"The theme of this Council is Congregational Churchmanship. Both Congregationalism with its emphasis upon individual liberty and Churchmanship, with its drive towards loyalty to the institution

95

and to fellowship, seem to us good. They appear to be important and not irreconcilable ideas. But are we sure that the world is not by our pre-occupation with ecclesiastical mechanisms luring us from our spiritual character and our primary task? As we dedicate these days to looking at Congregationalism and Chuchmanship as others might dedicate days to some other 'ism,' are we ready to see and confess, if we must, that these things may be primarily of men and of time and that they are not to be found at the heart of the Gospel of Christ? Does not our very theme seem to say that we are thinking that an historic, corporate, human instrument, beloved and rightly cherished, is more important to study than to study how we may, each one of us, be to 'the Eternal God what a man's hand is to a man'—and more importantly still—how the Eternal God can be to each of us what a man's heart and head are to his hands?"[13]

"Should we not warn ourselves against being committed to the egocentric effort to assess ourselves rather than to the theocentric effort of assessing and laying hold on God?"[14]

"We are to use long words like Congregationalism, Churchmanship, and words enjoying favour like oecumenicity—and others, I am sure. I remind you and myself that the great experiences of our life in time are elemental ones, and that the words which describe them and their areas are all short words: Earth and Sky, Sea and Sun, Day and Night, God and Man, Birth, Life, Death; Love and Hate, Good and Evil. We will do well to remember, too, that Christ's final query of the reputed founder of the Church was the simple but searching three-times repeated, 'Peter, lovest thou me?'

"Just as we would urge the secular world to look past factories and aeroplanes, past huge corporations and profits and politicians to justice and mercy, to freedom and peace, so I feel certain the secular world is asking, even longing, for us to look past our committees and our historic platforms to our timeless commission to declare God; past our measurables to our immeasurables; past our denominational machinery, excellent though it may be, to what should be our real product, Christ-like minds and men; to our own and other men's rootage in God; to what a sensitive and deeply-aware Scotsman, John Buchan, called 'our invisible means of support.' Only if our conference here on Churchmanship helps us discover and demonstrate God will men gratefully and long remember us."[15]

"To have the freedoms and the joys of fellowship, or the loyalties of Congregationalism and Churchmanship, but not truly to have Him, would be to be bereft of the one spiritual presence which can save us and help us do our share in saving the world.

"We are prone, in our neatly departmentalized world, to want to fit the Spirit, meant to be free and far ranging, and the Church, meant to be the way of Christ, into mechanisms and systems. Perhaps it is inevitable that we should dream of thorough organizations and committees, but we can recall that He dreamed of men loving Him enough to leave all and follow. Let us this week, beyond our care to define and describe our Churchmanship, take pains to deepen our discipleship."[16]

The Rev. H. F. Lovell Cocks, M.A., D.D. summed up in a paragraph the nub of the new polity proposal:

"By what right is the presence of Christ and the guidance of the Holy Spirit claimed for the local Church and denied to the county union, the provincial synod, the national assembly, or to this International Council? On what grounds can it be maintained that Christ is more surely present and the Spirit's guidance more authentically given to the individual Church than to the fellowship of Churches?"[17]

The Rev. John Huxtable, M.A., stated the policy problem rather neatly:

"If we are to come into closer association with one another, and still more if we are to come into more intimate relationships with other Communions, there is most urgent need for us to discover what is the logic of our clear doctrine of the gathered Church for such a Church's association with others like it, remembering . . . to address ourselves to our modern problems with the great abiding principle of our Churchmanship: how can we in this or that situation most adequately obey the great Head of the Church?"[18]

The Rev. Leslie E. Cooke, B.A., D.D., lauded the new proposal:

"We affirm the authority which belongs to the local Church Meeting, we are very diffident in defining what authority belongs to a Council or Assembly. In this matter Dr. Horton has by his recent studies rendered us all great service.

"A catholic principle of Churchmanship as far as we are concerned has never been worked out in terms of a catholic organization. While the principle permits us to share fully in the oecumenical movement, our failure to work out the implications of our principle for a catholic organization hinders our complete participation in that movement in so far that it is a stumbling block when actual negotiations for Church unity take place. Logically there is no one and no body which can negotiate Church union on behalf of a collocation of independent Churches.

"It may be that our greatest contribution to the conception of catholicity is yet to be made in the discovery of the way in which the local Churches may so express their corporate life that they can become, as it were, the Church without impairing for one moment the autonomy and freedom which belong to the local Church."[19]

I have quoted these speakers from the printed *Proceedings* of the St. Andrews Council. In actuality the spoken word was not always identical, as my notes testify. In particular, Dr. Stafford departed from his manuscript to indicate a prior critique of the manuscript "last night" as the reason for change. When I asked him about this he answered, "Henry, some of my friends thought I was too blunt, and I sometimes am. It was the kindly thing to nod in the direction of conciliar authority. That's all."[20]

With the plain quest in the very first address for a book which "might become normative for our Congregational world"[21] and a proposed "Message"[22] of five printed pages in *Proceedings* setting forth Congregational Polity in terms quite other than that which obtained in the U.S.A., I sought out Dr. Strang. He had seconded my motion to delay the vote on the "Message."

"Max," I said, "I have a strange feeling that Dr. Howard Stanley of Manchester and other staunch Congregational leaders aren't here for the same reason Fred Meek, Bill Keith, and kindred spirits in the United States aren't here."

"Something is very peculiar, all right."[23]

"What can we do? You are the one and only opponent of the merger who's here."

"I've got an idea, Henry. Stay right here." I stayed. Max returned with a handsome, open-faced Welshman. "Meet Dr. R. Tudur Jones. He wants to ask you what's behind the proposed message."

"Dr. Jones, here's my copy of the proposed Message to the churches. The numbers indicate specific wording which either champions one side in the CC/ER merger controversy, or which sets forth a concept of Congregational Polity unlike anything known in the Documents of our Churches, associations, conferences, or national bodies in the United States."

"Can you give me a specific example?"

"Surely. This 'Message' reads, 'In our Churchmanship the sole authority is the authority of Christ. We believe that the mind of Christ for his people is given to Councils by the same Spirit.' "[24]

"I've got it," he said. "Can you lads come around to our rooms for a spot of tea after tonight's meeting?"

I looked at Max. He nodded.

"Certainly. We'll be there."

When we arrived, the main room was filled with Welsh. All eleven delegates must have been contacted. About two dozen others were present. For over an hour Dr. Strang and I answered a hail of questions about the CC/ER merger. None had heard of the Polity and Unity Committee. I think it was Pennar Davies who brought us up short. "We Welsh thought it peculiar that *everyone* in America wanted to do away with Independency. We had blinders dropped over our eyes!" "Hear, hear," chorused the others. Someone said, "You must come back tomorrow night so we can learn more about this." Then the thoughtfulness and charm of the Welsh blossomed. "You know, Dr. Gray, neither you nor Dr. Strang is in a position to speak *against* the motion supported by your own general secretary. I think I express the mood of this meeting when I say 'Just leave it to the Welsh. We'll take care of the Message'." "Hear! Hear! Hear! Hear!" came a full-throated cheer! I thanked them and then asked if one of them would pray for us. Several prayed. Then they sang a Welsh benediction and Tudur Jones saw me to the corner to point the way to my rooms. Max had his in the same building with the Welsh.

The next night . . . more questions.

There remained but one business session of the Council.[25] Max Strang sat near me about the tenth row. The motion was made to approve the Message to the Churches; which had been improved, clarified and rendered more Congregational. It was seconded. Discussion was called for. *None came*! The chairman said, "Are you ready to vote?" From a row near the rear a tall Welshman arose, strolled rather diffidently down the center aisle to the front. "Mr. Chairman, I don't suppose the point is terribly important. And I'm sure you wish a Message to the Churches backed by unanimous approval. We Welsh would feel a bit happier in voting for this Message if the few words about the Christian spirit of love appeared immediately after 'the authority of Christ.' This would read, 'which can be exercised only by persuasion and in the spirit of love.' No doubt that's what is intended. In any case, we Welsh would be just a bit happier with those words added." He turned as if to go, then caught himself, "Oh yes, Mr. Chairman, I think I'll just move that these words be added as an amendment." There was a chorus from all over the hall, "Second the motion." The Welsh were well distributed! Again the speaker hesitated. "Of course, if the maker of the original motion could simply add these words, we could vote on the whole Message immediately." A torrent of amendments often comes on the heels of just one. The words were incorporated. The Welsh speaker called for the question. The vote was unanimous. And the Message to the Churches was buried.

Never once did I hear either it or the proposed normative book on polity referred to thereafter. But without the Welsh insertion the Message was tailor-made for presentation to the United States courts as THE word on Congregational Polity from the International Congregational Council!

As we celebrated at the Welsh rooms Max asked me, "Did you know HOW they were going to take care of it?"

"No, Max. I was ready to jump up and start a debate but a Welshman nearby whispered, 'Don't move.'"

Why should thirteen words make so much difference? Obviously, because they undid all the authority, control and power of the entire "Message," if all power could "be exercised only by persuasion and in the spirit of love."

Here is the core of the Message, WITHOUT THE WELSH ADDITION:

> "A weakness of our polity, in practice, is that it sometimes obscures the clear vision of the Great Church. Our recommendation about the place of Councils gives formal expression to a deep conviction that has been growing among us for many years. . . . [26]

> "Congregational Churchmanship is founded on the belief that where Christ is, there is the Church. In our history this fundamental principle has been specially expressed in the conviction that the local church is an embodiment or outcropping of the One Church of the Lord Jesus Christ. At the same time we have recognized although not always explicitly, that the local Church cannot be by itself the whole Catholic Church. As part of its obedience to Christ, the Lord of the Church, every local Church is committed to making actual its oneness with the wider Christian community. This fact, we consider, should be taken into serious account by all national Congregational Unions and by all Churches within these Unions. This means recognizing the authority of Christ both in the individual Church and in the Council (e.g., in meetings of Associations, Conferences, Provincial, County, State and National Unions) to which it sends delegates. In our Churchmanship the sole authority is the authority of Christ. We believe that the mind of Christ for His people is given to Councils by the same Spirit that guides the local Church." [27]

The Welsh addition substituted for the novel concept of Congregational Polity with the authority of Christ exercised by

Councils the time-honored New Testament practice of influence by persuasion in the spirit of love.

A Tale of Three Talks

The three talks were addresses by the Rev. Douglas Horton, D.D. The first was delivered June 22, 1950, in Dr. Horton's capacity as Minister of the General Council speaking to the Council at Cleveland. The second was a series of lectures delivered in May 1951 as moderator of the International Congregational Council speaking to the Annual Assembly of the Congregational Union of England and Wales at Oxford. This series was published in May 1952 by the Independent Press in London. The third talk was delivered as moderator of the International Congregational Council, speaking to that body on June 21, 1953, at St. Andrews. All three statements were versions of the notion that Congregational polity "recognized" the power of councils over Churches.

The 1950 address was not taken seriously except by those who were involved in the lawsuit of Brooklyn's Cadman Church against the General Council, in order to prevent the proposed merger of the CC/ER Churches. The 1951 addresses were not reported or discussed in the United States. The 1952 book containing the British lectures, though dedicated to "The Committee on Free Church Polity and Unity," was not presented to that Committee and was virtually unknown in the U.S.A. outside a few national officials. The 1953 address had as its goal issuance by the ICC of "a volume on *Congregational Churchmanship* which . . . might become normative for our Congregational world."[28] The Welsh amendment of the St. Andrews Message circumvented that purpose.

The content of all three talks directly dealt with Congregational Polity. IF Dr. Horton's theses were correct, then the Congregational Polity Committee should have found them in our contemporary basic documents, in our history, and in the current practice which was under study. If Dr. Horton were correct, the mediators were under obligation to find a way to unite the best in the noble heritage of the Pilgrims with what the Minister of the General Council perceived to be the essential needs of the twentieth century!

The question asked by Dr. Meek, one of the few who had read Dr. Horton's 1952 book, was "Does the book present Congregational Polity?" The answer requires study of the book, which is the most complete statement of the theses in the three talks. Then the theses of the book must be compared with Congregationalism in its chief historic documents and in the words of Congregational leaders in each era.

An Explanation of Nomenclature

The evidence from the major documents of historic Congregationalism must now be compared with that of the three talks delivered by the Rev. Douglas Horton.

I am reluctant to make this comparison for personal reasons. Each of the mediators counted Douglas Horton as a good friend. He had been most gracious to me when I became National Secretary for Young People's Work and Student Life in April, 1939. On my first official visit to the New York offices I asked Doug "what authority has a national officer in our fellowship?" His memorable reply etched itself into my mind, "He has all the authority that anybody will give him." This epic reply became more relevant and vital with every field trip. The authority of truth that shines in its own light and commends itself by its shining became the ONLY authority of importance to me.

In 1939, at the tail-end of the Great Depression, only two Congregational student programs, at the University of Connecticut and at Michigan State, were functioning. To re-relate Congregationally-founded Colleges to the fellowship I proposed week-long campus visitations, named embassies, by denominational leaders. Douglas Horton was one of the first to volunteer for service. With Ruth Isabel Seabury we were welcomed to such colleges as Beloit, Carleton, and Grinnell. Doug was a full participant and many were the hours we shared thinking through student/faculty/administration relationships, and the host of questions asked on campus.

When I became minister of the Oneonta Congregational Church in South Pasadena, California at Easter 1942 I was faced with the mammoth task of uniting a Church rent by dissension, deeply in debt, housed in a sanctuary more like a movie theater than a Meeting House. In October 1942 Doug made a special trip from New York to California to preach for me at the re-dedication of the newly re-constructed sanctuary.

In September 1945 he invited me to be a member of the small team to survey the war damage to the Churches in England, Scotland and Ireland. My report became that of the team and Doug pressed on with the million-dollar reconstruction fund, the youth service workers, the ministerial exchange and the enrollment of British theologs to study in Andover, Hartford, and Yale.

He visited Oneonta several times and invited me to deliver the theological discourse at the 1949 International Congregational Council meeting at Wellesley. Furthermore he backed 100% my convening of the first International Youth Assembly at the same time in other Wellesley College buildings.

Douglas Horton was the most perceptive architectural observer to visit Oneonta, both in the reconstructed sanctuary in 1942, and then at the new church campus in 1950. He had come to California for a series of lectures at Pomona College. His sole off-campus visit was to Oneonta. He understood on entering the new sanctuary exactly what we were seeking to "say in structure." It was he who encouraged me to write articles on church architecture and symbolism. For many years the guide book I wrote was sent to all church building committees by the offices of both the Congregational Christian Churches and those of the National Council of Churches.

I wrote this account because it is typical of the experiences of the mediators with the Rev. Douglas Horton, D.D. We were, and we still are, embarrassed and chagrined when opponents of the merger pilloried him. We were outraged at personal invective. It seemed unseemly to all of the mediators; those of us still alive continue to find it hard to bear.

This is difficult to write because the mediators had friends in both camps. The events of 1954 to 1957, yet to be chronicled, placed a terrible burden upon the spirits of the mediators.

Even now, I do not feel comfortable contrasting the polity of Congregationalism's historic documents with the polity theses of Dr. Horton. So, arbitrarily, I shall use the term "Mansfield Theses"; for Dr. Horton's Mansfield College lectures of 1951 are the fullest exposition of his polity. Our concern is with Congregational Polity; this nomenclature will help to keep that concern uppermost.

Congregational Polity According to the Mansfield Theses

The 96 pages of *Congregationalism* may be summed up under seven headings, each with wide significance.

"My thesis is that *a council is a kind of congregation.*"[29] This is elaborated to assert "Congregationalism stands for the Apostolic Succession of Congregations."[30] Further, the executive secretary of a council, such as of the General Council and the State

Conferences in the United States of America, is styled "Minister of the General Council," wears a pectoral cross of office, and is vested with ministerial, and by inference with sacradotal, authority.[31] Subsequently, "we have followed a widening way and laid upon our councils many duties other than teaching . . . Because the council stands between duties divine and human . . . it is no less a congregation than the local church."[32] Not only is a council endowed with the right, (as a church, to have a minister) it may also make "a place for bishops and presbyteries . . . when there is call for them."[33] In fact "By a system of assignment of responsibilities we may devise any type of organizaton which a situation may demand."[34] From the explication of "congregation" there is derived an ecumenical imperative: "Congregationalism is bound to co-operate with other denominations . . . because their people are obviously gathered into congregations which in principle answer to the Congregational definition."[35]

Concerning Word Usage

To examine the claims of the Mansfield Theses the first essential is to clarify the confused word usage. I capitalize Church in its chief New Testament usage. Eighty-six out of 105 times *ekklesia* means the particular Church, as, for example, the Church in Corinth. Nineteen times the New Testament *ekklesia* refers to the Church Universal in all eras and places, past, present, future . . . visible or invisible . . . militant on earth or triumphant in heaven. In no instance in the New Testeament does *ekklesia* refer to a denomination, council, conference, union, consistory or presbytery.

Secondly, in the interests of clarity, fellowship will be used to refer to the total company of all members of Congregational Churches. Where the denomination is intended, we shall use the terms current at the date and place under review, for example, Union referring to the Congregational Union of England and Wales, established in 1834, and National Council for the National Council of the Congregational Churches established in 1871. Whenever an organized body is intended, we shall use its name, as, "State Conference", or "General Council" or "Union".

Thirdly, the word "congregation" will be used to designate a company of Christians gathered for worship, not all of whom have covenanted with God and with each other to live and work together under the sole Lordship of Christ. Further definitions might prejudge the review of the Mansfield Theses.

A fundamental question is posed, "Is a council a Church?" The documents of Congregationalism NOWHERE IN NO ERA equate council and Church. As we examine them, I have modernized spelling for ease of reading.

The first document is the 1589 "True Description out of the Word of God of the visible Church."[36] "As it is seen in this present world (the Church) consists of a company and fellowship of faithful and holy people gathered in the name the Christ Jesus, their only King, Priest, and Prophet, worshipping him aright, being peaceably and quietly governed by his officers and laws, keeping the unity of faith in the bond of peace and love."[37]

The confession of the London/Amsterdam Church of 1592/ 1596 is very explicit. "Every Christian (Church) has power . . . to elect and ordain their own ministers" and determine their membership. "Christ has given this power . . . to the whole body together of every Christian (Church) and not . . . to any other Congregation."[38] "Ecclesiastical Assemblies . . . have not . . . neither can be . . . esteemed the true, orderly gathered, or constituted churches of Christ."[39] The distinct Churches "every one a compact City in itself"[40] are to seek "the counsel and help one of another in all needful affairs of the Church."[41]

When James I came to the English throne in 1603, Francis Johnson and Henry Ainsworth set forth an "Apology or Defence" for the early Congregationalists known as Brownists. The "Apology" states "every true visible Church, is a company of people called and separated from the world by the word of God, and joined together by voluntary profession of the faith of Christ, in the fellowship of the Gospel."[42] "All particular Churches ought to be so constituted . . . (that) the whole body of every Church may meet together in one place, and jointly perform their duties of God and one towards another."[43] "That the Church be not governed by Popish Canons, Courts, Classes, Custom or any human inventions, but by the laws and rules which Christ has appointed in his Testament."[44]

The Seven Articles of 1617 sent to the Council of state in England by the Leyden Church was uncompromising. "We believe that no synod, classes, convocation or assembly of Ecclesiastical Officers has any power or authority at all."[45]

It seems almost foolish to attest the nature of a Congregational Church and its relation to a council because the testimony of the historic documents varies so little. But it is exactly the basic proposition of the Mansfield Theses which is thereby contravened, therefore the point must be made by the evidence of the documents from 1589 to 1931. Hence we continue.

The Cambridge Platform of 1648 is the normative statement of Congregational Polity in seventeenth-century New England. Its position is forthright. "Ecclesiastical Polity . . . is . . . that form and order that is to be observed in the Church of Christ on earth."[46] "Particular Churches . . . (are) each one a distinct society of itself . . . (having a) *Visible Covenent*."[47] "This Voluntary Covenant"[48] is the basis for the life, work, discipline, and witness of the Church."[49] "Supreme and Lordly *power* over all the Churches upon earth, does only belong to Jesus Christ."[50] "Synods orderly assembled, and rightly proceeding according to the pattern, Acts 15, we acknowledge as the ordinance of Christ; and though not absolutely necessary to the being, yet many times . . . necessary to the well-being of Churches."[51] "The Synods, directions and determinations, so far as consonant to the word of God, are to be received with reverence and submission" but Synods must "Not exercise Church-censures by way of discipline, nor any other act of church-authority or jurisdiction."[52]

Parallel to the New England statement is "An Apologetical Narration"[53] of 1643 presented to the British Houses of Parliament by five prominent Congregationalists who were members of the Westminster Assembly of divines called together by Parliament. These leaders were Thomas Goodwin, Philip Nye, Sidrach Simpson, Jeremiah Burroughes, and William Bridge. In Dr. Paul's facsimile the basic position is "First, the supreme rule . . . was the Primitive pattern and example of the Churches erected by the Apostles."[54] Presbyterian power *over* Churches is explicitly described and found wanting. "We could not but imagine, that the first Churches planted by the Apostles, were ordinarily of . . . one city . . . ruled by their own Elders, that also preached to them."[55a] Therefore they state their conviction. "We could not therefore but judge it a safe . . . way to retain the government of our several congregations."[55b] The authority of councils is limited, even in case of scandal, to "withdrawing . . . all Christian communion with them until they . . . repent."[56]

The "Narration" goes further: "what further authority, or proceedings purely Ecclesiastical, of one or of many sister Churches towards another whole Church, or Churches offending, either the Scriptures do hold forth, or can rationally be put in execution . . . *for our parts we saw not then, nor do yet see*."[57] (italics mine). Not least in importance is the deliberate contrast drawn between the extreme independence of Brownism, "the authoritative Presbyterial Government in all the subordinations and proceedings of it"(24) and the Congregational "middle way."[58]

In his commentary Dr. Paul concludes:

"Here was obviously a distinguishable view of the Church for which others would not be slow to provide the names if they did not find one for themselves. Therefore, part of the significance of the pamphlet is that it reveals the general agreement of its authors with the Congregational churchmanship which Cotton, Hooker and their colleagues were developing experimentally in America."[59]

"A Declaration of the faith and order owned and practiced in the Congregational Churches in England; agreed upon and consented to by their elders and messengers in their meeting at the Savoy (Palace chapel), October 12, 1658" comes next, and is one of the clearest accounts ever written. Dr. Peel's book reprints this declaration in full. Here are the salient points:

"By the appointment of the Father all Power for the Calling, Institution, Order, or Government of the Church, is invested in a Supreme and Soverein maner in the Lord Jesus Christ, as King and Head thereof."[60]

"III. Those thus called (through the Ministery of the Word by his Spirit) he commandeth to walk together in particular Societies or Churches, for their mutual edification, and the due performance of that publique Worship, which he requireth of them in this world.

"IV. To each of these Churches thus gathered, according unto his minde declared in his Word, he hath given all that Power and Authority, which is any way needful for their carrying on that Order in Worship and Discipline, which he hath instituted for them to observe with Commands and Rules, for the due and right exerting and executing of that Power.

"V. These particular Churches thus appointed by the Authority of Christ, and entrusted with power from him for the ends before expressed, are each of them as unto those ends, the seat of that Power which he is pleased to communicate to his Saints or Subjects in this world, so that as such they receive it immediately from himself.

"VI. Besides these particular Churches, there is not instituted by Christ any Church more extensive or Catholique entrusted with power for the administration of his Ordinances, or the execution of any authority in his name."

* * *

"XI. The way appointed by Christ for the calling of any person, fitted and gifted by the Holy Ghost, unto the Office of Pastor, Teacher or Elder in a Church, is, that he be chosen thereunto by the common suffrage of the Church itself . . . "[61]

". . . they who are ingaged in the work of Publique Preaching, and enjoy the Publique Maintenance upon that account, are not thereby obliged to dispense the Seals to any other then such as . . . they stand related to, as Pastors or Teachers; . . . "[62]

"The Power of Censures being seated by Christ in a particular Church, is to be exercised only towards particular Members of each Church respectively as such; and there is no power given by him unto any Synods or Ecclesiastical Assemblies to Excommunicate, or by their publique Edicts to threaten Excommunication, or other Church-censures against Churches, Magistrates, or their people upon any account, no man being obnoxious to that Censure, but upon his personal miscarriage, as a Member of a particular Church."[63]

"As all Churches and all the Members of them are bound to pray continually for the good or prosperity of all the Churches of Christ in all places, and upon all occasions to further it; . . . So the Churches themselves . . . ought to hold communion amongst themselves for their peace, increase of love, and mutal edification."

* * *

". . . it is according to the minde of Christ, that many Churches holding communion together, do by their Messengers meet in a Synod or Councel, to consider and give their advice in, or about that matter in difference, to be reported to all the Churches concerned; Howbeit these Synods so assembled are not entrusted with any Church-Power, properly so called, or with any Jurisdiction over the Churches themselves, to exercise any Censures, either over any Churches or Persons, or to impose their determinations on the Churches or Officers.

"XXVII. Besides these occasional Synods or Councils, there are not instituted by Christ any stated Synods in a fixed Combination of Churches, or their Officers in lesser or greater Assemblies; nor are there any Synods appointed by Christ in a way of Subordination to one another."[64]

In New England the Westminster Assembly and the Savoy Declaration became grist for statements of faith on the one hand and polity on the other; though it should be noted that the Westminster Confession of Faith was modified to accord more closely with scripture.[65]

The mid 1600's were the years of New England disputes concerning the baptism of children only one of whose parents was a

Church member. These "Half-Way Covenant" synods or councils gave scant attention to polity. The chief polity effect was to accentuate the independence of the Churches, as illustrated by the gathering in October 1669 of the Third Church in Boston and the Second Church in Hartford, both later known as Old South Church. The latter stated Congregational Polity forthrightly.

"The Congregational way . . . as formerly settled, professed, and practiced, under the guidance of the first leaders of this church of Hartford, is the way of Christ."[66]

"Some main heads or principles of which Congregational way of church order are those that follow, viz:

"FIRST, That visible saints are the only fit matter, and confederation the form, of a visible church.

"SECOND, That a competent number of visible saints (with their seed) embodied by a particular covenant, are a true, distinct, and entire church of Christ.

"THIRD, That such a particular church being organized, . . . hath all the power and privileges of a church belonging to it; in special—1st, to admit or receive members; 2d, to deal with, and if need be, reject offenders; 3d, to administer and enjoy all other ecclesiastical ordinances within itself.

"FOURTH, That the power of guidance or leading, belongs only to the Eldership, and the power of judgment, consent, or privilege, belongs to the fraternity or brethren in full communion.

"FIFTH, That communion is carefully to be maintained between all the churches of Christ, according to his order.

"SIXTH, That counsel in cases of difficulty is to be sought and submitted to according to God."[67]

A Boston Synod met in 1679 and 1680. The two leading members, Rev. Urian Oakes of Cambridge and Rev. Increase Mather of Second Church, Boston, were in England while the Savoy assembly was in session, and were acquainted with both the Savoy Platform and those who had produced it. The preface to the 1680 Boston "Confession of Faith" affirms Savoy. "That which was consented unto by the Elders and Messengers of the Congregational Churches in England, who met at the Savoy . . . was twice publikly read, examined, and approved of . . . As to what concerns Church-government, we refer to the Cambridge Platform Anno. 1648."[68]

Again the scene shifts to England, following the 1662 ejection from pastorates of about 2,000 ministers who refused to obey the Act of Uniformity, the Five Mile Act and the Conventicle Act.

Most of these ministers were Presbyterian or Congregational. In 1691 ministers from both groups drew up "The Heads of Agreement." Here, if anywhere, one would expect to find support for the notion that "a council is a kind of congregation," but, the Heads of Agreement acknowledge the Universal Church as "all that are united to (Christ), whether in Heaven or Earth."[69] The united ministers "agree, that particular societies of visible saints, who under Christ their Head, are statedly joined together for ordinary communion with one another . . . are particular Churches."[70]

> ". . . none of *our* particular Churches shall be *subordinate* to one another; each being endued with *equality of Power* from Jesus Christ. And that none of the said particular Churches, their Officer, or Officers, shall exercise any *Power*, or have any *Superiority* over any other Church, or their Officers."[71]

> "6. That we are most willing and ready to give an account of our *Church Proceedings* to each other, when desired, for preventing or removing any offences that may arise among us. Likewise we shall be ready to give the right hand of fellowship, and walk together accoding to the *Gospel Rules* of *Communion of Churches*."[72]

> "1. WE agree, That in order to *concord*, and in any other *weighty* and *difficult* cases, it is needful, and according to the *mind of Christ*, that the Ministers of several Churches be consulted and advised with about such matters.

> "2. That such Meetings may consist of *smaller* or *greater Numbers*, as the matter shall require.

> "3. That *particular Churches*, their respective *Elders*, and *Members* ought to have a reverential regard to their judgment so given, and not dissent therefrom, without *apparent* grounds from the word of God."[73]

In New England the echo of the Heads of Agreement is "The Proposals of 1705, and the Saybrook Platform of 1708." The 1705 Massachusetts Proposals suggested that the informal ministers' meetings begun in Cambridge in 1643 become an "Association, that may meet at proper times to consider such things as may properly lie before them"[74] including trial of ministerial candidates so that pastorless Churches could have recommended to them "such persons as may be fit to be employed . . . for present supply, from whom they may in due time proceed to choose a Pastor."[75] A Church is fully in charge. If the associated ministers, "with a proper number of delegates from their several Churches, be formed into a standing or stated Council, which shall consult, advise and determine all affairs that shall be proper matter for the consideration of an Ecclesiastical Council within their respective limits."[76] These provisos are directed toward disorderly conduct, due to the moral turpitude of the times, as viewed by the ministers. And, even in this extremity the limit of a council's power is to recommend that the Churches withdraw communion with an offending Church or Pastor.[77] Nowhere in the Proposals is a council equated with a Church, or, endowed with church-power of any kind; even the "trial" of ministerial candidates is for *recommendation* to such Churches as seek advice.

An ecclesiastical historian would single out the Saybrook Platform of 1708, in Connecticut, for careful scrutiny. Here, if anywhere, one might expect support for the Mansfield Thesis that a council is a Church. From 1708 until 1784 Connecticut's Consociations were established by law. Their powers far exceeded those of any other Congregational councils before or since. Strangely the Saybrook Platform was drawn up by twelve ministers, eight of whom were trustees of the recently founded Yale College. There were also four Church members. The force of the Platform was derived from its adoption by the General Court of the Colony in October 1708.

The enacting motion read:

"The Reverend Ministers delegates from the elders and messengers of the churches in this government, met at Saybrook, September 9th, 1708, having presented to this Assembly a Confession of Faith, Heads of Agreement, and Regulations in the Administration of Church Discipline, as unanimously agreed and consented to by the elders and messengers of all the churches in this government: This Assembly do declare their great approbation of such a happy agreement, and do ordain that all the churches within this government that are or shall be thus united in doctrine, worship, and discipline, be, and for the future shall be owned and acknowledged established by law Provided always, that nothing herein shall be intended and construed to hinder or prevent any society or church that is or shall be allowed by the laws of this government, who soberly differ or dissent from the united churches hereby established, from exercising worship and discipline in their own way, according to their consciences."[78]

The provision for freedom of dissent negates the TOTAL imposition of authority over "the united churches."

The purpose of the regulations is stated "for the better regulation of the administration of Church discipline in relation to all cases ecclesiastical both in particular Churches and in councils."[79]

111

To achieve and activate the system of regulation "the Churches which are neighbouring each to other shall consociate for the mutual affording to each other such assistance as may be requisite upon all occasions ecclesiastical."[80]

In addition to discipline with regard to scandal or misconduct, the consociations "shall have power of examining and recommending the candidates of the ministry to the work thereof."[81]

The selection of pastors remains with the Churches but "the associated pastors shall also be consulted by bereaved Churches belonging to their association and recommend to such Churches such persons as may fit to be called and settled in the work of the gospel ministry among them."[82]

It is "recommended as expedient that all the associations of this colony do meet in the General Association by their respective delegates one or more out of each association once a year."[83]

With all its legal establishment the Saybrook Platform falls short of a mandate. The Consociations and the General Association are NEVER denominated Churches or Church. Nor do they claim the right to call pastors, baptize, celebrate the Lord's Supper, admit Church members, or perform the usual functions of a Church. The intent of the Platform is clearly stated as "the administration of Church discipline in relation to all cases ecclesiastical both in particular Churches and in Councils."[84] This wording *differentiates* between Church and council. The regulations are directed at good order, good administration, NOT at the sacramental, pastoral, preaching or other religious functions of either Churches or ministers.

I do not wish to leave the impression either that all Congregational Churches in Connecticut 1708-1784 submitted to the Saybrook regulations, or, that, on the other hand, the Platform was ignored. The facts are otherwise. Fairfield County Churches formed a Consociation with even stricter rules. New Haven County formed a Consociation which greatly diluted the Saybrook regulations. In Hardford's Old South Church successive pastors did little more than bow in the direction of the Consociation, which actually conducted its business like an association in Massachusetts.[85] There were also persecuted Congregational churches! Dexter tells the story of these Separatists.[86]

After the War of Independence the Consociation system was doomed. Deprived of its legal status it atrophied. The whole system collapsed with the attempt of the Hartford North Association to try Rev. Horace Bushnell, D.D., for heresy; the North Congregational Church simply withdrew from the Association![87]

The Plan of Union of 1801 betwixt Connecticut Congregational Churches and the Presbyterian Church in the United States is cited in support of delegation of power by Churches to councils or Presbyteries. All the Plan does is to provide that settlements west of the Hudson River may choose to be Presbyterian or Congregational. Here are its key provisos:

> "2. If in the new settlements any church of the Congregational order shall settle a minister of the Presbyterian order, that church may, if they choose, still conduct their discipline according to Congregational principles, settling their difficulties among themselves, or by a council mutually agreed upon for that purpose. But if any difficulty shall exist between the minister and the church, or any member of it, it shall be referred to the Presbytery to which the minister shall belong, provided both parties agree to it; if not, to a council consisting of an equal number of Presbyterians and Congregationalists, agreed upon by both parties."[88]

Furthermore,

> "If a Presbyterian church shall settle a minister of Congregational principles, that church may still conduct their discipline according to Presbyterian principles, excepting that if a difficulty arise between him and his church, or any member of it, the cause shall be tried by the Association to which the said minister shall belong, provided both parties agree to it; otherwise by a council, one-half Congregationalists and the other Presbyterians, mutually agreed upon by the parties."[89]

In actuality the agreement worked to the great disadvantage of the Congregational Churches.[90] The Presbyterians split over both the agreement and doctrine, into Old Lights and New Lights. In 1837 the Presbyterians abrogated the Plan of Union, and in 1852 the Congregationalists voted its demise.

Neither the Saybrook Platform of 1708 nor the 1801 Plan of Union encompassed church polity as a whole. Saybrook was directed chiefly to ways of correcting misconduct. The 1801 Plan was aimed at joint Presbyterian/Congregational ministry to the burgeoning population west of the Hudson. There is no hint of overall legislative or executive power over the Churches. Judicial review under the Saybrook Platform in Connecticut is strictly limited, with full provision for dissent.

National Congregational Councils first appear in Scotland May 6, 1813,[91] then in England May 8 & 11, 1831,[92] and in the United

States October 5-8, 1852.[93] The U.S. gathering was not organized as a periodic assembly until November 15-21, 1871.[94] Each of these bodies experienced considerable opposition. None claimed Churchly authority.

The polity principles of the Congregational Union of England and Wales, adopted in 1833, are summed up in the first four paragraphs:

"I. The Congregational Churches hold it to be the will of Christ that true believers should voluntarily assemble together to observe religious ordinances, to promote mutual edification and holiness, to perpetuate and propagate the gospel in the world, and to advance the glory and worship of God, through Jesus Christ; and that each Society of believers, having these objects in view in its formation, is properly a christian church.

"II. They believe that the New Testament contains, either in the form of express statute, or in the example and practice of apostles and apostolic churches, all the articles of faith necessary to be believed, and all the principles of order and discipline requisite for constituting and governing christian societies; and that human traditions, fathers and councils, canons and creeds, possess no authority over the faith and practice of Christians.

"III. They acknowledge Christ as the only Head of the church, and the officers of each church, under him, as ordained to administer his laws impartially to all; and their only appeal, in all questions touching their religious faith and practice, is to the Sacred Scriptures.

"IV. They believe that the New Testament authorizes every christian church to elect its own officers, to manage all its own affairs, and to stand independent of, and irresponsible to, all authority, saving that only of the supreme and divine Head of the church, the Lord Jesus Christ."[95]

The 1852 American paragraphs are equally explicit:

"*Resolved*, That this Council recognizes as distinctive of the Congregational polity—

"First, The principle that the local or Congregational Church derives its power and authority directly from Christ, and is not subject to any ecclesiastical government exterior or superior to itself.

"Second, That every local or Congregational Church is bound to observe the duties of mutual respect and charity which are included in the communion of Churches one with another; and that every Church which refuses to give an account of its proceedings, when kindly and orderly desired to do so by neighboring churches, violates the law of Christ.

"Third, That the ministry of the gospel by members of the Churches who have been duly called and set apart to that work implies in itself no power of government, and that ministers of the gospel not elected to office in any Church are not a hierarchy, nor are they invested with any official power in or over the Churches."[96]

The 1871 U.S. National Council set forth a classic statement on the relation of the Council to the Churches:

"The right of government resides in local Churches, who are responsible directly to the Lord Jesus Christ, the One Head of the Church universal and of all particular Churches; but that all Churches, being in communion one with another as parts of Christ's catholic Church, have mutual duties subsisting in the obligations of fellowship.

"The Churches, therefore, while establishing this National Council for the furtherance of the common interests and work of all the churches, do maintain the Scriptural and inalienable right of each Church to self-government and administration; and this National Council shall never exercise legislative or judicial authority, nor consent to act as a council of reference."[97]

The same Council appointed a large representative committee which, in 1883, published a Statement of Doctrine. Article 10 refers to the Church:

"X. We believe that the Church of Christ, invisible and spiritual, comprises all true believers, whose duty it is to associate themselves in churches, for the maintenance of worship, for the promotion of spiritual growth and fellowship, and for the conversion of men; that these churches, under the guidance of the Holy Scriptures and in fellowship with one another, may determine—each for itself—their organization, statements of belief, and forms of worship, may appoint and set apart their own ministers, and should co-operate in the work which Christ has committed to them for the furtherance of the gospel throughout the world."[98]

Fortunately a thorough compendium of actions taken by the U.S. National Council 1871-1930 was compiled and is in front of me as I write.[99]

The "Committee of Nineteen" report acted on by the 1913 Council was "concurred in by action of the American Board (ABCFM) at its annual meeting."[100] "The voting membership of the National Council was made the majority voting membership of the Board"[101] and provision was made in the Council by-laws that "the foreign missionary work of the Congregational Churches in the United States shall be carried on under the auspices of the American Board . . ."[102]

This action was to assure "representation of the churches in the Board" as sought in 1880.[103]

Most notably, the National Council By-Laws of 1913-1930 make the following specific statements:

1. The Secretary "shall be available for advice and help in matters of polity and constructive organization, and render to the churches such services as shall be appropriate to his office."[104]

2. The American Board (ABCFM) "shall be the agency of the Congregational churches for the extension of Christ's kingdom abroad."[105]

3. "The Home Societies . . . shall be the agencies of the Congregational Churches for the extenson of Christ's kingdom in the United States."[106]

The Home Societies included the Home Missionary Society, Church Building Society, Education Society, Sunday School and Publishing Societies, Board of Ministerial Relief, and Sunday School Extension Society.[107]

Of interest is the 1927 Council action with regard to publication of "statistics": "The Council will continue to make an annual compilation of statistics of the churches, and a list of such ministers as are reported by the several state organizations."[108] The National Council accepted the lists provided to it by the conferences, who accepted the lists provided by the associations—which were reported directly by the Churches.[109] The words "The Council urges upon the Churches"[110] echo the 1883 Council committee statement (see above) with regard to the authority of each Church to "appoint and set apart their own minister," and also the 1892 vote "That the Council give cordial recognition to the new churches which apply for admission to this Council, and extend to them the assurance of Christian fellowship."[111]

In 1925 the National Council voted with regard to the denomination known as the Evangelical Protestant Churches in North America, "That the Conference of the Evangelical Protestant Churches in North America be recognized as on a parity with Congregational State Conferences, with representation in the National Council accordingly."[112] What happened was that the E.P. Churches joined the National Council as a State Conference.

116

Plainly, there was no claim of control or authority over the Evangelical Protestant Churches by the National Council of the Congregational Churches. At the same time a working agreement was made with the General Association of German Congregational Churches.

In 1929 when the National Council affirmed "its constituent membership in the Federal Council of the Churches of Christ in America."[113] The report of the Federal Council was received "with expression of continued and growing confidence in this organization as a practical expression of the spiritual unity of American Protestant Christianity."[114]

At meetings of the National Council from at least 1886 onward resolutions were adopted favoring "a federation, without authority, of all bodies of Christian churches."[115] Special consideration was given to union of "Christian bodies, holding substantially the same faith and order"[116] by the 1886 Council.

Beginning in 1886 there was discussion of unions or proposed unions with the Free Baptists,[117] the Congregational Methodists,[118] the United Brethren,[119] the Presbyterian Churches in Cleveland,[120] Episcopalian,[121] the Disciples of Christ (the Christian Church),[122] and the Universalists.[123]

The Congregational Methodists "in a few states united with the Congregational associations" in 1887-1888.[124] None of the other consultations led to union.

Over the period from 1895 to 1929 there were sporadic discussions with the "Christian General Convention."[125] At the 1929 National Council meeting a resolution was voted providing for union. Its key provisions were as follows:

"*Voted*, That Section I, paragraphs 1 and 2, and Sections II and III, of the plan of Union between the National Council of the Congregational Churches and The General Convention of the Christian Church, as presented by the Commission on Interchurch Relations and amended by the Council, be approved and adopted, subject to concurrent action by The General Convention of the Christian Church.

"The Commission on Inter-church Relations presented the matter of the merger between the Congregational and Christian churches for further consideration. The first Enabling Act found in the minutes of Tuesday's proceedings (See above) was unanimously adopted by the Council, whereupon Doctor Denison, General Secretary of the Convention of Christian Churches, was called to the platform and responded fittingly on behalf of the Christian Churches.

117

"Upon recommendation of the Commission the following resolutions were voted seriatim:

"3. That the concurrence of The General Convention of the Christian Church in the provisions of sections I, paragraphs 1 and 2, II and III shall be sufficient to consummate the union; and that, when notified of such concurrence, the Executive Committee of the National Council is instructed to proceed with the responsible representatives of the General Convention of the Christian Church to plan for the next meeting of this Council as a constituent of the General Council of the Congregational and Christian Churches.

. . .

"6. To recommend the provisions of Sections XXII and XXIII to our Churches, Associations, and Conferences, urging their prompt and definite plans for such readjustments as may seem desirable.

"7. To recommend the provisions of Sections VI,VII, IX-XIV, XVII-XIX, to the favorable action of the various Societies concerned.

"8. To approve for substance the details involved in I, paragraphs 3-5, IV-VI, VIII, XV, XVI, XX, XXI, XXIV, and XXV and to authorize the Executive Committee of the Council to negotiate with the representatives of the Christian Convention for any necessary modifications.

"9. That such sections of the Plan as shall be approved by The General Convention of the Christian Church, and where their interests are involved, obtains the concurrence of the Congregational national missionary organizations and of the various local, state, and regional organizations, shall become effective at once, so far as this National Council is concerned.

"10. To recommend to the American Board of Commissioners for Foreign Missions that it make suitable provision, as early as practicable, in the membership of the prudential Committee for representation from the Christian Body.

"11. To recommend to the Home Board that it make suitable provision, as early as practicable in the membership of the Board of Directors (the Executive Committee of the A.M.A.) and its administrative Committees, for representation from the Christian body.

"12. To refer to the Executive Committee of the National Council with power any needed adjustments of detail in the Plan of Union.

"13. That the Commission on Inter-church Relations be empowered to develop plans looking toward the completion of this merger.

"14. That the Plan of Union as a whole, as presented by the Commission on Inter-church Relations, with its amendments, is hereby approved."[126]

In 1931 the National Council of the Congregational Churches and the General Convention of the Christian Church, acting separately in Seattle, adopted a constitution. Then in joint session the new constitution was adopted, creating the General Council of the Congregational and Christian Churches. Before many years the "and" was dropped. Following the conciliar merger the various national and state church-bodies unite.[127]

In the preamble to the constitution appears these paragraphs:

"The Congregational Christian Churches of the United States by delegates assembled, reserving all the rights and cherished memories of their historic past and affirming loyalty to the basic principles of unity and democracy in church polity, hereby set forth the principles of Christian fellowship immemorially held by these churches.

"We hold sacred the freedom of the individual soul and the right of private judgment. We stand for the autonomy of the local church and its independence of ecclesiastical control. We cherish the fellowship of churches, united in district, state and national bodies for counsel and co-operation. Affirming these convictions we hold to the unity of the Church of Christ, and will unite with all its branches in fellowship and hearty co-operation; and we earnestly seek that the prayer of our Lord for the unity of his followers may be speedily answered."[128]

Article II on Purpose is as follows:

"The purpose of the General Council is to foster and express the substantial unity of the Congregational Christian churches in faith, purpose, polity and work; to consult upon and devise measures and maintain agencies for the promotion of the common interests of the kingdom of God; to cooperate with any corporation or body under control of or affiliated with the Congregational or Christian churches or any of them; and to do and to promote the work of these churches in their national, international and interdenominational relations, and in general so far as legally possible to perform on behalf of the united churches the various functions hitherto performed by the National Council for the Congregational churches and by the General Convention for the Christian churches, it being understood that where technical legal questions may be involved the action of the separate bodies shall be secured."[129]

Any objective scholar must conclude from the historic documents of Congregationalism that a voluntarily gathered company whose members have covenanted with one another and with the God and Father of our Lord Jesus Christ to live, worship, work and witness together continuingly, is a true and entire Church of

Christ, that such a Church is fully competent to establish and maintain relationships of love and fellowship with other Churches, and may choose to co-operate with like-minded Churches in such matters and in such manner as each Church shall determine. Advice and counsel are to be sought in times of need but all power and responsibility remains with the Church.

Those Connecticut churches which accepted and followed the Saybrook 1708 rules are a limited exception; the Consociations exceeded "advice and counsel" in matters of discipline and possibly nomination of candidate ministers.

There really is no question as to the nature of Congregational Polity as seen in the historic documents. A council is NOT a Church.

The Mansfield Theses in Detail

The remainder of the 96-page book in which the Mansfield Theses appear may be gathered into seven groupings. First, and basic, is "My Thesis is that *a council is a kind of congregation*."[130] This claim has been considered above. Allied to it are the following: "Congregationalism stands for the Apostolic Succession of Congregations."[131] The sacradotal character of leaders of standing councils is seen in the change of title. "The name *Superintendent* . . . is now giving way . . . to one which has a richer Congregational connotation: *The Minister of the Conference*."[132] "Because the Council stands between duties divine and human . . . it is no less a congregation than is a local church."[133] "Congregationalism . . . (may make) a place for bishops and presbyteries . . . when there is call for them."[134] "Congregationalism is bound to co-operate with other denominations . . . because their people are obviously gathered into congregations which in principle answer to the Congregational definition."[135]

The first Mansfield Thesis is rather startling when the elements are joined. What emerges is: a church is a congregation; a council is a congregation, therefore a council is a church! The Apostolic Succession of the church universal is the congregation; all denominations have congregations, therefore all churches are Congregational Churches! Churches have ministers; councils are churches, therefore councils have ministers! Councils may be called presbyteries, and their officers bishops; Congregationalism has councils, therefore it may call the councils "presbyteries" and their officers "bishops."

Mansfield Thesis Number One claims to be the same as that of John Robinson, Henry Barrow, Henry Jacob and William Ames.

I invite the reader to make a personal assessment of this claim by comparing the Mansfield Thesis with John Robinson, William Ames, and Henry Barrow.[136] Here is a small, representative sample of statements from the writings of notable Congregationalists:

In John Robinson's *Of Religious Communion* published at Leyden (p. 17), the contrast between contemporary Protestant Christianity and true religion was drawn.

> "If the parrish assemblyes gathered by compulsion, of all the parrishioners promiscuously: the Provincial, Diocesan, & Lordly government: the Ministery thence derived, with the service-book, & administrations accordingly, be of God; then is our fellowship, onely of persons sanctifyed (at least owtwardly) ioyning themselves by voluntary profession under the government, & Ministry of an eldership; coceaving prayers & thanksgiveings, according to the Churches present occasions by the teachings of the spirit, & so administering the Sacraments accordeing to the simplicity of the gospell, not of God, nor from heaven. If one the contrary, ours be of God, & of his Christ; then is theyrs of anti-christ, Gods, & Christs adversary."[137]

> "This we hold and affirm, that a company, consisting though but of two or three, separated from the world—whether unchristian or anti-christian—and gathered into the name of Christ by a covenant made to walk in all the ways of God known unto them, is a Church, and so hath the whole power of Christ."[138]

> "A congregation, or particular Church, is a society of believers joined together by a special band among themselves, for the constant exercise of the communion of saints among themselves."[139]

> "The Apostolical office, as such, was personal and temporary; and therefore, according to its nature and design, not successive or communicable to others in perpetual descendence from them. It was, as such, in all respects extraordinary, conferred in a special manner, designed for special purposes, discharged by special aids, endowed with special privileges, as was needful for the propagation of Christianity, and founding of churches."[140]

> "The decree of a Council hath so much force as there is force in the reason of it."[141]

> "It is entirely consistent with *Reason and the Revelation of God's mind* in His Word, that there should be *Councils and Synods* called upon requisite Occasions . . . But there is great Danger, lest such Meetings should be *hurtful to the Principles and Liberties of particular Churches*, and so *degenerate from the good Ends* which

121

ought to be designed and pursued in them . . . Wherefore it is hoped, that *The Brethren* in these Churches *will always maintain their Right to sit and act in Councils and Synods*; but yet that they will *never think of* placing any juridical power in them, but will *always continue to assert the Powers and Privileges of Particular Churches, which are sacred Things, by no means to be slighted and undervalued, nor to be left at the Mercy of any Classes or Councils, Synods or General Meetings.*"[142]

"*Ecclesia did ever signify only one assembly, and never a dispersed multitude, holding many ordinary set meetings in remote places*, as diocesan and larger churches do. Now according to these, and other Greeks, living in the Apostle's days, do the Apostles speak."[143]

"To such a body"—a particular Church—"how many members may be added, is not limited expressly in the word, onely it is provided in the word, that they be no more than that all may meet in one congregation, that *all may heare, and all may be edified*. For the Apostle so describeth the whole Church as meeting in one place. I Cor xiv: 23. But if all cannot heare, all cannot be edified. Besides the Apostle requireth, that when the Church meeteth together for the celebrating of the Lord's Supper, *they shall tarry one for another*, 1 Cor. xi: 33, which argueth the Church then that all *might partake together of the Lord's Supper in one congregation*, and threfore such Parishes as consist of 15,000, though they were all fit materialls for Church fellowship, yet ought to be divided into many churches, as too large for one. When the hive is too full, bees swarme into a new hive; so should such excessive members of Christians issue forth into more churches. Whence it appeareth to be an error, to say there is no limitation or distinction of Parishes, meaning of churches (*jure divino*), for though a precise quotient, a number of hundreds and thousands be not limited to every Church, yet such a number is limited as falleth not *below seven*, nor riseth above the bulke of *one congregation, and such a congregation wherein all may meete, and all may heare, and all may partake, and all may be edified together.*"[144]

"The truth is, a particular congregation (Church) is the highest tribunall . . . If difficulties arise . . . the counsell of other churches should be sought to clear the truth, but the power . . . rests still in the congregation, where Christ placed it."[145]

The Second Mansfield Thesis

The second Mansfield Thesis is "No congregation is regarded as a member of the Congregational Christian fellowship in the United States . . . until its sister congregations in the fellowship

122

have acknowledged it as such,"[146] This thesis is generalized, Congregationalism is distinguished from Independency by "the chain of mutual recognitions which link the churches together."[147] From this base the thesis concludes, "Congregationalism tends toward mutual recognition, and so to co-operation and finally to organic union . . ."[148] The dogma is restated thus: "In order to fulfill the Congregational definition of a church in fellowship, a congregation must be recognized by the sister churches which it itself recognizes."[149] Point number two is summed up "Mutual recognition of a strongly supporting type is the bond which makes the Congregational Churches in America a communion. On that recognition the whole government of the denomination . . . is built."[150]

The second Mansfield Thesis is quite impossible to find in the writings of Congregationalism for an interesting reason. The key words used in this thesis are laden with legal significance given to them by merger proponents and their attorneys in the courtroom of New York's Judge Steinbrink. The words "fellowship," "recognition," "mutual recognition" and "communion," used in the technical Mansfield Thesis sense, simply do not appear in the literature of Congregationalism.

"Communion" is a precious word used for the Lord's Supper, for the intimate loving relationship of God to persons and peoples, and of godly persons and peoples to each other. I do not recall a single Congregational usage in the sense of "denomination" prior to 1940, and considerable research has failed to uncover any.

"Mutual recognition" and "recognition" are used quite often in Congregational literature especially the latter, without the slightest hint of legalism. I know of no instance in which "recognition" is said to be the foundation for "government of the denomination." Indeed one would not expect such use of the word since, by definition, "the whole government of the denomination" did not exist, as is crystal clear in the historic documents already quoted. The constitution of the General Council expressly disclaimed any such government.

"Fellowship" is found frequently in Congregational documents, and appears in the writings of our great exemplars. Usually "fellowship" means the family feeling and godly concern characteristic of our Churches and church-bodies at their best. Sometimes, especially in the twentieth century, "fellowship" is synonomous with the total body of all Congregational Christians,

Churches, church-bodies, and agencies. The use of "fellowship" as a synonym for an organizational chain of command has had no place in Congregational literature.

I was introduced to "fellowship" in Mansfield Thesis Two meaning in the early spring of 1952. A national fund to establish new Churches was faltering. The United States was divided into regions. Dr. Stanley U. North was appointed to head the Pacific Coast region.

At the request of State Superintendent Dr. Jesse Perrin I arranged to have him and Dr. North as my luncheon guests at the Pasadena Athletic Club. To my amazement, Dr. North launched into a virulent attack on me and on the Oneonta Congregational Church of which I was minister. "You are a traitor to the fellowship. We have honored you many times, and you have ignored your duty and you have led your Church to ignore its duty to the fellowship."[151] It was Lent. I was terribly busy and in no mood for a diatribe. As the waiter served the entre I responded "Stan, show me any Church in California which has given as much to new Churches as Oneonta has in San Marino and Arcadia." He retorted, "But not one cent of that is credited to the fellowship. It doesn't appear on my records so my quota is far below what it ought to be."

I replied, "Are you concerned about serving people by helping them to gather new Churches or are you worried about 'your quota'?"

He exploded, "It's time someone taught you a lesson. You're too d----- independent. You ignore me. But I don't need you to get at the potential givers in Oneonta. Aileen Ogier will give me their names and addresses."

Then *I* exploded. I put my napkin on the table, pushed back my chair, and said to Jesse, "I'll arrange for you to sign the bill for me. I refuse to eat with a person who threatens me and uses his previous pastoral relation with my secretary to fill some 'New York' quota. Oneonta is contributing $10,000 per year to gather the Arcadia Church. We have commissioned thirty of our members including a past-moderator to be charter members. Those thirty represent a loss to our budget of more than $3,000 a year, plus their larger capital gifts, work, and leadership. There is not a single Church in this conference—*not any*—which has done or is doing one quarter as much as Oneonta. This blackmail through my secretary is despicable. Good bye." And I left.

On the sidewalk, Jesse Perrin caught up with me. "Wait, Henry, Please! Lunch mustn't end like this. You and I have no quarrel. Don't go away mad."

"Look Jesse. You've known me and worked with me. You know I don't fly off easily. Of course I'm sorry I blew up but that doesn't make me ready to eat with a blackmailer in the name of 'fellowship'."

"All right. All right. It was a poor choice of words."

"No, Jesse. It was a wrong attitude and it stands for a dangerous trend in Congregationalism. I don't want to eat with Stan. In fact, I don't want to eat at all. Our Congregational fellowship is far too precious to be used as an organizational big club. And the guy's plumb wrong about new Churches. Oneonta has been doing the job, NOT talking about it and setting quotas. But I'm not going to argue here in the sidewalk."

"Look," Jesse pleaded, "At least consider *my* position as host superintendent to a national officer. Be courteous."

I liked Jesse Perrin. He'd been minister in Glendale. He had co-operated in joint ventures in student work, Pilgrim Fellowship, and Camp Pilgrim Pines.

"Jesse, this is final. I'll return and finish lunch on two conditions. First North will apologize for threatening to go behind my back, and *you* will give me *your* word that he won't do such an underhanded and un-Congregational thing. Second, we will NOT talk about his campaign for his quota of money for new Churches."

"That's pretty strong, Henry."

"That's it, Jesse. Take it or leave it. I'm too angry to do anything else."

"Will you come upstairs and wait 'till I talk to him?"

"Surely. I'll wait exactly sixty seconds."

When I returned to the table North apologized. I picked at my lunch. "Small talk" was the limit of our conversation.

Afterwards, downstairs, Jesse felt expansive. "Well," he said, "Let's you two shake hands." "What are we 'shaking *on*'?" I asked. He reddened, "J-j-u-st—just being friends." "Stan, if you'll promise never to threaten *any* minister and never to demean Congregationalism by using 'fellowship' as a whip, I'll shake hands and congratulate you."

He turned away.

Each of the mediators had to struggle with novel uses of old words like "fellowship." What disturbed me was the desecration of something very real, very beautiful, and very precious. I was sorry my temper flared up. It ought not to have done so. But I'd be dishonest if I did not add that the drive back to Oneonta was sad and lonely. Something infinitely priceless had been given a price tag. A majestic unity of spirit had been prostituted; "fellowship" meant "doing what you are told," "paying your quota." It had nothing to do with love and concern for the unchurched in San Marino or Arcadia or anywhere else.

With this background, with my detailed study of Congregational Polity in the Documents and Practice and with the love the REAL fellowship which was characteristic of the mediators, it should be easy to see why Mansfield Thesis Two was so foreign to our spirits—yes, so alien to Congregationalism.

Mansfield Thesis Three

The third Mansfield Thesis is initially stated rather mildly. "Standing councils," "permanent bodies of ministers and laymen"[152] differ in Church character from occasional meetings. Two questions are posed and answered in the affirmative. Can a council determine its membership and affiliation by itself? Has a council "church power?"[153] Regarding the latter it is asserted "All the arguments against the coercion of local churches by councils avail against the coercion of councils by churches."[154] The endpoint is quoted from Henry Jacobs, totally out of accord with Jacobs' steadfast testimony, "Let each council be . . . an entire and independent body politic spiritual . . . indeed with power in itself immediately under Christ."[155] A compelling proof of this thesis is said to be "The General Council of the Congregational Christian Churches in the United States was brought into being . . . without recourse to the churches at all. Councils are of the nature of 'committees with power'."[156]

This process of deduction is fascinating!

Let me state it boldly. The claim is that a permanent council, being a church, possesses "church power," can determine its membership and can choose its affiliations. Particular churches have no power over it because it is an independent body politic with power to act as it chooses. All this is supposed to be illustrated by the union of the General Convention of the Christian Churches and the National Council of the Congregational Churches in the U.S.A. in 1931.

Once stated clearly the fallacies are plain. Ask one question, "Could the General Council determine its membership if the Congregational Churches chose to elect no members?" Patently there were thousands of Congregational Churches before there was any General Council or National Council. The council is nothing but a meeting of persons from the Churches. Furthermore, as we shall document in another chapter, associations, conferences, boards, societies *and* the General Council are the *agents* of the Churches for specific purposes set forth in their respective basic documents. To expect an *agent* body to fulfill the mandate given it, *and no more*, is not coercion: it is the expected honorable discharge of duty. The quote from Henry Jacobs is instructive. Every mediator would laud Jacobs' description of a Council as a "body politic *spiritual*." That's exactly what we hoped for; spiritual guidance, "advice and counsel." The 1931 union is equally instructive. It was a national-level-only union. There should have been a referendum of the Churches. None was thought necessary because no change in faith or polity was proposed. The General Council constitution used almost the same words as the National Council consitution when it denied Council authority or control over the Churches.

In sum, with Congregationalists a "standing council" does not really exist. We use the legal fiction of a committee said to be the council *ad interim*, BUT every single act of the committee must be ratified by the General Council itself, and all honorable acts merely carry forward the instructions given by votes of the General Council.

The final collapse of Mansfield Thesis Three is sealed once we see that the power to elect the council members does not exist apart from the Churches, and further, while it is hoped that spiritual advice and counsel will be given to Churches by councils, the Churches have the sole right to determine, each Church for itself, whether or not, or to what extent, the advice and counsel given IS the Word of the Lord *for them*. *The ultimate dispostion of every recommendation rests with each Church.* Therefore, *no* council has "church-power;" it has, and should have, whatever spiritual weight there is in the worth of its advice and counsel no more, and, no less.

The Fourth Mansfield Thesis

The fourth Mansfield Thesis is "The written constitution of a modern council is an open covenent whereunto all the delegates particularly bind themselves when they accept membership according to its terms."[157]

Historical constitutions are few in Congregational history. The major extant ones have been quoted, that is, those of the Congregational Union of England and Wales, 1832, the National Council of the Congregational Churches of the U.S.A., 1871, and the General Council of the Congregational Christian Churches of 1931. These constitutions established the councils as agents of the Churches for specific purposes and prohibited legislative, judicial, or executive control of the Churches.

A constitution in the dictionary definition is the fundamental law of an organization. The Congregational Churches have never had an over-all fundamental law. Hence the novel proposal of Mansfield Thesis Four cannot be compared with prior documents or written statements of polity; for there are none.

Most astonishing therefore is the assertion that the constitution of a modern council is a covenant. Once more I am unable to compare this claim with other Congregational statements—because there are none.

It is obvious:

1. that a covenant is voluntarily entered into by personal choice rather than public election;
2. that a covenant in Congregational terms is a religious bond betwixt person and person, persons and God. Legalism is alien to a Congregational covenant;
3. that few delegates to a General Council have read the constitution, none as a covenant;
4. that no constitutional document in American Congregationalism up to and including 1954 contains one syllable claiming that it is a covenant, overt or implied.
5. that *any* council is a transient body, whose members are selected for a specified period. In the United States only a third or less serve more than one term, hence the essential covenant-relation in a continuing fellowship is missing; and so also is the week-by-week living, working, and witnessing which is the heart of a Congregational covenant.

Mansfield Thesis Four has no support in Congregational history, documents or practice. It attempts to clothe a council in the garb of a Church.

Mansfield Thesis Five

The fifth Mansfield Thesis is, The full meaning of the "call of the churches" is "the authorization of the churches."[158] That is, "essentially a council depends upon the authorization of all the other bodies of the fellowship, that is, basically, the churches."[159] The thesis is at once enlarged, "Authorization . . . means recognition and support."[160]

Throughout Congregational history Churches have called councils for advice and counsel. In Connecticut 1708-1784 many Churches authorized consociations or the statewide General Association to perform specific functions. There has never been, and is not now, any disagreement as to the power of Congregational Churches to call councils, or, to authorize them to perform any function which respects the self-completeness of each Church.

In no way does the limited authorization of a transient council mean "recognition and suppport" AS THESE WORDS ARE USED in Mansfield Five. *After* the New York trial in Judge Steinbrink's courtroom, the word "recognition" acquired legal nuances never before attributed to it. Note carefully the word "support:" this claim is precisely the basis for Dr. Stanley North's misinterpretation of "fellowship" referred to above.

According to Mansfield Thesis Five a council, by some legerdemain not known in Congregational history, is able to wield authority and demand support! Merely to state *that* proposition is to refute it. Witness the procedure by which most Congregational Churches in England authorized their council to exercise church-power. *First*, the Churches voted to form the Congregational Church in England, specifically authorized to unite with the Presbyterian Church in England, *THEN* the newly formed national church-body proceeded to effect a union of the Congregational and Presbyterian national Churches. In other words, Mansfield Five was rejected in England, and, to remedy the national Union's inherent lack of authority, a specific vote of each participating Church was required.

There is in the American Congress a vast difference between a vote to adopt a budget and a vote to appropriate the money to finance a program. All votes by all Congregational Councils, save in the Connecticut Saybrook years, are recommendations to the Churches, NOT a legal appropriation of funds or a compulsion to act. If an American council is true to its Congregational character even the monies from endowments are used in accord with the irrevocable trust requirements.

Just as the United States federal government cannot arrogate to itself powers not given to it by the people in the constitution, so, Congregational councils cannot arrogate to themselves powers not given to them by the Churches. Therefore, ultimate power resides in the Churches who may authorize or withdraw authorization with no inferred legal transfer of church-power to exercise "recognition" or require "support." This point will become clearer in the 1954 Polity Report.

Mansfield Thesis Six

The sixth Mansfield Thesis is "such is the freedom of congregations in a Congregational system that if they choose to set up an episcopal or presbyterial or other system, they may do so."[161] This follows a puzzling sentence, "The freedom of Congregationalism is . . . ampler than . . . non-Congregationalism . . . because the Congregation does not exert domination over so large an area . . . (as in any other) communion."[162]

It is not clear how freedom can be both "ampler" and more restricted simultaneously.

Whether a moral person is "free" to commit suicide is doubtful, in the extreme. It is equally implausible to contend that Congregational freedom is "free" to commit suicide by becoming presbyterial, episcopal or monarchial. Historically, even in the 1708-1784 Saybrook years in Connecticut, no claim was made to replace the power of the particular Churches by an inclusive governing body. True, I recall a map of Hartford c. 1820 with the designation "First Presbyterian Church" for the new Meeting of the First Church of Christ—Congregational—But there is no record that First Church EVER changed its name.[163]

Mansfield Thesis Six is as illogical as it would be to claim that God is free, therefore He can choose to become the devil! Which is impossible.

Mansfield Thesis Seven

Mansfield Thesis Seven is stated at some length, beginning "The ecumenical march for which the next decades are already calling must advance beyond the level of simple recognition toward that of supporting recognition which is the basis of organic union."[164]

Congregationalists are to lead "the ecumenical march" because "Every truly Congregational Church longs for the day when at least simple recognition will be given it by all other congregations in the Great Church."[165] "To believe that a single ecclesiastical constitution cannot include a plurality of polities is to be deluded by an outworn past."[166]

Thesis Seven is eventually stated thus:

"It is obviously necessary to have church government, rites and orders, if there is to be organized church fellowship, but whether they shall be democratical, aristocratical, presbyterical, episcopal, or even papal must depend upon many factors of time, place and culture, all of them being fully acceptable to Congregationalists as long as they do not extinguish the Congregation as a congregation according to Congregational definition. They are in fact tentatively acceptable even if they do abrogate the royal rights of the congregations *willing*, but don't abrogate those of congregations *unwilling*, to have it so."[167]

Expressed sequentially, Mansfield Thesis Seven posits "organic union" as the goal of "the ecumenical march." Organic union is to be under "a single ecclesiastical constitution" which provides for "church government, rites, and orders." The form of this government "must depend upon many factors of time, place, and culture, (all forms) being acceptable to Congregationalists." Those who do not espouse Thesis Seven are "deluded by an outworn past."

John Greenwood, Henry Barrow, and John Penry were hung in London in 1593 because they opposed "a single ecclesiastical constitution" in England based on "many factors of time, place, and culture." Erstwhile solicitor-general of the realm, John Cook, suffered a similar fate in 1660 for a similar reason.

Put bluntly, Mansfield Thesis Seven is blasphemy, because it puts expendiencies of "time, place, and culture" in the central determinative role reserved for the God and Father of our Lord Jesus Christ, and for Him alone.

The assumptions of Mansfield Thesis Seven are a cacophony of contradictions. The single phrase "as long as they do not extinguish the Congregation as a congregation according to Congregational definition" contradicts "It is obviously necessary to have (overall, organic) church government." Declaration of centralized over-body control by "presbyterial, episcopal or even papal" power contradicts "the royal rights of the" Churches even if the Churches are willing to be controlled!

Hundreds of years of Congregational history, and the history of the witness of the New Testament Churches, are contradicted by the assumed necessity of "church government, rites, and orders;" these are exactly what goaded Robert Browne, John Robinson, Francis Johnson and their fellow Congregationalists. We do not now and we never have accepted the undemocratic and non-New-Testament notion that there must be castes in Churches under the guise of "orders," or conformity of rites, or overall government.

131

The strangest contradiction of all is that "Congregational Churches long for" "recognition by Churches of other denominations" when, in fact, for centuries—certainly since John Robinson—Congregational Churches have lauded others, and have often been lauded by them. In the United States the contradiction is especially peculiar since *all* other church-bodies which entered New England sought "recognition" by the Congregational Churches!!

WHY the Mansfield Theses?

How is one to understand why the Mansfield Theses were propounded?

The answer does not lie in Congregational history, in our basic documents or in our literature.

Dr. Albert Peel and President Russell Stafford saw the "three talks" in the perspective of the World Council of Churches, the International Congregational Council and the exigiencies of the Cadman Memorial Church lawsuit to prevent the General Council from implementing the Basis of Union of the Congregational Christian Churches and the Evangelical Reformed Church in the United States.

The year was 1938, the place Beloit, and the occasion a meeting of the General Council of the Congregational Christian Churches of the United States. The Executive Committee had a nominee for the secretaryship, the Rev. Douglas Horton, D.D., minister of Chicago's Hyde Park Church, holding ministerial standing in both Congregational and Presbyterian bodies. In preparation for the secretaryship "Dr. Horton travelled round the world, meeting Congregationalists in every continent."[168] Quite naturally he also met leaders of the World Conference of Faith and Order, and the World Conference of Life and Work, both being predecessors of the yet-to-be-formed World Council of Churches. The Secretary-nominee "was greatly impressed by the world-wide range and opportunity of Congregationalism, and felt that, if only it could be focused, it had a vital contribution to make to the world."[169] 1937-1938 was a stirring time to be abroad in Europe, especially for one at home in the German language. (I had experienced this as a Tubingen University post doctoral student in 1935.)

To the surprise of ordinary 1938 Council delegates like myself the Secretary-nominee insisted that the office bear the title "Minister of the General Council," and that he be inducted into office in a ceremony patterned after a minister's installation as pastor and teacher, and that a pectoral cross of office be approved.

132

I had been the chief host minister to the 1936 General Council at Mount Holyoke College, and therefore knew personally nearly all the executives and committee members. The view expressed by men like Will Frazier was "I don't like it but it probably won't make much difference." On the lawn across from the sanctuary where there was some relief from the oppressive heat the commonest remark was "If that's the way he wants it, let him have it." The only real objections I heard were from state superintendents who had taken office since 1936. Dr. Horton wanted to induct them into office in the same manner, and some objected.

In retrospect it appears that the vision of focusing Congregationalism so that it could be a world force became a life purpose. Dr. Horton saw in 1938 that it would be nice to move among bishops, archbishops, partriarchs, and archimandrites in doctoral robe, with clerical collar, bands, a pectoral cross of office and the title "Minister of the General Council."

When the World Council of Churches was inaugurated Sunday August 22, 1948, in Amsterdam, the Rev. Dr. Douglas Horton was vice chairman of the Executive Committee, and chairman of the American Section. "It became increasingly evident that if International Congregationalism were to play its proper part in the world it must be more than a gathering of the clans once every ten years. Already it had become clear that its meetings must in some way be related to those of the World Council of Churches . . . Thus it was that in July 1947 an International Committee met in Bournemouth, England, at which it was decided to hold the next (International Congregational) Council at Wellesley College, in June 1949, to set up an International Office in London, and to invite Dr. Sidney M. Berry, the acting Moderator of the Council and the Secretary of the Congregational Union of England and Wales, to be the first Secretary."[170]

Earlier, in 1939, when war made postponement of the International Congregational Council scheduled for 1940 inevitable, "Dr. Horton invited an International Seminar to meet at Yale University in 1940. Its thirty members included a Chinese, a Japanese, an Indian, an Armenian, a Greek, a Slovak, a Mexican, a Filipino, a South African, an American negro, an Englishman, and American with varied European backgrounds. . . . The Seminar prepared a statement of Congregational views on the nature of the Church for the use of the World Conference of Faith and Order."[171] This statement is reproduced in chapter one of this book. It was published in 1951 under the chairmanship of Dr. George W.

Richards (E & R) in Vol. 3 of the American Theological Committee's report on *The Nature of the Church* as an "authoritative statement of beliefs as to the Church which are held in the (Congregationalist) communion."[172] The 1940 statement was NOT an "authoritative statement;" it was the report of 30 persons gathered at Yale by Dr. Horton, and had whatever weight there was in its worth, but no Congregational Churches or church-bodies ever approved it so far as I have discovered.

Dr. Peel's *Journal*[173] is the source of considerable information concerning Dr. Horton, since both men were at work on the calling of an International Congregational Council, though for somewhat different reasons. The distinguished English Congregational historian visited the United States in 1940, 1942, 1944 and 1946-1947. In 1942, 1944 and 1946-1947 he was our guest at the Oneonta parsonage in South Pasadena, preached at the Church, did research on John Penry in the Huntington Library, and spent many hours in the discussion of Congregational history, polity and theology. Albert Peel's lectures to the 1938 General Council were published under the title *Christian Freedom*.[174] The newly inducted Minister and Secretary of the General Council wrote the Introduction, with a concluding statement which I have quoted many times. I quote it again to contrast this 1938 statement with the Mansfield Theses.

> "God will presently be asking (who can fail to hear?) for those who will to take their stand for the freedom wherewith Christ has made them free. Weaker brethren will flee, in times of uncertainty, to the authoritarian churches and states, but not so, please God, shall we. We have a witness to bear. We shall stand for a free faith—because we know, like our fathers, that it is 'the hearts before God' that are important in time and eternity, 'and no thing els'."[175]

Albert Peel was an amazing person, quiet, almost shy, meticulous in scholarship, a delightful conversationalist and a warm-hearted English gentleman. When he preached or lectured, all shyness dropped away. In its place a strong voice, clear and urgent, fearlessly proclaimed the headship of Christ, the irrelevance of "sacraments,"[176] the call for the ministry of persons of mature experience rather than precise academic degrees,[177] the freeing of Churches from bondage to buildings,[178] and above all the freedom of each soul and the freedom of each Church.[179]

The alliance of Albert Peel and Douglas Horton helped to activate the International Congregational Council. It was one important thread in the weaving of substantial relations between the Congregational Churches in the United Kingdom and the United States, expressed by wartime fellowship, visiting, relief, and reconstruction.

Eleven years after the Beloit Council (1938) Drs. Peel and Horton published *International Congregationalism*,[180] the first 61 pages by Peel and the remaining 56 pages by Horton. Herein is found an otherwise missing link in the change of Dr. Horton from the author of the ringing challenge of freedom in the 1938 Introduction to *Christian Freedom* to the author of the Mansfield Theses.

"Some have dreamed that the International Congregational Council might become more than an organ for fellowship and the exchange of ideas. They have asked why it should not take the lead in Congregational evangelism and church extension.

* * *

"As the ranking organ of world Congregationalism, the International Council will eventually become the means through which the various Unions will recognize one another. Already the World Council of Churches has informally asked the International Congregational Council whether or not it considers a certain group of churches in Europe to be Congregational. The dangers connected with the development of a principle of recognition are too apparent. Free churches and free Unions do not want to be drawn into any time-wasting and spirit-desiccating controversies reagarding 'Orders'. The fact remains, however, that there is no body in the world better able to recognize a free church than a Union of free churches, and (it would seem to follow) none better able to recognize a free national Union than an international council of such Unions. As the denominations of Christendom, with the shrinking of all distances, become more aware of each other, the International Council is bound to be appealed to increasingly as a judge and arbiter in questions of recognition."[181]

Strangely, the same book states:

"The International Congregational Council can never boast itself to be the controlling force in world Congregationalism. That horrid contingency is eliminated by the very nature of Congregationalism, where the *locus* of all authority is the local church meeting. Congregationalism stakes its entire claim upon the truth that God in Christ is likely to speak more truly and directly to a group of devout worshippers than to a bishop, committee, or even a majority. . . . No Congregational church tries to control the life of any other church or group outside it, nor does any Board or representative body—or any International Congregational Council.

135

"The International Congregational Council is, however, a kind of church meeting itself. . . . The Council is the chief symbol of the unity of the churches, but it is more than a symbol: it is the agency *par excellence* to consider and devise measures to support the common interests of the churches around the world."[182.]

A Vision and a Voice

International Congregationalism is an early, eloquent espousal of a "United Church, Congregational" "against the world."[183] Dr. Horton, one of the leaders of the World Council of Churches in 1948, had a vision of Congregationalism as a prime leader in the "Great Church." Through that "Great Church" Congregationalism would have an important voice in the affairs of the world. This was no narrow yen for personal aggrandisment, as the Rev. Malcolm Burton often charged. Unbiased study of the record commends Dr. Horton's motives. He had become a Crusader for Christ lifting his voice in the name of Congregationalism to proclaim the vision of one "Great Church" pulling together a torn and shattered world. It seems best to quote the Crusader rather than paraphrase his words. Here then are the major sections of "Congregationalism Against the World:"

"Congregational is an adjective descriptive not only of a church, but of a civilization as well. Congregationalism has an effect upon its secular surroundings.

* * *

"That was in the seventeenth century, and within a single nation. We are concerned with the twentieth century, and are considering the place and prospects of a Council which operates at an international level. But the same principles hold. The work that was done by Congregational Independents for Britain and America and other countries now needs doing over again on the place of international politics. There is no more perfect principle to be found for the total organization of the nations of the world than the congregational 'Consociation, but not subordination.'

"There is a notable difference in the needed emphasis as the principle is applied to-day and that which was called for yesterday. . . . Among depressed and under-privileged classes the cry was necessarily for freedom, in Church and State. The consociation of the national body politic could be taken for granted.

"In the relationship between nations this is not so. Without giving up their decent sovereignty over their own inner affairs, the nations need to develop an international society. With them, for the moment, it is the other end of the Congregational principle which should be given greater weight: *'Consociation*—though not subordination.' And it is as an exponent and example of consociation that the International Congregational Council takes its place in the world to-day. As a matter of fact, wholly independent local churches are ill-equipped to speak a uniting word to the divided international world to-day, for their own dividedness and mutual isolation would speak so loudly that no one could hear what they said on the subject of international unity. . . . An International Council is itself in fellowship with other like bodies, each of them autonomous over its own concerns. It is therefore fitted in a double aspect to make plain to the nations the meaning of its own essential principle: "Consociation, but not subordination.'

"It must do its work in this realm first through the spoken and written word. The statements which the International Congregational Council, made up of representatives from the five continents, puts out to the public Press have their own *role* in moulding the thought of the day. As the Council grows, undoubtedly this part of its work will grow with it. One can look forward to a future in which the pronouncements of the Council, not only in politics, but in economics, in philosophy and theology—all of which have their own bearing upon politics—become part of the 'must' reading of all thoughtful people.

* * *

"The International Congregational Council has a work of demonstration to perform.

* * *

"There is no reason why it should not become to the world the mighty symbol of freedom in fellowship under Christ . . .

"The whole matter is summed up in a statement written in preparation for the meeting of the International Congregational Council at Wellesley, Massachusetts, in 1949, which describes Congregationalism in its essence, in its significance for the unviersal Church, and for the political life of the world. This statement discloses both the base on which the Council stands and the banner it unfurls to the world. It was the work of a committee consisting of Dr. Nathaniel Micklem (Chairman) and Dr. Peel of England, Dr. Walter Horton and Dean Luther Weigle of the United States, and Rev. Fr. Zdychynec of Czechoslovakia, and it was unanimously agreed to at Bournemouth. It reads:

* * *

" 'The distinctive element in the Congregational polity has been the local church, in which each member has his spiritual responsibility. The purpose of church polity is that Christ, and Christ alone, may rule in His Church. We believe that the instrument whereby Christ rules in the local church is the church meeting, at which all the convenant members of the church seek together by prayer and discussion to discover the will of Christ and are guided into a common mind by the Holy Spirit.

"'Local Congregational churches have united with other Congregational churches and with other communions for the purpose of wider fellowship and wider service. These wider unions are extensions of the principle of church government and church authority exemplified in the church meeting. It is Christ who rules in His Church; therefore to no individuals or courts is given coercive authority in the Church. Where Congregational churches have entered into union with other churches, it has been upon the principle that wider synods and courts of the church should have the same sort of authority as the church meeting; that is, that they should seek to find the will of Christ for His Church by prayer and discussion, and being led to a common mind should have the spiritual authority of the church meeting. It is our fundamental principle that in all the organization of the church at every level, all authority is spiritual or, as our fathers put it, ministerial, not legalistic, coercive and magisterial. We believe this to be the true principle of government and authority in the whole church catholic; this we regard as our essential contribution to the universal Church. We point out that this is a principle of unity and fellowship in the Spirit, not a principle of individualism, will-worship, sectarianism or anarchy. It is the principle of unity, of authority, and of obedience to Christ.

* * *

"'There has been historically, and there is in principle, a close connection between our polity and political institutions. Those who have known freedom and responsibility in the church meeting have not been tolerant of tyranny in the State. Democracy, as we understand it and desire to see it established, is government by discussion and consent. Our churchmanship is inconsistent not only with any form of State totalitarianism, but also with government by the mass-man or the mere power of majorities. The rights of man as the child of God and the rights of minorities must be respected. We stand for political government by the discussion of free men and by fundamental consent. Because of this respect for the individual, which we learn from Christ and practice in our church meeting, we stand for political and religious freedom, for economic justice, for racial equality, and for equality of the sexes. But we stand no less for the responsibility of every individual for the good of any fellowship of which he is a member. No one can take his rightful place in Church or State apart from the education and economic status which allow the development of full personality. Our concern for social righteousness therefore springs from our churchmanship and is integral to it.'

"In sum:

" 'First.   A Congregational church is a covenant fellowship, binding the members to God and to one another through Christ, the Head of the Church—a fellowship in faith, in worship, in mutual service and in the service of mankind. Its duty to the world is to spread the Gospel and to work for such political and economic conditions as are implied in the Gospel.

" 'Second.   The principle of spiritual authority exemplified in church meeting, where the whole fellowship is brought to a common mind by the Holy Spirit, is of universal application. Congregational churches have gone into unions with one another and with other churches on the basis that Christ rules in His Church only by the Spirit, and that He has not delegated coercive authority to individual officers of synods. We believe this to be the one principle of unity and authority for the universal Church. This principle is applicable not less in the political life of the world, involving government by persuasion, by discussion and by consent. Thus Christ rules in His Church and thus He must rule also in the world.' "[184]

Dr. Douglas Horton, with his vision of a kind of Congregationalism which would have a major voice in the "Great Church" and in the world of nations, returns us to the Amsterdam, 1948, inaugural meeting of the World Council of Churches.

A small book by Cecil Northcott, probably published in 1948, is titled *Answer From Amsterdam*, with the subtitle *Congregationalism and the World Church*.[185] This is the first of several little books bearing the imprint of both the British and American Congregational publishers. Herein is set forth vividly the impression made on Congregational publishers. Herein is set forth vividly the impression made on Congregationalists by the colorful garb and world sweep represented by churchly figures "the handsome bearded Syrian patriarch from South India . . . the

hatted bearded Orthodox men . . . archbishops and Congregationalists . . . archimandrites . . . the white robed figure of
D. T. Niles of Ceylon."[186]

Many of the world's notable scholars, church executives and a
few world-renowned church members were present. The roll
included Karl Barth, C. H. Dodd, Emil Brunner, Rheinhold
Niebuhr, Martin Niemoller, Dr. J. Hromadka, Mr. John Foster
Dulles (U.S. Secretary of State)—"Here for all practical purposes
were the churches of the world except the Roman Catholic Church
and a section of the Orthodox Church now living behind the high
barrier which marks East from West."[187] Among fellow members
of the Executive Committee the minister and secretary of the
General Council found the Most Rev. Archbishop Brilioth, the
Right Rev. Bishop Aulen, The Most Rev. Archbishop Germanos,
the Right Rev. Bishop Dun, The Right Rev. Bishop Fuglsang-
Damgaard, and Bishop Stahlin.[188] There is no need to assign
sinister significance to the adoption of gown, bands and pectoral
cross of office in such company. It was probably a simple way to
move among the distinguished company as an equal.

In the Tompkins book there is "an Ecumenical Glossary."[189]
Here the word usage of the Mansfield Theses shows its rootage in
the affairs of the World Council of Churches. "Church" is used in
three ways (i) "(in the singular and with a capital) to indicate . . .
One Holy Catholic and Apostolic Church."[190] (ii) "churches (in
the plural with small initial) is used for those organized forms into
which we are divided."[191] (iii) "*Churches* (or *Church* with a
capital) . . . whenever the word occurs as part of a proper title, e.g.,
Methodist Church, Greek Orthodox Church, World Council of
Churches."[192]

"*Catholic* Church (is used) to mean the Church spoken of in
the Creeds."[193]

"*Confession* (denotes) . . . the whole body of distincitve beliefs . . .
constituting a major Christian tradition,"[194] such as Orthodox,
Lutheran and Anglican. "*Communion* is a synonym for Anglicanism
as a confession."[195] "*Organic* union (or unity) is sometimes
opposed to *federation* or *federal* union (or unity) of churches."[196]
Reunion is to be "avoided because it presupposes union by *return*
to one particular form of church life."[197] "*Union* is a more appropriate word . . ."[198]

Thompkins reports several interpretations of church unity,
stressing "a new form of organic church life which would embody
all that is true in each of the diverse traditions—e.g. a church order

which embraced episcopal, presbyterian and congregational forms within a single church."[199] These words are almost identical with those in Mansfield Thesis Seven. Dr. Tompkins' office at the time of writing was at 297 Fourth Avenue, New York City, in the same building as 287 Fourth Avenue where was Dr. Horton's office. The offices were connected and the latter was chairman of the American Committee of the World Council of Churches. It would be strange if there had NOT been close collaboration on so important a study booklet. Tompkins was secretary of the committee of which Horton was chairman.

There are important words used by Tompkins in addition to those in the glossary: "*Liturgical worship*—the use of fixed forms."[200] "*Eucharist-centered worship*—This scriptural synonym for the Lord's Supper . . . (means that) all other worship (is seen) as preparation for . . . this central act. By a natural logic (this act is seen) as the central and most attended service of *every* Sunday."[201]

But at Amsterdam in 1948 *four separate* communion services had to be held to accommodate diversity of belief and practice.[202] In reporting this, Tompkins says, "The World Council must be scrupulous to avoid appearing 'to hold Communion services.' It is not the Church; it is not even a church."[203]

Let us add one more note from Northcott's Amsterdam book. To state "The position of Congregationalism in relation to union, it appears to me we have to say that the decisive marks of the Church are not in institutional continuity but in the Word and Sacraments of the Gospel."[204]

"Two remaining points need to be made. Modern Congregationalism as seen in Britain and America appears in danger of becoming 'just another denomination' with all the outward appearances of organization which go with ecclesiastical machinery. In doing so we must be careful not to submerge the distincitve experiences of our churchmanship, not for their own sake and for the glory of our confession but for the sake of the coming Great Church. A united church needs those gifts of Congregationalism which it has made its own treasure in Christ and whose united life will not be complete without them.

"It may be that of all sections of the Christian Church the Congregational as an organization must be ready to die to live."[205]

The "Great Church" and the Mansfield Theses

At last we are in a position to see that the Mansfield Theses were the fruit grown on the root of a vision of the "Great Church" healing a shattered world by uniting Christians everywhere into one powerful Voice speaking with power.

This is the only interpretation which makes sense to me. The man whom I knew and with whom I shared campus embassies, association meetings, state conferences, General Council meetings, and uncounted discussions, was filled with zeal for the "Great Church." He earnestly believed that it held the best hope for world order and world peace.

Among the mediators, dismay as to the content of the "three talks" was accompanied by admiration of the vision of the speaker, and puzzlement as to the forms and words introduced into Congregational Polity.

Yet it is obvious that those very words, in usages to which Congregationalists were not accustomed, came to the Mansfield Theses from discussions and writings of the World Council of Churches.

To say this is not to imply approval of the Mansfield Theses. It is only to shed light on the manner in which a spokesperson for Congregationalism had adopted the stance therein set forth.

Seeking Light

By the close of the St. Andrews International Congregational Council I was determined to seek more light and truth.

Intent study of great art clears my mind and refreshes my spirit; so I spent five days photographing in the Louvre. By the last day I was sure that two issues must be studied simultaneously. The first was the fruits of Christian devotion, the second, church polity as a hindrance or help to Christian living.

Aside from Congregational great-hearts like Bunyan, Milton, Brewster and Hooker I'd re-read year after year Sabatier's *Francis of Assisi*. Among saints not in free church tradition I had singled out Teresa of Avilla and her disciple John of the Cross whose active years corresponded to those of men like Fitz, Barrow, Greenwood and Penry in Great Britain. With their works in hand I made a pilgrimage to Spain to walk in their footsteps, reserving eight days thereafter to "sort out" polity and practice in the light gained from my pilgrimage. This meant hauling along a suitcase of books and reports, but E. Allison Peer's translations[206] were essential . . . and so were the polity books and reports.

Ten of Teresa's seventeen foundations were visited, and fortunately sisters who spoke English, French or German enabled me to listen to much testimony and history. John of the Cross impressed

142

me so deeply that I gave lectures and preached sermons on themes from his works. What impressed me was the practicality of these two great mystics. Both joined times of contemplation with periods of physical, mental and spiritual activity. Between them, they created classics of devotion like *The Ascent of Mt. Carmel* and *The Dark Night of the Soul* by John of the Cross and *The Interior Castle* and *The Way of Perfection* by Teresa of Avila.

Teresa and John were both rejected by the authorities of the Roman Catholic Church in Spain, both were persecuted, John was imprisoned for months. Both were physically weak. John was a diminutive 5'2" man, Teresa was ill for as long as three years at a time. Teresa had to seek the aid of King Philip II to secure a measure of freedom for both the new orders—the Discalced Carmelites. Assuredly those who claimed a saint withdrew from the world, was healed of bodily ills by divine intervention, and paid little heed to the mundane affairs of life were mistaken.

Teresa of Avila and John of the Cross were vital, clear-headed, dynamic and spiritually alive. They were all this, and more, despite the polity of the Church.

The then-obscure resort of Torremolinos near Malaga was my "thinking place." For eight days I ate little, walked a good deal, swam a little, and spent most of my time thinking and writing.

Two of many experiences which jolted me were a Sunday afternoon on the beach with the health officer from Gibralter. Police were arresting women of all ages whose garb did not reach to the knees and elbows. "What's happened?" I asked the health officer. "Oh," he replied, "I forgot you don't read Spanish. This morning the Archbishop of Malaga preached against over-exposure and announced rules for beach wear." "But is there a law about this?" He laughed. "In Spain the Church's word *is* law." "But, policemen are enforcing the Archbishop's ideas . . ." He held up his hand, "This is Spain, not U.S. Here, what the Archbishop says is enforced by the police."

The second experience took place July 8th at the hamlet of Alba de Tormes where Teresa died. An eager young Carmelite who wanted to talk showed me around. He was an attractive young man who had studied in England. "I'll show you things you never dreamed you would see," he told me after the service in the vast basilica. We crossed a road and entered the rather bare waiting room of the cloistered nuns. He turned to a rope-operated dumb waiter and tapped very loudly. Shortly there came an answering tap. Then he tapped a code. Up came the dumb waiter. He lifted the silver reliquary out of it. "Here," he said, "is the right arm of Teresa." I suppose I must have gasped. "*It is*," he continued, "Why don't you photograph it?" I did. Down went the arm. In answer to more taps, up came another silver reliquary, magnificently wrought. With triumph in his voice my Carmelite friend said, "Here is the heart of Saint Teresa, taken from her body shortly after she died, and wondrously preserved." That too, I photographed.

Outside, afterwards, the young man was full of questions about the U.S. and about my Church. He was plainly puzzled by the freedom of the U.S., the separation of Church and State and the fact that anyone could choose his vocation. "What do you do in Spain?" I asked. "How is it that a bright young man like you, and something of a cynic too, is here in this rural hamlet?"

"That's easy," he said. "In Spain there are two ways to become influential, the army and the Church. I prefer the Church. We own much more than half the land, our Orders are powerful. It's a good life with a great future." I thanked him.

Now, at Torremolinos I was faced with a land of saints repressed by a Church which had been described by a bright young Carmelite as one of the two roads to power in Spain.

I was totally persuaded that Teresa of Avilla and John of the Cross became saints because they were heretics aided by the discipline of the Church, especially by godly confessors and advisors.

I was equally sure that the dirty, ragged, hungry urchins on every street and all beaches but one, had not been helped by a wealthy, powerful Church.

Struggling with the *Mansfield Theses* I concluded that, in the light of my Spanish pilgrimage, acceptance of exterior authority ultimately led to a stratified Church with poor benighted beggars like those in Assisi and Malaga on one side and well-fed, over-dressed Archbishops on the other side. All this I recorded with great care, together with details of my Spanish pilgrimage, and an analysis of Congregational Polity in the light of St. Andrews. Each day the big envelopes were sent air mail to California.

Not one arrived. In 1953 Spain's mail was subject to the censorship of both Church and State. It required considerable investigation after my return to California, with the help of Thomas Cook and the U.S. Embassy to discover that all my notes and articles had been confiscated. No Mansfield Theses were needed to point out the harvest of unbounded church-power. The top question had become "Have the Congregational Churches drifted away from the polity of their basic documents IN PRACTICE?

CHAPTER 4 NOTES

1. All quotations are from Calder, R.F.G. (ed) *Proceedings*, 1953 Independent Press, London, p. 23, 30
2. *Proceedings*, p. 67
3. *Proceedings*, p. 69-70
4. Ibid, pp. 70-71
5. Ibid, p. 71
6. Ibid, p. 71
7. Ibid, p. 72
8. Ibid, p. 74
9. *Proceedings*, p. 76
10. Ibid, p. 77
11. Ibid, pp. 88-90
12. Ibid, p. 42
13. Ibid, pp. 42-43
14. *Proceedings,* p. 43
15. Ibid, p. 43
16. Ibid, pp. 43-44
17. Ibid, p. 54
18. *Proceedings*, p. 66
19. Ibid, pp. 85-86
20. Notes
21. *Proceedings*, p. 29
22. Ibid, pp. 158-162
23. All quotations in this section are re-constructed from hdg notes, letters, and log, unless otherwise indicated.
24. *Proceedings*, p. 160
25. *Proceedings* lists 2 business sessions. Hdg notes indicate completion of business Saturday morning, June 27, 1953, and a delay of lunch caused by a slightly longer-than-expected meeting.
26. *Proceedings*, p. 159
27. Ibid, pgs. 159-160
28. *Proceedings*, p. 21
29. Douglas Horton, *Congregationalism*, 1952, Independent Press, London, p. 1.
30. Ibid, p. 10
31. Ibid, p. 22
32. Ibid, p. 35-36
33. Ibid, p. 48
34. Ibid, p. 49
35. Ibid, p. 79
36. Williston Walker, *Creeds and Platforms of Congregationalism*, 1893, Charles Scribners, New York, p. 33
37. *Creeds and Platforms of Congregationalism*, p. 33
38. Ibid, p. 66
39. Ibid, p. 68
40. Ibid, p. 71
41. Ibid, p. 71
42. Ibid, p. 78

43. Ibid, p. 79
44. Ibid, p. 80
45. Ibid, p. 90
46. Walker, op. cit. p. 203
47. Ibid, p. 203
48. Ibid, p. 208
49. Ibid, p. 208
50. Walker, op. cit., p. 217
51. Ibid, p. 233
52. Ibid, p. 234
53. R. S. Paul (ed), *An Apologeticall Narration,* 1963, United Church Press, Philadelphia
54. Ibid, p. 9
55a. Ibid, p. 13
55b. Ibid, p. 14
56. Ibid, p. 17
57. Ibid, p. 15
58. Ibid, p. 24
59. Ibid, p. 66
60. Albert Peel, *The Savoy Declaration of Faith and Order*, 1939, Independent Press, London, p. 70
61. Peel, op. cit., p. 71
62. Ibid, p. 72
63. Ibid, p. 74
64. Ibid, p. 75
65. Peel, op cit., p. 20 ff.
66. E. P. Parker *History of the Second Church of Christ in Hartford*, 1892 Belknap & Warfield, Hartford, p. 46
67. Ibid, p. 46-47
68. Walker, op. cit., p. 439
69. Ibid, p. 457
70. Ibid, p. 457
71. Ibid, p. 460
72. Ibid, p. 460-1
73. Ibid, p. 461
74. Walker, op. cit. p. 487
75. Ibid, p. 487
76. Ibid, p. 488
77. Ibid, p. 489
78. Walker, op. cit., p. 507
79. Ibid, p. 503
80. Ibid, p. 503
81. Ibid, p. 506
82. Ibid, p. 506
83. Ibid, p. 506
84. Walker, op. cit., p. 503
85. E. P. Parker, op. cit., p. 97 ff.
86. H. M. Dexter, *Congregationalism As Seen in Its Literature*, see long note, p. 595
87. G. G. Atkins & F. L. Fagley, *History of American Congregationalism*, 1942, Pilgrim Press, Boston, p. 174. See T. Munger, *Life of Bushnell*

88. Walker, op. cit., pp. 530-531
89. Ibid, p. 531
90. Ibid, p. 532
91. Ibid, p. 543-544
92. Ibid, p. 545
93. Ibid, p. 538 ff.
94. Ibid, p. 570 ff.
95. Walker, op. cit., p. 551
96. Ibid, p. 567-568
97. Walker, op. cit. p. 573
98. Ibid, p. 581
99. Charles E. Burton (ed) *The National Council Digest*, 1930, Pilgrim Press, Boston
100. Ibid, p. 25
101. Ibid, p. 25
102. Ibid, p. 26
103. Ibid, p. 49
104. Ibid, p. 131
105. Ibid, p. 134
106. Burton, op. cit., p. 135
107. Ibid, p. 135
108. Ibid, p. 138
109. Ibid, p. 140 (1929 Council)
110. Ibid, p. 140
111. Ibid, p. 153
112. Ibid, p. 158
113. Burton, op. cit., p. 170
114. Ibid, p. 170
115. Ibid, p. 192 (1892)
116. Ibid, p. 193. See also 195
117. Ibid, p. 193 ff.
118. G. G. Atkins & F. L. Fagley, *History of American Congregationalism*, 1942 Pilgrim Press, Boston, p. 347
119. Burton, op. cit., p. 195
120. Ibid, p. 198 ff.
121. Ibid, p. 198
122. Atkins & Fagley, op. cit., p. 350
123. Ibid, p. 356
124. Ibid, p. 350 ff., 356 ff.
125. Ibid, p. 347
126. Burton, op. cit., pp. 200-201
127. Atkins & Fagley, op. cit., pp. 358-359
128. Minutes, General Council, etc., 1940, p. 117
129. Ibid, p. 117
130. Douglas Horton, *Congregationalism* 1952, Independent Press, London, p. 17
131. Ibid, p. 10
132. Ibid, p. 22
133. Ibid, p. 36
134. Ibid, p. 48
135. Ibid, p. 79

136. John Robinson, ed. R. Ashton, *Works*, 1851, London, Vol. ii, p. 132; William Ames, *Marrow of Sacred Divinity*, p. 135; Henry Jacob, Art. 8 in *Hanbury History* Vol. 1, p. 296; Henry Barrow, "A Brief Examination" etc., 1586, London; see H. M. Dexter, *Congregationalism In its Literature* 1880 Harper, NY, p. 211 ff.; see *Brief Discovery of the False Church*

137. J. Robinson, *Of Religious Communion*, Leyden, p. 17

138. J. Robinson, *Works*, Vol. ii, p. 132

139. Amesius, Medull, Theol. Cap. xxxii. Sec. 6

140. H. Barrow, "*Pope's Supremacy.*" *Works*, (Ed. 1845) Vol. iii., p. 115

141. R. Mather, "Church Government" (A.D. 1643), p. 66

142. S. Mather, "*Apology for the Liberties of the Churches in New England*" (A.D. 1738), pp. 109, 128

143. H. Jacob's "*Attentation*", (A.D. 1613), p. 209

144. J. Cotton, "*Way of the Churches*", p. 53, 54

145. T. Hooker, *Survey*, Part. iv, p. 19

146. Horton, op. cit., p. 9

147. Ibid, p. 9

148. Ibid, p. 61

149. Ibid, p. 83

150. Ibid

151. Reconstructed from 3 x 5 card notes

152. Horton, op. cit., p. 21

153. Ibid, p. 30,31

154. Ibid, p. 41

155. quoted Horton, p. 48

156. Ibid, p. 30

157. Horton, op. cit., p. 33

158. Horton, op. cit., p. 32

159. Ibid, p. 43-44

160. Ibid, p. 44

161. Horton, op. cit., p. 94

162. Ibid, p. 93

163. George L. Walker, *History of the First Church in Hartford*, 1884, n.p. Hartford also R. H. Potter, *Hartford's First Church*, 1932, First Church, Hartford, pgs. 37-48

164. Horton, op. cit., p. 84

165. Ibid, p. 83

166. Ibid, p. 90

167. Ibid, p. 95-96

168. Albert Peel, *International Congregationalism,* 1949, Independent Press, London, p. 58-59

169. Ibid, p. 59

170. Peel, op. cit., pp. 60-61

171. Ibid, p. 59

172. O. S. Tompkins, *The Church in the Purpose of God*, 1951?, N.Y., p. 35

173. Peel, op. cit., p. 59

174. Albert Peel, *Christian Freedom*, 1938, Independent Press, London

175. Peel, *Christian Freedom*, op. cit., p. 12

176. Ibid, p. 68 See all of Lecture III.

177. Ibid, pp. 102-103

178. Ibid, p. 96 "our property becomes our problem," quoted from E. G. Looseley.

179. Ibid, passion. This is the central theme of the book.

180. Albert Peel & Douglas Horton, *International Congregationalism*, 1949, Independent Press, London

181. Peel & Horton, op. cit., pp. 100-101

182. Ibid, pp. 96-97

183. Ibid, p. 110 ff.

184. Peel & Horton, op. cit., pp. 110-117

185. Cecil Northcott, *Answer from Amsterdam*, 1948 (?), Independent Press, London & Pilgrim Press, Boston.

186. Ibid, p. 11

187. Northcott, op. cit., p. 10

188. O. S. Tompkins, *The Church in the Purpose of God*, c. 1951 World Council of Churches, New York, p. 116

189. Ibid, p. 7

190. Ibid, p. 7

191. Ibid, p. 7

192. Ibid, p. 8

193. Ibid, p. 7

194. Ibid, p. 8

195. Ibid, p. 8

196. Tompkins, op. cit., p. 10

197. Ibid, p. 10

198. Ibid, p. 10

199. Ibid, p. 15

200. Ibid, p. 48

201. Ibid, p. 49

202. Ibid, p. 63

203. Ibid, p. 64. See also p. 95

204. Northcott, op. cit., p. 54

205. Northcott, op. cit., p. 58

206. E. Allison Peers, *Spirit of Flame*, SCM Press, London, 1943, *Mother of Carmel*, (3rd ed.) SCM Press, London, 1946, *The Works of Saint John of the Cross*, (2nd ed.) Burns, Oates & Washburn, London (tr), 1953. See also A Discalced Carmelite, *The Way of Perfection*, (3rd ed.) Leighton, Edinburgh, 1942.

CHAPTER FIVE

Consensus, Conflict and Conclusions

To arrive at a consensus concerning Congregational Polity as Practiced I had requested preliminary information from all state superintendents, geographic panel chairmen, and others whose names were suggested by superintendents or chairmen. The results were sketchy. After the presentation of the "Documents" study at the 1952 General Council, I suggested that a copy of the Documents Report be sent to all correspondents and that they be asked to direct their "Practice" comments to the numbered paragraphs of the Documents Report.

To sharpen forces, I sent the following letter,[1] January 9, 1953, to all:

"The Committee on Congregational Polity and Unity is going all-out to find an acceptable workable answer to the question, 'Can our Congregational Christian fellowship unite with other denominations?' The polity section of the Committee needs your help at two points.

"*First,* concerning 'Congregational Polity as it is presently practiced.' You have seen the enclosed 'Introductory Statement.' It is an objective study of our documents. Exactly what differences are there, if any, in the *practices* of your local churches, your association, your state conference, and any wider agencies of our churches with which you are connected? How do you care for ordination, calling a minister, ministerial standing, etc.?

"The existence, nature and meaning of 'Recognition' is one of the key questions in need of clarification. Is it your practice to regard the recognition of a church by an association as a recognition of the

151

Congregational character of the Church or as the recognition of the local church as a subdivision of the association (the conference and the General Council)? Is the authority given by a Congregational Christian Church to a wider agency the kind of authority which is given *for a specific purpose,* and which therefore can be withdrawn by the Church that gave it? For example, if a Church requests the superintendent to secure a minister, is this a delegation or specific authority given by, and subject to withdrawal by, the local church? Do you feel that money given to the Boards for their work or the General Council as per-capita giving is obligatory or in practice do the churches retain the right to give or withhold support? Do the churches feel that they retain any right of control over denominational organizations to which they give their money?

"What we are after on this first point is not opinions or generalizations. We need *facts,* concrete examples of *actual practice* which we can compare with our documentary study, and use as grist for our mill in producing a second study on 'Congregational Polity as it is presently practiced.'

"*The second point* on which we want help is just this. In your judgment, what is distinctive of our Congregational Christian Churches? Do you think of any statement of fundamental principles that you feel should be stated as a pre-condition to any plan of union with other churches? Here we specifically want your own opinion.

"I quite realize this is a long letter, and that a reply will take some real thought. Nevertheless, in view of the critical importance of the matter, I'm sure that I can count on you for a worthwhile contribution. The members of the Committee believe it is possible to find a way of responsible freedom which can guide our churches in all future plans of union, but we are keenly aware that that way can be found only with real digging for facts and the widest possible help in thinking through the meaning of the facts. We are determined to leave nothing undone that will help to give the next General Council a positive statement which can be a guide to us all in our ecumenical relationships.

"Your help is needed—much needed.

"Please let me hear from you by January 25—prior to the mid-winter meeting.

"Sincerely yours,

"Henry David Gray, Chairman
"Committee on Congregational Polity

"P.S. This letter has the unanimous approval of the Committee on Polity and Unity."

With the skilled assistance of Miss La Verne Davis, the replies were grouped, and I prepared a handwritten first draft. In an attempt to secure total response I wrote[2] on March 11, 1953, to those from whom no reply had been received.

"I wrote you some little time ago in relation to the Polity and Unity Committee, but have as yet received no reply. This is probably because I was late in getting letters out and needed as many answers as possible prior to a recent meeting in Boston. My apologies for the closeness of the time schedule for reply.

"Very thoughtful and extended answers came from half of those to whom I wrote, and became the basis for much worth-while discussion, and possibly for a line of thought which may hold the answer to our present and future ecumenical development.

"In view of the high value of the letters we have already received the committee urged me to seek a 100% reply. Can we not count on you to give us the benefit of your best thought on the two propositions:

"1.   Wherein does Congregationalism in practice differ from Congregationalism in our 'fundamental documents?'

"2.   What do you consider the foundation principles to be held to by the Congregational churches in any prospective union? Association by Fellowship with local freedom.

"Your help will be most deeply appreciated. We are trying to do a real, basic job and we need your help."

Thus, the June, 1953, meeting of the Polity and Unity Committee had in hand a 26-page mimeographed compilation titled, "A Study of Congregational Polity as it is Practiced in the United States." The manuscript was arranged topically, but, save for the introduction, the statements were copied from the replies of correspondents, with names attached thereto.

Because of the serious questions asked about polity statements in the report I reproduced the original quotations on "Ordination":

"ORDINATION:

"8.   In the three Conferences of the Southeast Convention there has been no satisfactory or well defined policy in respect to Ordination. Occasions are on record where local churches have proceeded to ordain a minister without a Council or reference to the Association or State Conference.—Rev. Thomas Anderson, Atlanta, Georgia.[3]

"In Oxford County, Maine, a church, locally, can ordain a minister, whether the conference endorses him or not.—Dixfield, Maine.[4]

"I have never known a local Congregational Church in Oregon either to license or ordain candidates for the ministry. Certainly it has not been done during my administration and in all my reading of past records I have never come across such a case. I hope that in any final report some such phrase as 'although very rarely done' may be added. . . .—Paul A. Davies, Portland, Oregon.[5]

"This is inconsistent with the practices of the Southern Convention and of all former Christian Churches. Although this was practiced to some extent in the former Congregational Churches many years ago, we raise the question,—Is this practiced anywhere within our churches today? . . .—Roy C. Helfenstein, for the South East Panel, Richmond, Virginia."[6]

Dr. Helfenstein's letter is an interesting contrast to that of Dr. Anderson since both are from the Southeast Region. Superintendent Davies' reply reflects the 1950 General Council debate regarding Oregon's North Willamette Association.

"Recognition" of a Church by an association was interpreted in a variety of ways: W.H. Davis of Santa Clara Association in California—[7]

"Our Association records indicate that recognition has been extended primarily on the basis of the Congregational character of the applicant organization."

Edward S. Treat of Fargo, North Dakota, spanned the variety:[8]

"The recognition of a church by an association would be regarded by some in our churches as a recognition of Congregational character of the church and by others as a recognition of the local church as a subdivision of the association."

Robert H. Reitinger of Connecticut stated practice with no documental standards:[9]

"In the matter of recognition of local churches, our Hartford East Association is prepared to recognize any local church meeting with our approval. Although no standards are provided in our Constitution for such recognition, I would assume that the Congregational character would have to be shown before it would be accepted. It would then become in some sense a subdivision of the Association, but first and foremost it is a local church with self-government and dedication to the general ideals of the Congregational Christian Churches."

Kenneth D. Claypool of Washington summed up a common view:[10]

"Recognition of a church by an association is both a recognition of the Congregational character of the church, and a receiving of that church into the fellowship (a fellowship of spirit and enterprize) of the other Congregational churches of an area. The same recognition makes it a part of the larger fellowship.

"That does not entail pre-commitment to support any project, but only a general acceptance to share with the other churches in advancing the cause of Christ and of the fellowship in so far as conscience will permit."

Distinctive Congregationalism

Each correspondent was requested to list points of view distinctive of Congregationalism.

Major emphases were expressed as follows:

"In my judgment some of the points of view distinctive of our churches are as follows:

"1. The complete autonomy of each local church.
"2. The 'Right of Private Judgment' for each individual in respect to theology and doctrine.
"3. The providing in society of a fellowship of people who desire to remain progressive in respect to religious faith and practice, and come to terms with new facts as they appear as the result of increase in human understanding.
"4. Complete freedom from ecclesiastical or theological domination for each church, and yet an expectation of cooperation in denominational activities in accordance with the decisions of each church in respect to the nature and degree of such cooperation.—Thomas Anderson, D.D., LL.D., Atlanta, Georgia."[11]

"The idea of greater centralization of power has gained ground in a great many areas of our common life today, and it is not surprising that it has entered into our thinking as Christian people. In Congregational procedure: We register our approval or disapproval through our choice of delegates. But final authority is at the bottom and not at the top. This is a fundamental concept with us. We recognize the right of Conference or Council to initiate but we accept the right of a local church to approve or disapprove.

"1. The basic question, as I view it, is this: Does the Union look in the direction of the Kingdom of God? Will it aid in uniting Christians in a more effective witness? Will it help to overcome the evils of division within the Christian family of churches?

"2.	I am for it if this can be done without sacrificing the freedom of the local church. I believe that it can be. We can join with people's of like tradition without losing the rights of the local church.

"3.	Such proposals should always be referred back to the local church for approval or disapproval. We recognize the right of any group to join or refrain from any union.—Francis C. Ellis, San Dimas, California."[12]

"Distinctive of our Congregational Christian Churches, we are free from ecclesiastical control, and the local church is free to govern its own affairs within the framework of fellowship ties and responsibilities.—Judson E. Fiebiger, Iowa."[13]

"The distinctive thing about our Congregational Christian Churches is that the authority which validates the whole denomination lies in their willingness to cooperate in a purposeful fellowship to get the things done which we can do together which we could not do separately. From the point of view of the State Conference, the Boards and Agencies of denomination, these churches cannot be supposed into any kind of an order or into any kind of an organization. They can only be won to a purposeful fellowship on the basis of common causes that are so well presented to them that they justify themselves in the mind of the churches. The whole thing forbids an ecclesia. It forbids an assumption by any of these bodies, Conferences, Boards or Agencies, or General Council, that simply because we have together at any time voting groups of people who are representative of these churches that these groups have any right to order the churches. These groups may simply formulate programs of purpose and must then always win the local church to full cooperation in their program. It cannot order. It cannot control. None of the Boards, Agencies, or Conferences can command. This certainly is distinctive. But any point at which we fail to try to win to a program rather than command, we are unlikely to get full cooperation.—Harold N. Skidmore, Michigan."[14]

"I would suggest the following points as being distinctive of our Congregational-Christian Churches:

"a.	Autonomy of local church with absence of external compulsion.

"b.	Absence of extensive creeds on any level.

"c.	Voluntary co-operation in wider work through suitable agencies.

"d.	Fellowship of co-operating churches.

"I believe that these principles should be a pre-condition to any plan of union with other churches.—Robert H. Reitinger, South Glastonbury, Connecticut."[15]

"It is neither freedom, period, nor fellowship, period. It is Freedom in Christ, and Fellowship in Christ. Each local church is a Church of Christ, not of the Minister, the deacons, the trustees, the young people or even the Ladies Aid! We belong to it in a real sense and while we are entrusted with its administration it is His. And further, the fellowship which we cherish has no meaning apart from Christ. This is the greatest foundation principle of them all and I am not being just pious about it. And I would add that I find many indications of the recognition of that principle.—Rev. James F. English, Hartford, Connecticut."[16]

"Personally I consider Congregationalism to be distinguished by the two features so often mentioned in your survey: (1) freedom from ecclesiastical authority and (2) the right of private judgment, each exercised with sincere devotion to Jesus Christ. These, as at once abolishing heresy and promoting continuous, constructive traditional views in accordance with changing insights and standards, and as alternatives to 'revelation,' authority, and dogma, are not merely precious denominational distinctions; they are Christian, basically human, ultimate, and therefore the hope of the world.—William Hawley Davis, Santa Clara, California."[17]

"A Congregational Christian church is one in which the individual within such church may believe in accordance with the dictates of his own conscience, so long as he believes and gives allegiance to the teachings of Jesus Christ. I, personally, would think that such a church should, also, be in fellowship with the other Congregational Christian churches in the local and in the state conference. Probably the majority of ministers and laymen of this Association would believe the same.—M.O. Skarsten, West Willamette Association, Portland, Oregon."[18]

Concerns Regarding Any Proposed Union

The intense concern of all correspondents with regard to the proposed Congregational Christian/Evangelical & Reformed merger was evident in lengthy, thoughtful and often incisive letters. What follows illustrates this concern:

"Hereunder are pertinent excerpts addressed to the question, What principles should be pre-condition to any plan of union?

" 1.   *Regarding a plan of union* with any other churches: It seems to me the money-element enters into this amalgamation quite definitely. Many of our churches have been established and functioning for a great many years, particularly in the eastern part of our country. My own church was built in 1826; is still standing and used every Sunday. During the

157

years bequests have been made to these churches. That is going to make it difficult to unite with other denominations unless some way can be provided wherein the Congregational groups can retain their own trust funds.—(Mrs. Frank) Alice H. McGouldrick, Dixfield, Maine.[19]

2. *Responsibility* is quite entirely a matter of moral obligation and Christian conviction rather than printed discipline and this is very obvious throughout the entire study made of the Constitutions of the various phases of our Fellowship. I do not feel capable of pointing out any particular statement which should be a pre-condition to any plan of union. I for one, would be very reluctant to lose any degree of autonomy now held by each factor in the Fellowship—the local church, the association, the Conference and National Boards and Agencies. I feel that the moral and Christian obligation to one another is far greater and of a much higher nature than rules and regulations agreed upon and imposed upon various and sundry groups. I realize that this leaves room for irresponsibility, indifference and political manipulation, nevertheless, even though there may be greater efficiency in dictatorship and much slower progress in democracies, I still would want any plan of union to be contingent upon our present freedoms within our divine obligations and Christian Fellowship.—Everett A. Babcock, Ohio.[20]

3. Missionary apportionments, per capita tax, and the like have never been accepted blindly by the individual churches, but are subject to individual vote. This has made us a denomination—if we can be called that—bulky and unwieldy at times. The Association, The State Conference, The General Council, the various Boards are subject to the will of the churches. Unfortunately the will of the churches is by no means unanimous. To solve such difficulties such as union of the denomination with another, it seems to me that each church will have to have in its by-laws a provision to be bound in such matters by the vote of the majority of the individual churches, Associations, and State Conferences— such is the price exacted by fellowship.—Alfred Paul Focht, Niles, California.[21]

4. I am inclined to think it would be unwise to try to draft 'any statement of fundamental principles that should be stated as a pre-condition to any plan of union with other churches.'— Paul A. Davies, Portland, Oregon.[22]

5. In any prospective union, it would be my hope that we could find enough things in common to work with like-minded groups without losing this autonomy at any of the levels.— David W. Shepherd, Chipley, Georgia.[23]

6. With reference to our possible union with other churches, I believe that it is very limited. Since we are not an organically united church in the traditional denominational sense, there seems to be only one possible course of union open to us. That is union on the basis of fellowship. Call it 'federation' (a word which our Ecumenicists do not like) or what will you, I believe that it is the only realistic and legal basis of union for our denomination. To try to make it otherwise, invites all the trouble which we have already experienced in the notorious E & R controversy. Therefore, the ecumenical torch, which some of our brethren are constantly brandishing around, should be aimed at those churches which are like-minded unto ourselves. Admittedly they are few. Personally, and I feel strongly about this, I believe that it will be more to the point if the members of our fellowship concentrate on how to restore the love of Christ to our denomination. Ecumenicity can, and I fear has, become just another panacea to restore that which should never have been lost.—Gerald G. Hallauer, Iowa.[24]

7. Christianity is fundamentally a matter of fellowship—that just as soon as legal compulsions enter in, the enjoyment of fellowship is jeopardized. The question then becomes not what the constitution says or what the courts decree but what the Christian conscience knows is right. We get into trouble when we cease to be Christian; we have glorious strength whenever the Spirit of Christ exists amongst us.—M.R. Boynton, Massachusetts.[25]

8. I think in a merger, it is imperative that we retain our freedom of individual action and do not delegate church authority to an overall church head.

   I too, have been studying 'The History of Congregationalism' and the breaking away from an overall Church head is what made us a Congregational group to begin with. We should not therefore plunge back into a similar condition.

   However, I do think a Merger plan possible of working out. To think otherwise would be presumptive of assuming that our present leaders are less intelligent than our forefathers.— Mrs. Hilmer Reed, Birchdale, Minnesota.[26]

9. One fundamental principle that we believe should be a precondition of union with other churches is that there shall be no coercion or threat of coercion over the life of any local church save the moral suasion of 'speaking the truth in love.'— N.F. Nordstrom, Walter Schlaretzki, Illinois.[27]

10. I do not know of any statement of fundamental principles that I feel should be stated as a pre-condition to any plan of

union with other churches. However, I personally would like to see one adopted, or suggested, as an affirmation of faith— to be used 'for substance of doctrine.' If this is inadvisable, why not have the uniting parties adopt a covenant? The English Congregationalists and Presbyterians recently did.— Arthur P. Colbourn, Rhode Island.[28]

11. Concerning the fundamental principles which Congregational churches would insist upon observing in any prospective union, the members of the Mid West Panel set down the following as probably including the major ones:

    1.   The right to call their own ministers.

    2.   The right to determine their own worship forms.

    3.   The right to hold and manage their own property.

    4.   The right to call a local church 'the church.'

    5.   The right to establish conditions of membership.

    6.   Freedom from external ecclesiastical controls.

    7.   The right to designate their benevolences.

    8.   The right to express fellowship concerns in voluntary organizations.

    9.   The right of churches to ordain.

    10. The right to insist upon the universal priesthood of the believers.

    11. Congregational control of all matters within any individual church.

    12. The freedom of thought and expression.

—Fred Hoskins, Chairman Mid-West Panel, April 21, 1953.[29]

12. The foundation principles of Congregationalism seem to me to be quite simple; the autonomy of the local congregation balanced with a spirit and practice of fellowship and full cooperation in the life and work of the denomination. I believe that the functions, powers and authority of higher bodies, or general bodies, such as conference and General Council (or whatever it is called) should be exercised (1) under a constitution that preserves the true autonomy of the local congregation as now enjoyed, and (2) by officers who are chosen by and responsible to the elected delegates of the churches. That is, here is involved a representative democracy. This is government and we have not had, in the ecclesiastical order, government outside the local congregation. In such an order, no ecclesiastical body would have authority over the congregation, but it would administer authority derived from the congregation over the activities, missionary and other, that the denomination as a whole carries on. This is the point at which we have arrived although we are still in a state of confusion because we have not clearly distinguished between the ecclesiastical and administrative functions.

I believe that we could unite with any other denomination that would accept this distinction, and agree to guarantee to the local congregational church its freedom before God. (autonomy is not too good a word, for it is really theonomy that we mean, and autonomy alone does not make a congregational church, but autonomy plus its correlate, full spiritual and practical fellowship with other churches).

I do not recognize the validity of the claim that an association or the General Council is, once constituted, an autonomous body in the same sense in which the congregation is. Such bodies are constituted *by* the congregations; they are morally responsible to the congregations. This does not mean that each delegate goes instructed on every or on any matter. Like all good representatives in a democracy the delegate, once elected, should act upon his own best judgment as to what is best for the whole church. Nevertheless, the General Council exists only to express the purpose and serve the true interests of the denomination. Its members act *for* the churches that elect them and have a moral responsibility, under God, to them. The General Council, in principle has no existence or meaning or validity, save as it seeks to express the common mind and purpose of the congregations. It is *their* creation but they are not *its* creation or servants in any sense. Now, this I take to be the nature of any General Council or Synod that heads or unifies a new denomination in which the Congregational churches are a constituent part. Such a body, could well, with this basis, assume the responsibility of administering missionary and other work on behalf of the whole denomination. In this sense it would have authority of an administrative nature, derived from the churches, over the programs of work. In this exercise of authority it would be responsible ultimately to the congregations.—Hugh Vernon White, Berkeley, California.[30]

13. I do think we must hold to the autonomy of the local church, and the avoidance of overhead control. But I think certain aspects of our denominational work can and should be delegated to our officers. However, our officers must not assume that they have delegated powers which they have not been given by vote of the local churches through proper procedure. I think herein lay some of our biggest difficulties in the recent merger effort.

The principle of liberality toward others who may be just as Christian as we but who may carry certain beliefs with which we may not personally agree. Too many of us in our own fellowship have acted as though those who could not go along with our so-called advance and 'liberal' views were therefore automatically barred from our fellowship.

'Freedom in Worship, but Fellowship in Service' to me carries a good deal of practical meaning. Frankly I think it is the kind of thing Stanley Jones' Federal Union might accomplish, and which I think would be better than one great organic Church Union.—W.P. Minton, Pennsylvania.[31]

14. The right to dissent is distinctive in Congregationalism. I still marvel at how we hold together in spite of its many manifestations, some of which cripple our effectiveness very seriously.

Can we ever hope to have any church union with any other body if we first set up a principle from which under no circumstances we will not depart.—Herbert C. Gans, Petaluma, California.[32]

15. Recognition should be made of such procedures which should be followed in any proposed merger of our fellowship with any other. We must, if at all possible, present some means by which such proposed mergers can be brought to a conclusion.—A.G. Swartz, Texas.[33]

16. The basic concept of a 'gathered church' whose members, under covenant, face the full responsibility for seeking to know and to do the will of God, just does not permit the delegation of that responsibility to anyone else. The duty to do God's will 'cannot be delegated.'

Any union or plan for a union that seeks to get from Congregational churches the delegation of authority to represent them in final commitments is a violation of the basic Congregational concept of a gathered church.—Harry W. Johnson, Idaho."[34]

The compilation of replies to inquiries regarding Congregational Polity in Practice were the focus of my thinking and writing at the St. Andrews International Congregational Council, and in Spain, summer 1953. Although the lengthy written reports were confiscated, the results of my mental/spiritual struggles were not.

Conflict

On my desk when I returned to California was a paper titled "Report for Educators' Panel," and shortly there arrived from Malcolm Burton a lengthy letter dated July 17, 1953, commenting thereon.

The Educators' Panel Report[35] proposed that, in history, Congregationalism had three characteristics:

1. The independence of each particular Church
2. Concern for "larger unity" and tolerance of types of Church polity other than Congregational, and
3. An understanding that all who follow the God and Father of our Lord Jesus Christ are spiritually one.

From the first premise the report concludes:[36]

> "insofar as historic precedent is a binding factor, such a deeply established concept would make impossible any type of participation in the ecumenical movement involving forced cooperation on the part of the local churches or the curtailment of their autonomy as self-governing institutions. The councils of Congregationalism have never been legislative bodies with powers of compulsion over local church life, and in this sense Congregational practice has differed throughout history from those polities of a more rigid character."

From the wide-armed inclusiveness of Richard Mather, John Robinson and John Cotton (?) and subsequent lack of Congregationalist claims to be THE ONLY CHURCH it is concluded[37] "the history of Congregationalism embodies as a characteristic a desire for larger unity in the Body of Christ, for this has been from the onset one of Congregationalism's major concerns." Just how John Robinson's goodwill toward all God's children metamorphized into "a desire for" the organic union of the Church of England from which he revolted is not made clear.

Next, the few recent unions with other denominations are cited to prove that the General Council may act "on its own"[38] to unite with whomsoever it will. Nothing is said as to HOW a National Council established by delegates from the Churches in 1871 COULD OR DID acquire the power to speak for the thousands of Churches gathered from 1620 to 1871! Citing the 1931 union of Congregational and Christian Churches is not much help since both groups of Churches espoused congregational polity, a common faith and similar practices, so that the declaration of the self-completeness of the particular Church in the 1871 Constitution was virtually transferred to the 1931 Constitution. In what manner this precedent sanctions a union *without* congregational polity, faith and practice is not evident.

The most puzzling facet of the proposed Educators' Panel Report is the conclusion that, because Robinson, Mather and Cotton (?) were tolerant they (and by inference all Congregationalists) support the establishment of One Big Church.[39] Does this mean that toleration of Hinduism proves that we wish to become Hindus? Does wide-armed goodwill indicate that we desire to trade our identity for that which we tolerate? John Cotton was not very tolerant of Presbyterians, but, if he had been, would that prove he wished to deny the Congregational polity he found in the New Testament?

Finally, the proposed Educators' Panel Report urged that "the fundamental essence of Congregationalism has existed in the realm of spirit rather than of form."[40] Therefore, Congregationalism is free to modify, adjust, and add to its forms as it desires. Exactly how A can become B without ceasing to be A is not explained.

The "Educators' Report" was similar to Professor Bainton in the stress on change. It was similar to the Mansfield Theses in its deductions. It had not been reviewed by the whole Polity and Unity Committee, hence I put it aside.

Then came Mr. Burton's letter,[41] dated July 17, 1953, the first page of which noted points similar to those just mentioned. But the second page had two polemical passages.

> "Some of these matters have come up frequently in our committee sessions, even if this particular report has not been considered. The report seems to me very carefully drawn. It is not something of hasty construction, and I would say that more than just the Educators Panel is back of it. Halverson, incidentally, told us the first time he was present that he would 'have to go outside of the panel members' to get real help on his subject. For the most part, it would seem, he has worked independently of the actual members of the panel as originally chosen and listed. Who the real personnel are, in putting this together, we cannot know. Von Rohr of Calif. has been mentioned as largely responsible, but if I were to make a guess I would say that persons around New York and New Haven have had as much or more to do with it. Its contents are something we shall yet have to reckon with, and I believe that some of its argument is the sort of thing which might come up as a defense in possible future law-suits, in case the organic union people decide to have a 'fight to the finish,'—as Merrill and Whittaker seemed to think they should.

> "Incidentally, I see in the final paragraph a trap for Fred Meek and Henry David Gray. Both of these men have been quick to criticize Halverson in the past and to make of no effect some of his previous efforts. But both are prone to argue for 'a theological basis' for Congregationalism, apparently believing that such a basis, and only such a basis, really matters. Such a line of argument leaves them wide open for this final suggestion in the Halverson report,— to the effect that Congregationalism is something quite other than

local autonomy and that its real essence, or distinctive quality, is to be found in the 'area of the spirit'."

The December 1953 Meeting

The Congregational Polity in Practice report now must embody the words, phrases, sentences and concepts of 140 correspondents. On the basis of it, and the documentary report, statements could be made as to the nature of Congregational Polity, the desirata for union, and procedures requisite to union. The report was needed for a meeting of the Central Committee.

The prelude to that meeting for me was receipt of a handwritten letter from Wendell Fifield, dated September 3, 1953.[42]

"Dear Henry:

"I have been giving a considerable amount of thought and study to the work of our committee this summer, and also to its future plans. By this time next year our committee, for better or worse, should be a matter of history. I am planning to have a meeting of the Central Committee, preferably in Boston, the week after Thanksgiving. This seems to be a reasonably quiet week for most churches. I have a great deal of difficulty visualizing the success of such a meeting without you. I am sure that you realize that you have been the most helpful member of the committee and are invaluable at its meetings. I realize that you have a very heavy schedule, and that naturally your first duty is to your church. But we have only one more meeting of the Central Committee and one more meeting of the entire committee so far as I can see. So I make bold to ask whether you could possibly come east for the Central Committee meeting. I have not yet canvassed the other members as to the date as I wanted to write to you first. If it just isn't possible for you to come do not hesitate to say so. But in the event that you can come I should like to ask the Executive Committee at its mid-September meeting to elect you an official member of the Central Committee. Then there will be no question about your standing and your vote. And in a possible close vote on some matters that might be very important. So will you drop me a line as to the possibilities.

"I have had an interesting time this summer writing a suggested section for our report dealing with 'organic union.' I have sent it on to Arthur Schwartz. A restudy of all that we have learned forced me to state that in our polity there is no possibility of organic union with connectional groups. I am very much interested to see what Arthur will develop. I think he has probably arrived at an opinion similar to my own. But no-one knows until he sends. You will be interested to know that Dr. *Walter* Horton in a comment upon the tentative

165

educators' report, which report has never been submitted to me and so is not before us, says that the report of our committee should in his judgment stress the 'covenant idea.' He says that in his opinion this is the genius of Congregationalism in its relationships. I have sent his complete statement on to Fred Meek for his committee. I received a letter from Fred a day or so ago indicating that he was hard at work on a statement of the covenant idea and would be sending me a statement soon. So all the wheels seem to be turning. I do not recall off-hand the further assignments of your committee. You, of course, have done the most of your work—and done it splendidly. The minutes which will reach you soon will outline all of the various committee assignments. As I recall it we were to have a statement from your committee of the relationship between Congregationalism in the documents and in practice either to preface or to summarize the material which the committee has already voted to include in its report."

A September 21 letter[43] addressed to all committee members stressed the urgency and importance of the P.U. Report.

"Dear Fellow Committee Members;

"I am enclosing a copy of the minutes of the Greenwich meeting as received from our secretary, Frederick W. Whittaker. I am sure we are all grateful to him for their completeness and clarity. If you have any corrections will you please send them to me?

"These minutes and the exhibits indicate the various assignments made to committees and individuals and so will serve as a reminder of the work ahead. I plan soon to call a meeting of the Central Committee for just after Thanksgiving to prepare a tentative draft of our report. All assigned work of committees and individuals should be in my hands prior to that meeting.

"As soon as possible thereafter, a copy of the tentative report will be sent to you for your study in preparation for our all-important meeting next February in Greenwich. I hope that any member of the Committee who has ideas which may prove helpful will send them as soon as possible to the proper committee chairman or individual as indicated by the assignments in our minutes.

"We now have less than a year for the preparation of our final report. The fine record of sacrificial service on the part of every member of the Committee insures that during the remaining months we will all strive to the utmost of our ability to produce a report measuring up to the importance of the matters with which we are concerned."

Another handwitten letter dated November 12, 1953:[44]

"Dear Henry:

"Thank you for your good letter. I am glad to know that we will have a further report from you. The work of your committee, which is largely *your* fine, wise and sacrificial work, furnishes the backbone for the entire body of our committee's report. We are all deeply appreciative of it. I have no suggestions as to its nature. I know how hard it is to find the time. I am devoting well over half of my time to it just now, and it is a struggle. I've just finished the first drafts of sections on 'Introduction' and 'The Work of the Committee' for the report. I have had to get extra secretarial help to get it done. If you find that it will help you to get similar help do not hesitate to do so and send the bill to Miss Debus. If you can get the material ready in time so that you can have 8 copies made it will be helpful for the use of the committee. Such expense should be billed to Miss Debus.

"I am having material mimeographed now which I hope will reach all members before our meeting for advance reading. I'm sure that all will find much of it of very considerable interest.

"I am so glad that you can come. Without your wise and willing work, we just would not have been able to reach our present position as a committee. I think that it is a pretty good one. The Court of Appeals' decision is expected on Nov. 19. If it wins I wonder what it will say and do."

Notice of the Central Committee meeting was dated November 23, 1953:[45]

"Dear Friends,

"I have been spending much of my time in preparation for our meeting on December 1st. I have re-read a very considerable amount of the material which has come before our committee since its inception. What a tremendous amount of it there is! And how interesting to re-read it in the light of the work of our group. I am also reading statements that are coming in now, which I will share with you in Boston.

"As a result of all this reading, together with my own thinking, a number of questions seem to me to come into sharp focus. I pass them on to you so that you may give them thought preparatory to our meeting.

"1. Is organic union, considered as on the organization level, possible or impossible under our Congregational polity? (This exempts the spiritual or fellowship concept of union.)

"2. If it is possible, is it practical or wise under present conditions?

"3. If it is impossible can our polity be changed to make it possible? If so how?

"4. If it is possible to change our polity to make it possible, would our principle of autonomy need to be partially modified or sacrificed, as the New England Panel suggests? If so are the values gained greater than the values lost? (I just received the new New England Panel report. I'll bring it with me.)

"5. Is the 'principle of progress' a basic principle of our Congregational polity? Can it or can it not be considered of sufficient authority to justify the modification or abandonment of the principle of 'the independence of the local church'?

"We cannot, of course, give final consideration to questions such as these until we have the reports from Swartz, Gray and Meek before us. But we can do some thinking about them for they seem to be questions which our committee must answer."

The Boston December 1, 2, 3, 1953 Central Committee meeting was determinate as to some sections of the final P.U. report, and events exterior to the committee raised questions concerning other sections.

It seemed wise to me to begin presentation of the 22-page report on Congregational Polity as Practiced (hereafter C.P.P.) with the following quotations from the Rev. James F. English, Connecticut State Superintendent.[46]

"I would say that Congregationalism in practice probably does not differ greatly from that which I have discovered in the 'fundamental documents.' I am quite confident that this is reasonably true as far as the local churches in Connecticut and New Hampshire are concerned. As I read the histories of the churches and observe their ways today I am impressed with the similarity of practices. . . . .

"I wonder if you would agree with me in the feeling that we are far away from both the spirit and the letter of such a document as the Saybrook Platform which failed for acceptance. . . .

"The development of the State Conference offices which Mr. Burton mistakingly identifies with the office of the Superintendent is of course relatively new. He makes the mistake of bringing in personalities as well as of being intensely unjust but I think he does well to call attention to the development. I doubt if the churches of Connecticut, for instance, are 'directed' as much by the Conference office as those which were founded and aided by the Missionary Society were a generation or two ago. In this conference no officer goes to a church or gives it advice in regard to its affairs unless requested to do so. My feeling is that the same is almost a universal rule."

Further, I called attention to the October 19, 1953 issue of the denominational periodical "Advance"[47] in which Professor Hugh Vernon White presented his carefully reasoned proposal for "two-level" thinking, e.g., ecclesiastical and administrative. The article elaborated suggestions made to the Polity Committee, some of which were incorporated in the final P.U. Report.

The Boston 1953 meeting examined all 22 pages of the C.P.P. report. The degree of common mind among us was striking. My "working copy" of the report shows:

1. a verbal change for clarification in p. 2
2. correction of two typographical errors on p. 3
3. correction of one typographical error on p. 5
4. deletion for re-study of paragraphs 56, 57, 58 on pages 13 & 14, which paragraphs dealt with the American Board (foreign missions)
5. on p. 16, deletion of three words in paragraph 73, and substitution of "responsible" for "reasonable" before "freedom"
6. one typographical error corrected on p. 20.

I list *all* of these corrections to underscore the remarkable degree to which very diverse minds had reached agreement by addressing the written testimony of 140 correspondents. The 74 paragraphs of C.P.P. use the words, phrases, sentences and ideas of the respondents.

Only where there was no response, that is, from the national boards, was there a lacuna.

Theology and Spirit

The most important addition to the P.U. Report given tentative approval at Boston, 1953, was Fred Meek's:[48]

"The essence of Congregationalism cannot be found adequately in documents, even in our own documents. Rather it is to be found and seen most clearly in the direction and quality and character of its spirit. Thus, its life, its polity, and its organizational structure are finally not of codification, but they are of the spirit, and they have both a surprising long-term uniformity and a suprising flexibility in the midst of changing circumstances. . . . .

"Congregationalism is a present living witness to the continuous on going existence of a particular pattern of Christian experience and practice which has definite New Testament rootage. Today, Congregationalism acknowledges that its experience and practice are one among many, for among the redeemed followers of Christ there are variance and variations in Christian experience and practice. Congregationalism does not deny the reality of any man's claim for his Christian experience, nor the reality of any Church's claim for its Christian experience and practice—if the fruits of Christian deed and character mark them—and if these claims are not exclusive in character, shutting other belivers out from some phase of God's grace and blessing. . . . We do not find in the New Testament any divine command about exclusiveness or uniformity of experience and of practice, when Christ's brethren gather together; but we do find an acknowledgement of the validity of variance, and we find an assurance of strength in the variance, if the units of gathered Christians are directed by a genuine desire for the fulfillment of Christ's purpose. . . .

"We believe that such a gathered group, gathered around the Christ Who said 'Wherever two or three are gathered together in may name, there am I in the midst,' has an essential completeness about it, so that the local church is the Church Universal, visible before men at a particular time and at a particular place. Thus the church is not present nor does it come into being, because there is a minister or a building or a bishop or an ecclesiastical administrative office. The Church is where two or three are gathered together in His name.

"We congregationalists give our final ecclesiastical authority into the hands of the congregation. We are willing to do this because of our emphasis upon the right of every Christian to have immediate access to God. Neither church nor clergy are necessary for this kind of access. . . .

"It is not accurate to say that the New Testament gives little substantiation for our kind of polity. . . .

"It needs to be remembered that frequently in the New Testament a differentiation was made between 'the church' and 'the churches.' For example, the New Testament speaks about 'the church in Corinth' and the 'Church in Thessalonica'; but it also speaks about 'the churches in Galatia.' The plural form is geographical describing the Church in multiplicity, but the phrase implies the closest spiritual and organic connection between the church in Corinth and any church in Galatia. This terminology, 'the church' and 'the churches,' which we Congregationalists use and insist upon, is of significant importance, because it testifies to a 'wholeness' and a universality in the life of the individual local Church, a kind of wholeness which churches of the Presbyterial order and of the Episcopal order do not concede to the individual local church. . . .

"Congregationalism, believing that Jesus Christ is the Head of the Church, has always found in that fact the already established unity of the Church and of the Churches. It has steadfastly refused to believe that there was ever any additional organic connection created with other Churches *through* Church officers *through* Church organizations. The unity (and it was an organic unity) in which our fathers were interested, was essentially the concept of the Body of Christ, which includes organically, integrally, spiritually all other bodies who claim Christ as Lord. Thus we are *not* exclusive, we are inclusive in our understanding of the Church Universal. And no one from any other Christian church, local or national or creedal, is excluded from membership, or from the Lord's Table. The acceptance and fulfillment of this inclusive pattern of church life is not a specious refuge from the active sharing of life together between ourselves and other churches and other denominations—it offers a genuine prospect for the fulfillment in fact of the unity of the Church of Christ.

"This practice of fellowship without compulsion of Christian Churches fellowshipping in Christ with each other, exerts the most profound demands on churches and people. . . .

"Fellowship in Christ, seeking to be led by the Holy Spirit gathering in the church meeting has been the matrix out of which have come some of the most creative Christian deeds and experience of the past four hundred years. And the little groups of people who so acted and so lived because they knew an essential completeness in their Church relationships, have provided within the vast secular setting within which their Churches have been set down, a more far reaching influence than perhaps any other religious group.

"When as Christians we live in this experience of fellowship, we want and we seek the fellowship and counsel of others in gathered churches like ourselves. Therefore we fellowship together in associations, in state conferences and in our General Council. . . . Because we have been neglecting this spiritual phase in our broader relations of fellowship, we have created a vacuum at the place where we have been organizing institutionally the life of our churches. Into that vacuum a relation of compulsion can very easily enter and be accepted. And then we would be transformed into something that is not our genus. The covenant relationship between our churches, such as we have between ourselves as individuals, is crucial in this day when so many of the secular pressures amid which we live in our society are pressures of power tending toward the creation of centralization.

"P. T. Forsyth has put it, 'The fundamental difference between a Church and a democracy lies in the principle that no numbers can create a real authority such as the Church confesses, whereas, democracy as such will listen to no authority but what its numbers and majorities do create.' Granted that this is a somewhat extreme statement, the fact is that the only authority to which congregationalists, when they are true to their genus, will submit, is the authority of the spirit manifest in individuals and in groups responsive to the will and purpose of Christ. This authority is most compelling of all. . . .

"The experience of the covenant may well be the method by which the Congregational Christian Churches can make their most effective contribution to the ecumenical movement. The expression of the covenant relation could bridge existing barriers of polity and tradition and could give the opportunity to objectify the fact which is so frequently overlooked, the fact of a deep already existing union between our Protestant Churches, an objectification possibly more significant than could be achieved by legalistic compulsions giving the outward appearance of unity.

"Acknowledgement of the fact that we are 'one in Christ' should be a primary emphasis. The failure of Protestantism as a united factor in the life of the world is not due to the fact that we are not 'one in Christ,' (it is Christ that made and makes us so) but to the fact that we have failed to realize this central fact and at times we have confused oneness in organization with oneness in Christ.

"One of the present contributions to unity which the Free Churches can make is to bear our particular witness to this 'oneness in Christ' as a present reality, and not as something yet to be achieved. . . .

"It would seem to be a primary function of the Free Churches to turn from these ecumenical pursuits which entangle them in their own polity and to emphasize for and in the ecumenical movement, the existing spiritual basis of union as embodied in the covenant relationship. This could give a profound fulfillment of our cherished purpose to fellowship in Christ, not only with ourselves but with all Christians."

Discussion did not materially change the substance or sentences of this paper as may be seen by comparing the quotations just given with the published P.U. Report.

The concluding two sections of the Rev. Frederick L. Meek's paper related to covenant union. The steps proposed were essentially those adopted by the Congregational Churches and the Presbyterian Church in England hereafter. Many English Congregational Churches voted to form the Congregational Church in England, authorized to draw up with the Presbyterian Church a constitution for a new denomination named the United Reformed Church. At Boston, 1953, both encouragement and scepticism were expressed.

The "suggested type of covenant"[49] met with unanimous approval and was remanded to the subsequent meeting of the whole Polity and Unity Committee.

According to my notes on December 3, 1953[50] attention centered on the organic union section, and I was directed to further re-word this section and send it to the Rev. Charles C. Merrill. Four areas were singled out as in need of additional writing viz. reasons for organic union, nature of organic union, procedure for advance of organic union by union of particular Churches "without let or hindrance," and the procedure in which a group of Churches call a national convention comparable to the 1871 Albany Convention.

December 1953 Rushes To A Close

Everything seemed to happen at once. On December 3, 1953 the State of New York Court of Appeals, in a split vote, set aside the Steinbrink decision on two grounds: (1) both parties agreed that no ecclesiastical question was presented and (2) since the funds were held by the boards, etc., rather than the General Council, and since the boards were not parties to the trial, no material interests were admitted for adjudication. This meant immediate pressure from some to press ahead with merger and let the P.U. Committee complete its study without bothering to consider its report—or, for that matter, the Claremont resolution.

I pressed on with the organic union assignment and sent copies to Drs. Merrill and Fifield. Wendell responded by hand, dated December 14, 1953:[51]

"Dear Henry:

"You did an excellent job on organic union. I hope that Charlie finds it possible to go along without much change. After studying your statement carefully I decided that it would be best to include a section on the Powers of the General Council outlining the two main ideas and then stating the processes for the realization of organic union which each would require. (1) If the General Council has the power at present, then I will pretty well follow Arthur's general plan. (2) If it does not,—then will follow my idea of unanimity which I am going to change to 'the substantial unity of the churches' using the actual phrase from the General Council Constitution. This should, I think, strengthen this approval.

"In order to make this section possible and provide the proper approach to it, I have taken the liberty of making some changes in the last two pages of your excellent statement. I enclose the two pages as I have revised them. My idea was to delete conclusions regarding the powers of the General Council until the matter is discussed in the following section.

"I am, of course, motivated in seeking this method by the desire to secure, if possible, a unanimous approval of the report. Possibly we will feel it advisable to express a judgment on 'organic union' versus 'covenant union' at the end of the report. I suppose there will be some divisions at that point. But if we can nail down our factual propositions by unanimous vote I feel this will be a great gain. And surely if we suggest what can be done if the General Council has the powers and also if it has *not* such a statement should be sufficiently objective for us all.

"I will send a copy of these 2 pages to Charles and suggest that they be substituted in your statement to propose the way for mine which incidentally I have already and am well satisfied with it.

"Thanks again for your splendid work. Without you the committee just couldn't function.

"Best always, Wendell

"P.S. If you have any suggestions or improvements or changes on what I have done, let me know."

A further handwritten letter dated December 21, 1953,[52] gives insight into the problems created for the P.U.C. by the appellate court decision:

"Dear Henry:

"The material came today. In fact it beat your letter in. I have now checked it over and it is in the works. Thanks for such a big job done so promptly and so well. Your letter came this afternoon.

"I talked to Charlie this morning over the phone. He is working on the statement. I assume from what he said that he's going to change it considerably. He now feels in view of the court decision that the way is clear and a ringing statement on 'organic union' is in place. He is very fair, however. Even said that if I wanted to edit what he wrote to do so. I do not however want to do it that way. I talked with him at great length and he may not change it as much as he had planned. However if he does I'm going to include both your statement and his in the report. He is agreeable to this. Then we'll have it out at Greenwich. I'm clear that this is the crucial issue so far as we are concerned and we must face it head on. But I think we have had enough intellectual and spiritual preparation to do it wisely and well. We will also face from some quarters the idea of modifying some of our present decisions in view of the opinion of the court. I do not discover in the majority decision anything that should lead to any modifications. But we must anticipate a certain amount of suggestions along this line. I am confident that with patience and goodwill we can work it out. Your work has furnished an excellent basis for it. I quite agree with you when you put 'in time' in caps. I think the timing is pretty good so far in that we can get copies of our report to the Executive Committee before they have a first meeting with the E. & R.'s. I wish we could have it before the Executive Committee itself meets. But that's expecting too much. I also wish this had all 'broken' closer to the General Council so that our report could have come officially before them before much had been done about the merger. But we'll press as rapidly as we can after February 5 to get it printed and mailed to the churches. That should help.

"All is quiet here. *Nothing* will be done until the meeting of the Executive Committee on January 28 so all is in orderly and proper procedure.

"I don't think Doug[53] believes there is a top secret to consider like situation. I can't for the life of me understand why. This certainly is. But in any case I suppose it would be expecting too much to have *no* statements now made that we are on our way in. Many such have been made. Many have assumed that it's all over. On the other hand many 'pro's' are urging that the whole matter be dropped in the interests of inner unity. There are strong currents both ways in the Executive Committee. That's going to be an extremely interesting and important meeting.

"I hope you can read this. My secretaries are too busy typing parts of our reports and Christmas programs to give me any time."

Dr. Merrill replied under date December 31, 1953:[54]

"Dear Henry:

"I am writing, for one main reason, to thank you for the fine way in which you enlarged and rewrote what I had said in my document headed 'Thoughts' about a united church. That was a swell job and I appreciated it very much.

"I also had the interesting experience of seeing in the hands of Horace Robson (who as you know is now Secretary of the Board of Pastoral Supply), as he was sitting opposite me at luncheon the other day, a copy of your latest Messenger. He was good enough to let me take it and as you will notice, I incorporated a couple of your phrases in my draft. I am afraid I didn't give you credit!

"After getting my draft the morning before Christmas Wendell spent the entire day, I judge, in going over it revising, making additions, etc. At least, he called me up and indicated how he was going to handle my paragraph on unanimity. What I had in mind was that my paragraph should be matched by a paragraph of his authorship which should state with equal strength the opposite point of view. It will be interesting to see what he worked out.

"He spoke of the report having now reached about one hundred typewritten pages. I am rather scared of its length. Historical scholars may read it in the future but how many will read it now?

"You remember that we were to send in suggestions for a definition of 'fellowship.' Hence my enclosure.

"Here's hoping that you and all your family will have good health and in every way a rewarding time during 1954. It has been good to get better acquainted with you during 1953 and the years before.

"Faithfully, yours, C.C.M."

The December "rush" was further complicated by a letter dated December 17, 1953, from Attorney Sargent H. Wellman,[55] counsel for the American Board taking issue with the "Introductory Statement . . . Congregational Polity in the Documents." Mr. Wellman wrote:

"Dear Wendell:

"I attended for a short while the other day a meeting of the Congregational Historical Society in which Rev. Charles C. Merrill gave a brief review of the work of the so called Fifield committee. At that time he gave us copies of your reports including the Introductory Statement. He also stated that he felt this was a very complete document which would probably be used as the basis for the new constitution of the United Church when it was formed.

"In view of these statements I write you regarding the provisions in the Introductory Statement relating to the American Board. As I understand it, the statement is an attempt to state the facts as they exist at present. If this is so, it seems to me that there are misleading statements in the four paragraphs about the American Board. It seems to me that the difficulty stems from the fact that the by-laws of the General Council are used as the source of information as to the American Board. The provisions from Article 4, Section 1 of the by-laws are quoted in the 44th paragraph of the Introductory Statement.

"From a legal point of view, this is not the correct way to approach the facts. The provisions of the General Council by-laws have absolutely no legal effect so far as the American Board is concerned. I think in some respects that they differ from the American Board's by-laws. The American Board, as you know, is incorporated in Massachussets. It is an independent legal body and its own constitution and by-laws are alone controlling in its organization and work. It is of course also true that the members of the General Council are considered as *nominated* for corporate membership on the American Board but their election by the remaining members of the corporation is required before they become corporate members. In practice of course this does make a close connection between the General Council and the American Board, but it still does not result in depriving the American Board of its separate corporate entity.

"You are aware I think also of the amendment to the American Board of Commissioners for Foreign Mission constitution which we secured in the early stages of the merger plans. This amendment would allow the American Board to amend its by-laws so that its corporate members could be elected by an outside body such as a Synod of the United Church. However, the amendment of the by-laws to accomplish this would have to be voted by the American Board itself.

"Dr. Merrill said at the meeting that the panel of lawyers under your commitee had not commenced to function, inasmuch as there was nothing for them to do until after the decision in the merger case. It seems to me however that if the Introductory Statement issued by your committee is to be used as the basis for further consideration it should be submitted to the legal committee and checked for accuracy in all respects. I have not studied the balance of the Statement with this in mind and have confined the few comments I make to the American Board situation with which I am more familiar. I am writing this letter to you and sending a copy to Dr. Merrill in the hope that it will be of some assistance.

"Sincerely yours, Sargent H. Wellman"

The problem which plagued the P.U.C. throughout four years was the legalese of the national level church-bodies. We all understood the fact that niceties of law are the business of the courts. Our goal was to write down what the documents said. Mr. Wellman was technically correct in saying that the General Council members are *nominated* for corporate membership in the American Board. But this neglects to remember that the corporate membership since 1913 had been the General Council members plus a varying number of others; the majority always being members of the General Council. It WAS true that in effecting the 1913 provision for General Council members as corporate members of the

American Board the Council members were purely nominated. Thereafter the corporate ABCFM membership was always predominately General Council members; those "carrying over" from one council to the next automatically elected new members. This was true when I was a General Council delegate in 1938, 1940, 1942, 1944, 1946, 1948, 1949, 1950, 1952, 1954 and 1956.

Nevertheless, the Wellman letter sent me back to my desk with the charters and by-laws of all national-level church bodies.

I must, by no means, leave the impression that ALL Lawyers disapproved of the Congregational Polity reports, both that on Documents and that on Practice. Roscoe W. Graves, Esq.,[56] finance chairman of the executive committee of the General Council, and a prominent Kansas lawyer, in a letter dated December 15, 1953, wrote:

"Dear Dr. Gray:

"This is to acknowledge your letter of December 18 enclosing the findings of your Committee, also your letter of January 12. I apologize for neglecting to reply to your first letter. Upon receipt of your letter this morning I picked up the report from my desk where press of business had caused me to lay it, and once started reading I could not stop until the end. It is a very fine statement.

"I have but one suggestion to make that is of no great consequence. In the closing sentence of Paragraph 7 you refer to church property, the title to which is held by a state conference or national society and conclude 'the local church is entirely free to use the property as it desires, except that the property cannot cease to be used by a Congregational Christian Church.' I wonder if the intention would be more clearly stated by saying, 'except the property cannot be used other than by a Congregational Christian Church.' Of course, it can cease to be used altogether whether by a Congregational Christian Church or otherwise.

"I have not been too enthusiastic over the work of the Committee on Free Church Polity and Unity, notwithstanding the fact that as I have become acquainted with Dr. Wendell Fifield I have come to admire him greatly and know that if the other members of the Committee have given the time and thought to it that has been given by you and Dr. Fifield, it would be a work well done. I have had the feeling that nothing constructive would be accomplished by the work of the Committee but after reading your report I realize that I was very wrong indeed.

"I do feel that the Committee should present to the General Council not only its report and findings of 'things as they are,' but

178

should make recommendations, where it appears proper, of 'what ought to be.'

"I think your Committee should give consideration to the printing of the final report and placing it in all of the churches as a handbook of Congregational Christian organization. Every person who unites with a Congregational Christian Church should be urged to read this report so they will know what kind of a church, organizationally, they are joining.

"We have received the court decision in the merger case and the question now is what to do and how to do it. I am fundamentally in favor of merger as I believe it is essential to the survival of Protestant Christianity in the years to come, but I am satisfied that many churches voted on the E. and R. merger not knowing what they were voting for. If our people had an opportunity to read the findings of your Committee they would be in a much better position to consider any future proposals of merger. I am saying that as a layman realizing how little we folks in the pews know about our Church organization and traditions out of which it has grown.

"In regard to the printing of the Committee report to the General Council, I cannot forget that I am chairman of the finance committee of the Executive Committee of the General Council and as such, I urge you to print no greater number of the report than will be actually used, as they will serve no good purpose stacked up in the wareroom at 287 Fourth Avenue, where too much of your Committee's previous printed matter has found its final resting place.

"I shall feel honored to be among the 'living bibliography' of your Committee report, although I have done nothing to deserve it.

"I hope that our entire denomination will feel the gratitude and sense of indebtedness to your Committee that it deserves for the monumental task it is accomplishing for our benefit.

"Sincerely, Roscoe Graves"

January 1954 Paper Blizzard

Under date December 22, 1953,Dr. Fifield[57] sent a letter to all P.U.C. members, the core of which was as follows:

"I have received several letters from members of our Committee on Free Church Polity and Unity asking about the effect of the opinion of the Court of Appeals on the work of our Committee. The answer is a simple one. It has very greatly increased the importance of our work.

"The Court in effect ruled that when no property rights are involved, 'the Courts cannot act in the internal affairs of religious bodies.' *This puts it squarely up to us.* If our problems as a fellowship are to be resolved it must be done by study among ourselves. This we are charged to do by the General Council."

"The opinion of the Court of Appeals will be considered at the meeting of the Executive Committee of the General Council on January 28th at Cleveland. There will be no special meeting of the Executive Committee. This indicates that the Executive Committee plans to proceed in a careful and dignified fashion in accordance with the Claremont resolution. There is *no* tendency to push nor to pressure the situation by anyone."

"The very great importance now attached to our report makes it more essential than ever that every member of the committee makes every possible effort to attend *our meeting at Greenwich, February 2nd to 5th.*"

"The report of our Committee will be completed on February 5th. It will be possible to have a copy of it in the hands of every member of the Executive Committee before any exploratory meeting with the E. & R. group is held. Hence the contents of our report can be used helpfully by the members of the Executive Committee in formulating their ideas concerning the future.

"It seems to me that the timing is working out very satisfactorily. It would indeed be unfortunate if the Executive Committee proceeded very far before reading our report. But this is not to happen. They will know from the beginning of negotiations what we have to say."

Wendell's notice of the February meeting crossed my December 18, 1953 letters[58] to (1) state superintendents, (2) association respondents, (3) panel chairmen and (4) 1951 respondents. To each was sent a copy of Congregational Polity in Practice (CPP) as revised at the December 1953 Boston Central Committee meeting.

Here is a copy of the letter addressed to the state superintendents:

"Rev. Frederick W. Alden
New Hampshire Congregational-Christian Conference
85 North State Street
Concord, New Hampshire

"My dear Dr. Alden:

"The Free Church Unity and Polity Committee is deeply grateful for the careful report which you sent to them. It has now been thoroughly studied, the results compiled, and these are enclosed herewith.

"Since the recent Court decision we have been given a January 15th deadline for a preliminary report to the Executive Committee of the General Council. Therefore, would you please give me your additional cooperation by going over the enclosed report and sending me any corrections or additions thereto. We trust it is satisfactory with you to include your name as one of those from whom this information has been received. Since nearly all the State Superintendents, all the Panel Chairmen, and a tremendous number of persons suggested by each of these are the 'living bibliography' of this report it was the judgment of our Central Committee that I should write to each of you asking further data and permission to list you as 'one of our living bibliography.'

"I, personally, want to thank you for the care with which you have answered our inquiries. Were it not for this cooperation the enclosed report would have been entirely impossible. It has been difficult in any instance, but I have done my very best to write it in accord with the material which you all have given me."

The letter to panel chairmen follows:[59]

"Rev. Roy C. Helfenstein,
3206 Grove Avenue,
Richmond 21, Virginia

"My dear Roy:

"You were Chairman of the Southeast Panel which discussed the report of Congregationalism as it appears in its documents issued by the Free Church Unity and Polity Committee. The reports which came in from the Panels were a great help. Enclosed is a copy of the present draft of the description of Congregationalism as it is practiced in the United States.

"Since there is obviously no documentary basis for this study, it has been thought well to return the document as it now stands to those who are 'human bibliography,' This is for a two-fold purpose: first, to receive from you such corrections and additions as you may wish to suggest as you see it in its more complete form, and, second, so that you may see what has resulted from your contribution.

"We trust that the use of the names of your Panel members in the document as those who constitute the 'human bibliography' will be entirely satisfactory to them. This implies no agreement on their part with the entire content of the report, but I have done my very best to compile it faithfully from the mass of material submitted to me by the Superintendents, the Panel Chairmen, the Panels, and all those names suggested to our Committee by any of the above.

"Your early comment will be much appreciated because we have been given a very difficult deadline since the new Court decision was rendered. In other words, I would like to hear from you by January first."

Letters to association correspondents and individuals were similar. This barrage of letters launched an all-out attempt to make our CPP report the most inclusive and precise study of Congregational Polity in Practice in the history of the fellowship.

The large majority of the 140 persons addressed responded by mid January. As each letter arrived it was carefully checked with the CPP working draft, errors were corrected, and changes in wording made, to make certain the CPP report was accurate. January 12[60] I sent another letter to all who had not yet responded, adding penned notes to each:

> "Replies to my request for help on 'Polity as Practiced' have been coming in steadily. These replies are so helpful that Wendell Fifield decided to send to the General Council Executive Committee copies of the draft you received. This gives me nine more days for additional revision.

> "We are determined to make this the clearest and best presentation possible. Also, we want you 'in' as one of the 'living bibliography'. May I urge you to MAKE TIME to give me your comments or suggestions—minor or major, brief or long. If your reply is brief, just write it on the back of this letter and put it in the enclosed stamped and addressed envelope.

> "I greatly dislike to add to your work load; for I know it must be as heavy as mine, but really, this is something we just *must* make as inclusive and active as our combined resources will permit.

> "Please let me hear from you—and write back the day you receive this letter if you possibly can."

January 21, 1954,[61] I sent a telegram to ten 1951 respondents and nine 1952-1954 respondents from whom no reply to the January 12th letter had been received. The latter read:

"NINE REPLIES TO POLITY REPORT NOT YET RECEIVED. PLEASE WIRE COLLECT PERMISSION TO USE YOUR NAME IN THE 'LIVING BIBLIOGRAPHY' OR SEND AIR-MAIL SUGGESTIONS FOR IMPROVEMENT.
   "HENRY DAVID GRAY
    ONEONTA CONGREGATIONAL CHURCH
    GARFIELD AND OAK
    SOUTH PASADENA, CALIFORNIA"

By January 29, 1954, we had received 109 replies. Among the important revisions made from the respondents on January 28 and

29 were the following: Congregational Polity in Documents (CPD) report paragraph 27 regarding fellowship bodies for men, women and youth was re-worded as subsequently printed. Paragraphs 78-82 on the International Congregational Council were re-worded. Tentative wording was prepared for CPP paragraphs 78 and 79 dealing with "Regional Meetings."

Personal letters were sent, dated December 29, 1953,[62] to the Rev. Drs. William Frazier, Ray Gibbons, Henry S. Leiper and Frank Scribner, and to Mr. Harold B. Belcher of the American Board

"Rev. Henry S. Leiper
General Council of the
Congregational Christian Churches
287 Fourth Avenue
New York 10, New York

"Dear Hank:

"Enclosed are copies of two facets of our Polity study before they come up for final discussion in January. We would like your careful study of them.

"First, the printed material is taken from the documentary description and I should like reference to documents for any changes which you feel need to be made. Second, the mimeograph material concerns present practice and I know the committee would like you to cite examples for any additions or corrections thereto since the material has been collected from virtually all the State Superintendents and a widely representative group suggested by them and by the Panel Chairmen.

"Unfortunately, the recent Court decision has placed a very tough deadline on me for this material and I have had a hard time getting it together in decent shape. I would need your answer by Janaury 8th, and I am fully aware that this is much too short a time but I know you will understand the difficult predicament I am in on time schedule."

Describing the Indescribable

One of the tasks assigned me at Boston December 1953 meeting was the writing of paragraphs on the three cardinal words of contemporary Congregationalism: Faith, Freedom, and Fellowship.

As soon as the Christmas and New Years programs and camps at Oneonta were over a full day was allotted to this challenging task. As Fred Meek's great paper made clear, the mediators regarded Faith as the foundation. I doubt that any of us would accept the triad, Faith, Freedom and Fellowship, as more than a very rough and limited description of the Congregational Way.

I had wrestled with "Faith" as a member and scribe of the committee of nine which drafted the "Message to the Churches" from the 1949 Wellesley meeting of the International Congregational Council. The statement which emerged read:[63]

"The word 'faith' is used by members of the Congregational Christian Churches to mean (1) the central Christian convictions, most especially as these are revealed in the life and teachings of Jesus Christ, and as these have been continuously re-expressed in statements of faith by succeeding councils of the Churches, or (2) the central Christian experience of allegiance to God as He is made known to us in Jesus Christ, as this experience is exemplified in Churches whose members are 'committed Christians' and in a fellowship of Churches which acknowledges Christ to be the sole Head of the Church, so that each community of believers is the universal Church in essence and is empowered by Christ to govern its life under the guidance of His Spirit.

The "Freedom" paragraph was complicated by the need to state the positive relationships of Churches and church-bodies. My scribbling, scratching out, and re-writing settled on the words "responsible freedom." The paragraph has been quoted in whole or in part many times, without acknowledgment of its source in the P.U. Report:[64]

"Responsible freedom describes the practical relation of the Congregational Christian Churches to one another, and to their wider agencies. The local Church voluntarily elects delegates to meetings of wider bodies, and takes responsibility for the work undertaken by those delegates, with the usual Congregational reservation, namely, that what is undertaken must *win* the support of the Churches, and that the Churches must win the support of their members. The wider bodies are expected to be sensitive to the will of the Churches, and, on the association and conference level, are directly controlled by delegates from the Churches and by directors elected by those delegates. On the national and international levels the control exerted by the Churches is very important in theory but necessarily quite removed in practice. *Responsible freedom, at its best, means voluntary partcipation in wider bodies on the part of the local Church and voluntary sensitivity to the will of the Churches on the part of the wider bodies.* It also means voluntary sharing by the local Church in the work carried on by the wider bodies, and voluntary responsiveness to the needs of the local Churches by the wider bodies. Responsibility and freedom are laid upon both local

Church and wider agency. No neat formula can express the meaning of responsible freedom, for it is a matter of moral obligation and Christian conviction. Fundamentally, it means that every Congregational Christian Church member is accountable to God for his creed and conduct and, accordingly, every Congregational Christian Church becomes likewise accountable to God and also to its members. Every wider agency is accountable to God for its creed and conduct, but it is also directly or indirectly accountable to the Churches which created it. What we have in practice is a system of direct delegate control by the Churches so far as associations and conferences are concerned, a system of indirect delegate control so far as the General Council is concerned, a system of tenuous delegate control so far as the national boards and agencies are concerned, and a system of no direct control at all so far as the missions council, the mid-winter meetings and the international council are concerned."

The third term "Fellowship"[65] has been used by Dr. Stanley V. North at the Pasadena Athletic Club as if it designated an authoritative body. I found it used in our studies with three chief meanings:

"The word 'fellowship' is a term much used by members of the Congregational Christian Churches. Its meanings are chiefly these (a) the inclusive body of those who share the Christian faith and recognize the Congregational way as the manner in which that faith expresses itself, (b) the totality of all the organized bodies of the Congregational Christian Churches, and of all groups of members acting together in the interest of the Congregational Christian Churches, and (c) the radiant personal and organizational relationships which characterize the life of those who acknowledge Jesus as Lord, who reverently seek to follow the leadings of the Holy Spirit, who join in common worship, whose kinship in Christian service bears fruit in mutual trust and deep friendship, and who have chosen to share together in the work and worship of the Congregational Christian Churches and the wider bodies created by them or by groups of their members."

On January 21, 1954, I completed revision of the typescript which included all changes made in the light of 109 responses, and a final pre-committee-meeting revision of the paragraphs on Faith, Freedom and Fellowship. Changes were made even after stencils had been cut. But the CPP report was ready for the General Committee.

Difficulties with the Home Board and American Board wording were surmounted by simplification of the statements and the inclusion of a NOTE as to the relationship of the P.U. Report statement and the legal charters of the boards.

In the CPP report, paragraph 57 read,[66] "The national societies ... are administered in accord with the provisions of their respective charters and by-laws (see documentary section IV, 3)." If several more months had been available it might have been possible to detail the practice of the boards.

Call to Greenwich, 1954

Two handwritten letters from Dr. Wendell Fifield furthered readiness to report to the General Committee.

Under date, December 24, 1953,[67] he wrote regarding the organic union section as follows:

"Dear Henry:

"I received 'C.C.''s version of Organic Union this morning. I read it with care several times. . . . I called Charlie up this afternoon. We had a good visit about it and reached this agreement: We will terminate his part of the 'Organic Union' with section 3 on page 9. Then I will add the material which I sent you. . . .

"We can now consider that the section on 'Organic Union' comes from him, or at least has his benediction and blessing. . . .

"I feel that between all of us, and especially because of you, we now have a reasonably fair, well-balanced, and non-loaded section on Organic Union. I really think we've come out much better than I thought we could on so debatable a point.

"I'll be interested in your reactions. At least I've done my best in this key controversial matter."

With reference to the report as a whole Wendell wrote under date January 4, 1954:[68]

"Dear Henry:

"Thank you for your recent letter received here. The material from Charlie Merrill is now being mimeographed so any changes will need to be made now at Greenwich. I turned all the tentative report over to Miss Debus before I left yesterday . . . She hopes to get it all mimeographed and mailed to the committee on January 15 so they will have time to study it before February 2. . . . If there are any major changes indicated, it would be a good idea for you to have substitute sheets made before you come east and bring them with you. Any cost is a proper charge to our committee. . . . I have been wondering whether we really need to include the sections on the Boards. Apparently there is considerable confusion and conflict about them. . . .

"I find much hope that there can be a *new* way brought into the 'union' picture. 'Must we be dragged through it all again?' I am so often asked. Plan to make a strong presentation of the covenant idea to the Executive Committee as a way that will bring back a real glow and radiance to the whole business.

"Best always, Wendell"

The general letter dated January 12, 1954,[69] reviewed overall progress and outlined the Greenwich meeting agenda:

"Dear Fellow Committee Member,

"*Well, here it is! The tentative report of our Committee.* It represents a tremendous amount of work by all of us.

"I hope that it will reach you in time to permit you to study it carefully before the Greenwich meeting. I am sending you two copies so that you can mark up one and still have the other one for reference.

"To achieve at our meeting the final approval of so extensive a report as this will be a considerable undertaking. However, if each member has marked in advance the parts he or she feels should be discussed, we can concentrate on those matters and so eliminate the necessity of taking up every paragraph in the report. Furthermore the sections which have already been discussed at length and approved should be disposed of quite rapidly.

"I hope that we can hold our discussions to the principles involved and not become too engrossed in matters of words and phrases unless they influence meanings.

"In my opinion the sections dealing with Organic Union, the Powers of the General Council, the Spiritual Basis and the Covenant idea will require the most careful consideration by the Committee. Very soon after our first session starts we will turn directly to these sections.

"The section on Organic Union has been rewritten many times. The final version came to me from Dr. Merrill. In his copy he had an additional point at the end dealing with the principle of unanimity. After reading it I talked with him over the phone and read to him much of the section on 'The General Council' which I had written.

"We agreed that his material should not be included in the section on Organic Union as it stated a value judgment on which the Committee may well be divided. And that the body of the report should be made as objective as possible. However, I feel it only right to send you a copy of Dr. Merrill's statement for your study since it was submitted to the Committee.

"We will need to consider at our Greenwich meeting whether we as a Committee will in a concluding section express any judgments

187

relative to the body of our report. There would probably be differences in opinion expressed at this point. For example the section on the Powers of the General Council indicates objectively possible divergent opinion. Our Committee may wish to express, even by a majority and minority vote, its judgment on this vital matter.

"The Committee may also wish to express its judgment as to the relative values of future procedure along the line of federation, organic union, or covenant union. There may be other matters also, concerning which we may feel that we should speak out.

"Matters such as these must await our careful and prayerful consideration at our meeting. Such a statement as that of Dr. Merrill's referred to above and sent with this report, should be considered in this connection.

"In editing this entire report, a matter to which I have devoted most of my time for the past two months, I have sought to keep it very definitely objective at every point so far as it was humanly possible. *I have no doubt that at points I have failed.* These points we shall discover at our Greenwich meeting and deal with in proper fashion.

"In view of the fact that the decision of the Court of Appeals is now available, I have taken the responsibility of interpolating certain comments and references. All such references are wholly on my own responsibility. The Central Committee has not seen them. They may, of course, be included or deleted as the Committee desires.

"I shall not take the space here to acknowledge the special work of those who prepared the various sections of the report. This I will do at our Greenwich meeting. While it represents the sacrificial and capable work of many, it is to be the report of all of us. I hope and pray that we may be given in our meeting the wisdom to make it so.

"Our final report should be completed when we adjourn on February 5th. I am making preparation to have it mimeographed in sufficient numbers so that every member of the Executive Committee of the General Council will have a copy before their first conference with the E. and R. leaders.

"You will recall that such a joint conference was provided for by the resolution adopted by the General Council at Claremont. I am very glad that our Executive Committee will have the benefit of our report before they discuss with the E. and R.'s wisdom of proceeding further in the merger program.

"I cannot refrain as I bring this letter to close from telling you how great a joy it is to work with you, and how proud I am of the Committee, each and every one.

"My best wishes always, L. Wendell Fifield"

The only unresolved issue was the CPP statements regarding the American Board and the Home Board. Atty. Wellman, Dr. William Frazier, Dr. Truman Douglass and ABCFM treasurer Mr. Harold Belcher insisted that both the American Board and the Home Board were separate, independent, self-governing bodies, subject only to their own charters and by-laws. I was unable to get *them* to write substitute sections. This is quite understandable in view of the grilling these officers had been subjected to in the New York Superior Court Cadman case. Wendell worried about it more than I did. We both wanted the P.U. Report to be complete, but accuracy seemed to me the top priority; complete if possible, if not then accuracy up to the limit of available data.

The anamolous position of the boards may be explained by facts called to my attention in a letter from the Rev. Malcolm Burton dated February 8, 1954:[70]

> "At the National Council of 1927 a phrase was added to the description of the relation of the national societies. Figure out for yourself WHY, but I suspect it had to do with the ruckus over the amalgamation of the Boards in 1925, when the American Board double-crossed everybody and stayed out after pretending they were going to join with the home societies to make one missionary board. I will italicize the phrase that was added at this time:

>> "'With the consent of our National Missionary Societies, whose approval is a necessary preliminary, *and whose constitutional right to withdraw such consent by due process is recognized*, the following shall define the relation of these societies to the National Council.' (By-Law X, 1927, page 292 of Nat. Coun. Minutes)

> "I traced this phrase on down to see what happened to it. It was carried over into the new constitution for the union with the Christians in 1931 and persisted until 1942. What happened was this: when the union took place there were added about four temporary paragraphs, dealing with relationships between the Christian Boards and ours until such time as corporate mergers could be accomplished. In 1942 all of these paragraphs were deleted because the necessary steps had been taken. At the same time, and apparently thinking that this phrase had come in at the same time, the above was removed. Actually it appears to me as an evidence of the same pretense of independence which the American Board now stresses. Or maybe with the American Board officials we should admit the technical independence, but remember the promises or 'covenant' made in 1913, which the American Board has never been at pains to repudiate publicly. If they want the churches to think they are giving

189

their money to an 'agency' when it comes to gifts then the officers of the American Board had better plan on *being* an agency all the time. Otherwise quit pretending."

Wendell Fifield's handwritten letter[71] (1/16/54, Fifield to Gray) sets the stage for the Greenwich meeting:

"Dear Henry:

"After very careful thought I have decided to place before the Executive Committee at its meeting on January 28 the Covenant Union Plan. I realize that this is 'jumping the gun' on the meeting of our committee. But I shall do it on my own responsibility. I have already asked for and been accorded sufficient time to do this. More and more I feel that any further procedure along the line of the basis of union or a constitution modeled after it would be a great mistake. The Cadman Church has already filed a request for a rehearing before the Court of Appeals. How long this will keep us in the courts I do not know. But of this I am certain: if we do not get away from the whole procedure of organic union we will be in the courts the rest of our lives and then some. The majority decision of the Court of Appeals as you have doubtless noted gives permission for us to join with the E. & R. only on the ground that the Basis of Union is in accordance with Congregational Polity. *This I do not believe*, but in any event it limits the area of our ecumenical outreach to those who will accept Congregational Polity in order to unite with us. I suspect this number is nil. Rather than promoting our participation in the ecumenical movement it definitely limits it.

"Most of the people with whom I talk say in substance, 'Must we drag through this again?' The radiance of the merger vision is gone. As one of our top officials, whose name I cannot use, but who gets about among the churches constantly, said to me the other day 'The merger is a wilted flower and it will never be anything else.'

"In the covenant idea we have a procedure that will give new radiance and meaning to the whole business. I have a specific plan worked out now for it which is just as definite as any plan for organic union. So far as my mind is able to determine it has all the values of 'o. u.' with not any of the complicating disadvantages.

"In preparing my statement for the Executive Committee I need to check my accuracy just at one point. To me the crux of this entire matter is Section IV, Part 4, Propositions IV and V. My impression is that these two propositions are aptly suggested by, and in truth grow out of, the material which you have assembled in Congregationalism in the Documents and in Practice. My recollection is that all existing documents suggest these two propositions and that further, all of those who wrote in to you also support them as indicated by Proposition 73 in the appendix 3. In this connection would I be justified in saying that 140 (or whatever the number is) of our leading Congregationalists support these propositions. That, in addition to the complete statement, has been re-verified by our 90 who have already replied after having been sent the entire statement. I want to be absolutely accurate in what I say at every point.

"I met with 12 of the Miami ministers to discuss this the other day. Not one of them accepted Congregationalism B and when I pointed out that unless Congregationalism B was accepted the merger had no chance, aside from chicanery, they all declared themselves for the Covenant Plan including the only E. & R. minister in Florida who was a guest.

"I would be greateful if you would 'hurl' me back an answer to my question just as soon as possible. I leave for Cleveland on January 26 and I want to go loaded,—and believe me I am. but I do need a check in this one point.

"Best wishes always, Wendell

"P.S. Have you seen Wagner's statement in the Messenger? If he holds to that I see no chance for the present merger unless someone engages in some linguistic acrobatics to an incredible degree."

Perseverence In Search of Precision

When the General Committee met at Seabury House, Greenwich, February 2-5, 1954, each member was intent on fashioning a report which should commend itself by precision, balance, accuracy, and wisdom—a formidable undertaking.

On Wednesday afternoon the General Committee divided into three working units on Organic Union, Covenant Union and Congregational Polity in Practice. Due to assertions, chiefly by denominational officials, that the CPP report was inaccurate, as reported at length by the Rev. Arthur Gray, Chairman of the General Council Executive Commitee, I invited anyone to inspect the letters and panel reports which backed up every phrase of every paragraph. Arthur Gray, Atty. Ed Williams, Superintendent Rev. William D. Pratt, and Rev. Alfred Hurst volunteered or were appointed.

My notes show that the quiz continued for three hours, 2:30 to 5:30 p.m. It began rather preemptively. Arthur said, "There isn't any association which accepts ordination by a church, is there?"

I spoke to all four, "Do you mind if, instead of answering questions, I produce the letters and reports from which the text is drawn? You can then compare the wording for yourselves."

"That is the proper way to review this," Williams said. "As an attorney I view the actual letters and reports as critical. They must back up every single disputed item in the CPP report."

"All right," said Arthur. "Show me ANY letter or report which backs up paragraph 6, 'A Congregational Christian Church may license or ordain its own candidates for the ministry.'"

"Okay, Arthur." I extracted papers from my bulging files (in two briefcases). "Here is the report of the Oxford Association, from Dixfield, Maine, on April 8, 1953. Mrs. Alice McGouldrick says, 'In Oxford County, Maine, a church, locally, can ordain a minister, whether the conference endorses him or not.'" I handed over the two-page, single-spaced, typewritten letter.

Arthur read it, handed it on. When all had read it there was no comment. It appeared as if it had been expected that THIS could NOT be supported. In the silence I volunteered. "Would you like to see more data on this point?" Bill said, "I would."

"I believe you all know Dr. Thomas Anderson of Atlanta. Here is his letter: (Anderson to Gray, 4/15/53) 'In the three Conferences of the Southeast Convention there has been no satisfactory or well defined policy in respect to Ordination. Occasions are on record where local churches have proceeded to ordain a minister without a Council or reference to the Association or State Conference.'"

"Let me see that Henry. I know Tom," Hurst requested. He read all three single-spaced typewritten pages slowly.

As he handed them to Arthur he remarked, "There are little churches throughout the South and along the Wabash in Illinois and Indiana which do pretty much as they please. Somehow, I never thought of *them* as part of this study . . . " His voice drifted off at the end.

Arthur's review was more rapid. Bill's took even less time.

Arthur commented, "I'd have to agree that these reports authenticate paragraph 6. But that doesn't mean they represent our whole fellowship."

Williams hadn't spoken. "There is a basic issue here. Is this CPP report supposed to say WHAT IS, or WHAT OUGHT TO BE?"

"Ed," I replied, "Our steadfast aim has been to say exactly *what is*. I'm prepared to alter *any* statement which cannot be backed up by these letters and reports. I'm not prepared to return to the General Committee saying the CPP report needs to be changed to conform to my personal views . . . or to anyone else's personal views. These statements encompass the span of variety in our practice—and nothing more."

Arthur mollified. "Henry, we're not questioning your integrity. It's just that many of the statements seem incorrect."

"Fine," I replied. "We are five reasonable people. Name every statement which seems incorrect, examine the record on which it is based, and then *you* tell me how to say anything other than what we have said."

"Don't get so upset," Bill responded. "I've been through this with you, especially since Claremont. I can tell Arthur I've seen every word of the report except the corrections and additions made in the past couple of weeks. *I'm* satisfied that what it says is accurate, though there's a lot of it I don't like."

Arthur was pensive. He slowly turned the pages of the CPP report. "Henry," he said, "Sometimes *how* a statement is worded bothers me. In the paragraphs about the assocations why do you use *may* in paragraphs like 18, 19, and 25 and then positive words in connection with local churches in 2, 3, and 4?"

"Let's glance down *all* the paragraphs on Churches and associations. Regarding Churches, in paragraphs 1, 5, and 6 *may* is used. In 2, 3, 4, and 7 the verbs are positive. In 8 and 9 the governing word is *voluntarily*. With regard to the associations 18. 19 and 25 use *may*, 10, 11, 12, 13, 14 15, 16 17, 20, 21, 23, 24 and 26 use positive verbs; *customarily* governs 22, and 27 simply lists concerns stated in the letters and reports. What, exactly, is the problem?"

Bill Pratt spoke up. "I asked this question in our Congregational Polity Committee. The problem is in 18 which says, 'The association *may* withdraw fellowship from a local Church for spiritual and moral reasons.' This reads AS IF there were strict boundaries to an association's actions regarding a church. But are there?"

"Bill, you are a conference superintendent. Whom among your colleagues do you wish to hear from on this point?"

"Fred Alden of New Hampshire is pretty thoughtful, and Jim English of Connecticut. Then Everett Babcock of Ohio and Tom Goodwin of Minnesota—and somebody from the Christian connection, maybe Butterfield."

I thumbed through my files. "Okay, let's see what they say. Each man has the printed Documentary report, and a copy of an earlier version of the Practice report. The paragraph numbers are alike. Here's Alden's 6-page report (Alden to Gray, 1/16/53). On #18 he writes, 'This is correct.' Butterfield asked Tom Anderson of Atlanta to write his reply (Anderson to Gray, 4/15/53). Butter-field reviewed the report and okayed it. You'll have to read the letter because the Southeast Convention is in the process of re-organization. In essence what Tom reports is NO existing, customary practice; a situation the re-organization aims to cor-rect. The word *may* is obviously an understatement so far as the Southeast Convention is concerned."

"Let me read Tom's report," Bill requested. While he was reading I passed Alden's two documents around.

Bill looked up. "What about the rest?"

"Everett Babcock's (Babcock to Gray, 1/15/53) first lengthy paragraph says that practice in Ohio does not 'differ with the *Introductory Statement* except possibly in paragraph 17 under *Associations*. In Ohio actions of a vicinage council in ordination would not confer ministerial membership in an association: this appears to be covered in 19, 20, 21."

Hurst reached out his hand. "Go on with the papers while I read this," he suggested.

"Jim English of Connecticut (English to Gray, 4/3/53) also wrote at length. The nub of what he says is that all relations of Churches, associations and conferences 'is perhaps best described by the word cooperation.' His report has no hint of authority exer-cised by associations over Churches. He points out that Connecticut Congregational Churches are 'freer than in the seventeenth and eighteenth centuries.'"

"What about Tom Goodwin," Bill Pratt asked. "In his letter (Goodwin to Gray, 1/15/53) Tom wrote that the association has 'no authority over any church, except that for due cause, the association may withdraw fellowship from the offending church exactly as a local church may withdraw fellowship from an indi-vidual member, for adequate cause. But how often is it done? The whole genius of our fellowship is inclusive rather than exclusive. We make every effort to win over the member who offends against the fellowship, so that if the final result is separation, it has really been by the choice of the offender.'"

"That's the way I size things up," commented Bill.

"Suppose I give each of you a dozen of these replies in alpha-betical order. Why not read them through, compare what's in the CPP report, and then show me whatever needs to be changed."

Williams said, "Give me a dozen beginning at the *end* of the alphabet."

I took a break while the reading proceeded.

After the reading Arthur Gray began, "What's in the report often repeats word for word whole sentences of my letters. I'm satisfied that the CPP reflects the sample I read."

Williams added, "So am I."

Pratt's comment was, "I've been over most of this in the committee, and it reads better now than ever."

Hurst agreed. "There is no question in my mind about the statements. I DO question the last two paragraphs of the introduction, which seem to me to leave the impression that all 140 who participated have approved the whole document. I don't even know whether or not they have read the whole report. Have they?"

I replied, "There's no way I can guarantee that each person read the entire report. It was sent to them, both a first draft which they revised, and then the edition you are reading, except for minor improvements made in the past few weeks. 109 of the 140 wrote saying they had read it. Every name used is used by written permission of the person."

"I still don't like it," said Hurst.

"It's almost time to return to the General Committee. Why don't I try to compose a substitute reading, then we could submit the wording to the General Committee."

"That would suit me," responded Hurst.

I looked at Arthur. "Who's going to report from our review to the General Committee?"

"Why look at me?"

"You're chairman of the Executive Committee which appointed us."

"So I am. I'll do it."

Discussion and Decision

At 5:30 the General Committee assembled. Chairman Fifield called for the report of the Congregational Polity Committee. I outlined how we had proceeded, then stated that Arthur Gray was reporting for the committee review. Arthur was brief. He said the review was thorough, that each had examined the primary source letters and reports, and that he didn't like what they had found. "The CPP report, with some minor exceptions in wording, now corrected, is accurate. The last paragraph of the introduction is probably okay as to its facts but we think it leaves a wrong impression so a new paragraph will be ready after dinner."

The chairman smiled. "Then you are ready to approve the CPP statement for inclusion in the P.U. report, with the exception of the introduction."

"Not so fast, Wendell. I didn't say that. I do not like the emphasis on freedom, or the boundaries placed around associations, conferences, the General Council and the national societies. There must be some way to make the statements say what they ought to say."

Malcolm Burton cut in, "That's *your* problem, Arthur. All *we* have to do is make sure WE say what the sources say." Whitehouse added, "Why do we come back to WHAT IS versus WHAT OUGHT TO BE? We decided several times that WE HAD TO BE a true reflection of Congregational Polity as it is practiced."

Merrill said, "The problem is that there are words like 'may' which leave the impression that the association, conference or national body *may not* act for itself. Everybody knows that parliamentary procedure gives every body the right to run its own affairs." Bainton, Cannon and Halfaker explicated along the same line. Then we recessed for dinner at 6:20.

The committee re-assembled at 7:55 to continue consideration of the report on *Congregationalism in Practice* and *Congregationalism in the Documents*. It was a long and strenuous evening till recess at 10:30.

The chairman began by reminding us that we were to report what we found, not what we hoped to find. Then he asked me, "How do you want to proceed?"

"There are three points at which we need to make decisions. First is the text of the CPD and CPP, second is the introduction to the CPP, third is the inclusion of the national church-bodies. I'd propose dealing with all questions about the text first."

The afternoon process was repeated for nearly three fourths of an hour, and less than a dozen small changes were made, most of them enhancing the position of the Churches. Each is marked on the working copies in front of me. Malcolm Burton wanted to eliminate the words "standing" and "recognition." In the primary sources the word "membership" appears often, and "recognition" is frequently omitted. Thus # 1 did not need the phrase crossed out, "a Church may become a Congregational Church . . ." All agreed that # 2 was improved when it read a Church could "apply for and receive *membership* in an association."

No substantial changes are noted in the working copy. By 9 p.m. I suggested a new wording for the introduction, which was agreed

196

upon and approval voted for inclusion of the Congregational Polity Documents and Practice. The minutes mistakenly read "Documents" only. The subsequent record refers back to *both* Documents and Practice.

The exception was the wording concerning national church-bodies.

Discussion of both documents and practice of national church-bodies was prolonged, chiefly directed toward *how* officials of Home Board and American Board could be persuaded to provide substitute statements where they thought the CPP inaccurate. It was voted to postpone final vote on these church-bodies. At the same time it was agreed to retain the Documents statements. Thus many Practice paragraphs simply referred to the corresponding paragraph in the Documents.

With the working paper on practice approved as corrected, 2/3/54 at Greenwich, in front of me, I wonder 28 years later what was objectionable! Here is the statement excised from the introduction.[72]

> "In view of the nature of this report, and of the importance attached to it, we have thought it well to include here the names of our correspondents, though it needs to be remembered that the report as a whole is not necessarily identical with the description of Congregational polity given by any individual correspondent. They are simply 'The living bibliography' of this practice report. And it ought also to be noted that a few correspondents, and some members of one panel, expressed the opinion that at certain points Congregational practice *ought to be different from what it is.*"

The deleted paragraph is a statement of fact, in exact wording already approved in writing by the correspondents.

Fear of the weight of the names which was voiced in the discussion led to the removal of the last sentence of the introduction. In the draft it read, "Whatever merit the study may have is due in large measure to them." I intended it to be a well-earned acknowledgment of our committee's debt. Arthur Gray and Mrs. Robert Williams led the chorus; so I took out the acknowledgment and substituted "the committee itself is responsible for compiling these statements"—later we removed "compiling."[73]

There was unanimous approval of the statements of Faith, Freedom, and Fellowship, with warm commendation of the phrase *responsible freedom.*

Thursday morning (2/4/54) my "Summary of Polity Principles" was approved, with one dissenting vote. My "Definitions" section was unanimously approved. "The Powers of the General Council" was approved except for further editing. "The Spiritual and Theological Basis of Unity in Congregationalism" was referred to the Central Committee for further editing with Fred Whittaker asked to prepare wording in the light of the discussion.

Friday morning two papers on ecumenical history were placed in the appendix, as was the section on the organization of the P.U. Committee.

With adjournment at 11:30 a.m. I thought my work on the Polity and Unity Committee was completed. I was wrong.

Wendell called me aside and said, "Henry, I want you to edit the whole report. I'm not well enough to do that and struggle with the national officers too."

"But won't that raise objections? Why not circulate the completed manuscript to several?"

"That could be done. Whittaker is prompt. So is Burton. But I'd want you to do the writing."

"I really thought today would end my commitment, Wendell."

He grew grim. "We have come a long way, Henry. I'll need you right to the end. You *will* do it, won't you?"

"I'll do the best I can."

Working Under Pressure

The editorial task felt added pressure because of meetings between the E. & R. Executive Council/C.C. Executive Committee and communications related thereto provided confused signals.

Dr. Wendell Fifield reported the February 9, 1954, E. & R. Administrative Committee and the C.C. Advisory Committee[74] to the Polity and Unity Committee members on February 15:

"Two specific actions were taken that will be of interest to our Committee:

"1. The joint meeting of our Executive Committee and their General Council has been postponed until April 26th. This was done so that this joint meeting will be held after our Committee report has been completed.

2. At this meeting I am to present the 'Covenant Plan of Union' as a definite part of the agenda.

"This arrangement was by concurrent unanimous action of both groups.

"The following is my own personal evaluation of the meeting: This meeting could take no official actions, though the meeting on the 26th can. Early in the meeting, Dr. Wagner, President of the Evangelical and Reformed Church made a statement on behalf of the Evangelical and Reformed Church which seemed definitely to close the door to any further negotiations looking toward union. As the top officials of the Evangelical and Reformed Church were present and no dissent to his statement was made, it was assumed that he spoke for them all. Among other things he said, 'It would be a great relief to the Evangelical and Reformed Church to be out from under the merger matter.' No representative of the Evangelical and Reformed Church spoke a word of encouragement for the consummation of the proposed merger.

"It seemed obvious that what has happened is this. During the past four years the leadership of the Evangelical and Reformed Church has changed. The present leadership is interested only in the presbyterial type of polity. They told us they had tightened this type within themselves in the past four years. They now regret they ever consented to the Interpretations to the Basis of Union. They are not in accord with certain statements of the Basis of Union introduced by the General Council in the present litigation. Dr. Wagner called this a third document or an interpretation of the Interpretations. Furthermore, they have a plan for considerable development within their own church in which their present leadership seems greatly interested and to which they wish to give their complete attention.

"It is obvious that in the face of this attitude toward the proposed merger on the basis of the Basis of Union, further action is not only unwise but almost impossible.

"After the position of the Evangelical and Reformed Church relative to the proposed union had been made clear, I then outlined the idea of covenant union, wholly on my own responsibility. Several of the E. & R's expressed an interest in it. They felt that it contained sufficient possibilities to have it presented to their General Council. Hence the meeting on April 26th.

"I personally very much doubt if there is enough present interest and enthusiasm on the part of the E. & R's for any form of union with us. I am convinced equally that it is now the 'Covenant Plan' or nothing.

"If negotiations are terminated entirely there will be a vast vacuum of frustration and disappointment in the hearts of large numbers of those attending the Yale meeting of the General Council. It is my deep conviction that our report will help to fill this vacuum and so chart the way in the light of our recent experiences for our future procedure as a free fellowship in relation to the ecumenical movement.

"It should be *definitely* stated that no official action has yet been taken nor can any action be assumed as official until it has been taken, but all signs point to the probability that when the report of the Committee on Free Church Polity and Unity is given, there will be no merger negotiations with the Evangelical and Reformed Church before us unless there be an exploration of the covenant idea.

"It would seem to me that this probable situation creates a greater significance and importance for our report and places upon us a very deep responsibility to do everything possible to make it worthy of this opportunity.

"The above statement is in accordance with the appraisal of the situation sent by Douglas Horton to the Executive Committee of the General Council of the Congregational Christian Churches.

"L. WENDELL FIFIELD"

This was followed by a second report dated February 23, 1954:[75]

"TO THE MEMBERS OF THE COMMITTEE ON FREE CHURCH POLITY AND UNITY:

"Dear Fellow Member,

"There has now been time to consider the bearing of the joint conference of February 9th, which I reported to you in an earlier letter, on the work of our Committee. If the indications of that meeting are carried out and the merger negotiations broken off, then our report will be considered by our fellowship against one of three possible backgrounds:

"1. Further negotiations with the Evangelical and Reformed Church relative to the covenant idea.

"2. No merger negotiations with any fellowship or denomination.

"3. Possible exploratory conversations with some fellowship of congregational polity. In this connection it should be remembered that a committee of the Disciples of Christ, a fellowship with congregational polity, took action expressing a purpose to approach our fellowship when our negotiations with the Evangelical and Reformed Church were terminated. No one can prophesy at this time, but such an approach might be made to us.

"These three alternatives indicate that an organic union with a Church of connectional or presbyterial polity will not be imminent when our report is presented. This may well have some influence upon our report.

"We have stated in parts of our report already approved that the problem of union between free churches of like polity does not

200

possess most of the problems of union which exist when polities are dissimilar. Procedures must, of course, be proper but since such unions in no way effect the polity and so the autonomy of the local church, serious problems are avoided.

"You will recall that at Greenwich the main difficulty in formulating the section on organic union was not to find a way for churches with free church polity to unite but how to bridge the separation between the free churches and the connectional churches. Many of the Committee have reached the conclusion that the only way to do this is on the spititual level which led to the development of the covenant idea.

"In view of the probable situation for some time to come—that such organic unions as we shall attempt will be within the area of congregational polity—I am wondering whether the thing for us to do is to say very frankly that we have not discovered the way in which we can 'bridge the gap' on the basis of organic union. Then deal in the organic union section with the development of organic union within the free fellowships as the next step in the organic union approach to ecumenicity. Then present the covenant idea as a method that would immediately operate either between free fellowships or free fellowships and connectional groups. Thus we would cover both areas in constructive fashion.

"This would mean that we would suggest for the present that free fellowships unite organically and that connectional denominations unite organically. There are no serious poilty problems here. Then we suggest that simultaneously covenant unions be developed between free fellowships and connectional denominations thus starting the process of bridging the gap.

"To take this position would not involve saying that a way to move across organically might not sometime develop. But it would suggest that for the reasonable future this two-fold approach represented the sound and sensible approach of the churches with free polity to the ecumenical movement.

"None of our report which is in final form now precludes this approach. If it seemed to be a wise one then those who are again rewriting the section on organic union could write it from this point of view. It would produce a far stronger and less controversial statement.

"The only other major changes would involve certain restatements in the section on the powers of the General Council. This would mean placing a different emphasis on the present material. It would not be difficult to do and would produce a more constructive and less controversial section. I will be glad to do this if it seems wise.

"Will you consider this suggestion carefully? Re-read our tentative report with this idea in mind. Then will you write me your reactions to the idea, or if it is not clear, write and ask further questions. I personally want to give it more thought and study while you are doing the same.

"If I find that your reactions do *not* indicate a generally favorable attitude toward the idea, then we will drop it. If they do, then I will ask the various members of the committee who are working on the sections on organic union, the covenant union, and the spiritual and theological basis, to have this idea in mind. Meantime I will rewrite the section on the General Council, seeking to beam it toward this idea of a two-fold conclusion.

"I know how busy you all are. At the same time we may have something here which will help us to improve the wisdom and acceptability of our report. Will you, therefore, write your frank reactions as soon as possible, so that those of us who have work to do on the report will know the thinking of the Committee in view of this apparently new background situation?

"Best wishes always, L. Wendell Fifield

"P.S. Please send answers directly to me at 75 Hicks Street, Brooklyn 1, New York."

Dated February 22, 1954,[76] came a handwritten letter from Wendell showing the inter-relationship of the P.U. report, the hesitancy of the home and foreign board executives and the C.C./E.R. merger negotiations.

"Dear Henry:

"You will recall that one of the arrangements I made with the Board to get rid of that letter (refers to Atty. Wellman's letter re. American Board) was that I would ask for a meeting of the Panel of Executives to talk over our report. I wrote Dr. Horton about it, and arrangements are now in process for such a meeting. It will be held the middle of March or thereafter. I want to be very sure that I have full information about your sections of the report for that meeting. This applies especially, of course, to just what is to be included in the section on 'Congregationalism in the Documents' about the Boards. Will you keep me advised as to your progress with the officials of the Boards in accordance with the resolution we passed at Greenwich. I just want to be very sure that I am completely informed when I meet with them. I just wish you lived close by so that you could share the meeting with me.

"I've just spent the afternoon of this holiday with Douglas Horton at '287'. He received a telegram from Wagner containing a resolution adopted by their General Council last week. It seems quite ambiguous at points and difficult to understand as to meaning or motive. But it is clear from it that the attitude of the Administrative Committee with whom we met at Cleveland was not sustained so far as its finality was concerned. When we left Cleveland we all were convinced that it was all over. Now,however, while none of the objections are withdrawn there is the apparent attitude, 'lets talk it over further.'' Possibly the E. & R's felt that the onus of healing up the merger was upon them. But apparently they are not willing to take the responsibility of having the negotiations terminated on April 26 on their initiative.

"Naturally I am amazed and disappointed. Not by any fundamental change in their position they say nothing, for example, about writing a constitution which is all we can discuss with them. They also say that they do not like the idea of a 'watered down' union or covenant. But that if necessary they will refer it to their synods.

"My disappointment is that apparently now this matter is going to drag along into the Yale Council and beyond. I'm certainly glad I made it clear in my recent statement that anything might happen on April 26th for I guess it will. This turn of events will probably mean that the 'pros' will take heart and go at it again.

"In the present I'm not going to send word of this to our committee. Things change too rapidly—and who knows what will come next. So this is just between the two of us. But it sure gives me 'chairman's headache'. What if now the brethren get together and work out a formula for the General Council and at the same time our report says you can't do it. That would be something. Just now I envy anyone who is 3,000 miles from '287'. I still see *no* possibility of both groups getting together. But it may take them longer to separate.

"Sorry to unload all this onto you. But I'm just back from '287' and I must say something to someone—and who is more wise and understanding than you.

"Best always, Wendell"

Elusive Descriptions

December 19, 1953,[77] I wrote to the following officials of the national bodies requesting THEIR OWN wording for any or all of the paragraphs referring to the national bodies in the Congregational Polity reports, both Documents and Practice: American Board—Mr. Harold Belcher, Treasurer; Home Board—Rev. William F. Frazier, Treasurer; Council for Social Action—Rev. Ray Gibbons, Director; Missions Council—Rev. Henry S. Leiper,

Minister and Executive Secretary; The Annuity Fund for Congregational Ministers—Rev. Frank J. Scribner, General Secretary.

One major complaint was that our committee used *both* the General Council constitution and by-laws *and* the charters, by-laws or other basic documents of the national bodies.

"Dear Henry:[78]

"I am sorry that I had to send the telegram that I did, for I know that you are in a jam with the pressure put on you by the Central Committee. The difficulty which we have found in the statement is so basic that it seemed impossible to work out on such short notice the changes which we felt should be made.

"The basic difficulty is this. The statement of relationship between the Board and the General Council seems to be based wholly on the by-laws of the General Council. The by-laws which control an organization are its own by-laws, not the by-laws of another organizaton with which it has a relationship. If this statement is supposed to be a documentary statement, it should be legally correct. In the court case there were too many questions arising because of the quoting of statements that were not legally correct. If the work of your Committee is going to be an important stage in the development of the denomination, any documentary statement put out by the Committee should be such that it could not be legally challenged at any time. That is why we feel that any change in the proposed statement should be very correctly drawn up.

"I am sorry that we have upset your work and that of the Committee, but it seems that the matter of accuracy is so important that it would be much better to be sure of that, even though the matter was delayed.

"Yours sincerely,
"Harold B. Belcher, Treasurer."

A second major complaint resulted from a phrase in one of my letters stating that the documents were secured from the Steinbrink court record. In 1951-1952 I repeatedly asked for copies of charters, by-laws, etc., in the New York offices. Again and again I was told, "We can't give you that without the approval of the Board, the executive vice-president, etc." Finally I remembered that copies of all the charters, by-laws and other basic documents were in the Steinbrink court record, so, I secured a copy of that record and detatched the official documents, which are in front of me as I write. The Congregational Polity Committee did not quote or paraphrase a single phrase of the voluminous testimony. The Committee confined itself to the Documents for the CPD report.

For the Practice report (CPP) the Committee confined itself to the actual data given by 140 correspondents, 6 panels, the state superintendents and the national officers. The aim was to describe the national bodies AS EACH OF THEM WAS PERCEIVED IN *PRACTICE*. And this is exactly that to which objections were raised by a few officials.

The reason for the uneasiness of the national officers was chiefly the badgering to which they had been subjected in the New York Superior Court. Furthermore, they felt they were pilloried by the Rev. Maclcolm Burton in his book, *Destiny for Congregationalism* and by additional printed and mimeographed circulars written by opponents of the C.C./E.R. merger.

It is beside the point to consider whether or not the critics were fair and well-mannered. Each of the mediators deeply regretted *all* elements of villification, on *all* sides. But we had to accept the plain fact that the chief proponents and opponents were very, very sensitive. Over a quarter of a century later most are still sensitive. Therefore the factual record which follows will be in the words of the executives, except for connecting links to make clear that which is under discussion.

Working Descriptions of the National Societies[79]

The Congregational Polity compiled from the basic documents and from 140 correspondents the following description of the national societies and the relationship to them of the Churches:

"(The relation of the General Council to the national societies is stated in the by-laws of the Council as follows:

"The foreign missionary work of the Congregational Christian Churches shall be carried on under the auspices of the American Board of Commissioners for Foreign Missions; and home missionary and educational work of these churches under the auspices of the Board of Home Missions.)

"57. The Churches and all the wider bodies of the Congregational Christian fellowship have their respective inner polity structures set forth in charters, constitutions, by-laws, or rules of procedure under which each particular Church or wider body is organized.

"Polity relationships between Churches and wider bodies are frequently set forth in the basic written documents of the Congregational Christian fellowship e.g. in certain local Churches, association, and state conference constitutions; and there are general statements of polity relationships in the basic documents of the General Council. All these inter-Church wider body polity statements describe the relationships of the various bodies of a voluntary fellowship; they do not compel conformity; they simply state the polity relationship which is regarded as desirable *by the body making the statement*; they gain acceptance on the basis of inherent worth.

"A local Congregational Christian body is initiated by men and women who covenant together as a Church. Wider bodies of the fellowship are initiated by (1) The united action of two or more Churches. (2) The united action of two or more Church members. (3) The united action of two or more wider bodies. Thus certain wider bodies, for example, the association, are clearly and directly the responsible agents of the Churches whereas other wider bodies, for example, the Annuity Fund for Congregational Ministers, are clearly and directly responsible to their own Boards of Control. The unity of the Congregational Christian fellowship is achieved chiefly by good-will, and by working agreements which are mutually accepted by the agreeing bodies, for example, the American Board, voluntarily agrees under its own charter, to meet at the same time as the General Council, and to elect the members of the General Council as corporate members of the American Board. By this voluntary agreement the foreign missionary work of the fellowship becomes a concern of the General Council and of the Churches, associations, and conferences from which have come the delegates to the General Council. What we have in some of our wider bodies is an extension of the principle of the 'gathered' Church; i.e. those Congregational Christians who were concerned about foreign missions simply 'gathered' themselves together as the American Board and proceeded to solicit the support of others both as individuals and as Churches. The 1913 re-organization plan, adopted unanimously by the General Council, created a framework of voluntary relationships between the General Council and other wider bodies such as the American Board, in order to establish a closer tie between the Churches and the many wider bodies through which are channeled the concerns of the Churches and their members.

THE AMERICAN BOARD

"58. The American Board is regarded by our fellowship as the agency of the Congregational Christian Churches for the extension of Christ's Kingdom abroad.

"59. The American Board's important decisions regarding the missionary outreach are made by the prudential committee, on recommendation of various committees or officers of the board. Decisions regarding apportionment are made by the executive committee of the General Council on recommendations of a survey committee appointed by them. The American Board is regarded as the foreign missions arm of the Churches, whose chief decisions are made at meetings held in connection with the biennial General Council meeting. In practice the work of the Board has to be directed by the prudential committee of 39 members; and is governed by its Charter and by-laws, by its trust agreements with donors, by its inter-board agreements made through the missions council and by the sensitivity of its officers to the views of the state superintendents and others present at the mid-winter meetings.

"60. The American Board is, in practice, the chief administrative agency through which our Churches contribute to foreign missions. The board is related to the Churches (a) by those delegates who attend annual meetings of the board, (b) by those members who sit on the prudential committee, (c) by giving or whitholding of financial support by a Church or Churches, or (d) by the direct consultation of churches or church members with responsible representatives of the board.

THE BOARD OF HOME MISSIONS

"61. The Board of Home Missions is regarded by our fellowship as the 'agency of the Congregational and Christian Churches for the extension of Christ's Kingdom in the United States except as such activities are administered locally.' 'It carries on the work and inherits the property and other rights of the following agencies: The American Missionary Association, the Congregational Church Building Society, the Congregational Home Missionary Society, the Congregational Sunday School Extension Society, the Congregational Education Society, the Congregational Publishing Society, and the Congregational Board of Ministerial Relief. It is authorized by charter to 'cooperate with any other societies or agencies under the charge and control of churches of the Congregational and Christian order in the United States.'

"62. The Board of Home Missions elects its chief executive officers at those annual meetings which are held in connection with meetings of the General Council. Its work is planned and conducted by departments and divisions responsible to a 40 member board of directors which meets regularly, and which manages and conducts the affairs of the board, determines the policies, authorizes expenditures, and provides for employment of personnel. The directors are elected by the board at the time of the biennial meeting of the General Council. The Churches nominate delegates who are elected to the General Council by associations or conferences. These delegates are elected corporate members of the Board, which elects directors who determine the policies and program for a manifold work which effects every local Congregational Christian Church.

"63. The Board of Home Missions is, in practice, the most powerful single organization in the Congregational Christian fellowship, because of its huge funds, large personnel, and wide charter of activity.

THE COUNCIL FOR SOCIAL ACTION

"64. The Council for Social Action is the agency of the Congregational Christian Churches for helping to make the Christian gospel more effective in society, national and world-wide,through research, education, and action, in cooperation with the Churches and their missionary agencies.

"65. The Council for Social Action is a body created by and responsible to the General Council. It is required to make a full and accurate report of its condition and work to the General Council at each stated meeting of that body. It comprises a council of 18 persons elected for six-year terms and serving on a volunteer basis.

"66. The Council for Social Action has been studied by a 'Board of Review' appointed by the executive committee of the General Council. The report of the board of review, together with the recommendations of the executive committee, is to be presented at the 1954 meeting of the General Council. Therefore, no reference is made to it here.

THE ANNUITY FUNDS AND RETIREMENT FUND

"67. These funds are administered in accord with the provisions of their charters and by-laws. Suggestions from the Churches may be made by delegates to meetings of the General Council, or by consultation with the authorized officers of the funds.

THE MISSIONS COUNCIL

"68. The Missions Council is a joint agency for missionary education, stewardship, and promotion of income for the American Board, the Board of Home Missions, the Council for Social Action, the State Conferences, Relief and Reconstruction, and the Congregational Service Committee. To it are assigned the performance of varied special services for the Churches and their cooperative agencies. It is an inter-board agency whose functions are strictly interpretative and educational and it has no responsibility for the making of missionary policy or for the administration of missionary work.

"69. The Missions Council members are responsible to the boards or agencies they represent. Its officers are responsible to the Missions Council itself. A responsible relation to the Churches is maintained indirectly through the several boards and agencies.

"70. The mid-winter meetings correlate into a single program simultaneous 'called' meetings of the following agencies and organizations of the Congregational Christian Churches: The Missions Council, the prudential committee of the American Board, directors of the Board of Home Missions, members of the Council for Social Action, Superintendents' Conference, Conference of Women State Pesidents, Presidents of Laymen's State Fellowships, secretaries of the Boards, members of the national committee of our Christian World Mission, executive committee of the General Council. In addition 'others attending associated meetings, are usually invited to sit in as corresponding members.' (1952 Blue Book) This includes members of the Christian Education Council (conference directors of education and staffs of Pilgrim Press and Christian Education Division), members of divisional or departmental committees, the Pilgrim Fellowship (youth) executive committee, and numerous other committees such as General Council nominating committee, Congregational Christian Service Committee, allocations committee, survey committee, etc. ('All of us are involved in the meeting of *each agency*, as voting or as corresponding members.' (1952 Blue Book.)

"71. The mid-winter meetings are scheduled by co-operative action through the missions council, ad interim committee, or joint cabinet.

"72. The program planned at the mid-winter meetings becomes the official program of the national and state agencies of the Congregational Christian Churches through action of the several bodies represented in or meeting in connection with the missions council.

"73. The mid-winter meetings have become a very influential gathering of the Congregational Christian fellowship, at which important decisions are made, Missions Council officers are elected, new emphases are debated, schedules of work are cleared, and fundamental policies are proposed. The Churches have no direct representation at these meetings, although those who attend are the elected or employed officials of the various conferences, boards, agencies, committees and associated bodies listed in Statement 70.

"74. The mid-winter meetings gain in their influence from the structural inter-linkage of the national boards and agencies and from the presence of conference superintendents and other officers, as noted in Statement 70. The decisions made have no power to compel local Church action, but they can do much to determine what is presented to a meeting of the General Council, what promotional literature is to be published, what speakers are to be made available for state conference and association meetings, how the apportionment dollar is to be divided, and whether or not work in one field or another is to be given special support. In short, many of the chief administrative decisions affecting the life and work of our Churches are made at the mid-winter meetings."

Concerning the above description, Rev. William F. Frazier,[80] treasurer of the Board of Home Missions wrote, January 4, 1954:

"Dear Henry:

"I find numerous points of inaccuracy in the material you sent me on the Board of Home Missions. I note there are many quotations, but since the source of the quotes are not given I cannot check them to know whether there are simply errors in quotation, or the sources are in error.

"Nothing plagued me so much when I was on the witness stand at the first trial as to be confronted with one printed statement after another bearing the name of the General Council or some committee or commission of the Council, and I would have to say that it was untrue. Truth and accuracy are far more important in what you are getting out than meeting any deadline whatsoever. It would be far better to say nothing than at this stage to have any inaccuracies.

"I cannot correct this material in a moment. Truman Douglass is not here, being in the field somewhere, St. Louis, I think. I will organize my comments as rapidly as possible, but I feel sure they will not reach you before the 8th.

"Your material was only delivered here a couple of hours ago.
"Truly your friend
"WM. F. FRAZIER, Treasurer"

"January 11, 1954
"Dear Mr. Gray:[81]

"I think Truman Douglass, as Executive Vice President of the Board of Home Missions, ought to be responsible for any general reply commenting on the material you sent us. It will be the latter part of this week before he is back here. I do not want to be uncooperative but this is the first time I ever saw any of this printed material. If it was presented at Claremont, I certainly did not see it and no part of it, nor any question connected with it, was ever referred to me.

"If I were attempting comments, I would have to begin with the first paragraph and go through all of it. I think there are three statements in the first pargraph (45) which are essentially, and in one case, absolutely in error: (a) The Board of Home Missions has a multiple charter granted by the states of New York, Connectictut,

210

and Massachusetts. For the purposes of its business, I suppose the New York charter is the most important of the three. (b) The organization of the Board of Home Missions was pursuant to Acts not by the General Council but by seven boards. The General Council did no more than advise. The incorporators were the directors and executive vice president of the seven boards. It is not important to say who incorporated the Board of Home Missions; but it is important that no one should say that the General Council incorporated the Board of Home Missions. There should perhaps be four national corporations instead of two which were founded persuant to votes of the General Council (or National Council). This amendment to the above shows again how easy it is to be in error and how carefully all statements ought to be examined. There are two national corporations which the General Council did create but the Board of Home Missions was not one of them. (c) The absolutely erroneous statement in this paragraph is 'for objects "exclusively charitable, educational and literary."' I am completely at a loss to know where that quotation could have come from. It certainly omits the chief purpose of the board which is religious and secondarily missionary. This is perhaps sufficient to show the sort of questions I would raise regarding all that is said here.

"Denominational policy does not come within the scope of my work since I became Treasurer and Dr. Douglass Executive Vice President. I do find myself questioning the proprietary of the language used and many statements which, I believe, to be entirely contrary to fact, and some of the omissions which seem to me to be much more important than some of the things included. The relationship, for example, described between the Board of Home Missions and the old corporations is of fundamental importance and, it is not at all what is stated here. They have lost none of their rights or property. Relationship is a matter of the utmost importance. Now this whole discussion is one for Dr. Douglass and not for me, so I am going to put it all before him as soon as he gets back.

"I may say that having dug around the General Council I have found the brochure from which much of your material was clipped. I find the whole document full of similar inaccuracies.

"I could have been of more help, perhaps, if I had seen this material or known what was going on many months ago.

"With best regards,

"Sincerely yours,
"WM. F. FRAZIER, Treasurer"

The Rev. Ray Gibbons, Director of the Council for Social Action, wrote, January 4, 1954:[82]

"Dear Henry:

"New Year's Greetings!

"I gather you are in a hurry to have answer about the CSA Polity. Here it is.

"First, the printed material is substantially correct but needs revision in Article 55. The General Council at Claremont voted to change the by-law affecting CSA Associates. (See Vote 52 G-39). Second, the mimeographed articles are satisfactory. I am rather surprised you used the word 'official.' Why not have the first sentence read, 'The Council for Social Action has been studied by a Board of Review appointed by the Executive Committee of the General Council.'

"Cordial regards, Ray Gibbons"

The Rev. Henry Smith Leiper, minister and executive secretary of the Missions Council, wrote, January 4, 1954:[83]

"Dear Henry:

"Your letter of the 29th is on my desk this morning and must have an immediate answer. My secretary is ill and so I am typing this myself. Errors there will be and I trust you will pardon them!

"It seems to me that the language of the two clippings you send is very clear in most points but not in the respect to what the Missions Council is and how it is responsible to the Churches.

"I would quote the actual wording of the Rules of the Missions Council as pubilshed in the Blue Book. It was created by action of the delegates of the General Council at South Hadley in 1936. Its sole purpose is 'to keep before its constituency the Home and Foreign missionary and educational work of the Congregational Christian Churches, with a view to increasing interest, enlarging annual contributions and securing legacies, conditional gifts, endowments, and special gifts for the entire work: state, national and foreign.'

"It is clear that the Council promotes the apportionment and the states secure their main support from it. Thus it serves the states directly and indirectly in other ways.

"But it is only indirectly a creation of the state conferences. It is the joint agency of the American Board, the Board of Home Missions, and the Council for Social Action. Corresponding members without vote are designated by the Superintendents' Conference, the Conference of Women's State Presidents, the Directors of the Laymen's Committee, the Secretaries of the (member) boards, the members of the National Committee of our Christian World Mission, and the Executive Committee of the General Council.

212

"Therefore, paragraph 66 might better read:

"'The Missions Council is a joint agency for missionary education, stewardship and promotion of income for the American Board, the Board of Home Missions, the Council for Social Action, the State Conferences, Relief and Reconstruction, and the Congregational Service Committee. To it are assigned the performance of varied special services for the Churches and their cooperative agencies.'

"67 as it stands is very misleading. I would suggest that it would be more accurate to say: 'The Missions Council membership although chosen in differing ways is responsible to the Boards it represents. Its officers are responsible to the Missions Council itself.'

"Somewhere it ought to be spelled out that the Missions Council has no responsibility for the making of missionary policy or the administration of missionary work. Its functions are strictly interpretive and educational. It is so organized that no one board can dictate the policy to be followed in the performance of its functions.

"This you may feel is indicated in the substance of paragraphs 60 and 61. But it ought to be made more explicit.

"I trust this gives you what you need.

"Happy New Year!
Yours fraternally, Henry Smith Leiper"

The Rev. Frank J. Scribner of the Annuity Fund for Congregational Ministers wrote, January 5, 1954:[84]

"Dear Henry David:

"Your letter of December 29th reached me yesterday. I spent a good part of the day upon it, but am stumped as to how to reply.

"I cannot give my approval to the material regarding 'the annuity funds' which you enclose. If I make corrections here and there of detail, it would imply that I approved the rest of it. I could not possibly prepare an accurate statement of the organization and operation of the Annuity Fund and Retirement Fund in time to reach you by January 8th.

"I am terribly sorry to be uncooperative in this matter. I know the pressure under which you are working. But it is extremely important that any statement bearing the approval of the officers of both Funds should be accurate in all details. I will do my best to make an adequate reply as soon as I can do so, but I simply cannot prepare one within the time limit that you have set.

"Very regretfully yours,
"Frank"

213

and added on January 18, 1954:[85]

"Dear Henry:

"I have given careful attention to the material you sent me and am enclosing what seems to me a more correct statement. You will notice the following changes.

"Printed Material.

"Title. There is no such thing as 'the annuity funds,' either as corporate bodies or as a term in general use.

"You will note that in each case I have put the word 'corporation' in lower case. When the word is capitalized it is most naturally taken to refer to The Corporation for the General Council.

"b. The By-Law which you quote defines eligibility for membership, not membership itself, hence the slight change.

"d. You have quoted directly from the By-Law which puts the making of reports in the future tense. Elsewhere in the material you have removed the word 'shall' and substituted the present. I have done the same here.

"e. 'All' lay workers is hardly correct. I have quoted from the Charter of the Retirement Fund.

"Mimeographed Material.

"The Annuity Fund has no constitution. I have, therefore, removed the word. The concluding sentence of your mimeographed material is not true to fact and should be deleted.

"With apologies for the delay in preparing this material, I am

"Cordially yours,
"Frank"

On January 18, 1954, I wrote[86] to the Rev. Truman B. Douglass, Executive Vice Pesident of the Board for Home Missions:

"Dear Truman:

"I have been in correspondence with Will Frazier concerning the material printed in the Polity Committee Report to the Claremont Council and covering the mimeographed 'tentative' material to be issued by the committee for the New Haven Council.

"He informs me that this correspondence should be directed to you. It was sent to Will in order to save you the trouble of digging into the details, since we were not concerned with developing new policy. In the printed document our effort was to set the polity relations of the Board of Home Missions according to charter and General Council constitution. Actually, this is merely the academic

214

task of putting in the clearest possible language that which is put in many pages of the charters.

"The brief mimeographed statement was simply designed to say in the fewest possible words what the particular polity and relations of the Board of Home Missions is. This may or may not correspond to the documentary picture. As a matter of fact, I have not carefully examined the two in relation to each other.

"It was my instruction from the committee, and has been my steadfast endeavour, to produce the studies on as objective a basis as was humanly possible.

"*The printed study*, presented at Claremont, was based on the General Council constitution and the charters of the Boards and Agencies, and the constitutions of all State Conferences which possess constitutions, and the constitutions of one-third of the associations in the country. This was a long, involved and extremely difficult job fully shared in by our committee. It has been in print for almost two years. I made the mistake of assuming that those of you in positions of national leadership might have seen it. The mimeographed document is based on our correspondence with and questionnaires to 146 individuals, of whom 140 replied. These including all State Superintendents, all Panel Chairmen, and all persons suggested by either of the above. A copy of the tentative mimeographed report was sent to each of the individuals who replied to our earlier communications. In addition it was sent to representative persons in the various Boards and Agencies.

"All this has involved an enormous amount of work, especially for a local pastor already overloaded. It has been done because I believed it was worth doing for the denomination.

"I am a bit dismayed that the only two persons who have failed to help me make the material accurate represent two national agencies. This may be because I somehow did not rightly approach them. If so, I am sorry. I hope that this lengthy explanation will draw from you the earliest possible reply. If you wish to rewrite *the printed section* to correspond to the charters in all three states in which you are chartered I shall be most happy to insert such a substitute documentary statement. Every one of us on the committee wants to make this thing accurate. If you wish to send me detailed suggestions for the revision of *the mimeographed material* I shall submit them to the committee on February 1st. I cannot promise that these will be accepted *in toto* since the mimeographed document deals with practice as people all over the country see it and not simply as you or I or our Boards or committees see it. I have no notion as to whether or not what is printed is or is not what any individual Church, Agency or Board may think 'ought to be practiced' the latter is entirely out of my province.

"This entire study, so far as our committee is concerned, is decidedly apart from our individual opinions. It is an honest and straight-forward attempt to study the denomination as it purports to be in its fundamental documents and as it is felt to be by representative folk throughout the entire nation.

"I am sure that you, being a scholar, have some idea of the enormous task we have been trying to bring to a conclusion. Therefore, I feel certain that you will give me the material which we need to make the sections dealing with the Board of Home Missions what they ought to be.

"Very sincerely yours,
"Henry David Gray"

Dr. Douglass wrote[87] (Douglass to Gray, 1/19/54):

"Dear Henry:

"Will Frazier has shown me your letters of December 29 and January 8 together with his replies. I do not think I have anything important to add within the limits of the time I have to consider these materials. I am just back from a succession of field trips and about to leave for Cleveland.

"Will is correct in saying that the statement about the Board of Home Missions—both in the printed document and the mimeographed sheet—contain a number of inaccuracies. How many there are I shall not attempt to say until I can find more time to examine the language carefully.

"Your comment in your letter of January 8 that the material in the Introductory Statement was all taken from documents in the Court record does not seem to me to solve the problem of accuracy. A great many documents went into the record. Some of them contain statements that are ambiguous, untrue, and even ridiculous.

"In general it is a sound principle that statements descripitve of the organization and relationships of the Board of Home Missions and the Societies for which it acts as agent and attorney should be taken from the charters and by-laws of these bodies, not from the constitution of the General Council nor from unauthorized statements originating in other organizations.

"Best regards.

"Sincerely,
"Truman B. Douglass"

On January 18, 1954, I wrote[88] to Mr. Harold B. Belcher, treasurer of the American Board of Commissioners for Foreign Missions:

"Dear Harold:

"Thanks for your reply to my letter.

"In the printed document our effort was to set the polity relations of the American Board according to charter and General Council constitution. Actually, this is merely the academic task of putting in the clearest possible language that which is put in many pages of the charters.

"The brief mimeographed statement was simply designed to say in the fewest possible words what the particular polity and relations of the American Board is. This may or may not correspond to the documentary picture. As a matter of fact, I have not carefully examined the two in relation to each other.

"It was my instruction from the committee and has been my steadfast endeavour, to produce the studies on as objective a basis as was humanly possible.

"*The printed study*, pesented at Claremont, was based on the General Council constitution and the charters of the Boards and Agencies, and the constitutions of all State Conferences which possess constitutions, and the constitutions of one-third of the Associations in the country. This was a long, involved and extremely difficult job fully shared in by our committee. It has been in print for almost two years. I made the mistake of assuming that those of you in positions of national leadership might have seen it. The mimeographed document is based on our correspondence with and questionnaires to 146 individuals, of whom 140 replied. These including all State Superintendents, all Panel Chairmen, and all persons were suggested by either of the above. A copy of the tentative mimeographed report was sent to each of the individuals who replied to our earlier communications. In addition, it was sent to representative persons in the various Boards and Agencies.

"All this has involved an enormous amount of work, especially for a local pastor already overloaded. It has been done because I believed it was worth doing for the denomination.

"I hope that this lengthy explanation will draw from you the earliest possible reply. If you wish to rewrite *the printed section* to correspond to your charter, I shall be most happy to insert such a substitute documentary statement. Every one of us on the committee wants to make this thing accurate. If you wish to send me detailed suggestions for the revision of *the mimeographed material* I shall submit them to the committee on February 1st. I cannot promise that these will be accepted *in toto* since the mimeographed document deals with practice as people all over the country see it and not simply as you or I or our Boards or committees see it. I have no notion as to whether or not what is printed is or is not what any individual Church, Agency or Board may think 'ought to be practiced.' The latter is entirely out of my province.

"This entire study, so far as our committee is concerned, is decidedly apart from our individual opinions. It is an honest and straight-forward attempt to study the denomination as it purports to be in its fundamental documents and as it is felt to be by representative folk throughout the entire nation.

"I am sure that you have some idea of the enormous task we have been trying to bring to a conclusion. Therefore, I feel certain that you will give me the material which we need to make the sections dealing with the American Board what they ought to be.

"Very sincerely yours,
"Henry David Gray

"P.S. The February 1st meeting of our committee is in Greenwich. I am to bring to it mimeographed copies of all propsed revisions in the material for which my Polity Comittee is responsible. Obviously, this is a tight schedule."

On February 19, 1954,[89] I wrote again to Dr. Douglass and Mr. Belcher as follows:

"Dear Truman:

"Pursuant to our discussion when I was in New York and following the discussions of the Polity Committee at Greenwich, I am writing to ask your cooperation in the preparation of our report which is to be presented to the Executive Committee of the General Council immediately after Easter.

"As it now stands we have in the practice document the following statement regarding the National Societies 'The National Societies related to the Congregational Christian Churches are adminstered in accord with the provisions of their charters and by-laws. (See documentary section).' The following generalized statement is under the heading Some General Organizations:

"The Churches and all the wider bodies of the Congregational Christian fellowship have their respective inner polity structures set forth in charters, constitutions, by-laws, or rules of procedure under which each particular Church or wider body is organized.

"Polity relationships between Churches and wider bodies are frequently set forth in the basic written documents of the

Congregational Christian fellowship e.g. in certain local Church, association, and state conference constitutions; and there are general statements of polity relationships in the basic documents of the General Council. All these inter-Church-wider body polity statements describe the relationships of the various bodies of a voluntary fellowship; they do not compel conformity; they simply state the polity relationship which is regarded as desirable *by the body making the statement*; they gain acceptance on the basis of inherent worth.

"Thus certain wider bodies, (for example, the association), are clearly and directly the responsible agents of the Churches whereas other wider bodies (for example, the Annuity Fund for Congregational Ministers), are clearly and directly responsible to their own boards of control. The unity of the Congregational Christian fellowship is achieved chiefly by good-will, and by working agreements which are mutually accepted by the agreeing bodies, (for example, the American Board, voluntarily agrees under its own charter, to meet at the same time as the General Council, and to elect members of the General Council as corporate members of the American Board). By voluntary agreement the foreign missionary work of the fellowship becomes a concern of the General Council and of the Churches, associations, and conferences from which have come the delegates to the General Council. What we have in some of our wider bodies is an extension of the principle of the 'gathered' Church; i.e. those Congregational Christians who were concerned about foreign missions simply 'gathered' themselves together as the American Board and proceeded to solicit the support of others both as individuals and as Churches. The 1913 re-organization plan, adopted by the General Council, created a framework of voluntary relationships between the General Council and other wider bodies such as the American Board, in order to establish a closer tie between the Churches and the many wider bodies through which are channeled the concerns of the Churches and their members.

"I am enclosing a copy of the printed Introductory Statement, which will appear as our documentary statement, with the request that you prepare and send to me the material as you would like to have it stand for the Board of Home Missions section numbers 45 through 52.

"It is our intention to go over these and so far as is humanly possible to keep them in precisely the form in which you give them to us. I do not know what we shall do about the statement in the General Council constitution but we want these things all to be as accurate as human care can make them so I shall appreciate your help in this regard.

> "Sincerely yours,
> "Henry David Gray"

On the same day the Rev. L. Wendell Fifield,[90] at my request, wrote to leaders of the national bodies (Fifield to Douglass et. al. 2/19/54):

"At the recent meeting of the Committee on Free Church Polity and Unity, the material dealing with the Boards in the section on 'Congregationalism in Practice' was deleted from the report.

"Relative to the section on 'Congregationalism in the Documents' the Committee passed this motion:

> "The Committee wishes to express its thanks to its chairman for his courteous dealing with national society leaders in its behalf. In the interests of the greatest possible authenticity in its report, the Committee welcomes accurate statements from the national societies concerning their respective bodies, and will give them full consideration in consultation with the executives of the Boards.

"I have written Dr. Horton, chairman of the Panel of Executives, asking him to arrange a meeting at your convenience sometime before April 1st. At this time I will welcome the opportunity of meeting with the Panel and answering questions concerning any part of the report.

"If ideas of helpfulness or concern come to you at any time relative to the work of our Committee I hope that you will feel free to get in touch with me."

Dr. Douglass replied[91] (Douglass to Gray, n.d.):

"Dear Henry—

"I am sorry you have been ill. I also have been out of action—first with a virus, then with a case of shingles. Am getting back on the job.

"On February 19 Wendell Fifield wrote me that his committee had voted to delete the material dealing with the Boards. I thought that ended the matter.

"I am seeing Wendell tomorrow and will find out what he wants us to do.

> "Regards,
> "Truman"

Dr. Leiper[92] replied (Leiper to Fifield, 3/4/54):

"My dear Wendell:

"I agreed some time ago to send you the exact, official description of the Missions Council taken from the Rules of the Missions Council and published in the Blue Book.

"It seems to me any other description would be subject to question and debate. This is, at least, the official description of our form of organization, function and authority.

"Yours fraternally,
"Henry Smith Leiper"

"Dear Henry:

"I think this belongs to you so I am sending it on at once.

"Wendell"

Then Mr. Belcher answered[93] (Belcher to Gray, 3/26/54):

"Dear Henry:

"This letter is brief because I am very much rushed to day, but I did want to get it off to you as quickly as possible. I am enclosing a copy of the statement regarding the American Board, which Mr. Wellman has drawn up, and which I have gone over with him. We have not put it into the system of paragraphs, but if you want to do so, we will not object.

"I realize that you have had a hard job to get ready for the Committee Meeting this material, and I am sorry if delays on our part have made it any more difficult.

"Yours sincerely,

"Harold B. Belcher,
"Treasurer.

"*P.S.*—The statement at the beginning of the section on the missionary societies should be corrected to indicate that their organization and operations are defined by *their own* Charter and By-Laws, and not by the By-Laws of the General Council."

Comparison of the Statement compiled by the Congregational Polity Committee with that in my letters to Dr. Douglass and Mr. Belcher (2/19/54) makes clear the great hesitancy of the board executives to put on paper anything at all! If something must be written, let it be easy to defend in court. This, of course, is readily understandable. But it is not what our committee was commissioned to do. There seemed to be a difference concerning the "practice" of the national bodies as between the view from an east coast office, and, the perception of state superintendents, association registrars, and geographic panel correspondents. This might be strange under normal circumstances, but the mileau in the late winter of 53-54 was tangled. There was conflicting views *within* the CC/ER negotiating groups.

As Dr. Fifield worked on his section of the final report he wrote[94] (Fifield to Gray, 2/25/54) by pen:

"Dear Henry:

"I have revised this section in the light of the ideas sent out in my most recent letter to my committee. I have also incorporated the suggestions made at our Greenwich meeting. We will be studying this at the April meeting of the Central Committee which you do not plan to attend. I am therefore sending you this copy in advance. When you have time will you read it over and send me your ideas, comments, criticisms of it.

"We, our committee, is to have one of the seminars 3—two-hour periods. I hope that you can be present to share with me in its leadership. Especially I hope you will bring all those fine letters. I suspect that much of the discussion will hinge on the sections of the Documents and the Practice. So I'm writing this early to ask for your help.

"I wrote to Dr. Wagner asking him to explain the resolution adopted by the E. & R. General Council. The more I read and study it the more confused I get. It can either be an approval of or a repudiation of the position of their administrative committee. I hope a letter from Jim Wagner will make its meaning clear. I think we need a committee on semantics.

"Copy of your letter to Belcher and Douglas crossed my recent one to you. It is an excellent letter and should do the job. When you hear from them will you drop me a line so I'll be fully satisfied when I go into conference with the Panel of Executives.

"Best always,
"Wendell"

Rev. Charles C. Merrill[95] states clearly some of the objections of those who wished the report to say that they thought to be "Congregationalism." (Merrill to Gray, 2/25/54):

"Dear Henry:

"I got back from Florida Thursday night but didn't get quite the rest which I hoped for, hence my delay in writing you until today. I am somewhat at a loss to know how to write you about the printed document which begins with the 'introductory statement.' I am particularly concerned with the section on the local church in which I believe that you emphasize independence at the expense of the fellowship. When one reads paragraphs 2, 3, and 4 he gets the impression that Congregational churches are apt to do pretty much as they please and in subsequent paragraphs the same impression seems to be continued. For example, in paragraph 7 you use the word *may* with regard to a request for a council. The fact is that it usually does make such a request.

"In paragraph 8 you say a local Congregational church *may* license and ordain. In 57 years of experience in the Congregational ministry I can't recall a single instance where this has been done. Why call so marked attention to so rare a thing?

"At the very end of this section on the local church you speak of churches 'which do not participate actively in (its) organizational life.' Is that any peculiarity in the Congregational denomination? I don't see why it needs to be emphasized.

"Going on to the next section on 'the association.' In paragraph 16 you practically repeat what has been said in paragraph 1 of the 'local church.' In paragraph 18 you refer to the association calling an ecclesiastical council. You already have referred to that in paragraph 13. This is also referred to in paragraph 17. Is such repetition necessary?

"Looking through the State Conference I find again the use of the word *may* in the first paragraph. Why not make it positive? As a matter of fact, the churches *do* act together. In paragraph 28 you speak of the State Conference being financed by 'endowments or gifts.' Why put 'endowments' first? Couldn't it be put more briefly by saying:

"'The State Conference is financed chiefly by the giving of the local churches supplemented by income from endowments which differ widely in the different states.'

"To tell the truth, Henry, I have sometimes wondered why Wendell kept me off your Polity Committee. Doubtless he had a perfectly good reason for doing so. However, I think I might have been of some assistance to you. I think that perhaps I have a right to be in a somewhat independent position in criticizing the work of your Committee because although I have not seen the particular documents that you have seen, I have seen other similar documents and have given a good deal of study and thought to the whole situation for at least 40 years.

"Please understand that I am not saying this in any spirit of sour grapes. I hope I have gotten beyond that stage. The upshot is that probably your report had better go in as it is and I had better make some kind of demur, perhaps in a minority report which will, of course, not be confined to this particular section. My conception of Congregationalism is given on page 4 of my Southworth Lecture. I will venture to quote:

> "'The two fundamental principles of Congregational Polity, the two foci of the Congregational ellipse, as it is sometimes put, are freedom and fellowship, and it is the interplay of these two principles which particularly distinguishes Congregationalism. If you undertake to describe our polity, at least as it has developed on this continent, don't say that it is merely an 'Adventure in Liberty,' as is sometimes affirmed, but that it is an adventure in liberty and union, in freedom and fellowship.'

"I cannot let my name go in an endorsement of any document which doesn't put freedom and fellowship side by side emphasizing neither at the expense of the other.

"Faithfully yours,
"C.C.M."

In due time Dr. Fifield met with the executives and wrote by pen[96] (Fifield to Gray, 3/27/54):

"Dear Henry:

"I met with the Executives on Thursday. It was only a fairly satisfactory meeting. Apparently on the part of some there is feeling because they have not been widely consulted in the work of the committee. Some others had heard rumours of what the report was to contain and were alarmed by them. The rumors were in no instance correct. However we had a frank and, of course, friendly discussion which may be productive of some values. Time will tell. You will doubtless receive a statement from Harold Belcher very soon. So the only other one is that from the Home Boards. Truman Douglass is not apparently willing to furnish a statement. But he did say that he would take the material which is already in 'Congregationalism in the Documents' and write you about the statements that he considers uncorrect and I assume indicate what he feels to be the correct ones. Our meeting was a confidential one. But since it involves your work I think I should say in confidence, that the difficulty with the Home Boards seems to be an unwillingless to assume responsibility for any part of our report without knowing what is in all of it. This, of course, is impossible as we ourselves do not yet know its entire contents. Nor do I see how any report could ever be made if no information were supplied until the entire report was prepared. There would be no material with which to prepare a report. On the other hand it should be said that as a result of the materials used especially about the Home Boards in the Cadman Case, they are very much concerned *not* to be even remotely a party to any position about the nature of Congregationalism which they have not seen and fully approved. I see the dilemma clearly and think that the argument we now have is the best possible solution. Truman Douglass said he will write you soon about it. We thus received the material we need. But we include it in our report on our own responsibility. Thus the Home Boards are in a position to repudiate the whole business if they so desire. This whole merger business has created many problems for the Boards and their Executives have heavy burdens as a consequence. They probably more than any others have a rightful anxiety as to what effect our report may have upon their Boards. Next it was obvious from talking with them that they had the idea that we were going to deal far more extensively with the Boards than we have ever had the slightest idea of doing. I am sure that I was able to unburden their concerns on that point. If the material does not come along from the Home Boards soon I suggest you let *me* know rather than write again to Truman and I'll go over and work it out with him personally.

"Matters relative to the merger are in a state of confusion. Now that the leaders of the E & R church have postponed any meeting until fall even to discuss with us what can be done many questions arise. What should we do at Yale? What is back of all this? Who thinks what about who and what? etc., and amid it all there is, of course, a genuine 'heart sickness' on the part of many that their great dream now seems to be very very dim. While I have not agreed with them in most points I have always believed in their sincere consecration to their ideal, and share to a considerable degree with them in sympathetic ideas—standing of their present sadness. It's tough to see what was to be the crowning glory of a life time of Christian leaderships assume the tarnished and tattered aspects which the Proposed Union now presents.

"Next week I go up to New Haven to tackle the matter up there. I am certain that our officials have no more desire that this N.H. proposal came up for debate or action at Yale than I do. What will develop I do not know. It should be an interesting day.

"Then the following week in Boston. It's not going to seem right not to have you there. Yet I am sure it is right, especially in view of your health, for you not to come. Soon it will be April 20 and I hope on the 22 we can write 'finis' to our report and that I can turn it over to the Executive Committee on April 26 and then get a good night's sleep.

"Best wishes always,
"Wendell"

As early as March 8, 1954, Rev. L. Wendell Fifield[97] sent notice of the April meeting, 1954, in New York:

"TO MEMBERS OF THE COMMITTEE ON FREE CHURCH POLITY AND UNITY

"Dear Fellow Member,

"You have by this time received a copy of 'Possible Forms of Union' written by Malcolm Burton at the request of the Committee. I hope that you will read it with care. It suggests a new approach to the presentation of the forms of union in our report. As it will be discussed at length by the Central Committee at the Boston meeting on April 6th, I hope that I may have your reactions prior to that time.

"If this approach commends itself to the Committee, the ideas suggested in my most recent circular letter would not be germane.

"We have a fine response for the attendance at the meeting on April 20th. It looks as if again we would have close to 100% attendance.

"What a committee! How proud and pleased I am to be a member.

"Best wishes always,
"L. Wendell Fifield"

By now I had complete drafts of nearly all segments of the report, including that on different forms of union as mentioned in Mr. Burton's letter (Burton-Fifield-Gray, 2/24/54 & 3/13/54):[98]

"Dear Wendell,

"Here is the first draft of my proposed section on different forms of union. Aside from the adjustments necessary for the part on Covenant union, which I have not yet gone over in this regard, I would say that this represents very much what I had in mind at Greenwich. I may think of some items I have forgotten, but otherwise I would be prepared to let this go out to the committee pretty much as it is. I hope to be able to start cutting stencils on it soon, preparatory to keeping my mind on getting it out to all members of the Polity Committee.

"To my mind this is the part of our report that many people will look to as the heart of the whole thing. Actually the ground work we have done is probably much more important. But average people will not realize that at first. We simply must give evidence of having thought about *all* different kinds of relationships for the free churches in the ecumenical movement, and this brief outline of eight different forms of union will be more likely to make them think that we have really considered the matter than as though we were to come up with just one pet idea of our own, or with two or three possibilities offered.

"Let me know what you think of this if you have any major suggestions to offer.

"Cordially,

"Dear Henry:

"I would greatly appreciate your turning your logical and systematic mind to the enclosed and letting me know what you think of it.

"Sincerely,
"Malcolm K. Burton"

"To the members of the Committee on Free Church Polity and Unity:[99]

"At our last meeting at Greenwich it was agreed that I was to take the materials on the Covenant Union plan and on Organic Union and work them into a general section on possible forms of union, after which I was to send the results out directly to all members.

"The Central Committee will meet at Boston on April 6-8. Comments in general on this material should be sent to Dr. L. Wendell Fifield, 75 Hicks St., Brooklyn 2, N.Y. Comments on organic union, especially any suggested additions, should be sent to Arthur Swartz, 5139 Ridgedale St., Dallas 6, Texas. This was what we agreed. The material will be gone over by the Central Committee and then by our full committee April 20-22.

"A few afterthoughts of my own appear at end of page 15, but read the material for yourself first so as to get your own impressions without any coloration from me.

"To my way of thinking the importance of some such section as this is very great. People want to know that we have surveyed the whole field. Whether all the forms of union will strike people as having practicality or not is less important than a feeling that we have at least tried to present the whole picture.

"If you wish to express your reactions to me I shall enjoy receiving them, but I feel it more important that Dr. Fifield hear from you on it.

"Cordially,
"Malcolm K. Burton"

April 18, 1954, was Easter. Some idea of the pressure under which we all worked is indicated by the fact that on Easter I led seven services, preached to 4021, received 99 new members, and baptized 31 adults and 42 children. Then it was necessary to emplane for New York at 7:30 Monday morning.

I do not find a copy of the April 20-22 meeting minutes in either my personal file or in the photocopies of the official records in the Congregational Library. I do have my dated notes.

Initially three sections were considered, slightly revised and adopted. These were:

Section 8—Forms of Union of Special Interest including Covenant Union and Organic Union

Section 9—Powers of the General Council

Section 10—Recommendations for use of the Report.

On April 22, 1954, all sections had been "hammered on the anvil" 'till acceptable. At that point the chairman gave a brief, eloquent testimony to the importance of the task and requested that we vote on transmittal of the entire document as it stood on 4/22/54. The vote was unanimous, though one person expressed reservations but did not present them.

After the meeting Wendell and I reviewed the sections with a view to editorial needs, format, type font and cover. His parting word was "I'm sorry this is our last meeting in one way: we won't see as much of each other as we have."

Into Print And . . .

May 7, 1954, the chairman wrote to all of us as follows:[100]

"TO MEMBERS OF THE COMMITTEE ON FREE CHURCH POLITY AND UNITY

"Dear Fellow Committee Members,

"On the morning of April 27th I presented our report to the Executive Committee. I was accorded a cordial and attentive hearing. After I had finished, the Committee decided (and I think very properly) that they would not discuss the contents of the report but rather its method of distribution. There was considerable discussion at this point.

"The final decision led to the withdrawal of the motion of the last meeting that the report should be handled as had the report of the Board of Review. In its place a motion was made that copies of the report be sent in advance to the delegates to the General Council for their information only. This means, as I understand it, that the final presentation of the report to the General Council will be made when the chairman reports on Thursday morning, since this Committee was appointed by the General Council. The General Council will

228

then act on the recommendations of our Committee. What the Council chooses to do will then determine the future uses of the report. This is the original method for the release of the report determined a considerable time ago. Most of our Committee think the report should be made directly to the Council. This will now be done.

"This arrangement determines the type of report which I will make. The whole arrangement seems to me a sound one and can now be regarded as final. My offer to cooperate with Miss Debus and the Council staff in checking the report and the proof was accepted. I shall therefore keep an eye on the proceedings until the printed copies are ready.

"On your behalf I asked that a minute of appreciation for the fine cooperation of Miss Debus and Mrs. Wilsey be placed in the Executive Committee minutes. This was done.

"At our last meeting I failed to mention the seminar which our Committee is to conduct. I have been asked to serve as leader, but all members of the Committee are invited to have a part in them. If you come to Yale, and do not have other appointments during the time of our seminar, I should greatly appreciate it, if you would attend. This will give me the opportunity to distribute the questions asked to those best fitted to answer them. It will also permit those who came to the seminar to become acquainted with the Committee. Will you please regard this as a very cordial invitation to participate?

"We all realize that the first reactions to our report will be mixed. Very naturally those who expect that it will support their personal point of view will be dissappointed—and may give expression to their feelings. But the report is right and good and after initial reactions it will win its way.

"I have these suggestions to make:

"1.   When disappointment is expressed, suggest a further study of the report. I've already seen this work amazingly, in the past couple of days.

"2.   Some may seek to minimize sections of the report by saying that 'certain people' wrote them. Let us always have in mind that regardless of who did the initial work on any section, this is *now* the report of the entire Committee. No sections belongs to any one person. They all belong to us all. I mention this because it has already happened to me. Concerning a section with which the speaker was not in agreement he would say 'of course, that section was written by ———, and naturally he just didn't know.' Interestingly enough in every instance of such a conversation the speaker was *wrong* about the author of the critized material.

229

"My experience leads me to pass on to you the fact that our report will meet with an initial mixed reception and that recommendation for further study as well as an insistance that this is the report of all of us without negative vote will help to gain support for the report itself. In all fairness I shall say that *none* of the attitudes encountered above were on the part of any members of the Executive Committee.

"In concluding this, which may be my last letter to you, I would be remiss if I did not again express my very deep personal appreciation for your fine personal work on the Committee. In retrospect the values of our report grow. Those who read it, free from any prejudice, have used such words as 'monumental, stupendous, possessing permanent value and significance, a tremendous piece of research, etc.' With all these I agree. And I know the hard work, the loyal endeavor, the unbiased point of view, the complete selflessness which you gave to make it possible. So once more, my deepest thanks.

"I hope I'll see you at Yale.

> "Best ever,
> "L. Wendell Fifield"

Written by hand (Fifield to Gray, 4/29/54) he wrote to me:[101]

"Dear Henry:

"I have asked Miss Debus to arrange to have a copy of the page proof of our report sent to you directly from the printers. I hope that you will be able upon its arrival to steal a couple of hours to look it over. Of course, the contents cannot now be changed but you can greatly help us in catching mistakes—spelling, punctuations, and capitalization. More important you can help us check to be sure that all the changes voted in our last meeting have been properly made. Then if you will send the report back directly to Miss Debus, airmail within 24 hours, your help will be greatly appreciated. I am making similar requests of Malcolm and Fred Whittaker. Miss Debus and I will both do it here. Between all of us we should surely catch everything.

"The Executive Committee changed the method of procedure relative to the handling of our report again. This is final. I am sending out a letter to all the committee describing the exact procedure, so will not outline it here. It reverts to the first method which we worked out, and accords more closely with the wishes of the committee than the more recent plan.

"Unfortunately I have been sick in bed for the past week and was permitted only to get up long enough to present the report to the Executive Committee and then go back to bed again. As a result I did not hear the discussion of the invitation of the E & R's to meet with them in October. I am told it was accepted however. Further, I am informed it was voted to prepare a statement of the exact status of our situation relative to the merger for prior submission to them. I was informed that this resolution made it very specific that this statement was to make *no* offers *nor* to contain any commitments. If all this be true it certainly is not in the minds of our executive committee, nor our leaders that the merger issue will come up at Yale. They are making too definite plans for beyond Yale. This leads me,—though I realize that anything can happen—to feel that the main peril to our report at Yale will come through side issues such as the Center Church plan.

"I would say in confidence to you that some of the brethren were quite upset by the report. I had a long talk with Mr. Wood about it. He was greatly disturbed especially by Section V, Part 6 (I believe it was) and in that the statement that the General Council did not have the power to unite the one that Ross Cannon commented on. These people have keen minds and see at once the implications of some parts of our report. But I find no tendency, as some of our committee feared, to sabotage it. I tell these brethren the more you study it the better you'll like it. It must be quite a shock to those who expected something quite different.

"So much for now. But I cannot close without saying, what every member of the committee would say, that the report just wouldn't have been possible without you. You made an unmeasurable contribution to it. Beyond that I must say that the deep friendship which you and I came to have as we worked together will always be very precious to me.

"Best always,
"Wendell"

Then on May 26, 1954 (Fifield to Gray) Wendell reported by pen:[102]

"Dear Henry:

"The word went to the printer today to go ahead and print the report. This was necessary to get the printed copies sometime next week and get them out in time to reach the delegates. The long weekend complicates things. We had not received the last part of your corrections but I felt that we must go ahead. I think between all of us we have the copy in good shape. In certain instances where suggestions were made that would improve the report, but which did not correct mistakes in type-setting or actual errors of statement, we did not make the suggested changes. This would have again involved added time and expense. I explain this so you will understand why some of your suggestions were not complied with. This applied to the suggestions made by all who worked on the proof including myself. In several instances making an apparently single improvement would have involved the resetting of an entire page, resubmission of proof, etc., which would slow things down.

"Most of the corrections were, however, incorporated. I feel that with all of us working on it, we probably have a pretty 'clean' job. Thanks so much for your help.

"The air hereabouts is full of rumors. Many of the brethren are presently upset by Truman Douglas's speech in Mass. All sorts of ideas as to what may happen at Yale are floating around. I am sure that anything can happen. But I have a feeling that the statement of the Executive Committee in the last advance, our report, a degree of Christian common sense on the part of the delegates, and possibly God's guidance, if we are worthy, will think about wisdom rather than hysteria. Hope so.

> "Best always,
> "Wendell"

I wrote to him, May 28, 1954:[103]

"Dear Wendell:

"Thanks ever so much for your notes about the script. I have sent them all back and I am sorry some of them did not get there in time. There just were not enough hours in the day to get it all done.

"I believe that we have done the best that could be done by the Report in the time which was available for it. Certainly it is an enormous task to get that amount of printed material out, even if it is done without checking with four people in all parts of the United States.

"I look forward eagerly to receiving of the full document.

"I shall be in New Haven on the Monday before the Council starts I hope, and I also hope that somehow my room will not be too far distant from yours. Maybe if you know who is making the arrangments you could do something about that! At any rate, we shall have to work closely there.

"My very best to you.

> "Sincerely,
> "Henry David Gray"

My letter of thanks to the 109 correspondents who had continued to reply right to the end was as follows:

To Those Who Shared In The
Study of Congregational Polity[104]

"Dear Friends:

"One hundred and nine of you sent valuable material to our committee since Christmas! Thanks ever so much.

"You will want to know what happened to your letters.

"1. I revised the whole 'Practice' document using ideas, sentences, phrases—even individual words from your material.

"2. Three other members of our committee spent a full, hardworking afternoon discussing and checking what I had done.

"3. The full committee (from all over the U.S.A.) considered, revised, and adopted the material for inclusion in our report to the General Council when the remainder of our report is ready.

"4. The sections dealing with the national societies have been largely dropped from the practice document, though they are covered in a prior documentary study which we completed in 1952 and which is presently being revised with help from the national society officers.

"5. The paragraph which preceeds the list of our 'living bibliography' was interpreted by some readers to mean that each of you 'approved' the whole report!! We have tried to make the intent as clear as possible in the following substitute paragraph:

> "This report, describes Congregational Christian polity as it is practiced currently and does not presume to say whether or not *what is* is *what ought to be.* With these words of interpretation, we pay grateful acknowledgment to the following for their careful, detailed, and thoughtful responses to our request for guidance. It needs to be remembered that the report as a whole is not necessarily identical with the description of Congregational polity given by any individual correspondent, but the committee itself is responsible for compiling these statements.

"A bibliography simply identifies the books, articles, or other sources whence material is derived. A 'living bibliography' is in precisely the same category.

"I want you to know that your recent suggestions have greatly improved the document and will increase its value for our fellowship. Assembling, checking, re-writing, re-checking and re-checking this important material has taken us almost four years, but we are satisfied that what we now have is as accurate as human care can make it. Without your help the whole job would have been impossible.

"You will want to know that our committee expects to be able to place its full report in the hands of the Executive Committee of the General Council about ten days after Easter.

"Very sincerely yours,
"Henry David Gray"

CHAPTER 5 NOTES

1. H. D. Gray to 140 correspondents, 1-9-53
2. H. D. Gray to 37 correspondents, 3-11-53
3. T. Anderson to Gray, 4-15-53
4. Mrs. Alice McGouldrick to Gray, 4-8-53
5. P. A. Davies to Gray, 1-19-53
6. Helfenstein for SE Panel to Gray, p. 4, 3-24-53
7. Davis to Gray, 1-23-53
8. Treat to Gray, 1-16-53
9. Reitinger to Gray, 1-21-53
10. Claypool to Gray, 1-24-53
11. T. Anderson to Gray, 4-15-53
12. Ellis to Gray, 4-21-53
13. Fiebiger to Gray, p. 3, 1-17-53
14. Skidmore to Gray, p. 2, 1-20-53
15. Reitinger to Gray, p. 2, 1-20-53
16. English to Gray, p. 2, 4-3-53
17. Davis to Gray, p. 2, 1-23-53
18. Skarsten to Gray, 1-22-53
19. McGouldrick to Gray, p. 2, 4-8-53
20. Babcock to Gray, p. 4, 1-19-53
21. Niles to Gray, p. 3, 1-22-53
22. Davies to Gray, p. 4, 1-19-53
23. Shepherd to Gray, 4-6-53
24. Hallauer to Gray, p. 3, 1-21-53
25. Boynton to Gray, p. 2, 1-3-53, p. 2, 1-21-53
26. Reed to Gray, p. 2, 1-23-53
27. Nordstrom & Schlaretzki to Gray
28. Colbourn to Gray, p. 3, 2-26-53
29. Hoskins to Gray, for Mid-West Panel, pgs. 3, 4, 4-21-53
30. White to Gray, pgs. 2-3, 3-24-53
31. Minton to Gray, p. 2, 3-30-53
32. Gans to Gray, pgs. 1, 2, 3-24-53
33. Swartz to Gray, p. 3, 1-28-53
34. Johnson to Gray, p. 2, 1-12-53
35. First draft, Educators Panel Report, July 1953
36. Ibid, 3
37. Ibid, 4
38. Ibid, 5
39. Op. cit, pgs. 3, 4
40. Op. cit, p. 6
41. M. K. Burton to Gray, p. 2, 7-17-53
42. Fifield to Gray, 9-3-53
43. Fifield to Gray, 9-21-53
44. Fifield to Gray, 11-12-53
45. Fifield to Gray, 11-23-53
46. English to Gray, pgs. 1, 2, 4-3-53
47. H. V. White, *Advance*, 10-19-53, Board of Home Missions, NY

48. F. M. Meek, on Congregational Theology and Polity, 16 pages in length, 12-2-53 quotations are from pages 1, 2, 3, 4, 5, 7, 10, 11, 12, 13
49. Meek, op. cit., pgs. 15-16
50. H. D. Gray, notes 12-3-53, Boston
51. Fifield to Gray, 12-14-53
52. Fifield to Gray, 12-21-53
53. Douglas Horton
54. Charles C. Merrill to Gray, 12-31-53
55. S. H. Wellman to Fifield, 12-17-53
56. R. W. Graves to Gray, 12-15-53
57. Fifield to Gray, 12-22-53
58. Gray to those indicated in text, 12-18-53
59. Gray to panel chairman, 12-18-53
61. Gray to respondents as noted in text, by Western Union, 1-21-54
62. Gray to named national officers, 12-29-53
63. Revised Report, Congregational Polity as Practiced, etc. 2-2-54, p. 21
64. Ibid, 21
65. Polity as Practiced, op. cit, 21-22
66. CPP, Op. cit, 15
67. Fifield to Gray, 12-24-53
68. Fifield to Gray, 1-4-54
69. Fifield to Gray, et al., 1-12-54
70. M. K. Burton to Gray, 2-8-54
71. Fifield to Gray, 1-16-54
72. Polity & Unity Report, June 1954, p. 37, 38, General Council, NY
73. CPP, 2-2-54, revision, p. 1
74. Fifield to Gray, et al., 2-15-54
75. Fifield to Gray, 2-23-54
76. Fifield to Gray, 2-22-54
77. Gray to antional officials, 12-29-53, see page 180
78. H. B. Belcher to Gray, 1-11-54
79. CPP. 12-2-53 version, paragraphs 56-72 inclusive. This is the only accurate documented description of the relation of the National Societies to the fellowship. At the insistence of national officials it was NOT printed.
80. Frazier to Gray, 1-4-54
81. Frazier to Gray, 1-11-54
82. Gibbons to Gray, 1-4-54
83. Leiper to Gray, 1-4-54
84. Scribner to Gray, 1-5-53
85. Scribner to Gray, 1-18-54
86. Gray to Douglass, 1-18-54
87. Douglass to Gray, 1-19-54
88. Gray to Belcher, 1-18-54
89. Gray to Douglass, 2-19-54
90. Fifield to national officials, 2-19-54
91. Douglass to Gray, n.d., Feb./Mar. 1954
92. Leiper to Fifield, 3-4-54
93. Belcher to Gray, 3-26-54
94. Fifield to Gray, 2-25-54
95. Merrill to Gray, 2-25-54

96. Fifield to Gray, 3-27-54
97. Fifield to Gray, et al., 3-8-54
98. Burton to Fifield and Gray, 2-24-54
99. Burton to Gray, et al., 3-3-54
100. Fifield to Gray, et al., 5-7-54
101. Fifield to Gray, 4-29-54
102. Fifield to Gray, 5-26-54
103. Gray to Fifield, 5-28-54
104. Gray to all correspondents, 2-10-54

CHAPTER SIX

Expectations and Actions

There were three hopes for the 1954 General Council. The mediators expected additional time to negotiate, to temper extreme advocates, to think through the Polity and Unity Report, and to devise a method of union for the CC/ER which would combine freedom, faith and fellowship in some as yet undiscovered way. The Rev. Alfred Grant Walton used his considerable persuasive powers and the propinquity of his Brooklyn home to the General Council offices, to press for full acceptance by the E&R of the liberalizing "Interpretations" adopted at the 1948 Oberlin General Council. The Rev. Roy L. Minich skillfully directed the attention of Massachusetts leaders to the positive aspects of the Claremont resolution. The Rev. Wallace Anderson championed the idea "Let's see what the Polity and Unity Report says." The latter was the dominant position of the mediators in the late spring of 1954.

Many of the proponents and opponents of the CC/ER merger were prepared to "wait and see." The more ardent advocates were not. They were determined to use whatever means would achieve their goal.

It was with considerable relief that the mediators hailed the general letter of the Chairman of the Executive Committee of the General Council (A. D. Gray to Congregational Christian Churches, 4-27-54).

"The Executive Committee of the General Council
   to the Congregational Christian Churches

"Sends greeting:

"Pursuant to the instructions of the General Council the Executive Committee is carrying forward conversations with the Evangelical and Reformed Church.

"On February 9th the six members of our Executive Committee who constitute the Advisory Committee met with the Evangelical and Reformed Administrative Committee. The impression we gathered at that time was discouraging in regard to the possibilities of union.

"The following week, however, we received a telegram from the Evangelical and Reformed General Council, the body corresponding to our Executive Committee, which indicated their desire for further conversations and made clear their point of view on several matters.

"The possibility of further legal action, though remote, is not yet eliminated.

"In view of this situation the Executive Committee makes the following statements.

"1. Acting upon the instructions of the General Council the Executive Committee will hold a joint meeting with the Evangelical and Reformed General Council on October 12th and 13th of this year.

"2. It is desirable to have further time to study the problems related to the proposed union.

"3. The Executive Committee will see to it that variant points of view among us are represented on our committees as the study proceeds.

"4. The Executive Committee does not propose that any action on the matter be taken at the forthcoming meeting of the General Council in New Haven.

"5. The Executive Committee does not anticipate that it will have any recommendations to present to the General Council until the meeting of 1956.

"Wishing you grace, mercy, and peace, we remain

"Yours faithfully,

"The Executive Committee of the General Council
Arthur D. Gray, Chairman"

The five points appeared to assure further study with all viewpoints considered and no action at New Haven.

The opponents of the CC/ER Merger did not accept the letter. Rev. Joseph J. Russell expressed their view in the June, 1954 "Free Lance."

"IS THE MERGER DEAD?

"Rev. Joseph J. Russell, Holbrook, Mass.

"'WHY DO YOU TROUBLE-MAKERS keep digging up the merger when everybody else knows it is a dead issue! Don't you know that the E and R people have lost interest? Don't you know that our General Council Executive Committee has decided not to ask any action on it at New Haven?' Such questions as these have been thrown at members of the Continuation Committee in recent weeks. That there has been some reason behind the questions we do not deny, but before we assume that the matter may be considered as safely buried, it is well to examine the evidence. A study of the statements, official and semi-official, from leaders of the two denominations may serve as an eye-opener.

"It is true that last February Dr. Douglas Horton stated in a personal letter to a member of an Illinois church that a change in E & R leadership had made it unnecessary for opponents of the merger to have any further fears as to its consummation. It is true that shortly before that a joint meeting of the Advisory Committee of our General Council and the Administrative Committee of the Evangelical and Reformed Church was held, at which there were indications that the E & R leaders had, quite understandably, grown impatient with delay, and that since they were ready to carry their presbyterianism further in consolidating the original merger (1934) which had constituted their Church, they were ready to withdraw from negotiations with the Congregationalists. The statement by Dr. Horton referred to above apparently reflects the attitude taken in that joint meeting by Dr. James E. Wagner, new President of the E & R Church. . . .

"It is further true that on April 28 the Congregational Christian News Bureau issued a news release, stating that the proposed joint meeting of the E & R General Council and our Executive Committee, originally slated for late winter, had been postponed until October 12-13, and that the Executive Committee 'does not propose that any action be taken on the matter of the merger at the forthcoming meeting of the General Council at Yale University', and that it 'does not anticipate that it will have any recommendations on the proposed merger to present to the General Council until the Council meeting of 1956'. All these things have led many people to the honest conclusion that the issue is a dead one, at least so far as this year's General Council is concerned.

"Is It A Dead Issue?

"Dr. Wagner Says No! In the April issue of the *Messenger,* (E & R journal) Dr. James E. Wagner, President of the Evangelical and Reformed Church, writes, 'The possibility of the merger of the Evangelical and Reformed Church with the Congregational Christian Churches is not by any means a dead issue. It is true that our General Council has adopted a statement insisting on a very realistic appraisal of the situation as it now exists in both communions. It is just as true that our General Council holds itself in readiness to resume conversations with the Congregational Christian Executive Committee, to explore every possible move forward, and to take any step which offers promise of achieving real organic union on the basis of the principles found in the Basis of Union." (Again no mention of the Interpretations!)

"Dr. Scotford Says No! Two weeks prior to the publication of the above, the *Messenger* published a letter from Dr. John R. Scotford, who was editor of *Advance* during the period when the merger first came up before our churches for action. Dr. Scotford says in part, 'The two groups need each other. The Congregational Christian Churches need the painstaking responsible democracy of the E & R churches, and also the deep devotion which the people feel to the local churches. The E & R churches need the community outlook and the "public-mindedness" characteristic of the Congregational Christians. . . . The ecumenical movement needs this particular union. . . At present the E & Rs and the Congregational Christians are the only differing groups that have any inclination to get together. . . In the process of the merger the unexpected has always happened! On at least half a dozen occasions a small group thought they had the matter all quietly buried, only to have it spring to life once more *when it came before a larger body.'* (Emphasis added.)

"Facts from the Field Says No! The May, 1954 issue of *Facts from the Field,* (Missions Council publication) says, 'In line with Congregational democratic procedures no advance blueprint can be drawn of what will transpire (at the 1954 General Council) . . . but a few of the issues sure to engage the delegates are . . . the proposed merger with the E & R Church'. Surely this statement comes from a source close to our denominational headquarters."

Shadow of the Law

Viewed with hindsight, the enlistment of attorney Loren Wood of New York by the proponents should have been a portend of the attempt to discredit the Polity and Unity Report in order to proceed with the CC/ER Merger. It did not seem so in January when

240

Rev. Douglas Horton wrote to Rev. L. Wendell Fifield (1-18-54).

"Dear Wendell,

"Mr. Wood this morning received from Mr. Crawford, the chairman of the Legal Panel, a copy of his response to a letter from you which had apparently been sent to the members of the Legal Panel but which he himself had not received. Mr. Wood wanted a copy of the original letter so I asked for it and gave it to him.

"As he read your original letter and the accompanying statement, Mr. Wood began to be apprehensive about the draft report of your Committee. He will undoubtedly be writing you about that. I very much hope to give the report a thorough reading myself though I daresay I know much of what it contains from what you have told me. At the moment I am busy preparing lectures for Bangor in two weeks.

"I hope you have had a grand two weeks and look forward to seeing you soon.

"Ever thine,

"Douglas Horton"

Beyond the USA

The mediators were chagrined by the amount of money, time and energy diverted from the main work of the Churches by the Merger. The Congregational witness was seriously impaired in the United States and not just in the United States. The proponents were motivated by a majestic goal; the Merger of two dissimilar polities, and the merger of Anglo-Saxon rooted Congregational Churches with Continental based Evangelical and Reformed Church.

The U.S. CC/ER Merger was a step in the grand design of a United Kingdom Merger and a new kind of International Congregational Council powerful enough to influence the World Council of Churches.

The inter-weaving of all these threads is chronicled in successive "Advance Reports" and "Council Minutes" beginning in 1938. Of quite special importance are the records of travels, attendance at conferences in Tokyo (1945), Lund (1953), Toronto (1950) and Evanston (1954). Clearly the Minister and Secretary of the General Council viewed the world as his parish, gained financial and personal support for his world vision from the Executive Committee, and regarded the consummation of the CC/ER

Merger as a prelude to uniting Anglo-Saxon and Continental church bodies, and a demonstration of how denominations with disparate polity (e.g., congregational and presbyterian) could be united.

Beginning in Advance Reports, 1946 (p. 72) a "Report of the World Council of Churches" became an integral part of the General Council Minister's personal accounting. A continuing web of relationships was woven, both personal and organizational; for example in Japan, October (1945) and Geneva (1946). This devotion to the ecumenical movement is recorded as follows: "It is to the American Committee of the World Council of Churches that for the last year I have given all my extra working hours. . . . I have done this in the firm belief that the General Council is committed to the ecumenical movement and desires to participate in its development."[1]

Leadership in World Church affairs led to public status, which is illustrated by one event promoted by the American Committee for the WCC, chaired by Rev. Douglas Horton. He reported, "In the spring of 1954 it brought to America three leaders of the ecumenical movements—Dr. W. A. Visser't Hooft of Geneva, Dr. Marc Boegner of Paris and the Bishop of Chichester (England). A large ecumenical service was held in the Cathedral of St. John the Divine (New York) in May when these leaders spoke."[2] This stately occasion which called public attention to the Chairman's efforts to revive the WCC was reported by press, radio, and television.

Meetings of the Executive Committee began to give time and money to the ICC and WCC. Advance Reports for the 1950 General Council[3] reports selection of delegates (Feb. 4-9 meeting) for both WCC and ICC, and undergirds the finances of both bodies.

A sense of the meaning of these world relationships to Dr. Horton as conveyed by his 1950 report, merits close study,[4]

"...I have devoted not a little time in the last two years to the developing World Council. I attended the meeting of the Assembly in the late summer of 1948, served as chairman of the Nominating Committee at the meeting of its Central Committee immediately thereafter, and have from time to time since then sat in at the meetings at which its United States unit, the 'Conference of U.S.A. Member Churches', has been slowly brought into being.

"No one can attend meetings of the Assembly for any length of time without becoming aware that, though its members are the individual denominations of the various nations, its objectives are shaped largely through the impact of the groups of denominations having similar faith and polity—world Angelicanism, world Lutheranism, world Presbyterianism, and the like.

"It was in part because the voice of world Congregationalism needs to be heard clearly and not brokenly in the conclaves of the World Council but also, and more importantly, because the various segments of Congregationalism throughout the world need each other for counsel, inspiration, and mutual support that in your behalf I have also devoted a good deal of time to the re-constituting of the International Congregational Council. Previously a mere mass meeting called together every ten years on the two sides of the Atlantic by turn, it is now a body comparable to the General Council itself, with a headquarters in London and a full-time Minister and Secretary who visits the isolated outposts of Congregationalism, arranges for the visits of Congregational ministers and laymen, students and social workers to Britain, to the United States, and elsewhere, and in every way seeks to cultivate international understanding among us in the name of our common witness. The new constitution of the International Council was formally adopted at a series of meetings in Wellesley, Massachusetts, covering a week of June in 1949, the arrangements for which were a chief concern of our headquarters in New York.

"The World Council of Churches differs from the Federal Council of the Churches of Christ in America in this, that its purpose is to provide not only a means for interdenominational cooperation but also a medium through which closer and stronger types of union may be studied and, when found acceptable, promoted. The Federal Council is constituted for cooperation alone: it is not intended at all to reduce the number of the 250 sects in this country, or even of the 27 communions which compose it. It is for this reason that those denominations of the country which are the most sensitive to the need for greater Protestant unity responded with gladness to the appeal sent out by this Council from Grinnell in 1946 and entered into the negotiations which culminated in an official meeting held at Greenwich, Connecticut, in December of last year. An organization is now set up whose purpose, complementary to that of the Federal Council, will be to draw together in the most effective union possible those denominations whose faith and practice are sufficiently similar to permit it. This includes almost all of those that lie between Angelicanism and Eastern Orthodoxy on the one hand and Fundamentalism on the other. One reporter from New York called up while the meeting was in progress in Greenwich and asked to be informed of the exact moment the next day when American Protestantism was to become united! The goal lies far in the future,

243

but it will be recorded in history that the first step toward it was taken by this Council. Though I have had to give relatively little time to this movement, I have felt that it was all time well spent.

"Before the meeting of the World Council Assembly in Amsterdam, I was able briefly to visit some of the centers in Europe. . ."

Following the 1950 Cleveland Council meeting which concluded on June 28th, the Minister of the General Council proceeded (July 8-15) to Toronto as a member of the Central Committee of the WCC, to plan for the next *World Assembly*.[5] Meantime Mrs. Douglas Horton (Mildred McAfee Horton) became Vice President of the U.S. National Council of Churches. Together, Dr. and Mrs. Horton were delegates to a WCC Conference on Arab Refugees, held in Beirut, Lebanon, May 4-8, 1951. The same year there were other major conferences at Paris, Cleveland, Beirut, Bad Boll, New York, Geneva, Rolle, Clarens, and elsewhere in Switzerland.[6] Then came Lund, Sweden in August, 1952 at the Faith and Order Conference of the WCC, followed by visitation in Stockholm. A swing around the world took place at the end of 1952, to the Central Committee of the WCC at Lucknow, India, with visitations in India, Australia and New Zealand.[7] Rev. Henry Smith Leiper was now executive of the New York WCC office and reported, "the budget for 1951 has been fully raised. . ." There has been a contribution "from the U.S.A. of $240,000 toward the central budget of the World Council. . ."[8]

July 4, 1953 brought the International Congregational Council at St. Andrews which was reported in Chapter Five. The 1953 ICC polity report was rather misleading but that scarcely mattered, since it was given no publicity. As reported, the findings stressed "where Christ is, there is the Church. . . . This means recognizing the authority of Christ in the individual church and in the Council. . .to which it sends delegates. . . ."[9]

The place of this polity theory and of the ICC in the unfolding grand design of the Minister and Secretary of the General Council is indicated in his report.

"The purposes of the International Congregational Council are not exhausted in the meetings held every five years. The permanent headquarters in London is the center of unremitting activity, as the report of the Council to be given at New Haven will show.

"It is under the approval of the International Congregational Council that our project with Australian and New Zealand Congregationalism is being arranged. With like approval we are also

244

expecting that the Evanston delegate from the Remonstrant Brotherhood in the Netherlands, the Rev. N. van Gelder of Utrecht, will spend two months with us after the close of the Assembly of the World Council of Churches. This idea was first broached at the meeting at St. Andrews.''[10]

Visits added to the impact of Dr. Horton's 1951 lectures at Oxford, his 1952 book on polity, and his 1953 address on polity at the St. Andrews International Congregational Council. English Congregational/Presbyterian union was the immediate goal to which the new policy was directed.

Influence in England

The Rev. Harold Bickley, an English "moderator," that is "superintendent" in U.S. terms, one of my British friends, wrote to me on April 21, 1954 indicating English response to St. Andrews and to "a new sense of denominational responsibility."

"My dear Gray,

"It was good to receive your letter telling me of the things that are happening in the denomination and in your own church. My latest news of the situation in your country is that some new turn has been given to events, which at the moment isn't public news, but this may only be a matter of hearsay. . .and this may mean the end of union. I haven't any details of this, but have only heard a whisper. I am most interested to see how events turn out in your country. Your letter was most illuminating. I hope that Evanston will prove more helpful than St. Andrews. I personally was rather disappointed in St. Andrews, I felt that we were empasising (sic) fundamental dogmas held by all churches and rather getting no further than theological generalities. Perhaps I am pessimistic. The report makes interesting reading, underlining what most of us believed. In this country we are passing through a difficult period for our denomination. Someone has said that all crises in English Congregationalism have been occasioned by finance. We are facing this crisis now, and I think we shall win through and set our denomination upon a sound collective basis. A committee has been meeting preparing a total budget for complete denominational expenditure, the chief item is the guaranteeing of the minimum basic stipend for our ministers. . .the county unions rose against administration on a provincial basis. . .and insisted on administration on a county basis. Now the county unions have made themselves responsible for raising the £130 thousand we need, and have agreed to work hard and find this acceptance of their quotas for this total financial fund. This does not include the London Missionary Society which by its constitution is interdenominational, even though nearly all its money comes from Congregational churches. At the assembly in May we shall vote on this important matter. And I am sure it will go through and be taken up by the churches. There seems to be a rising tide of enthusiasm in our county assemblies and a new sense of denominational responsibility, for unless we can maintain the ministry on a denominational level we shall perish for lack of interdependency. Leslie Cooke has had a hard furrow to plough during his years of office, but he has done excellent work and Howard Stanley has proved himself a real administrator. We still record a declining membership, but the decline is not so steep. I think that there are signs that a revival of our churches is beginning, and it has been long over due. I find my churches in the province are much more spiritually concerned and ready to go forward than they were four years ago. I often think of the tide of religion in your land. . .and am thrilled to hear of the wonderful work you are doing in your amazing church. You must be thrilled by it. It is a great tribute to you and your leadership."

The influence of the St. Andrews ICC meeting is evident. I replied (Gray/Bickley 5-7-54).

"My dear Harold:

"The joy and delight of reading what you did with the things Miss Busch had packed with the help of the women is unbounded. I am more than glad that this sharing has been possible.

"I trust that everything is going well in your May meetings. They will be over, I expect, by the time you receive this letter, but I am sure that good sense will prevail and proper action will be taken to under gird the work of the churches through the county Unions, since that seems to be the manner of administration which meets with the approval of the largest number.

"Our Polity and Unity report has now been presented to the Executive Committee of the General Council, has been received by them, is being printed, and will be sent to all the ministers and to all the delegates to the General Council meeting this forthcoming June. As soon as sufficient copies are off the press, I hope to send one to you. There has been, as we anticipated, some disappointment on both sides in regard to the report. We did not take sides for or against this particular merger which is still up in the air. Instead, we chose to present a rather lengthy and careful study of Congregationalism as it is in the documentary sources of our present day organizations and in the practice in the denomination as a whole. We followed this by a very careful analysis of the types of union and of what is needed by way of adaption and by way of procedure in order to accomplish union in any particular manner. We then made certain minimal recommendations including the establishment of a new committee

246

to define carefully, the powers of our General Council. This seems to be one of the very crucial issues on which the denomination as a whole is not especially clear in its thinking.

"It is, of course, clear from our documents and from our practice that we are what we are and cannot unite with other groups except by modification of what we are. Whether this can be done and in what way it can be done is spelled out in great detail, and we feel, with considerable clarity. However, all this will come to you as soon as I have any copies off the press. I have not yet received the proofs from the printer, so you can see that we are still some little way off.

"Give my very best regards to your dear wife and as you visit Plymouth or Bath carry our love and affection to the people who so graciously made us feel at home and who have written to us over the years. We value these friendships highly."

When the English Congregational paper *Christian World* (5-20-54 issue) arrived the report of the Rev. Leslie Cooke's address was as follows (only longer!).

"The theme of Dr. Cooke's address was that 'the whole is more than the sum of its parts'; that is to say, that the Union is more than an aggregation of the separate churches and associations which make it up. Something new entered into the life of Congregationalism when churches and County Unions entered into association for the achievement together of certain purposes beyond the power of each several part. . . . If in domestic affairs it was essential that the Congregational churches should act together, it became absolutely vital in our dealings with other Churches, with other Congregational Unions and with the Free Church Federal Council and British Council of Churches. *To engage in these relationships at all,* said Dr. Cooke with great emphasis, *this Union of Congregational churches has to act as though it were a Church.*

* * * * *

"Even the 'as though' of that statement would not be enough to prevent any Separatists or Isolationists from feeling a shock of horror, but it was received without audible sounds of dissent—in a thoughtful silence. This was not all, for Dr. Cooke had something to say about the question of Free Church unity which had been reopened at the last Congress of the Free Church Federal Council at Worthing. 'The Reformed and Evangelical witness in this country is suffering because of divisions among the Free Churches, and consequent misuse of resources. I think both the Pope and the Devil are rubbing their hands over the fact. . .'"

Obviously the world was indeed the parish of the Minister and Secretary of the General Council!

Other Voices

The Minister of the General Council was by no means the only prominent Congregational advocate of organized ecumenicity. He was the most deeply involved in international church affairs, and an idealist in search of a church body which would shape the world. There were numerous other proponents of the UCC/ER Merger. The Rev. Joseph J. Russell of Massachusetts mailed (5-20-54) copies of notes taken at the Massachusetts State Conference Meeting May 18, 1954. These recorded a powerful address by the Rev. Truman B. Douglass, Executive Vice President of the Board of Home Missions, as follows (in part):

"Congregationalism has shown itself adaptable to many ways of church life. . . . It is easier to honor the Pilgrim Fathers than to be pilgrims. . . . All efforts to define Congregationalism are futile—has to be lived out in possibly ways. It is absurd to be a Continuing Congregationalist, as sons of the Reformation we know that no church is a continuing church. Must hope to be renovated, reformed. Anyone who hopes to be a Continuing Congregationalist in the static sense will find that Congregationalism has moved on to something else. I urge a clear recognition of new patterns. . . . We have been in the forefront of the ecumenical movement. Are we now to defend ourselves against a self-parading denominationalism? Is there a new fundamentalism in church polity? . . . We must not substitute forms for discipleship. (We) must remind ourselves that no particular form of the church is the whole. Bear witness to (the) power of new forms of church life. (We) must be ready to repudiate forms, even our own. This is a recognition of the sovereignty of God. . . . (The) free way of church life develops into eccentricities unless we accept disciplines. Autonomy can become anarchy. Theological freedom can become the setting up of trivial expressions in place of noble creeds of ages. Autonomy must be balanced by articulation in bodies like State Conferences etc."

Revs. Shirley Greene, Albert Penner, Clifford Simpson, Ned McKenney, Joseph King, and many others pressed for merger approval at New Haven.

Storm Signal

The need for mediating influence became more urgent as the time before the Council shortened. All members of the Polity and

Unity Committee with the possible exception of Rev. Charles Merrill and Rev. Malcolm Burton continued to hope the four years of research, discussion, writing, and editing would give guidance to the fellowship. Mr. Merrill was the sole member to abstain from voting to approve the final report; he thought Congregational polity had changed, and ought to adapt to the merger. Mr. Burton's view was that no attention would be given to the report.

Then came the Rev. L. Wendell Fifield's general letter of May 25, 1954 with its unsettling content. The letter read:

"Dear Fellow Committee Member,

"When you receive your copy of our report, there will be three matters which require explanation.

"1. On the cover will be a statement to the effect that the Executive Committee has neither approved nor disapproved the report. Of course, we know that our report makes an affirmative or negative action on it impossible. We state this clearly in the 'Foreword.' But, I have found that many do not read the 'Foreword.'

"As a member of the Executive Committee who sat through the Cadman trial, I know the problem and embarrassment which can be created by documents sent out from '287', which have never been approved by the Executive Committee or the General Council. If they came from '287' and there is no statement to the contrary, it can be asserted that they are official pronouncements of the Council. The Executive Committee in the future is going to be very careful to designate clearly whether or not any printed statement sent out from '287' has been officially approved. They have properly done this in the case of our report, since they merely assumed the responsibility of sending it to the delegates.

"2. Because so many have not read the 'Foreword,' I have inserted the statement concerning it on the title page of the report. Since this does not relate to the body of the report but will help in the understanding of it, I felt that it was a proper thing to do.

"3. The other matter relates to the first of our recommendations. In thinking the matter over and studying the proof, I realized that the matter of making it clear that this report had been neither approved nor disapproved by the General Council and that affirmative or negative action is impossible because of the nature of the report would arise again when the report comes before the General Council. Unless a specific statement covering this is presented in advance, a considerable debate may get under way on the floor drawing attention away from the contents of the report (which is the important part of it) or possibly even resulting in postponement of action while statements are prepared.

"It seemed to me that the best way to contribute to what I hope will be prompt acceptance of our resolutions was to cover the situation in the resolutions themselves. Therefore, I wrote the statement which you will find in parenthesis under our first recommendation. I phrased it so that the responsibility would be mine rather than that of the Committee as the Committee cannot act upon it. However, before I authorized its inclusion, I did check with a majority of the Central Committee. I had to reach those I could in a hurry as the report is being printed. I cleared the statement with Fred Whittaker, Henry David Gray, Fred Meek and Malcolm Burton. These, with me, constitute a majority.

"I also talked the matter over with Louise Williams at the New York State Conference meeting. She was in agreement. This group, whom I was able to contact quickly, represented a cross section of the Committee, and verified my judgment that the inclusion of this recommendation was both wise and strategic.

"Had it been possible to hold a meeting or even poll the Committee by mail, I would, of course, have done so. But, neither was possible. Nor did I even have the available time to poll by phone the entire Central Committee. I am sending this explanation to you in advance of the report so you will understand these three matters when the report is received.

"I had expected that once our report was completed and sent to the printers there would be nothing more to do, but I find that problems relative to its adequate and proper distribution do arise. I am doing my utmost to handle them to the best of my ability and in a manner which I feel would be the wish and judgment of the Committee.

"Best wishes always,

"L. Wendell Fifield

"P.S. I have just finished reading the page proof of our report. It looks well. It reads well. Upon this reading of it in its printed completion, I feel more satisfied with it and prouder of it than ever.

"W."

I talked with Wendell by phone on June 1st. He was both elated and discouraged; elated that the printed Polity Report read better the second time through; discouraged that the unusual "label" had been required on the cover. "I guess we can live with it. It's what's inside that counts." I hoped he was right.

Whenever I could I reviewed the basic documents, marked them for ready reference, and filed them. Then the same thing was done for the hundreds of letters from our 140 correspondents. June 16, 1954 I wrote to Wendell.

"Dear Wendell:

"I am looking for a copy of the Report one of these days, and shall sit down and leaf it through with a good deal of joy in the completion of the job, and memory of the wonderful friendships which we have developed while doing the job under your chairmanship.

"The material which I have on hand is being got into some kind of order for Yale but, frankly, I do not have the time nor can I spare my secretary's time to do it the way I had hoped to do it so that it might be referred to with ease by anybody. That will have to be done over the summer.

"You can count on me to be in the Seminar however, and to do what I can throughout the conference Council time, as you may wish to call on me, to further the acceptance of the Report and its use as a basis for denominational thinking and strategy.

"There are many, many cross-currents in California relative to merger, social action, and general denominational principles. This I suspect is simply a reflection of what is general throughout the nation.

"May we pray and hope that our Report will give some direction to all of the confusion.

"Best to you.

"Sincerely yours,

"Henry David Gray"

Wendell's last letter to me before the New Haven Council was penned, dated June 4. It caught the mood in which we approached the 1954 General Council.

"Dear Henry:

"Thank you for your good letter. I called Florence to see if she could get you room in the building with ours. (Mrs. F. will be with me.) Florence is not handling the reservations this time. But she said she would do her best, which I have found is usually sufficient.

"All seems quiet here. Possibly this is the core of peace at the center of the hurricane. I do not know. Hope not. I'm meeting with a committee of the Executive Committee this afternoon to discuss the presentation of our report to the General Council. I am very anxious if possible to have the support of the Ex. Committee for our recommendations. It is made up, the Committee, of my best friends on the Ex. Committee so I anticipate a very friendly session.

"Center Church is going to propose some amendments for *1956*. That's O.K. by me. So I guess I got that cared for.

"Best always

"Wendell"

Settled and Unsettled

New Haven had long been anticipated. Four years of arduous work was finished. The documents, reference works and hundreds of letters and comments in my briefcases were immediately available to confirm the accuracy of the Congregational Polity Committee Report. How would it be received?

I settled in at the Taft Hotel, then headed for the registration desk at Woolsey Commons. Wendell hailed me. I crossed the street to meet him. "Have you seen this?" he said, brandishing a slim yellow jacketed pamphlet. "No, I just got here." He motioned to a shaded spot. Then I saw the sparks in his eyes. He was livid. I had never before seen Wendell angry. "What *is* it?" I asked. " .'s a lawyer's brief against our report. Never in all the years have I heard of lawyers being employed to discredit an official study commissioned by the Council at a cost of $30,000 to $40,000! And it's being handed out with our report *before the Council has even received the report.* Why wasn't I told about this? Why didn't Atty. Loren Wood advise the Polity and Unity Committee? Why was I 'led on' by the Executive Committee to think since we had made all the adjustments they suggested, that the presentation of our study was just like any other major report? Why?" He buried his great bushy head and luminous eyes in his big strong hands.

Why? The only glimmer of an answer I had was the long involved trail of world bodies, colorful conferences, and one man's vision of a world of peace and justice under the influence of One Great Church. There wasn't much comfort in that fleeting thought. Then another idea emerged, the same hope that leads me to write this account of the mediators. . .of whom Wendell Fifield was the noblest.

"Wendell" I suggested "Maybe Mr. Wood has done us a favor. My greatest fear was that the Polity and Unity report would be quietly received and then be ignored. Somebody has made sure it won't be ignored. *If it is read,* it will tell its story more convincingly than any speech. Besides, Wendell, that report is history. Never before, in all the centuries, have Documents and Practice been collected and systematized. From today forward nobody can claim to discuss Congregational Polity intelligently without grappling with the Fifield Committee's report."

He looked straight at me. "Do you really think I'm making too much of this?" and he shook the booklet.

"Wendell, I haven't read it. I haven't seen it. In fact, I haven't yet seen a bound copy of our own report. I don't like the idea of a lawyer's brief against any report, but I sure enough think attention will be focused on Polity and Unity because of it. And I think your great task is to capitalize on that attention. Don't fight it. Carry the cause of the report *on its merits*. Take for granted the receptiveness all our letters indicated. Include Mr. Wood's pamphlet in our recommended report distribution. People can read. Legalese won't hurt the report; it turns people off."

"You might be right," he said very thoughtfully. Then he stood up. "I've got some thinking to do," and he was gone.

Within minutes I met other members of our committee. All were angry. It did seem a strange proceeding, since Mr. Wood and other lawyers had been either unable or unwilling to advise the committee, or meet to discuss the issues for four years. Nevertheless anger hardly seemed likely to remedy the situation. My comment to each was "Let me register. When I get my copy of the booklet and our report, I'll sit down on the grass and read all of it—at least twice."

That seemed to pacify. And that's what I did. The *content* of the Wood booklet can best be reviewed in a later chapter: the *attitude* revealed in it, and the *effect* of it upon the Council are of immediate concern. The attitude was condemnation of the Polity and Unity study on legal grounds. The effect was multiple. Some were scandalized at a legal attack on a study committee of the General Council by attorneys of the General Council. Others were overjoyed, feeling that, no matter what the PU report said, the way to merger was legally open. Most were confused; for most, as always, were first timers. A few had been oblivious to polity; now they wanted "to know what it was all about." The chief effect of the Wood booklet was to focus attention on the PU report.

Announced Intentions

The 1954 General Council was called to order at 2:00 p.m. Wednesday, June 23, in Woolsey Hall, Yale University, New Haven.

The preliminaries were scarcely over before "Mr. Ronald Bridges of Maine announced the intention of the officers of the

American Board of Commissioners for Foreign Missions and of the Board of Home Missions of the Congregational Christian Churches to present certain amendments to the By-Laws."[11] The process of tailoring the By-Laws and Standing Rules to the theories of executives had been transposed into new "rules" across the years, beginning, if my memory is accurate, with a 1949 Council provision that the General Council "recognized" a Conference as being a Conference of the Congregational Christian Churches! In 1954 Mr. Bridges' main amendment related to the status of Council delegates as corporate members of the foreign and home mission boards, ABCFM and BHM.[12]

The New Haven meeting demonstrated the capacity of proponents of merger to pass or reject proposals with ease. It was obvious that Puerto Rico Churches of the United Evangelical Church were not "identical in status and function with the Congregational Christian Conference of Puerto Rico"[13] but a motion claiming they were identical passed, though the resolution recognized a parallel action by the General Conference of the Evangelical United Brethren Church!

"Christ On His Throne"

By late Wednesday it became clear that the novel polity theories of the Mansfield Theses were to be declared the New Gospel.

As the theme for the opening address of the 1954 General Council Rev. Douglas Horton chose the title of a 1640 anonymous British book on Congregational Polity. So doing he elected to talk about polity the day before the scheduled report of the Committee on Free Church Polity and Unity. The reason was clear. Here is the background of the address.

On April 17, 1953 the Minister of the Council addressed the Centennial celebration of the Chicago Congregational Association on the subject *The Association,* theorizing that a new type of church body was needed by the Congregational Churches because the New England state governments had functioned as regulatory bodies until 1818 in Connecticut and 1834 in Massachusetts, and thereafter left a void.

He asserted "development of the new communion among the churches has been. . .breath-takingly rapid."[14] Further, he claimed "In the Congregational Christian system the Association has long since taken the place occupied by the bishop of the episcopal systems of church government. . . . The Association. . .has the power of electing whether or not it will cooperate with this church or that;

in its constitution is written the authorization to admit or expel churches from its membership on adequate cause."[15]

Now, at New Haven, the theory of Congregational Polity created by Mr. Horton was given triumphant expression. Hence it is necessary to set forth his address in some detail, beginning with its introductory thrust.

"I have come to look forward to meetings of the General Council with eagerness. They give opportunity, which to some of us is becoming dearer with the years, of meeting old friends. They open a shining door to new and growing friendships. They provide an arena for the lusty clash of thoughts as we take the lists for truth. They become a mirror, in the person of our guests and members from afar and in the interest that we embrace, of the whole complex, baffling, and infinitely alluring world of people.

"Dismiss your fears, if you have any, of what may happen here. Time and again, as at Claremont just two years ago, we have entered into such a meeting as this in an atmosphere dark with presentiment, but presently, as the hours together have given us understanding, an insight has been lighted in the minds of some one here, another in the mind of some one there, until, the brightness being caught by many, the place has become spiritually ablaze and the shadows faint and few.

. . . . .

"Christ on his throne casts the radiance of eternity upon us. Here Dr. R. W. Dale's oft-quoted words have their occasion:

"'To be at a church meeting, apart from any prayer that is offered, any hymn that is sung, any words that are spoken, is for me one of the chief means of grace. To know that I am surrounded by men and women who dwell in God, who have received the Holy Ghost, with whom I am to share the eternal. . .life to come, this is blessedness.'

"Here the secular is transfigured. When one remembers that he meets here with others upon whom the light of immortality already begins to shine, he is rescued from the false belief that this is a mere political gathering. It is a political gathering, to be sure, but how different the politics of immortal souls from that of time-servers!

"Because Christ is on his throne, our traffic here is not with petty compromise or sly personal achievement but with the things of souls—truth, and justice, and whatsoever things are lovely and of good report. In so far as we are believers, we are on a search for verities on which the whole weight of belief may be based, and we have no stomach for the shifts and dodges that are virtues in some parliaments.

"It is from the spiritual experience of a meeting of the Church like this that our polity derives. That polity is not an invention of our forefathers. They did not spin abstractions, weave them together into a pattern, and call the result Congregationalism. They did not choose Congregationalism as one picks out a hat to wear or a car to ride in. Congregationalism chose them: that is to say, they found the association with Christ in the congregation of the Christian friends so rich, so unrefusable, so requisite to the more abundant life that they became exultant slaves to it. Once having known, seen, felt the congregation of believers as the throne room of Christ, they knew they could not be happy in any polity which even suggested that this was not the heart of Christ's kingdom on earth. From their early conventicles in London they went out with a sure step to witness to their discovery before the whole world as those who had washed in a mystical Pool of Siloam saying, 'Whereas we were blind, now we see.'

"Let me set before you in brief propositions—no ninety-five Lutheran theses this afternoon, but just six—certain phases of our polity which grow directly out of this experience of encountering Christ in the congregation precisely as he said we might—where two or three are gathered together in his name. I do this because the subject of polity has been happily so much to the fore during the last years and because it is likely to arrest our attention to this meeting. Indeed I hope it will, and accordingly make my contribution to it.

"I. *The Church of Jesus Christ is one.*

. . . .

"II. *The Congregational Christian Churches are one.*

. . . .

"III. *The Church is before all Officers, and may be without them.*

. . . .

"IV. *Each congregation represents the Catholic Church.*

. . . .

"V. *Every congregation is bound to every other by ties of mutual recognition.*

. . . .

"As an instrument to set forth our mutual recognitions of each other's rights and responsibilities, it is proposed that at this meeting you appoint a committee which, cooperating with subcommittees in various parts of the country, would begin work on a constitution for our communion. For over a hundred years we have been operating on precedent, on a constitution not written. But the need is being felt for something more definite. The demand is coming from many quarters.

"a. Dr. Fifield's Committee is asking for a committee to determine the powers of the General Council. Our whole denominational life moves in a conciliar system, to which the General Council is central. To describe our Council's relationship to the churches, therefore, would be to write a denominational constitution.

"b. The Board of Review of the Council for Social Action has spoken of a constitution as a major need of the communion.

"c. Some of our best thinkers, like Dr. Hugh Vernon White, have asked for a constitution.

"d. One of the first questions a layman asks, as he begins interestedly to enquire into the structure of our denomination, is as to how our parts are constitutionally related to each other.

"e. For the first two hundred years of our existence we had a constitution—the Cambridge Platform, which John Wise, that apostle of liberty, regarded as the bed rock of our freedoms.

"f. For decades the Congregational Union of England and Wales, operating under an over-all constitution, has derived only strength from it.

"It will be for you, listening to the voice of him who speaks to the conscience, to decide whether the writing of a constitution, binding only upon those who accept it, is the best means for helping our churches and all our organizations mutually to understand the relationships which have grown up in our highly complicated modern communion.

"VI. *The Church is the instrument through which Christ promises the redemption of the world.*"[16]

Anent Address of Minister

One can have nothing but condemnation for the laudatory remarks about the nature of the Church Meeting in a Congregational Church. The presence of Christ amongst His people gathered by choice as a continuing covenanted people of God is, indeed, a central and cherished Congregational conviction. Dr. R. W. Dale of Birmingham gave this view of a Church Meeting classic expression.

What puzzles and dismays an enquiring mind is the extraordinary leap of illogic by which Dr. Dale's shining words are claimed as a description of the 1954 General Council meeting at New

Haven! We delegates were at least two-thirds first timers. The process of selection *excluded* all who were unable to finance attendance, nearly all who did not have the approval of Conference Superintendents, and all whose vocation prevented taking a week's vacation by choice. The process of selection *included* officials—national, conference, boards and agencies—ministers known to be organizational supporters, a few hardy opponents of either the CC/ER merger or the political, social and economic activities of the Council for Social Action, and a small number of the mediators. Furthermore the Assembly was neither A Church nor THE Church; it was a body of delegates *from* Churches, met in council for a few days, then adjourned. . .in practice dissolved. Nothing could be farther removed from Dr. Dale's conception of a Church, as indeed, was pointed out by President R. H. Stafford of Hartford Seminary at St. Andrews.[17]

Mr. Horton's six points are intended to have, and did have on most delegates, a cumulative impact. All rest on the basically uncongregational claim that the General Council is a Church.

Mr. Horton begins with the oneness of the Church, quoting Dr. P. T. Forsyth out of context. The organizational unification sought by Mr. Horton was the opposite of the spiritual union espoused by Dr. Forsyth. ALL—proponents, opponents and mediators—agreed that the invisible Church of Jesus Christ in all times and climes is ONE. Its oneness is not organizational, though it may be seen in institutions. The "marks" of the Church are (1) the shared spirit of Christ (2) the reincarnation in individual and corporate life of the holiness of God in Christ (3) the wide armed inclusiveness of a fellowship of love not using rules to exclude race, class, creed, culture or code and (4) vitally alive with the awareness of grace, faith, zeal and witness which characterized the twelve disciples.

Mr. Horton next says, "The Congregational Christian Churches are one."[18] Their oneness is akin to that of the Church Universal—PLUS. The "plus" concerns a family identity with shared roots, emphasis on intellectual integrity, education, justice, and service. The leap from CC oneness of family spirit in the Lord to "unified structure of our denominational life"[19] is chasmic. If "This is the basic reason why we are interested in union with the Evangelical and Reformed Church"[20] then the yen is expediential not experiential: it is an organizational convenience rather than a spiritual adventure at the behest of conviction.

Point three wears the garb of appeal to the emergent democracy advanced by the Rev. Thomas Hooker of Hartford. In 1954 access to many of Mr. Hooker's writings was difficult, so perhaps the speaker had not read them. In the 1970's Professor George H. Williams of Harvard University, and colleagues, produced a valuable collection of Mr. Hooker's works.[21] And a number of good analyses have followed, especially that of Professor Frank Shuffelton.[22] But even in 1954 there were available enough source materials to clearly exhibit Mr. Hooker's abhorrence of the kind of Church government championed by Mr. Horton. Mr. Hooker's summary of church polity is well known. Here are the applicable paragraphs,[23] so that the reader may judge personally whether or not Mr. Hooker could properly be quoted in favor of the overall governing constitution called for by Mr. Horton.

"'If the Reader shall demand how far this way of church-proceeding receives approbation by any common concurrence amongst us: I shall plainly and punctually express myself in a word of truth, in these following points, viz.

"'Visible saints are the only true and meet matter, whereof a visible church should be gathered, and confederation is the form.

"'The church as *totum essentiale,* is, and may be, before officers.

"'There is no Presbyteriall church (i.e., a church made up of the elders of many Congregations appointed classickwise, to rule all those Congregations) in the New Testament.

"'A church Congregational is the first subject of the keys.

"'Each congregation completely constituted of all officers, hath sufficient power in herself, to exercise the power of the keys and all church discipline, in all the censures thereof.

. . . . .

"'Consociation of churches should be used, as occasion doth require.

"'Such consociations and synods have allowance to counsel and admonish other churches, as the case may require.

"'And if they grow obstinate in error or sinful miscarriages, they should renounce the right hand of fellowship with them.

"'But they have no power to excommunicate.

"'Nor do their constitutions bind formaliter & juridice.''

Mr. Hooker was expressing more than his personal preference: His manuscript had been examined and approved by a general meeting of Congregational ministers in Cambridge, July, 1645. It is extremely difficult to discern the mind processes by which Mr.

Hooker's views could become the basis for the alien concept that "The essential Church (Council) is before all officers"[24] WHEN "CHURCH" is skewered to mean a national organization. This is exactly what Mr. Hooker denied!

Point four is "Each congregation represents the Catholic Church."[25] It would be hard to find a Congregational thinker of any era who did not agree IF POINT FOUR MEANS the invisible Church Universal. But that's not what is intended here. By some legerdemain, not readily apparent, only the *legal* independence of a Church in a limited sphere is approved, *but* interdependence (if not *dependence*) obtains in the fellowship. By this means what *appears to be* an affirmation of inherent self-completeness becomes an indictment of the General Council's Committee on Free Church Polity and Unity.[26]

> "Because the Committee on Free Church Polity and Unity under the chairmanship of Dr. L. Wendell Fifield has devoted itself with whole-hearted concern and great generosity of time and effort to the studies assigned it by the General Council and because it has sought by such means as were at its disposal to pursue a course at once mediating and educational, I know that as the committee now brings its work to a close you will want to extend to all of its members an expression of gratitude for their services. In my first reading of the report of the committee I seem to detect that it gives weight to the theory that autonomy comes first and fellowship second. I do not feel in it emphasis upon the fundamental Congregational doctrine that fellowship in Christ is the very essence of the Church and freedom comes as part and parcel of that fellowship. If that emphasis is lacking, it should surely be added, for it is not only good historical Congregationalism but is regarded as the gist of our polity by Congregational peoples around the world today. Each congregation represents the whole Church of Christ: this is the nature of our fellowship: we are members one of another."

This extraordinary paragraph criticizes the P&U Report for failure to make fellowship "the fundamental Congregational doctrine," as if the Committee were free to write ITS view of Congregational Polity! *In actual fact* the P&U Report even in the "first reading" of the Minister of the General Council states plainly, "This report describes Congregational Polity as it is currently practiced and does not presume to say whether or not *what is* is *what ought to be.*"[27] Apparently the Minister of the General Council did not feel limited to Congregational Polity as recorded in the basic documents, or as attested by practice throughout the length and breadth of the United States.

Point five is "Every congregation is bound to every other by ties of mutual recognition."[28] This proclamation violates both basic documents and recorded practices. A Church is something quite other than a chance collection gathered in assembly and called a "congregation," as has been pointed out.[29] The word "bound" hardly fits the voluntary nature of all inter-Church and Church-wider-body relationships. The word "recognition" is here used in the specialized, legal, authoritative, binding sense given to it by merger proponents in the Cadman/General Council trial in Judge Steinbrink's court. That meaning is the invention of those seeking, by some means, to secure organic union. This is made clear by Mr. Horton:

> "As an instrument to set forth our mutual recognitions of each other's rights and responsibilities, it is proposed that at this meeting you appoint a committee which, cooperating with subcommittees in various parts of the country, would begin work on a constitution for our communion. For over a hundred years we have been operating on precedent, on a constitution not written. But the need is being felt for something more definite. The demand is coming from many quarters.
>
> "a. Dr. Fifield's Committee is asking for a committee to determine the powers of the General Council. Our whole denominational life moves in a conciliar system, to which the General Council is central. To describe our Council's relationship to the churches, therefore, would be to write a denominational constitution.
>
> "b. The Board of Review of the Council for Social Action has spoken of a constitution as a major need of the communion.
>
> "c. Some of our best thinkers, like Dr. Hugh Vernon White, have asked for a constitution.
>
> "d. One of the first questions a layman asks, as he begins interestedly to enquire into the structure of our denomination, is as to how our parts are constitutionally related to each other.
>
> "e. For the first two hundred years of our existence we had a constitution—the Cambridge Platform, which John Wise, that apostle of liberty, regarded as the bed rock of our freedoms.
>
> "f. For decades the Congregational Union of England and Wales, operating under an over-all constitution, has derived only strength from it.
>
> "It will be for you, listening to the voice of him who speaks to the conscience, to decide whether the writing of a constitution, binding

only upon those who accept it, is the best means for helping our churches and all our organizations mutually to understand the relationships which have grown up in our highly complicated modern communion."[29b]

It is exceedingly difficult to perceive the intricate mind processes by which the brotherly fellowship of Churches could be a demand for an overall constitution! It requires dangerous stretching of the imagination to name our boldest apostle of independent Churches, Rev. John Wise of Ipswich, as the advocate of the Cambridge Platform as a modern governing constitution, which it neither was nor pretended to be.[30] Exactly how could Rev. Hugh Vernon White's plea for ecclesiastical independence and administrative efficiency be a "demand" for "a constitution for our communion" when Dr. White specified that he meant ecclesiastical freedom and administrative machinery responsive to the churches? And by what reasoning could the request of the P&U Report for a commission to study the constitutional problems be taken as a "demand" for a "constitution"?

Point six is "The Church is the instrument through which Christ promises the redemption of the world,"[31] and that may be the key to the meaning behind the address.

Behind the Address

The address roused the proponents of merger to fever pitch; for them it was the brave new gospel. The opponents were angered and skeptical. The mediators were shocked and puzzled.

Many years later, the address seems understandable in the context of the Council Minister's activities from 1938 to 1954, especially 1948-1954.

Conferences, committee meetings, and celebrations in Lund, Stockholm, Geneva, Oxford, Beirut, Lucknow, Australia, New Zealand, the Central Committee of the WCC at Toronto; the ICC World Assembly at St. Andrews and the summer 1954 Evanston Meeting of the World Council of Churches contributed to the content of the address. So did the court cases, first in Judge Steinbrink's NY courtroom, and then in the court of appeals.

Toronto should have been a guide toward federation of free Churches. At the WCC Central Committee meeting in Toronto the ancient Orthodox Churches of the East insisted, as a precondition of their participation, that the World Council of Churches was NOT and NEVER COULD BE a *Church*. By this insistence they inadvertently allied themselves with the Free Churches!! But of this there is nary an echo in the New Haven address.

After the New Haven General Council, came the WCC assembly at Evanston. To it the "churchly issue" raised at Toronto was referred and the position of the Orthodox Churches was adopted by the World Council of Churches. If one takes seriously Mr. Horton's final point "the redemption of the world," as I am persuaded he did, then it seems important that he be able to appear and speak in the councils of the WCC at Evanston as the "Minister of the Congregational Christian Church," something he had aspired to be since at least 1940.[32]

IF the Congregational Christian Churches of the United States could lead the world's Congregationalists to accept themselves as "a Church", then, might there not be real hope that the World Council of Churches might become "THE CHURCH", through which the redemption of the world might be wrought.

Like all the mediators, I was appalled by the content of the New Haven address, and equally, by captious, even scurrilous, interpretations of it. I am unable to see Mr. Horton as a scheming montebank; a characterization which does not explain his words or deeds. The interpretation suggested here seems to me to do more justice to his broad vision of world service, his sense of *making* history, and his profound desire to fly a flag called Congregationalism from a lofty mast to which to rally the Christian peoples of the world.

Polity and Unity Report Presented

About midmorning on Thursday, June 24, the Rev. L. Wendell Fifield, chairman, presented the Polity and Unity Report, stressing the unanimity reached by 21 persons of widely divergent views. A prolonged debate ensued directed to the words "approved", "received" and "referred."[33] At 12:08 p.m. the meeting was recessed 'till 4:15 p.m.

Between noon and 4:15 p.m. Wendell and I reworded the six sections of the recommendation. With indefatigable patience he sought out proponents and opponents, produced acceptable language, and offered a substitute motion covering all previous suggestions. Mr. Ronald Bridges agreed to second the motion, and did. As accepted by the General Council the recommendation read:[34]

263

"1.   That this study be received and one copy sent to each church and that on a proper financial basis it be made generally available for study; and that on the cover and on the title page there be printed this statement: 'This report is sent to the churches for their information and study only. It has neither been approved nor disapproved by the Executive Committee or the General Council.'

"2.   That the legal statement prepared by Wood, Werner, France and Tully be sent to the churches for their study with the report of the Committee on Free Church Polity and Unity. It shall have on its cover this statement: 'This opinion of our counsel is sent to the churches for their information.'

"3.   That the further use of the study be directed by the Executive Committee of the General Council of the Congregational Christian Churches.

"4.   That provisions be made by the Executive Committee for the preservation of the considerable bodies of source materials gathered by the Committee, and that these materials and this report be made available to the committees and commissions studying Congregational Christian polity and considering church union.

"5.   That a special committee be elected by the Executive Committee to study the question of the powers of the General Council and to report at the General Council meeting in 1956. That this committee shall not only study the problem for itself but shall also set up and oversee study of the problem throughout our fellowship. It should be noted that such material bearing on this subject as this report contains is directed entirely to the subject of unity and does not constitute a complete study of this vital subject, (Mr. Fifield pointed out that if the proposed 'committee on the constitutional problem' were set up, that committee would serve the purposes of this recommendation.)

"6.   That the Committee on Free Church Polity and Unity be discharged at the close of the 1954 General Council. It is understood that members of the Committee will be glad thereafter to give whatever assistance they can."

Once again L. Wendell Fifield had demonstrated his tremendous skill and deep devotion. The accomplishments of the Committee on Free Church Polity and Unity are a monument to him.

When the Rev. Arthur D. Gray, chairman of the Executive Committee of the General Council "expressed appreciation and deep gratitude to the Committee on Free Church Polity and Unity" the assembly's enthusiastic approval of his motion was a fitting tribute to a great man.

Thursday afternoon's verbal fireworks were not over! The Executive Committee chairman immediately followed the Polity and Unity Report vote by introducing "a resolution to provide for a study commission on a constitution for the fellowship and moved its adoption."[35]

A torrent of words followed, with the Rev. Malcolm Burton demanding that the Executive Committee "keep its word, as mailed to the Churches on April 27, 1954."[36] Rev. Arthur Gray vigorously denied the allegation. Rev. David G. Coldwell of Colorado and the Rev. David H. Beach of New Haven called for immediate passage of the resolution. Rev. Harry R. Butman and Mr. Kenneth W. Greenawalt of New York protested both the content and the timing of the resolution. A vote was called for. The 383 ayes and 250 noes fell short of the necessary two-thirds to close off debate, but it was evident that only a sense of fair play motivated many noes. The Council was effectively controlled by the executives, the committees and their allies.

In a sensitive effort to ease tension and remove from the proposal the assumption that the General Council possessed the power to write a "constitution for the fellowship," one of the mediators, the Rev. W. A. Keith of Michigan offered an amendment. A merger opponent moved to table both resolution and amendment but lost by an overwhelming voice vote. Mr. Keith's motion was then voted down. Mr. Burton then proposed a substitute motion "that a commission to study the constitutional problem as it relates to the General Council and the fellowship be authorized, the members of which would be appointed and other details dealt with by the Executive Committee.[37] In short order the Chairman of the Executive Committee indicated that the substitute motion was acceptable and it was voted by voice.

As if to keep tempers simmering Rev. Charles C. Merrill, Chairman of the Commission on Interchurch Relations and Christian Unity then presented a resolution "to proceed with the union with the Evangelical and Reformed Church."[38] By vote this was referred to the Executive Committee, whose letter of April 4, 1954 had given assurance that there would be no "action on the" CC/ER merger at New Haven!

The Friday Merger Wrangel

Overnight there had been much consultation among proponents, opponents and some mediators.

Mr. Merrill re-introduced his resolution as follows:

"WHEREAS the final judgment of the New York State Court of Appeals in the case of the Cadman Church v. the General Council has now been rendered; and

"WHEREAS the Executive Committee of the General Council has arranged a meeting for the coming fall with the corresponding body (known as the General Council) of the Evangelical and Reformed Church;

"THEREFORE BE IT RESOLVED, in view of these facts, that the General Council of the Congregational Christian Churches of the United States, meeting in New Haven, Connecticut June 23-30, 1954.

"1) *Reaffirms* its earnest desire as expressed in the first resolution at the meeting of the General Council held at Claremont, Calif., in June, 1952, to continue 'to look forward to a united fellowship of the Evangelical and Reformed and the Congregational Christian communions'; and to that end

"2) *Renews* its instructions as previously given to the Executive Committee in the subsequent resolutions adopted by the Claremont General Council of 1952 with regard to the Union of the Congregational Christian Churches with the Evangelical and Reformed Church, so far as they still are applicable."[39]

Mr. George E. Gullen, Jr., of Michigan moved that the resolution be postponed indefinitely after which vociferous debate took place accompanied by noisy crowd reactions. Many were impatient, thwarted and angry. Rev. Bedros Baharian of Massachusetts called for a close to debate, and it was so voted. Then in rapid fire order an end to debate on Mr. Merrill's motion was called for and voted; on the CC/ER merger vote a massive chorus cried "yes." No count was made, but I doubt that there were more than 200 noes, if that many.

Quick to take advantage of the mood of impatience, the Executive Committee then reported adversely on Mr. Burton's proposed amendment to the By-laws concerning the method of electing secretaries. Three brief comments supported the Committee, debate cut off was called for and voted, down by loud "yeas." It was difficult to estimate how many of the 1494 registered voting delegates were present but there wasn't the slightest doubt as to the thorough control of the Council by those favoring the CC/ER merger.

Social Action

At least one major issue in the acrimonious social action debate centered on Congregational Polity. Can a wider church-body "speak for" the entire fellowship? If the spate of important statements swept through the Council during the afternoons of Saturday, Monday, and Wednesday do not "speak for the denomination," then, what value do they have? The mediators answer, The Council's votes express the majority opinion of those present and voting; beyond that their weight derives from their worth.

To the New Haven Council majority this was inadequate, and it is not clear that the polity implications mattered to them. What counted was the "voice of the church" speaking to crucial social, economic, racial, political and technical issues of contemporary life.

Many, if not most, of the mediators agreed wholeheartedly with the noble purposes of the social action resolutions. The overpowering of Council minorities by the majority, and the flouting of individual conscience appeared to contradict the high ends espoused.

The "Association"

From the perspective of twenty-eight years there would seem to be no sound precedent in history, no authority in document, and no example in practice for the trial of an Association by any wider body. The Associations were formed by and are responsible to the Churches, certainly not to the General Council.

The acids of power had eaten away the initiative of the Churches. The result was an unseemly rejection of a Church formed Association on the grounds that a Conference had not "recognized" it. Once again the Mansfield Theses, which had never been presented to the Churches, were blandly decreed to be "Congregational Polity," which they were not and never had been.

As long ago as 1890, the Rev. Alonzo H. Quint, one of the stalwarts of the National Council, stated Congregational Polity regarding Churches and Associations. He points out that the council of 1892 "Resolved, That affiliation with our denomination of churches not now upon our rolls should be welcomed upon the basis of common evangelical faith, substantial Congregational polity and free communion of Christians, without regard to forms or minor differences."[40]

To make doubly sure his concept of Congregational Polity is clear, Dr. Quint says, "The fellowship of the Congregational churches is. . .one of sentiment. They neither need nor desire a formal external authority. . . . Indifferent to non-essentials, and reverential to conscientious convictions, they hold that no true unity can exist except by the spontaneous affiliation of Christians. Christian love is the bond of union. . . . The churches include in their (Associations). . .those., who in faith and order voluntarily recognize the claims of such unity."[41] Congregational Churches "recognize" each other ONLY by voluntary self-affiliation moved by a shared faith, love, and polity. The idea of an Association as a law making legislature, a judge, or police power enforcing "standards" is totally foreign to the genius of the Congregational Way.

A Subtle Offensive

At New Haven the introduction of fraternal visitors was not confined to the customary opening session. Presentations occurred daily, compelling the Council to be aware of organized ecumenicity. *Wednesday* presented fraternal delegates from England, France, Holland, Japan, Italy and the Philippines. *Thursday* morning greetings were read from the Armenian Churches and from the Congregational Union of England and Wales. *Friday* afternoon there were greetings from L'Eglise Chritienne Missionaire Belge. *Saturday* the director of Accueil Fraternal in France gave an address. *Sunday* afternoon Miss Dorothy J. Biggs of the International Congregational Council addressed "all women." *Monday* the American Board presented its work round-the-world. *Tuesday* Miss Biggs addressed the Council, greetings of the Remonstrant Brotherhood were read; it was voted that "Our Christian World Mission" be the 1954-1956 denominational emphasis; and Dr. W. A. Visser 't Hooft of the World Council of Churches was the featured evening speaker. *Wednesday* a lengthy resolution on "Free Church Contributions to the Ecumenical Movement through Councils of Churches" was debated and referred to the Executive Committee for action at the 1956 Council.

Finally the Council voted to authorize the Executive Committee to make one resolution out of the following two.[42]

"Free Church Contributions to the Ecumenical Movement Through Councils of Churches

"1.   The General Council of Congregational Christian Churches rejoices in the unique part played by the churches of its fellowship in the formation of city, state, regional, national and world councils of churches and in the rapid rise and growing strength of these bodies.

"2.   We would remind our churches that the fundamental contribution of the free churches to the basic philosophy of these councils has been the principle of 'unity without uniformity.'

"3. We would affirm as our conviction born out of centuries of experimentation and experience that Christian togetherness can achieve historic endurance only through a freedom which grants a mutual respect for differences. Growing and lasting unity in Christ must be of the spirit.

"4. We would commend the Remonstrant Brotherhood of the Netherlands and other member churches of the World Council of Churches which have a concern for a change in the 'basis' formula of the World Council of Churches.

"5. We would ask our delegates to the Evanston Assembly of the World Council of Churches to request that the matter of the 'basis' be kept open for further study.

"Proposed Substitute Resolution

"1. The Congregational Christian Churches of the United States have been blessed by their participation in the World Council of Churches through many years.

"2. Furthermore, the World Council has achieved, under the Holy Spirit, an extraordinary and effective working community consisting of some 160 Christian communions.

"3. Again, that cooperation has, in large part, been dependent upon a mutual acceptance of the Biblical and apostolic faith in Jesus Christ—a faith which we have affirmed in many documents throughout our history.

"4. Therefore, this General Council reiterates its own allegiance to that faith and recognizes the desirability of maintaining in substance the prevailing theological basis of the World Council of Churches, regardless of the merits or demerits of the present wording and changes which may later be made in it."

"Editorial changes," chiefly the inserting of "or were adopted by, a polity" in the following resolution changed a declaration of authority into a statement of response to God's leading. The resolution titled "Purposeful Polity"[43] was as follows:

"Purposeful Polity

"WHEREAS our spiritual ancestors, in their concern for the free working of the Spirit of God in their midst, adopted, or were adopted by, a polity for the ordering of their church affairs through which they believed God could most effectively speak, and

"WHEREAS their concern was not primarily polity, and

"WHEREAS the witness of the church is strongest when least conscious of polity,

269

"BE IT RESOLVED THAT we seek the guidance of the Holy
Spirit in this our day, to develop and exercise such understanding of
polity as shall best express the Spirit of Christ among us, and so
order our affairs that we may be united on ever wider fronts with
other welcoming bodies, not thinking of polity as the end in itself."

At the 1954 General Council it was impossible to escape the
drums beating the march of organized ecumenicity.

Beyond the Council Sessions

Our overview recounts the public consideration of polity by the
New Haven Council. But the real debate on the Report of the Committee on Free Church Polity and Unity had two additional loci.
First, the Polity Report was uppermost in the daily discussions
beyond Woolsey Hall. Second, the Report was tested in special
afternoon seminars on Thursday, Friday and Monday. The seminar
sessions were so seminal that the next chapters are devoted to
them.

CHAPTER 6 NOTES

1. 1946 Advance Reports, General Council, NY, p. 21.
2. Ibid, p. 73.
3. 1950 Advance Reports, General Council, NY, p. 12 ff.
4. Ibid, pp. 26-27.
5. 1950 Advance Reports, op. cit., p. 61.
6. 1952 Advance Reports, General Council, NY, p. 68.
7. Ibid, p. 25.
8. Ibid, p. 72.
9. 1954 Advance Reports, General Council, NY, pp. 28-29.
10. Ibid, p. 29.
11. 1954 Minutes, *General Council,* NY n.d., p. 13.
12. 1954 Council Minutes, op. cit., p. 16.
13. Ibid, p. 17.
14. The Chicago Theological Seminary Register, Chicago, 1953, p. 12.
15. Ibid, p. 14.
16. 1954 Minutes, op. cit., pp. 76-82.
17. *Supra.*
18. 1954 Minutes, op. cit., p. 71.
19. Ibid, p. 71.
20. Ibid, p. 72.
21. George H. Williams, et al., *Thomas Hooker,* Writings, 1626-33, 1975 Harvard Univ. Press, Cambridge.
22. Frank Shuffelton, *Thomas Hooker,* 1977 Princeton Univ. Press, Princeton,
NJ.
23. Printed in A. E. Dunnings, *Congregationalists,* 1894 J. A. Hill & Co., NY, pp.
141-142.

24. 1954 Minutes, op. cit., p. 79.
25. Ibid, p. 79.
26. 1954 Minutes, op. cit., p. 80.
27. Free Church Polity & Unity, 1954 General Council, NY, p. 38.
28. 1954 Minutes, op. cit., p. 80.
29. *Supra,* esp. Chapter 4.
29b. 1954 Minutes, op. cit., p. 81.
30. *Supra,* esp. Chapters 2 & 3.
31. 1954 Minutes, op. cit., p. 81.
32. 1940 Minutes, General Council, NY, p. 59.
33. 1954 General Council Minutes, op. cit., p. 18.
34. Ibid, p. 19.
35. 1954 General Council Minutes, op. cit., p. 19.
36. Arthur Gray to the Churches, 4-27-54.
37. 1954 General Council Minutes, op. cit., p. 20.
38. Ibid, p. 20.
39. 1954 General Council Minutes, op. cit., pp. 21-22.
40. Alonzo H. Quint, in A. E. Dunning, *Congregationalists in America,* 1894, J. A. Hill & Co., NY, p. 524.
41. Ibid, p. 493.
42. 1954 General Council Minutes, op. cit., p. 48.
43. 1954 General Council Minutes, op. cit., p. 38.

CHAPTER SEVEN

Testing Time

Three two-hour seminars at the 1954 General Council were testing time for the Report of the Committee on Free Church Polity and Unity. Chairman, Rev. L. Wendell Fifield presided. I sat beside him with two bulging briefcases containing all documents and all respondent replies, in case they should be needed. They were.

Thursday at two the first session opened with an immediate upthrust of hands, many waving copies of the Legal Opinion of Wood, Werner, France and Tully. Wendell put his hand over the microphone and said to me, "Mr. Loren Wood, the General Council attorney, is seated about half way back in the aisle seat to your extreme right."

Agent or Not?

Rev. Roy Helfenstein was recognized. He berated the Committee for not following exactly what he had written in his letters to me, and ended by saying, "This is what I mean. The lawyers say the General Council, Boards, Conferences and Associations are NOT *agents* of the churches. This report says they are. After *four years* study we are handed a report which doesn't stand up to the law. Who's responsible for this?"

Wendell looked at me. I nodded.

"I'll ask Dr. Gray to reply to Dr. Helfenstein," he announced.

"The Congregational Polity Committee is responsible for this Report, though every sentence has been scrutinized by every member of the entire Polity and Unity Committee."

Dr. Helfenstein interrupted, "What we want to know is, how you bungled the statement on 'agent'. This booklet says your Report is all wrong."

"Doctor, I'll let you judge that for yourself. Turn your 'Advance Reports' to the AMENDMENT to the By Laws PROPOSED by the American Board and the Home Board. By Laws, Section IV 'National Societies' in paragraph 1 relating to the American Board reads, 'This Board *shall be the agency of the Congregational Christian Churches* for the extension of Christ's Kingdom abroad.' Paragraph 2 says the same thing regarding the Board of Home Missions: 'This Board *shall be the agency of the Congregational Christian Churches. . . .*'"

"The Conference constitutions. The constitutions themselves are open for examination. The constitutions say:

New York: "To promote the general interest and agencies of the Congregational Churches in New York."

Minnesota: The Conference is "the agency of the Congregational Christian Churches of the state for the accomplishment of the work they wish to do co-operatively."

Iowa: The Conference is established "to be the agent of and instrument for carrying on such. . .work as the Churches may desire to undertake in common."

Kansas: "to promote the general interests and agencies of the Congregational and Christian Churches of Kansas, to be their instrument for carrying on such religious, educational and philanthropic work as they may desire to undertake in common. . ."

Montana: "to be the agent and instrument of the Congregational Christian Churches of Montana for carrying on. . . ."

Washington: Conference object is "the coordination under one management of the general interests of the churches by means of agencies constituted and controlled by the churches themselves through representation in this body."

Wyoming: "to be the agent and instrument of the Congregational Christian Churches of Wyoming. . ."

North Dakota: "to be the agent and instrument of the Congregational Christian Churches of North Dakota. . ."

Utah: "to be the instrument of the Utah Congregational Churches for the carrying on of whatever work the churches may desire to undertake in common. . ."

Pennsylvania: "the coordination under one management of the general interests of the churches by means of agencies constituted and controlled by the churches themselves. . ."

Oregon: "to be the agent and instrument of the Congregational Churches of Oregon for the carrying on. . ."

Missouri: "by means of agencies constituted and controlled by the churches themselves. . ."

The gentleman beside Dr. Helfenstein stood up and held up his hand. I waited. He spoke "How many more do you have to read?"

"There are 39 Conferences, but one doesn't have a constitution, Oklahoma-Texas. I've read 12. There are 26 more."

"How many of them say the conference is the agent of the Churches?"

"All but the Southeast and Puerto Rico say the Conference is the agent, instrument, exists to promote the work of, or some similar phrase. The wordings differ but all indicate that the Churches consider the wider bodies their agents. Of course, there are over 140 replies in the *Practice* section too."

"Let's get on with the seminar."

I sat down. Wendell took the podium.

Administering the Sacraments

A belligerent voice demanded, "This #4 on page 23 of the Polity Report says a Church can give *anybody* the right to administer the sacraments. I never heard of such a thing. It's absurd."

Wendell stepped back and I replied,

"In Connecticut, by state law, even a marriage can be performed by any member elected by a Church. So far as Baptism and the Lord's Supper are concerned, there are Churches in isolated areas in nearly every section of the country which provide for this exceptional contingency. The First Congregational Church of South Hadley, Massachusetts customarily requests a deacon to preside at communion once a year, just to symbolize the priesthood of all believers. If you wish me to list each instance it will take some time, but I'll do it."

"Never mind. This is worse. #8 on page 2 of the Report says a Church may ordain its own minister. I challenge you. Is there *anywhere* in the United States *any* Church that does this?"

"Of course there is, otherwise it wouldn't be in the Report. Half a minute and I'll find it. Here we are. The report of the Oxford County Association in Maine is signed by Mrs. Alice McGouldrick of Dixfield, Maine. The only provision in that Association for ordination is by each Church. In the Practice section it is reported that most Churches ask neighbors to share in the ordination. Then, here's a fairly long report by Dr. Thomas Anderson of Atlanta: he says the practice of ordination by a single Church is a real problem in the Southeast. In Robinson County, Illinois there is only one minister who was ordained in any other way than by the Church itself."

Polity Report Versus Lawyers Opinion

At this point my eye caught sight of Mr. Loren Wood, gathering up his papers to exit, so I interjected, "Mr. Wood, you are the attorney for the General Council. Your name is signed to the Legal Opinion. Would you like to explain your claim that the Report is inaccurate? Better still! Here are the constitutions of all State Conferences, and of about one-third of the Association constitutions. Come up and examine them. Do they, or do they not, state that the Conferences and Associations are 'agents' of the Churches?"

All eyes focused on Mr. Wood. He hesitated not an instant, but walked straight out of the auditorium. So far as I could hear he made no comment.

But one woman near the front stood up, with blazing eyes and cried, "This is impertinent. Challenging Mr. Wood like that! It's cheap grand standing! It's shameful."

As she stopped to get a breath I inquired, "If I am incorrect, Madam, please prove it by the facts. Our business here is serious."

"I refuse to be spoken to in such a fashion."

"I'm sorry, Madam. Could you direct your criticism to the facts please?"

Suddenly she calmed.

"Young man," she said, "how do *you* have 'facts' that one of the finest New York lawyers doesn't have?" She sat down triumphantly and there was a smattering of applause.

I looked at Wendell. He just smiled his deep beneficent smile and said quietly, "Go on, you can't do any more harm!"

"Ladies and gentlemen," I began. "This question is embarrassing, very embarrassing. I understand from Dr. Fifield that Mr. Loren Wood, like his father before him, is a distinguished member of the New York Bar. I am not a lawyer. I did not study to become a lawyer. I do not *wish* to be a lawyer. I am a minister because God called me, and a kindly people invited me to serve them.

"The fundamental defect of the Legal Opinion may be stated quite simply. It is not the work of a scholar.

"The Legal Opinion begins with preconceived theories and then attacks Polity Report findings which do not correspond to these assumptions. A scholar begins with the basic documents of

276

Churches, Associations, Conferences, General Council, National Boards and other wider bodies recording *what the documents themselves say.* A scholar gathers representative statements of practice from experts in all sectors of the land, from knowledgeable ministers and members, Association registrars, Conference Superintendents and from General Council, Board and agency officers. Persons consulted were not *selected by the researchers* but by the Superintendents and the General Council Executive Committee. The Polity Report lists the names of the respondents on pages 38 to 40. What is recorded is the testimony of a broad spectrum of knowledgeable officers, most of whom have had many years of intimate involvement on Association, Conference or national level, or all three.

"The Legal Opinion was submitted to no Congregational body for scrutiny and revision. The Polity Report was THRICE submitted (1) the Documents section to the 1952 General Council, (2) the Documents and a first draft of the Practice sections to ALL respondents and panels including ALL Superintendents, (3) The final Practice section was revised to accord with responses and was then re-submitted to all respondents and panels. *In addition* each and every phrase; often, each and every word, was studied by the Congregational Polity Committee, and by the entire Committee on Free Church Polity and Unity. I have the manuscripts at each stage, which prove conclusively that the Polity Report was reviewed and revised, not once, but *at least five times.* THE ONLY 'AUTHORITY' POSSESSED BY THE 'LEGAL OPINION' IS THE 'OPINION' OF TWO LAWYERS WHO HAD NOT READ THE BASIC DOCUMENTS, AND WHO HAD NOT SEEN THE VOLUMINOUS REPORTS ON CONTEMPORARY CONGREGATIONALISM.

"On the one hand stands the only in-depth scholarly study of Congregational Polity ever made in the United States: the product of 21 dedicated searchers for truth, with the participation of 140 persons of exceptional knowledge.

"On the other hand stands an opinion with no basis in Congregational history, basic documental study, or research into contemporary Congregational practice.

"The Legal Opinion proclaims its preconceived bias even in details of word usage. Beginning in the second paragraph of the 'cover letter' to Rev. Arthur D. Gray, Chairman of the General Council Executive Committee, CAPITALS are reserved for *A*ssociations, *C*onferences, *G*eneral *C*ouncil, and the *B*oards, with a small 'c' for the 'churches'!! Throughout the Legal Opinion the gathered Church of Jesus Christ is downgraded, restricted, and defined as 'local'. John Wesley's aphorism 'the world is my parish' is beyond the scope of the Legal Opinion. In utter defiance of the charters, by-laws, rules, and established usage, wider bodies are declared irresponsible to the Churches to which they owe their origin, their continuance, their commission, and their support.

"The lady's question goes to the heart of this discussion. The Committee on Free Church Polity and Unity was charged by the 1950 General Council to make an exhaustive study of Polity and Unity. This is what we have done. The Committee was NOT charged with a legal review of Congregational Polity. The lawyers panel *was* requested to provide opinions. Dr. Fifield personally invited Mr. Loren Wood to assist the Committee. Mr. Wood refused on grounds that a court case (Cadman Church against General Council) was pending. When the pending case had been decided, Mr. Wood continued to refuse. The central question is, Are we in search of the spiritual, religious and actual bases of Congregational Polity, OR, Are we seeking a legal ground on which to act in the CC/ER Merger?"

To my great surprise there was scattered applause.

Dr. Fifield moved quickly, "Suppose we ask specific questions directed to the Report. Let us begin with both Document and Practice sections regarding the Churches."

It was past 4:00 o'clock and someone called attention to this, so the meeting recessed 'till Friday. It took at least ten minutes for the auditorium to empty and for persons with comments or questions to talk to us. Then Wendell said "I'm glad *you* were answering those questions. . ." he hesitated, almost in meditation, "If most of the emotion has been vented, it may be that we can turn these meetings into a real sharing of experience. Little was accomplished this afternoon. There was no positive contribution." He was thinking aloud, so I kept quiet. "There must be a better way to conduct this seminar. There has to be. Let's meet early to-morrow after we've slept on it." And he was gone.

I met Rev. William Keith on my way to the Taft Hotel. Bill commented astutely, "Henry, the problem isn't the Polity Report. A lot of prominent people like Al Penner, Cliff Simpson, Truman Douglass and Doug Horton already have their minds made up. What the pro merger people hoped for from the Polity and Unity Committee was a way to do what they want to do." "Bill," I replied, "You may be right. You're a keen observer. . . Would you do something for me to-morrow?"

"I'd have to know what you wanted before I committed myself."

"Sit in the middle of the next seminar. Afterwards, tell me what we're doing wrong, and what people are saying."

"Why?"

"We are probably going to try a different approach. I'd like to know if we have found a useful tact."

"Oh sure," was the answer, "I'll do *that*. Just don't involve me in the Report. That's not my *thing*."

Into the Depths

Friday, June 25, 1954 at two o'clock the Chairman suggested to the seminar of about 75 persons that attention seemed to focus on the Legal Opinion. He reviewed the lack of constructive exchange on Thursday, and invited suggestions as to how best to proceed.

I think it was the Rev. Roy Helfenstein who spoke up, saying, "Since interest centered on the Legal Opinion, why not discuss *that*, it may be more important than the Report?"

Several members of the Polity and Unity Committee objected, since the seminar's theme was the Report. Both Wendell and I had examined the Legal Opinion with great care. I believed we could and should answer every point in it. Wendell thought this procedure would lead to nothing but argument. Therefore I was unprepared when he announced, "The Chair will entertain questions or comments directed to the first two paragraphs of the Legal Opinion."[1]

"We address ourselves primarily to the factual and legal findings contained in Chapters IV, 3 through IV, 6, which appear to be the premises for many of the conclusions which follow and which accordingly constitute the heart of the Report.

"The Report contains statements in fields other than the legal phases of Congregational polity which we do not pass upon. We desire to confine ourselves to the legal relations to each other of the churches, Associations, Conferences, Boards and General Council raised by the Report. In this connection it is noted that no meetings of the Panel of Executives or Superintendents were held and also that 'no meeting of the legal panel has been held' and the Committee 'has not been able to make a thorough study of the legal methods.'"

Someone queried, "Why weren't meetings held for Executives, Superintendents and for the legal panel?" Dr. Fifield replied, "I met with the Executives personally. Superintendents Minton and Babcock compiled the Superintendent's Report. I personally met with Mr. Wood: but both he and other lawyers advised us it was inappropriate for them to participate while cases were pending in court. Attorney Edwin Williams was a member of the Polity and Unity Committee and shared fully in its work."

"What happened to the Superintendent's Report?" demanded a lady in the second row. Wendell nodded. "Madam, it's here. It was used in compiling the very first draft of the Documents Report and also the Practice Report. All letters from Superintendents Minton and Babcock, as chairmen, are also here."

The lady did not give up easily! "What was done with the letters?"

"They were used in refining successive drafts of the Reports."

She persisted, "Then, how could it happen that the Legal Opinion says no meetings were held?"

"That, Madam, is out of my venue. The Legal Opinion authors did not, EVER, inquire whether or not there were Superintendent's Reports or Executive's letters. I am unable to answer your question, but the facts are verifiable, if you care to examine the reports and letters right now."

There was a momentary pause, then a thoughtful man stood and inquired, "What is meant by 'a thorough study of legal methods'?"

Dr. Fifield replied, "I wrote that phrase in the 'covering letter': it is not in the Report itself. What I meant is explained in the preceding paragraph. The two paragraphs have to be read together.[2]

"Because the litigation in the Cadman case, which inevitably dealt with many of the legal points involved in the work of the Committee, has extended over most of the period of the Committee's work, it has been impossible to get the answers to many legal questions involved in this study. The lawyers composing the legal panel in the main doubted that they should express opinions with regard to legal matters until the final legal word relative to the Cadman case had been spoken by the Courts. Therefore, no meeting of the legal panel has been held. However, a number of the members of the panel acting purely in a personal and unofficial capacity did furnish helpful suggestions at various points.

"This report, therefore, confines itself primarily to the statement of principles and polity of Congregationalism and to general considerations about the ecumenical movement and our place in it, rather than to the application of these principles and this polity to specific instances. The Committee regrets that its work was limited by this situation and that therefore, it has not been able to make a thorough study of the legal methods. It feels, however, that the General Council can at any future time use this report and apply its principles to specific issues and actions."

When Wendell finished I asked if I might add. He nodded.

I began, "The Legal Opinion makes the members of your Committee on Free Church Polity and Unity very sad. I have alluded to the absence of scholarship. But there are two more basic considerations. First, it is sad when two uninformed persons permit their opinions to cause consternation in this General Council, and in our fellowship. Second, the Legal Opinion addresses 'the factual and legal findings'[3] supposed to be presented in the Report. Then 'the legal phases'[4] are made the basis for the entire Legal Opinion.

"Congregationalism has never been, and is not now, based on legalities. It was precisely *against* legalities that Congregationalists protested. The test of validity for Congregational Polity is not civil law but Christian conviction. There are no relations of Churches apart from the gathered company of faithful followers of Jesus Christ. There are no 'legal phases' of Congregational Polity which take precedence over the voluntary covenanted, continuing body of believers. It is the presence of the Spirit of God in Christ which unifies Congregational Churches; our unity does not depend upon the General Council, Conference, or Association. The Congregational Church is quite incidentally an organization; it is basically a band of believers whose only headquarters is heaven. The one foundation of Congregational Polity is the God and Father of our Lord Jesus Christ. It is futile to posit supposed legalities as the basis of the Congregational Christian fellowship, and there is no support whatsoever for this heresy in the Documents or Contemporary Practice of our Churches on any level—local, associational, conference or national."

"That was a speech," said Chairman Fifield. "Let's try to keep both questions and answers as brief as possible so that everyone may be heard. Could we address the third paragraph of the Legal Opinion.[5] As we do I want to report that disagreements were talked over 'till changes in wording of the Report was unanimous. At the very end, one person refrained from voting to approve the Report as a whole. I state that to set the record straight. The Minutes attest the fact."

"We understand the Report will be filed with the General Council without being submitted for its approval, because there are many areas of disagreement within the Committee itself. Notwithstanding

281

this circumstance, the Report should be subjected to penetrating analysis and study and any criticism should be filed with the Report to avoid the appearance that the views expressed in the Report are the commonly accepted views of the fellowship. Moreover, there are many portions of the Report which describe themselves as matters which the Committee has found to be the fact and many matters which are stated as the expressions of the opinion of apparently the entire membership of the Committee. As a result, even though the General Council may not approve the Report, nevertheless present and future readers may, by reason of the filing of the Report, ascribe to these portions qualities of legal authenticity which they do not possess."

"Question! Do you agree that the General Council shouldn't be asked to approve or reject the Polity and Unity Report?"

The Chairman answered, "The Committee believes its findings are matters of fact. It welcomes analysis and study rather than casual debate. The Committee recommends that a constitutional commission be established by the General Council to further explore the powers of the General Council."

"Question! What validity does the Polity and Unity Report have, with a Legal Opinion which calls its findings 'unsound'?"

The Chairman turned to me.

"Ladies and gentlemen, there has never before been a complete review of our polity history, basic documents and contemporary practice. Therefore, the authenticity of the Report has a threefold attestation. First, the synods, councils, and other historical testimonies support the Report. Second, the *complete* file of basic Documents is open to public scrutiny; in the judgment of your Committee, selected by the Executive Committee of the General Council, the record is accurate. Third, the Practice Report is backed by over 200 letters from Conference Superintendents, Association Registrars, national officers, ministers and Church members—from every geographic area. Thus we state unequivocally, so far as it is humanly possible, this Practice Report IS 'the commonly accepted views of the fellowship.'"[6]

President Fredrick Whittaker added, "I personally collected material from about twenty-five leaders in the Northeast. The Report is not exactly what the Rev. Tom Cornish of Maine wrote, or Mr. Gurney Edwards of Rhode Island, or Mrs. Ellis L. Hemingway of New Jersey, or Rev. Nathaniel Guptill of Maine. The Report is the clearest, most condensed statement the Committee could devise to rightly represent *all* the letters from *all* geographic areas."

The Rev. Alfred Hurst stood up to say, "I was one of those from the Christian side of Congregational Christian," which caused a ripple of laughter. "The Report does not exactly agree with the Manual of the Southern Convention, and those of us from the Christian Churches would have preferred other wording in a few instances. But the Report *includes* us; it correctly describes the degree of difference which exists to the satisfaction of the three committee members who became Congregational long after they became Christian."

The Chairman called for consideration of the two-sentence paragraph near the top of page four of the Legal Opinion.[7]

> "It is noted that the Report does not cite the sources of its premises but treats them as established facts. The following analysis is submitted to show that they are not facts but are legal conclusions which are unsound."

A young person rose and asked if she was permitted to speak since she was not a General Council delegate. Assured of her welcome she said, "Probably I'm just showing my ignorance, in college we always cited our sources. Is there some reason why that wasn't done in the Polity Report?"

I replied, "The Association, Conference and national church bodies are described in words or phrases from their own charters, by laws, or standing rules, and the Report states this.[8] Let me direct your attention to one item which has been disputed, regarding the Board of Home Missions. There are 15 statements in the Documents Report.[9] Six statements are exact quotations from the charters; seven are abridged in the words of the charters or by laws; one is an exact quotation from the General Council Constitution; and one is a statement listing the exact charters by name. Contrary to the Legal Opinion the Report DOES cite all the sources used; the Legal Opinion cites FOUR!"

The young lady was still standing. "Sir," she said, "aren't you referring to the Documentary section? What about the Practice section? There are no footnotes."

"You are on the way to becoming a scholar! There are no footnotes, but a list of names of all respondents who read the final draft and gave us permission to use their names appears before the first word in the Practice Statements.[10] The list of names is introduced by an exposition of method used in 'the normal scholarly manner.'"

She persisted, "But there are no footnotes just as the lawyers say."

"You are more of a scholar than the lawyers! *They* didn't ask for footnotes; they blandly asserted, 'The Report does not cite the sources,' which is incorrect.

"There were two reasons for omitting the identity of the author of each phrase (or word). First, the Committee sought to use language which accurately reflects Congregational Usage, according to all correspondents, not narrowly limited to any one or more correspondents. We did not wish debate to arise as to the authority of one correspondent, or another. Second, contrary to expectation, the Committee discovered an extraordinary degree of agreement, so that footnoting every phrase was repetitive."

She continued! "*You* may think the words in the Report reflect the way Congregationalism is practiced, but how do *I* know that?"

"The only way you can know what the letters say *in your own right* is by study of them. You are invited to inspect them. Anyone may do so."

"Sir," she asked, a bit plaintively, "Isn't there any other way?"

"Miss, so far as I am aware, accurate knowledge is best found by personal examination of the record. The Legal Opinion was written without examination of the record."

President Frederick Whittaker spoke up, "Dr. Gray, I think the young lady deserves at least one other answer." He turned toward her. "I read all of these records. Each member of the Congregational Polity Committee read them. If you are not able personally to study all the originals you *may* be willing to accept the testimony of the members of the Congregational Polity Committee, that is, of Superintendent William D. Pratt of Northern California, Mr. Veo Small, a Seattle educator, Rev. Arthur G. Swartz of Texas, Rev. Malcolm Burton of Michigan, and Rev. Henry David Gray of Southern California. I served on the Committee 1950 to 1952. And the entire Polity and Unity Committee reviewed, revised, and authorized the Report in your hands. Could these persons not provide reasonable assurance as to the reliability of the Report?"

A minister with a Southern accent interjected, "I think I'd just like to support the young lady. I'm looking at paragraph one under 'The Local Church.'[11] Exactly who agreed with this statement?"

I looked at Wendell. He was a bit grim. "You'll have to answer that one," he said.

"Here are the correspondents' words regarding the final draft, which is what is printed.

"*Rev. Thomas Anderson, Atlanta, December 26, 1953:* 'I have no suggestions relative to any additions or deletions. It (Polity as Practiced Report) seems to me to comprehend the actual situation very accurately.'

"*Superintendent Frederick W. Alden, N.H., December 24, 1953:* 'I have nothing to criticize nor to add to the report of the committee but rather. . .want to offer my commendation to the committee in this effort to give the picture of the fellowship as it works at various levels. . .the reporting of information has been faithful and complete.'

"*Superintendent Everett Babcock, Ohio, January 15, 1953:* 'I am in receipt of your inquiry asking what practices there are in our churches, associations, and the Conference which differ (from the Documents Report). None. Except possibly one in paragraph 17.'

"*Rev. David Nelson Beach, Connecticut, 17 January 1954:* 'I am impressed by the identity of what you outline with what I have lived with in my 35 years in the parish ministry in five states.'

"*Rev. Zdenek F. Bednar, Vermont, January 22, 1954:* 'I think the report shows clearly the official polity of the Congregational church as it is practiced in our churches.'

"*Rev. Robert L. Blakesley, Ohio, January 21, 1954:* 'I find it. . .difficult to understand just what you want by way of comment or additional corrections. The report seems to be a composite of the replies which you have received.'

"*Rev. Harold R. Browne, Colorado, January 7, 1954:* 'I checked over the content of the report and approve of it most heartily.'

"*Rev. Harold R. Bruce, New Hampshire, December 24, 1953:* 'You are to be highly commended for your work in analyzing the individual statements and in preparing this very systematic and clearly phrased report. I have no further comments for. . .the final statement.'

"*Superintendent Robert H. Bruce, New York, December 31, 1954:* 'As a report of what many different people believe to be the practice in actual operation of the churches I think it is an excellent report.'

"*Rev. Harry R. Butman, Southern California, January 14, 1954:* 'it is an invaluable summary of the status of congregationalism at the present time.'

"*Superintendent Erston M. Butterfield, So'east Convention, January 1954:* 'The committee's 'Polity as Practiced' is one of the finest documents to be developed in recent years! It's findings should provide a good basis for further progress toward true 'Congregationalism'.'

"*Rev. Kenneth D. Claypool, Seattle, January 9, 1954:* 'a fine piece of work. . . . I like the whole tone of it, the obvious comprehensiveness and the clear concise form.'

"*Superintendent Albert B. Coe, Massachusetts, January 7, 1954:* 'You have put an immense amount of time and intelligent effort into this study. For that we shall all be grateful. I have only one suggestion. . .in paragraph 31. . .could it not be said positively rather than negatively?'

"*Rev. Arthur P. Colbourn, Rhode Island, December 28, 1953:* 'Congregational Polity as it is Practiced. . .is an excellent piece of work. . . . Is Congregationalism a polity for. . .the mid-twentieth century?'

"*Rev. Thos. J. W. Cornish, Maine, January 2, 1954:* 'the report. . .seems to me to cover all the necessary points.'

"*Rev. Gardner D. Cottle, Vermont, 18 January 54:* 'A careful reading. . .compels the comment "this is an excellent piece of material. I wish that such a digest might have been available to us earlier" . . . a grand job.'

"*Rev. Robert E. Crawford, Massachusetts, January 1954:* 'No suggestions for revision. . .an impressive job. . .useful. . .in church membership instruction too.' ' "

From the rear of the room came a voice, "How long does this go on?"

I replied, "I've just completed the C's. The next letter begins the D's. We've only heard from 18 of about 140."

"Are there *any* which disagree with the Report?"

"Yes. Many persons made excellent editorial suggestions, which we adopted. A few had substantial concerns, but none concerned Paragraph One."

"Then why do you have to read them?"

"Because the young lady in the second row wanted proof that the statements are accurate. She has a right to know. You all do."

"Maybe she's satisfied now."

I addressed the young lady, "Do you wish me to continue, or would you prefer to examine these personally?"

"I'm satisfied," she replied.

"Nevertheless," I rejoined, "the Committee would consider it a favor if you were willing to examine the records and report your findings on Monday."

"I just might do that," was the reply.

The Congregational Church

A New Englander suggested that the seminar might address the paragraphs relating to the Congregational Church. "First Church was gathered in 1733," he said, "before any Massachusetts Association or Conference existed, and nearly a century and a half prior to the institution of the General Council. The Church is more important to us than anything else."

The Chairman inquired whether or not the seminar members approved of the suggested procedure. They did.

"May I suggest that you all compare three accounts: the first 30 statements in the Document Report, the first 37 statements in the Practice Report, and the entire section, "The 'Real Denominational Autonomy'" in the Legal Opinion.

"The 'Real Denominational Autonomy'

1. "To develop a correct analysis of the relationships within the fellowship, we start with a premise upon which *all* agree: The Associations, Conferences, General Council and Boards have no power or authority of any kind over the temporal or spiritual affairs of the churches. The respective churches within their membership possess the sole power and authority in the sphere of their individual affairs. However, it does not follow from this that the *sole* source of power within the denomination is in the churches. The total power, authority and influence of the Congregational Christian denomination is more than the sum of the individual powers of the 5600 churches.

2. "Only a few of the outward manifestations of this proposition need be cited: (a) The *Associations* are the custodians of the standing of our ministers. A church must be accepted by an Association to become a part of the fellowship. As the Committee found, (IV, 4, pars. 13, 17 and 18), the Association elects its officers, establishes its procedures, writes its own constitution, holds and administers its own property, establishes its own rules of membership, plans its own program, orders all its affairs, and may withdraw fellowship from a local church. (b) The *Conferences* perform wide functions in channeling the giving of the churches, investing funds, holding property, training ministers, establishing standards which it recommends to the churches, and having written statements of membership (IV, 4, pars. 31, 37). (c) The *General Council* determines its own program, seeks to express the common mind and to exercise leadership (IV, 4, pars. 52 and 54), all in addition to broad constitutional powers. (d) The Boards have the power to direct the investment and

use of vast sums of money for missionary and other purposes, limited only by their charters and, where they exist, express trusts.

3. "The General Council, Associations and Conferences are all authorized by their constitutions to 'promote' and 'foster' the fellowship of the churches; and all of these bodies express the opinion and the will of their members and make recommendations to the other bodies whether the same are adopted or not. All manage their own property, conduct their own affairs, and amend their constitutions by sole action of their own members. All of these are recognized as powers and functions of these wider bodies and not as functions of the individual church, nor are the churches bound by or responsible for their actions.

4. "The difficulty in Chapters IV, 3 through IV, 6 lies in the assumption that there is but a single mass of power in the fellowship for which a source must be found and barring the wider bodies as a source, the authors of those Sections concluded that it comes from the churches. This theory, however, fails to explain the existence of powers within the fellowship which the churches never had and could not exercise effectively.

5. "The fact is that there are many distinct and separate powers and each has its individual source. The power to control a local church is obviously in that church. The power to give denominational recognition to a church is in the Association. The power to promote fellowship is in the Associations, Conferences and the General Council. The power to study church union, to report and to draw up plans of union is in the General Council. The power to seek, hold, invest, and expend missionary funds and pension funds, and to seek through wills, trust instruments, foundations and from any other source, funds for any of their corporate purposes, is in the Boards.

6. "No local church has the power to grant denominational recognition to a sister church and therefore cannot delegate that power. No local church has the custody of ministerial standing within the denomination and therefore cannot delegate that power. The list can be extended by reciting all of the functions and activities within the fellowship which are generally recognized as not within the purpose, function or competence of the local church. It then becomes clear that the total power of a local church, added to that of the other 5600 churches with like power, does not begin to equal the sum of the total powers found within the fellowship.

7. "It is therefore necessary to conclude that there are powers within the denomination which do not have their source in the local church. Stated differently, there are autonomies within the denomination other than the autonomy of the local church. These powers and autonomies relate not to the control of or by the individual

church but to the wider aims and purposes of the fellowship. To epitomize—within the area of local church function, each church is autonomous; within the area of Congregational outreach and of inter-church function, there are other autonomies which reside in the various wider bodies. In both areas the autonomy of each body is premised upon its lack of power to disturb the autonomy of any other body. Accordingly, the autonomies which exist in the wider bodies do not pretend to limit the autonomy of the local church or of the various other wider bodies. Likewise, the autonomy of the local church does not pretend to limit the autonomies of its sister churches or, for that matter, of groups of sister churches as they may be collected in Associations, Conferences and Councils. In the very nature of Congregationalism, there is no such thing as dictatorship of one body over another, or of one person over another. 'Power' no more rises from the bottom up than descends from the top down.

8. "The powers which reside in the wider bodies originate with them and arise from the very existence of the organization and its purposes and functions. They are not old powers which theretofore resided in the churches and were delegated to the wider bodies. The Report itself found powers which, rather than being delegated, have developed out of the necessities of the situation (IV, 4, par. 51) and from usages and 'commonly accepted practices' over the years (IV, 4, first paragraph). See also Burton's Manual, p. 40.

9. "Another difficulty in parts of the Report is the inclination to think of the churches as one organism which can delegate and withhold, commit and withdraw, possess and control. Actually they are 5600 individual bodies and no church or group of churches can speak for them with authority. Any effort so to speak would be presumptuous and can be ignored or repudiated at the sole discretion of the local church.

10. "Nor is the Report correct in finding that the powers of the Associations, Conferences and General Council are specific. In most instances their powers are to 'promote' or 'foster' fellowship and thus are the utmost in generality and include all matters which, in the conscience of *that* body, tend to promote the fellowship. A typical example is the by-law of the Southern California and Southwest Conference, which provides:
   " 'The purposes of this Conference shall be to advance the Kingdom of Jesus Christ by promoting through the fellowship of the Congregational Churches of Southern California and the Southwest and by cooperating with our National Congregational Benevolent Societies.' (By-Laws, Article I, 'Purposes'.)

11. "William E. Barton in his *Law of Congregational Usage* recognized the differing areas of function and purpose within the

denomination and the autonomies pertaining to each when he wrote (page 291):

> " 'As the local church has its own autonomy and all rights belonging to it as a local body are jealously to be guarded, so the churches in their district grouping have an autonomy. There are certain matters wherein the autonomy of the group is quite as sacred as the autonomy of the local congregation.'

* * * *

> " 'Congregationalism is conscious of a real denominational autonomy; the autonomy of the local church, independent within its sphere; the autonomy of district and state bodies through which the churches effect their united work and fellowship; and the autonomy of our national church organization, the National Council, and the societies, a controlling majority of whose voting members are members of the National Council.' (p. 454-55)

12. "Throughout denominational literature can be found examples of legitimate activities of the wider bodies performed under the auspices of the will of the uninstructed delegates which composed its meetings. For example, *Burton's Manual,* page 53 states:

> " 'It (the General Council) also bears testimony to its faith through approved statements or resolutions on various topics *at its own will.'*

"*Atkins and Fagley* at page 341 state the competence of the wider bodies to act for themselves:

> " 'Hence, as the agencies outside the local church are neither legislative nor judicial, but only administrative, any proposal for church union affects only the agency taking action. For example, when the National Council has voted to merge with the national organization of another religious body, it has not followed that the local units of either body were merged but that the cooperative agency of the Congregational churches—that is, its National Council—united with a similar agency in some other body for coordination and mutual enrichment of both.'

"The Working Arrangement Between the Various Autonomies

13. "Does all of the foregoing mean that the Associations, Conferences, the General Council and the Boards are without control and can, in the expression of their autonomy, whittle away at the autonomy of the churches or act without regard for the interests of the majority of the individuals and churches in the fellowship? The answer, as the history of our fellowship shows, is a categorical negative.

14. "In the first place, a basic limitation upon the autonomies of the wider bodies is the existence of the universally recognized premise that the autonomy exists only to the extent that it does not tread upon the autonomy of the other bodies and of Congregational Christian individuals. In the second place, each of the wider bodies is controlled by a majority of its members. These members are representative of the conscience of the majority of the individuals in the fellowship throughout the nation and it is that conscience which has invariably aligned the regional and national bodies with the predominate local and national viewpoint within the fellowship at any given time. In the third place, no Association, Conference or Council can long ignore or depart from the collective will of the individuals in the fellowship without losing both their financial and moral support.

15. "Factually and from a legal point of view, the sole control of the wider bodies rests in a majority of its members present and voting in a meeting. There is no control of those bodies in a church acting individually or in a group of churches acting as such. A church can be said to control them only in the indirect sense that its representatives in an Association or Conference may at any given time be in agreement with other members and they may together constitute a majority of the membership voting in a meeting. This circumstance does not make the Associations and Conferences an agent of a church or of the churches as a group.

16. "If Chapters IV, 3 and IV, 4 of the Report had been limited to demonstrating these practical indirect controls within the denomination, it would have been factually and legally sound. The Report, however, goes on to translate them into legal concepts, to state the legal relationships within the denomination and to apply to them such legal terms as 'agents,' 'limited power,' 'delegated power' and 'specific power.' In so doing, the authors of those Sections have presented a form of Congregationalism which has never existed, which is contrary to the documents of the denomination, and which leads to patently unworkable conclusions and insurmountable paradoxes in denominational life.

"The Impossibilities and Paradoxes Suggested by the Report

17. "If, as the Report says, the 'wider bodies' are the agents of the churches, then these bodies are governed by 5600 principals, each of which admittedly is free to select its own Christian theology, determine its own practices and hold its own views of its relation to the wider bodies. If the Report is correct, then to which of these principals is the 'wider body' 'responsible'? If not all of the 5600 agree, then which conflicting view should it accept? If 1 or 100 disagree,

should the 'wider bodies' be 'accountable' to those 'Principals' or to the 5599 or 5500 which approve? Attention is drawn to a specific situation. In the case of *Cadman v. Kenyon*, the New York Congregational Christian Conference sought to file a brief in the Court of Appeals as a friend of the court for the purpose of presenting its views. 83% of its members and 79.93% of the 332 churches in the Conference had voted in favor of the Plan in The Basis of Union. Nevertheless, counsel for the Cadman Church argued that the Conference was a representative body of the churches in New York State, was 'supposed to be operated for the benefit of all of them' and since, counsel alleged, five of the 'large and prominent churches' in Brooklyn were of a contrary position, the Conference should not be permitted to file the brief. Here was an attempt by an individual church to create enforced 'responsibility' to its views to the exclusion of the views of the other churches concerned. (The attempt failed since the Court permitted the filing of the brief.) This of course is but one example of the application of these premises to our denominational life; yet it evidences the confusion and frustration which would prevail in the organs of our fellowship.

18. "It can therefore be seen that there is no limit to the use which could be made of the premises in this Report. The consequences are not confined to denominational unions and the ecumenical movement, but will invade every facet of denominational life. If accepted, the functioning of the Associations, Conferences, the General Council and the Boards would become impossible."

Now, from "Congregational Polity as Seen in the Documents":

"The Local Church

"1. A Congregational Christian church originates as a body of Christians in a particular community. It writes or chooses its own statement of purpose, belief, covenant, or creed, adopts its own constitution, or other governing rules, and is subject to no external ecclesiastical authority for the substance of them. In practice there is often consultation with representative Congregational Christian individuals or organizations. Provisions for extending fellowship to a church by an association vary, but in no instance do they or can they prevent a church from governing itself according to its own desires. 'Recognition' is recognition of a church that already exists; it is not the 'creating' or 'constituting' of a church which had no prior existence. But recognition by other Congregational Christian churches is a prerequisite of denominational standing.

"2. A Congregational Christian church sets its own standards for membership. These may or may not require baptism or assent to a creed. Many churches have adopted the Kansas City Statement of

Faith as formulated by the National Council of 1913. Reception of members is by confession of faith, by letter of transfer from other Christian churches, or by re-affirmation of faith, but each church exercises the right to set forth the specific meaning of these three modes of reception.

"3. A Congregational Christian church orders its worship as it believes to be most fitting. In actual practice the individual minister leads the regular Sunday services, and is expected to win the approval of the members when significant changes are to be made in the order of worship. Normally, the board of deacons or similar committee is charged with concern for the worship of the church.

"4. A Congregational Christian church administers the sacraments and holy rites on conditions and after such manner as it chooses so to do. Although laymen may preside at the Lord's Table, the sacraments are customarily administered by ministers. The right to administer the sacraments may be granted to a student-pastor or lay reader by vote of the individual church.

"5. A Congregational Christian church is free to adopt and follow its own program of education, fellowship, community service, missionary action, music, pastoral work, and kindred religious and civic activities.

"6. A Congregational Christian church calls its minister, sets his compensation and tenure, and makes all other business arrangements. Some parishes still maintain an ecclesiastical society which performs some of these functions.

"7. A Congregational Christian church may request that a council (association or vicinage) either 'install' or 'recognize' its minister. The council may withhold 'recognition' or 'installation' or may give counsel, but the final decision as to whether or not the candidate will be its minister rests with the local church. The holding of a council (if any) is at the request of the church. The minister may exercise his ministerial duties whether or not he is 'installed' or 'recognized.'

"8. While a local Congregational Christian church, in its own right and by itself, may license and ordain candidates for its own Christian ministry, such licensure or ordination need not be accepted as valid by an association (or conference, where conference is the body in which ministerial standing is held).

"9. A Congregational Christian church or 'ecclesiastical society' holds title to property in its own right; and when title is held by a conference or board because of gifts or loans, it is assumed that the local church will gain title at the earliest possible moment, and will, in the interim, be free to conduct its business affairs according to the dictates of its members. In some instances local church property is held in trust by the conference, on request of the church.

"10. A Congregational Christian church expresses concern for Christian out-reach by voluntary acceptance of responsibilities in associations, conferences, boards, the General Council, Councils of Churches, and innumerable other organizations.

"11. A Congregational Christian church cherishes the fellowship of its sister churches. The personality, ability, and Christian character of leaders (local, associational, conference, board, national) does much to determine the meaning of 'the fellowship' at any given time, in any given situation, or throughout the nation. The 'fellowship' always and everywhere means a sincere concern

"(1) for the well being of each church by other churches,

"(2) for the furtherance of common concerns; educational, inspirational, missionary, or other, and

"(3) for the nurture of the Christian faith in all by the sharing of the faith of each.

"Nevertheless, every conference includes churches which do not participate actively in its organizational life.

"The Association

"There are almost 250 associations in the United States, composed of an average of 23 churches each. The 'association' is sometimes called a 'conference,' 'union,' or 'district association.'

"12. An association of Congregational Christian churches is a voluntary association of 'churches' or 'churches and ministers.' Most associations appear to be unincorporated bodies consisting of elected representatives, both lay and ministerial, from the constituent churches. In at least four states no association exists, but the small state conference takes its place.

"13. Although constitutional provisions vary, an association customarily meets at least once a year for counsel, inspiration, fellowship, the sharing of information, and review of or action upon questions relating to church or ministerial standing. It performs the functions of an ecclesiastical council on request.

"14. An association elects its own officers, establishes its own rules of procedure, writes its own constitution, may hold and administer its own property, establishes its own rules for membership, chooses its own paid personnel (if any), plans its own program, and orders all its affairs.

"15. The association credentials committee (variously named), when requested to do so by a local church, examines candidates for ministerial standing and recommends to the association the extending (or not) of such standing. The association usually specifies requirements for the granting of ministerial standing which are designed to assure the association of the Christian character, training and belief of the applicant. Membership in a local church of the association, is a pre-condition of any ministerial status; it is not possible to be a member of the association, conference, or General Council apart from membership in a local church. The Congregational Christian minister possesses dual status as a member of the local church, and as a minister with standing in an association (or conference where conference performs this function).

"16. A group of Christian people gathered together in a neighborhood constitute themselves a congregationally organized church, write their own constitution, call (or even ordain) their own minister, and subsequently ask to be received into the fellowship of an association. When received into fellowship, the church becomes listed as a member of the Congregational Christian denomination. The local churches will be permitted to join them. The conditions are designed to assure the association of the Christian character and belief, congregational organization, and stability of the applicant body. There is no provision for refusal of fellowship to any applicant church on the basis of creed, acceptance of financial or legal obligations to the denomination, vows of allegiance to authority, or other similar requirements.

"17. The credentials committee or the association acting through its executive or advisory committee, on request of a local church, may call a 'council,' either associational or vicinage, for the purpose of examination; give ministerial status 'in care of association,' 'approbation to preach,' licensure, ordination, recognition, or installation; adjudicate disputes; extend fellowship to a church; and for 'other purposes historically served by ecclesiastical councils.' Provision is made for councils called at the request of a minister or local church member, acting individually.

"18. As custodian of the ecclesiastical standing of churches and ministers the association seeks to guard the faith and purity of its fellowship. Called as an ecclesiastical council it inquires into matters of dispute and gives advice and assistance in adjusting any unhappy differences within a church, between churches, or concerning conduct unbecoming to a minister or church. An association may withdraw fellowship for reasons of non-attendance, 'or other sufficient reasons.'

"19. Some associations enter into comity arrangements with other denominations regarding the locating of new churches. Further, certain associations take the initiative in stimulating the formation of new churches.

"20. The association cooperates with the state conference, the General Council and other boards and agencies in their programs. It may establish its own committees on religious education, missions, social action, evangelism, men's work, women's work, young people's work, etc. As the local organization of the churches, it elects delegates to the General Council and, when requested to do so by the conference, nominates members for the conference board of directors.

"The State Conference

"21. The state conference is usually a legally incorporated body, with a salaried superintendent and staff, through which the churches may act together in church extension, missions, social action, education, counsel, ministerial training, standing and placement, investment of funds, holding of property, fellowship, and matters of area-wide concern. (N. B. Four conferences permit ministerial standing to be held in the conference by consent of the association.)

"22. The state conference performs its functions within defined limits. As a typical instance of definite limitations, Massachusetts uses these words to describe the relationship: 'Following Congregational principles, this Conference shall under no circumstances exercise authority over churches or individuals or interfere with the government or discipline of the churches. It shall advise and counsel the churches when requested, but it is recognized that each church has the power of self-determination in all matters.'

"23. The voting membership of the state conference is made up of at least one lay and one ministerial representative of each local church. Some conference constitutions provide for representation from educational institutions of Congregational origin or relationship, and for inclusion of conference officers and committee chairmen as voting members of the conference meetings.

"24. The state conference elects its own officers, including a board of directors (or trustees) which functions as an executive committee to carry out the will of the churches as expressed at the conference meeting. In many states each association nominates one member of the board of directors. Some boards of directors are also empowered 'to initiate new forms of work and to provide for their prosecution.'

"25. The work of the state conference is carried on by means of departments, boards, or committees, such as missionary, education, fraternal service, social action, new work, student work, evangelistic, ministerial etc. All such departments, boards, or com-

296

mittees are normally responsible to the board of directors, and function within the constitution and by-laws of the state conference.

"26.   The superintendent (or otherwise named officer with similar duties) is the chief executive officer of the conference and serves as its representative at various denominational and inter-denominational meetings. He serves as an advisory member of conference committees and counsels with the local churches as requested. He keeps himself broadly informed regarding every phase of the work undertaken by the conference and seeks to coordinate it effectively. He exercises general supervision over other employees of the conference. He may be assisted in these duties by members of his staff.

"27.   The Laymen's Fellowship, the Fellowship of Congregational Christian Women, and the Pilgrim Fellowship (for youth) are sometimes listed as department activities of a state conference. They are recognized as an integral part of the fellowship in the written programs of many conferences, and of the Mid-winter Meetings of the Missions Council.

"28.   The state conference is financed by endowments or gifts; but in most cases chiefly by the giving of the local churches. In many instances the conference acts as collection agency for the association per capita, the General Council per capita, the General Council mileage fund, the apportionment giving to missions, and many other funds. But in no case does a church cease to be a Congregational Christian church because it fails to pay per capita, apportionment or other monies. Giving is voluntary.

"29.   The conference acts as the representative of the General Council, boards and agencies in presenting their several programs and needs to the churches. At the same time it seeks to function as the servant of the churches both in their area-wide work and in the strengthening of their own local work.

"30.   The state conference relation to the churches is well described by Dr. Charles C. Merrill as follows: 'This many-sided work is carried on without a book of discipline or a canon law, or a government. There is a minimum of authority. There is a maximum of fraternity. It is a fine illustration of what may be called "free cooperation."'"

Now, from "Congregational Polity in Contemporary Practice":

"The Local Church

"1.   A Church may become a Congregational Christian Church in a variety of ways, but in all instances the church exists as an organized Christian fellowship prior to its recognition by the area association of Congregational Christian Churches (or Churches and Ministers). While the applicant body is not constituted a church by recognition, it is clearly understood among us that recognition establishes a responsible relationship between the applicant church and the association. To become recognized, an applicant body must be organized as a Christian Church, according to the principles of a Congregational polity, must request recognition of an association, and must accept the responsibility of mutual counsel and advice.

"2. A Congregational Christian Church has entered or may now enter the fellowship in one of the following ways:

"a. By traditional relationship with other Congregational Christian churches, as in New England churches which pre-date the organization of associations.

"b. By action of a local group of Christians who organize a church, and then apply for and receive membership in an association.

"c. By action of a 'community church' which applies for and receives membership in an association.

"d. By action of a conference or association which initiates the organization of a local group into a church, after which the church then formally applies for and receives membership in an association.

"3. A Congregational Christian church assumes complete freedom to determine its own covenant, basis of membership, statement of faith (if any), forms of worship, programs of religious education, ownership and administration of property, choice of minister or other leadership, programs of community service, fellowship, music, pastoral work, and all other local religious and civic activities. It is customary among us for the minister to preach the Word and administer the sacraments and holy rites, although the local church may call upon other members to fulfill any or all of these functions.

"4. A Congregational Christian church calls its own minister, and in consultation with him, makes all business agreements associated with his acceptance of service as its minister. When a church requests a conference superintendent (or other officer) to help it to find a minister there is no permanent delegation of authority; the superintendent simply makes a recommendation and brings minister and church together, while the church retains the sole power of decision in the matter.

"5. A Congregational Christian church may request that an ecclesiastical council 'install' or 'recognize' an ordained minister as its pastor and teacher (or assistant pastor or minister of education or other ministerial officer), and this practice is now common among our churches. When the council is called by action of an association, at the request of the local church (which is a widespread practice), the minister's recognition or installation by the council also gives him ministerial standing in the association. When the council is called by action of the local church, acting for itself, the minister applies to an association for ministerial standing there, even though he is the minister of a local Congregational Christian church. The vicinage council called by action of the local church is in as good favor among us as the associational council.

"6. A Congregational Christian church may license or ordain its own candidates for the ministry, but while the right to do so is maintained, occurrence is rare; and a locally licensed or ordained minister may exercise his ministry only in a local church which recognizes him as a minister. His local license or ordination does not confer ministerial standing in an association.

"7. A Congregational Christian church, or 'ecclesiastical society,' normally holds title to its property in its own right, and exercises its own discretion in the administration of all its real property or financial interests. But it is now the practice of some churches to place title to their property in the care of the state conference or of one of the national boards, and in several states, all real and personal property of an extinct church becomes the property of the state religious body with which the church was associated. When title to property is vested in a state conference or national board the local church is entirely free to use the property as it desires, except that the property must continue to be used by a Congregational Christian church. However, the building department mortgage application forms and the administrative rules of the Board of Home Missions and of certain conferences require that a church receiving loans, grants, or other financial aid perform such acts as consultation regarding choice of a pastor, pledge annually to the building department, conduct business affairs in a systematic manner, insure and repair the church property, and remain in fellowship with the denomination.

"8. A Congregational Christian church voluntarily accepts responsibilities in connection with the life and work of the associations, conferences, councils, boards, and other organizations outside itself. The local church in our fellowship ordinarily takes its responsibilities to wider agencies quite seriously, particularly with reference to (a) representation at meetings, (b) financial contributions, and (c) dissemination of information. Persuasion is the only authority exerted on a local church to accept responsibilities in wider bodies. There is general recognition of the fact that united efforts to further over-all objectives can do much for the cause of Christ which the local church cannot do alone.

"9. A Congregational Christian church voluntarily gives to agencies beyond itself the authority to act on its behalf for the achievement of specific objectives, e.g., home missions, foreign missions. Any authority delegated by a Congregational Christian church to any other body or person can be withdrawn by the local church.

"THE ASSOCIATION

"(Sometimes called a 'local conference,' 'union,' or 'district association.')

"(There are 259 associations listed in the 1952 yearbook.)

"10. An association of Congregational Christian churches is a voluntary fellowship of churches, or churches and ministers. The large majority of associations are unincorporated. All meetings of an association are composed of delegates (or 'messengers') from the associated churches. A good number also extend membership to all ordained Congregational Christian ministers who hold standing in the association. Most associations are geographically contiguous.

"11. An association ordinarily meets at least once a year. The chief business relates to questions concerning church or ministerial membership. In addition, addresses are given, usually by representatives of the conference, missionary boards, or other agencies of Christian life and work beyond the local church. Worship, fellowship, mutual counsel, and sometimes common action form the substance of the association meeting.

"12. An association meeting attracts the attendance of delegates by virtue of (a) the sense of responsibility to attend on the part of the local church (b) the fairly common rule (frequently unenforced) that ministers must annually report to the association in person or in writing in order to retain ministerial standing, (c) the strength of the program for the meeting, and (d) the need for fellowship in areas where Congregational Christian churches are few in number. Attendance varies widely, with a majority of the churches represented at most meetings.

"13. An association elects its own officers, establishes its own rules of procedure, writes its own constitution, is the custodian of the membership and credentials of its ministerial members, may hold and administer its own property, establishes its own rules for membership, chooses its own paid personnel (if any), plans its own program, and orders all its affairs.

"14. The association credentials committee (variously named) is the body before which are brought matters relating to church or ministerial standing. In several conferences one or more of the associations has designated the conference, or a conference committee, to perform these functions on behalf of the association, e.g. Northern California, Vermont; and there are several states in which the conference and association are identical, e.g. Wyoming.

"15. The association, acting on the advice of its credentials committee, and in response to the request of a local church, makes provision for the reception of churches into membership in the association, for the care of candidates for the ministry, for the installation or recognition of pastors, for the transfer of ministerial standing from association to association, and for the holding of associational councils in connection with all the aforementioned.

"16. The association receives into fellowship as a Congregational Christian church a group of Christian people who have constituted themselves a congregationally organized church with (a) a constitution, (b) a roll of members, (c) officers, (d) a statement of Christian faith or purpose, (e) a stable business condition, and (f) provision for adequate leadership. Many associations, e.g. Hartford East, Connecticut, and Rockingham, New Hampshire, have no constitutional standards for recognition, but in practice apply the above-mentioned criteria.

"17. When the association has received an applicant local church into its membership, listing as a Congregational Christian church follows. Such an acceptance into membership is the means by which a fellowship of churches organized as an association, admits new members, by determining whether or not the faith and order of the applicant body are in line with the main stream of our Congregational heritage, and whether or not the applicant body is ready to share with the Congregational Christian Churches in advancing the cause of Christ and of the fellowship of the churches, in so far as conscience will permit. Acceptance into the fellowship has a dual character among us: (1) The association acceptance of the applicant body into membership, and (2) the local church acceptance of the association as its agency of fellowship and concern.

"18. The association may withdraw fellowship from a local church for spiritual and moral reasons. While other grounds are provided in our written documents, there appears to be no application of these in practice.

"19. The association may cease to be the wider body in which a local church finds fellowship. The most widespread reason for this is change in the theological viewpoint of the local body, often because of changes in its ministry. Ordinarily, a sustained effort is made to keep the church in the fellowship, but when such efforts fail, and if there are not property rights of the association or other wider body involved, the association ceases to list the local church as a member. The church then is no longer listed by the conference or other wider agencies of the Congregational Christian fellowship.

"20. The association is the chief agency of the churches for the holding of ministerial standing, and the general practice of our churches is to request the association to act as an ecclesiastical council in connection with 'in care of association' status, licensure, ordination, installation or recognition. The applicant person is proposed to the association by the local church of which he is a member, a committee examines him and/or his credentials, a council of the association is called (often jointly by local church and association), and the action of the council is automatically accepted as the action of the association.

"21. The association is not bound to accept the ministerial standing conferred by a council which has been called by a local Congregational Christian church, acting apart from the association, even though the minister thus given standing may continue to exercise his ministry in whatever church is willing to accept him as its minister.

"22. The association customarily accepts into membership a minister who has been ordained by another Congregational Christian association, even though its constitution stipulates its freedom to do otherwise.

"23. The association examines applicant ministers whose standing is in non-Congregational Christian church bodies, and accepts them into membership unless there are strong moral, spiritual or educational reasons for doing otherwise.

"24. The association, on request of a local church, calls a council for the installation or recognition of an ordained minister, and by action of this council, a minister is given standing in the association. There is among our churches no commonly accepted practice concerning the installing or the recognizing of an ordained minister, nor is there universal agreement as to its meaning. Larger churches or older churches generally hold such services, although not always as an ecclesiastical council, and often as a vicinage gathering. These services symbolize the local church's concern for the approbation of its sister churches, and indicate the interest of the fellowship in the well-being of the local church.

"25. The association may act as an advisory council concerning any matter on which council is requested by a local church. This practice is very infrequent, but it is sometimes of great significance. It may result in 'loss of standing' for a minister guilty of misconduct, or in 'withdrawal of fellowship' from a church which 'walks disorderly' (to use the time-honored phrase). The association has the right and duty to be responsible for the membership and credentials of the churches and ministers in its fellowship.

"26. The association meeting is one of the chief means of communication between the churches and the wider agencies of the fellowship, since it is the churches assembled together in council. The association officers cooperate with the state conference leaders, and with the educational, missionary, service, or other wider agencies of the churches.

"27. The association, its nature, functions and future, is a matter of widespread concern among the committee's correspondents. Few are satisfied with the association as it now functions, and many experiments are being made concerning: (a) matters of church and ministerial standing, (b) the relationship of association committees to those of the conferences, (c) the channeling of financial help to needy churches through the association, (d) the holding of meetings on Sundays, in the evenings, and at times which will encourage large lay attendance, (e) the improvement of meeting programs, (f) the promotion of between-meeting fellowship and other activities, (g) the collection of an associational 'per capita' contribution from member churches, (h) the merging of activities of the association with those of the state conference, and (i) the provision of travel-expense money for delegates in order to increase the ministerial and lay participation, particularly in such activities as councils of ordination.

"THE STATE CONFERENCE

(Usually a legally incorporated body with salaried leadership. Sometimes called a 'Convention' or 'union.' With a few exceptions our correspondents report that the conference includes all local churches in a geographic area. There are 39 conferences listed in the 1952 yearbook.)

"28. The state conference is an administrative agency of the churches, responsible to an annual meeting of delegates from the churches, and to a board of directors (sometimes differently titled) elected by the annual meeting delegates. The responsibilities possessed by the conferences are such as have been given to them by the churches which created and maintain them.

"29. The state conference chief executive is the minister of the conference or superintendent (sometimes differently titled). He is responsible for general oversight of all the conference-wide work of the churches, and is often assisted by a professional staff, or by an office staff, or by both. The superintendent is expected to be 'minister to the ministers' and counselor to the churches, especially in matters relating to the ministry. He represents the churches at denominational and interdenominational gatherings on the state level, and frequently in a metropolitan or on a national level. The General Council, the national boards and agencies, and the inter-denominational bodies with which our churches are associated all regard the superintendent as the 'key-man' through whose office their relations with the local churches are channeled. He is, by virtue of office, a full delegate to the General Council and a member of the Mid-Winter meetings (see below). The superintendent also serves as a liaison person for the churches in relation to governmental and private agencies engaged in socio-humanitarian or educational work. Often he serves as home missions director for the area, and always he is expected to give special advice and help in the development of home missionary projects.

"30. The state conference exercises considerable influence among our churches by virtue of its representative character, and in proportion to the competency of its leadership, the adequacy of its financial resources, the cooperativeness of the constituent churches, and the nature of its geographic area. Its powers are administrative rather than ecclesiastical. For a great number of our churches it is the most important and influential link with the Congregational Christian fellowship.

"31. The state conference is the cooperative agency of the associated churches for church extension, missions, aid to weaker churches, social action, education, mutual counsel, ministerial training, standing and placement, investment of funds, holding of property, fellowship and other matters of area-wide concern. Therefore, the churches expect the officers of the conference to act on their behalf, with the power both to plan and to execute all that is necessary to accomplish the above-mentioned ends. The administrative power given to the conference by the Churches can be withdrawn by the Churches which gave it; either by action according to the conference articles of incorporation (in which case the entire program may be altered), or by individual church action (in which case the action taken is effective only for that particular church).

"32. The state conference has no authority over the local church. Its present relation to the Churches is well described by Dr. Charles C. Merrill as follows: 'This many-sided work is carried on without a book of discipline or a canon law, or a government. There is a minimum of authority. There is a maximum of fraternity. It is a fine illustration of what may be called "free cooperation."'

"33. The state conference is a vital link in the organizational programs of the Fellowship of Congregational Christian Women, the Laymen's Fellowship, and the Pilgrim Fellowship for youth. The promotion of the national and conference missionary objectives, the calling of meetings for study and inspiration, and the holding of retreats, camps, or conferences constitute the main functions of the fellowships for men, women and youth. Often paid executive leadership is provided at the national and state levels. All three fellowships are national organizations. In addition the men and the women are organized throughout the world under the International Congregational Council.

"34.   The state conference is financed by endowments or gifts, but chiefly by the voluntary giving of local churches. 'Goals' are suggested to churches by some conferences, but no church is known to have been refused full participation in the life and work of a conference because of failure to pay the per capita, apportionment, or other monies. The superintendents report unanimously that churches retain the right to give or to withhold financial support.

"35.   The state conference receives the financial support of the local churches for the purpose of carrying out specific objectives. Its stewardship of monies given to it is governed by those objectives, and its stewardship accounting is made to the board of directors elected by the annual meeting of the conference and to the annual meeting itself. The conference is free to expend the monies entrusted to it in accord with its own rules of procedure. In every day practice our churches feel that they retain control over the state conference through delegates, directors, persuasion, and support or non-support. If monies are expended for purposes other than those designated in the articles of incorporation, constitution, by-laws or other fundamental document of the conference, such expenditures may be called in question by the board of directors, the annual meeting, or by such legal processes as are provided by the individual state government with reference to violations of trust agreements.

"36.   The state conference, on request, acts on behalf of an association in such matters as (1) collection of an association per capita, and (2) making arrangements for speakers at association meetings (though in more than one state the association collects a per capita on behalf of the conference, e.g. Illinois.)

"37.   The state conference is the state-level administrative agency of the churches for specific and limited purposes just as the association is the area-wide agency of the churches for specific and limited purposes. State conferences possess written standards for membership of churches, and recognize themselves as the creation of the churches. Their relationship to the associations varies from the single example of the Southern Convention which has the right to 'determine the bounds of local conferences' (i.e. associations), to the general practice of mutual voluntary agreement between conference and association concerning such matters as boundaries and functions. In practice, churches have re-aligned themselves into associations by mutual consent, without reference to the conference, and the churches of at least one association (Los Angeles) are considering re-grouping themselves into three new associations. In practice, a group of churches unite in an association and then arrange to participate in the life and work of a conference. The association is the only universally recognized credential-holding body among us, except in those instances where the conference, by specific request of an association or acting as an association exercises this power. While some conference constitutions speak of 'recognizing' the associations, the word 'recognizing' is not here used as a formal or legal term. Recognition means voluntary acceptance of responsibility for consultation, cooperation, and mutual helpfulness between the state level conference and the area-level association created by the churches as organs of common life and work in their respective spheres. The relationship between these organizations defies legal definition because its essence is the moral and spiritual concern of each unit for all other units. What is 'recognized' is the moral and spiritual responsibility of a conference and an association which agree to walk with each other in ways of fellowship and service."

The First Question

The first question was, if "we start with a premise on which *all* agree"[12] how is it possible to disagree so completely on so many matters?

Compare paragraphs 1, 4, 5, 6 in the Legal Opinion with the evidence in our Documents and Practice. The Legal Opinion invents a series of limits to the life and work of a Congregational Church. The "individual affairs" of the Second Church in Hartford have no "sphere" of limitation. Before there was an Association, the Church existed; at no time did it ever need to be "accepted by an Association to become a part of the fellowship." The exact opposite is the fact. The *Association* had to be accepted by the Church to become part of the fellowship. The approximately 1/3 of all Congregational Christian Churches in U.S.A. which are in New England are comparable to Second Hartford. In December 1869 in Ventura, California, the Ventura, Los Angeles, San Bernardino, and Santa Barbara Churches "by delegates assembled" *created and recognized* the Southern California Association.

The odd notion that "the churches never had '*unlisted*' powers"[13] and that these unspecified powers spontaneously arose in the

Rev. Douglas V. Maclean, CT.[119]

"Congratulations on the most difficult task well done! I have no quarrel with the presentation made of 'Congregational Polity As It Is Practiced In The United States.' Since it is concerned with facts and not with opinions or general propositions, I can give it my hearty approval."

Superintendent Walter Schlaretzki, IL.[120]

"Thank you for sending me the report on how we Congregational Christian people actually conduct our fellowship's affairs. It reveals an immense and constructive labor and we owe you much thanks for it.

"It seems to me that it is a careful description, as factual as the situations which it describes, and as exhaustive as one could wish, or is useful for our study. I have not thought of anything to add, nor do I find anything which requires serious restatement."

How Can These Things Be?

The reaction of the Friday seminar at the New Haven General Council varied from shock to anger. It was capsuled by the question, "How can these things be?" How can the opinion of two lawyers have been received by the Executive Committee, printed and distributed when it contradicts the thorough, painstaking and extensive study of Congregational Polity in Practice?

My reply that afternoon was, "I don't know."

After the session, which lasted till almost five o'clock, the Rev. William Keith said something very revealing, "Henry, I don't think Mr. Loren Wood knew the extent of Wendell's work. I'm wondering if somebody else wrote a preliminary paper."

"Wait, Bill," I replied. "What you're saying is that the whole Legal Opinion, and not just the sentence on which I commented, may not be the work of the lawyer?"

"That goes too far, Henry. All I'm saying is there has to be *some* answer to that last question. How did it happen that we got the Polity Report *and* the Legal Opinion? Do your remember *ever* having a lawyer's official Opinion *against* a General Council Committee's Report?"

"No, Bill, I never even *read* of such a thing happening. But let's think a bit about the answer. You may have it. Suppose you were the Minister of the General Council; suppose you had to face a Polity Report which shattered your dream of church union; suppose you were convinced that *your* interpretation (Congregational

339

'B', or The Mansfield Theses) was the only possible basis for union; suppose you felt bound to tell the General Council that the Polity Committee Report was wrong and you were right—could you think of any way to tell the Council *better* than a Legal Opinion?''

"But that means. . . . "

"It's easy for us to *think* it means something sinister, but does it? Isn't it just the best way to shelve an unwelcome Report?"

"I'll have to think about that."

All of the mediators had to think about the astonishing juxtaposition of the clear and almost unanimous testimony of Congregational Polity in History in Document and in Practice facing the opinion of one (or two) laywers. It was a tough assignment.

CHAPTER 7 NOTES

1. Wood, Werner, France & Tully, *A Legal Opinion*, 1954 no pub. NY 5 and *Ibid*, 1954 General Council NY 3
2. Report, Free Church Polity & Unity, 1954 General Council, NY, p. V
3. Op cit, p. 3
4. *Ibid*, p. 3
5. Op cit, 3.
6. Op cit, 3
7. Op. cit. 4
8. Polity & Unity Report, op. cit. 22, 27
9. *Ibid*, 32, 33
10. Polity and Unity Report, pp. 38-40
11. Polity and Unity Report, p. 40
12. Legal Opinion, op cit, p. 4
13. Legal Opinion, op cit, p. 4
14. Ibid, pp. 3, 4
15. Polity Report, op cit, p. 47
16. Polity Report, op cit, p. 25
17. Legal Opinion, op cit, p. 4
18. Ibid, p. 5
19. Legal Opinion, op cit, p. 6 (#8)
20. Ibid, p. 8 (#16)
21. Ante Chapter Four
22. *Cambridge Platform of 1648*, 1948 General Council, NY
23. Op cit, pp. 3, 4
24. Ibid, pp. 13, 14
25. Ibid, p. 18
26. Op cit, p. 19
27. Ibid, pp. 27, 28, 29
28. Cambridge Platform, op cit, p. 30, 31
29. Op cit, p. 30
30. C. E. Burton, *National Council Digest*, 1930 National Council, NY, Summaries pp. 14-19

31. *National Council Digest*, op cit, p. 118-119
32. Ibid, p. 118
33. Ibid, 119, Rules I, II, 1, 2
34. Polity and Unity Report, pp. 22ff.
35. Charter, Congregational and Christian Conference of Illinois, p. 2, 1947, Office of the Conference, Chicago
36. Legal Opinion, op cit, p. 8 (#16)
37. Op cit, p. 6 (#9)
38. Polity & Unity Report, op cit, p. 56
39. Polity & Unity Report, op cit, p. 56-57
40. Legal Opinion, op cit, 5 (#5)
41. Polity Report, op cit, p. 40, also p. 47 #37
42. Ibid, p. 25
43. Legal Opinion, op cit, p. 6
44. Polity Report, op cit, p. 43
45. Ibid, p. 45
46. Ibid, p. 46
47. Ibid, p. 47
48. Polity Report, op cit, p. 50
49. Ibid, p. 51-52
50. Ibid, p. 49
51. Legal Opinion, op cit, p. 7
52. Council Digest, op cit, p. 118
53. W. E. Barton, *Law of Congregational Usage*, p. 291
54. Ibid, p. 9, from Barton 454
55. Legal Opinion, op cit, quoting from Atkins & Fagley *History of American Congregationalism*, p. 341
56. Alden to Gray, Jan. 15, 1953
57. Anderson to Gray, Apr. 15, 1953
58. Bednar to Gray, Jan. 22, 1953
59. Boynton to Gray, Jan. 23, 1953
60. Bruce to Butman, Oct. 22, 1952
61. Babcock to Gray, Jan. 15, 1953
62. Claypool to Gray, Jan. 24, 1953
63. Coe to Gray, June 9, 1953
64. Colbourn to Gray, Feb. 26, 1953
65. Cottle to Gray, n.d. (before Mar. 1, 1953)
66. Davies to Gray, Jan. 19, 1953
67. Davies to Gray, Jan. 23, 1953
68. Deems to Gray, Feb. 2, 1953
69. Ellis to Gray, Apr. 21, 1953
70. Fiebiger to Gray, Jan. 17, 1953
71. Focht to Gray, Jan. 22, 1953
72. Gans to Gray, Mar. 24, 1953
73. Goodwin to Gray, Jan. 15, 1953
74. Hallauer to Gray, Jan. 21, 1953
75. Hayer to Whittaker, n.d. (received before 4-30-51)
76. Hemmingway to Whittaker, Apr. 6, 1952
77. Hulbert to Gray, Mar. 25, 1953
78. Hurst to Gray, Jun. 4, 1951
79. Johnson to Gray, Jan. 12, 1953

80. Lightbourne to Gray, Jan. 19, 1953
81. Lewis to Whittaker, n.d. (received before 4-30-51)
82. Mager to Gray, Apr. 7, 1951
83. McGouldrick to Gray, Apr. 8, 1953
84. McKendrick to Feaster (and Butman), Oct. 8, 1952
85. Minton to Gray, Mar. 30, 1953
86. Norenberg to Gray, Jan. 15, 1953
87. Perrin to Gray, Jan. 19, 1953
88. Reed to Gray, Jan. 23, 1953
89. Reitinger to Gray, Jan. 22, 1953
90. Reynard to Gray, 14 Oct. 1952
91. Rowe to Gray, n.d. (before 4-30-53)
92. Rymph to Gray, Jan. 19, 1953
93. Sangree to Gray, Jan. 9, 1953
94. Schlaretzki/Nordstrom to Gray, Jan. 21, 1953
95. Scott to Gray, Jun. 1, 1953
96. Shepherd to Gray, Apr. 6, 1953
97. Sill to Gray, Mar. 28, 1951
98. Skarsten to Gray, Jan. 22, 1953
99. Skidmore to Gray, Jan. 20, 1953
100. Towle to Gray, July 29, 1953
101. Treat to Gray, Jan. 16, 1953
102. Tuttle to Gray, Jan. 20, 1953
103. Walker to Whittaker, n.d. (before 4-30-51)
104. White to Gray, Mar. 24, 1953
105. Beach to Gray, 17 Jan. 1954
106. Butman to Gray, Jan. 14, 1954
107. English to Gray, Jan. 8, 1954
108. Johnson to Gray, Dec. 23, 1953
109. Rowe to Gray, n.d. (recd. Jan. 1954)
110. Shepherd to Gray, received Jan. 6, 1954 and phone call recorded
111. Simpson to Gray, Friday, January 1954
112. Gregg to Gray, Dec. 24, 1953
113. Hook to Gray, Dec. 21, 1953
114. Hoskins to Gray, Dec. 26, 1953
115. Kettelle to Gray, Jan. 1, 1954
116. Lewis to Gray, 16 Jan. 1954
117. Lightbourne to Gray, 1/11th/1953
118. McKenney to Gray, recd. Jan. 1954
119. Maclean to Gray, Jan. 8, 1954
120. Schlaretzki to Gray, Dec. 26, 1953

CHAPTER EIGHT

From Test to Testimony

The mood of the New Haven General Council on Saturday and Sunday was impatience.

Social action issues were divisive and emotional. Both proponents and opponents of the CC/ER merger were frustrated. The initial address by the Minister of the General Council left little negotiating space for the mediators.

Among those with whom I conferred was Rev. Wallace Anderson. Wally was a member of the Executive Committee. He was concerned, "What troubles me is absence of reasoning. I have doubts about continuance of the 'Associates in Reading and Thinking.' Nobody appears to be interested in *thinking*." I asked, "Aren't there good minds on the Executive Committee?" He looked at me in his quizzical way then said, slowly, "There are, but they don't stand a chance against the emotional fervor for the merger and for social action. I'm worried . . . not just about the merger. I'm worried about the intellectual awareness which used to be synonomous with New England and Congregationalism."

Later that Saturday (my notes do not say when) I met Rev. Alfred Grant Walton, who was in a hurry. "I'm on my way home to Brooklyn to preach tomorrow, but I'll be back. All the good work done by Wendell (Fifield) and his committee is being swept aside. Those who want the merger are determined to have it, and there's no way to stop them. The seminars are window dressing."

The Rev. Rockwell Harmon Potter was more explosive. His great voice boomed across the campus, "This merger was a mistake from the beginning, and your committee won't change

343

anything. H-e-n-r-y don't waste time on polity. Keep the faith. That will outlast the polity."

Rev. Arthur Bradford stressed the fellowship. "The unity of the fellowship takes first place. Most of my friends agree but continue to press for merger with the Evangelical and Reformed. They are embarrassed by the delay. They gave their word that the union would proceed and feel betrayed by hinderances. Our Report is viewed as one more hurdle, and is therefore resented. I think you know how the executives feel, and they have much support. The support may not be as widespread as they suppose it to be since they listen to those who agree with them."

"Arthur, do you think Monday's Polity seminar can help to ease tension?"

"I have only been present at the Thursday and Friday seminars for a few minutes because of other commitments. It seems to me that the only positive contributions our polity committee can now make are in the realm of historical records and perhaps in enunciating the content of universally accepted principles like fellowship, faith and freedom." The Rev. Walter Giersbach was blunt, "You're wasting time. They've got their minds made up." (referring to General Council leaders.)

When I met with the Rev. William A. Keith my discouragement must have been evident. He volunteered, "From what I hear it's not all 'in the bag.' The 'Interpretations' (of the Basis of Union) added at Oberlin in 1948 are still unacceptable to the E&R."

"Bill, that doesn't mean much at this council. If everything's decided what's the use of holding seminars?"

"Henry, Friday afternoon woke up a few. The men sitting around me were asking good questions. That Legal Opinion troubles some pretty thoughtful people. Keep on the way you are going this afternoon."

The Rev. L. Wendell Fifield was pensive as he and I compared notes on our personal conferences in preparation for the Monday seminar. Wendell mused, "This is really my 'swan song.' My term on the Executive Committee ends with this General Council. I retire within a year. I'm very tired." Then his eyes lit up, "Since this *is* our last day, let's see to it that the meaning of the Report is clearly understood. I *still* believe in what the committee has done. Let's go."

Is There Any Way?

The Chairman opened the seminar by noting that most discussion had focused on the meaning of 'agent,' 'control,' and 'power,' especially, in relation to the Churches, Associations and Conferences. "Which leaves much yet to be considered. Where do you wish to begin this afternoon?"

A man who said he was from Seattle asked, "Isn't there some way to sort out all this stuff so we can talk about it in sections?" Wendell replied, "That should be possible. Would you like Dr. Gray to suggest how this might be done?" At least two-thirds of the fifty or so present nodded.

Major Points

I began, "Suppose you look through the Legal Opinion from subhead 'Impossibilities and Paradoxes' to the signatures. The major points appear to be (1) The alleged impossibility of Churches acting together, (2) concerns about properties, (3) powers of the General Council and Boards, and (4) what is meant by the word 'responsible.' The previous seminars have dealt at length with 'agent,' 'source of power' and 'control.' I'd suggest we address these four points giving a half hour to each one."

The Chairman asked for comments. There were three. Have a brief introduction to each point. Give as many people as possible the opportunity to speak. Indicate the paragraphs in which each point is covered.

"Very well," said Wendell, "if no one objects I'll ask the Congregational Polity Committee Chairman to introduce the first point."

Acting Together

"May I invite you to read the *Legal Opinion* Paragraphs 17, 18. Compare these with the *Documents Report* paragraphs 31, 39 (Nat'l Soc. p. 31), 41, 45, 52, 53, 54, 58, 69-73, and the *Practice Report* paragraphs 48, 53, 57, 66, 69-72, and 82. Additional paragraphs in the Documents and Practice Reports elaborate in detail these 22 paragraphs. Here is the Legal Opinion."

"Acting Together" As Seen In The Legal Opinion

17. "If, as the Report says, the 'wider bodies' are the agents of the churches, then these bodies are governed by 5,600 principals, each of which admittedly is free to select its own theology, determine its own practices and hold its own views of its relations to the wider bodies. If the Report is correct, then to which of these principals is the 'wider body' 'responsible?' If not all of the 5,600 agree, then

which conflicting view should it accept? If 1 or 100 disagree, should the 'wider bodies' be 'accountable' to those 'Principals' or to the 5,599 or the 5,500 which approve? Attention is drawn to a specific situation. In the case of *Cadman v. Kenyon*, the New York Congregational Christian Conference sought to file a brief in the Court of Appeals as a friend of the court for the purpose of presenting its views. 83% of its members and 79.93% of the 332 churches in the Conference had voted in favor of the Plan in The Basis of Union. Nevertheless, counsel for the Cadman Church argued that the Conference was a representative body of the churches in New York State, was 'supposed to be operated for the benefit of all of them' and since, counsel alleged, five of the 'large and prominent churches' in Brooklyn were of a contrary position, the Conference should not be permitted to file the brief. Here was an attempt by an individual church to create enforced 'responsibility' to its views to the exclusion of the views of the other churches concerned. (The attempt failed since the Court permitted the filing of the brief.) This of course is but one example of the application of these premises to our denominational life; yet it evidences the confusion and frustration which would prevail in the organs of our felowship.

18. "It can therefore be seen that there is no limit to the use of which could be made of the premises in this Report. The consequences are not confined to denominational unions and the ecumenical movement, but will invade every facet of denominational life. If accepted, the functioning of the Associations, Conferences, the General Council and the Boards would become impossible."

Compare this opinion with the detailed provisions for Acting Together which appear in the basic Documents of Congregationalism.

"Acting Together" As Seen In The Documents

"31. The General Council of the Congregational Christian Churches of the United States is a voluntary organization of the Congregational Christian churches. Its purpose is 'to foster and express the substantial unity of the Congregational Christian Churches in faith, purpose, polity and work; to consult upon and devise measures and maintain agencies for the promotion of the common interests of the kingdom of God; to cooperate with any corporation or body under control of or affiliated with the Congregational or Christian churches or any of them; and to do and to promote the work of these churches in their national, international, and interdenominational relations."

"39. The General Council is not a legislative body with ecclesiastical authority over the churches, associations or conferences, but states general objectives and makes recommendations which carry the authority of their inherent wisdom and value and are considered and acted upon on the basis of their practical moral and spiritual appeal. 'We hold sacred the freedom of the individual soul and the right of private judgment. We stand for the autonomy of the local church and its independence of ecclesiastical control. We cherish the fellowship of churches united in district, state and national bodies for counsel and cooperation."

"41. The purpose of the American Board of Commissioners for Foreign Missions as stated in its charter is that 'of propagating the Gospel in heathen lands, by supporting missionaries and diffusing a knowledge of the holy scriptures'."

"45. The Board of Home Missions of the Congregational and Christian Churches is a corporation chartered under the laws of Massachusetts (1937), Connecticut (1937), New York (1937), pursuant to action by the General Council at its 1936 meeting for objects 'exclusively charitable, educational and literary,' as follows:

"a. To conduct missionary and educational operations and diffuse a knowledge of the Holy Scriptures, in the United States and in other countries, and promote Christian civilization by endowing, assisting or establishing academic, collegiate, or theological institutions of learning therein, and assisting persons of either sex seeking an education.

"b. To establish, aid and promote churches, Sunday schools, Bible schools and kindred institutions, either directly or through other corporations having similar objects in the United States and other countries.

"c. To promote the building of meeting-houses, parsonages and other buildings by the Congregational and Christian Churches of the United States and its possessions.

"d. To secure, hold, manage and distribute funds for the relief of needy Congregational and Christian ministers and the needy families of deceased Congregational and Christian ministers.

"e. To publish, purchase, sell, circulate and distribute, in such manner as they shall deem expedient, any and all publications, books, tracts, papers or periodicals, calculated to promote good morals and pure Christianity and the spread and extension of the gospel of Jesus Christ.

"f. And in general to extend the gospel and the means of Christian education, and to do and promote charitable and Christian work for the advancement of the general interests of the Congregational and Christian churches in the United

States and elsewhere; and the corporation hereby created may cooperate with any other societies or agencies under the charge and control of churches of the Congregational and Christian order in the United States.

"The Board of Home Missions carries on the work, is authorized to accept and receive, and inherits the property and other rights of the following agencies: The American Missionary Association, the Congregational Church Building Society, the Congregational Home Missionary Society, the Congregational Sunday School Extension Society, the Congregational Education Society, the Congregational Publishing Society, and the Congregational Board of Ministerial Relief. The Board is the agent and attorney of all these organizations."

"52. The Board of Home Missions is designated in the Constitution of the General Council as the recognized body 'of the Congregational and Christian Churches for the extension of Christ's kingdom in the United States except as such activities are administered locally.'"

"53. The Council for Social Action is the agency of the Congregational Christian Churches for helping to make the Christian gospel more effective in society, national and world-wide, through research, education, and action, in co-operation with the churches and their missionary agencies."

"54. The Council for Social Action is a body created by and responsibile to the General Council. The Council for Social Action is required to make a full and accurate report of its condition and work to the General Council at each stated meeting of that body. It comprises 18 persons elected for six-year terms and serving on a volunteer basis."

"58. The Missions Council has for its function the task of keeping before its constituency the Home and Foreign missionary and educational work of the Congregational Christian Churches, with a view to increasing interest, enlarging the annual contributions and securing legacies, conditional gifts, endowments, and special gifts for the entire work: state, national and foreign."

"69. The International Congregational Council consists of not more than 235 members from the constituent churches, 75 from U.S.A., 75 from the British Isles, 75 from all other lands. Not more than ten additional members may be elected by the Council on nomination of its executive committee.

"70. The International council delegates are elected by the constituent bodies from which they come, in accord with electoral procedures set by these bodies.

"71. The International Council ordinarily meets at intervals of five years.

"72. The purpose of the International Council is 'to promote regular consultation and effective cooperation among its constituent churches; to devise measures and maintain agencies for the advancement of their common witness; and to strengthen the Congregational contribution to the World Council of Churches and to the ecumenical movement generally.'

"73. The constituent churches of the International Council are evangelical and reformed churches of the world which are organized (a) in national unions of Congregational Churches, or (b) in communions which in part spring from Congregational Churches and maintain the principles of Congregational churchmanship, or (c) as communions or groups of churches ordered after the Christian faith and Congregational polity."

Clearly, the churches have created organs by which they act together. This is affirmed by the Polity and Unity Survey of Practice.

Churches Acting Together In Practice

"48. The General Council biennial meeting is (a) *the churches of our order in council assembled*, (b) *a gathering for fellowship*, counsel and discussions, (c) *a business session* of delegates for the transaction of such business as may come before a General Council by virtue of its charter or other fundamental documents; and (d) *a corporate meeting* of those boards and agencies of our churches which are related to or controlled by the General Council. Its powers in each of these capacities are defined by the charters, constitutions, by-laws or other fundamental documents of (a) the General Council, or (b) the associated bodies whose official meetings are being held, or (c) the special instructions or memorials of churches, conferences, associations, or other agencies of the Congregational Christian Churches."

"53. The General Council has no written standards for the 'recognition' of a conference. Recognition is taken for granted, and describes the relation of mutual responsibility which exists between the state conference-level and the national-level agencies of the churches. It is to be defined in terms of mutual obligations and spiritual fellowship rather than in legal phrases or in a printed discipline. A conference which is the state-level agency of a group of Congregational Christian churches asks for and receives (by virtue of its nature) the privilege of participation in the life and work of the General Council, and voluntarily covenants with the General

Council to cooperate in the national-level life and work of the fellowship, unless prevented by conscience from so doing."

"57. The churches and all the wider bodies of the Congregational Christian fellowship have their respective inner polity structures set forth in charters, constitutions, by-laws, or rules of procedure under which each particular church or wider body is organized.

"Polity relationships between churches and wider bodies are frequently set forth in the basic written documents of the Congregational Christian Fellowship, e.g. in certain local church, association, and state conference constitutions; and there are general statements of polity relationships in the basic documents of the General Council. All these inter-church-wider-body polity statements describe the relationships of the various bodies of a voluntary fellowship; they do not compel conformity; they simply state the polity relationship which is regarded as desirable *by the body making the statement*; they gain acceptance on the basis of inherent worth.

"Thus certain wider bodies, for example, the association, are clearly and directly the responsible agents of the churches, whereas other wider bodies, for example the Annuity Fund for Congregational Ministers, are clearly and directly responsible to their own Boards of Control. The unity of the Congregational Christian fellowship is achieved chiefly by goodwill, and by working agreements which are mutually accepted by the agreeing bodies, for example, the American Board, voluntarily agrees under its own charter, to meet at the same time as the General Council, and to elect the members of the General Council as corporate members of the American Board. By this voluntary agreement the foreign missionary work of the fellowship becomes a concern of the General Council and of the churches, associations, and conferences from which have come the delegates to the General Council. What we have in some of our wider bodies is an extension of the principle of the 'gathered' Church; i.e. those Congregational Christians who were concerned about foreign missions simply 'gathered' themselves together as the American Board and proceeded to solicit the support of others both as individuals and as churches. The 1913 reorganization plan, adopted by the National Council, created a framework of voluntary relationships between the General Council and other wider bodies such as the American Board, in order to establish a closer tie between the churches and the many wider bodies through which are channeled the concerns of the churches and their members."

"66. The program planned at the Mid-Winter meetings becomes the official program of the national and state agencies of the

350

Congregational Christian churches through action of the several bodies represented in or meeting in connection with the Missions Council."

"69.   The International Congregational Council is described in our documentary statement. It is primarily a world-wide fellowship organization for national bodies which recognize their kinship with Congregational principles and polity.

"70.   The International Council presently has its headquarters in Memorial Hall, London, England. This office acts under the Minister and Secretary, the Associate Secretary and their assistants as a center for inspiration, information, exchange of groups and preachers between national bodies, stimulation of interest among lay women, laymen, and young people, holding of conferences, and furtherance of certain world ecumenical relationships.

"71.   The International Council customarily has met alternately in the British Isles and in the United States. Its moderators also have been chosen from these two areas.

"72.   The International Council is a practical means of promoting understanding fellowship, thinking and a measure of united action among its constituent groups. Each meeting issues a "Message to the Churches" which seeks to gather up the chief concerns of the delegates in a framework of Christian conviction. These 'Messages' are circulated generally by many of the constituent bodies."

"82.   The word 'fellowship' is a term much used by members of the Congregational Christian churches. Its meanings are chiefly these: (a) the inclusive body of those who share the Christian faith and recognize the Congregational way as the manner in which that faith expresses itself, (b) the totality of all the organized bodies of the Congregational Christian churches, and of all groups of members acting together in the interest of the Congregational Christian churches, and (c) the radiant personal and organizational relationships which characterize the life of those who acknowledge Jesus as Lord, who reverently seek to follow the leadings of the Holy Spirit, who join in common worship, whose kinship in Christian service bears fruit in mutual trust and deep friendship, and who have chosen to share together in the work and worship of the Congregational Christian churches and of the wider bodies created by them or by groups of their members."

I had hardly finished reviewing Legal Opinion, Documents and Practice when a hand shot up, "Yes, sir." I said. "What's the issue in Legal Opinion paragraph 17?", he asked. I replied,

"The seminar has noted in detail the fact that all wider bodies are agents of the Churches. *This paragraph disowns the fun-*

351

damental character of Congregationalism when it denies the testimony of almost 400 years, the written evidence of synods and councils, and the present witness of the Congregational Way in America. The issue here is much more than legal. The Congregational Churches are quite incidentally an organized denomination; they are a fellowship. From 1620 to 1871 no national organization existed but the Congregational *fellowship* already existed, and has never ceased! Practice Report, paragraph 82 reads as follows:

> "82. The word 'fellowship' is a term much used by members of the Congregational Christian churches. Its meanings are chiefly these: (a)the inclusive body of those who share the Christian faith and recognize the Congregational Way as the manner in which that faith expresses itself, (b) the totality of all the organized bodies of the Congregational Christian churches, and of all groups of members acting together in the interest of the Congregational Christian churches, and (c)the radiant personal and organizational relationships which characterize the life of those who acknowledge Jesus as Lord, who reverently seek to follow the leadings of the Holy Spirit, who join in common worship, whose kinship in Christian service bears fruit in mutual trust and deep friendship, and who have chosen to share together in the work and worship of the Congregational Christian churches and of the wider bodies created by them or by groups of their members."[1]

Typical of the understanding expressed in all basic documents are these statements from Conference constitutions across the country.

1. *No. California.*
    "The object of this Conference is the fellowship and cooperation of the Congregational churches and ministers of Northern California."[2]

2. *Colorado*
    "It shall be the object of this organization to express the fellowship and promote the practical cooperation of the churches . . ."[3]

3. *Connecticut*
    Object: "The development of brotherly intercourse and cooperation among the Congregational Christian Churches of the State."[4]

4. *South Dakota*
    First object "shall be to express and promote the fellowship and practical union of the churches . . ."[5]

5. *North Dakota*
   Identical to South Dakota.[6]

6. *Florida*
   Identical to South Dakota.[7]

7. *Hawaiian Evangelical Association*
   Purposes: "to provide its members with opportunities for mutual counsel and assistance in the great work of propogating the Christian Gospel. . . ."[8]

8. *Idaho*
   "The purpose of this Conference shall be to increase the efficiency of the churches and ministers of the Conference by fellowship and counsel, and to promote unity of feeling and consert of action in every good work."[9]

9. *Illinois*
   Objects: "the promotion of fellowship . . ."[10]

10. *Indiana*
    "to secure a more perfect union and better co-operation between the membership and the churches, and to promote fellowship and understanding among the churches and ministers for the upbuilding of the Kingdom."[11]

11. *Iowa*
    "To foster and express the practical unity and fellowship of the churches connected with this body; to gather and disseminate information relative to the work and fellowship of these churches."[12]

12. *Kansas*
    "The purposes for which this corporation is formed are: to promote the general interests and agencies of the C. C. Churches of Kansas; to be their instrument for carrying on such . . . work as they may desire to undertake in common . . ."[13]

13. *Maine*
    "To promote . intercourse and fellowship among the Congregational Christian churches of Maine."
    "It accepts the two principles of American Congregationalism; viz., independence in matters of local concern, fellowship in matters of common concern."[14]

14. *Massachusetts*
    "Advise and counsel the churches when requested, but it is recognized that each church has the power of self-determination in all matters."[15]

15. *Michigan*
    "The object . . . is . . . the propogation of the religious faith and ecclesiastical polity of the Congregational . Christian Churches . . ."

"Purposes within the scope of the Conference (are) more particularly" ten items, the tenth being a 'catch-all' "doing of whatever else may foster the growth, or promote the welfare or the interests of (the) faith and order" of the Congregational Christian Churches.[16]

16. *Middle Atlantic*
Object "to extend within the membership a brotherly acquaintance and fellowship; to promote unity of spirit and practice . . . "[17]

17. *Minnesota*
"This Conference shall be incorporated and shall be the agency of the Congregational Christian churches of the state for the accomplishment of the work they wish to do co-operatively. It shall seek to coordinate the several forms of denominational activity engaged in by the churches of the Conference and . . . promote the benevolent interests of the domination within the state in fellowship with the General Council."[18]

18. *Missouri*
"The objects and purposes . . . shall be: Section 1. To promote Christian fellowship among the Congregational Christian churches of Missouri . . . by means of agencies constituted and controlled by the churches themselves."[19]

19. *Montana*
"The object . . . shall be to express the fellowship and promote the practical union of the churches . . . and to be the agent and instrument of the Congregational Christian Churches of Montana for the carrying on of such religious work as the said churches may desire to undertake in common."[20]

20. *Nebraska*
"The constitutive principle of this Conference is that of representative democracy, which recognizes the autonomy of the local church and its independence of all ecclesiastical control."
"The object . . . shall be to co-ordinate . . . the common activities of its members . . . This Conference shall be composed of . churches and ministers" of the Congregational Christian Churches in Nebraska.[21]

21. *New Hampshire*
Objects: "the promotion of . . . brotherly intercourse and harmony among the Congregational and Christian churches of the state . . ."[22]
"This Conference . . . maintains the right and duty of churches to unite in local, state, and national bodies for fellowship, counsel, and co-operation in all matters of common concern. And this Conference exists in part to promote said fellowship and

counsel and to make effective such co-operation among the churches of the State and between them and the General Council and our national and state missionary enterprises."[23]

22. *New York*
Objects: "To carry on such . . . work . . . as the churches may desire to undertake in common through representation in this body."[24]

23. *Ohio*
"Basis of Fellowship
"The Congregational Christian Churches of Ohio, united through the grace of our Lord, Jesus Christ, finding in the Bible the supreme rule of faith and life, but recognizing that there is wide room for differences of interpretation among Christians, do confidently declare our fellowship to be based upon the acceptance of Christianity as primarily The Way of Life and not upon uniformity of theological opinion or any uniform practice of ordinances.

"We humbly depend, as did our fathers, on the continued guidance of the Holy Spirit to lead us into all truth, enabling us to walk in the ways of the Lord, made known or to be made known to us."[25]

24. *Oregon*
"The object . . . shall be to promote Christian Fellowship among its members . . . and to be the agent and instrument of the Congregational Christian Churches of Oregon for the carrying on of such . . . work as the churches . . . may desire to undertake in common."[26]

25. *Pennsylvania*
"The objects of this conference shall be in general those stated in the Articles of Incorporation, and in particular the promotion of fellowship among the churches and ministers, and the coordination under one management of the general interests of the churches by means of agencies constituted and controlled by the churches themselves through representation in this body.

"The conference will labor for the propagation of the faith and polity of the Congregational and Christian churches of the State of Pennsylvania, working in fellowship with them and with the district associations which they compose, and with the General Council of the Congregational and Christian Churches of the United States. It will seek to promote the welfare of the churches and ministers, and to advance the interests of the kingdom of Christ."[27]

26. *Puerto Rico*
"The purpose . . . to assure the close brotherhood among the churches."[28]

27. *Rhode Island*

Objects: "the promotion of unity, harmony and fellowship among our Congregational Christian Churches of this state; their cooperation in religious, missionary and charitable work, the propogation of the religious faith and polity of the Congregational Christian Churches . . ."[29]

28. *Southern Convention*

"The purpose . . . is to build the kingdom of God, and to that end it shall have general supervision of all the enterprises of the denomination within" (the geographic area described in Article II).[30]

29. *Southeast Convention*

"organized to the end that there shall be a more vital fellowship among the churches . . ." "The name of the fellowship shall be . . ."[31]

30. *Utah*

"The purpose . . . to increase the efficiency of the churches and ministers . . . by fellowship and counsel, to promote unity of interest . . . , and to be the instrument of the Utah churches for the carrying on of whatever work the churches may desire to undertake in common."[32]

31. *Vermont*

"to promote the harmony, fellowship, efficiency and cooperation of the Congregational . . . churches and ministers in Vermont."[33]

32. *Washington*

"the promotion of fellowhship among the churches and ministers, and the co-ordination under one management of the general interests of the churches by means of agencies constituted and controlled by the churches themselves through representation in this body."[34]

33. *Wisconsin*

Object: "to express the fellowship and promote the practical union of the churches connected with this body."[35]

34. *Wyoming*

"The object of this conference shall be to promote and express the fellowship of the Congregational Christian Churches in Wyoming."[36]

35. *Oklahoma-Texas*

Was in the process of writing a constitution in 1952-1954.

36. *German Conference*

Was a language group unlike other "state" conferences, and had no formal constitution.

37. "Conferences" in Alabama, Mississippi, Georgia, South Carolina, North Carolina and Virginia were grouped as "Convention of the South" for which no constitution was available.

38 & 39. The Southwest and Southern California Conferences united to form the "Congregational Conference of Southern California and the Southwest."

Unaware of the singularity of that Conference statement of purpose the Legal Opinion quotes the old version, "The purposes of this conference shall be to advance the Kingdom of God by prompting the fellowship of the Congregational Churches . . ."[37] Ironically, I was at the time Chairman of a Committee to draft a new Constitution and By-Laws for Southern California and Southwest! The lengthy article on Purposes begins, "The general purpose of this Conference shall be to express the fellowship and to further the work of the Congregational Churches"[38] in the geographic area. The original manuscript, with innumerable crossings-out, additions, and corrections is open to inspection.

"Acting Together" In The Fellowship

The thirty-five available documents have been quoted. The alleged notion of inability to act cooperatively is contradicted by the documents, and by actions taken by the Churches from the Salem Council of 1629 to 1954.

The word *fellowship* is the central purpose or object in 26 of the 35 constitutions. The same idea is phrased as "development of *brotherly love* and cooperation among the Congregational Churches" in *Connecticut*, and *Puerto Rico. Hawaii* provides for "mutual counsel and assistance," *Kansas'* purpose is "to promote the general interests of the Congregational Christian Churches . . ." In *Massachusetts* the object is "advice and counsel (to) the churches when requested." In *Michigan* the main purpose is "doing . whatever . may foster the growth, or promote the welfare or the interests of . . . the churches." In *Nebraska* "the object . . . shall be to co-ordinate . . . the common activities" of the Congregational Churches and ministers. Thus, in *all but one* constitution the Conference exists for fellowship, brotherly love, cooperation, advice, counsel and doing whatever will foster the growth, welfare and interests of the Churches.

The Southern Convention is a hold-over from the 1931 union with the Christian Churches. Its entire constitution is authoritative, unlike all of 34 other Conference documents.

The issue of the nature of the inter-relations of Churches and wider bodies in Congregationalism is clear in the Legal Opinion under the heading "The Impossibilities and Paradoxes Suggested by the Report." "Impossibility" refers to the astonishing way in which the Congregational Christian fellowship acts as one body! Possibly the "Paradox" refers to the way the Churches act in fellowship as Associations, Conferences, General Council or Boards.

Review of all extant fundamental Documents, Congregational History and Practice (testimony of experts throughout the land) lies behind the following statement on *fellowship*.

"82.   The word 'fellowship' is a term much used by members of the Congregational Christian churches. Its meanings are chiefly these: (a) the inclusive body of those who share the Christian faith and recognize the Congregational way as the manner in which that faith expresses itself, (b) the totality of all the organized bodies of the Congregational Christian churches, and of all groups of members acting together in the interest of the Congregational Christian churches, and (c) the radiant personal and organizational relationships which characterize the life of those who acknowledge Jesus as Lord, who reverently seek to follow the leadings of the Holy Spirit, who join in common worship, whose kinship in Christian service bears fruit in mutual trust and deep friendship, and who have chosen to share together in the work and worship of the Congregational Christian churches and the wider bodies created by them or by groups of their numbers."[39]

Brotherly love, cooperation, mutual counsel and devout dedication to the God and Father of our Lord Jesus Christ produced the incredible missionary, educational, societal, and religious work of the Congregational Churches.

Unusual Words In the Legal Opinion

One is curious to know how a lawyer came to use the words, "Impossibilities and Paradoxes." The phrase is redolent of Karl Barth's "Doctrine of the Word of God" which was translated into English by the Rev. Douglas Horton; this was the book which first emphasized *paradox* and *impossibility* in 20th Century Christianity. What appears to be quite *"impossible"* by puny legal power has always been accomplished with joy by the power of the Spirit of God made manifest in and through the Churches of God.From the *impossible* action by thousands of Congregational Churches the state of California received its first elected official,

358

Rev. Walter Colton, its first public school in San Francisco, its first College out of which grew the University of California, its first newspaper at Monterey, Churches dotting the state and Colleges of high quality like Pomona, Scripps, Claremont, and Mills. Many times Missionary Agent Warren had to act *in accord with the Spirit and in defiance of the "Board"* to do what the loving heart of the Churches wished to do. In the 20th Century Sam Coles and Dr. Mary Cushman of Angola have had to do the same, Frank Laubach too!

Fellowship produces whatever organization is needed to accomplish God's purposes through His Churches. *Organization* is not an assurance of fellowship; it may indeed, destroy fellowship. Legalism is no substitute for love, as the mediators have said again and again.

The Association constitutions bear unanimous testimony to the reason for their existence—fellowship, brotherly counsel and advice. Congregational Churches were "recognized" by sister churches, mutually, before there were associations. What was "recognized" was each other's spiritual allegiance and shared ways of expressing that devotion, eschewing all legal or arbitrary rules. There is no provision whatever for the approval or disapproval, the acceptance or non-acceptance of one Church by sister Churches for organizational reasons. The first National Council enunciated the standard.

> "*Resolved*, That affiliation with our denomination of churches not now upon our roll, should be welcomed upon the basis of common evangelical faith, substantial Congregational polity and free communion of Christians, without regard to forms or minor differences."[40]

Perhaps the most telling example of the true nature of the Council is seen in its origin in 1871, and the limited powers given to it by the Churches.

> "'The Congregational churches of the United States, by elders and messengers assembled, do now associate themselves in National Council, to express and foster their substantial unity in doctrine, polity and work: and to consult upon the common interests of all the churches, their duties in the work of evangelization, the united development of their resources and their relations to all parts of the kingdom of Christ."[41]

Congregational freedom *encouraged* the consultation and missionary action of the New Testament Churches. Of this fact the Council at Jerusalem described in Acts 15 one of many testimonies.

Voluntary cooperation created and sustained all the consultations and actions of the Church bodies created by the Churches
in the United States . . . and in the Colonies prior to 1776. Of this,
the origin, nature and nurture of the National Council in 1871 is a
prime example. The Congregational Churches have acted together
through organs of fellowship and love.

Property Rights

Mediators like Professor Matthew Spinka, Rev. Roy Minich,
Superintendent Harley Gill and Rev. Arthur Bradford rarely
wrote or talked about property rights. Devout Christians like Professor Benjamin D. Scott of Pomona College believed that it *must*
be possible to settle all material questions amicably if spiritual
misunderstandings and differences were resolved. The issue of
"property rights" was viewed as an undesirable intrusion into the
CC/ER merger discussions. When great souls like President
James A. Blaisdell wrote[42] about "property rights" they did so
with great reluctance.

I was shocked when legal action was threatened by stalwarts like
Rev. Malcolm Burton and Rev. James Fifield. This was the initial
reaction of every one of the Mediators. The lawyers of the General
Council, Wood, Werner, France, and Tully, were joined by
merger proponents like Rev. Truman Douglass, Rev. Frank
Scribner, Rev. William Frazier (who, by now, had switched sides
under tremendous pressure, being ousted as Home Board Executive Vice-President and installed as Treasurer), and Rev. Albert
Penner. The result was dismay among the Mediators. The possibility of reconciliation now faced entrenched opposing parties and
a new kind of acrimony in spoken and written words. I can state
categorically, that this acrimony saddened us beyond my power
to express.

The Property Issues

The property issues were real, and varied. Properties owned by
each Church were quickly seen by CC/ER Merger proponents and
opponents to be under the control of each Church.

The hundreds of million dollars accumulated from trusts,
bequests, gifts, contributions of Churches and individuals over
centuries were technically vested in many church bodies. For
example, assets of the "Six Societies," Church Building, Education, etc. are held, since 1936, by the Home Board through the

360

legal devise of powers-of-attorney. Vast monies have been invested by the Churches and individual Congregationalists through State Conferences, some Associations, some City Missionary Societies, and kindred bodies.

A third type of property is illustrated by those bodies which were controlled by their membership, such as, the Ministers Annuity Fund and the American Congregational Association, the latter being the owner of Congregational House in Boston and proprietor of the great Congregational Library. Technically, court decisions recognized the self-governing character of these bodies, with certain important provisios.

Property dispute centered chiefly on the assets of national and state bodies. It was this issue which was addressed in the Monday seminar at the New Haven Council in 1954.

One Lawyer's View of Property Rights

The property rights represented by the trusts, Church and individual contributions, etc. over many, many decades are discussed in paragraphs 23 and 24 of the Legal Opinion.[43]

23.   "The Report (IV, 6, par. V) speaks of the 'joint properties of our present fellowship' and 'common property rights.' If the words were used in a legal sense, they evidence a misapprehension of the law. There are no joint properties or common property rights. The decisions of the Appellate Division and the Court of Appeals of the State of New York, after full submission of the facts, categorically denied the existence of such properties or rights. The Court of Appeals said:

"'Notwithstanding that the above listed Boards and agencies are corporations authorized and existing under the laws of several different states the plaintiffs nonetheless contend that such boards and agencies have in fact no separate and independent status because their boards of trustees, officers and administrators are drawn from the membership of the General Council and that their activities are for all practical purposes, controlled and supervised by the General Council— that diversion of their funds and assets and mingling of same with the funds of others is in interference to its detriment in a property interest belonging to the Cadman Church and other non-assenting churches. This, however, *is not established in fact* as the proof shows and it is conceded, the Cadman Church has not contributed any funds, except as we have seen, for other than a general corporate purpose and these voluntarily and without restriction as to use or application.

Under such circumstances it must be assumed that such funds
were general gifts for use by the corporations in connection
with their general corporate purposes. Such voluntary unre-
stricted contributions for a general charitable and religious
purpose *create no proprietary or beneficial interest* warranting
the civil courts in interferring in their expenditure so long as it
appears that such use and application is not violative of charter
purposes.' (Italics ours.)

24. "The Committee believes in the principle that the General
Council has no *right* to unite *itself* with other bodies where such
action vitally affects the interests of the Churches (IV, 6, par. III).
The difficulty with this criterion is that it means different things to
different persons. To some, the Churches are vitally affected as
soon as the Council departs from their individual views as to its
proper conduct. We have already discussed the consequences of the
theory of control which arises from this line of thought. Others still
adhere to the view that the Churches have property interests in the
funds of the Boards. This theory has been entirely destroyed by the
decision of the New York Court of Appeals as noted above. The
only acceptable interpretation, legally, is that the interests of the
Churches are affected when their properties or operations are disturbed. If the Committee means this, then it is stating a near axiom
of Congregationalism which all proposals for union have recognized."

Contrast the statement of the churches' control of wider bodies
in the documents.

Property Rights In The Basic Documents

The General Council in 1954 was not itself a body with large
properties. A Corporation for the General Council held the assets.
The American Board (foreign missions), the Home Board, other
national level bodies, and State Conferences held title to the major
assets of the Congregational fellowship.

In the documents property rights are dealt with quite incidentally since the fellowship is spiritual in nature, with its "powers"
derived from and depended upon the Churches. Here are the
passages to compare with the Legal Opinion.

The General Council[44] (from its constitution and by-laws)

"31. The General Council of the Congregational Christian
Churches of the United States is a voluntary organization of the
Congregational Christian churches. Its purpose is 'to foster and
express the substantial unity of the Congregational Christian
Churches in faith, purpose, polity and work; to consult upon and

devise measures and maintain agencies for the promotion of the Common interests of the kingdom of God; to cooperate with any corporation or body under control of or affiliated with the Congregational or Christian churches or any of them; and to do and to promote the work of these churches in their national, international, and interdenominational relations.'"

"33. The General Council meets 'biennially in the even-numbered years, the exact time and place to be fixed by the Executive Committee, unless otherwise ordered by the Council.' Special meetings may be called by the Executive Committee or when as many as seven state organizations request it. The primary concern of the biennial meeting is the transaction of the business entrusted to the Council by the churches.

"34. The Executive Committee of the General Council is composed of 18 elected members serving six-year terms and the Moderator, *ex-officio*. It acts as the General Council *ad interim* and is required to make a full report of all its doings at biennial meetings. Questions of polity not clearly defined by the Council may be determined by the Executive Committee *ad interim*. While it is not charged with details of administration of the several national agencies, it seeks to correlate their work, and may make such recommendations to the Council as it may deem wise for the more economical and efficient administration of the several organizations. It studies the relative needs of the several denominational agencies and recommends apportionment percentages. An Advisory Committee may act for the Executive Committee between meetings 'with such limitations and powers as the Executive Committee may direct.'

"35. The Business Committee of the General Council is charged with preparation of the docket for business sessions, and all Council business is first presented to it, except the reports of the Executive, Nominating, and Resolutions Committees. The Council may consider any item presented or suppressed by the Business Committee. The Executive Committee shall serve as the Business Committee of all regular and special meetings.

"36. The Corporation for the General Council of the Congregational Christian Churches of the United States consists of 15 persons elected by the Council in addition to the Moderator and Secretary of the Council, *ex officio*. The object of the Corporation is to do and promote religious, educational and charitable work for the advancement of the general interests and purposes of the Congregational and Christian Churches. It may receive, hold, and administer, in trust or otherwise, funds and property for the use of the General Council, or of churches or other institutions of the Congregational or Christian order.

"37. The Moderator (elected by the General Council for a two-year term) shall preside over meetings of the General Council, may deliver an opening address to the Council over which he presides, and exercise the 'representative functions . . . of visiting and addressing churches, conferences, associations, and conventions upon their invitation, and of representing the Council in the wider relations of Christian fellowship so far as they may be able and disposed.' It is understood that his personal acts and utterances have no authority from or upon the General Council or its constituent groups.

"38. The Secretary (elected by the General Council for a two-year term) is also the 'Minister of the council,' and shall be available to the committees and commissions 'for advice and help in matters of policy and constructive organization.'

"39. The General Council is not a legislative body with ecclesiastical authority over the churches, associations or conferences, but states general objectives and makes recommendations which carry the authority of their inherent wisdom and value and are considered and acted upon on the basis of their practical moral and spiritual appeal. 'We hold sacred the freedom of the individual soul and the right of private judgment. We stand for the autonomy of the local church and its independence of ecclesiastical control. We cherish the fellowship of churches united in district, state and national bodies for counsel and cooperation.'

"40. There are various committees and commissions of the General Council such as the Commission on Stewardship, the Commission on the Ministry and the Commission on Interchurch Relations and Christian Unity. The purpose of the Commission on Interchurch Relations and Christian Unity is to 'devote itself to a careful study of all phases of inter-church relations including local and general expressions of Christian fraternity and cooperation such as federated churches, federations of churches, cooperative enterprises, and comity in educational and missionary work'; to 'make a study of church union, including its objectives, its feasibility, and its processes'; to 'cultivate friendly relations with other bodies of Christians for the sake of those relations in themselves and in the hope of consummating further union'; and to 'cooperate with bodies of other denominations in fostering the spirit of oneness among the followers of Christ.'"

The American Board[45]

"Note: The American Board of Commissioners for Foreign Missions was incorporated in 1812 by Special Act (Chap. 21) of the Commonwealth of Massachusetts. From time to time amendments have been made by the legislature. Under authority of this charter, the corporation has made by-laws which have been amended from

364

time to time. The following statements as to certain provisions as to the organization and operation of the corporation are intended merely as a general summary and the legislative acts which constitute the charter and the by-laws adopted under its authority should be referred to for a complete and accurate statement.

"41.   The purpose of the American Board of Commissioners for Foreign Missions as stated in its charter is that 'of propagating the Gospel in heathen lands, by supporting missionaries and diffusing a knowledge of the holy scriptures'.

"42.   The corporate members of the corporation are elected as provided in the charter and by-laws by the corporation itself. There is no requirement as to their membership in any particular denomination. When the Board was originally organized, the membership contained persons belonging to several denominations and the corporation received support from individuals who belonged to different denominations. With the passage of time, various denominations organized their own foreign mission boards and the American Board became more closely associated with the Congregational denomination and received a large portion of its support from the Congregational Christian Churches, although still receiving support from other sources. This led in 1913 to a change in the by-laws by which it was provided that all delegates to the National Council of the Congregational Churches (now General Council) should be considered as nominated for corporate membership in the American Board. Their election by the corporation is still necessary. There is in addition another group of corporate members, also elected by the corporation known as the members at large.

"43.   The American Board has the usual officers of a corporation, elected by the corporation. The Prudential Committee performs the functions and duties generally exercised by a board of directors or trustees. The chief executive and administrative officer is the Executive Vice-President and under him are the various secretaries, associate and assistant Secretaries.

"44.   While there is no requirement to that effect, the American Board customarily holds its annual meetings every other year in conjunction with the meeting of the General Council and it makes report of its work to the meetings of the General Council."

The Board of Home Missions[46]

"45.   The Board of Home Missions of the Congregational and Christian Churches is a corporation chartered under the laws of Massachusetts (1937), Connecticut (1937), New York (1937), pursuant to action by the General Council at its 1936 meeting for objects 'exclusively charitable, educational and literary,' as follows:

"a. To conduct missionary and educational operations and diffuse a knowledge of the Holy Scriptures, in the United States and in other countries, and promote Christian civilization by endowing, assisting or establishing academic, collegiate, or theological institutions of learning therein, and assisting persons of either sex seeking an education.

"b. To establish, aid and promote churches, Sunday schools, Bible schools and kindred institutions, either directly or through other corporations having similar objects in the United States and other countries.

"c. To promote the building of meeting-houses, parsonages and other buildings by the Congregational and Christian Churches of the United States and its possessions.

"d. To secure, hold, manage and distribute funds for the relief of needy Congregational and Christian ministers and the needy families of deceased Congregational and Christian ministers.

"e. To publish, purchase, sell, circulate and distribute, in such manner as they shall deem expedient, any and all publications, books, tracts, papers or periodicals, calculated to promote good morals and pure Christianity and the spread and extension of the gospel of Jesus Christ.

"f. And in general to extend the gospel and the means of Christian education, and to do and promote charitable and Christian work for the advancement of the general interests of the Congregational and Christian churches in the United States and elsewhere; and the corporation hereby created may cooperate with any other societies or agencies under the charge and control of churches of the Congregational and Christian order in the United States.

"The Board of Home Missions carries on the work, is authorized to accept and receive, and inherits the property and other rights of the following agencies: The American Missionary Association, the Congregational Church Building Society, the Congregational Home Missionary Society, the Congregational Sunday School Extension Society, the Congregational Publishing Society, and the Congregational Board of Ministerial Relief. The Board is the agent and the attorney of all these organizations.

"46. The corporate membership of the Board of Home Missions consists of the voting life members of the seven organizations named above, the directors of the Board of Home Missions, the members of the General Council of the Congregational Christian Churches, and 250 members-at-large elected by the Board at meetings held in connection with the General Council for terms of four years.

"47.   The officers of the corporation are a president, three vice-presidents and an executive vice-president, a secretary and a treasurer, general secretaries, and a board of directors.

"48.   The Board of Directors numbering 36 persons, elected for terms of four years, plus the president and three vice-presidents, manages and conducts the business and affairs of the corporation.

"49.   The Executive Vice-President is the executive of the Board of Directors and a member of all standing committees, but may not vote in the Nominating Committee or the Committee on Personnel and Salaries. There are as many general secretaries as the requirements of the work make necessary, the number being determined by the Board of Directors.

"50.   The Division Committees give aid and counsel and make recommendations to the Board of Directors concerning the work of the several Divisions: viz, American Missionary Association, Church Extension and Evangelism, Ministerial Relief, Pilgrim Press, Christian Education, Promotion and Missionary Education.

"51.   The departments within each Division are established for the execution of work (i.e. Youth, Children, etc.), but responsibility rests with the Board of Directors, under the instructions of the Board.

"52.   The Board of Home Missions is designated in the Constitution of the General Council as the recognized body 'of the Congregational and Christian Churches for the extension of Christ's kingdom in the United States except as such activities are administered locally.' "

The Council for Social Action[47]

"53.   The Council for Social Action is the agency of the Congregational Christian Churches for helping to make the Christian gospel more effective in society, national and world-wide, through research, education, and action, in co-operation with the churches and their missionary agencies.

"54.   The Council for Social Action is a body created by and responsible to the General Council. The Council for Social Action is required to make a full and accurate report of its condition and work to the General Council at each stated meeting of that body. It comprises 18 persons elected for six-year terms and serving on a volunteer basis.

"55.   A consultative and supporting Body of Associates of not more than 250 created by the General Council may attend the

367

General Council and may speak but not vote, except as they are full members of the Council."

The Annuity Fund[48]

"56.   The Annuity Fund for Congregational ministers is an incorportated body under New Jersey law whose purpose is, as stated in its charter, 'the maintenance of a society for beneficial and protective purposes to its members . . . and to provide for the relief of disabled members, or their families, and to maintain a fund or funds for that purpose, and to contract with its members to pay death benefits, and to pay the same to the member's widow, minor children, or persons dependent upon him, or to his legal representatives, after his death.'

"a.   The business of the Annuity Fund is managed by a Board of Trustees, twelve in number, who have the power to elect officers and to make, alter or amend the Rules and By-Laws of the Corporation.

"b.   The members of the Annuity Fund are those ministers of the Congregational Christian Churches in the United States of America or of a religious denomination or order affiliated, merged or consolidated with such Congregational Christian Churches who are enrolled in the Fund in accordance with its rules and by-laws.

"c.   The Trustees are elected by the members at the annual meeting of the Corporation, and are chosen from the names of eligible persons presented to and approved by the General Council of the Congregational Christian Churches of the United States.

"d.   The Trustees report to the General Council of the Congregational Christian Churches of the United States at its regular sessions, including a full review of the condition of the corporation and the report of the Treasurer.

"e.   The Retirement Fund for Lay Workers is a corporation similarly organized and directed for all lay workers employed by Congregational Christian Churches or by religious, charitable or educational bodies or organizations affiliated, merged or consolidated with such Congregational Christian Churches. Its officers and trustees are identical with those of the Annuity Fund for Congregational ministers."

The Missions Council[49]

"57.   The name of this organization is the Missions Council of the Congregational Christian Churches. (This name was adopted by the Joint Meeting of the Directors of the Home Boards and the

368

Prudential Committee of the American Board of Commissioners for Foreign Missions, at South Hadley, Mass., in June 1936; which meeting was held in accordance with actions of the General Council of Congregational and Christian Churches, the Home Societies, and the American Board at their meetings in June 1936.)

"58. The Missions Council has for its function the task of keeping before its constituency the Home and Foreign missionary and educational work of the Congregational Christian Churches, with a view to increasing interest, enlarging the annual contributions and securing legacies, conditional gifts, endowments, and special gifts for the entire work: state, national and foreign.

"59. The members of the Missions Council are the thirty-six elected members of the Board of Directors and the President and Vice Presidents of the Board of Home Missions; and the thirty-six elected members of the Prudential Committee and the President and Vice Presidents of the American Board; and the eighteen members of the Council for Social Action; and the Secretary of the General Council *ex officio*.

"60. The Missions Council at its annual meeting may elect as corresponding members of that meeting the members of the Executive Committee of the General Council, secretaries of the national societies, the superintendent or chief executive officer of each state conference, the presidents of women's state organizations, non-board members of standing committees of the national societies, any others whom the Council may deem appropriate to sit as corresponding members, and who may be recommended by the Business Committee.

"61. The Missions Council shall meet at least once each year at such time and place as shall be determined by the Council from year to year. Other meetings may be held as voted by the Council or by the Board of Directors of the Board of Home Missions and the Prudential Committee of the American Board of Commissioners for Foreign Missions, and the Council for Social Action, acting separately on recommendation of the Ad Interim Committee of the Missions Council hereinafter provided.

"62. The officers of the Missions Council shall be a Chairman, a Vice Chairman, a Recording Secretary and a Treasurer. These officers shall be elected at the annual meeting and shall serve for a period of one year, or until their successors shall have been elected and qualified.

"63. The Ad Interim Committee of the Missions Council shall consist of the following persons or their alternates: two members of the Prudential Committee of the American Board to be chosen by the Prudential Committee, two members of the Board of Directors

369

of the Board of Home Missions to be chosen by the Board of Home Missions; the Chairman of the Council for Social Action; the Chairman of the Missions Council, *ex officio*; and two Superintendents serving on the Joint Staff; and the Chairman of the Women State Presidents. The Minister of the General Council, the Executive Vice Presidents of the Boards, the Director of the Council for Social Action, the Ministers and Associate Executive Secretary of the Missions Council are corresponding members. Meetings of the Ad Interim Committee may be called by the Cabinet or the Chairman whenever they deem it advisable.

"64.   The Minister of the Missions Council has the responsibility of an executive secretary and is elected biennially by the Missions Council. He is responsible to the Missions Council and to the Ad Interim Committee when the former is not in session. He gives leadership in developing a program to acquaint the churches with the total task of the fellowship and to create a spiritual understanding and an increased devotion to missions. He is in general charge of relating the interests of the mission boards with the conferences, the churches and individuals.

"65.   A Joint Cabinet representing the several national agencies (and the State Superintendent's Conference) constitutes the Cabinet of the Missions Council as 'the connecting link between the Executive or Ad Interim Committee and the promotional staff.' (1952 Blue Book)

"66.   A Joint Staff representing the several national agencies and the general promotional interests of the denomination 'implements the promotional plans and policies as determined from time to time by the cabinet or adopted at the annual meetings.' (1952 Blue Book)

"67.   The Business Committee of three, appointed either by the Ad Interim Committee or by the Joint Cabinet prepares the docket for the annual meeting but the Council is free to call for business not placed on the agenda by the Business Committee.

"68.   The Mid-Winter Meetings, scheduled by cooperative action through the Missions Council, Ad Interim Committee, or Joint Cabinet, are the means of developing a unified program which becomes the official program."

The International Congregational Council[50]

"69.   The International Congregational Council consists of not more than 235 members from the constituent churches, 75 from U.S.A., 75 from the British Isles, 75 from all other lands. Not more than ten additional members may be elected by the Council on nomination of its executive committee.

"70.   The Inernational Council delegates are elected by the constituent bodies from which they come, in accord with electoral procedures set by these bodies.

"71.   The International Council ordinarily meets at intervals of five years.

"72.   The purpose of the International Council is 'to promote regular consultation and effective cooperation among its constitutent churches; to devise measures and maintain agencies for the advancement of their common witness; and to strengthen the Congregational contribution to the World Council of Churches and to the ecumenical movement generally.'

"73.   The constituent churches of the International Council are evangelical and reformed churches of the world which are organized (a) in national unions of Congregational Churches, or (b) in communions which in part spring from Congregational Churches and maintain the principles of Congregational churchmanship, or (c) as communions or groups of churches ordered after the Christian faith and Congregational polity."

Obviously the Congregational Churches made ample provision to "act together"!

Re Property Rights In Practice

As with the Documents, so, likewise, in Practice property rights are subsidary to the co-operative life and work of the fellowship. Understanding of the *nature* of fellowship and awareness of the *co-operative procedures* evolved to achieve great results is essential in order to set in perspective any and all property concerns. Here is the summary of congregational Christian national level Polity as Practiced.

The General Council[51]

"38.   The General Council of the Congregational Christian Churches of the United States is a voluntary national-level organization of the Congregational Christian Churches. Its purpose is stated in the documentary section, IV, 3.

"39.   The voting membership of the General Council is made up as indicated in the 'documentary' section of this report.

"40.   The General Council meets 'biennially in the even-numbered years, the exact time and place to be fixed by the Executive Committee, unless otherwise ordered by the Council.' Special meetings are called by the executive committee or when as many as seven state conferences request it. While the primary con-

371

cern of the biennial meeting is the transaction of the business entrusted to the Council by the fellowship, consideration is also given to matters of common concern.

"41.   The Executive Committee of the General Council is composed of 18 elected members serving six-year-terms, and the moderator, *ex officio*. It acts as the General Council *ad interim* and is required to make a full report of all its doings at biennial meetings. Questions of policy not clearly defined by the Council may be determined by the Executive Committee *ad interim*. While it is not charged with details of administration of the several national agencies, it seeks to correlate their work, and makes such recommendations to the Council as it may deem wise for the more economical and efficient administration of the wider agencies of the churches. It studies the relative needs of the national level denominational agencies and establishes apportionment percentages. An Advisory Committee acts for the Executive Committee between meetings 'with such limitations and powers as the Executive Committee may direct.' The advisory committee meets at least once each month, and is 'on call' to consider any urgent business of the denomination.

"42.   The business committee of the General Council is charged with preparation of the docket for business sessions, and all Council business is first presented to it, except the reports of the executive, nominating and resolutions committees. The Council has the right to consider any item presented or suppressed by the business committee, but in practice the crowded schedule discourages actions which are not given a scheduled place on the agenda. The Executive Committee serves as the business committee of all regular and special meetings, and meets on call (sometimes several times a day during a council meeting) to transact business.

"43.   One of the problems of the General Council meeting is its large size, or its organization (or both): which makes it hard to achieve the kind of consideration and directive action envisioned by the General Council's constitution, its leaders, and its members, and worthy of its representative character.

"44.   The corporation for the General Council of the Congregational Christian Churches of the United States is described in the documentary section, IV, 3. The corporation is simply the legal body which carries out the purposes or instructions of the General Council.

"45.   The moderator (elected by the General Council for a two-year term) presides over meetings of the General Council, delivers an opening address to the Council over which he presides, and exercises the 'representative functions . . . of visiting and addressing churches, conferences, associations, and conventions upon their invitation, and of representing the Council in the wider relations of Christian fellowship so far as they may be able and disposed.' While it is understood that his personal acts and utterances have no authority from or upon the General Council or its constituent groups, nevertheless our churches put great value on the advice of the moderator, his influence beyond our fellowship is quite considerable, and his methods of leadership have a profound effect upon committee and Council meetings.

"46. The secretary (elected by the General Council for a two-year term) is, since 1938, also the 'Minister of the Council.' He is available to the committees and commissions for 'advice and help in matters of policy and constructive organization.' The secretary and minister is the continuing administrative leader of the General Council, whose words and acts are interpreted as representative of our churches. He takes counsel with the Advisory Committee and with the Executive Committee in matters of major importance. In his capacity as minister he seeks to be a spiritual guide to the churches, and to all their agencies. As the chief officer of the entire fellowship it is his privilege and duty to follow the stated or implied instructions of the General Council, and of the Executive Committee between sessions of the Council itself.

"47. The associate minister and secretary and the treasurer of the General Council are also elected by the biennial meeting of the Council. They are the professional staff of the General Council under the general direction of the secretary and minister. In practice each officer fulfills the functions associated with his office, and consultation concerning special problems is held with each other and with the secretary and minister, with the Executive Committee, Advisory Committee or other agencies of the churches.

"48. The General Council biennial meeting is (a) *the churches* of our order in council assembled, (b) *a gathering for fellowship*, counsel, and discussions, (c) *a business session* of delegates for the transaction of such business as may come before a General Council by virtue of its charter or other fundamental documents; and (d) *a corporate meeting* of those boards and agencies of our churches which are related to or controlled by the General Council. Its powers in each of these capacities are defined by the charters, constitutions, by-laws or other fundamental documents of (a) the General Council, or (b) the associated bodies whose official meetings are being held, or (c) the special instructions or memorials of churches, conferences, associations, or other agencies of the Congregational Christian Churches.

"49. The General Council is not a legislative body with ecclesiastical authority over the churches, associations or conferences, but states general objectives and makes recommendations which carry the authority of their inherent wisdom and value, and are considered and acted upon on the basis of their practical, moral, and spiritual appeal.

"The control of the General Council by the churches is through delegates, the Executive Committee, the Advisory Committee and direct persuasion. More than ninety percent of the delegates to the General Council are now *elected* by conferences and associations in which the churches have direct representation. Some are directly nominated by local churches, others are not. The General Council is, therefore, in practice, *an organization* which is *composed of persons* who are members of Congregational Christian churches rather than an organization *directly* controlled by the churches themselves through their own elected delegates.

"50.   The General Council is described in its constitution as 'a voluntary organization of the Congregational Christian Churches.' In the opinion of our correspondents this means that no coercion or threat of coercion of any type may be used to compel a local church to comply with the wishes of General Council leaders, or with resolutions voted by the General Council itself. The conferences, associations, other wider bodies, and churches may accept or reject, amend or neglect any proposal made to them.

"51.   The General Council possesses all the powers specifically given to it by the churches. In addition, due to the lack of clearly defined representative bodies with power to act for the churches, the General Council (and other wider agencies) has had to assume the administration of important work involving large funds, ownership of property and considerable working personnel.

"52.   The General Council is the national-level organization through which the Congregational Christian churches of the United States guide and administer their common work on this level. It is not independent of the churches; it is the nation-wide responsible organ of the fellowship morally and spiritually bound to the churches and to their other wider bodies; it seeks to express the common mind, interests, and purposes of the churches; its delegates are members of the churches, responsible to the churches, associations, conferences or other agencies but supremely responsible to God as He makes Himself known to them in convictions of conscience; its powers are moral, declaratory and administrative. The General Council is a representative agency of the churches through delegates elected by associations, conferences or other agencies in accord with its own constitutional provisions.

"53.   The General Council has no written standards for the "recognition" of a conference. Recognition is taken for granted, and describes the relation of mutual responsibility which exists between the state conference-level and the national-level agencies of the churches. It is to be defined in terms of mutual obligations and spiritual fellowship rather than in legal phrases or in a printed discipline. A conference which is the state-level agency of a group of Congregational Christian churches asks for and receives (by virtue of its nature) the privilege of participation in the life and work of the General Council to cooperate in the national-level life and work of the fellowship, unless prevented by conscience from so doing.

"54. The General Council exercises leadership on behalf of the Congregational Christian churches through the following commissions: Commission on Interchurch Relations and Christian Unity, Commission on Stewardship, Commission on the Ministry; the Council for Social Action; and the following standing committees: The Nominating Committee, Committee on Credentials, Committee on Resolutions. Other *ad hoc* committees are elected or appointed for specific purposes and definite terms of service. Each performs those functions associated with its descriptive title. In addition the General Council is the organ through which our fellowship shares in interdenominational or interfaith activities on a national or world level.

"55. The Commission on Interchurch Relations and Christian Unity represents the viewpoint of our churches at all ecumenical meetings, fosters good working relations with other church bodies than our own, and cultivates moves toward union of our churches with other Christian bodies. It is not empowered to act for our churches, or for any of the association, conference, or national bodies of our churches, but is responsible for the initiation of projects in the field of interchurch relations. The 'Manual' of the Congregational Christian churches 1947 states what is the general opinion of our correspondents: 'Since in Congregationalism whatever organizations there are beyond the local congregation, whether the association, the state conference, or the General Council, are merely administrative or advisory organizations without infringement on local autonomy, no authority exists to unite the churches of the denomination *en bloc* with those of another.'

"56. The General Council chief executive officers are elected by the biennial meeting of the Council, report to that meeting, and are responsible to it and to its elected Executive Committee and to the Advisory Committee. The report to the biennial meeting is printed and a formal address is given. The Executive Committee meets at least three times a year as the 'Council *ad interim*' to transact the business of the General Council."

Some General Organizations[52]

"57. The churches and all the wider bodies of the Congregational Christian fellowship have their respective inner polity structures set forth in charters, constitutions, by-laws, or rules of procedure under which each particular church or wider body is organized.

"Polity relationships between churches and wider bodies are frequently set forth in the basic written documents of the Congregational Christian fellowship, e.g. in certain local church, association, and state conference constitutions; and there are general statements of policy relationships in the basic documents of the General Council. All these inter-church-wider-body polity statements describe the relationships of the various bodies of a voluntary fellowship; they do not compel conformity; they simply state the polity relationship which is regarded as desirable *by the body making the statement;* they gain acceptance on the basis of inherent worth.

"Thus certain wider bodies, for example, the association, are clearly and directly the responsible agents of the churches, whereas other wider bodies, for example, the Annuity Fund for Congregational Ministers, are clearly and directly responsible to their own Boards of Control. The unity of the Congregational Christian fellowship is achieved chiefly by goodwill, and by working agreements which are mutually accepted by the agreeing bodies, for example, the American Board, voluntarily agrees under its own charter, to meet at the same time as the General Council, and to elect the members of the General Council as corporate members of the American Board. By this voluntary agreement the foreign missionary work of the fellowhsip becomes a concern of the General Council and of the churches, associations, and conferences from which have come the delegates to the General Council. What we have in some of our wider bodies is an extension of the principle of the 'gathered' Church; i.e. those Congregational Christians who were concerned about foreign missions simply 'gathered' themselves together as the American Board and proceeded to solicit the support of others both as individuals and as churches. The 1913 reorganization plan, adopted by the National Council, created a framework of voluntary relationships between the General Council and other wider bodies such as the American Board, in order to establish a closer tie between the churches and the many wider bodies through which are channeled the concerns of the churches and their members.

"58. The national societies related to the Congregational Christian churches are administered in accord with the provisions of their respective charters and by-laws (see documentary section, IV, 3)."

The Council for Social Action[53]

"59. The Council for Social Action is the agency of the Congregational Christian churches for helping to make the Christian gospel more effective in society, national and world-wide, through research, education, and action, in cooperation with the churches and their missionary agencies.

"60. The Council for Social Action is a body created by and responsible to the General Council. It is required to make a full and accurate report of its condition and work to the General Council at each stated meeting of that body. It comprises a council of 18 persons elected for six-year terms and serving on a volunteer basis.

"61. The Council for Social Action has been studied by a 'Board of Review' appointed by the Executive Committee of the General Council. The report of the Board of Review, together with the recommendations of the Executive Committee, is to be presented at the 1954 meeting of the General Council. Therefore, no reference is made to it here."

The Missions Council[54]

"62. The Missions Council is a joint agency for missionary education, stewardship, and promotion of income for the American Board, the Board of Home Missions, the Council for Social Action, the State Conferences, Relief and Reconstruction, and the Congregational Christian Service Committee. To it is assigned the performance of varied special services for the churches and their cooperative agencies. It is an inter-board agency whose functions are strictly interpretative and educational and it has no responsibility for the making of missionary policy or for the administration of missionary work.

"63. The Missions Council members are responsible to the boards or agencies they represent. Its officers are responsible to the Missions Council itself. A responsible relation to the churches is maintained indirectly through the several boards and agencies."

The Mid-Winter Meetings[55]

"64. The Mid-Winter meetings correlate into a single program simultaneous 'called' meetings of the following agencies and organizations of the Congregational Christian Churches: The Missions Council, the Prudential Committee of the American Board, directors of the Board of Home Missions, members of the Council for Social Action, Superintendents' Conference, Conference of Women State Presidents, Presidents of Laymen's State Fellowships, secretaries of the boards, members of the national committee of our Christian World Mission, Executive Committee of the General Council. In addition 'others attending associated meetings, are usually invited to sit in as corresponding members.' (1952 Blue Book) This includes members of the Christian Education Council (conference directors of education and staffs of Pilgrim Press and

Christian Education Division), members of divisional or departmental committees, the Pilgrim Fellowship (youth) executive committee, and numerous other committees such as General Council, Nominating Committee, Congregational Christian Service Committee, Allocations Committee, Survey Committee, etc. (*'All* of us are involved in the meeting of *each agency*, as voting or as corresponding members.' (1952 Blue Book)

"65.   The Mid-Winter meetings are scheduled by cooperative action through the Missions Council, *ad interim* committee, or joint cabinet.

"66.   The program planned at the Mid-Winter meetings becomes the official program of the national and state agencies of the Congregational Christian churches through action of the several bodies represented in or meeting in connection with the Missions Council.

"67.   The Mid-Winter meetings have become a very influential gathering of the Congregational Christian fellowship, at which important decisions are made, Missions Council officers are elected, new emphases are debated, schedules of work are cleared, and fundamental policies are proposed. The churches have no direct representation at these meetings, although those who attend are the elected or employed officials of the various conferences, boards, agencies, committees and associated bodies listed in statement 64.

"68.   The Mid-Winter meetings gain their influence from the structural inter-linkage of the national boards and agencies and from the presence of conference superintendents and other officers, as noted in statement 64. The decisions made have no power to compel local church action, but they can do much to determine what is presented to a meeting of the General Council, what promotional literature is to be published, what speakers are to be made available for state conference and association meetings, how the apportionment dollar is to be divided, and whether or not work in one field or another is to be given special support. In short, many of the chief administrative decisions affecting the life and work of our churches are made at the Mid-Winter meetings."

International Congregational Council[56]

"69.   The International Congregational Council is described in our documentary statement. It is primarily a world-wide fellowship organization for national bodies which recognize their kinship with congregational principles and polity.

"70.   The International Council presently has its headquarters in Memorial Hall, London, England. This office acts under the Minister and Secretary, the Associate Secretary and their assistants as a center for inspiration, information, exchange of groups and preachers between national bodies, stimulation of interest among lay women, laymen, and young people, holding of conferences, and furtherance of certain world ecumenical relationships.

"71.   The International Council customarily has met alternately in the British Isles and in the United States. Its moderators also have been chosen from these two areas.

"72.   The International Council is a practical means of promoting understanding, fellowship, thinking and a measure of united action among its constituent groups. Each meeting issues a 'Message to the Churches' which seeks to gather up the chief concerns of the delegates in a framework of Christian conviction. These 'Messages' are circulated generally by many of the constituent bodies."

The Service Committee[57]

"73.   The Congregational Christian Service Committee is an agency of the Congregational Christian fellowship for certain relief and reconstruction work, including centers of service in Lebanon, Greece, Italy, France, Germany, India and England; a displaced persons resettlement program; a work camp program in conjunction with the youth department of the World Council of Churches; and an International Service Center (and hostel) in New York City.

"74.   The Congregational Christian Service Committee is incorporated, the corporation being composed of twenty-four members of the Prudential Committee of the American Board.

"75.   The Congregational Christian Service Committee board of directors is elected by the corporation. Other officers are elected by the board, and are responsible to the board and corporation. Leaders of the Board of Home Missions, Council for Social Action, General Council and youth departments are listed as *ex-officio* directors."

Pastoral Supply[58]

"76.   The Congregational Board of Pastoral Supply and the Midwest Pastoral Relations Committee are agencies which assist Congregational Christian churches in finding suitable pastors.

"77.   The pastoral supply agencies are maintained by cooperative action of eastern and midwestern groups of conferences respectively. They are responsible to these conferences, and cooperate with the General Council Department of the Ministry."

Regional Meetings[59]

"78.   Regional meetings of the Congregational Christian churches are held annually in the New England, Mid-West and Northwest geographical areas. The American Board, the Board of Home Missions and the Council for Social Action hold annual meetings at the time of the eastern and midwestern regional meetings (each board alternates between east and midwest). Primary responsibility for program planning rests with a regional committee cooperating with the Missions Council. The national boards share in this responsibility in those years when their annual meetings are held in the regions. These meetings have gained considerable importance in matters of fellowship and inspiration. In addition there is some guidance given to the Missions Council in educational and promotional matters.

"79. There are societies and organizations on all levels of our fellowship (such as the Congregational Christian Historical Society and the Congregational Library) whose constituency and control are substantially or exclusively Congregational Christian. These bodies are governed in accord with their own charters, constitutions, by-laws, or other rules of procedure. Their relation to the churches and to other wider bodies is largely determined by their leaders."

The Seminar Compares

What has required many pages to record took about twenty minutes to compare in the seminar, since each person had in hand the data herein reproduced.

The initial question after comparison was, "Why does the Practice Report omit consideration of the American Board and the Home Board?" When the question was asked Rev. Wendell Fifield, chairman, gave a big audible sigh. "The question is very perceptive," he replied, "I was personally involved in a rather persistent effort to secure written statements from the Rev. Truman Douglass, Mr. Harold Belcher, and the attorneys for the home and foreign boards. Dr. Gray's correspondence and personal inquiries were followed by my own personal visits and letters. Neither of us was able to enlist the cooperation of the officers or attorneys of the boards. At the last possible moment before the printing of the Polity and Unity Report, I polled the Committee and it was agreed to print what you have read. The decision was made because the Committee *retained* in the Documents Report the exact language of the constitutions, charters, and by-laws of the Boards."

"But what about 'Practice,' are not the Boards the very agencies through which most of the work of the fellowship is done?", asked a young man who identified himself only as a minister from Michigan.

"That's a question for the Congregational Polity Committee Chairman," said Wendell.

"The Congregational Polity Committee gathered data on national bodies in precisely the same manner as was used for all other Practice data. The responses were tabulated and submitted to the Claremont General Council in 1952, which Council received them with enthusiasm. The paragraphs were revised to include references as late as January 1954. The Committee substituted the paragraphs headed 'Some National Bodies' when answers from the American Board and Home Board were refused. However, the responses are available. They reflect the view of the Legal Opinion only in one or two instances of persons involved in the legal process."

A lady from Maine inquired, "Would you please share with us several *representative* comments with regard to property rights?"

Dr. Fifield responded, "Are there particular persons whose names appear on pages 38 to 40 of the Polity and Unity Report whose responses you wish to hear?"

The lady from Maine replied, "Well, I'd like one from Maine."

Dr. Fifield nodded to me.

"The New England Panel included five Maine representatives, Bridges, Hayes, Roundy, Bull, and Cornish. They first met June 17 and 18, 1953 in Newbury, Vermont, with Roundy, Bull and Cornish present. The Panel reported that they considered the General Council to be 'maintained by the Congregational Churches.' Of the Boards, Dr. Rockwell Harmon Potter was supported in the statement 'When each agency accepted the advice of the (1913) Committee of 19 each member of the (National) Council became a member of the American Board. From this time on Congregationalism was a representative democracy. The Churches gained control of the Board.'[60]

"Frederick D. Hayes[61] of Auburn wrote January 14, 1954, 'I think this is a grand job, well done' (the Practice Report). He added later his approbation of the statements on the national level. Perhaps you know the past president of the Women's Fellowship of Maine, Mrs. Charles A. Haynes,[62] who wrote, 'Polity as Practiced seems to me to be a complete and satisfactory statement (of Congregationalism) as I have seen it work . . .' Would you like to hear more?"

A dry Yankee voice replied, "No, thank you. I am Mrs. Haynes."

When the seminar chuckle subsided the Chairman inquired, "Do you wish to have read any other responses?"

Rev. Roy Helfenstein spoke up, "I do. I'd like to hear what someone from the *Christian* Church had to say."

I asked, "Will a report of conversations with Superintendent Archie Hook be satisfactory?"

"Yes sir! He's a good man."

"Superintendent Hook responded with several letters, and added much in conversations. He views the closer-knit organization of the Christian Southern Convention as more practical than the Congregational Way. The Southern Convention holds title to joint properties and even to certain individual Church properties. Dr. Hook pointed out last Thursday that the new Puerto Rico Conference shared some characteristics of the Christian Churches, and so to a lesser degree, does Hawaii. The Washington State Conference has adopted some Christian Church practices regarding ordination but not in connection with property during Mr. Hook's superintendency."

Dr. Helfenstein broke in, "What I want to know is Archie Hook's views about who owns the Board assets."

"So far as I understand him, he sees the national assets as a sort of trust held for use in whatever mission or service the Churches want and will support."

"*That's* what I thought he'd say. It's what any of the Christian 'connection' would say. We don't haggle over who *holds* the assets! What's important to us is how they are used."

The contrast between the attitude toward merger of proponents, opponents and the mediators is revealed sharply in the property issue. The notion that legal nicities should determine the disposition of assets dedicted to the life and work of Congregational Christian Churches appeared to be shared by proponents and opponents of the CC/ER merger. The mediators sensed spiritual defeat in legal action.

Not least tragic to the mediators was the loss to the Kingdom of God of the material resources, the time of a whole generation, and the thought power of the leaders of our fellowship of Churches. We could not but grieve that missionary outreach, church expansion, membership enlistment, training of ministers, support of education and publication of forefront books and articles languished. Decrease in Christian work and witness paralled increase in the spending of time, talent and treasure on the material aspects of the CC/ER Merger.

Of all deprivations none was more devastating than loss of intellectual pioneering. Prior to about 1945 nearly every major publisher in America issued books by Congregational authors which were at the cutting edge of biblical, theological, societal, psychological and philosophical thinking. Our own Pilgrim Press was one of the chief publishers of forefront thought. The proportion of America's notable authors who were Congregational far exceeded the proportion of Congregationalists in the population. The roll included authors across the spectrum of thought, such as Lloyd Douglas, Rollo May, Sidney Weston, Theodore Soares, Washington Gladden, Robert A. Millikan, Lewis B. Paton. These are only a handful. The giants of intellectual advance from Cotton Mather to Amos and Thornton Wilder have been an outstanding aspect of the Congregational Way in America.

The mediators included intellectual pioneers like Frederick Meek, James A. Blaisdell, Matthew Spinka. *All* of the mediators valued highly the quest for intellectual excellence. The precipitous decline in this field was, and is, one of the most serious results of the CC/ER merger and the drain of brain-power to unification of denominations into "One Great Church."

The mediators quickly grasped the alleged significance of the legal battles. Which body is the "successor" to the Pilgrims? Are not the descendents of those whose funds were given in trust morally bound to do all possible to carry out those trusts? Will not the loss of conference buildings, camps, and all the series of funds for church building, education, students, missions, etc. cripple the work and witness of the Churches?

The mediators saw another facet of the property rights issue. If, as we believed, the CC/ER merger represented the culmination of efforts toward centralization and overt political and economic action *which had already taken place* within the CC fellowship, then, why not let the CC/ER merger be a purging from Congregationalism of those who no longer wished to walk the Congregational Way?

In England, Canada, New Zealand and Australia representatives of varying points of view within Congregationalism were able to divide the assets in accord with trust deeds and numerical strength. United States law differs from British law, but Christian love and goodwill do not differ from one land to another. There was, and is no legal requirement that approximately 70% of the Churches affiliated with the General Council of the Congregational Christian Churches should claim 100% of the assets.

In view of the alleged support of the new denomination, the United Church of Christ, for social justice, for corporate stewardship of capital funds in the interest of fair play for, for example, blacks in South Africa, many of the mediators have been puzzled by UCC failure to deal justly with its own minorities—the non-voting Churches, the National Association, and the Conservative Conference. What mystifies is that persons whom we know and admire seem to be totally oblivious to a gross injustice on their doorstep while they militantly (and oft times courageously) campaign for justice at a distance. As Mediators, we do not have the slightest interest in seeking to pressure the UCC to do justly; only voluntary recognition of minority rights is morally and spiritually convincing.

Many of us believe a fresh moral and spiritual awakening in the UCC would be generated by an initiative in proportional sharing with the vibrant minorities of the Congregational Way. Can conscience be clear while the take-all possessor of assets continues to ignore or deny the common sense rights of Congregational minorities?

The Chairman stood, "Unless there is urgent request for more reading of responses regarding property rights, I'd like to move on to 'the powers of the General Council.'" The murmer of agreement was general so we turned to a comparison of the Powers of the General Council in the Legal Opinion, the Documents and the Practice Reports.

Powers of the General Council

The Legal Opinion section is titled, "The Theories of General Council Power"[63] as follows:

"In Chapter VII, the Report lists six theories of the power of the General Council which it has discovered during its studies. There is yet another theory which the Report did not list, to wit: the position taken by the General Council in the litigation in the New York courts.

"This position holds that the General Council has the power 1) to initiate, promote and promulgate plans of union, and 2) to consummate that portion of the plan which may call for its own union with the national body of another denomination.[1] This power is found in

"(1) As a practical matter, the plan should provide for the continued existence of the General Council, as was true under The Basis of Union, for 'The Corporation of the General Council', which is trustee of various trusts, is by its charter subject to the direction of the General Council and a disappearance of the Council would create legal questions as to whether the identity or nature of the trustee of those trusts has changed.

384

the usages of the fellowship, in the clear implications of the Council's stated constitutional powers and in the inherent powers which reside in all bodies, but particularly in ecclesiastical bodies that are not governed by judicatories.

"This position presupposes that the General Council does not consummate for the Churches, Associations, Conferences and Boards, nor are they bound to accept the plan. They may, if they choose, evidence their respective approvals or ratifications by vote or by merely continuing to support the Council and the new body which carries out the plan. Moreover, continued support does not necessarily imply that they approve of all phases of the plan or that they are committing themselves, temporarily or permanently to any procedures under the plan.

"It is assumed that those who prepared Chapter VII believed they were stating the General Council's position in the 'third theory' and also in the 'fourth theory.' If so, they have been under a misapprehension. The differences are substantial and important. Both the 'third theory' and 'fourth theory' hold that the Council has the power to act for the fellowship in matters of union and they suggest no limitation of that power, except paradoxically that it is not binding on the individual church. Under these theories, the Council could not only promulgate but it could consummate the portions of the plan applying to the other bodies; and the Council's negotiations, phraseology, procedures and statements would be considered those of the churches and would be binding on them. *Such a position was not and never has been taken by the General Council*, despite repeated attempts to characterize its position as such."

In The Documents

The constitution and by-laws of the General Council nowhere describe in detail "the powers" of the Council, since the Council's purpose is not executive, judicial or legislative.[64]

"31. The General Council of the Congregational Christian Churches of the United States is a voluntary organization of the Congregational Christian churches. Its purpose is 'to foster and express the substantial unity of the Congregational Christian Churches in faith, purpose, polity and work; to consult upon and advise measures and maintain agencies for the promotion of the Common interests of the kingdom of God; to cooperate with any corporation or body under control of or affiliated with the Congregational or Christian churches or any of them; and to do and to promote the work of these churches in their national, international, and interdenominational relations.'"

The wording of that constitutional statement is clear, viz. *the Council is the body through which the work of the Churches is to be promoted.* Paragraph 34 specifies the advisory character of the Council regarding other agencies of the Churches, and, with reference to the money voluntarily given by the Churches.

In no place is the strictly advisory role of the Council more apparent than in the office of the Moderator, whose personal acts and utterances 'have no authority from or upon the General Council or its constituent groups.'[65]

The Document stance is summed up in paragraph 39.[66]

"39. The General Council is not a legislative body with ecclesiastical authority over the churches, associations or conferences, but states general objectives and makes recommendations which carry the authority of their inherent widsom and value and are considered and acted upon on the basis of their practical moral and spiritual appeal."

In Practice

There was general agreement on the powers of the General Council *in practice.* This is expressed in the Polity and Unity Report.[67]

"48. The General Council biennial meeting is (1) *the churches* of our order in council assembled, (b) *a gathering for fellowship,* counsel, and discussions, (c) *a business session* of delegates for the transaction of such business as may come before a General Council by virtue of its charter or other fundamental documents; and (d) *a corporate meeting* of those boards and agencies of our churches which are related to or controlled by the General Council. Its powers in each of these capacities are defined by the charters, constitutions, by-laws or other fundamental documents of (a) the General Council, or (b) the associated bodies whose official meetings are being held, or (c) the special instructions or other agencies of the Congregational Christian Churches.

"49. The General Council is not a legislative body with ecclesiastical authority over the churches, associations or conferences, but states general objectives and makes recommendations which carry the authority of their inherent wisdom and value, and are considered and acted upon on the basis of their practical, moral, and spiritual appeal.

"The control of the General Council by the churches is through delegates, the Executive Committee, the Advisory Committee and direct persuasion. More than ninety percent of the delegates to the General Council are now *elected* by conferences and associations in which the churches have direct representation. Some are directly nominated by local churches, others are not. The General Council is, therefore, in practice, *an organization* which is *composed of persons* who are members of Congregational Christian churches rather than an organization *directly* controlled by the churches themselves through their own elected delegates.

"50. The General Council is described in its constitution as 'a voluntary organization of the Congregational Christian Churches.' In the opinion of our correspondents this means that no coercion or threat of coercion of any type may be used to compel a local church to comply with the wishes of General Council leaders, or with resolutions voted by the General Council itself. The conferences, associations, other wider bodies, and churches may accept or reject, amend or neglect any proposal made to them.

"51. The General Council possesses all the powers specifically given to it by the churches. In addition, due to the lack of clearly defined representative bodies with power to act for the churches, the General Council (and other wider agencies) has had to assume the administration of important work involving large funds, ownership of property and considerable working personnel.

"52. The General Council is the national-level organization through which the Congregational Christian churches of the United States guide and administer their common work on this level. It is not independent of the churches; it is the nation-wide responsible organ of the fellowship morally and spiritually bound to the churches and to their other wider bodies; it seeks to express the common mind, interests, and purposes of the churches; its delegates are members of the churches, responsible to the churches, associations, conferences or other agencies but supremely responsible to God as He makes Himself known to them in convictions of conscience; its powers are moral, declaratory and administrative. The General Council is a representative agency of the churches through delegates elected by associations, conferences or other agencies in accord with its own constitutional provisions."

The Legal Opinion, without benefit of research, gathering of contemporary data, and historical study, posits the view of the Mansfield Theses. According to this theory the Council has the power, quite independent of the Churches, "to initiate, promote and promulgate plans of union."[68] The General Council has power to do whatever it wants to do, "except paradoxically that it is not binding on the individual church."[69] The *paradox* is in the mind of the author of the Legal Opinion. The Congregational Christian fellowship is a living organism; sever the Council from the Churches and it ceases to exist, with no delegates to attend, no money to support it, no "reasons for being!"

The Chairman rapped on the table and admonished me, "Mr. Gray, you have added your own peroration to the outline of the powers of the General Council. In fact, the Polity and Unity Committee found disagreement among its members as to whether or not the powers of the Council were deliniated with enough clarity to be described. The Committee concluded that more study was needed and recommended that a special Commission be appointed by the General Council to pursue the matter. This 1954 Council accepted that recommendation. Unless there is serious objection, the Chair will rule that discussion of the powers of the General Council is out of order until the New Commission shall have made its report in 1956."

The ruling was unexcepted, but the seminar *applauded*!

Dr. Fifield continued, "The meaning of 'responsible' appears to be the final point for our seminar. May I ask Dr. Gray to introduce it, *briefly*."

The Meaning of "Responsible"

The Legal Opinion

Paragraph 22 of the Legal Opinion is as follows:[70]

"The Report speaks of the Associations, Conferences and General Council as being 'responsible' to the churches. The word 'responsible' may have been used figuratively to convey the fact that they seek to know the views of the members of the churches and to act in harmony with prevailing opinion. However, if it was used to connote legal responsibility enforceable by law the Report is in error."

In The Documents

There is in the Documents no definition of the word *responsible*. It is used in the constitutions and/or by-laws or both of Associations, Conferences, and national bodies.

In Practice

In practice your committee found the word *responsible* used by officials to mean *required obedience*, to which there was strong objection. After prolonged discussion, and much perusal of suggestions from the study panels and expert correspondents, the following emerged.[71]

"81. Responsible freedom describes the practical relation of the Congregational Christian churches to one another, and to their wider agencies. The local church voluntarily elects delegates to meetings of wider bodies, and takes responsibility for the work undertaken by those delegates, with the usual Congregational reservation, namely, that what is undertaken must *win* the support of the churches, and that the churches must win the support of their members. The wider bodies are expected to be sensitive to the will of the churches, and, on the association and conference level, are directly controlled by delegates from the churches and by directors elected by those delegates. On the national and international levels the control exerted by the churches is very important in theory but necessarily quite removed in practice. *Responsible freedom, at its best, means voluntary participation in wider bodies on the part of the local church and voluntary sensitivity to the will of the churches on the part of the wider bodies.* It also means voluntary sharing by the local church in the work carried on by the wider bodies, and voluntary responsiveness to the needs of the local churches by the wider bodies. Responsibility and freedom are laid upon both local church and wider agency. No neat formula can express the meaning of responsible freedom, for it is a matter of moral obligation and Christian conviction. Fundamentally, it means that every Congregational Christian church member is accountable to God for his creed and conduct and, accordingly, every Congregational Christian church becomes likewise accountable to God and also to its members. Every wider body is accountable to God for its creed and conduct, but it is also directly or indirectly accountable to the churches which created it. What we have in practice is a system of direct delegate control by the churches so far as associations and conferences are concerned, a system of indirect delegate control so far as the General Council is concerned, a system of tenuous delegate control so far as the national boards and agencies are concerned, and a system of no direct control at all so far as the Missions Council, the Mid-Winter meetings and the Inernational Council are concerned."

Wendell smiled, "That *was* shorter. Are there questions?"

President Whittaker stood up, "I'd like to add that the statement of *responsible freedom* is regarded by all of us as one of paramount importance. Responses to this statement were commendatory, perhaps unanimously; for I do not recall any dissent. I thought the seminar should know this."

A number of heads nodded assent. Dr. Fifield caught the mood, "This is an appropriate note on which to terminate our seminar. I want to thank you for participating. And I want to express my personal delight that what began on Thursday with tension and argument has progessed by exploration of all the complexities of Congregational Polity until there appeared among us a common appreciation of the meaning of *responsible freedom*. It may be that this fulfills the purpose of the seminar. I would like the privilege of closing with the benediction."

Everyone rose spontaneously. The benediction was pronounced. Out doors about ten minutes later the Rev. William A. Keith spoke for many when he commented, "It's too bad the right people were not present at this seminar."

CHAPTER 8 NOTES

1. Polity and Unity Report, 1954, General Council, NY p. 56
2. No. California Congregational Conference, By-Laws, Art. II 5-19-51
3. Colorado Congregational Conference Constitution, Art. II c. 1952
4. Connecticut Congregational Constitution, Art. II n.d. c. 1951
5. So. Dakota Congregational Conference, By-Laws, Art. II 5-1-41
6. No. Dakota Congregational Conference, By-Laws, Art. II, 1950
7. Florida Congregational Christian Conference, Charter, Art. II, 1922/1945
8. Hawaiian Evangelical Assn. Constitution, Art. II, 1952
9. Idaho Conference etc., Constitution, Art. II c. 1952
10. Illinois Conference etc. Constitution, Art. II May, 1947
11. Indiana Conf. etc. Constitution, Art. II, 1933/1935
12. Iowa Conf. etc. Constitution, Art. II c. 1952
13. Kansas Conference etc., Arts. of Inc. 1910, 1932, 1938, 1946
14. Maine Conference etc. Arts. II & III, 1871-1943
15. Massachusetts Conference etc. Art. II, 1950 yearbook of Conf.
16. Michigan Conference etc. Articles of Association, Art. II, 1934
17. Middle Atlantic Conference etc. By-Laws Art. II, 1947
18. Minnesota Conference etc., Constitution, Art. II, c. 1951
19. Missouri Conference etc. Articles of Association, Art. II c. 1951
20. Montana Conference etc., Constitution, Art. II 1944/1950
21. Nebraska Conference etc. Constitution, Arts. II, III, IV 1950
22. New Hampshire Conference etc., Charter, Objects, 1914, 1919, 1933, 1939
23. Ibid, By-Laws Art. II, Section 2 1939
24. New York Conference etc., Arts. of Incorporation "Objects," 1909-1947
25. Ohio Conference etc., Basis of Fellowship and Rules, 1943, 44, 49
26. Oregon Conference etc. Constitution, Art II Object 1950
27. Pennsylvania Conference, etc. Constitution, Art. II, 1948
28. Puerto Rico Conference, etc. Constitution, Art. II c. 1951
29. Rhode Island Conference, etc. Constitution, Art. II, 1947
30. Southern Convention etc., Constitution, Art. III c. 1951
31. Southeast Convention, etc. Constitution, Preamble, Name, 1949
32. Utah Conference etc., Constitution, Art. II, 1926
33. Vermont Conference etc., Charter, Section I, 1945
34. Washington Conference Constitution, 1948, Art. II
35. Wisconsin Conference etc. Constitution, Art. II, 1948
36. Wyoming Conference etc. Constitution, Art. I, Sec. 2, c. 1931

37. Legal Opinion, paragraph 10
38. Southern California and Southwest Conference By-Laws, Art. II, 1954/55
39. Polity Report, op.cit. 56-57
40. A. E. Dunning, *Congregationalists in America*, 1894, J. A. Hill, New York, p. 524.
41. Ibid, pp. 523-524
42. J. A. Blaisdell, c. 1956, privately published pamphlet
43. Legal Opinion, op.cit., pp. 13, 14
44. Polity & Unity Report, op.cit., p. 27, ff.
45. Polity and Unity Report, op.cit., 31 f.
46. Polity and Unity Report, op.cit., 32. f.
47. Polity and Unity Report, op.cit., 33 f.
48. Polity and Unity Report, op.cit., 34
49. Polity and Unity Report, op.cit., 34-36
50. Polity and Unity Report, op.cit., 36
51. Polity and Unity Report, op.cit., 47-51
52. Polity and Unity Report, op.cit., pp. 47-51
53. Ibid, p. 51-58
54. Polity and Unity Report, op.cit., p. 52-53
55. Ibid, p. 53-54
56. Polity and Unity Report, op.cit., p. 54
57. Ibid, p. 54-55
58. Polity and Unity Report, op.cit., p. 55
59. Ibid, p. 55
60. Report of the New England Panel
61. Hayes to Gray, Jan. 14, 1954
62. Haynes to Gray, Jan. 17, 1954
63. Legal Opinion, op.cit. paragraphs 25, 26, 27, 28
64. Polity and Unity Report, op.cit., p. 27
65. Ibid, p. 31, paragraph 37
66. Ibid., p. 31, paragraph 37
67. Polity and Unity Report, op.cit., pp. 49-50, paragraphs 48, 49, 50, 51, 52
68. Legal Opinion, op. cit., paragraph 26
69. Ibid, paragraph 28
70. Legal Opinion, op.cit., paragraph 22
71. Polity & Unity Report, op. cit., p. 56, paragraph 81

CHAPTER NINE

Last Stand for Study

One slim hope remained to the CC/ER Merger Mediators at the close of the 1954 New Haven General Council meeting of the Congregational Christian Churches. That was "the Claremont Resolution" of 1952, reaffirmed in 1954. The resolution read:[1]

"BE IT RESOLVED that this General Council of Congregational Christian Churches continues to look forward to a united fellowship of the Evangelical and Reformed and the Congregational Christian communions; and

"BE IT FURTHER RESOLVED that the Executive Committee be instructed to seek joint meetings with the General Council of the evangelical and Reformed Church; that the resolutions submitted by the Massachusetts Congregational Conference and the New York Congregational Christian Conference be referred to those two bodies meeting jointly; and that all other resolutions and suggestions originating in our fellowship which are of common interest to the two communions be likewise referred to them; and"

"BE IT FURTHER RESOLVED that those two bodies meeting jointly be requested, if both approve, to be responsible for the preparation of a draft proposed constitution for the General Synod of the united fellowship to be made available to the membership of both communions for discussion and suggestions."

"BE IT RESOLVED that on all the Congregational Christian bodies responsible for the implementing of the resolution above there be representatives of the different points of view among us; and that the process of cooption be employed whenever desirable; and

"BE IT FURTHER RESOLVED that the executive Committee is requested to establish a consulting relationship with the Committee on Free Church Polity and Unity during the drafting of the proposed constitution; and

"BE IT FURTHER RESOLVED that in the preparation of such a draft every effort be made to preserve all the spiritual and temporal freedoms and rights now possessed by the individuals, churches, associations, conferences, and boards of this communion."

"(and) BE IT FURTHER RESOLVED that pending the final judgment of the New York Court of Appeals concerning the present appeal of the Cadman Church to that court no action should be taken which would in any way conflict with the due process of law or jeopardize the rights and standing of the General Council in the eyes of the law."

The reaffirmation in 1954 read:[2]

"WHEREAS the final judgment of the New York State Court of Appeals in the case of the Cadman Church VS. the General Council has now been rendered; and

"WHEREAS the Executive Committee of the General Council has arranged a meeting for the coming fall with the corresponding body (known as the General Council of the Evangelical and Reformed Church;

"THEREFORE BE IT RESOLVED, in view of these facts, that the General Council of the Congregational Christian Churches of the United States, meeting in New Haven, Connecticut June 23-30, 1954.

"1) *Reaffirms* its earnest desire as expressed in the first resolution adopted at the meeting of the General Council held at Claremont, Calif., in June 1952, to continue 'to look forward to a united fellowship of the Evangelical and Reformed and the Congregational Christian communions;' and to that end

"2) *Renews* its instructions as previously given to the Executive Committee in the subsequent resolutions adopted by the Claremont General Council of 1952 with regard to the Union of the Congregational Christian Churches with the Evangelical and Reformed Church, so far as they still are applicable."

Such hope as we had for an unbroken Congregational Christian fellowship centered in these two resolutions. I believe it is accurate to say that all of the Mediators were reasonably comfortable with the prospect of a national-level-only union, a joining in fellowship on the basis of a constitution for the national body prepared by a

394

committee representative of all the major viewpoints amongst us.

The 1952 Clarement Resolution *could be* a pathway to wider cooperative witness and work *together*. Among those who shared this hope were Rev. William A. Keith, Rev. Arthur Bradford, President Frederick Whittaker, Rev. Frederick Meek and Rev. John Webster.

Others shared the same hope, with a high degree of scepticism. Among the skeptics were Professor Matthew Spinka, Rev. Alfred Grant Walton, Rev. Rockwell Harmon Potter, and Rev. Wallace Anderson. Mr. Anderson spoke for all of them when he said, "It's too late. Minds are made up. All we can hope for is moderation."

Amid Extra Work

Summer and Autumn 1954 brought the building of Oneonta's Hall, Youth Center, and classrooms; the furlough of my assistant the Rev. John R. Elmore for a year of study, and an incredible deluge of weddings (80 in one year), baptisms, funerals, and speaking appointments. In addition there was unusually persistent solicitation to accept the ministry of Pitt Street Congregational Church in Sydney, Australia, the South Congregational Church in Hartford, or the presidency of Illinois College. Pres. Walter Giersbach had pressed upon me the presidency of Pacific School of Religion during the Polity and Unity years, on condition that I support the merger. Rev. Frederick L. Meek, chairman of the "Search Committee" of Andover Newton Theological School had urged me to accept the Deanship. Then there were Churches in several states making persistent inquiry. In other words, 1954-1955 was a year of decision making. Following the New Haven General Council I tried to avoid polity in the hope that the guidelines of the 1952 Claremont Resolution, reaffirmed by the 1954 General Council would be honored.

Known later[3] was an Evanston meeting of CC/ER leaders described as follows:

"At a conference four of us—Drs. Wagner, Grauer, Coe, and myself—were able to hold one perspiring noon in August at Evanston, the thought was introduced that bilateral committees might be set up to consider and prepare findings on each one of the more important matters concerning which there remains any doubt on the part of either communion as to the attitude of the other. One such committee, it was suggested, might study and report briefly or at length on the Nature of the Church, another on Fundamental Belief—questions which it would be profitable for us to take up under any circumstances. The attempt would be to arrive at a common, not necessarily a uniform, mind on these subjects. If this course were followed I should hope that we might have a competent national committee on each question and local committees which would keep in close rapport with the national committee. On these committees could be placed persons representing various schools of thought.

"This is a procedure which the Church of South India in the days before its union found most fruitful.

"The magazines and literature of the two denominations might be exchanged, all in the interest of developing mutual understanding. . . .

"Some attention might be paid to increasing the number of those, now too few, who are familiar with the practice of both denominations. . . .

". . . (I)f we are to go forward with the proposed union, let us do so in a large way, the needs and opportunities of the whole world being our axes of reference. In the very difficulty of our task, in the practical proving that groups of different ecclesiastical and even cultural backgrounds may be harmonized in Christ, lies part of our challenge. If we move ahead at all, it should be in the consciousness of the part our two communions have played in history and with a sense of the new age just beginning. Only so, I believe, can we dream, plan, and build adequately."

News of this conference was not made public 'till early 1955. The Mediators learned of it in late October, from Rev. Wallace Anderson, a member of the Executive Committee.

Improvised or Inspired?

October 12-13, 1954 in Cleveland there was held a joint meeting of the CC Executive Committee and its counterpart the ER General Council.

Accounts of this meeting differ. The account in *Die Entstehung der "United Church of Christ" (USA)*[4] is somewhat more balanced than others. Hans Keiling visited me in Hartford, on March 22, 1966. As a doctoral candidate he showed no desire to study the documents on Congregational Polity, but had great interest in gathering reports and court documents for a file in Germany. I wasn't always sure that he understood what was being said, even though we used both English and German interchangeably. His steadfast aim was to buttress his thesis that the USA United Church of Christ was an expression of a drift toward church-union beginning as early as Schleiermacher and represented by the union in Germany of various Lutheran and Calvinist bodies.

Keiling's account of the October '54 meeting is worth reading. The crucial gathering began with two statements, one by the Rev. Douglas Horton as secretary of the CC Executive Committe, and the other by Rev. James E. Wagner as President of the ER Church.

Mr. Horton began with his interpretation of legal and ecclessiastical events prior to the meeting. The tone is indicated by an account of the 1954 New Haven General Council meeting which caused Rev. Wallace Anderson to shake his head and say, "Is he talking about *New Haven?*" Mr. Horton's words follow:

> ". . . (I)f we are to go forward with the proposed union, let us do so in a large way, the needs and opportunities of the whole world being our axes of reference. In the very difficulty of our task, in the practical proving that groups of different ecclesiastical and even cultural backgrounds may be harmonized in Christ, lies part of our challenge. If we move ahead at all, it should be in the consciousness of the part our two communions have played in history and with a sense of the new age just beginning. Only so, I believe, can we dream, plan, and build adequately."[5]

Mr. Wagner summarized "actions taken by the Evangelical and Reformed Church with regard to the proposed merger with the Congregational Christian Churches."[6] He then proceeded to outline "Present Evangelical and Reformed Concerns" forthrightly, so as to state clearly the stance of the ER.

"The statement adopted at the ER General Council's meeting in February, 1954, together with conversations and correspondence between interested persons as well as a few published articles and communications, all reflect some major concerns, if they are not profound misgivings, on the part of the Evangelical and Reformed Church. Chief among these concerns or misgivings are the following:

"1. The composite resolutions adopted by the ER General Council in September-November, 1948, really echo the reluctance and the reservations with which we voted to approve the Interpretations. It must not be forgotten that we voted this approval only because at that time the merger proceedings had gone so far that it seemed worth paying ANY price, worth making ANY FURTHER, concession, rather than assume responsibility for bringing those proceedings to an abrupt halt. It is not inaccurate to observe, however, that the substance of the Interpretations was essentially repugnant to the Evangelical and Reformed Church in the light of the full organic union to which it had committed itself from the beginning.

"2. We are troubled by the proposal of the 1952 CC General Council at Claremont providing for 'the preparation of a draft of a proposed constitution for the General Synod of the united fellowship.' Our clearest clue to the implications of that proposal is found in the address of the Moderator at Claremont, in which he said:

" 'The Council will consider setting up a Committee in which differing points of view on the merger are represented. Its function will be to propose a constitution for the merged Churches. SOME WILL DESIRE TO MOVE FORWARD ALONG THE BASIC PROVISIONS SET FORTH IN THE "BASIS OF UNION." Our Evangelical and Reformed friends may resist any change at this point. OTHERS WILL BE INTERESTED IN EXPLORING THE POSSIBILITY OF MAKING THE MERGER ONLY AT THE NATIONAL LEVEL WITH THE GENERAL COUNCIL AND OUR OTHER NATIONAL AGENCIES OF BOTH DENOMINATIONS. This would allow the states and local churches to follow the unification process as and when they elect. The American Board would regain approximately the status with which it was launched. The "Basis of Union" as it might be developed would then serve as a model constitition to be altered as states might elect. At some points our youth have already moved into such a unity. Judging from past attitudes, states like Ohio where both denominations are in great power would probably move swiftly toward merger at the state level. Other states, like Illinois, where differences of point of view are acute, might take some years to work out a pattern of unification. Meanwhile, there seems to be no particular reason why the sixty-six Evangelical and Reformed churches of Texas with their 16,000 members should undergo an organizational revolution to accommodate themselves to our three churches in that state with their total of 250 members. Nor does it seem sensible to ask our New England states of Vermont, New Hampshire, Maine, and Massachusetts to undergo the full force of such a major revolution as the "Basis of Union" stipulates, to make themselves acceptable to the small Evangelical and Reformed Churches which are found in this area where 20 per cent of all Congregational Christians live. Union at the national level is a realistic recognition that the states and local churches must in the last analysis determine their life under our system.'

"If what is now sought is only a top-level administrative merger, it is quite doubtful whether the Evangelical and Reformed Church would be interested in further negotiations. We want to be 'one body,' not just 'one head.'

"3. A third concern resides in what we have come to call the 'Explanations' which counsel for the CC General Council presented to the Court in an early brief and which seem to us to eviscerate the Basis of Union much more than the Interpretations had already done. Our concern is this: Since these 'Explanations' were part of the grounds on which a dissolution of the injunction was secured, do they now, to borrow a phrase from the Chairman of the Committee on Free Church Polity and Unity, constitute a mandate within the limits of which, from now on, merger negotiations must of necessity be conducted?

"4. A fourth concern hinges on how extensive the opposition to the proposed merger is within the CC fellowship. The overwhelmingly favorable vote at each CC General Council is impressive; but so is the persistent and apparently well-financed organized opposition. Is there, in addition to this organized opposition, any considerable distribution of churches, associations and conferences which have been just completely indifferent, but whose very indifference up to this point might prove to be fertile ground from now on for seed-sowing by the already organized opposition? If this is a real possibility, do we, having proceeded to effect a merger, then face the twin prospects of leaving perhaps a thousand or more congregations to constitute a continuing denomination so that there would still be two denominations where there had been two before; and, further, a possible sequence of litigation to harass us for years to come? If either or both of these prospects were to ensue, it is difficult to see how the cause of Christian union would have profited:—it might even have suffered by our proceeding in the face of these prospects."

There is no room for speculation as to Mr. Wagner's intent. The words are strong "profound misgivings," "reluctance;" "essentially repugnant;" "troubled;" the Explanations given by CC counsel to the courts "seem to us to eviscerate the Basis of Union." The crux of Mr. Wagner's statement bears repeating.[7]

"If what is now sought is only a top-level administrative merger, it is quite doubtful whether the Evangelical and Reformed Church would be interested in further negotiations. We want to be 'one body,' not just 'one head'."

Keiling selects several descriptive words and phrases to depict the gloom which enveloped the meeting[8] as follows: "confusion," "reluctance," "reservations," "disillusionment," "frustration," "with virtually every fear or question ever heard by either denominational group placed clearly before the joint meeting,"[9] "our spirits reached an ultimate low," "twelve years of efforts seemed to be ending in futility." This continued to be the mood of the meeting from October 12th on into October 13th.

A findings committee was appointed to couch the failure of the meeting in acceptable language. In the sentiments of Mrs. Claude Kennedy, it appeared as though the merger were dead.[10]

What happened on October 13th, as reported by Rev. Wallace Anderson,[11] is as follows: "Wagner, president of the E&R felt at breakfast time on October 13th nothing would be done definitely. He told me so. Then a special committee brought in the 1, 2, 3 etc. of the letter missive. We met, by ourselves, and the voting began. It seemed to me like a 'tired political convention' with almost everyone hopping on the band wagon and not seeing the *whole denominational picture....* I . . . voted negatively throughout the whole matter.

"I felt like resigning, in fact I did offer to resign as chairman of the Advisory Committee that morning—but they said 'no' and I realized nothing would be gained by quitting."

Keilings's account of the situation reads, " 'And then something happened!' als das tags zuvor beauftragte, 'Findings Committee' nach durchwachten Nachtstuden betrat. Sein Vorsitzender, Dr. Ben Herbster . . . erstattete Bericht."[12]

So, after a night consideration the committee's "erstattete Bericht" was reported as follows:[13]

"1) 'Christ calls us to mission and unity.' This challenge becomes ever more insistent as we live and labor in these disturbed days. The church must minister more effectively to the needs of our time. To this end we believe that the Spirit of God is leading us in the direction of re-uniting the divided body of Christ.

"2) We believe that when the Congregational Christian Churches and the Evangelical and Reformed Church voted to enter into a union, this action was taken in response to this imperative. In consummating this union we believe that we are following the leadership of the Holy Spirit.

"3) In accordance with actions of the General Council of the Congregational Christian Churches and the General Synod of the Evangelical and Reformed Church, we re-assert the validity of the Basis of Union with the Interpretations as the basis for this merger. We feel that the matter of the drafting of a constitution is adequately provided for in this instrument. We look forward to the holding of the Convening General Synod in 1957.

"4) We authorize the chairmen (of the Executive Committee and the Evangelical and Reformed General Council) to appoint a joint committee of lawyers to counsel with the Executive Committee of the General Council of the Congregational Christian Churches and the General Council of the Evangelical and Reformed Church as may be requested.

"5) We authorize a joint project in some such area as stewardship or evangelism to help demonstrate the added strength which a united church will have. To this end a joint committee of three from each group shall be appointed.

"6) We authorize a program to be launched to acquaint the members of the Congregational Christian Churches and the Evangelical and Reformed Church with the advantages that will accrue with union. To this end a joint committee of three from each group shall be appointed.

"7) We recommend that local churches, commissions, boards, conferences, synods, associations, and similar denominational groups be urged to invite fraternal delegates and observers from the other group to their meetings, to foster fellowship and understanding.

"8) We recommend that the Executive Committee of the General Council of the Congregational Christian Churches provide subscriptions to *Advance* for the members of the General Council of the Evangelical and Reformed Church and that the General Council of the Evangelical and Reformed Church provide subscriptions to *The Messenger* to the members of the Executive Committee.

"9) We agree that the Executive Committee of the General Council of the Congregational Christian Churches and the General Council of the Evangelical and Reformed Church shall meet jointly within approximately six months to hear reports, to study the Basis of Union, and to take whatever further steps may be necessary. The time and place shall be left to the Administrative Committee of the Evangelical and Reformed Church and the Advisory Committee of the Executive Committee.

"10) We refer the primary implementation of items 4, 5 and 6 to the Commission on Interchurch Relations and Christian Unity of the Congregational Christian Churches and the Committee on Closer Relations with Other Churches of the Evangelical and Reformed Church in consultation with the Executive Committee of the Congregational Christian General Council and the General Council of the Evangelical and Reformed Church.

"11) We are encouraged by the spirit of understanding and mutual trust evident in this meeting. With faith in God and confidence in each other we look forward to the consummation of this union. We are certain that any problems arising out of the union can be solved through God's grace and Christian love.

"It was agreed to discuss the report paragraph by paragraph, and this procedure was followed.

"VOTED: To approve the report as a whole (with minor editorial changes) by a vote of 14 yes, 3 no; by Executive Committee members."

A general letter (Letter Missive October 18, 1954) embodying these findings was sent by the Executive Committee to the Congregational Christian Churches and Ministers. It arrived on my desk October 22, 1954. In reply I wrote my sharpest letter.[14]

"To say that this Letter Missive is disturbing is to put it mildly. It is incredible. Two General Councils have voted on a carefully reasoned compromise means by which we could move forward in our ecumenical relations, namely, what has been called 'The Claremont Resolution.' This was set down by the General Council meeting at New Haven by reaffirmation as the orderly means for our forward movement into wider ecumenical relationsips. It is now, apparently, blandly disregarded. This is incredible.

"As an individual, I am shocked. What action will be taken by those of us who feel that ecumenical relations must move forward in an orderly, thoughtful, and Christian manner I do not know. For myself, I can and will have no part whatsoever in any union which is approached in such a method.

"To say, 'In consummating this union we believe that we are following the leadership of the Holy Spirit' is a desecration. How can the Holy Spirit possibly encourage a divisive, unkind, and flagrant disregard of what has been so prayerfully, and thoughtfully arrived at as 'The Claremont Resolution?'

"What I shall write or do, or what other people will write or do, as greater time is available for thought I do not know. But the immediate reaction is one of complete outrage.

"I sincerely and prayerfully urge that the Executive Committee reconsider again 'The Claremont Resolution' and the actions of two successful General Council meetings upon that, and that you, one and all, search your consciences as to how you can move forward and take all of us with you and not split the body of Christ again and again needlessly, fruitlessly, hopelessly. Wishing you the guidance of the Holy Spirit, I am

"Sincerely yours,

"Henry David Gray"

The Holy Spirit

Before the chronicle of the Mediator's responses to the October, 1954 meeting one needs to consider the statement "In consummating this union we believe that we are following the leadership of the Holy Spirit."

If, as Rev. Raymond B. Walker claimed, "The spirit of a new Pentecost fell upon the baffled company,"[15] the consistent Congregational usage of centuries attestated that the Spirit's voice was authoritative FOR THOSE WHO HEARD IT. Not a scintilla of support could be adduced for the idea that a 14 to 3 vote of *any* committee is the voice of the Holy Spirit speaking to the Congregational Christian fellowship.

Three points are noteworthy. First, in the entire CC/ER merger process the guidance of the Spirit was always claimed when that guidance supported the wishes of those in favor of merger. The only vote of the General Council which approached the constitutional norm of "substantial unity" was the 95% approval of the 1952 Claremont Resolution WHICH RESOLUTION WAS NOW DISCARDED. Was the October 1954 "Findings Committee" report *improvised* or *inspired*? And if inspired, inspired for whom? Certainly not for the more than 900 delegates who supported the discarded Claremont Resolution.

Second, the results of the October 1954 meeting were hardly the "fruits of the spirit" of the New Testament. Division, bitterness and distrust followed, rather than unity, joy, peace, kindness and love.

Third, the October 1954 Meeting allegedly spirit-guided, deliberately rejected the explicit instructions of the 1954 General Council to appoint a Constitutional Commission, and in fact, robbed that Commission, when it was tardily appointed, of a primary function, that is, the consideration of a United Church Constitution.

From the standpoint of the Mediators these were some of the preliminary questions raised by the Letter Missive in which the Executive Committee vote was announced. This statement is illustrated by the following letters of Mediators.

Rev. Wallace W. Anderson[16]

"Rev. Henry David Gray,
Oneonta Congregational Church
Garfield Avenue at Oak Street,
South Pasadena, California

"Dear Henry:

"Thank you for your good letter of October 22nd which was addressed to the members of the Executive Committee. I have been disturbed as you are. All I can say to you is that I put in a very miserable session at Cleveland. You may recall that the vote on the final action was 30 to 2. My vote was one of those two negative votes.

"When this matter came before us for discussion, when our Executive Committee was meeting by itself, I brought out the fact that the Claremont Resolution was made with the understanding that there first be the draft of a proposed constitution submitted to our denomination. This constitution was to be prepared by those representing all sides of the merger question. I mentioned your name personally as one who seconded that resolution with the understanding that it was a compromise and an attempt to bring all of our groups into closer harmony.

"The General Council minutes of 1952 were opened to page 20 and I was told by the Chairman of the Executive Committee that on line 9 of that resolution I would note the phrase 'if both approve.' Our Executive Committee was not approving and the General Council of the E. & R. Church was not approving, therefore we had a perfect right to go ahead and proceed with the merger without the proposed constitution.

"I admitted that, technically, we could 'wiggle' out of the promise because of that phrase 'if both approve,' but I maintained that we were playing false to our commitments and that the overwhelming majority of delegates at Claremont and again at New Haven felt that no steps would be taken until a proposed constitution was submitted.

"I had the experience of voting 'no' and then having the Chairman address a few remarks to me as to why I shouldn't have voted 'no.'

"I knew I could write this to you, personally, and I know you will treat it as confidential but I was so heartsick over the speed with which things were done at Cleveland that I left in a mood that I felt was not entirely Christian.

"Thank you for your comment about 'the guidance of the Holy Spirit.' I had to smile inwardly when I read on the second page of the Letter Missive 'this action was taken by a joint vote of 30 to 2 with one abstention.' Then, in the very next line you will note that 'the Executive Committee took this action in the confidence that it was both following the guidance of the Holy Spirit' etc. It certainly left Mrs. Kennedy of Minneapolis and Mr. Doane who abstained from voting and myself out 'on the limb' without any contact with the Holy Spirit!

"Power to you and thank you again for writing in the spirit that you did to all of us.

"Ever faithfully,

"Wally

"WWA:pyb

"P.S. I'm prompted to add this because you say 'It puzzles me.' On Oct. 12th our C-C differences were obvious to the E & R group. I know Wagner, president of E & R felt at breakfast time on Oct. 13th nothing would be done definitely. He told me so. Then a special committee brought in the 1, 2, 3 etc. of the letter Missive. We met, by ourselves, and the voting began. It seemed to me like a 'tired political convention' with almost everyone hopping on the band wagon and not seeing the *whole denominational picture*. It was in our denominational group meeting I voted against #1—and to be consistent voted negatively through out the whole matter.

"I felt like resigning, in fact I did offer to resign as chairman of the Advisory Committee that morning—but they said 'no' and then I realized nothing would be gained by quitting.

"WWA."

Rev. Arthur H. Bradford[17]

"Dr. Douglas Horton
The General Council,
Congregational Christian Churches
287 Fourth Avenue
New York 10, New York

"Dear Douglas:

"I want to send this word to you, and, if I may, through you to the Executive Committee of our General Council. As you know, I was a member of the Executive Committee for twelve years, serving for two full six-year terms, and an interval of two years between them.

"I write at this time because I am concerned for our Fellowship of Churches, its unity and peace and spiritual strength.

"I write out of my four years of experience as a member of the Committee on Free Church Polity and Unity (pages vi and vii) I want to call to your attention now, and to the attention of the Executive Committee. These paragraphs are as follows:

"'Although our Committee was not authorized to give special study to the proposed merger of the Congregational Christian Churches and the Evangelical and Reformed Church, this matter has been much in our thoughts during all our work together. Fully realizing how widely we have differed in our convictions about the merger we have learned to value more than ever the privilege of belonging to a free church fellowship. We are profoundly thankful that while we freely and radically disagree on a matter so important to us all we can study together as we have done on this Committee,

405

helping one another to understand more fully the character of our Congregational Christian heritage in the common purpose to help our denomination make its greatest possible contribution to the cause of Christian unity in our time.

"'We have been increasingly concerned to keep unbroken the free fellowship to which we all belong. We are a Christian fellowship. This means we are a family group—a Church family—whose members are bound together by common memories and ideals—faith and friendship and love for one another in the name of Christ, our Lord.

"'We believe it is possible and always will be possible for a majority and a minority in our fellowship to study and confer together as members of the Committee have done and that ways will be found in which our denomination can boldly act in service to the ideal of Christian unity. The time required for such procedure will, we believe, always be justified.'

"The spirit expressed in these paragraphs from the Report of the Committee on Free Church Polity and Unity is, I believe, the spirit needed in the leadership of our denomination at the present time. The action of the Executive Committee at Cleveland, in October, 1954, seems to me to be of a contrary spirit. This action could lead to a serious break in our Fellowship.

"Therefore, I hope and pray that the Executive Committee will rescind its October vote. I hope that it will then arrange for an unhurried meeting of itself with such a widely representative group such as that which served on the Committee on Free Church Polity and Unity. Out of such a conference, and only so, in my judgment, can we hope to find the right way forward for our whole fellowship— the way forward to a more Christian Unity.

"'Life is not so short,' as Emerson tells us, 'but that there is always time enough for courtesy.'

"Faithfully yours,

"Arthur H. Bradford

"P.S. I am sending copies of this letter to a few fellow ministers with the hope that the expression of my own convictions may be helpful to them, and through them, to others."

Rev. Frederick M. Meek[18]

"Rev. Raymond B. Walker, D.D.
First Congregational Church
1126 S.W. Park Avenue
Portland 5, Oregon

"Dear Raymond:

"I have just received your letter addressed to the members of the Free Church Polity Committee, and I read it with amazement because of the complete misunderstanding of the point at issue.

"The members of the Free Church Polity Committee are *not* disturbed about the possibility of being overlooked *personally*. But I know that many of them are seriously disturbed that our leaders and the Executive Committee should ignore so completely the report of the Free Church Polity Committee—a Committee appointed by the General Council, and representative of the whole denomination in thought and attitude. It is the *report and not the individual personnel* of the Committee that has importance. And it is the ignoring of the *report, not the people*, that is the matter for the gravest concern and questioning.

"Nowhere in your letter do you mention or take into consideration the basic reason for the appointment of the Free Church Polity Committee—the fact of our denominational confusion as to who we Congregationalists are, and what, under our polity, we can do in matters of church union.

"As soon as the report (as unbiased a document as a group of intelligent, consecrated representative men and women could produce) came out, it was evident that it did not find favor with some of our influential leaders. The sorry spectacle of attempting to slit the report's throat before it ever got to the people, by attaching a legal opinion to it when it was given to the delegates in New Haven, indicated in advance what might be the reasoning contained in any forthcoming explanatory letter about why the importance of the report and the necessity for its study were to be ignored. Then came the attempt on the part of leaders to discourage sending the report to the churches—a move which did not prevail at the General Council. The sending of Mr. Wood's opinion along with the report to all our churches (even though with General Council approval) is part of the same pattern of trying to kill the report. That is what the Executive Committee would do as it shies away from urging a study of the report by the churches, before this move toward union with the Evangelical and Reformed Church is projected.

"The understood purpose behind all that the Committee did in our years of concentrated study and work, was that a study of the report would be fostered in all churches. If that were not the purpose, the Committee members would certainly never have given the long hours which the Committee's work demanded. The only way in which a litigation-free attempt to unite with the Evangelical and Reformed Church can ever be hoped for, is on the basis of what this Committee has impartially found. If the report is ignored and not used constructively, the Executive Committee will be hard put to it to explain that neglect in future days.

"The Executive Committee is acting as if this were still 1948 and not the year of our Lord 1954. There has been much discussion in our fellowship; there have been many changes in point of view; there has been, most significant of all, the printing of the report of the Free Church Polity Committee. To undertake to lead our denomination into an immediate union without a more adequate consultation with our churches on the basis of a study of this polity report is to attempt to force action roughshod without regard.

"The Free Church Polity Committee members, as well as the denomination, are entitled to a different kind of explanation (an explanation relevant to the basic facts of the Committee's appointment) for this current avoidance of the report than your letter provides. And that explanation should deal with *the report*, not the personnel of the Committee—a matter entirely avoided in your recent letter to the Committee members.

"Sincerely yours,

"Frederick M. Meek"

Rev. L. Wendell Fifield[19]

"The Members of the Executive Committee.

"Dear Friends:

"For a variety of reasons, including certain physical limitations, I will not take an active part in the bitter controversy created by the action of your committee on October 12 and 13 relative to the merger.

"I would not, however, wish my non-participation to indicate to you or to my friends in our Fellowship my acceptance of or acquiescence to the proposals set forth in your 'Letter Missive' of October 18, 1954.

"I write, therefore, to express my most emphatic protest against the statements relative to the merger and also the failure to appoint 'a Commission on Constitutional Problems' as you were instructed to do.

"I have read with care the explanations as sent out with the 'Letter Missive' and feel them to be wholly unsound and in no way a sufficient justification for disregarding the mandate placed upon you by the General Council in the Claremont Resolution.

"As I understand it, you took the position that since the General Council of the Evangelical and Reformed Church and you did not agree that a constitution should be written, the Claremont Resolution was inoperative. In view of this decision on your part you undertook to work out a new plan of procedure with no authority from the General Council, a procedure in direct contradiction with the definite instructions given you by the General Council. Such a procedure was in violation of the rights and duties of the Executive Committee as set forth in the General Council Constitution. (See section on Executive Committee.)

"As a matter of proper procedure, since you found that the two groups 'did not agree' on the advisability of writing a constitution, you had no alternative except to report this fact back to the General Council and ask for further instructions.

"Instead, you took the actions which you have reported. These actions violate the instructions of the General Council in the following particulars:

"1. The Basis of Union with Interpretations is reintroduced. One of the purposes of the Claremont Resolution was to secure a new document, which would profit by what had been learned during our unfortunate controversy. It was hoped and expected that the submission of such a 'consititution' to the churches as provided in the Claremont Resolution would produce the harmony in our Fellowship which the Basis of Union and Interpretations failed to secure. Your action defeats this purpose which was the expressed will of the General Council voted at two Councils and mandatory upon the Executive Committee.

"2. The Claremont Resolution's limitation of the Constitution to 'the General Synod' is removed by the reintroduction of the Basis of Union as a prior document. The phrase relative to the General Synod was included in the Claremont Resolution to make it very clear that this proposed union could not involve any individual church without the independent action of that church. This is in accordance with the pleadings of the General Council in the Cadman case, and the decision of the Court of Appeals which makes further merger procedure possible on the basis of their decision. It is in accordance with the report of the Committee on Free Church Polity and Unity. And most important of all, such a limitation of the constitution 'to the General Synod' is made madatory upon the Executive Committee by the Claremont Resolution itself. To sub-stitute 'the Basis of Union and Inerpretations' for a 'constitution for the General Synod of the united fellowship to be made available to the membership of both communions for discussions and sugges-tions' is to alter completely the instructions to the Executive Committee given by the General Council. It changes the entire purpose and plan of the General Council. This the Executive Com-mittee had no right to do. I question seriously whether any proposal for the merger which does not stipulate clearly the freedom of every church to determine its relationship to the proposed United Church by its independent action, is legal and permissible in view of the decision of the Court of Appeals. Even if the Basis of Union were used, the fact that union can be had only on the national level would have to be officially stated.

"3.   The General Council instructed that in the executing of the Claremont Resolution 'there be representatives of the different points of view.' The presence of three opponents of the merger on the Executive Committee in no way meets this mandate of the General Council. Certainly one of the very extensive points of view in this whole matter is that of those who are friendly to the report of the Committee on Free Church Polity and Unity. None of them was involved nor consulted. Nor were the conclusions of this four-year unanimous report of twenty-one of your Congregational brethren given any consideration. While the Committee on Free Church Polity and Unity has ceased to exist, it did signify its willingness to be of further assistance to the Executive Committee. The primary purpose of this offer was to make possible the section of the Claremont Resolution which refers specificially to a consulting relationship. The Committee on Free Church Polity and Unity believed that the instructions in the Claremont Resolution would be faithfully followed. The disillusionment is great and disheartening.

"It is incredible that a report representing so careful a study by so important a committee, produced at a very considerable financial cost, and at an even greater cost of sacrificial service on the part of the committee should be blandly dismissed. This report is a true and accurate and impartial statement of our Congregational polity. Whether you like it or not, it tells the truth. It must here be stated with the deepest regret that your proposals for merger procedure are in direct violation of the principles set forth, with the unanimous approval of the committee, in section 4. Sooner or later our Fellowship must decide between your 'over-night' solution of the problem and this four-year study of the Committee on Free Church Polity and Unity.

"4.   The failure to appoint the Commission on Constitutional Problems is a direct defiance of the instructions of the General Council. The assertion that the action of the Executive Committee relative to the merger renders such a Commission unnecessary is contrary to fact. Indeed such a Commission is now all the more necessary to deal with the violations of the Constitution of the General Council involved in your merger proposal.

"The Claremont Resolution, the report of the Committee on Free Church Polity and Unity and the work of the Commission on Congregational Problems constituted a carefully worked-out program for a proper, sound and Christian approach to the whole matter of the relationship of our Congregational Christian Churches to the ecumenical Movement. It was developed over years of sacrificial study by consecrated people of all points of view. Your action jeopardizes this whole carefully worked-out program by an action which I understand was hastily arrived at overnight. With all the earnestness which I command I protest this action.

"As one who worked for years upon this problem I feel especially keenly the statement 'in consumating this Union we believe that we are following the leadership of the Holy Spirit.' The implication that the hundreds who have worked in a spirit of consecrated sacrifice, that the General Council in voting and revoting the Claremont Resolution were *not* guided by the Holy Spirit but that you were, seems to me a statement that should never have been made. Personally, I still believe that the guidance of God's spirit was with those who for months and years sought to work out this problem, and with the General Council as well. The assumption that a program worked out in a few short hours, based upon the wish-thinking of a preponderant majority, expresses the guidance of God's spirit, seems to me the greatest tragedy of this whole tragic business.

"I raise one more point. Why did the Executive Committee feel that they should yield to the desires of the Evangelical and Reformed Church rather than steadfastly stand upon the instructions of the General Council, of which you are a part and which it is your duty properly to represent? I have had sufficient experience to know that your proposals of October 12 and 13 represent in the main the suggestions of the Evangelical and Reformed Church (for I have often heard them make them) rather than the official actions of our General Council. Your proposals seem to represent more nearly an effort to circumvent the instructions of the General Council in the Claremont Resolution than steadfastly to uphold them.

"I write this with what I feel to be a sense of righteous indignation but also of deep sorrow. I know the more bitter controversy which lies ahead, its loss in money, in friendship, in Christian good-will and achievement. I feel sure that further court actions will ensue.

"This time the issue is different. It's not the 'merger' that is the question. It is whether our Executive Committee can alter, negate and disregard the specific instructions and madates of the General Council. On this issue, so far as I can see, there is no mediating position. There is no middle ground. Many who have been pro-merger will be anti-usurpation. I know this because many have written me already. My mail has been flooded with letters all protesting the fact that the Executive Committee has 'misinterpreted,' 'ignored,' 'by-passed,' 'defied' the Claremont Resolution, and so the General Council. (These are not my words but theirs.) The rising tide of opposition, especially from pro-merger adherents, has startled me by its size and intensity. I cannot tell you how sadly I view this new struggle in a Christian group which was just moving back to genuine fellowship again.

"I regret more than I can say the conviction on my part which makes this letter necessary. I have struggled with the matter for weeks. But since I shall feel free to make these statements herein recorded to others, I feel that I should, in all fairness, send them to you.

"I feel sincerely that the whole Ecumenical Movement insofar as our Fellowship is concerned, has suffered a severe setback as the result of this action. If your action of October continues in force and is not repudiated by your committee or the 1956 General Council, our Ecumenical progress will be retarded for many years. I am confident that it will be repudiated by the General Council. Then where will we be after two years of turmoil between now and then?

"I have been a Congregational minister for over thirty-five years. As you know, I have served our Fellowship in many capacities. I have never begged before. But I do now. I beg you to give this matter further consideration before it is too late. I urge you to reassert your proper position as an Executive Committee in relationship to the mandates of the General Council and proceed in accordance with its instructions.

"Most of us, you and I, have worked together. I have always considered, and do now, that regardless of our differences of opinion we are Christian friends. I have written with utmost frankness. Yet I assure you there is no spirit in my heart but that of personal friendship and good-will toward each of you. That this attitude does not extend to your action of October 12 and 13 is, of course, fully clear.

"Some who have been disillusioned by your action will remain sad and silent. Some will speak out. But as the word gets around, and it will, and the true nature of the action becomes clear, there will be, at the heart of our Fellowship, on the part of those who are for and those who are against the merger, a sadness which Congregationalism has never known before.

"Sincerely,

"L. Wendell Fifield"

Of the pro-merger responses to my letter, I report those of Mary Fiebiger and those of Chairman Raymond B. Walker. Mrs. Fiebiger was a member of the October 13 Findings Committee; Rev. Wallace Anderson credited her with the idea that the Claremont Resolution phrase "if both approve" meant that, since both did *not*

412

approve, the Committee was free to act as it pleased. Her letter, and that of Mr. Walker, together with my replies, state the issue.

Mrs. Judson Fiebiger[20]

"Dr. Henry David Gray
The Oneonta Congregational Church
Garfield Avenue and Oak St.
South Pasadena, Calif.

"Dear Henry:

"Your letter to the members of the Executive Committee came and I am dismayed at your reaction. I only wish that you and a million other Congregational Christians might have been the unseen guests, looking in on our Cleveland meeting, feeling the power of God moving in our midst.

"Mayhap you suspect that the meeting was 'packed,' that certain persons, at least, went with definite goals to put through. My friend, this is far, far from the truth. I honestly believe that our folks—and theirs, went with a deep sense of responsibility and wondered honestly where we would arrive in our two days together. I feel sure that regardless of our own personal opinions, we wanted to do what was right and best toward advancing the Kingdom of God in the world.

"We had many documents before us, including the Claremont Resolution, which we studied carefully and discussed thoroughly. We talked over many things, asked numerous questions of each other, pondered prayerfully the mandates of several General Councils and the issues before us. We met jointly and separately. The Claremont Resolution was not 'blandly disregarded' I assure you. It was taken into account very definitely and we continue 'to look forward to a united fellowship of the E&R and the CC communions.'

"Never have I felt the leading of the Holy Spirit more keenly than in this meeting and it hurts me deeply to have you say that this very statement is a desecration. No one at our meeting, either pro or con was 'outraged,' as you describe your feeling. Please read again the final paragraph of the statement we adopted. All present would testify, I feel sure, to the spirit evident there.

"Henry, I do not know what you will write further or what you will do, but I hope you will not see fit to disrupt and divide. I hope you may work with us, take each step of the way beside us—and if a step should come that you just can't take, let's work that one out as we come to it. We spelled out the fears of some, when we wrote the Interpretations and the E&Rs adopted these. We trust each other—and are not afraid of losing our freedoms.

413

"Thank you for your prayers. We—and you—all of us, need the guidance of the Holy Spirit.

"Cordially,

"Mary Fiebiger"

Rev. Raymond B. Walker[21]

"Dr. Henry David Gray
Garfield Avenue at Oak Street
Pasadena, California

"Dear Dr. Gray:

"I have before me your letter of October 22nd addressed to members of the Executive Committee. I am much disturbed by your apparent misunderstanding of our 'Letter Missive.' At all times we had the Claremont Resolution before us and believed that we were charting our course within its directives. How, specifically, do you feel that we have violated this resolution?

"It is, first, a re-affirmation of the purpose of the General Council to unite with the Evangelical and Reformed Communion. Second, it instructs the Executive Committee to seek joint meetings with the General Council of the Evangelical and Reformed Church and specifies that resolutions and suggestions originating in our fellowship and which are of common interest to the two communions be referred to such joint meetings. This includes the resolutions presented by the Massachusetts Congregational Conference and the New York Congregational Christian Conference. Third, it provides that the two bodies meeting jointly, IF BOTH APPROVE, be responsible for the preparation of a draft of a PROPOSED constitution for the General Synod of the united fellowship and that this PROPOSED constitution is to be made available to the members of both communions for discussion and suggestions. Please note—whether or not the constitution should be drafted at this time is left to the discretion of the two bodies meeting jointly. It was our feeling that the first step should not be drafting of a proposed constitution, but a program designed to develop understanding, fellowship and a common spiritual forward movement. The Basis of Union with Interpretations, wisely, we believe, postpones the adoption of a constitution until after the consummation of the union and 'that the spirit of a union in Christ with full trust in one another might be jeopardized if ecclesiastical legalities were put to the fore.' In other words, we felt that the basis of union is psychological rather than merely legal. This does not, however, preclude the appointment at any place in our program of a joint commission to begin the study of a constitution, to draft the same and to submit it as a proposal to the churches of both communions. Perhaps that is what we ought to do.

414

Perhaps that is what we shall do. You will note that the next joint meeting is to be held within approximately six months to hear reports, to study the basis of union 'and to take whatever further steps may be necessary.' I was very happy to receive a copy of the resolution of the Los Angeles Association adopted October 19th and its constructive suggestions will most certainly be presented to the next joint meeting. Fourth, the Claremont Resolution also provided that there be representatives of the different points of view on all the Congregational Christian bodies 'responsible for the implementing of the resolution above.' The resolution above refers, of course, to the drafting of the proposed constitution. We did not consider the resolution as implying that members of the dissident minority should be seated in the joint meeting of the Executive Committee and the General Council. As you know, this was demanded by members of the Continuing Committee. And, of course, you also know that two members of our Executive Committee were elected because they represent the non-merger point of view.

"It is my earnest desire that we may move forward toward the consummation of this union in a spirit of Christian fellowship, no one impugning the motives of the others or passing judgement without every attempt at understanding. In such a spirit it would be possible for us to move together. I am shocked and saddened by your question, 'how can the Holy Spirit possibly encourage a divisive, unkind, and flagrant disregard of what has been so prayerfully, and thoughtfully arrived at as "The Claremont Resolution"?'

"Sincerely yours,

"Raymond B. Walker, Chairman
Executive Committee, General Council
Congregational Christian Churches"

Mr. Walker was not present, so far as I recall, when we framed the Claremont Resolution. He had participated neither in the studies of the Free Church Polity and Unity Committee, nor in the CC/ER consultations. Hence it must have been very difficult for him to see the significance or understand the background of the Claremont Resolution, the Polity and Unity Report, or the "Explanations" given to the court by counsel for the General Council. I tried to provide part of a frame of reference in my reply.[22]

"Rev. Raymond B. Walker, D.D.
First Congregational Church
1126 S. W. Park Avenue
Portland 5, Oregon

415

"Thank you for your prompt reply to my letter concerning the action of the Executive Committee. Oddly enough, in the same mail came a letter from Jesse Perrin with a copy of your reply to him concerning the Los Angeles Association Resolution. I wrote that Resolution.

"I wrote the Resolution before I had seen the Letter Missive. What is incredible in the Letter Missive is that we all know that the Claremont Resolution was intended to set up a careful, deliberate, and helpful process by which all viewpoints could be represented, a constitution written, and deliberate action taken. It is true that it does not *say* in the Claremont Resolution that you were to follow this if the E & R did not agree to it. The reason was simple, it was *understood* in our conferences that the thing (merger) would be dropped if they did not agree to it. This of course was not put down for the reason that the more ardent pros did not want it put down, which is quite understandable because it would have closed the door.

"I find my desk covered with letters from all over the country expressing great indignation, and the interesting thing is that they come from people in all stratas, not just from those who are violent anti folk. My own viewpoint is that we should merge with whomsoever we can merge with provided we do so with the guarantees of freedom which are in your mind as you write in your October 26th letter. To leave the squabbles until afterwards is a futile process. There needs to be a constitutional document, and as you point out it could be produced now. I am perfectly sure that I for one will never go into any union of any kind until such a document is available. I am also equally sure that I am ready to go into any union in which the things mentioned in your letter are safe-guarded. I am far and away in favor of cooperation.

"It should be pointed out however that only the grossest misrepresentation could construe two people out of a total executive group of twenty-four as being representative of the total opinion in this country concerning the merger. Never at any time have more than between 50 and 60% of the churches voted favorably. Many have not voted at all. One thousand one hundred and sixty-two voted against. This means that two people were sent to represent approximately 40% of the denomination. This obviously is impossible.

"It was the intent of all of us who worked so long, so hard on the Polity and Unity Committee that we might be helpful and constructive and by being objectively interested in the problem give a solid foundation on which to carry forward 98 or 99% of the denomination. This I believe was accomplished in the past 4½ years. I am not sure just now what is going to occur, but I am certain that we are in for a much more bitter struggle than was the case over the basis of union, for the reason that many people now feel that they have not been kept faith with, and that the action taken in Cleveland was the response of folk to a warm, friendly, emotionally favorable situation and not to the total fellowship behind them in the Congregational Christian Churches. We have clear and good guidance in the Claremont Resolution. If it is followed, I believe we can carry 99% of the people (or thereabouts) with us. If it is flouted, I see nothing ahead of us but great difficulties and I am frankly *terribly* concerned.

"God be with you.

"Sincerely yours,

"Henry David Gray"

Probably because of Rev. L. Wendell Fifield's letter, Mr. Walker directed the following to the members of the Polity and Unity Committee.[23]

"Dr. Henry David Gray
Oneonta Congregational Church
South Pasadena, California

"Dear Dr. Gray:

"This letter is being sent to members of the former committee on Free Church Polity and Unity. I regret the necessity of mimeographing the body of the letter. My own inadequate office facilities make it necessary. Please consider it as personal as tho (sic) it were typed.

"Word has come to us that some members of the Committee on Free Church Polity and Unity are inclined to feel that their four years of work in behalf of the General Council has been disregarded by the Executive Committee in its recent addition anticipating the consummation of the union with the Evangelical and Reformed Church. I am sure that I speak for the Executive Committee when I say that we are genuinely sorry to hear this. I hope that we have been misinformed. In any case, let me review the facts.

"We of the Executive Committee had no thought that the work of the Committee on Free Church Polity and Unity had anything to do with the basic commitment made by the General Council in 1949 to merge with the Evangelical and Reformed Church. The resolution by which the General Council constituted the Committee on Free Church Polity and Unity in 1950 was specific on this point:

"'The constituting of this committee is not to be interpreted as affecting any past decisions of the General Council.'

417

"That the basic commitment to unite was recognized as a past decision of the General Council is confirmed by Dr. Arthur Gray, my predecessor as Chairman of the Executive Committee, who helped to draft this part of the resolution. This was further confirmed, as the record shows, by what was said from the platform of the General Council just before the vote was taken.

"In the Claremont Resolution of 1952, the General Council again referred to the Committee on Free Church Polity and Unity:

"'THE EXECUTIVE COMMITTEE IS REQUESTED TO ESTABLISH A CONSULTING RELATIONSHIP WITH THE COMMITTEE ON FREE CHURCH POLITY AND UNITY DURING THE DRAFTING OF THE PROPOSED CONSTITUTION.'

"(The Claremont Resolution, as you will remember, states that the General Council 'continues to look forward to a united fellowship,' instructs the 'Executive Committee to seek joint meetings with the General Council of the Evangelical and Reformed Church,' and 'those two bodies meeting jointly be requested, if both approve, to be responsible for the preparation of a draft of a proposed constitution for the General Synod of the united fellowship to be made available to the membership of both communions for discussion and suggestions,' that 'on all the Congregational Christian bodies responsible for the implementing of the resolution above there be representatives of the different points of view among us; and that the process of cooption be employed whenever desirable.')

"In 1954 at New Haven, the General Council reaffirmed the entire resolution from which the paragraphs above are quoted SO FAR AS THIS RESOLUTION WAS STILL APPLICABLE. By that time, however, the committee on Free Church Polity and Unity at its own request had ceased to exist. No current reference to it was therefore applicable.

"The Committee on Free Church Polity and Unity, in relinquishing its duties, had kindly tendered to the General Council the good offices of those who had been its members for any services for which their studies had given them special ability. In this connection it is natural to think of the writing of a constitution.

"At the joint meeting of our Executive Committee and the General Council of the Evangelical and Reformed Church last month, the following action was taken:

"'In accordance with actions of the General Council of the Congregational Christian Churches and the General Synod of the Evangelical and Reformed Church, we

418

reassert the validity of the "Basis of Union with the Interpretations" AS THE BASIS FOR THIS MERGER. We feel that the matter of drafting a constitution is adequately provided for in this instrument.'

"This would mean that no constitution would be presented to the denominations for ratification before the union is effected. We do not yet know whether a beginning may not be made, however, in WRITING a constitution in the near future. This matter will undoubtedly be before the next joint meeting of the Executive Committee and the General Council.

"In any case, whenever the constitution is written—now or later—I feel certain that the Executive Committee will desire to avail itself of the offer made by the Committee on Free Church Polity and Unity, and utilize the wisdom of its former members. It would be difficult for all the twenty-two members to serve on a constitution-making committee, but doubtless all would be somehow involved in the process. I say 'somehow' because we do not yet know the form the constitution-making will take.

"Furthermore, constitution-making is only one of several important projects for which, in accomplishing the union, we should want to draw upon your experience.

"I trust, therefore, that instead of holding any untoward feelings about the action of the Executive Committee, all members of the Committee on Free Church Polity and Unity will keep themselves in readiness to assist us. We should know more about the whole matter after our next joint meeting with the Evangelical and Reformed General Council in April.

> "Cordially yours,
> "Raymond B. Walker, Chairman
> Executive Committee of the General
> Council of Congregational Christian Churches"

The Claremont Resolution/Gray to Walker[24]

"Dr. Raymond B. Walker
First Congregational Church
1126 S. W. Park Avenue
Portland 5, Oregon

"My Dear Dr. Walker:

"Thanks for your thoughtful letter regarding the interpretation of 'The Claremont Resolution.'

"On the floor of the Council at Claremont I described that Resolution as 'a bridge between opposing viewpoints.' This is precisely what it was intended to be, and this is why I supported it whole-heartedly at Claremont, and took a considerable part in gathering support for its re-affirmation at Yale.

"Why is the Resolution a bridge? Because it provides an orderly procedure into union which protects our freedom and yet promises hope of ecumenical advance. This is done in several ways.

"1. The Resolution limits the constitution to the General Synod, thus saying plainly that we are a fellowship of Churches and not a monolithic organization at all. After meticulous, (and I mean meticulous) study for four years, I became convinced that if an over-all constitution could be written, it would be of such general nature as to be almost value-less. A General Synod constitution could be very specific, and could be written well and quickly by informed members of the Congregational Churches and E. & R.

"2. The Resolution insists that the constitution be written *first*, thus saying plainly what kind of polity *is* to obtain in the General Synod. Without that, there is no guarantee whatever, for the reason that our people do not trust each other! There is no way to allay these widely-shared fears except the plain, honest, clear statement of what is intended in a constitution NOW. And if it be true, as I hope it is, that you are right in saying none of our essential freedoms *will* be lost, then certainly it should be very easy to put that down in a constitutional document, and no one should fear so to do.

"3. The Resolution provides that all the varying viewpoints among us shall be represented on the negotiating committee, thus saying plainly, that no high-handed action is intended. It should be understood that much of the objection to the merger is objection to the degree of overhead authority and centralization which has come to exist *among us*, in our own present conference and wider relationships. Many are quite unwilling to see these seemingly self-assumed powers crystallized into a government of the Churches and ministers. This objection can be met only by integrity of the highest order on the part of the Executive Committee, made crystal clear by the co-opting of men of all viewpoints. There must be no 'pushing the business through,' if all the sincere Churches and ministers are to be carried along. This was a very important point at Claremont, and by no stretch of the imagination could it be said that the present Executive Committee represents, in fair proportion, 'all viewpoints.'

"If you will turn to the Minutes of the Yale council, you will see *in actual words*, with no inference needed to interpret their meaning, that *two kinds of action were taken at Yale* with regard to the Clare-mont Resolution. One, very rightly, I believe, once again re-affirmed our desire to work for union with the Evangelical and Reformed Church. *That one* the Executive Committee 'Letter Missive' quoted. *But the second half of the Resolution* was a deliberate, straight-forward instruction to the Executive Committee; *and it was not quoted,* nor was it followed. The expedient used was to interpret the earlier phrase, 'if both approve,' as an escape clause, which it was never intended to be.

"The Claremont Resolution was an honest attempt to build a bridge. Why blow up the bridge?

"I shall have to be frank and say that I cannot and will not enter any union founded on uncertainly, varying interpretations of the uniting articles, and general chaos. It *might* be best for the Execu-tive Committee to appoint an entirely new group to negotiate, one that is fully representative and at the same time sincerely interested in free church union. Or, it might be desirable for the Executive Committee to co-opt a goodly number of persons 'representing all viewpoints among us.' The constitutional issues are difficult and complex. They will need exacting thought; but they are far from insoluble. They can be met, at least so I believe. *But they must not be avoided.* They must be met fairly and representatively.

"There are a very large number of us who are absolutely deter-mined to be sure *before we unite,* that what we are getting into *is* a free church union. We share *neither* ultra extreme position. We just believe we should know what we are doing *before* we do it, and we are not going to unite with anybody unless we know *beforehand* what is the constitution of the new body. I rather imagine that we are going to be compelled to organize ourselves into a 'center group' if our fellowship is to follow some orderly procedure like that set forth in the Claremont Resolution. Certain it is that we shall not sit idly by. The issue involved in blowing up the bridge is critical. The Executive Committee, as the Council ad interim had the *legal* right to do this, but *the Committee certainly did not follow either the plain words of both sections of the Resolution at Yale, nor the equally plain intent of the entire action at Claremont.* Legally, the action is unimpeachable—but—?

"These issues loom so large that many of us believe we will simply have to take time, and our own money, to organize, to visit the Churches, and to represent the sort of constructive, fair, orderly procedure which would appear to be the way into free Church union—and not into schism.

"Excuse the length of this letter; I wish I could talk with you for some time instead. Few of those who share my concern agree in the slightest with the 'angry' words you report being addressed to you. We feel far more 'sad' than 'angry.'

"God be with you.

> "Sincerely yours,
>
> "Henry David Gray"

March 15, 1955 Petition

Dissent from the October 1954 action of the CC Executive Committee was so widespread that I framed a tentative "petition," circulated and revised it, and then presented it to the CC Executive Committee signed by the following twenty-six persons:

Perry Avery, Federated Churches, Corvallis, Oregon

Reginald Dwight Avery, Kensington Congregational Church, Kensington, Connecticut

Harold E. Barr, First Congregational Church, Danbury, Connecticut

Whitmore E. Beardsley, Hollywood Congregational Church, Hollywood, California

Oliver K. Black, First Congregational Church, Moline, Illinois

Dwight L. Cart, First Congregational Church, Winchester, Massachusetts

Howard Conn, Plymouth Church, Minneapolis, Minnesota

Ronald W. Dickson, First Congregational Church, Marshalltown, Iowa

L. Wendell Fifield, Plymouth Church of the Pilgrims, Brooklyn, New York

Henry David Gray, Oneonta Congregational Church, South Pasadena, California

Charles M. Houser, Plymouth Church, Des Moines, Iowa

Richard R. Hulbert, Pilgrim Heights Community Church, Minneapolis, Minnesota

Edwin C. Johnson, Anthony Park Congregational Church, St. Paul, Minnesota

William A. Keith, First Congregational Church, Kalamazoo, Michigan

Einau M. Martinson, Union Congregational Church, Minneapolis, Minnesota

Frederick M. Meek, Old South Church in Boston, Boston Massachusetts

Harold Rekstad, First Congregational Church, Winona, Minnesota

Kenneth E. Sims, The Colonial Church of Edina, Minneapolis, Minnesota

Matthew Spinka, Hartford Seminary Foundation, Hartford, Connecticut

Fred B. Spyker, First Congregational Church, Great Barrington, Massachusetts

Fred A. Stever (retired Pastor) Registrar, Twin Cities Association, Minneapolis, Minnesota

Neil H. Swanson, Jr., First Congregational Church Wauwatosa, Wisconsin

Alfred Grant Walton, Flatbush-Tompkins Congregational Church, Brooklyn, New York

Lawrence J. Weinert, La Canada Congregational Church, California

Frederick W. Whittaker, Bangor Theological School

Walter W. Witt

"A PETITION TO THE EXECUTIVE COMMITTEE

"We, the undersigned Congregational Christian pastors are concerned with the well-being of our fellowship of Churches.

"We do not identify ourselves with any present group among us, official or unofficial.

"We earnestly desire to see our Congregational Christian Churches enter into the largest possible union of free Churches.

"We are, however, distressed by the action of the Executive Committee at Cleveland, in October, 1954, because it takes us back to the controversies of six years ago.

"We feel that this is *1954* and not *1948*.

"A fresh approach to union with the Evangelical Reformed Church is needed, one which begins with the present situation. To this end we petition the Executive Committee to rescind its October 1954 vote, and to institute a new representative joint committee with the Evangelical Reformed Church. This new committee should, forthwith, prepare the fundamental document that explicitly sets forth the polity of the proposed United Church, so that the document may be submitted to the Church for their own individual action."[25]

Reply to Petition

The reply to the petition affirms concepts which are opposite.[26]

"Dr. Henry David Gray
Garfield Avenue at Oak Street
South Pasadena, California

"Dear Dr. Gray:

"I have just received yours of the 15th.

"The Executive Committee met in Cleveland January 27th. The next meeting has been set for June 20th. There is, however, a possibility that a meeting may be held in New York late in April. In any event, at the next meeting of the Executive Committee I shall present your communications and the copies of your petition.

"Personally, and I feel that members of the Executive Committee assume a like position, it is my conviction that the union can be achieved within the framework of the free church; however, when it comes to the achievement of this 'without undue division in our own fellowship,' that is a matter quite beyond the control of the Executive Committee.

"We feel that we are moving under the mandate of the General Council. As our recent publications have stated, we regard the 'Basis of Union and Interpretations;' as our only charter. Actually, this document is a statement of principles and a working agreement. We believe that it contains the guarantee of a union within the framework of a free church. While it is not a constitution, as such, to all intents and purposes it IS a constitution since it lays down the methods we must follow and the principles to which we must adhere.

"In your letter of December 6th there is a phrase which has disturbed me greatly. You state that without a constitution first, 'there is no guarantee whatever, for the reason that our people do not trust each other!' Do you believe that ANY document, constitution or otherwise, can hold people together who do not trust each other? If the followers of Jesus cannot trust one another, who in the world can?

"I have had some experience in labor relations; during the war I served as a public member of the 12th Regional War Labor Board. I have learned that no dispute is ever SETTLED legally; it is SETTLED psychologically. Legal actions may be necessary but finally it is mutual confidence and trust that affects the settlement. The proposed constitution, either for the United Church or its General Synod would certainly provide for amendment. How could people who do not trust each other feel secure under such a document? Only, of course, as they maintained a balance of power. In such an atmosphere could people work in Christian fellowship?

"You ask for the 'plain, honest, clear statement of what is intended in a constitution' and you ask for it 'NOW.' We feel that you have it

424

in the Basis of Union and Interpretations. Is objection to this document based upon intellectual doubt as much as emotional resentment? I cannot see any way to go forward with the union apart from the one charter adopted by both communions and sanctioned by the Courts. Is there a way whereby going forward even so, the principles set forth can be restated or reaffirmed so as to meet what appears to be a psychological need, i.e., reassurance?

"At the January meeting of the Executive Committee I presented every letter of protest I had received, not reading them in their entirety but setting forth in substance the position of the writers. Yours of October 22nd was presented to the Committee and members are conversant with your position. It is, of course, regrettable that your petitions did not reach me for presentation.

"You state your position as out of step with extremists on both ends. There seem to be some who are unwilling to unite under any circumstances. Evidently, no assurances will satisfy them. If a constitution were written NOW, they would resist it just as they have resisted the Basis of Union and Interpretations. You mention also those 'who wish to unite at any cost.' I do not know any people whom I would place in this category. I have repeatedly said that personally I stand for Congregational rights and freedoms. My statement to the Continuation Committee in Chicago last December emphasized this. And in it I am confident that I articulated the mind of the members of the Executive Committee. Who are these people who want to unite at any cost—who are willing to abrogate the principles of Congregationalism? I feel that in the union we would be sharing these principles; and that into such a free church other communions could be drawn. Indeed, it is my personal conviction that the wave of the future for the ecumenical movement is basic Congregational principles. However, I do not insist that they shall be labelled Congregational. It is the spiritual essence and not the word which constitutes the principles.

"Since your kindly letter of December 6th I have had in mind writing and presenting these thots (sic). With sincere reciprocation of your 'God be with you,' I am

"Sincerely yours,

"Raymond B. Walker"

Reply to the Reply!

The Mediators continued to hope that direct conversations with ER Church leaders might produce an acceptable Basis of Union. Hindsight suggests that we were wrong. However, hindsight also reveals the high degree of commitment to One Big Church with administrative power and ecclessiastical standing in the World Council of Churches. Hence, this was my reply to Rev. Raymond B. Walker.[27]

"Dr. Raymond B. Walker
First Congregational Church
1126 S. W. Park Avenue
Portland 5, Oregon

"My dear Ray:

"When I look at the date on your letter, March 17th—St. Patrick's Day—I fully realize that an Irishman should have answered that letter immediately!

"Unfortunately, I have been up against a serious staff shortage in the absence of my associate finishing his last year at seminary all this last year. Now that he is back I realize even more how much I missed him.

"I do want to go back to your letter to make some comments which may be helpful in the present situation.

"In the first place, I hope it is clear in everybody's mind that there are a very small number who want union at any cost, a very small number who want no union at all no matter what kind it is, and a very large number of us who have no aversion whatever to union but would, as a matter of fact, welcome it, provided only that it shall be done in an orderly and free church way.

"What I mean by an orderly way, is that the Committee on Information should provide *information*. When they quote a Claremont Resolution they should quote it in its entirely so that it is clear that a constitution for the General Synod was intended by that particular Council. I believe they will do us much more service, and I believe that the goal of union will be furthered by careful balanced presentation of information as such and only as such.

"Orderly also means that the kind of thing that has been done in the recent Letter Missive will be done periodically and continuously throughout the entire period of negotiation toward union. I think it would be much wiser to use the word proposed union than union as a matter of honesty. There is no union until it is actually accomplished. But orderly means simply that you keep on sending out Letters Missive well-worded, clear, in laymen's language, and attractively printed like the recent brochure. It also means that everything be done to encourage free discussion in a orderly, decent, Christian way.

"What I mean by free church in my statement above is of course related more to freedom of conscience than anything else. There is

426

no reason at all that I can think of why a 'for instance' constitution could not be drawn up at once. True, it would bind no one, but it would certainly be able to say in very few words exactly what is intended. The basic problem with the Basis of Union is its lack of clarity. It is ambiguous, often saying two quite different things in the same paragraph like for example the paragraph concerning the ministry where a standard procedure and another possible procedure are presented side by side. James Wagner's article inlcuded in the Letter Missive makes clear the concern of the E. & R. at this point. I wonder if it might not be wise, at this point, to take some persons like myself and like Fred Meek who have questions in their minds and let us sit down with James Wagner and others in the E. & R. I am not at all sure that we are as far apart as some people think we are. I sense back of Wagner's statement a concern for freedom as real as my own. Perhaps the terms in which it is stated are not quite the same as my own, but it seems to me that the concern is the same. At any rate, a 'for instance' constitution could be drawn up.

"The real problem is the one on which you placed your finger in this letter of March 17th—lack of trust. There are people who simply will not trust any document but they are not the majority, nevertheless, they can influence the majority so long as there is no document to which the majority can cling as being very simple and very clear in its intent. The Basis of Union is neither simple nor clear. I thoroughly agree with you that nothing is ever settled legally. There will, I think inevitably, be legal action. If I sense the attitude of a great many people on the Continuation group with whom I associate occasionally, though not regularly, this is likely to be the case. I personally have never been too strong for that sort of thing. I feel that we could resolve a lot of these difficulties by writing a very simple document now.

"You ask who are the people who want to unite at the cost of abrogating principles of Congregationalism. Well, I suppose that my brilliant and esteemed friend Truman Douglass is a leader in that to judge by the article which he wrote about Bishops in Congregationalism in a national magazine.

"Best regards.

"Very sincerely yours,
"Henry David Gray"

The Core Question

The core question of the Mediators concerning the October '54 vote of the CC Executive Committee was, *What is a Church?* Can there be a national church in the Congregational understanding of the New Testament.

On April 2, 1955 the Rev. James E. Wagner addressed an illuminating statement to the ER Synod Meetings.[28] The nature of the proposed United Church is stated explicitly. "The Basis of Union does provide (IV-A) that 'the General Synod shall initiate action for the preparation of a constitution of the *United Church*.' Not only the *General Synod* of the United Church,—this was a matter on which clear understanding was reached." In proclaiming this concept of *the Church* Mr. Wagner quotes Congregationalists. Rev. Daniel Jenkins has never been closely associated with the Congregational Union of England; he is a brilliant, stimulating gadfly. P. T. Forsyth's famous phrase "outcrop of the great Church" is wrenched from the context of Forsyth's theology.

We need, therefore, to re-examine the core question at its roots, in the interpretation made by Rev. Douglas Horton in the Mansfield Theses, most especially the fundamental appeal to the 15/16 century founders of modern Congregationalism. The question then becomes, *Did* Henry Barrowe, Francis Johnson, Henry Jacobs, William Bradshaw, and Dr. William Ames profess a Church other than the particular gathered fellowship. In CC/ER Merger terms, Can the Congregational Way *exist* under a constitution for the entire fellowhsip, members, Church, associations, conferences, national bodies and kindred agencies?

From the Sources

Dr. Williams Library in London preserves the sources, including the martyred Henry Barrowe's *Platform*[29] & *Brief Summe*[30] etc. As an able and well educated lawyer Henry Barrowe wrote with precision. What he has to say is, "a true planted and rightly established church of Christ is a company of faithful persons, separated from unbelievers, gathered in the name of Christ whom they truly worship and readily obey. They are a brotherhood, a communion of saints, each one of them standing in and for their Christian liberty to practice whatsoever God hath commanded and revealed unto them in His Holy Word." Barrowe recommended elders within each Church, elected by the people to serve at the will of the people. In April 1593 Henry Barrowe died for his Congregational convictions. I find it singularly distasteful to find "Barrowism" misinterpreted; he was a heroic martyr for his independent churchmanship. In the *Defence of the Churches and Ministry*[31] he writes with candor and tolerance. "The faithful servants of Christ (denying the whole constitution and government of the Church of England) may instantly deny the people whilst they

428

remain in that constitution to be members of a true constituted church, yet hereby do not condemn them." The attitude of the Mediators was akin to the irenic spirit of Henry Barrowe.

Francis Johnson

Rev. Francis Johnson's testimony is well represented in the book which also contains some of Henry Barrowe, the *Defence*.[32] Johnson condemns the state Church of England as the "antichristian abomination yet retained in England."[33] After a detailed tirade against bishops, "Popist vestments, as Roches, Horned cap, Tipper, the Surplice, . . . and cape . . . ,"[34] Johnson roundly excoriates the centralized, constitutional idea of the church, saying the "Whole ecclessiastical constitution is such, as they worship God in a false manner."[35] Here is Johnson's word on the true church, "the true visible church of Christ (is) a company of persons called and separated from the world by the word of God, and joined together in fellowship of the Gospel, by voluntary profession of the faith and obedience of Christ."[36] Each particular Church *is* the Church, according to Johnson.

Henry Jacob

Rev. Douglas Horton quoted Jacob in favor of a council or synod being "a kind of church," as has been noted in "Mansfield Thesis Three" in chapter four. In conversation, he pressed the importance of Jacobs and William Ames. The supposition of Congregational "connectionalism," said to be rooted in Jacob/Ames was the historical foundation for espousal of a denominational constitution. Mr. Horton had great success in gaining acceptance for this novel idea among proponents like Rev. Albert Penner, Rev. Raymond B. Walker, and Mr. Ronald Bridges.

Jacob wrote a lot. One of his writing techniques, as, for example, in *Divine Beginning*[37] etc. is to present ideas AGAINST WHICH he wishes to argue. Many readers fail to distinguish Jacob's presentation of the OPPOSITE view and his own view. This appears to be Mr. Horton's problem. In the *Divine Beginning* appears the following: "Although he (Christ) did appoint by his apostles a certain particular form in the primitive age, (namely, that each Church was a particular congregation) yet the Holy Ghost meant not that this should be the perpetual form of Christ's Church." This is precisely the argument adduced by Mr. Horton and expressed by Rev. James E. Wagner in his report to the ER Synods in April 1955. The problem arises when one *continues* to read what Jacob said, "It is simply impossible that any thing should be only in the general nature thereof . . . if Christ did appoint primitively a certain form, then the same still even unto us is a Divine Ordinance . . . unchangeable by men." Lest a reader doubt what Jacob meant by an unchangeable Divine Ordinance here is what follows, "a true visible . . . Church of Christ is a number of faithful people joyned by their willing consent in a spiritual outward society or body, politic, ordinarily coming together in one place, instituted by Christ in his New Testament, and have(ing) the power to exercise ecclesiastical government and all God's other spiritual ordinances (the means of salvation) in and for itself immediately from Christ."[38]

After a lengthy exposition of the Greek *ekklesia* Jacob concludes "this very word *ekklesia*, a Church, . . . doth show evermore a certain form and matter of this Visible Church; namely, that it is a particular ordinary congregation only, as before we observed also."[39] In more than one hundred pages of detailed discussion of the nature of the church, there is no mention of synods or councils.

Rev. Douglas Horton writes, "Let each council be what Jacob in 1613 declared a church to be, 'an entire and independent body politic spiritual . . . indued with power in itself immediately under Christ,' and it will be a body of people at once legally free and morally responsible."[40] What Henry Jacob wrote is not amenable to this reinterpretation. Mr. Horton could have read some pages later in the *Attestation*, "The congregations free consent, is their ancient right . . . as they are Churches of Christ."[41] Or this, "the Church of Bishops . . . is no other Church than such as the Prophet named Maligmant."[42]

In *Reasons* Jacob states unequivocally, "a greater ecclessiastical government than the churches we know none."[43] Jacob agrees with Zwingli, "this man of God, Zwingli, . . . reproves . . . the very nature of those Synods which are held to be a representative Church."[44] Again he agrees with Dr. Belson, "A general Council is not the Church."[45]

An objective scholar reading the over 2,000 pages of Henry Jacob in Dr. Williams Library is compelled to conclude that Jacob was a forthright, dedicated, clear-minded defender of the New Testament Churches as *the* Christian Churches.

Nowhere is this clearer than in his dicussion of the word *"Episcopus."* Mr. Horton writes, "Henry Jocob made a place for bishops and presbyteries, and so do we."[46] He claims "the name

430

'Moderator,' used of a bishop, is found in Henry Jocob's writings of 1604."[47] Mr. Horton's reference is to page 89 of Jacob's *Attestation*. This is part of an extended discussion of biblical word usages. Mr. Horton might have continued to read on 'till he reached Henry Jacob's conclusions. On page 97 "the government of Diocesan Bishops (though of the best sort) is not so good or safe . . . (as)consociation."[48] And on page 100 "the Church government ought always to be with the people's free consent,"[49] and "Synods . . . can not be approved which rule imperiously over the Congregations."[50] If the *Attestation* had been read clear through Jacob's conclusions would have been plain "a Universal Synod for Unity, alas, how vain it is."[51] "Councils . . . we allow . . . and . . . acknowledge great benefit by them, so that their Decrees may be examined and tried (by God's Word) of them to whom God's word appertaineth."[52] This was the standpoint of the Mediators.

Unfortunately, Mr. Horton never points out what Henry Jacob meant by "bishop" or "presbytery." As to *episkopos*, Jacob meticulously traces the New Testament identification of bishop, minister, and presbyter. Jacob's bishop is the minister of a particular Church. Mr. Horton's "bishop" is a synodical officer with power. On page 94 of *Attestation*, Jacob calls the "Deocesan Bishop" a mistake. "They were begun . . . out of good intention; yet it is as plain as may be that error always accompanied them from the first. The best of their Bishops . . . at last . . . got the power of Government absolutely into their hands, clean excluding all power of the people."[53] THAT'S what Henry Jacob thought of bishops.

Reasons summarizes as follows, "For the space of 200 years after Christ visible Churches . . . were not diocesan Churches, but particular ordinary congregations only; and the bishops were only parishonal not diocesan bishops, differing from other pastors only in priority of order not in majority of rule."[54] He *cannot* be quoted in favor of either overhead government or CC/ER merger. "The ordinary form of Church government set forth in the New Testament, ought necessarily to be kept still by us; it is not changeable by men."[55]

A novel interpretation of Jacob's use of presbytery appears in Rev. Douglas Horton's *Congregationalism*,[56] in support of inclusion in one potpourri the episcopal, presbyterial and congregational forms of government. However, in *Divine Beginning* Jacob wrote, "All men know that these kinds of government, viz., Democracy, Aristocracy, and Monarchy, do differ formally and essentially one

431

from the other . . . the Christian Churches true and right government doth differ formally and essentially from the government
diocesan, provincal and catholic."[57] Presbytery, in Jacob's usage
refers to a body of elected persons in a particular Church, what
we might term a "Church Committe," "Church Council," or
"Church Board."

I researched the following writings of Henry Jacob in Dr.
Williams Library:

1599 *A Defence of the Churches and Ministry*
1604 *Reasons Taken Out of God's Word*
1605 *Shortly Dialogues* (Sam'l Hieron also?)
1605 *Abridgment*
1606 *Christian and Modest Offer*
1606 *Myld and*
1607 (1599) *Defence* (1st part)
1608 *Defence - The Second Part*
1608 *A Dispute*
1610 *Divine Beginning and Institution of Christ's True Visible Church*
1610 *Confession of Faith? (with Barrowe)*
1613 *Attestation*
1616 *Confession of Faith*

Faced with these ancient books, I was forced to conclude that in
the entire *corpus* of Henry Jacob a Church is always a particular
Church and never a Council or Synod. Nowhere can Jacob be
quoted in favor of a General Synod, a bishop, or a ruling presbytery.

William Bradshaw

Explicating the nature of a council, Rev. Douglas Horton quotes
William Bradshaw,[58] and, by associating him with John Robinson,
arrives at the novel opinion that "a synod was a church."[59] We
have established Robinson's teaching in chapter four. Bradshaw is
blunt "every . . . assembly of men, ordinarily journeying together
in the true worship of God, is a true visible Church of Christ; and,
the same title is improperly attributed to any other Consociation,
Synods, Societies, Combinations, or assemblies whatsoever,"[60]
"All such Churches . . . are in all ecclessiastical matters equal and
of the same power and authority . . . (and) ought to have the same
spiritual priviledges, perogatives, officers, administratives, orders,
and forms of worship."[61] To all of which the Mediators would say

432

"Amen." There's more in Bradshaw, especially in *Of Divine Worship*[62] and *A Protestation*.[63] There is not the slightest, tiniest glimmer of an over-body Church in William Bradshaw.

The Learned Dr. Ames

Rev. Douglas Horton had an unfeigned delight in William Ames. At one point when he was Dean of Harvard's Divinity School, I chanced to mention a study of Ames I had undertaken. His excitement glowed, "Henry, there's a forgotten scholar. Harvard's study of divinity *was* Ames." "*The Medulla?*," I inquired. "Yes, indeed," he replied, "And it remains a theological masterpiece today."

Mr. Horton's *Congregationalism* claims kinship with Ames,[64] described as one "whose lengthened shadow lies over all of early Congregationalism."[65] In his hundreds of pages of close packed theological aphorisms, Ames presents "a particular church (which) is a society of believers joyned together in a special band among themselves, for the constant exercise of the communion of the saints among themselves."[66] What Ames stressed was the *covenant* relationship.[67] In his chapter 32 "Of the Church instituted" the accent is on the particular, local, worshipping body of saints. Ames is a theologian, so he expostulates on the headship of Christ, and the validity of the covenanted fellowship; "such a company and not larger is . . . (an) *ekklesia*."[68]

Careful analysis of William Ames is essential to an understanding of the CC/ER events of 1954-1956. Rev. Douglas Horton was immersed in Ames, in the CC/ER Merger, in the World Council of Churches, and in the deanship of Harvard Divinity School to which he moved July 1, 1955. While at Harvard Mr. Horton translated and published Ames "Exhortation to Students of Theology" (1958), The Harvard Divinity School Library published a facsimile edition of Ames' 1922 Inaugural Lecture (1964), and Mr. Horton's article, "Let Us Not Forget the Mighty William Ames" was published in *Religion In Life*, XXIX (1960).

Mr. Horton indicates that Ames was *Congregational* but not *Separatist*,[69] and this is correct *so far as toleration* of other Christians is concerned. But it is not possible to deduce from Ames toleration *approval and espousal* of Presbyterial or other centralist forms of church government.[70] Nor will it do to blandly assert that "History has shown that Separatism swings into a fissiparous course which leads in the end to the atomizing of the Church, whereas Congregationalism tends toward mutual recognition, and so to co-operation, and so finally to organic union."[71] The

433

fullest account of Ames points out that Nonconformity has no stopping point except separation.[72] And while there are very sharp criticisms of Separatist by Ames, for example in his two *Manuductions for Mr. Robinson*,[73] the later writings became increasingly critical of national churches. His last work is an almost violent denunciation against human ceremonies in God's worship.[74] In his final year, 1633, Ames accepted a call to become a minister with Rev. Hugh Peter of the avowedly Congregational Church at Rotterdam. It is not accurate to quote from Ames' early works as if they were his mature thinking.

What has happened in Mr. Horton's interpretation of William Ames may be explained by his personal reading back into the seventeenth century of ecumenical ideas and involvements of the twentieth century. He writes, "Only those historians who are unfamiliar with our contemporary ecumenical movement are likely to minimize the difference between the Congregational Puritans and the Separatists of the seventeenth century.[75] Among the criticized historians is Professor Perry Miller!

Next there is made one of those mental leaps characteristic of Mr. Horton, "The Jacobs and the Ames and those who followed them . . . knew they had hold of an idea with a future, an idea which would create history."[76] But neither Henry Jacob nor William Ames ever espoused the notion that a council was a church, or, indeed, that there could exist any Church other than the particular, covenanted, meeting-regularly-together fellowship of Christ-followers. The "idea which would create history" belonged to Mr. Horton, not to William Ames. And the "history" created by it in the CC/ER Merger spawned *four* sets of church groupings where there were *two*; the CC and ER became the United Church of Christ, the National Association of Congregational Christian Churches, the Conservative Congregational Christian Churches and perhaps as many as 500 to 1000 independent Churches.

Relevance of Ames to CC/ER Merger

Ames was quoted to support the October 1954 vote of the executive committees to merge the Congregational Christian Churches and the Evangelical and Reformed Church. First, Mr. Horton claimed, and Rev. James E. Wagner accepted the claim, that there was "something deep in the view of life"[77] of Ames and his followers because of which "the Congregationalists came honestly and naturally by their interest in ecumenicity."[78]

434

Mr. Wagner, and I suppose nearly everyone else, accepted this assertion as meaning that Congregationalism's leading 17th century theologian was expressing an "ecumenicity" *latent* in Congregationalism, and that, in the CC/ER Merger that which *had been Congregationalism from the beginning* was being fulfilled.

The "special language" of the twentieth century ecumenicals fosters such misconceptions. Ames, like *all* other early Congregationalists, honestly and naturally based his polity on the New Testament. He found there only an invisible Church Universal, or, a visible particular, covenanted, on-going, worshipping society of Christ-followers. With Ames, a tolerant view of others must not be misread as "interest in ecumenicity." Ames had no interest in organized ecumenicity.

Secondly, Mr. Horton claimed, and had the claim allowed, that non-Separatist Congregationalists evolved a connectional polity in New England founded on Ames. Of Jacob and Ames Mr. Horton writes, "These men were the fathers in God of the younger generation of John Cottons, Thomas Hookers, and John Davenports, who settled New England and wrought the principles of Congregationalism into a practically viable polity."[79] The notion that any of these great heroes of the Congregational Way ever advocated connectionalism is gainsaid by the record reported in chapter four.

Ames, specifically, opposed the kind of "constitution for the whole" denomination which people like Mr. Wagner had been led to believe was "a Amesian contribution" to New England. Churches are particular congregations and neither constitutions nor hierarchies—"merely human creations brought into the church without divine precept or example"—nor synods dare rob the Churches of their authority and freedom under the sole Headship of Christ.[80] Later in the *Marrow* Ames explicitly denies that *any* body can have greater authority than the particular Church "all Christian Churches have altogether one and the same right, that one doth no more depend upon another, than another upon it. . . . it is most convenient that one particular Church does not consist of more members than may meet together in one place . . . such a company and not larger is . . . (an) *ekklesia*."[81]

Ames scathingly denounces synods, classes, and their bureaucracy, "the hierarchy are merely human creatures . . . They rob the Churches of their liberty, which they excuse as it were, a regal, or rather tyrannical dominion over the Churches themselves and their pastors."[82]

Ames does not recognize any such title as "Minister of the General Council." He says, "the right of calling a minister is in the Church to whom he is to serve"[83] and outside the particular Church there are no "Ministers."

Ames was equally clear in his rejection of the entire concept of a synod, council or classes as a church. Synods are by "common consent (for) mutual help as much as fitly may be, in those things especially, which are of great moment, but that combination doth neither constitute a new form of a Church, neither ought it to take away, or diminish any way, that liberty and power which Christ has left to his Churches, for the directing and furthering whereof it only serves."[84]

The evidence does not support any claim whatever that there was a latent organic ecumenicity in early Congregationalism.

What then of the second major proposition claimed in support of the CC Executive Committee action in October 1954, namely, that twentieth century Congregationalism had "adapted itself to new conditions" and that the CC/ER Merger merely sought to regularize an already emergent polity?

The Constitutional Problem

On January 29, 1955 the following telegram was received.[85]

"DR HENRY DAVID GRAY=

"=ONEONTA CONGREGATIONAL CHURCH
SOUTH PASADENA CALIF=

"YESTERDAY THE EXECUTIVE COMMITTEE UNANI-
MOUSLY VOTED TO ASK YOU TO SERVE ON THE COM-
MISSION ON THE STUDY OF THE CONSTITUTIONAL
PROBLEM OF THE CONGREGATIONAL CHURCHES
GREATLY HOPE YOU WILL SERVE LETTER FOLLOWS
SOONEST=

"DOUGLAS HORTON=."

Under date, February 4, 1955, the Rev. Douglas Horton wrote as follows:[86]

"Dear Henry:

"At the last meeting of the General Council, held in New Haven in June of 1954, it was

436

"VOTED (54 G 33) that a commission to study the constitutional problem as it relates to the General Council and the fellowship be authorized, the members of which would be appointed and other details dealt with by the Executive Committee.

"Last week, the Executive Committee, meeting in Cleveland, appointed to this commission, to be called The Commission on the Study of the Constitutional Problem, nine persons:

"Dr. Hugh Vernon White of California, Chairman
Dr. Ronald Bridges of Maine
Mr. Clarence R. Chaney of Minnesota
Mrs. Robert J. Crossen of Missouri
David K. Ford, Esq., of Ohio
Dr. Henry David Gray of California
Dr. Ervine P. Inglis of Missouri
Mrs. Claude C. Kennedy of Minnesota
Lucius E. Thayer, Esq. of Massachusetts

"According to directions of the General Council the Commission will have to determine whether or not a constitution for the entire denomination should be written and whether or not a number of amendments to our present General Council constitution and changes in our present general procedures should be recommended for adoption.

"The Commission will probably meet in Chicago, since that is the most accessible center for this particular group. It will probably meet for two days at a time but not more than once or twice a year. I shall suggest to the chairman that from the point of view of the general denominational calendar it would be well to hold the first meeting as soon after Easter of this year as possible. When I hear from him I shall write you again.

"In the meantime let me express the hope that you will be able to serve us in this important capacity. The questions to come before the Commission are basic and insistent. A card is enclosed for convenience in reply.

"Ever yours faithfully,

"Douglas Horton"

"Dr. Henry David Gray
Oneonta Congregational Church
South Pasadena, California

"This is the follow-up to my note. Do help me at this point: it is really important.

"D."

I call attention to the penned note on this letter, "Do help me at this point; it is really important," in order to make two observations. First, the inclusion of only one person from the 21-member Polity and Unity Committee and the inclusion of at least four persons with little knowledge or experience hardly seemed propitious. Second, on October 13, 1954 the CC Executive Committee *had already decided* that no United Church constitution was needed prior to union, and, I suppose as a corollary, had not appointed the commission mandated by the 1954 General Council. The temptation to avoid the task was overcome only by the words of Rev. L. Wendell Fifield, "I nominated you, because this may be the last chance we have to moderate the merger people. You owe the Polity and Unity Committee this representation."

One point was clear. Mr. Horton wrote accurately, "The questions to come before the Commission are basic and insistent."[87]

The April 18 & 19, 1955 Meeting

March 7, 1955 was the date of the following call to the first meeting.

"The Chairman of the Commission on the Study of the Constitutional Problem has asked me to call you to its first meeting to be held at the LaSalle Hotel, Chicago, beginning at 2:00 P.M. on Monday April 18th and running through that afternoon and evening and the following morning and afternoon of April 19th.

"Some time before the meeting, I shall plan to send you a copy of the various actions of the General Council and its Executive Committee which constitute the charter of the Commission."[88]

The call was followed, under date March 24, by a five-page recital of the New Haven General Council, reviewed in chapter six.

The initial sessions of the Constitutional Commission were exploratory, due to the inexperience of the members. Eight of the nine members were present, in the La-Salle Hotel, Chicago, with Rev. Douglas Horton as secretary.

Chairman, Professor Hugh Vernon White of Pacific School of Religion, read the Commissions Charter from the 1954 General Council Minutes.[89]

"From this it was judged that the main task of the Commission is as follows:

"1) To consider the fundamental constitutional problem, answering such questions as

438

"a) Is it theoretically possible for the CC Churches to adopt an overall Constitution?

"b) If theoretically possible, is such a Constitution desirable at the present time?

"c) If desirable, what kind of Constitution should it be?

"2) To take up incidental *ad hoc* questions which have been or shall be referred to the Commission."

Seven communications regarding polity, and five proposed amendments to the General Council Constitution were presented. At the evening session the following votes were recorded.[90]

"It was

"AGREED   That the evening be given to the *ad hoc* questions
55-4CP3   referred to the commission.

"The history of the amendment desired by the Southeast Convention was given by Mr. Gray and it was

"VOTED   (one abstention) That the Executive Com-
55-4CP4   mittee be requested to take
                    under consideration the ap-
                    pointment of an *ad hoc* com-
                    mittee to study the polity and
                    practices of the fellowship,
                    approximately once every six
                    years.

"It was

"VOTED   That it is the sense of this Commission that the
55-4CP5   Memorandum to be prepared by this Commis-
                  sion accords with the intent of the first part of the
                  Resolution from the Southeast Convention and
                  represents the extent to which this Commission
                  can profitably go at the moment in carrying out
                  the Resolution.

"It was

"VOTED   To assign to a sub-committee consisting of Messrs.
55-4CP6   Bridges, Ford and Thayer the matter of studying
                  the Burton and American Board proposed amend-
                  ments to Article IV, Sections 1 and 2, with the
                  request that they bring this Commission a pro-
                  posed recommendation on the subject for the
                  General Council.

"It was

"VOTED   To approve tentatively the Executive Commit-
55-4CP7   tee's amendment to the proposed amendment from

the Massachusetts Conference, the Secretary to learn from Massachusetts the reason for the suggested change and to report before final decision is made.

"Correspondence from the Rev. David N. Beach of New Haven was now brought up and discussed at length. At the conclusion of the evening, Mr. Gray was asked to draw up a vote regarding it."

The chief discussion of the morning session on April 19 concerned the nature of the Commission's report to the General Council. The Minutes do not agree with my notes. Here are the substansitive parts of Mr. Horton's minutes.[91]

"The session began at 9:00 A.M. with prayer by Mr. Gray.

"It was

| "VOTED 55-4CP8 | That the Secretary be asked to write an informal letter to Mr. Beach of New Haven embodying the gist of the following statement prepared by Mr. Gray. (The Secretary has written the letter requested to Mr. Beach.) |

"'This Commission finds that the Constitution of the General Council defines as members thereof those persons who are delegates sent by Associations and Conferences, together with certain designated ex officio members. It is the judgment of the Commission that each CC Church, as a member of the fellowship of Churches, is spiritually represented in conciliary gatherings, whether they are meetings of the General Council, the State Conferences, the Association, or meetings of *ad hoc* councils. The General Council is *a meeting of delegates* in an organization of the CC Churches; the fellowship is *the spiritual union of the Churches.* Our churches are held together by Christian fellowship and not by law.'

"Neither Mr. Avery's amendment nor the Essex North Association question were taken up at this meeting. Neither was Mr. Kimball's amendment since it arrived after the meeting.

"The Chairman presented a letter from the Rev. A. Vaughn Abercrombie of Rhode Island dealing with problems directly connected with the proposed United Church of Christ. After thorough discussion it was

| "VOTED 55-4CP9 | That the Secretary be asked to communicate informally with Mr. Abercrombie, to thank him for his letter, to tell him of the discussion which had taken place in the Commission regarding it . . . |

"It was tentatively

"AGREED   The the report of the Commission to the General
55-4CP10   Council would begin in substance as follows:

"1)   This Commission believes it undesirable to attempt to write a
Constitution for the CC Churches at this time.

"2)   It recommends the manual of the CC Churches as embodying
the features of our polity and practice.

"3)   To the specific question referred to in the Report of the Committee on Free Church Polity and Unity as to the powers of
the General Council, the Commission offers the following
Memorandum"

"MEMORANDUM ON THE POWERS
OF THE GENERAL COUNCIL, etc.

"The Commission now considered various propositions which might go
into the Memorandum and it was

"VOTED   To approve the proposition that the General
55-4CP11   Council has complete power over itself, and only
itself, as defined in its constitution and by-laws,
and that it is the nationwide organ morally and
spiritually responsible to the total fellowship and
to every constituent part of it.

"It was further

"VOTED   To approve the proposition that the members of
55-4CP12   the General Council must be elected and approved
in such manner as is set forth in its own constitution; and that the Council has the power of recognizing conferences on behalf of the fellowship.

"It was

"VOTED   To approve the proposition that the General
55-4CP13   Council has the power to act in ecumenical and
other matters for each church, association or conference, only insofar as its action is acceptable
to that church, association or conference.

. . .

"Considerable time was spent upon the question as to whether the
State Conference has power to recognize a group of churches as an
Association and belonging to it. Mr. Chaney pointed out that
'recognition' technically has to do with recognition of membership.

"The Chairman suggested that the existence and functioning of the
General Council was made possible by mutual cooperation of the
Conferences, Associations and Churches. . . .

"It was

| "AGREED
55-4CP15 | That Mr. Gray and the Secretary be asked to pre-
pare a preliminary statement on the powers of the
General Council. |

"It was

| "VOTED
55-4CP13 | That at the opening of the next meeting of the
commission, Vote 55-4CP13 be recon-
sidered . . ." |

I was irked by the intrusion of the secretary who was not a member of the Commission. The notion of a supposed power of the General Council to "recognize" conferences on behalf of the fellowship" was neither approved nor discussed. The Commission members agreed that the General Council was governed by its own constitution. The minutes were all tentative at the first meeting and the November 8, 1955 session stipulated, *That the votes taken by the Commission at its meeting of April 18-19 as to statements to be included in its report to the General Council were of a tentative nature!!"*

Professor White talked to me at length on the night of April 18th. The gist of his concern was "we are not yet dealing with the critical issues. Perhaps it would be wise if (we) had an agenda and some proposals to direct discussion and action to the constitutional issue itself."

"I like that," I replied, "I'm unhappy with the secretary's part in setting the agenda. If anything worthwhile is to be accomplished, we need less opinion and more fact."

"Now, Henry," replied Vernon, "Don't be impatient."

With that admonition I went to my room to frame the resolution which appears in the minutes concerning the Rev. David N. Beach correspondence.

The Chairman Prepares

Under date July 15, 1955 Professor White sent to the Constitutional Commission members a vitally important letter and memorandum which are abridged as follows:[92]

"In view of the limited time allowed for our work, if we are to report to the General Council at Omaha next June, it will be necessary for us to proceed at once by correspondence with our study. Accordingly I am writing this letter with suggestions for our further discussion. . . .

. . .

"I should like to have an agenda prepared and agreed upon well in advance of the next meeting. This was impossible for the first one which was necessarily devoted to an exploratory and preliminary discussion. But our conference by mail ought to make it possible to plan an agenda for November. There is also a distinct advantage in writing down one's thoughts and in being able to consider the thoughts of others as they have written them. . . . (I)n order to keep our flow of communications centralized I suggest that all general contributions be sent to me. I shall see that they are promptly duplicated and mailed to each of you. . . . .

. . .

"As a beginning I am enclosing an analysis of our problem and a statement which I hope will further the discussion. I should appreciate comments on these notes and any additional contribution to the basic problem.

"Cordially yours,

"Hugh Vernon White"

"THE CONSTITUTIONAL PROBLEM
Hugh Vernon White—July 1955

"1. Although the 'constitution' with which we are concerned is not that of the proposed United Church, but of the Congregational Christian churches, still the 'problem' has arisen as a result of the proposed merger. The problem is whether Congregationalism can set forth its unity in terms of a constitution. As I understand it this is our basic subject of consideration, more important than any dealing with details of a present or future constitution. As I have reflected on our discussions at Chicago certain questions arise in my mind. I shall try to state them for your consideration.

"2. In his 'Minister's Address' at New Haven (G. C. Minutes 1954, p. 81) Dr. Horton made a plea for the writing of a constitution, giving six specific considerations supporting the proposal. However, when the matter came up in our Chicago meeting it was agreed almost without discussion that it was not desirable to attempt the writing of a constitution because the working unity of the denomination is based on voluntary participation rather than authoritatively imposed procedure. We agreed that we should recommend the 'Manual' as descriptive of this procedure and then make a series of statements setting forth the actual nature of relationships within the denomination on this point. I thought there would be some who would feel that an over all constitution is desirable, as seemed to be the intent of Dr. Horton's address; and that there would be some who would take the position that any constitution would conflict with congregational freedom. I am sure now that this lack of dif-

443

ference means that we must go more deeply and more discriminatingly into the meaning of a 'constitution.' Two questions arise:-

"3.   The first has to do with the constitution of the proposed United Church. If it is not possible now for the Congregational-Christian denomination to adopt a constitution without abandoning the essentially congregational attribute of freedom (however construed), how can that freedom be conserved in the constitution of a United Church? Perhaps this is another way of stating the 'problem.' Or it may point to the diverse meanings of 'constitution.' I have duly consulted Webster's New International Dictionary and find several meanings. I shall not quote them; you also have a dictionary!

"4.   The second question, then, is What meaning shall we give to 'constitution?' Or, if there are several *kinds* of constitution, which kind can the Congregational Christian churches adopt as workable and also consistent with their essential character as free churches? Or must *all* constitutions be rejected on principle, in which case, how are our churches ever to agree upon a constitution for a United Church? Two documents have been put into our possession designated as constitutions, (1) the Cambridge Platform and, (2) the Constitution of the Congregational Union of England and Wales. Another very interesting document enclosed with the minutes that you received is the Management Audit of the American Baptist Convention. These documents are deserving of careful study. I shall set down some notes on each of them.

"(1)   The Cambridge Platform is in the main a careful statement of the 'autonomy' of the *church* which is the local congregation, under the absolute authority of Christ or the Word. It contemplates no permanent churchly organization beyond the church. A Snyod is to be called when needed and constituted of delegates sent direct by the several churches. The findings of the Synod are to be received by the churches only 'so far as consonant with the word of God.' Presumably each 'church' must determine what findings are so consonant. At any rate no provision is made for compulsion since 'it belongeth to Synods and counsils (sic). . . . not to exercise Church-censures in way of discipline, nor any other act of church-authority or jurisdiction.' This document, therefore, is a carefully formulated statement of the traditional freedom of the (local) church, what we now call autonomy. (It is not really autonomy but theonomy, for the freedom is from any ecclesiastical or civil authority in order that the church may be abolutely subject to Christ as known through his Word. Negatively it is the explicit rejection of presbyterianism.)

"(2)   The Constitution of the Congregational Union of England and Wales is an 'over-all' constitution which asserts the units of the churches as a fellowship with mutual interests and moral responsibilities. It provides for meetings of an Assembly made up of representatives of the churches and congregational colleges, and states common objectives. It is a sort of 'declarative' constitution, but does not in any sense constitute a 'fundamental law' for the churches of the Union, nor prescribe authoritative regulations for the life of churches or County Unions. In short it is descriptive of the voluntary participation of technically autonomous bodies such as we are familiar with in (sic) our present denominational life.

"(3)   The Management Audit of the A.I.M. recommends . . . a 'proposed organization structure.' This system is proposed in the interest of efficiency and unification of management. On paper it is startlingly simple and reasonable. I haven't any idea how the Baptist people have responded to it. But since their problem is so much like our own let us consider this proposal. It is asserted that 'under the plan no change is made in the participation of state conventions and standard Baptist city societies, etc.' The question is, could we substitute for 'American Baptist Convention,' 'General Council; (sic) and for 'General Council,' 'Executive Committee' and adopt substantially this scheme so far as administration is concerned? Note that this is not a Plan for the government of local churches, State Conventions or City Societies. Apparently it is felt that the free action of these church bodies is not involved, but that they are to be provided with a method by which their elected representatives constituting the 'Convention' will have over-all authority over the common work and agencies of the denomination.

"(4)   This is the thing I had in mind in the proposal first made in a letter to Dr. L. Wendell Fifield . . . I am enclosing a copy of my letter to Dr. Fifield herewith. Let me say that this proposal was made in good faith but with the full realization that it raised a basic question rather than settling one, namely, it is possible to combine in a single constitution these two orders, the *ecclesiastical* and the *administrative* and so serve the two interests, *freedom* and *efficiency*? Also the further question is involved whether the 'government' involved can exist in the sense of the administrative authority of the General Council over denominational enterprises, without becoming also an ecclesiastical authority over the churches. My proposal is that the churches through their delegates should control (act through) the General Council but that the General Council should have no power to legislate for the churches. This 'constitutional question' I had hoped to have dealt with by those more competent in the making of constitutions that I am, and now, ironically enough, I am a member of the Commission to which the problem comes! . . . Therefore I submit to members of the Commission this proposal for discussion. If it is, in fact, impracticable, let us dismiss it. If it does point the way to the kind of a constitution that Congregationalism can adopt without ceasing to be in the basic (ecclesiastical) sense congregational, let us have a sub-committee appointed to draw up a draft of such a constitution. My own mind is completely open on the matter and my feelings will not be hurt if the whole scheme is found unwordable and dropped.

"THE CONSTITUTIONAL PROBLEM II

"1.   Constitutions in the full sense of governing documents exist in—

"The Local Church
"The Associations
"The Conferences
"The General Council
"The Boards, Councils, Societies, etc.

"But the powers or applications of such constitutions are limited to the bodies that adopt them and are constituted by them. There seems to be complete agreement on this point.

"2.   The problem arises when we seek to create a constitution for the Fellowship, or Denomination or whole body of churches, i.e., an over-all constitution. The need for such a constitution arises from the call to act *as a denomination*. At present no single representative body has power to act for the denomination. This is the dilemma presented by the Merger. The basic fact has always been there; there is no organ of responsible and competent authority to speak for or act for the denomination. It now appears that the merging of the General Council and the General Synod in the General Synod is not the Union of the Congregational Churches and the Evangelical and Reformed Church, and apparently if and when it occurs union of the two denominations will still be a thing of the future. The reiterated provision that all the rights and liberties of the churches shall be preserved in the United Church means that the writing of a constitution for the United Church will come smack up against the same problem that confronts us as a denomination. (No similar problem confronts the E. & R.) If I understand aright the task assigned to our commission it is to deal with this dilemma and to see if any constructive proposal can be made that will prepare us to go into the task of constitution writing for the United Church with a clear definition of what kind of a constitution we can accept and even perhaps with a rought (sic) draft of such a constitution. It seems to me that there are certain alternatives, as follows,—(there may be others)

"(1)   To present the present practice of the Congregational Christian churches as in fact a constitution in the sense admissable to our churches. This is a voluntary cooperation which actually works externally *like* an authoritatively ordered whole under a con-

446

stitution but which basically has no foundation in legislation or the authority of any central or supreme body over others. As I read the Basis of Union and the Interpretations it seems to call for such a 'constitution.' Like our General Council the General Synod will have formal power over its own acts and membership, but none over the conferences, associations and churches.

"This constitutes a dual type 'constitution.' It is a constitution in the ordinary sense of fundamental law for the General Synod, but a purely advisory or descriptive document (hardly to be called a Constitution) for the total Fellowship.

"(2) To present a constitution such as suggested in my letter to Dr. Fifield—if we can devise one that we believe really succeeds in combining ecclesiastical freedom in the traditional congregational sense and administrative control and efficiency. If we find that it is not possible to produce such a constitution, then a third alternative exists.

"(3) The third alternative is to present a true over-all constitution of a legislative character. This will mean a system of control vested in a General Council will be exercized (sic) over all the churches according to the constitutionally specified powers and limitations. All ambiguity as to the meaning of 'constitution' would be eliminated in this case; it would be the fundamental law of the denomination and would embody legislative and judicial powers which are the essential marks of government. This is really hardly an alternative for (a) it is precisely this that Congregationalists have rejected and sought to provide against all along and (b) every congregation, association, and conference would have to voluntarily reorganize itself or revise its own constitution to make such a constitution valid. There is no remote possibility of this. However, I think it is in order for us, in surveying the whole problem to look squarely at this alternative, define it clearly and state the case for and against it.

"3. It seems to me that our action, which I take to be wholly tentative, at our first meeting, in saying that it is not desirable at this time to try to write a constitution and in recommending the Handbook as descriptive of denominational practice, in effect points to the first alternative. If that is true we ought to make explicit statement to that effect both for the sake of our own understanding and the information of the E. & R. Church. In any case we should make an unambiguous statement as to the specific sense in which 'constitution' is used in any discussion and also, if possible, present a definite proposal as to a valid form of constitution for our denomination, or valid forms if there are more than one."

Professor White's memorandum rightly focuses on the *nature* of a constitution, and, on the impossibility of *a governing constitution* for the entire CC fellowship. He is entirely clear that "At present no single representative body has power to act for the denomination."[93] With regard to a constitution as the 'fundamental law of the denomination' Professor White states categorically "This is really hardly an alternative for (a) it is precisely this that Congregationalists have rejected and sought to provide against all along and (b) every congregation, association, and conference would have to voluntarily reorganize itself . . . to make such a constitution valid. There is no remote possibility of this."[94]

Return to Administrative/Ecclesiastical

Professor White proposed administrative control by the Churches without ecclesiastical rule by wider church bodies.[95]

"We . have today two systems: (1) the primary ecclesiastical order of congregations, associations and General Council and (2) the administrative order of state conferences and national boards. A large part of our problem of polity centers in the attempts to unify these two systems. And the heart of the problem lies in the fact that in principle an ecclesiastical order is not a 'government' but a voluntary association of autonomous congregations, while the administration of the 'work' of the denomination through the conferences and boards requries government, the ownership of property and the power to use income in activities subject to their direction and control.

"In these essentially administrative agencies, with programs of work, endowments and budgets, a paid secretariat and corps of workers, questions of ownership and authority are involved. Here administrative authority is necessary and the problem of its source and the limits to be imposed upon it becomes important. *In this respect* our denomination has moved toward the function of a governing body. As a purely ecclesiastical fellowship no government is involved . . .

. . .

"Such representative bodies, however, should have direct control, for the churches as such, overall joint enterprises, in the conferences and in the nation. They should be incorporated with full legal power to act for the churches, and under a constitution that would specify how the churches through their elected representatives are to exercise ultimate power over them. It seems to me that this would remove the ambiguity of our present makeshift conbimation (sic) of the two systems. It ought to be clear that this constitution would regularize and make explicit the fact that state and national work organizations are the creatures of the churches and under their ultimate control in definitely specified ways. Authority would be exercised in the administrative order and from the bottom up; in the ecclesiastical order authority would arise in the congregation and be exercised in the joint bodies but no authority from any 'higher' body would be exercised over the congregations.

"I do not believe it a valid claim that an association or the General Council, once constituted, is an autonomous body in the same sense in which the congregation is one. Such bodies are constituted by the congregations; they are morally responsible *to* the congregations. . . . the General Council exists only to express the purpose and serve the interests of the denomination. Its members act *for* the churches that elect them and have a moral responsibility, under God, to them. The General Council, in principle, has no existence, or meaning, or validity, save as it seeks to express the common mind and purpose of the congregations which are the denomination. It is *their* creation and they are not *its* creation or servants in any sense.

"I believe that a General Council, or Synod, so constituted could be given the full authority to administer the common enterprises of the denomination. As such, however, it would have no authority of an ecclesiastical or any other nature over its constituent congregations. . . . ."

Rev. Douglas Horton's Paper

Under date June 18, 1955 the following communication accompanied a thirteen-page paper titled "The Powers of the General Council of the Congregational Christian Churches."[96] Since the paper was discarded by the Commission, its value as a statement of Mr. Horton's views; which is considerable.

The paper begins with the specious proposition that the General Council "enjoys a certain sovereignty in Christ . . . because, there is no appeal beyond Christ." This is predicated on the notion that the Council is a church, which we disposed of in chapter four. As a temporary, delegate, church-body any and every action of the General Council represented an appeal to the Churches for funds, for personnel,—for everything needful.

The paper is confused. Here is its wording.[97]

449

"Our fundamental criticism of the constitution of the General Council as it now stands is that it is almost barren of theology. To our mind the constitution for a part of the Church of Jesus Christ should expressly state not only that it derives from basic Christian faith, but how it so derives. The casual reader could hardly distinguish the form of our present constitution from that of any secular society.

"What powers has the General Council over itself?

"The General Council is part of the Church of Jesus Christ. Jesus Christ is in the midst of it. 'When two or three are gathered together in my name, that am I in the midst of them.' Because, therefore, there is no appeal beyond Christ, the General Council enjoys a certain sovereignty in Christ. This is a spiritual matter of great importance, deriving directly from the presuppositions of Congregational polity.

"The Council's spiritual freedom to obey the living Christ in its midst is reflected in the legal power of the Council."

The novel idea that the Council is a church directly under Christ and not amenable to the Churches from which its members came, leads to a stark assertion that the Council's loyalty is not to the Churches.

"One test of whether a proposed action is beneficial or inimical to the Church as a whole may be made by asking whether the action would tend to consolidate or divide the Congregational Christian Fellowship. Action which would seriously split the communion can seldom be called beneficial to the Church as a whole, and yet it must be remembered that the ultimate loyalty is to Christ and not the communion. A decision taken in loyalty to Him would in the end benefit the communion, in spite of the apparent immediate untoward results. This test is therefore useful and generally available, but not absolute."[98]

Of some interest is the realization that the Council has no direct power over associations or conferences, since power to "recognize" a conference was one of Mr. Horton's chief claims for the Council at the April meeting noted above.

"(T)he General Council has no direct legal power over the churches and by implication, no direct legal power over associations or conferences."[99]

This positive position is immediately followed by gymnastic logic which I am unable to fathom, whereby each of the agencies created by, responsible to, sustained by, and *unable to exist* apart

450

from the Churches whence come their members and support is said to be independent.

"Each group in the Congregational Christian Fellowship has the power of remaining in the Fellowship or leaving it without charge of schism if the decision to leave is made on grounds of loyalty to Christ; and correspondingly the Fellowship has the power of remaining in correspondence with any of the churches or breaking that correspondence. This is technically called the power of recognition.

"Theoretically, the entire Fellowship has a right to say whether or not a person should belong to it, but as a practicable legal procedure it accepts every individual admitted by a local church to membership in the Fellowship. Similarly, it admits every church recognized by an association as part of the Fellowship. Similarly, it admits every association recognized by a conference, and every conference recognized by the General Council, as part of the Fellowship."[100]

This statement invents an entity designated as "The Fellowship" with all sorts of powers. We have already seen in chapter five that the very essence of fellowship in Congregationalism is its voluntary nature. Capitalization does not change that fact.

The device proposed to strip some of the power of the Churches over the General Council *claims* as "essentially disorderly" a practice with centuries of sanction.

"This Commission regards the practice of instructing delegates as undesirable and essentially disorderly, and this for a good Congregational Christian reason. The practice robs the delegate of the full freedom of voting in accordance with the leading of Christ discoverable at the meeting to which he is sent. The Congregational Christian way is to appoint a delegate in which the group has confidence and then trust him to be faithful, in Christ, to the group."[101]

My notes attached to this paper state "the reality and unity of the denomination arises from the voluntary participation of the Churches and their members." I further wrote "The Churches and electing bodies (of delegates to the General Council) entrust to the delegates the responsibility of representing their convictions and concerns. This is a far deeper moral and spiritual task than the technical practice of 'instruction'. . . (but) the electing body possesses the power to instruct."[102]

Fortunately, in September, Mr. Horton wrote again.[103]

"Dear Henry:

"The most exciting news I have heard since my return from Europe is that you are going to the South Church in Hartford. I am

451

more than delighted. You will have hard work there—but you were never the one to look for an easy job.

. . .

"Just before I left for Europe I asked that a paper I had dictated on 'The Powers of the General Council of the Congregational Christian Churches' be sent to you. This was to help fulfill the instructions given to you and me as a subcommittee to prepare a paper on that subject to be reviewed by the Commission on the study of the constitutional problem when it next met this autumn.

"I am not at all proud of the paper as it now stands. I hope that you will either correct it or write an entirely new one which I can have mimeographed and sent around to all the members of the Commission as soon as possible. The only other one besides yourself who has seen the copy of my first draft is our chairman, Dr. Hugh Vernon White."

By the time this letter was received I had written "an entirely new one"!

Chairman's Initiative and Leadership

Mrs. Claude C. Kennedy[104] and Mr. Clarence R. Chaney[105] objected to items in the circulated April 18-19 Minutes. Mr. Chaney stated an important weakness of the CC General Council.

"I hope that at our next meeting we can get to a discussion of the composition of the General Council which many of us feel does not in its present form fairly represent the substantial business and professional people who make up the bulk of our laity. This would have to do with the constitution of our General Council and would be property within our province.

"Your wish that our agenda for the next meeting may be well worked out in advance seems easy of accomplishment with the outline adopted at our first meeting plus suggestions for filling it out which may grow out of correspondence. I hope that all matters mentioned in writing by the members of our group will be on such an agenda for discussion at the meeting."[106]

Professor White called the second Commission meeting for November 8-10 at Chicago's La Salle Hotel.[107]

Shortly thereafter he wrote in detail in answer to my letter of chagrin at the form and content of Mr. Horton's paper as referred to in his September 9, 1955 letter. Because of its quality and importance I quote the letter in its entirety.[108]

452

"Dr. Henry David Gray,
The Oneonta Congregational Church,
South Pasadena, Cal.

"Dear Henry:

"I appreciate very much your letter of Sept. 15. It crossed my letter to you. Now that the matter of Hartford is settled I imagine that a certain strain is relaxed. What I am now writing you is 'off the record.' I want to tell you what I have in mind and hope to see the Commission do. If you feel that I am on the right track your help will be invaluable in getting it done. And if you think that my plan needs change or amendment at any point your criticism will be equally valuable. To begin with, I hope that we can adopt a brief report. Weeks ago, after an intensive absorption in the whole matter I typed two pages which sems to me to sum up the facts and true definition of our denominational situation as regards a constitution. Now I take it out and change a few words. It is in the hands of the mimeographer and I plan to send it out to our Commission members and say that I offer it as the basic form of our report, subject, of course, to amendment and correction. I should greatly appreciate it if you could look it over and let me know if you feel that this is the kind of thing that would be usable—not in detail but 'for substance of doctrine.' I am greatly hoping that we can concentrate on such a document rather than undertake to work out rewordings for the minute revision of the constitution of the General Council. I wonder if the essential problem that you and Douglas Horton are working on cannot be comprehended in such a statement. That is, cannot your report consist of 'material' for this final statement which ought to put precisely the meaning of it? You, of course, will have to write the report. I hope you will not feel at all bound by Doug's dissertation.

"Our task, after all, is to study and report on the constitutional problem and we must decide what the problem is and what we can say about it. If we do have to mention some specific points as regards the General Council constitution I would hope that we could append them as addenda to the basic document. My concern for this basic document is that, despite all the published statements, we still seem to lack a comprehensive and brief account of Congregational polity as it works. My effort contains nothing new; if it has any virtue it is because it seeks to state precisely what the principles are of our actual practice. I would preface this two pages with a short paragraph stating that the 'problem' of a constitution for Congregationalism lies in the fact that the usual meaning of constitution is a basic law and prescribes rules for all to whom it applies and that this is impossible with free churches. In fact, after that preface I should be happy if some such brief statement as I have prepared would constitute the entire report of the Commission.

453

"I may say, again off the record, that I have a certain feeling of floating in the air in this job. It is clearly the program for the G. C. to vote to proceed with the Merger next June. The church public still does not realize that all that can be accomplished will be a merger of the two top bodies in 'The United Church' and that the whole organization of both denominations must be preserved and will constitute the legal realities of the two. The first task of the United Church will be the writing of a constitution. This has always seemed to me to be putting the cart before the horse. I thought that the appointing of our Commission might mean that some delay would be in order so that we might help to clarify the thought of the denomination on the matter of a constitution. Even now, I can see that if we do a good job it may have some influence on the writing of a constitution for the United Church. At any rate I would like to conclude our work with a precise and brief statement that will touch upon every relevant point and be immediately understandable to everyone.

"You will be interested to know that I got a communication from Dave Beach and the Senior Deacon of the New Haven church saying that they had received a letter from Dr. Horton in answer to their proposed amendment and that they were disturbed by it. They wanted to appear before our Commission. I wrote them saying that we were not having hearings and simply quoting the paragraph that you formulated at Chicago, also interpreting our discussion. I have heard nothing further from them. What I suspect is that Dougles (sic) did not quote the statement but put it in his own words with the result that there was a certain blurring of the idea. I think your statement satisfied them.

"I know that you will be in the midst of a great change at the time of our Chicago meeting but I trust that you will be able to be with us all through it. And if it is not pushing you too much could I have a line from you in answer to my main question: Do you think this plan of proceedure (sic) and this particular statement are basically right. You have been much nearer to the whole matter than I and I will appreciate your counsel.

"Cordially yours,

"Hugh Vernon White

"P.S. I have written in *Headings* which indicate definitions in each section. This is my suggestion for a 'Memorandum' which we agreed to write.

"V"

At the end of October I mailed to Mr. White my memorandum on "The Powers of the General Council." He replied.[109]

Professor Hugh Vernon White's Memorandum

The two pages to which Mr. White referred in his October 4 letter read as follows:

"(The following is suggested as the basic form of the Memorandum to be submitted to the General Council by the Commission. H.V.W.)

"I. The Churches

"The congregation is a *church*. As a local, continuing body of believers it is a congregation of the universal Church of Christ. As a fellowship of faith it is subject to no civil or ecclesiastical authority, but is autonomous under God.

"II. The Denomination

"The Congregational Christian churches constitute a Christian Denomination. The unity and reality arise from the voluntary participation of free churches. The freedom of the churches exists (1) under the direct and absolute sovereignty of God revealed in Christ and (2) with full responsibility for sharing in the fellowship, counsel and common work of the Denomination.

"III. The Organization

"1. Congregational Christian churches form Associations, Conferences and a General Council for mutual counsel and encouragement, and to facilitate common activities.

"2. Each of these joint bodies is essentially an organ of the churches through which their fellowship is made real and fruitful, and their Christian purpose of witness and service made effective.

"3. These bodies are constituted by delegates—however elected—from the churches, and represent the churches. The delegates are not merely individual Christians seeking personal objectives or expressing personal opinions, but responsible representatives of the churches.

"4. These bodies, whether incorporated or not, are legally competent to speak and act only for themselves and within the provisions of their own constitutions. They cannot bind the churches by any act or judgment. But this technical, procedural autonomy is wholly subordinate to the substantial fact of their responsibility to the churches, and their fundamental status as organs of the churches.

"They are thus technically free bodies to which are entrusted the interests and purposes of the denomination. This is their constitutive character; they actualize the unity of the churches not under law but in trust. In this way they have their true existence and validity under the principle of Congregational order.

"IV. The Polity

"The foregoing sections are descriptive of the historically developed unity of the Congregational Christian churches. They are not statements of a 'constitution' in a prescriptive or authoritative sense, but are descriptive of the way denominational life and unity have developed historically. A detailed exposition of this way is contained in the 'Manual.' Externally it is a working order which operates much like that of an authoritatively constituted denomination. But it is actually a way 'constituted' in freedom.

"V. The Work

"Each organ of the common life of the Denomination—Association, Conference, General Council, or any other that may be formed—is competent, as representative of the churches, to carry on such activities as will express their common purpose, and has full legal powers to hold funds and properties and to administer work. Such work can either be carried on directly, or by the creation of special agencies, or by assuming ultimate control and direction of existing agencies insofar as the agencies may agree to such control and make their charters or constitution consistent with it.

"No power is or can be vested in any church body—association, conference, General Council, or other—to exercise legislative or judicial control over the churches. The authority and control such bodies can be empowered to exercise, or can exercise is administrative and not ecclesiastical and has to do with denominational agencies and not the churches or church bodies."

When Professor White's Memorandum reached the General Council executive secretary, Dr. Buschmeyer requested legal advice thereon. Attorney Loren T. Wood thereupon sent the Rev. Douglas Horton the letter here reproduced.[110]

"Dear Dr. Horton:

"Dr. Buschmeyer has asked us to comment upon the 'basic form' of the Memorandum to be submitted to the General Council by the Commission on the Constitutional Problem and to forward our comments to you:

"There are several points at which the Memorandum causes us concern. The Memorandum is capable of and will be interpreted as a description, in secular terms, of legal relationships within the denomination as well as a description, in theological terms, of the spiritual relationship within the denomination. As a result the Memorandum in its present form can cause difficulty in future litigation, if any, and also in the day to day interpretation of their own polity by Congregational Christians themselves.

456

"A. *The statement that the delegates are responsible represen-*
tatives of the churches. (Article III, paragraph 3.)

"The delegates to the joint bodies (Associations, Conferences, and the General Council) are undoubtedly conscious that their position depends upon the will of their own churches and that the churches may refuse to elect delegates who will not express the views of the churches. Likewise, the churches may refuse to re-elect delegates whose performance is not satisfactory. In this sense, there exists a responsibility to represent the local church and the church possesses a means to enforce this responsibility. However, this cannot be interpreted, as some Congregationalists have attempted, as a legal power in the church to direct the delegates in their voting, or to command the joint bodies to express the will of the church. The statement in Article III, paragraph 3 is susceptible of interpretation in terms of agency and a legal power in the local church to dictate to the joint bodies. Accordingly it is our opinion that it should be stated differently.

"Parenthetically, the Congregational polity imposes its own particular limitations upon the representative character of the joint bodies. Each delegate to such bodies goes uninstructed by his church. We question whether the significance of this element of the Congregational Christian polity has been fully reflected in the memorandum.

"We suggest that paragraph 3 of Article III will cause less difficulty if it were to read as follows:

"'These bodies are constituted by delegates—however elected—from churches and in some cases by delegates from other joint bodies. While the delegates undoubtedly, and quite properly, represent the viewpoint of their own church or joint body—and the church or joint body, by its power to elect and re-elect, possesses the means of insuring such responsiveness—nevertheless the delegates are free to be guided by their own judgment and conscience in performing the business of the association.'

"B. *The statement regarding the technical, procedural autonomy*
wholly subordinated to responsibility to the churches. (Article
III, Paragraph 4.)

"The foregoing discussion suggests the limitations of this Article III, paragraph 4. The joint bodies have substantial powers of their own which although consistent with the freedom of the individual church, define a realm or sphere within which the joint bodies must act. (See our Opinion dated June, 1954 on the Report of the Committee on Free Church Polity and Unity for an amplification.) For several reasons, not the least of which is the provisions of their own

457

constitutions or charters, the joint bodies cannot control or direct the churches. At the same time they can act in fields in which the single church cannot act. Accordingly, they possess useful and substantial purposes which are neither technical nor procedural. Just as the joint bodies have neither the function nor the power to invade the realm of the churches so individual churches have neither the function nor the power to invade the real or sphere of the joint bodies. Accordingly each has autonomy suited to its purpose and scope and neither autonomy can be fairly described as technical or procedural.

"Legally, the joint bodies are not 'wholly subordinated' but possess an autonomy having boundaries which are well recognized. The statement in Article III, paragraph 4, can be interpreted as holding that the joint bodies are the agents of the churches. Such an interpretation is not correct and would be devastating to the future operation of the denomination.

"We suggest that paragraph 4 of Article III will cause less difficulty if it were to read as follows:

"'The function of the joint bodies is defined by their constitutions and charters and by the practical consideration that they will fail to receive the support of the churches if they exceed their proper function. They cannot bind the churches by any act or judgment, nor can the individual churches directly dictate or control the action of the joint bodies. The autonomy of the joint bodies is complete within their proper sphere as set forth in their governing documents, but it must of necessity be exercised with recognition that it will become useless if it does not reflect the will of the majority of the churches. The joint bodies are thus free to express the wider interests and purposes of the denominations. This is their constitutive character; they actualize the unity of the churches in spirit and in fact. In this way they have their true existence and validity under the principle of Congregational order.'

"C. *The satement in Article IV that 'externally it is a working order which operates much like that of an authoritatively constituted denomination.*

"We are unable to see any similarity between the working order of the Congregational Christian denominations and authoritatively constituted denominations. There is no semblance of intra-denominational authority and control in the operation of the fellowship. It is our opinion that this sentence could be clarified or omitted.

"Very truly yours,

"SIGNED
"(Wood, Werner, France & Tully)

"LTW/MC"

458

It will be noted that Mr. Wood, who had never read the charters, constitutions and by-laws on which the *Documents* section of the Polity and Unity Report, was based or, the panel reports and voluminous correspondence on which the *Practice* section was based, and, who had not researched Congregational polity history, herein proceeds to pontificate as to facts about which he could have no knowledge apart from the sources just mentioned which have not been consulted.

As with the Polity and Unity Committee Report, so here, too, legal opinions thought to be essential to the Mansfield Theses and/ or "Congregationalism B" are interjected to discredit the wise, thoughtful, careful Memorandum of an excellent scholar in a leading Theological School.

Decision at Chicago

Present in Chicago were Mr. White, Chairman, Messrs. Bridges, Chaney, Ford, Gray, Inglis and Mrs. Kennedy. The secretary was Mr. Horton. We met from 2 p.m. on November 8 to 9 p.m. November 9.

The substantive sections of the Minutes are as follows.[111]

"The Chairman now presented the draft of the Memorandum which he had prepared and sent out to the members in advance of this meeting. This was discussed paragraph by paragraph and remitted to him for re-editing.

. . .

"The second session was called to order at 7:15 P.M.

"This session was wholly taken up with the discussion of the Memorandum by the Chairman and the paper on the Powers of the General Council by Mr. Gray, at the conclusion of which the two men were

"REQUESTED   To re-edit their work in the light of the com-
55-11CP3   ments made around the table and present the
               new editions to the Commission on the follow-
               ing morning.

. . .

"The morning session was given chiefly to a review of the new redaction of the Chairman's draft of the Memorandum.

"Copies of the re-edited draft of Mr. Gray's paper on the Powers of the General Council were distributed to the members of the Commission.

"The third session recessed at noon.

"The fourth session was called to order about 12:30 P.M.

"The review of the Chairman's Memorandum continued. The following procedure was

"VOTED
55-11CP6

The Chairman again to edit his Memorandum after the conclusion of the meeting; Mr. Gray again to edit his paper on the Powers of the General Council and send the new edition to the Chairman by December 1; the Chairman to have both his Memorandum and Mr. Gray's paper mimeographed and distributed (2 copies each), together with copies of a proposed Covering Report, to the General Council, to the members of the Commission, the Secretary of the Committee and the Acting Secretary of the General Council by December 10; the members to correct and return their copies to the Chairman by January 1, those who do not respond being considered to approve the copies in the form submitted; if the suggested corrections are not mutually incompatible, the Chairman to re-edit both the Memorandum, the paper on the Powers and the Covering Report in the light of the suggestions and transmit them (two copies each) to the members of the Commission and the two secretaries before January 10; the members to send to him their written approval by January 20; the Chairman to mimeograph and send to the secretary of the Executive Committee 50 copies of the approved documents by January 25 for reading by the Executive Committee, if desired, and for inclusion in the Advance Reports; and if the procedure breaks down at any point, as for instance would be the case if the written corrections of the members could not be correlated, the Chairman to consider the possibility of calling another meeting of the Commission.

. . .

"Before the fourth session recessed at 6:15 P.M. a beginning was made on the consideration of Mr. Gray's second edition of his paper on the Powers of the General Council.

"The fifth session convened at 7:30 P.M.

"It was unanimously

"VOTED   That this Commission holds that the General
55-11CP9   Council has the power to determine its own
                membership and to decide with what bodies it
                shall be in fellowship.

. . .

"Before the session came to an end, it was

"VOTED   That other matters which have been before the
55-11CP11   Commission but not voted upon, viz: the con-
                stitutional amendment submitted by the Reverend
                R. D. Avery of Connecticut, the question raised
                by the Essex North Association of Massachusetts,
                and the constitutional amendment proposed by
                Mr. Irving Kimball of Massachusetts, being con-
                cerned either with details of administration or
                with changes in established procedure, lie out-
                side the charter of the Commission.

"The Commission has considered and acted upon

"1)   The fundamental constitutional problems of the communion
       as they relate to the General Council and also
"2)   Matters on which judgment by the General Council is required
       for a clarification of its present procedures, but has favored as
       little constitutional change at this time as possible.

. . .

"The Final Session was adjourned at 9:00 P.M. with prayer by
the Secretary.

                          "Douglas Horton
                          Secretary"

The White Memorandum

Professor White's paper was discussed section by section, sentence by sentence and word by word. In front of me is a copy with
penned in changes in wordings, deletions, and additions including
notations as to the Commission members advocating the new
wording. Seven of Mr. Ford's perceptive suggestions were adopted,[112] the written comments of attorneys Thayer and Wood were
discussed and rejected. An improvement in language by Mr.
Chaney was adopted. Four language improvemens by Mr. Gray
were adopted. The form and substance of Professor White's
Memorandum was re-submitted on Wednesday (November 9) and
accepted as the best judgment of the Commission.

461

Discussion of the Gray Memorandum on "The Powers of the General Council" proceeded from session to session on a sentence, phrase and word basis. In front of me are thirty-three pages of re-wordings, mostly on LaSalle Hotel stationary, including the third complete redaction which was written during the night November 9 and 10.

Mrs. Kennedy requested a statement as to the meaning of "substantial unity" as it appears in the CC General Council constitution. At the request of the Commission I submitted the following, which was accepted in the form here presented by unanimous agreement but does not appear in Mr. Horton's Minutes.

Substantial Unity[113]

" 'Substantial unity,' as it appears in the constitution of the General Council, means true to the essential nature of our Congregational Christian way, based upon ample agreement in the fellowship, and founded on principles which have been proven to have solid worth (or substance). The phrase 'substantial unity' is not the same as the phrase 'virtually unanimous,' even though both are valid aims in the work of church bodies. The former refers to a deeper, foundational unity, an inner one-ness in matters of primary importance; the latter refers to a count of votes in which nearly all votes cast support one proposition. In any action of major importance, such as union with another fellowship or denomination, the General Council has a very grave responsibility to seek, to find, and to follow the way of 'substantial unity'."

Mr. Ronald Bridges, a staunch and determined protagonist of the CC/ER Merger supported the substantial unity statement. "We need to try to understand what was meant by the fellows who wrote the constitution, and this comes as close to the meaning of 'substantial' or 'substantive' as we are likely to get. The Latin is *substantialis* which I take to pertain to *essence* or *inherent nature*. I'll accept this statement." Mr. Horton suggested "Substantial now means simply majority agreement . . ." Mr. Bridges broke in rather dryly, "Doug, that's what I would *like* it to mean, but is not what it *does* mean." The Bridges-Horton dialogue completed discussion on this point. The Commission agreed that "substantial unity" meant what the above statement says.

The Recognition Question

Legal authority had been claimed on the basis of "recognition" of Conferences by the General Council, Associations by the Conferences, and Churches by the Associations. This was the nub of the Mansfield Theses, "Congregational B," and attorney Wood's "court case."

Mr. Chaney was adamant, "The General Council is just a group of elected people who meet for two or three days. *It* is recognized by the Churches, Associations and Conferences, but it's the Churches that count for they elect the people who meet and pay their bills. If the Council is some kind of superbody it could make all kinds of rash statements. It could refuse to "recognize" a Conference because the Conference did not agree with one of their pronouncements."

Mr. Ford responded, "I agree in substance with Mr. Chaney, but the issue here is not pronouncements. It is simply orderly procedure from the local to the district, to the state, to the national. That's all."

Mrs. Kennedy commented, "Not quite *all*, Mr. Ford. The Executive Committee of the CC voted on October 13 last year *to merge the whole fellowship* on the basis of this idea of recognition."

I scribbled various versions, four of which illustrate the comprehensiveness of the Commission's work.[114]

1. "The *G.C.* recognizes the state conference as the organization through which the *G.C.* will certify its delegates. Certification is simply attestation to orderly election of delegates by the association."

2. "By the process of co-operation the G.C. recognizes the state conference as one of the church bodies of the denomination."

3. "Moved that the G.C. has the power to recognize the Conference as a church body within the CC fellowship. This recognition carries with it no control by the GC over the Conference."

4. "The G.C. has the power to determine its own membership, and to decide with what bodies it will be in fellowship."

Number four appears in the Commission's report to the General Council. Number four was an attempt to state what the Commission thought to be the constitutional, legal, situation, *not* the ecclesiastical, moral or spiritual relationship, as is paragraph two of the final report.

The view of the Commission as to the normative relationship of Council, Conference, Association . . . of all church-bodies in the CC fellowship was eventually phrased as follows.[115]

"No church-body can bind or control the churches, other church-bodies or the affiliated organizations. Polity statements which refer

463

to the inter-relationships of church bodies simply describe the relation regarded as desirable by the church-body making the statement; they gain acceptance in the CC fellowship on the basis of inherent worth."

Is The Council A Church?

Of consumate interest is the fact that no Commission member thought the General Council was a *church*. Included in my pen script is the following which was unanimously approved.[116]

"The Council is not *a Church*, since its members are chosen *not* by a covenant relation with God and with each other *but* by a process of election (or by virtue of office) from other bodies, as set forth in its constitution and by-laws. The Council *is a church-body*, since it was created by, is *spiritually* the organ of, and is morally responsible to express the substantial unity of the churches in life and work."

After eighty-four changes by the Commission the report was thoroughly revised by Professor White and by me, mailed to all Commission members, and then, with the additional suggestions received by mail was submitted by the Commission to the 1956 General Council which approved the report as presented. The record is as follows.[117]

"The report of the Commission on the Study of the Congregational Problem was introduced by the Rev. Hugh Vernon White, of California, as printed in the Advance Reports, pages 58-63. Chairman White commented that despite wide divergencies of opinions on the part of individual members of the Commission, the report had been unanimously approved by the Commission. It was moved that the report be received.

"In the discussion that followed, the Rev. Neil Swanson of Wisconsin, the Rev. Malcolm Burton of Michigan, the Rev. David Nelson Beach of Connecticut, Mr. Henry Baldwin of Wisconsin, the Rev. Walter Schilling of Iowa, the Rev. George Gullen of Michigan, the Rev. Frederick A. Meyer of Minnesota, Mr. Ashby Bladen of New Jersey, the Rev. Henry David Gray of Connecticut, the Rev. Judson Fiebiger of Iowa, the Rev. Hugh Vernon White of California, the Rev. Thomas Anderson of Georgia, the Rev. Douglas Horton and the Rev. William Knox of Massachusetts participated.

"Mr. Burton moved to amend the original motion to include the words 'and approved.' The question being called for, the amendment was put to a vote.

"56 G 12. VOTED: To amend the original motion by adding the words 'and approved.'

"56 G 13. VOTED: That the amended motion be adopted to wit: 'that the report of the Commission on the Study of the Constitutional Problem be received and approved.'"

Our chairman wrote concerning the meetings November 8-10 as follows.[118]

"Dear Henry:

"I am returning the Statement by Dr. Wagner. You did not make an overstatement when you said that it was a remarkable document.

"I cannot tell you how much I appreciate your contribution to the work of the Commission on the Study of the Constitutional Problem. You carried a major load both in the discussion and in the writing. If, as I hope will be the case, our report is approved by the Executive Committee and by the General Council, even 'adopted' by the latter, it will be something of a recognized result of all the labor you put into the work of the Committee on Free Church Polity and Unity. It has been an especially heavy burden for you to carry during this time of your change from South Pasadena to Hartford.

"As soon as I get your final draft on the powers of the General Council I shall get out the total document to the members of the Commission. If it comes along all right in the return of the copies to me we may advance our time schedule a bit. But there is no pressure on the members as they get the document and I hope they will not call for any real revision.

"Cordially,

"Vernon"

And after the thorough re-write he wrote:[119]

"Dear Henry:

"Here is the final result. You did an excellent job of revision. It all hangs together. I am hoping that no material revision will be called for.

"With best wishes,

"Vernon"

The Rev. L. Wendell Fifield

I sent a copy of the "December revision" of the Constitutional Commission's report to Rev. L. Wendell Fifield, since he had performed such exemplary service as Chairman of the Polity and Unity Committee.

His reply is of great interest.[120]

"Dear Henry

"When I went into town from Claremont yesterday I found your letter. As we are only out here part of the time my mail is *not* forwarded. Hence the delay in my reply. The document which reached me was of great interest to me. It seems to me excellent and certainly is in line with our polity report. How the Executive Committee can make the statement they did in their last letter Missive in the face of the statements in this document, the polity report, the pleadings of the General Council, the decision of the Court of Appeals, the Constitution of the General Council is a complete mystery to me. It really infuriates me. This seldom happens. And there is nothing I can do about it all. How I long to be back in the Executive Committee where I could speak up though I realize that my health would no longer permit such tensions!

"Now concerning the one sentence about which you asked me. I'm pretty rusty on this kind of business. The only thing I can figure out is "As an administrative organization the membership and fellowship powers of the General Council *are limited* to determining its own membership and to deciding with what bodies it will be in fellowship in accordance with *the restrictions* of its own Constitution and by-laws." However I find no fault with the statement as you have revised it to read. Probably the negative approach as indicated above would be even less acceptable to your committee.

"I would appreciate it if when this statement in final form can be released you send me a copy. Apparently I am to be a delegate to Omaha—though I would prefer not to be. I'm planning however what I might helpfully say, however, if I got the floor. There is much in this I would like to quote if I could.

"I had a hernia operation in December. When I am over the effects of it, I hope to feel much better than for a long time. My modest work, to which I returned last week, goes well.

"Best always,

"Wendell"

Here is the complete text of the Constitutional Commission report as approved by the 1956 General Council.[121]

"THE CONGREGATIONAL CHRISTIAN CHURCHES

"1. The Church is a historic fellowship created by the act of Christ and sustained by His indwelling Spirit. It is constituted by faith in Christ and mutual love among its members.

"The term 'church' has two basic biblical meanings: It designates (1) the one universal fellowship which includes all Christians, and (2) the local congregation of Christian believers. In the Congregational Christian order the *church*[1] is the local continuing body of believers which is a congregation of the universal *Church of Christ.*

"2. *The Congregational Christian Churches*[2] form together an evangelical protestant *denomination.*[3] Its basic unity is in Christ as head. Humanly speaking, it is a unity arising from voluntary participation of the churches. The freedom of the churches exists (1) under the direct and absolute authority of God revealed in Christ and (2) with responsibility for sharing in the fellowship, counsel, and common work of the denomination.

"3. The denomination embraces two *orders,*[4] the ecclesiastical and the administrative. The ecclesiastical order represents the life and relationships of churches and *church bodies*[5] in their character as spiritual fellowship constituted by direct relation to Christ. The administrative order represents churches, church bodies, and other organizations in their functional character. It designates the denomination at work.

"4. The churches have joined themselves together in associations, conferences and a General Council. These are primarily church bodies and form an *ecclesiastical order.* Each of the church bodies is essentially an organ of the churches through which their fellowship is made real and fruitful, and their Christian purpose of witness and service made effective. In this order the principles of

---

"[1] The word 'church' has a variety of meanings. As used herein it is spelled with a small 'c' when the local church is meant, and with a capital 'C' when it designates the universal Church of Christ, or the Church Universal. The capital 'C' is used at the beginning of paragrah 2 because 'Churches' here is a part of the *name* of the fellowship.

"[2] *The Congregational Christian Churches* is the common and official name of our total fellowship as distinguished from other denominations, communions, sects, etc.

"[3] The term 'denomination,' which simply means 'name,' is used of the total fellowship. It has no connotations of authority or form. It is used instead of 'fellowship' because it embraces both the primary aspect of fellowship and the secondary aspect of functional organization.

"[4] 'Order' is used here in its general sense of 'system' or 'aspect.' It has only such specific connotations as are stated in the text.

"[5] 'Church body' is a term used in the Cambridge Platform (Ch. X,2) of the congregation as 'the Company of professed believers.' It is used here as a simpler expression for 'ecclesiastical body' generally and applied to associations, etc., as constituting the larger fellowship of the Congregational Christian churches.

freedom and fellowship prevail. The congregation or church, and the church bodies are self-governing, but they recognize a mutual moral obligation to cooperate, and to respect each other's counsel. All are under the constraint of Christ to participate in the common witness to His gospel and in service to God and man.

"5. The administrative order has emerged from the primary ecclesiastical fellowship. It is concerned with the work of the churches in their own upbuilding, in their participation in the Church Universal, in their evangelistic witness, and in works of human service.

"In its administrative function each church and church body becomes a working organization operating according to its own constitution. Each carries on its own work and the work of the denomination and has full legal powers to own funds and properties, and to employ and direct the activities of its personnel. It may or may not be incorporated, but in any case it constitutes an entity with legal rights and duties, and is subject to civil authority like any other organization. However, even in its administrative aspect, no church or church body is subject to any other save as such control is provided for in its own constitution or by its own free action.

"6. There are also organizations such as the missionary societies formed by the free action of individual Christians which have become integral parts of the total administrative order of the denomination. And a church body may create organizations which are then subject to its authority and countrol, as for example the commissions of the General council. Further, there are affiliated bodies such as colleges that cooperate with the denomination and participate in its life.

"7. *The Congregational Christian Churches* is the official name of the denomination in its totality, embracing both ecclesiastical and administrative orders. Although plural in form the name represents a denominational unity of churches, church bodies and affiliated organizations. As a whole it seeks to fulfill the meaning of the Church as the body of Christ and the fellowship of faith, and also to carry on all the activities to which the Church is led by faith in God and love for men.

"The distinction between the ecclesiastical and the administrative orders is real and important but these are ultimately two aspects of one total reality. In the ecclesiastical order the rule of Christ is direct; its human correlates are freedom of the individual mind and conscience, and absence of legislative authority. In the administrative order full ownership and authority are exercised by each of the organizations over its own properties, finances and employed personnel.

468

"In the ecclesiastical order the rule of Christ calls for brotherly love and participation in the common fellowship of the churches. In the administrative order each organization is under moral obligations to cooperate in the common task and to strive earnestly for working unity among all parts of the denomination.

"Thus in the two orders unity is sought, under God, in faith and work.

"8. Church bodies—associations, conferences, and the General Council—are composed of delegates chosen directly or indirectly from the churches and in some cases from other church bodies. While delegates represent the churches and express their common purposes and convictions, they act in the end according to their own judgment of what the common purpose requires at any point of decision. Here not formal instruction but confidence and good faith realize the Congregational Christian principle of freedom and responsibility.

"9. Joint bodies, in their action as representative of the churches, both ecclesiastically and administratively, are formally governed by their own constitutions and by-laws. They are responsible for their own acts and judgments in seeking to carry out the common purpose. No infallibility of judgment can be claimed. Actions by majority vote always call for profound seriousness and humility. Minority opinion is to be respected and freely expressed, and the possibility recognized that the leading of the Spirit may result in its vindication or in decisions diffferent from those of both majority and minority.

"THE POWERS OF THE GENERAL COUNCIL

"1. The General Council of the Congregational Christian Churches is an unincorporated association which performs, so far as is possible legally, the various functions formerly performed by the National Council of the Congregational Churches and by the General Convention of the Christian Churches. The National Council was created by action of delegates or messengers sent to a constituting convention by Congregational churches. The General Convention was created by the voluntary association of several 'ministerial conferences,' and of several 'local conferences' composed of elders and delegates sent by Christian churches.

"2. The nature of its origin gives to the General Council power to foster and express the substantial unity of the churches in faith, in polity, and in ecclesiastical relationships with non-Congregational Christian Church bodies. The Council possesses power to nuture fellowship, to recommend statements of faith, to suggest standards of procedure in matters of polity, and to advise the local churches, corporations or other bodies concerning all matters of faith and order. Its power in these church matters 'is simply friendly advice— having so much force as there may be force in the reason of it' (Dexter, Handbook p. 66). The Council possesses no legislative or judicial power over the local churches, or over the corporations or other bodies under the control of or affiliated with the churches.

"3. The General Council is, therefore, essentially a church body which derives its religious character from its central allegiance to God in Christ, and its corporate character from its relationship to the churches, church members, and church-related organizations. All the powers of the General Council are assumed to be exercised under God, in obedience to the guidance of His spirit, and as an organ of fellowship and hearty cooperation. The Council is not a *church*, since its members are chosen by a process of election or by virtue of office, as set forth in the Council's constitution and by-laws. The Council *is a church body*, since it was created by, is spiritually the organ of, and is morally responsible for the fostering and expression of the substantial unity of the churches in life and work. The General Council is the national body by means of which the local churches can manifest most completely their unity in faith, purpose, polity, and work. In a primary sense, it is a church body seeking to give counsel, and to implement cooperation in matters of common concern in the fellowship.

"4. In its ecclesiastical capacity as a church body, the General Council acts as a part of the universal Church of Jesus Christ in all ages. In its ecclesiastical capacity, the Council possesses power to call meetings through which the churches may express themselves, to proclaim the reciprocal duties and obligations of fellowship among all Congregational Christian bodies, and to declare what it understands to be 'the mind of Christ' on any matter of common concern to the churches. The self-completeness under Christ of the local church (sometimes called the headship of Christ), limits the power of the General Council or of any other church body to speak for the whole fellowship in matters in which the guidance of the Holy Spirit is variously understood among us.

"5. The General Council has the *legal power* to unite itself with any body or bodies that share its general purpose, provided only that its action be taken in accordance with such parliamentary procedure as may be required by its constitution, by-laws, and standing rules. It also has the *moral and spiritual obligation* to unite *only* with such body or bodies as share its general purposes, and grave responsibility so to act as to express the substantial unity of the churches.

"6. In a secondary sense, the General Council of the Congregational Churches is an organization governed by its own constitution and by-laws. Its constitution provides that it shall consult upon and devise measures and create agencies 'for the promotion of the common interests of the Kingdom of God; cooperate with any corporation or body under the control of or affiliated with' the Congregational Christian Churches or any church or churches among them, and promote 'the work of these churches in their national, international and interdenominational relations.' In this administrative sense the local churches, and the corporations and other bodies affiliated with the Congregational Christian Churches, have entrusted to the General Council some measure of general concern for the promotion of their common interests as a fellowship. As an administrative organization the General Council has the power to determine its own membership and to decide with what bodies it will be in fellowship, within the limits of its own constitution and by-laws and without infringing upon the rights and powers of the churches and church bodies whose delegates constitute its membership.

"7.   From its secondary character as an organization governed by its own constitution, the General Council derives power to perform such functions as are 'in the common interest' of the fellowship. It has the power to do everything useful to carryout the purposes stated in its constitution and by-laws, *provided* that it shall in no way *impose* its will on any local church, corporation or body under the control of or affiliated with the Congregational or Christian Churches or any of them:' (Constitution). Within these limits, the General Council has the administrative power to further and promote the life and work of the fellowship. It can commit itself, and only itself, to any course of action. Further, because its 'commitment' is certain to affect the life and work of the entire fellowship, the General Council has a duty to weigh its decisions in the light of its moral and spiritual relationship to the churches, corporations, and other bodies, over and beyond its legal powers.

"8.   Negatively, the General Council possesses no power to do anything contrary to the best interests of the churches, corporations and affiliated bodies, or contrary to the mind of Christ, or contrary to the purposes of its own constitution or by-laws, or contrary to the charters, constitutions, by-laws, or other rules of the churches, corporations, or affiliated bodies which cooperate with the General Council by their own voluntary action. The General Council has the power or act for the entire fellowship as it wins support by free cooperation on the part of the churches, corporations, and affiliated bodies. At its best, this means keen sensitivity to the needs of the fellowship so that the measures devised and the actions initiated gain the voluntary support of the churches, corporations, and affiliated bodies. In pioneer activities this means creative work of

471

clearly Christian purpose and high minded leadership such as will commend the work and win support for it.

"9. In smmary: The General Council is, at one and the same time, (1) a body of representative churchmen who in Christ's name seek the guidance of God, and (2) a church body designed to manifest the substantial unity of the churches in matter of faith and order, and (3) an organization designed to further the work of an entire fellowship composed of churches, corporations, and affiliated bodies. Its powers are derived from and are limited by its three-fold nature.

"10. It should be noted that the three-fold nature of the General Council lays upon delegates a varied responsibility.

"(1) They are men and women whose ultimate and supreme allegiance is to God as made known in Jesus Christ. Therefore they recognize that on *all matters* their first duty is to 'hear what the Spirit says to the churches.' (Rev. 2:7)

"(2) They are members of Congregational Christian churches who 'agree in the belief that the right of government resides in lcoal churches, or congregations of believers, who are responsible directly to the Lord Jesus Christ, the One Head of the church universal and of all particular churches, but that all churches, being in communion with one another as parts of Christ's catholic church, have mutual duties subsisting in the obligations of fellowship.' (1871 Constitution of the National Council). Therefore they recognize that all measures and actions relating to faith and order are matters of import earnestly commended to the consideration of the churches.

"(3) They are delegates who are church members, elected by groups of churches united in associations, conferences, or other bodies, or they are delegates by virtue of office. Therefore they recognize that their measures and actions on matters of life and work should seek to express the will of the bodies which they represent.

"11. When the duties of delegates on these three levels conflict, the primary loyalty is to God in Christ, although delegates should be aware that they are both *individuals* acting for themselves and also *representative individuals* acting on behalf of a spiritual fellowship.

"12. No action of the General Council can commit the bodies from which the delegates are elected or appointed. Each body must act in accord with its own constitution and by-laws, and all bodies must win the support of the members of the churches if their recommendations are to be effective for the work of the Kingdom.

"13. The word 'representative' here means that the purpose, spirit, and aspirations of the electing or appointing bodies are to be

472

present in, and are to be furthered by the delegates in Council assembled. The manner in which the churches, corporations, and affiliated bodies are 'represented' in the General Council is more significant than the representation of an instructed delegate in a non-church body. In our fellowship, while the power to instruct may be exercised, a representative is expected to be a dedicated Christian who will sincerely seek to act according to the mind of Christ made known or yet to be made known in the common spirit of the body to which he is elected or by insight into the common spirit of the entire fellowship."

"It Really Infuriates Me."

The words are from Rev. L. Wendell Fifield's January 23, 1956 letter. And, as he adds, "This seldom happens" to him.

What is now before us is an action taken by the CC Executive Committee on October 13, 1954 which is a complete denial of the clear testimony of the classic early Congregationalists, a reversal of the expressed will of the 1952 and 1954 General Councils, *and* contrary to what the Council's own Polity and Unity Committee *and Constitutional Commission* found to be, in fact, contemporary Congregationalism.

How can these things be? What has to be kept in mind is the mood of the proponents and the opponents, the "ecumenical climate" of 1956, and the great desire of Rev. Douglas Horton to achieve his dream. The position of the Mediators was well expressed by the Rev. Frederick W. Whittaker.

"Crisis and Choice for Congregationalism[122]

"On May 2, 1955, it was my privilege to address the annual meeting of the Massachusetts Convention of Congregational Ministers, held in Boston, on the assigned subject of the proposed merger between the Congregational Christian Churches and the Evangelical and Reformed Church. . . .

"As a Congregationalist I am concerned that our churches shall participate with all possible effectiveness in the modern ecumenical movement. Thus I am in favor of the merger if it can be accomplished without denominational schism. My qualifications for discussing this subject include the fact that I am President and Professor of Ecclesiastical History of Bangor Theological Seminary, and that I was a member and secretary of the General Council's Committee on Free Church Polity and Unity.

. . .

473

"The American denomination of churches known as Congregational Christian (Churches) now faces a crisis. The word 'crisis' is used advisedly in the sense described by Webster's dictionary as a 'point of time when it is decided whether any affair or course of action must go on, or be modified, or terminated.' The affair is the proposed merger of the Congregational Christian Churches and Evangelical and Reformed Church to form the United Church of Christ. The course of action is the plan sponsored by the Executive Committee of the General Council to consummate the merger in 1957 in accordance with the provisions of The Basis of Union and Interpretations. The decision or choice to proceed, or to modify, or to terminate, is one which will be made not later than June, 1956, when the General Council meets in Omaha. Thus I speak to you on the pertinent subject, 'Crisis and Choice for Congregationalism.'

. . .

"There are some among us who hold that the issue of this particular merger has already been settled by action of the Executive Committee of the General Council. There are others, however, who contend that the crisis and the choice lie just ahead of us. . . .

". . . with increasing tempo throughout the denomination, new and serious consideration is being given by thoughtful people to the proposed church union . . .

"In order to comprehend Congregationalism's present crisis and choice it is necessary for us to understand the meaning of such terms as 'Basis of Union and Interpretations,' 'Directives at Claremont and New Haven,' 'Executive Committee Action' and 'Committee upon Free Church Polity and Unity'. . . .

. . .

"May I call to your attention now two facts which are pertinent here and upon which I shall elaborate later in another context: (1) The General Council which met at New Haven in June, 1954, did not vote to proceed toward union with the Evangelical and Reformed Church through the instrument of The Basis of Union and Interpretations, although it was legally free to do so if its members were so minded. Rather, it renewed the instructions given to the Executive Committee by the Claremont General Council of 1952, which included a provision for the drafting of a proposed constitution for the General Synod of the united fellowship. (2) On October 13, 1954, the Executive Committee of the General Council, meeting at Cleveland with the corresponding body of the Evangelical and Reformed Church, re-asserted the validity of The Basis of Union and Interpretations as a proper instrument for merger, and suggested that the convening General Synod be held in 1957. In taking this action the Executive Committee claimed that it was 'carrying into effect the desire of the Congregational Christian Churches as they have expressed themselves through their delegates to the General Council for many years.' This claim is now in dispute.

. . .

"CLAREMONT AND NEW HAVEN DIRECTIVES

"The re-introduction of The Basis of Union and Interpretations has followed the inability of the Executive Committee of the present General Council to reach agreement with the corresponding body of the Evangelical and Reformed Church on another plan of union sponsored by the General Councils of 1952 and 1954. This plan differed from the original Basis of Union in that it called for the drafting of a proposed constitution for the General Synod prior to the union rather than after the United Church was formed. This alternative plan was first approved by the General Council at Claremont in June, 1952, at a time when The Basis of Union and Interpretations was being tested in the courts.

"The . 'Claremont Resolution' provided in part 'that the Executive Committee be instructed to seek joint meetings with the General Council of the Evangelical and Reformed Church' and 'that those two bodies meeting jointly be requested, if both approve, to be responsible for the preparation of a draft of a proposed constitution for the General Synod of the united fellowship.' (The clause, 'if both approve,' should be remembered for future reference.) When the General Council met at New Haven in June, 1954, it renewed these instructions to the Executive Committee at a time, I remind you, when it could have rescinded them and re-introduced The Basis of Union and Interpretations.

"EXECUTIVE COMMITTEE ACTION

"The joint meeting called for by the Claremont and New Haven directives was held in Cleveland on October 12th and 13th, 1954. The chairman of the Executive Committee issued a 'Letter Missive' on October 18th which has provoked vigorous and extended discussion of the merger issue within the denomination. . . .

"The Letter Missive described the conclusions reached at the joint meeting of the Congregational Christian Executive Committee and the General Council of the Evangelical and Reformed Church. By a vote of 30 to 2, with one abstention, it was agreed to 'reassert the validity of the Basis of Union with the Interpretations' and 'to look forward to the holding of the Convening General Synod in 1957.' . . .

475

"In explaining why the joint meeting did not carry out the instructions given to the Executive Committee by the General Councils of 1952 and 1954, the Letter Missive stated: 'The two bodies did not approve preparation of a draft of a proposed constitution for the General Synod of the united fellowship. After prayerful discussions of the subject it was felt . . . that the Basis of Union with the Interpretations adequately provides for the drafting of such constitutional instruments as will be needed, and that the spirit of a union in Christ with full trust in one another might be jeopardized if ecclesiastical legalities were put to the fore.' Later in a brochure entitled, 'Speaking to our Condition . . . ,' the Executive Committee called particular attention to the clause in the Claremont Resolution, 'if both approve,' and then added this comment: 'Since the writing of the constitution was to proceed only if BOTH groups agreed, the writing of the constitution was dropped.' Both groups then voted to proceed with the union on the original Basis of Union and Interpretations.

. . .

". . . The question being asked in many quarters is whether or not the Executive Committee was justified in taking the action it did in reasserting the validity of the Basis of Union and Interpretations. The premise adopted by the Executive Committee is set forth in the following quotation from 'Questions and Answers,' an official publication of this Committee through its so-called Information Committee: 'The General Council has never modified or rescinded the covenant with the Evangelical and Reformed Church, voted in 1948 and reaffirmed in 1949, to enter into the union on the Basis of Union and Interpretations.' If this premise is valid then the Executive Committee was fully justified in taking action as it did. If the premise is not valid, then the Committee's action is subject to reconsideration.

"In my opinion, the premise is not valid, and I refer to the words of the Committee's own document to support my position. In 'Questions and Answers,' the answer to question No. 16 reads in part: 'Actions of General Councils remain in force unless they are revised or rescinded by subsequent councils. Each council has the right to legislate for itself and, in so doing, to modify the votes of its predecessors.' . . . The obvious conclusion is that . . . the General Council directives of 1948 and 1949 . . . have certainly been 'revised' and 'modified.' . . .

"There are other factors which can be overlooked or disregarded only in the peril of schism within Congregationalism. In spite of the legal sanction given by the courts, there is evidence that even proponents of the Basis of Union and Interpretations do not look upon it now with the same favor they bestowed six years ago. Further, there is a divided opinion within the denomination concerning the powers of the General Council, and the Council itself voted in 1954 to authorize a study and report on this crucial question. Again, there is considerable demand for the preparation and approval of a constitution for the proposed United Church before the union is consummated; as early at 1952 the General Council received and referred to its Executive Committee a resolution from the Massachusetts Congregational Conference asking for the preparation of tentative constitution for union with the Evangelical and Reformed Church which would be 'consistent with the principles enunciated by the Committee on Free Church Polity and Unity.' Moreover, a result of the publication of the report on this latter committee there is now available to our churches an opportunity to study Congregational polity as it now exists and to determine which form of union is more desirable for our participation in the ecumenical movement.

"In view of this ambiguous situation, and in the interest of denominational harmony, the whole issue should be referred for discussion to the General Council of 1956. In order that this Council may be prepared to make a proper decision it seems to me essential that the people of our churches should not only re-study the Basis of Union and Interpretations but should also carefully consider . . . A Study by the Committee on Free Church Polity and Unity.

"FREE CHURCH POLITY AND UNITY

"The Study is a 122-page report by a committee of twenty-one lay people and ministers of our denomination with Dr. L. Wendell Fifield of Brooklyn, N.Y., as its chairman. In June, 1950, the General Council at Cleveland authorized the establishment of this committee and charged it with the responsibility of making a careful study and report 'of the principles and polity of Congregationalism' with 'particular reference to the spiritual and legal methods for the participation of the free autonomous fellowships in the ecumenical movement.' After four years of work the committee presented its report to the General Council at New Haven in June, 1954. The report was received by the Council, which voted to send one copy to each church for 'information and study' and to make additional copies 'generally available' on a 'proper financial basis.' The further use of the study was left to the direction of the Executive Committee with the provision that source materials be preserved and made available with the report to 'committees and commissions studying Congregational Christian polity and considering church union.' This then, is a vital document and one which deserves thorough consideration by the people of our churches. . . .

" 'The Fifield Report,' as it is affectionately known (at least by its authors), is less than a year old . . . In its brief life thus far, it has not

477

yet gained full recognition and favor in all Congregational Christian quarters. On its birthday in the General Council last June it was 'spanked' with a legal opinion by the lawyers for the Council, and an unsuccessful attempt was made on the Council platform to prevent its free circulation among the churches. However, it has not been banned in Boston, and I proceed now to present it to you. The following quotation from the 'Foreword' to the report will establish the proper mood for our consideration: 'The Committee as a whole does not regard itself as an advocate or sponsor of any specific proposals or positions. Such value judgments . . . must rest entirely with the churches. The committee has endeavored to discover all of the pertinent material bearing upon "free church polity and unity" and then present it in as clear, complete, and objective fashion as possible.'

"The heart of the report with regard to source materials is found in sections 3 and 4 of chapter four. Section 3 is a description of Congregationalism as set forth in contemporary documents. A sub-committee spent three years gathering, studying, and collating the constitutions, by-laws, and charters of the national-level organizations, the state conferences, and one third of the associations. Local church documents were also consulted by individual members of the sub-committee. The results are stated in 73 propositions . . .

"As a counterpart to this documentary account, section 4 describes Congregational polity as it is currently practiced in the United States. This information was secured by various methods. When widely distributed questionnaires failed to produce conclusive evidence, a syllabus . . . was sent to chairmen of geographical panels for study, discussion and report. These panels were located in New England, the southeast, the midwest, the northwest, and the southwest, and consisted of a total of 53 persons appointed as consultants for the committee. Later the sub-committee sent the statement on documentary Congregational polity to all state superintendents, all panel chairmen, and to a list of individuals whose names had been suggested; these persons were requested to report all known significant deviations in Congregational practice as compared with documentary polity; 140 replies were received. A tentative statement was then prepared by the sub-committee, re-submitted to the consultants for correction and amendment, and finally adopted in its present form after full consideration by the whole committee.

"This section 4, then, describes in 84 propositions Congregational Christian polity as it was practiced in the year A.D. 1954 at the various denominational levels and it also includes an exposition of the terms 'Faith,' 'Freedom' and 'Fellowship.' It is clearly indicated that the report does not presume to say whether or not what is is what ought to be. . . .

. . .

"The relationship between the local churches and General Council with reference to participation in the ecumenical movement is the subject matter of chapter eight in the report. The committee discovered that as many as six different theories of this relationship are held by Congregationalists; this fact led it to make the recommendation, adopted by the General Council in 1954, that the Executive Committee elect a special committee 'to study the question of the powers of the General Council and report at the General Council meeting in 1956.' . . .

". . . Churchmen interested in theology will want to read chapter three on 'The Spiritual and Theological Basis of Congregationalism as Related to Christian Unity.' To whet your interest I take time to read . . : 'The essence of Congregationalism cannot be found adequately in documents, even in its own documents. Rather it is to be found and seen most clearly in the direction and quality and character of its spirit. Congregationalism is a defninte type of Christian experience, finding visible practical expression in our churches and in our polity. Thus our church life, our polity and our organizational structure are finally not of codification, but they are of the spirit. And they have both a surprising, long-term uniformity and a surprising flexibility in the midst of continually changing circumstances.'

"Those who are interested in Christian unity would do well to come first to an understanding of the nature of the church. Suggestive and helpful ideas are contained in this chapter, for example the following:

"'Congregationalism believes that the church begins with redeemed individuals. We do not become Christian by the acceptance of the content of any document or by any ecclesiastical ceremony. Rather we become Christian through our personal relationship with Jesus Christ. That experience in which we find Him our Saviour and our Lord brings us into closest fellowship with Him, and it brings us also into fellowship with others of like experience, so that we come to know the strengthening experience of the fellowship that is His church. In that relation, the experience which first brought us into the fellowship of the church is further purified and re-enforced.'

. . .

. . ."(There) is a chapter of the Fifield report equalled in importance only by the previously-described sections on polity in the documents and in practice. It is chapter seven on 'Forms of Special Present Interest.' Without advocating the adoption of either plan the committe singled out 'Covenant Union' and 'Organic Union' as 'particularly significant' . . . 'in the framework of our present historical situation.' I commend them . . . as possible alternatives when the General Council comes to its hour of decision.

"COVENANT UNION

"There is a school of thought within Congregationalism which believes that the experience of covenanting together with other groups of Christians 'may be the method by which Congregational Christian churches can make their most effective contribution to the ecumenical movement.'

. . .

". . . The following is one suggested form of the covenant:

" 'Holding sacred the treasures of faith and freedom to which we are heirs, and recognizing our common loyalty to Jesus Christ, the great Head of the church, we do solemnly covenant before God and with each other to walk together in Christian love and fellowship, and to share in promoting the common interests of the Kingdom of God.'

"You have now . a resume and analysis of a document . officially before the Congregational Christian churches for study. It was prepared by Congregationalists who held many shades of opinion concerning polity and unity, but all of them were anxious to present to the denomination factual source materials as a guide for its participation in the ecumenical movement. The report was completed only after literally thousands of hours of work by the committee members and their consultants. The General Council spent an estimated $40,000 to support this work. Perhaps this will explain why many Congregationalists are disturbed by the opinion of the Executive Committee that this report is irrelevant in our present time of denomination decision.

"Under date of November 15, 1954, members of the Fifield committee received a letter from the chairman of the Executive Committee which read in part: 'We of the Executive Committee had no thought that the work of the Committee on Free Church Polity and Unity had anything to do with the basic commitment made by the General Council in 1949 to merge with the Evangelical and Reformed Church. The resolution by which the General Council constituted the Committee on Free Church Polity and Unity in 1950 was specific on this point: "The constituting of this committee is not to be interpreted as affecting any past decisions of the General Council."' One reply to this contention is the following clause in the Claremont Resolution adopted by the General Council in 1952 and reaffirmed in 1954: 'The Executive Committee is requested to establish a consulting relationship with the Committee on Free Church Polity and Unity during the drafting of the proposed constitution.' Another is that conditions surrounding the proposed merger have changed since 1949 and Congregationalism is now faced with new decisions for the future. Certainly the Fifield committee report has an important role to play on the contemporary scene.

. . .

"I close with this thought: As Congregationalists prepare for the General Council meeting of 1956 may they be strengthened and guided by the sentiment expressed in these words from the report of the Committee on Free Church Polity and Unity: 'We have been increasingly concerned to keep unbroken the free fellowship to which we all belong. We are a Christian fellowship. This means we are a family group—a Church family—whose members are bound together by common memories and ideals—faith and friendship and love for one another in the name of Christ, our Lord. We believe it is possible and always will be possible for a majority and a minority in our fellowship to study and confer together, as members of the Committee have done, and that ways will be found in which our denomination can boldly act in service to the ideal of Christian unity.'"

CHAPTER 9 NOTES

1. Minutes, 1952 General Council, NY n.d. pp. 19-22
2. Minutes, 1954 General Council, NY, n.d., p. 21-22
3. Douglas Horton *Statement*, Oct. 12, 1954, pp. 3, 4
4. H. P. Keiling, 1969, Lettner-Verlag, Berlin, pp. 157-159.
5. Horton Statement, op.cit., p. 4
6. James E. Wagner, *Preliminary Statement*, Oct. 12, 13, 1954, p. 1
7. Wagner, op.cit., p. 3
8. Keiling, op.cit., p. 158
9. Minutes—Joint Meeting CC/ER, p. 2 (Keiling 158)
10. Malcolm K. Burton, *Disorders in the Kingdom*
11. Anderson to Gray, Oct. 28, 1954
12. Keiling, op.cit., p. 159
13. 1956 Advance Reports, 1956 General Council, NY pp. 9-10
14. Gray to CC General Council Executive Committee, 10-22-54
15. Keiling, op.cit., p. 159, footnote 35
16. Anderson to Gray, 10-28-54
17. Bradford to Horton, 11-15-54
18. Meek to R. B. Walker, 11-18-54
19. Fifield to Executive Committee, 11-15-54
20. Mrs. Fiebiger to Gray, 10-30-54
21. Walker to Gray, 10-26-54
22. Gray to Walker, 11-2-54
23. Walker to Gray, 11-15-54
24. Gray to Walker, 12-7-54
25. Gray to Walker, 3-15-55

26. Walker to Gray, 3-17-55
27. Gray to Walker, 6-23-55
28. James E. Wagner, *Looking Forward To The United Church of Christ*
29. Barrowe, *Platform*, 1593, "Printed for the year of better hope." Barrowe and his work are well recorded in E. J. Powicke, *Henry Barrowe Separatist*, 1900, London, n.d.
30. Barrowe, *Brief Summe* etc. 1588, probably printed in Holland.
31. Barrowe, *Defence etc.*, 1599, Schilders, Zealand, 81
32. Francis Johnson, *A Deference of the Churches and Ministry*, 1599, Schilders, Zealand See esp. pgs. 26-78.
33. Ibid, 26
34. Ibid, 28
35. Ibid, 50
36. Ibid, 78
37. Henry Jacob, *Divine Beginning and Institution of Christ's True Visible Church*, 1610, Hastings, Leyden. (The document is not long. There were no page numbers.)
38. Jacob, op.cit., *Divine Beginning*
39. Ibid.
40. Douglas Horton, *Congregationalism*, 1952 Independent Press, London, 48
41. Henry Jacob *An Attestation*, 1613, Schilders, Middleburg
42. Ibid, 102
43. Henry Jacob *Reasons Taken Out of God's Word,* 1604 R. Schilders, Middleburg, 30
44. Jacob *Attestation*, 105
45. Ibid, 107
46. Horton, op.cit. 48
47. Ibid, 49
48. Jacob *Attestation*, op.cit. 97
49. Ibid, 100
50. Ibid, 100
51. Ibid, 178
52. Ibid, 178-179
53. Jacob *Attestation*, 94-95
54. Henry Jacob, *Reasons Out of God's Word*, 1604 (Schilders, Middleburg) 57
55. Ibid, 70
56. Ibid, 48
57. Jacob, *Divine Beginning*, op. cit.
58. William Bradshaw, *English Puritanisme* 1605 (Holland)
59. Horton, op.cit. 25
60. Bradshaw, op.cit. 5
61. Ibid, 5
62. William Bradshaw, *Of Divine Worship* 1604, n. publ., n.d.
63. William Bradshaw *A Protestation* 1605 (Holland)
64. Horton, op.cit. 34
65. Williams Ames, *The Marrow of Divinity*, 1642 (edit) Griffen, London, published by order of the House of Commons
66. Ibid, 157-158
67. Ibid, 159
68. Ibid, 202
69. Horton, op.cit. 19

70. Ibid., 60-61
71. Ibid, 61
72. Keith L. Sprunger, *The Learned Dr. William Ames* 1972, U. of Illinois Press, Urbana, IL 230
73. William Ames, *A Manuduction for Mr. Robinson*, 1614, *Dort A Second Manuduction for Mr. Robinson,* 1615, n.p.
74. *A Fresh Suit Against Human Ceremonies in God's Worship*, 1 633, n.p.
75. Horton, op. cit, 61
76. Horton, op.cit., 61-2
77. Ibid, 62
78. Ibid, 61
79. Horton, op.cit., 59
80. William Ames Marrow, 1:20, 27, 79, 33, 39
81. Ibid, 201-202
82. Ames, Marrrow, 203
83. Ibid, 204
84. Ibid, 203
85. Horton to Gray, *Western Union*, 1-29-55
86. Horton to Gray, 2-4-55
87. Horton to Gray, 2-4-55
88. Horton to Gray, 3-7-55
89. Constitutional Commission Minutes, Apr. 18-19, 1955, 1
90. Ibid, 2, 3
91. Constitutional Commission Minutes, op.cit., 3, 4, 5, 6
92. White to Gray, 7-15-55
93. White to Gray op.cit., under II
94. Ibid, II p. 3
95. Ibid, White to Fifield letter, 5-14-53
96. Horton to Gray, 6-28-55
97. Horton, op. cit., 1-2
98. Ibid, 2
99. Horton, op.cit., 4
100. Ibid, 5
101. Ibid, 6
102. Gray, attached to Horton, op.cit.
103. Horton to Gray, 9-9-55
104. Kennedy to White, 8-10-55
105. Chaney to White, 8-11-55
106. Chaney to White, op.cit., 2
107. White to Gray, 9-19-55
108. White to Gray, 10-4-55
109. White to Gray, 11-2-55
110. Wood to Horton, 11-7-55
111. Constitutional Commission Minutes, November 8-9, 1955
112. Gray copy of White Memorandum, 11-8-55
113. Gray, Commission Meeting, 11-8-55, paper #2
114. Gray, op.cit, paper #14
115. Gray, op.cit., paper #15
116. Gray, op.cit., paper #19
117. Minutes, 1956 General Council, NY, 14.
118. White to Gray, 11-12-55

119. White to Gray, 12-8-55
120. Fifield to Gray, 1-23-56
121. Advance Reports, General Council, NY, 78-82
122. President Frederick W. Whittaker, *Crisis And Choice for Congregationalism*, May 2, 1955, Old South Church, Boston

CHAPTER TEN

The Quest For Spirit And Truth

While the Constitutional Commission was at work the Mediators sought to make room for reason and religion in the CC/ER Merger proceedings. The Revs. Carl Martinsen of Grand Rapids, Elden Mills of West Hartford, Alan Jones of Indiana, Perry D. Avery of Oregon and President Frederick W. Whittaker of Maine were among those who wished to avoid fragmentation of the fellowship. It seemed to most mediators that a split could be avoided by a reasonable and spiritual approach rather than legal and organizational procedures. We believed the quest for church union should be an outward expression of a spiritual fellowship acting with sensitive awareness of the very real differences which needed to be reconciled. Our view was that *any* compulsory merger would hinder rather than help the cause of Christ. Most of us espoused the concept of merged national bodies, assured direct *Church* control over the proposed national synod, with an unamendable preamble to the national-level constitution containing a Bill of Rights which stated concisely the facts of Congregational liberty which have been presented herein, in our history, in our documents, and in practice.

1955 was a year of conferences, correspondence, resolutions—and hopes. My sentiments in January 1955 were expressed as follows:

"The Free Churches and Christian Unity"[1]

"The Congregational Churches belong to the company of all those who follow Christ in freedom of worship, belief, creed, and

485

self-government. And through nearly four hundred years they have raised the standard of freedom under God.

"As would be expected, free churches have been eager to defend the rights of others, and have recognized the validity and worth of all paths to the presence of God. All co-operative Christian efforts have been given continuous and vigorous support by the Congregational Christian Churches. They have ever been proponents of unity in Christ.

"When in the course of events, there comes a conflict between support of freedom under God on the one hand, and organizational church union on the other hand, our churches have been mentally and spiritually distraught. And no wonder; for allegiance to the rulership of Christ alone is one of our cardinal principles, and desire for co-operative Christian life and work is one of our cherished dreams. Our problem is how to unite and remain free.

"An answer to our present predicament is to be found in union of spirit and action rather than in uniformity of creed and organization. In this direction lies the best contribution the Congregational Christian Churches can make to Christian unity. No monolithic, centralized organization is either desirable or necessary in order to unite with others in Christian life and work. The historic method of the Scriptures and of the early Congregationalists was unity by covenant agreement. On Mt. Sinai God and man covenanted together. In the cabin of the Mayflower a group of men covenanted with each other, under God. Again and again, vital religious work has been made possible by covenant agreement. There is no reason why our Churches can not follow this well proven path into larger united worship and service.

"The trend toward highly centralized government over the Churches is a mistaken notion of what constitutes Christian unity. We need both freedom and fellowship if we are to be true to our faith."

Committee For the Continuation

Following the 1947 Evanston Meeting the vigorous opponents of the CC/ER Merger organized "The Committee for the Continuation of the Congregational Christian Churches" with Revs. Howell D. Davies and Malcolm K. Burton as spokespersons. Soon after the CC General Council Executive Committee Meeting in Cleveland,[2] October 12-14, 1954, the Continuation Committee met in Chicago, November 4-5, to consider an appropriate response to the "rush to merge."

Under date January 15, 1955[3] the proposal to form state and national associations of Congregational Churches determined to be free was proposed.

"At our Chicago meeting on Nov. 4 and 5 we talked of encouraging the formation of fellowship groups in the various states with definite thought of having some organizations ready for our churches when and if the merger takes place.

"It should be remembered that the Continuation Committee is not an organization in which churches hold actual membership. Ours is an advisory type of committee.

"The free fellowships in the local states would envisage actual church membership. Churches would not withdraw from their associations or conferences just yet. They would, instead, adopt a dual standing relationship. A precedent for this can be found in the Riverside Church in New York, which has full standing in a Baptist Association and then was admitted, with blessings of our denominational top brass, into full standing with our New York City Association of Congregational Christian Churches. In each state, then, we could develop new 'associations' with actual church membership.

"Now the suggestion has come in for a national association as well, again on a dual standing basis. Such an organization might be known as the 'National Association of Churches That Intend to Remain Congregational Christian.' Such a title would be provisional only, to carry over the present emergency. Later it could be changed. Or the title might be from the start. 'National Association (or "Conference," or "Council") of Congregational Christian Churches.' By using the word 'Association' on national and state levels we would not now conflict with other existing names.

"It has been strongly urged that we ought to prepare the call for such a national meeting, with the plan of definitely organizing within the months lying just ahead. Then churches could start voting membership therein and making provision for the election of delegates to it.

"Advantages of Setting Up National Association

"So far we have had little to offer churches that wanted to 'do something' in their opposititon to the merger. We have given them 'protecting resolutions' to adopt, and these would safeguard them against having their delegates to association or conference carry them into the merger. But we have offered the churches no other place to go, once they take the position that their associations have 'left them' behind. We should fill that gap. By having them join 'stand-by' organizations, which are not 'official' as yet, we would be ready when the time comes with the organizations which would be official for the churches remaining in C.C. fellowship.

"Much might be said in favor of starting with a national Association, instead of feeling that we must get a state association set up for each group of churches that want some place to go or to be when other churches leave us to enter the United Church. By having one national Assocation in the very near future we would answer the question at once for all churches that wonder where their 'standing' would be after the merger takes place. One 'National Association of Congregational Christian Churches,' receiving individual churches into its membership, could give 'standing' in the continuing Congregational Christian denomination. State organizations could be formed as the need developes (sic).

. . .

"Incidentally we want to guard against the mistakes now evident with existing organizations. We never want any future officialdom to say that the new organization, which we are thinking of setting up, is not made up of the churches or controlled by them. From the start it should be a direct membership organization, with each church an actual member."

In September the *Continuation Committee* and an organization, chiefly Church members rather than ministers, called the *League to Uphold Congregational Principles* voted to issue "a call for a national meeting of churches, to be held presumably in Detroit, Michigan, on November 9 and 10 . . . for the purpose of forming a permanent national association of Congregational Christian Churches for fellowship and mutual counsel . . . It will be a direct membership body."[4]

The meeting was held at the Fort Shelby Hotel in Detroit, a National Association was formed, Articles of Association were written for submission to the Churches, officers were elected, an executive secretary was employed, and a national office was established. The history of the National Association is not within the scope of this book. Announcement of the Detroit meeting, formation of the Association by about 100 Churches, and establishment of a secretariat spurred the Mediators into action.

The annual meeting of the Massachusetts Convention of Congregational Ministers, held in Boston, on May 2, 1955 heard and discussed the summary and suggestions of President Frederick W. Whittaker of Bangor Theological School as reported in Chapter Nine.

The Mediators, led by Rev. Frederick M. Meek, inserted display advertisements in *Advance* and *Christian Century*. The theme of these inserts was "Let us reason together and pray together in order to act together." Mr. Meek was just recovering from months of enforced silence due to a severe throat ailment. He arranged by letter for a reporter from *The Christian Science Monitor* to interview me in Hartford with the result that a very well written, balanced account of the CC/ER Merger issues appeared in the *Monitor*. But even as prominent a minister as Dr. Meek found it hard to secure accurate information on the proceedings of the various committees established at the Oct. 14, 1954 meeting of the CC Executive Committee.

Information Lacking

June 21, 1955 the Rev. Frederick M. Meek wrote to me.[5]

"Rev. Henry David Gray, Ph.D.
Oneonta Congregational Church
South Pasadena, California

"Dear Henry:

"I am wondering what information you may have about the present status of the merger situation. The strange thing is that here in Boston I find myself virtually isolated from any contact with the situation whatsoever, and apparently completely shut off from all sources of information. No one discusses the matter with me, and the feeling in favor of the merger is strong here in the old Commonwealth because of Bert Coe's personal influence.

"I should be grateful if you would talk into your dictating machine for a little while about the situation, so that I could have at least some orientation.

"I have had some word that our advertisements are producing some effect. A good many people are reading them and some questions are being asked.

"Would there be any point in a letter being sent out to the churches as a whole indicating the action of the First Church in Columbus, Ohio, the action of Plymouth Church in Minneapolis, (I could not arouse any interest on the part of Howard Conn in my Polity Report project) the attitudes of churches like your own, First Pomona, Old South, Wendell Fifield's church and so on? If it were evident that a sufficient number of these churches had reservations and at least wanted to see the constitution, it might have some effect on the thinking of wavering churches.

"I presume that by now you have seen a copy of Whittaker's address which he gave at my invitation here in Boston. Our good friend Bert Coe sat directly in front of Whittaker and took copious notes during the address.

"In answer to a question during the question period Charlie Merrill said that we did not have time to go into the Polity Report,

489

and that was the reason no attention was being paid to it! We are certainly in a bad way if a merger has to be carried through so quickly that an examination of basic congregational polity and of our documents cannot be carried through because 'there is not time enough.'

"I think we are in for difficulties. Certainly it should be possible to obtain, should we be reduced to this said extremity, a legal injunction to prevent the General Council acting on the basis that it is carrying the churches in with it.

"What was the spirit and the thinking at the meeting which you attended a little while ago in connection with the constitution?

"All good wishes.

"Sincerely yours,

"Frederick M. Meek

"P.S.   I am only within the last few days beginning to get back energy which enables me to do things over and above keeping my head above water. But by the time fall comes around I shall be in a position to lend some time and effort to pressing matters.

"F.M.M."

Lack of information was widespread, creating ever increasing inquiries by moderates, such as this July letter.[6]

"Dr. Henry David Gray
1830 Spruce Street
South Pasadena, California

"Dear Henry:

"Is anything happening, looking forward to the next General Council, which will furnish a program of action for the 'moderates' who are gravely concerned over the present trend in merger proceedings?

"As I see the picture, the ardent 'pros' are determined to present the Council with a 'fait accompli.' The 'antis' cry 'ultra vires' and will have no part of it. What about those of us who have been friendly toward the idea of union, but who feel that the present pressure to 'ram it through' does not take account realistically of the present sentiment of the churches, and does not adequately safeguard cherished Congregational principles and practices? Is there any constructive action we can undertake together which will help to prevent further disruption and chaos in our fellowship?

"I for one have not been, and do not care to be identified with the Committee for the Continuation of General Council Christian Churches, nor with the League to Uphold Congregational Principles. But I do feel that the only hope now for our denomination is for the reasonable moderates, like yourself, to have a constructive voice at Omaha which will demand the Congregational Churches be heard, and that their interests and desires be respected, before any union is consummated. Do you feel as I do, that it is a mistake for the Executive Committee and the 'top brass' to surge ahead on the basis of the 1948 vote of the Special Meeting of General Council—ignoring all the court suits, polity studies and heart-searchings that have taken place since in the churches?

"I do not have a program, nor any of the answers, but would welcome any sign that people, like yourself, are thinking together and evolving a strategy. Who is to be the 'voice' of the churches and of the 'moderates' at Omaha?—One of you to whom I am writing? Wendell Fifield? Who? I'd like to get behind that person to encourage him in the task that lies ahead.

"Oregon, where I now serve, has only a few E & R Churches. The Conference will be swept into the Merger, when and if it is consummated. Those of us who have misgivings, however, do not find ourselves in sympathy with the recalcitrant opposition under the Rev. Horace L. Bachelder of Oregon City. If we are to be spared, it will have to come out of what happens at General Council.

"Your reactions and suggestions would be greatly appreciated.

"Sincerely yours,

"Perry"

The Douglass Article

In the September 21, 1955 issue of the CC monthly *Advance* there appeared an *apologia* for the CC/ER merger on an intellectual and mildly theological basis. . . . *for the first and only time*! Its author was the brilliant brains of much merger strategy, the Rev. Truman Douglass, executive vice-president of the Board of Home Missions. The title was taken from Governor Bradford's account of *Plimouth Plantation*, "Great and Honorable Actions (and) Answerable Courages."

Mr. Douglass' eloquent statement adduced seven points. The first four repeated the misinterpretation of John 17, "that they all may be one" in organizational rather than spiritual terms, and argued that "the world" did not take the Churches seriously because they spoke with varied voices. The nub of the first four points is in the following paragraph.[7]

"The world will begin to look toward the church with hope and expectancy when there is visible evidence that the church believes

491

and embodies in its own life the unitive, community-making power of the truth it proclaims.

"In (the CC/ER) union the gospel word of reconciliation which we preach will become real, acquire substantiality and be authenticated by our life."

Douglass' point five is a vigorous claim to pioneering initiative in ecumenicity. The essence of his position is as follows.[8]

"The union will give hope and encouragement to a vast company of Christians outside our two denominations who are similarly desirous of setting forward the cause of union among the people of God.

"It will put new heart in an American Protestantism that at one moment sincerely mourns the unhappiness of its divisions and at the next seems to acknowledge that it is stuck fast in them and sees no likelihood of finding the way to wholeness.

"The plain truth is that the Protestant bodies in this country desperately need a few ecumenical successes. . . . In some quarters there is a dismal sense that American Protestantism is impotent to alter what it repeatedly acknowledges as wrong. . . .

". . . It may be that 'answerable courages' have been wanting because the intended actions were not sufficiently 'great & honorable' in their significance for the Christian future.

"The union to which we are committed will be for American Protestantism the crossing of a divide which it has not previously surmounted and will open a vast new prospect before all denominations. . . .

"As encouragement in the search for unity there is needed a major breakthrough that will carry the whole endeavor beyond the stage of thinking almost entirely in terms of the 'reunion' of traditional ecclesiastical groupings. Our two denominations will have the honor of this accomplishment."

The sixth point is puzzling. It claims that the CC/ER Merger is *not* a *merger*, like that of a business corporation, but is a *union*. Since the position of Mr. Douglass and his associates in their court testimony invariably claimed *corporate rights* to all CC assets for all national bodies, it is a bit disconcerting to square the *merger*, even if it were on a national level, of CC/ER bodies as a *union*. Mr. Douglass' elaboration of point six increases the puzzlement.[9]

"So far as I know, no organization of either denomination—no local church, no board, no corporation, no institution is at this time contemplating merger with anyone. We are looking forward to union. If mergers ever take place, they will be by-products of this union. A union is not, like a merger, mathematical or mechanical; it is organic—an activity of living, remembering, purposing communities of persons. . . .

"We hold that it is important not only for us to demonstrate the possibility of union among Protestants but also to commend this kind of union—commodious, democratic, rejoicing in the rich variety of life and experience in the Christian fellowship—a union in which in very truth we have combined 'indestructible union of the whole with indestructible life in the parts.'"

In the September 1955 *Advance* article by Mr. Douglass the final point returns to the standard ecumenical *will of God* argument. But Douglass assays to prove that organizational unification *is* the New Testament goal. His is a closely reasoned, intellectually honest, drastic reapprisal of the theological meaning of "the Church."[10]

"*The supreme gift of union is none other than that which is always and everywhere the sovereign good of the church. It is the clearer apprehension in faith and the fuller expession in fact and action of the true nature of this fellowship—the meaning of what must in the end be the one life of this one covenant people, brought into existence by the act of the one God, the gracious giver; sustained, governed and renewed by the presence of the one Christ, the redeemer; led in its pilgrimage by the one Spirit, the guide, the comforter, the revealer.*

"The church is to be this people, not merely in the inward conviction of its members but in such outward and visible form that it shall be a witness—that men may see it for what it is in God's intent—and 'that the world may believe.'

"For this the 'spirit of unity' is not enough. There are those who assert that the petition of Jesus for the oneness of his followers has nothing to do with the visible and objective union of separated churches. But the commission given to Christians that they be one people is not dependent on this or any other individual proof-text of Scripture; it comes from the living gospel which Scripture enshrines and communicates.

"It is, in fact, because church union has to do with the gospel that the 'great & honourable actions' taken in its behalf are often accompanied by 'great difficulties.' They involve a fresh encounter with the gospel and the gospel is generally disturbing before it is comforting. It is no sign of weakness or confusion that in recent years we of the Congregational Christian churches have been probing deeply into the meaning of our denominational life, the nature of our church-manship and the character of our mission as a family of churches. It is the kind of drastic self-appraisal in the light of the gospel which we believe every denomination will be obliged sooner or later to undertake. Our great concern should be to make certain that it shall culminate fruitfully and creatively.

. . .

"Out of this testing of the church by the gospel comes the conviction that the oneness to which Christians are called is actual, visible, substantial, not merely 'spiritual.' In fact it was in paganism, with which the gospel was in early conflict, that all things were spiritualized. To separate the spiritual from the corporeal was to 'think like pagans.'

. . .

"Christianity is not spiritualism and the claim upon Christians to live in unity is not to be spiritualized into thin air. Every description and symbol of it in the New Testament is such as to make clear the objective and corporate meaning of this oneness. We are to live together as 'brethren' in the real life of a family. There is to be 'one fold,' 'one flock' under one shepherd. The Christian fellowship is a 'body' or a 'building'—'all the members fitly framed together.'

"In all the New Testament's infinite variety of form and symbol, the meaning is the same. The church is not an idea or ideal, insubstantial and immaterial. It is a community, a movement in history, a common life to be proclaimed, experienced and shared. It is called to be one people who not only know their oneness among themselves but also are known for what they are, 'that the world may believe.'

. . .

"For a church or a family of churches there is only one relevant question: whether it will respond to a present leading of the spirit and answer the here and now summons of its Lord. . . .

"Two Protestant bodies in the United States cannot by their union make visible their unity within that church. And that is all that God requries of us for now. . . .

"Are the meanings and hopes implicit in this union sufficiently commanding to call forth from us the requisite 'great & honourable actions' and the 'answerable courages'?"

The Douglass article was hailed by proponents of the CC/ER Merger as the gospel for our times. It was viewed as grandiose eloquence and even "doubletalk" by CC/ER opponents. The Mediators welcomed the article as a solid contribution to sensible thinking about some of the basic issues.

494

An invitation to address the mid October, 1955 meeting of the Twin Cities Association in Minneapolis stimuated my thinking and led to a reply to Rev. Truman Douglass entitled "Central Convictions . . . Daring Deeds" expressing the plea of the Mediators for reason and religion. The manuscript of that address was written under intense pressure. October 16 I concluded a nearly 14-year ministry at Oneonta Congregational Church in South Pasadena. In September and October weddings, baptisms, new members and planning two "Church Years," one for Oneonta, one for South Congregational Church in Hartford restricted severely the time available for preparation of the Twin Cities Address. Further, Rev. Howard Conn cautioned me, "Many ministers in the area are strong supporters of the Merger. You will have a good hearing, but don't expect a warm welcome." Pressure of time and awareness of, at best, a lukewarm audience may well have shaped the words. We stopped overnight Monday October 17, in Denver and I wrote and revised at white heat. The long "puddle-jumper" flight on Tuesday 18, Denver to Minneapolis was low and bumpy, so I gave up writing and centered down on content. The final revisions were made in Minneapolis.

Twenty-seven years later, the Twin Cities address continues to be a reasonable presentation of the position of the Mediators.

The great issues at stake in the proposed union of the Congregational Christian Churches with Evangelical and Reformed Church are religious. They concern our central Christian convictions. It is strange that there has been no debate on these issues; and that instead our discussions have dealt chiefly with organization. Dr. Truman Douglass' September article in "Advance," which modified very considerably the earlier position in his other statements, such as the Feb. 4, 1948 "Christian Century," is a first mild attempt to seek theological justification for a type of church union which is primarily a rather late example of the sociological tendency to centralization characteristic of the twentieth century.

Since the aim of all church union is the furtherance of God's purpose for His people, it follows that we should consider the value of any church union in the light of "central convictions" which inspire "daring deeds" for Christ and His Kingdom.

Points of Beginning

It needs to be stated clearly and unequivocally that what we Congregationalists are concerned about is the Church as the fellowship of those who worship the God and Father of our Lord Jesus Christ.

It needs to be said, also, that like our forefathers, we turn to the New Testament for our understanding of *how* we are to further the life and work of Christ's Church.

It needs to be added that we rely upon the guidance of the Holy Spirit in the New Testament sense, as the Spirit of God that was in Christ, now present in those who are Christ-like; yielding "the fruits of the Spirit" which are "love, joy, peace, good temper, kindliness, generosity, fidelity, gentleness, and self-control."

It needs to be proclaimed that our Christian Hope, for this world or for the next, is *not* in belonging to any organization at all—church or otherwise—but is in faithfulness to God who, in Christ, has promised that those who believe in Him shall experience a new life here and now so glorious in character that we can begin to live, and can continue to live a life that is eternal.

These points of beginning bring us directly to the central convictions of our Churches, and the daring deeds into which these convictions should lead us.

God and Man

The first central conviction to be faced in the proposed union of the Christian Congregational Churches and the Evangelical and Reformed Church concerns the Christian concept of God and of man's relationsip to God.

We believe in the God and Father of Our Lord Jesus Christ.

This means that a moderator of the General Council who assures a court that the Council may unite at will with a Jewish synagogue is talking foolishly, on the basis of a thin legal misinterpretation of a basic Christian fact. We *can* unite with any person or group of persons who have in them the same mind and spirit of God which is made known to us in Christ— and with *no others*. Our Christian dedication is more fundamental than our legal rights.

The centrality of allegiance to God "in Christ" means that the one-ness of the Church of Christ is *not* institutional or organizational. The oneness of Christ's Church is the shared spirit of Christ. "Wherever the Spirit of Christ is *there* is the Church." Dr. Douglass characterizes spiritual unity as "thin air." But Jesus himself said "Worship the Father in spirit," and the New Testament bears ample witness to the reality of the Spirit. The plain fact seems to be that many people are no longer willing to accept the teaching of Jesus concerning spiritual one-ness. They no longer *believe* that the best way to "stay together" is to be *drawn together* by a common allegiance to a common Lord. They *say* that the one-ness of the Church must be outward and visible; but *in fact* the only one-ness

496

worth having is one-ness in Christ. Any and all outward *forms of union* are empty shells unless and until there is a consecrated heart; unless and until there is a "unity of the spirit in the bonds of peace." So long as we remain committed to the conviction that we are related to the God and Father of our Lord Jesus Christ, our *one-ness is spiritual*; it will of necessity, be one-ness "in Christ." If it is not, no amount of organizational unification will either create or sustain real one-ness.

Christ's Church

The second central conviction concerns the question, "What is Christ's Church?" "What is the measure of its power and what is its task?"

The Church is the fellowship of those who follow Christ, seeking to do His will in at least three ways: (1) through ever richer experiences of worship; (2) through enlarging experiences of personal growth; (3) through the proclamation of the Gospel "into all the world." Just to state this Congregational concept of the Church is to declare that with us churchmanship and discipleship are identical. We believe that the Church is the fellowship of believers committed to Christ. This view has roots in the New Testament. There are just two meanings of "Church" in the New Testament. The word is used 105 times; 86 of these clearly refer to the local Church, and 18 refer to the universal company of believers in all ages and places. Not one refers to any denomination or to any body comparable to the united Protestant or Roman Catholic, or Eastern Orthodox Churches.

The vitality and power of the Church of Christ is to be measured by the worth of the worship, work, and witness of His followers. When the people of Christ are living their faith daily, when the worship of the Churches is sincere, when the ministry of the Churches is the eager dedication of men and women to the service of their Master, when the extension of Christ's Kingdom is gladly accepted as a privilege of discipleship, when the life of contemporary society is permeated by Christ-like standards in human relationships—when these things are true, then "the vast company of Christians outside our two denominations," for whom Dr. Douglass pleads, will be given *real hope* and *real encouragement*, for then our Churches will be going forward in the power of the Spirit of God in Christ, and not the weakness of ecclesiastical machinery.

Both the New Testament and Christian history testify to the truth that the work and witness of the Church of Christ depends upon Christian commitment rather than ecclesiastical unification. When Kenneth Scott Latourette wrote his monumental *"History of the Expansion of Christianity"* two full volumes, were devoted to

497

"The Great Century." That Century was the nineteenth in which the Gospel spread more rapidly than in many other centuries combined. In that century the London Missionary Society, The American Board, the American Missionary Society, the Y.M.C.A., and uncounted other Christian enterprises arose. The record of their work and witness makes us feel humble and unworthy. Now, mark you, this very same century saw the rise of many denominations. It was not an era of ecclesiasticism; it was a time of evangelism; it was a day when central convictions bore fruit in daring deeds.

If what we seek is a fresh endowment of the Spirit and new power for Christian witness, as Dr. Douglass suggests, then, what we most need is *new consecration* and *not added centralization*. Suppose we contrast the daring deeds of the nineteenth century Congregationalists with the record of our Churches in the decades just passed, in which there has been a drift away from a voluntary fellowship of Churches toward central organization with wide powers affecting the life and work of the Churches. Has centralization strengthened and extended the work of the free Congregational Churches? The answer is NO.

The answer NO needs to be stated in specific terms. In the decades just passed the Congregational Christian Churches have rarely had the vitality to produce even one-half the leaders needed for ministerial and missionary service. In the 1930-1940 decade we had ebbed as low as to have only 50% of our ministers, 40% of our foreign missionaries, and 33% of our home missionaries coming from our own Churches. Our former leadership in publication of religious literature has almost disappeared. The number of our Churches, missionaries, and local ministers has decreased in about the same ratio as the number of our national and conference officials has increased. Where we have retained a vigorous Christian witness, it has been as much or more due to the work of individuals and local Churches, as it has been to the work of wider bodies. And the lost opportunities in expanding America are, in very large measure, the result of our inner confusion and our tendency to leave to the conference or national bodies tasks which we ought to have done as individuals, and Churches, or as Associations of Churches.

There is a lesson in the fact that the Park Street Church in Boston and the Lake Avenue Church in Pasadena, both of which do their work spontaneously, have *expanded* their direct and independent work at home, have founded new missions abroad, and are contributing to such causes much more in dedicated leaders and in dollars than any other Churches of our order.

In short, the claim that ecumenicity is the modern equivalent of evangelism is false. Yet, if you study the "answerable courages"

498

said to emanate from ecumenicity you will see that union of denominations is being heralded *as if it were the Gospel for our day.*

The fact seems to be that desire for union is a counsel of despair, a desire to trust size of organization to lend influence and create prestige; when the only real power of the Church of Christ (as our forefathers, and presently the Quakers amply demonstrate) lies in utter dependence on God. It staggers the imagination to think of what God might have wrought through our Churches in the past decade if we had given to the worship, work and witness of Christ all the time, energy and money which we have devoted to the organizational type of ecumenicity, a form which has no rootage in the gospel and which in our own fellowship, has brought division and distress instead of refreshment and power.

The Church and its Lord

A third central conviction concerns the question: How is Christ's Church related to its Lord?

"Modern Congregationalism is the legitimate outcome of a consistent application to Church polity of the principles of the Reformation;" these are the opening words of Williston Walker's authoritative collection of *"The Creeds and Platforms of Congregationalism."*

What is here stressed is the fact that *we believe Christ is the sole Head of the Church.* Congregationalists reject *all* authority save that of the Word of God, the living, personal Word known in the teachings, the work, and the life of Jesus Christ.

Jesus himself said, "No man can have two masters." This is as true of Churches as it is of individual Christians. *If* we profess to believe in "the triumph of an idea, a movement, a spirit, a style of life," then we ought *to trust that idea and trust that spirit.* The Pilgrim tradition is a present adventure which the great, learned, and lovable Albert Peel, foremost Congregational historian of the century, described as "the most courageous and most scriptural venture of faith possible to Christian communities, for it takes the promises of God seriously and, depriving believers of all external support or control, casts them wholly upon the Spirit. The depths to which it can fall corresponds to the heights to which it aspires. It gives full, practical expession to the undeniably scriptural view that the Church is the people, and holds it better to run all risks than to sacrifice the principles which makes the congregation of believers responsible for the quality of their own spiritual life." Dr. Peel accurately reflects the influence of a lifetime spent with the diaries of Congregational leaders, the findings of Councils, and the study of the Scriptures.

"One is your Master, and you are all brothers"—that One is the God and Father of our Lord Jesus Christ. We *can own* NO other Master, not even our own Association, Conference or General Council.

If our Churches are true to the principle of the sole Headship of Christ, then locally there will be no test of membership except the sincere desire of the applicant to accept the covenant or statement of purpose which testifies to the allegiance of a people to God. No "dues" or "assessments" are in order in such a fellowship. When sole allegiance is to Christ, then *responsibility* means being true, at all costs, to the voice of God in Christ as the Spirit speaks to conscience. We are false to our convictions when we fail to fulfill our Christian duties, NOT because we have broken an ecclesiastical rule, BUT because we have been untrue to our Lord Himself. We are false to our convictions when we do whatever we are told to do by ecclesiastical organizations unless we believe that we are called of God so to act.

To put Dr. Douglass' words in fitting context, the "spiritual toughness, organizational resiliency, (and) capacity for adaptation" which makes our Congregational way "relevant and serviceable to the deepest needs of men and to the supreme tasks of the Church in the present," or in any other generation, is rooted in the conviction that Christ, and Christ alone is Head of the Church.

It is for this religious reason that we hold each local Church to be a true Church in its own right, "Where Christ is—there is the Church."

To accept the *sole* Headship of Christ in His Church means to deny any *other* Headship.

When Baptism is set down as a condition of Church membership, as it is in the "Basis of Union," it symbolizes a fundamental change in our concept of Church membership as a covenant relationship of Christian people in a community for worship, work, and witness. Allegiance shifts from Christ as Head to Sacrament or Creed as Head. Nearly all our members are baptized but when a conscientious person from the Society of Friends wishes to join one of our Churches his sincerity is likely to be accepted in place of baptism.

When the relationships of pastor to people are supposed to conform to a "standard" procedure, then allegiance shifts from Christ as Head to the Placement Bureau as Head.

When program planning in Churches, in the youth, women's and men's fellowships, and in the associations of Churches is the acceptance of what has been planned at a "Mid-Winter Meeting" at which the Churches as such are not even represented, then allegiance shifts from Christ as Head to "the Board" as Head.

500

When theological schools, orphanages, and other institutions are under the control of a Synod, so that curricula, faculty, administration, student body, licenture, and ordination are subject to central oversight, then allegiance shifts from Christ as Head to Synod as Head.

When *any* constitution or other fundamental documents subject to amendment by *any* body outside the local fellowship is accepted by a Church, then that local Church has shifted its responsible relation from Christ as Head to the constitutional body as Head. Once *any* such constitution is accepted by a local Church, power is thereby given *over* the local Church.

A precise illustration may make clear this transfer *from* allegiance to God in Christ *to* allegiance to a body outside the local Church. A few years ago a nationally known Presbyterian leader was minister of a nearby Church. One day he called to ask if I would perform a marriage between two members of his Church, one a divorced man whose wife had gone to live with other men. The session of his church and the ministers of that Church unanimously agreed that the young man and his bride-to-be were just the sincere earnest kind of a couple whose marriage should be performed in the Church. The Presbytery disagreed. The wedding took place in a Congregational Church where God's love for his children took precedence over the powers of any ecclesiastical body.

The sole Headship of Christ is the true source of stamina for our Congregational Way. Our strength is in Him. The true resiliency of our Churches is their ministry to the needs of men and communities as Christ speaks to their consciences. The true relevance of our Churches to the needs of our age is our eagerness to adventure in ever new ways of service in response to the inner leading of the Holy Spirit.

There is lack of nerve and courage in the weak assumption that we cannot trust the Headship of Christ in a super-organized age. "Why are you afraid, have you still no faith?"—no faith, after the witness of all the ages since Jesus was here among men, a witness often made most clearly (as in St. Francis, St. Teresa, Grenfell, or Frank Laubach) when it most defies organizational circumscription. Why are we running for cover under the roof of ecclesiasticism in the face of the example of the ages in an over-organized Church of Rome or Roman Empire, and in the light of the principle of decentralization already evident in contemporary society? The yen for "one big organization" is the sociological backwash of a secular practice which has had its day and is presently being modified in business and government to resemble more closely the kind of voluntary fellowship which is the native climate of our free Churches.

As one who has been interested in history from childhood days, and as one who has had some relation to the polity developments in our Churches in recent years, I have been rather surprised at the attempt which has been made to re-write Congregational history in order to provide a setting for mid-twentieth-century ideas of "one big Church." The names of Jacob, Barrow, Cotton, and sometimes Owen are often quoted. And the name of a modern English Congregationalist, who holds no position of importance among English Congregationalists, Jenkins, is added for good measure. Much is said in some circles about the years of "Consociation" in Connecticut. It is almost incredible that careful scholars should allow themselves to speak of a somewhat Puritan thread as if it were the whole cloth of Congregationalism.

There are *many* threads in our history. But if you wish to follow the central pattern then turn to the great Councils, to the records of the Churches themselves, and to the balanced scholarship of men like Williston Walker. Or, if you wish, turn to the carefully documented study made by the Committee on Polity and Unity which gives you the *actual documentary position of our Churches* as of the year 1954. When careful scholarship is applied, either to our history or to our contemporary documents, there is no doubt but that we have been, and that we say we still are, a voluntary fellowship of free Churches, organized "to do and to promote the work of these Churches."

The Headship of Christ has been and is a conviction so central to our Congregational way that a change in this allegiance represents a fundamental change from our historic witness and from our present way of working.

One, Holy, Catholic, Apostolic

A fourth central conviction is raised by this question: What do we mean when we say that Christ's Church is one, holy, catholic, and apostolic.

These are ancient words, but they are words with which we shall have to become familiar in the years of great Church power into which the American Churches have now entered.

One-ness means a common allegiance to Our Lord as we have already pointed out.

Holiness means that the Church of Christ is righteous and just, like its Lord. Its "great and honorable actions" are *honorable*.

When a local Church mistreats its organist, its minister, or its caretaker it is not *holy*. When a minister fails to keep his high trust as an ambassador of Christ, both he and the Church he serves are *not holy.* When "officials" introduce favortism or power-politics into Church affairs the Church is not holy.

So, too, in the wider relations of our Churches, fairness, honesty, integrity, and honor are the marks of righteousness. When printed assurance is given that a ballot will be taken and that 75% approval will be required to consummate a union, that assurance should be scrupulously kept. No "tenth inning" should be played because only 63% have scored "yes." No "umpire's decision" to make 72.8% acceptable instead of 75% should be made. No funds given by all should be used to bring even 27% "into line." No "Committee on Information" should function as a bureau of propaganda for one viewpoint. Honesty is honesty. "Honorable actions" must be *honorable.* The Church local *and* the wider representatives of the Churches must be *holy,* if their "answerable courage" is to be other than a hollow pretense.

The Church is to be *catholic.* In the New Testament the word Church is used 18 times to refer to the Church universal. Catholic means universal, not only world-wide today, but in all previous times, and for all ages to come. The Church universal is far more than the small sized ecumenical goal of those who seem hungry for organizational power and for the false safety of size.

To be catholic or universal the Church needs to include in its fellowship all who choose to follow Christ. This is the Church as a universal fellowship—not as a world-wide organization. The Church Universal is not made up of many denominations, Protestant, Roman Catholic, or Eastern Orthodox; it is created by God and depends solely upon the Spirit of Christ which upholds, strengthens, and guides the representatives of the Churches in Council.

Church Councils are a means of fellowship. Their powers are moral and declarative. It is deplorable that most of our recent Council meetings have been "business sessions" devoted to everything but the great Christian convictions and their relevance to the needs of our time. The Churches in Council have all the powers that inhere in the intrinsic worth of their actions and recommendations. They have no power over the Church. *They are not the Church Catholic. They are not even a Church at all in the New Testament* sense of the word "Church." If we choose to speak of the General Council as a "Church" we should honestly state that we are changing the New Testament usage, the usage of our Churches for hundreds of years; and that we are re-defining the word "Church" to mean a body of people elected for two years by other bodies, and passing out of existence every two years.

Apostolic. The word means that we share the same faith as did the apostles. It can be, and is, twisted to mean that chosen men, ordained by some set procedure, are *the* representatives of Christ among men. And there has been a tendency toward this view among us in recent years. Early Congregationalists ordained their ministers in *a* Church to serve *that* Church, and only that Church. This is still practiced among us, though very rarely. We ordain most men now by the invitation of the Church, through the Association of Churches, and such ordinations are customarily accepted by other Associations. An Association could, however, refuse to accept the credentials offered, and once in a long time this actually occurs.

Our ministers are men and women, called of God in their own consciences, and called by a group of Christian followers to minister to them. The apostolic power of a Congregational minister is his Christ-like character—as much or as little of it as he possesses.

These are the ways in which the Church of Christ is *one, holy catholic, and apostolic.*

Summary

To sum up, let me say again that Church union is essentially related to our central convictions—

(1) Our belief in God, the Father of our Lord Jesus Christ
(2) Our belief that the Church is Christ's Church, and its task is his work
(3) Our belief that the Church can hold no other allegiance than that which it has to Jesus Christ as Lord.
(4) Our belief that the Church must be one in Christ, holy in character, catholic in inclusive witness, and apostolic in its faith.

Reasons for Union

In conclusion, then, let us ask, For what reasons would anyone want union with the Evangelical and Reformed Church, or with any other fellowship or denomination?

Much of the discussion of the issue before us, on all sides, has seemed to move on the plane of expediency, and has been related to overhead costs, size, publication ventures, and lobby influence on government, on the one side; and to institutional responsibilities and safe guarding of funds on the other. These issues are important, but they are not as important as the ends they are designed to serve. What do we want the union for?

Surely there could be only one basic reason for any church union, namely to help men and women to become Christians, or to become better Christians.

Church order is important not to provide an efficient organization, or dignified assemblies, or even adequate sustentation and church extension funds, but in order to bear witness to the gospel. The criterion by which it is judged should always be the gospel; but the Congregational Christian fellowship is in no condition to act under sure guidance of God's Spirit. Yet, it is only as we are able to follow that Spirit that we shall rise from level of expediency to the level of Christian action. Too often power has gone out of our church Councils because we have sought to settle matters with our own judgment in terms of what seems to us to be the best policy at the moment, rather than to probe the apparent issues to their proper depth and submit them to Christ's judgment. We talk about finding and following the guidance of God's Spirit. Our goal seems to be to "get our own way" rather than to find and follow Christ's way.

Over the months and years of our difference, debate has seemed to center on the issues of procedures which are the expression of principles, rather than on the principles themselves. Some of us have longed for and pleaded for some word which would rise above our selfish fears and cares. There is yet time to face the fundamental issues with wisdom, understanding, and charity. Nothing is ever lost when honest men face their differences and take time to find God's answer to their needs. Conclusions are too often only the point at which we grow weary of thinking.

Surely our unhappy divisions are to be healed, not by search for a lowest common denominator, or by any device of expedience, but rather by universal penitence, by a common understanding of the things we most surely believe and by a more faithful obedience to the Word and Will of God.

In the final analysis all church unions must be spiritual unions. That we all have failed to find the guidance of the Spirit in the proposed Union of the Congregational Christian Churches and the Evangelical and Reformed Church is painfully clear. On every side the fruit of our controversy has been bickering, misunderstanding, impatience, strife, bitterness, and broken personal relationships. But the "fruit of the Spirit is love, joy, peace, good temper, kindliness, generosity, fidelity, gentleness, self-control." Those who belong to Christ have crucified the flesh with its emotions and passions. "As we live by the Spirit let us be guided by the Spirit." So reads the book we all profess to follow. Here is the central conviction which leads to daring deeds for Christ and His Church.[11a]

This address is reasonably representative of the Mediators. Of it Mediator Rev. Howard Conn said, "These things should have been said sooner." Mediator Rev. L. Wendell Fifield's penned response was:[11b]

"Dear Henry:

"I have just read 'Central Convictions—Daring Deeds.' It is excellent, clear, concise and convincing. How in the light of so irenic an analysis, the 'pro-Mergerites' can procede in good conscience I do not understand. Possibly the answer is that it is not in 'good conscience.' From some things I hear clear out here, I gain the impression that they are really beginning to think—some of them. Harry Butman reported to a group of us here about the conference in N.Y. He spoke in the highest terms of your fine, courageous leadership. All the time he was talking I had a sense of inner pride and the voice within kept saying, 'He is my friend.' It is good to know that the point of view which some of us have shared has so able and eloquent a spokesman.

"After much searching of heart I have decided *not* to attend the Omaha convention. I came very near to sacrificing all my future usefulness during the 6 years that I was rather at the center of things. I've just reached the stage where the mention of the word 'Merger' no longer kills my appetite or ruins my sleep, and sends up my blood pressure! I just don't dare get back into that condition again. If I felt that I could really accomplish something at Omaha I would take the risk. But all that I can do, I have done. I no longer have any official position that would give me a chance to make a speech. I'd just be another delegate with a chance possibly to be recognized for 3 minutes in limited debate. I think my ghost in the memories of the past when I did have the platform, etc. will be more effective than my presence lurking around the outskirts of things.

"Furthermore such leadership as I have been able to exercise must be taken by others. I'll be 65 before the Council. My withdrawal from active controversy is inevitable. Better to do it before I blow up or break down under it.

"All of this reverts back to my very deep joy at reading your statement and hearing of your fine leadership. Such 'mantle of leadership' as I have worn seems to me very properly to fall upon you. As a member of the constitutional committee you should have easy platform access. You know the whole subject better than anyone else on either side. And have the gift of clear, concise, conciliatory presentation. I hope and pray that you will assume the leadership of the 'moderate' opposition where I think the hope lies. My mail constantly brings testimony to the fact that many earnest 'pros' are anti Executive Committee. They are outraged by the usurpation of power by the committee, as well as its obtuse attitude toward the whole situation. I believe that a motion to accept the report of the Executive Committee, except for *those parts relative to their merger activities*, would have a fair chance to pass. Of course, such a motion must be attempted, for a routine approval of their minutes would settle the whole matter before it was even discussed. If I can be of any help or give any advice I will be glad to do so. I shall watch the developments at Omaha with prayerful interest and deep concern.

"All goes incredibly well for me here. My work is made to order for my interests and my physical capacities. I love every minute of it. James' health is improving and he has now taken over the extra things I had done to help him for awhile. So I have a normal and not too heavy schedule. My outside lecture program is rapidly approaching saturation. We greatly enjoy our double system of living—our lovely little home—Claremont and our attractive apartment here at the Bryson just 4 blocks from the church.

"I'm glad to receive your bulletin and to hear such splendid reports of your new work.

"Best always,

"Wendell"

Rev. Raymond A. Waser wrote:[11c]

"Dear Henry:

"Your new book on Truman Douglass is the best thing out on the merger. When I remember all the words that have been written to date, I want you to know that it is a very genuine compliment. You got down to the basic issues and, I believe, set them on fire for the first time. More courage and power to you. As for strategy, the only strategy I know of now is to keep the pro-merger group on the defensive. We do that mainly by keeping our banner high.

"I regret this rather long delay in answering your kind letter inviting me to preach at the South Church on June 17. The delay was due to the fact that I tried to work out a schedule. I find now that I must leave the East on the 14th of June to return to California.

"Rockwell Harmon reports great and good news of your ministry in South Church.

"With every blessing to you, Helen and the family,

"Sincerely yours,

"Raymond A. Waser"

The fact that many merger opponents and proponents welcomed "Central Convictions—Daring Deeds" illustrates wide support for the viewpoint of the Mediators. Merger opponent, Rev. Malcolm K. Burton wrote,[12] "I am much impressed with your Minneapolis presentation." And superintendent James English remarked, "That needed to be said after Truman's article was printed."

507

During 1955 a carefully planned series of actions was taken under the supervision of the CC Executive Committee. These actions included speech-making, publications, planning committees for the 1956 General Council at Omaha, consultations between educational, national, international and other bodies of CC/ER, and "strategy" sessions. The heretofore mentioned Ex. Com. CC October 1954 Minutes outlined these procedures in advance.

An opposing series of actions and reactions included "protective resolutions," voted by over a hundred Churches to assure continued possession of all local assets. Associations, Conferences, and ministers' meetings passed resolutions. The viewpoints expressed are typified by the following two resolutions.

Illinois Central West Association

"WHEREAS, the first meeting of the General Synod of the United Church of Christ will not take place until June 1957 and

"WHEREAS a committee will be appointed at that meeting to draw up a constitution for the United Church and present it at its next Biennial Meeting in 1959, and

"WHEREAS in the meantime the 'BASIS OF UNION' will only be a temporary guide for the United Church and cannot be made binding upon local autonomous churches, autonomous associations, and autonomous conferences without definite action on their part, and

"WHEREAS, we cherish our CONGREGATIONAL and CHRISTIAN hereitage (sic) and freedoms and hope they may be preserved and become an integral part of the United Church, and

"WHEREAS we desire to save our fellowship from disintegration and yet not surrender those cherished freedoms,

"WE THEREFORE sincerely urge that final judgement on the merger be delayed so long as we prudently may and at least until a constitution for the UNITED CHURCH is offered to the churches.

"THEREFORE BE IT RESOLVED:

"I.— That the Central West Association of Congregational and Christian Churches recommends to its local constituent churches that they take no definitive action on the merger until after the constitution of the United Church has been submitted to them.

"II.—That the Central West Association of Congregational and Christian Churches shall take no definitive action regarding the Merger until after said constitution has been presented to it.

"III.—That we recommend that our sister associations in the Illinois Conference give this resolution considerate thought at their respective association meetings and that if deemed wise by them that they take similar action.

"IV.—That we recommend that the Illinois Conference of Congregational and Christian Churches take similar action in its annual meeting in 1956."

New York City Congregational Church Association, Inc.[14]

"WHEREAS, on May 13, 1948, this Association, namely the NEW YORK CITY CONGREGATIONAL CHURCH ASSOCIATION, INC., approved the proposed union with the Evangelical and Reformed Church on the terms set forth in the *Basis of Union* by a vote of 144 to 91, and this Association is planning to enter the union upon its consummation; and

"WHEREAS, it is probable that the General Council will take the necessary steps, in 1956, for the consummation of the said union; and

"WHEREAS, a number of the churches in this Association have, in good faith, raised serious questions over the possible loss of some of their traditional autonomy if they become a part of the union; and

"WHEREAS, under the well recognized form of organization of our denominational fellowship, a church becomes and remains a Congregational Christian church only by virtue of its admission to and continued membership in a local or district Association, and without any possible interference by the General Council or the State Conference, and always possesses the right, at any time, to withdraw from the Association and, thereupon, to cease to be a part of our fellowship; and

"WHEREAS, this power to determine the conditions of a church's admission into, and continued membership in, the Congregational Christian fellowship is peculiarly and solely the function and sphere of the local or district Association and

"WHEREAS, *The Interpretations of the Basis of Union* specifically recognize the autonomy of the local or district Associations in their own spheres; and

"WHEREAS, *The Interpretations of the Basis of Union, impliedly, if not expressly, recognize the continued existence of the local churches as "churches" and not as mere "congregations" of a single national church; and*

"WHEREAS, *The Basis of Union* contains recommendations for the adoption of certain procedures as normal or standard, which are regarded by many of our churches as unacceptable or uncongregational, but such procedures are merely recommended and may or may not be put into effect by local or district Associations, as they deem proper; and

"WHEREAS, this Association desires to preserve unbroken the integrity of the roll of churches now in its membership, and intends to exercise its autonomy in its own sphere by giving certain assurances and guarantees to such churches; now it is

"RESOLVED, that this Association guarantees to each of its member-churches, present and future, a continuance of its existing right to withdraw from membership in this Association and thus cease to be a part of the United Church of Christ, retaining the complete, unconditional ownership, control and use of its property, whenever it shall see fit to do so, and regardless of its reason for taking such action; and it is further

"RESOLVED, that, as a condition of any future reorganization of this Association, or consolidation thereof, with any synod, conference, or other group or organization of the United Church of Christ, this Association will require a guarantee of the said right of withdrawal by every church, as hereinbefore set forth; and it is further

"RESOLVED, that, without in any way irrevocably binding its actions for the indefinite future, this Association declares that it has no intention of putting into effect any uncongregational procedure, or of becoming a party thereto; and it is further

"RESOLVED, that, in the light of the foregoing assurances and guarantees this Association sincerely and affectionately hopes and believes that every church will remain a member of this Association; and it is further

"RESOLVED, that copies of these resolutions be forwarded to all the churches which are members of the Association, to the General Council of the Congregational Christian Conference, Inc..."

The efforts of Mediators, Whittaker, Meek, Walton, Bradford, Keith, Webster, Potter, Avery, and others were directed to the meetings of both proponents and opponents of the CC/ER Merger in 1955. The results were not encouraging. Announcements by the Ex. Comm. CC and by the newly formed National Association of Congregational Christian Churches indicated a hardening of positions. By the end of 1955 the Mediators resolved, each independently and then collectively, to seek a meeting with the CC Executive Committee.

January to June 1956 was a period of intense negotiations focused in a post Easter (April) meeting with the CC Executive Committee in New York City, and then in a delegated meeting of leaders in early June in Cleveland. The first of these gatherings was sparked by vigorous support of the Twin Cities Address (Oct. 1955), now circulated in pamphlet form together with an appeal for a hearing, under date January 5, 1956.[15]

The many who responded wrote statements so clear and forceful, and so contrary to false rumors of their positions, that it is important to record them word for word.

The Rev. Frederick L. Fagley, for many years Associate Secretary of the General Council, one of our prime historians, and the most loved person in the CC denomination, wrote[16]

"Dear Henry:

"Thank you ever so much for sending me this copy of your fine address. A copy came to me some time ago and I read it with great interest.

"You have spoken brave and true words and I hope the booklet will have wide circulation.

"This whole movement has brought to us all many moments of sorrow. The object has never been made clear to our people and many things have been done and many words spoken that do not harmonize with our ideas of brotherhood and Christian teachings.

"What good can come from all of it no one knows. But surely we have a task of reconciliation before us.

"With high regard and all good wishes

"Fred Fagley"

Mr. D. Howard Doane, CC Ex. Com. member from St. Louis succinctly stated the idea that the CC/ER Merger proponents were captives "of a great idea," as elucidated in Chapter Six.[17]

"I feel that your letter has expressed a very effective and well considered viewpoint. The one thing that I have made clear, as I have expressed myself from time to time before the Executive Committee, is that I am dedicated to some kind of a plan that will minimize the break in our denomination which now seems inevitable as a result of the proposed merger program. I have made it clear on many occasions that only a minimum effort is being devoted to finding ways and means for areas of agreement, compromise and a give-and-take attitude that might pull us along together. I am confident that most of the officials of our denomination are determined to go forward with the merger. One of the most unfortunate aspects of current plans seems to be a feeling that some of our churches are expendable and they must be charged off as one of the costs for the consummation of a great idea."

President Frederick W. Whittaker wrote[18]

"Although I am much in favor of the formation of a 'middle party' in the present merger controversy I am not free to take action on this matter during the month of January. . . . Perhaps we can await developments at the mid-winter meeting and then take some concerted action in February if that seems advisable. I had luncheon with Wally Anderson recently and I feel certain he would be interested in a conciliatory approach to the controversy which is now spreading throughout the denomination.

"I have just read your reply to the editorial which appeared recently in *Advance* magazine. It is very well done and I certainly hope it will be published."

Rev. Frederick Groetsema of Newton Highlands expressed widespread sentiments.[19]

"Dear Henry:

"I have just read your very clear statement in the paper which came today containing the announcement of the new organization of C.C. Chrs. I did not read the 'Advance' artical (sic) simply because I have long since quit reading it, I get mad when I do . . . and there are other reasons too; but your clear, Christian refutation was a gem. Thank you for it.

"At the moment my own church, which voted in favor of the Merger, would not do so again, nor would I, on the grounds that you haven't gained anything for a 'united Church' if you split a group to do so. There are two areas in this whole field of a United Protestantism which need further clarification: one is that we need to provide for types by which I mean, that there are folk who need ritual and symbolism . . . others do not. The second thought is that any real uniting must come from the grass roots, it must be a genuine feeling and desire on the part of the individual Christian . . . in other words until the Spirit of Our Lord is everywhere so evident and so present as to 'move' the individual everywhere, we work at the wrong end of the stick.

"Blessings on your new work.

"Cordially yours,

"Fred"

Letters and conversations prior to the CC general "Mid-Winter Meeting," held January 28-29 at Buck Hill Falls led to the following invitation extended by Rev. Raymond B. Walker.[20]

"Dear Dr. Gray:

"If our anticipations are realized, at the conclusion of our next Executive Committee meeting and joint meeting with the General Council of the Evangelical and Reformed Church (April 3 to 5), we shall be in a position to answer many of the questions which you and other Congregational Christians, officials of the Evangelical and Reformed Church, as well as ourselves, have been asking.

"By unanimous action of the Executive Committee I am instructed to extend to you and three others, also considered representative of churches opposed to or hesitant regarding the proposed Union but who are not affiliated with one of the organized opposition groups, an invitation to spend a day with us. We are also inviting four representatives from The Continuation Committee, The League to Uphold Congregational Principles, and The National Association of Congregational Christian Churches. Others in your category are: Dr. Frederick M. Meek, Dr. Howard J. Conn and Dr. Frederick W. Whittaker. We expect to complete our sessions on April 5th and would like to devote all the next day, Friday, April 6th, to this proposed meeting.

. . .

"We believe that such a conference could be mutually pleasant and productive. It would spend little or no time on the past, but rather center attention on problems before us. We will, to the best of our ability, answer questions regarding the proposed Union which you have already submitted or may wish to submit. We hope that we may have the privilege of asking you questions also.

. . .

"We should like you to be our guest for lunch and dinner on Friday, April 6th. We are proposing that the meeting be held at 287 Fourth Avenue, New York City, commencing at 9:30 a.m., and continuing into the evening if mutually requested.

"Mr. D. Howard Doane would be thoroughly acceptable to us as moderator of the proposed meeting, but we are willing to leave the selection of chairman to the meeting itself. I shall appreciate your comment as to this."

I replied.[21]

"The Rev. Mr. Raymond B. Walker
1126 W. Park Avenue
Portland 5, Oregon

"Dear Mr. Walker:

"Your letter of February 28th is welcomed. It comes at a time when all of us are even more deeply concerned than we have been about the future of our fellowship.

"I shall be happy to accept your invitation.

"I would be less than frank if I did not say that the invitation sent to me is rather awkward in its timing. Ordinarily one would assume that it would be desirable to have a meeting of minds in our Congregational fellowship *before* the Executive Committee met again with the leaders of the Evangical (sic) and Reformed Church. I cannot but wonder if the meeting is called simply for the purpose of pacification, in which instance it can have little conceivable value.

"As one who had considerable part in both the Claremont resolution and in reaffirmation of that resolution at New Haven, I am inclined to feel that what we need is a representation of all points of view in a meeting with the E and R leaders.

"As you know, the superficial issues do not seem to me important and the name calling seems to me completely out of order. The fundamental principles involved are important. These should be on the agenda. Here I will list a few of them for that agenda. (1) Is there assurance from both the Executive Committee of our fellowship and the General Council of the E and R Church that a constitution will be written forthwith, that it will be for the general synod alone, and that it will be submitted to the churches for their approval? (2) Is there assurance from both sides that control will not be exercised over seminary, ordination, licensure, etc.? (This is now provided for in the present E and R constitution) (3) Is there assurance that no 'standard' procedures will be set up which can be interpreted as authoritative, such as the basis of union requirement of baptism for all church members, and the basis of union provision for a standard procedure with regard to ministerial placement? (4) Is there assurance from both sides that the general synod is to be aware of its relations to the churches and is to recognize the representative control which the churches possess over it through their members who are delegates to it?

"There are many other issues, but those would be a good starting point.

"May I, however, urge you to make provisions for a meeting of the kind of group outlined in your letter with the E and R leaders *prior* to the meeting of the Executive Committee with them.

"I would like to see a free church union. I believe we can get such a union. I am irrevocably opposed to any authoritative kind of union.

"Very sincerely yours,

"Henry David Gray"

President Frederick W. Whittaker's answer read:[22]

"I am very happy to accept your invitation and shall plan to be present. Perhaps I should point out, however, that I am neither opposed to nor hesitant about the proposed union itself. I have been and am an ardent proponent of the United Church of Christ if it can be consummated without schism among the Congregational Christian Churches. In my opinion, some of the procedures adopted by the Executive Committee of the General Council in seeking to effect the union have unnecessarily divided our denomination; therefore, I have opposed some of the procedures rather than the union itself. It is my hope that the proposed meeting in New York will help all interested parties to find a way toward union without schism.

"The 'ground rules' which you outline in your letter seem quite appropriate to me, and I am also in accord with your suggestion that Mr. D. Howard Doane be named chairman of the meeting. I do have misgivings at one important point: it seems to me that the meeting which you have planned would be much more effective if it were held prior to rather than after the joint meeting of the Executive Committee with the General Council of the Evangelical and Reformed Church. If the Executive Committee is to make use of the information and opinions to be presented by those who have been invited to attend the meeting on April 6th, I should think that the Executive Committee would like to have these data before it meets with the representatives of the Evangelical and Reformed Church. . . . I am taking the liberty of listing very briefly in this letter my own beliefs concerning proper procedures which should be adopted if the projected United Church of Christ is to become a reality without schism in our own denomination. . . .

"1. Before the proposed United Church of Christ or any other form of church union is consummated, the Executive Committee should sponsor a study among our churches of the report of the Committee on Free Church Polity and Unity.

"2. The Basis of Union and Interpretations should be modified, amended or re-written so as to provide clear answers to the many questions which have been asked during the past eight years concerning details of the proposed merger; preferably, a constitution for the United Church of Christ should be prepared and voted upon before the union is consummated.

"3. The General Council, the boards, agencies, and individual local churches should have an opportunity to vote again on the question of union before any definite steps are taken to establish the United Church of Christ; the situation today is much different from the situation which prevailed when the first vote was taken.

"Please be assured that I look forward with pleasure to the privilege of meeting with you and your colleagues in New York next month."

The CC Executive Committee acceded to our request.[23]

"I note your suggestion that we change the day of the conference between the Executive Committee and representatives of The League to Uphold Congregational Principles, The Committee for the Continuation of Congregational Christian Churches, The National Association of Congregational Christian Churches and Drs. Meek, Conn, Whittaker and Gray. I have the consent of the Executive Committee to this change. We shall therefore, hold the meeting in New York City on Wednesday, April 4th, 9:30 a.m., the day BEFORE the next joint meeting of the Executive Committee and the General Council of the Evangelical and Reformed Church rather than the day following this meeting as originally announced. I trust that the change at this late date will not cause you inconvenience.

. . .

"We are earnestly trying to find a way for fair counsel with people of variant points of view. Studies and conferences with our Evangelical and Reformed brethern are evolving a program for the implementation of the Basis of Union With the Interpretations, both as to principles and schedule, which we propose to recommend to the General Council at its forthcoming meeting. As I implied in my previous letter, this we shall be glad to discuss with you on April 4th."

Rev. Howard Conn called a meeting with Meek, Whittaker and Gray in New York 9:30 p.m. Easter evening.[24] Meantime on March 22, 1956 the Hartford Association of Congregational Ministers arrived at a proposed course of action designed to lead to CC/ER union without splitting the CC fellowship. This proposal was sent to the CC Executive Committee[25] prior to the consultation, beginning Wednesday, April 4, 1956 in New York City.

The April '56 Consultation

I cannot stress too strongly the representative character of the April '56 Consultation. Here, at last, forty-three persons representing all viewpoints on the CC/ER merger were assembled.

Those present included:

General Council Officers: Rev. Albert B. Coe, Moderator; Rev. Fred S. Buschmeyer, Acting Minister and Secretary; Rev. Charles S. Sowder, Secretary; Mr. John T. Beach, Treasurer.

Executive Committee Members: Rev. Wallace W. Anderson, Mr. Ashby E. Bladen, Mrs. Arthur T. Calvert, Mrs. Lyman T.

Crossman, Mr. D. Howard Doane, Rev. Jesse H. Dollar, Mrs. Judson E. Fiebiger, Mr. Roscoe Graves, Pres. Charles S. Johnson, Mrs. Claude C. Kennedy, Rev. Carl Martenson, Mr. William Peterson, Mr. Nathaniel A. Talmage, Rev. Jerry W. Trexler, Rev. John C. Walker, Rev. Raymond B. Walker, and Mrs. Edgar A. Bark, President of the Women's Fellowship.

Employed Officials: Rev. Truman Douglass, Rev. Ray Gibbons, Rev. Everett Parker, Rev. Fred Hoskins.

Laymen's League: Messers Bailey, Harlow, Heaney, Slocum and Greenawalt.

Continuation Committee: Rev. Marion Bradshaw, Rev. Malcolm K. Burton, Rev. Harry R. Butman, Rev. H. D. Davies, Rev. Russell Clinchy.

Mediators: Rev. Howard Conn, Rev. H. D. Gray, Rev. Frederick Meek, Pres. Frederick Whittaker.

There were in addition Superintendent W. Wilder Towle of Missouri and I think Rev. Philip G. Scott, Superintendent Cornelius E. Clark, and Mr. Russell Graham. (I did not record full names of Scott, Clark and Graham.) No minutes were recorded. (My notes and those of Rev. Harry R. Butman are before me as I write.)

A Cosmetic Consultation

In reviewing 12 pages of single-spaced typed notes and 9 3x5 note cards, what stands out is the cosmetic character of the consultation. This was clear when Rev. Raymond B. Walker distributed a 5-page memorandum on behalf of the CC Executive Committee. Here are the salient paragraphs of the Statement.[26]

"The Executive Committee of the General Council has called this conference in the hope of achieving greater mutuality of understanding and agreement concerning the proposed union as set forth in the Basis of Union published in January of 1947, as approved by the General Council in June of 1948 with the addition of the Interpretations. . . .

"We may or we may not be in complete agreement about details of past procedures or in interpretation of these procedures. It is our understanding however that we are mutually interested, in this conference, in arriving at a mutual understanding of what is now proposed, and to achieve a maximum agreement among ourselves as members of the Congregational Christian family fellowship concerning what these proposed procedures may mean for the future life and work of the various parts of our fellowship. It is to achieve as

517

much mutuality of understanding and agreement in these areas as possible that we are met today.

"In setting forth the procedures as proposed, the Executive Committee does not speak as merely so many individuals expressing their personal preferences. The proposed procedures have been evolved by a committee seeking to act responsibly under the charter and votes passed on to the Executive Committee by the General Council properly convened in regular session. It is to a similarly convened meeting of the General Council that the Executive Committee must report its conclusions or recommendations concerning the matter placed in its hands by the General Council. In the discharging of these responsibilities, the Executive Committee has been and is eager to receive, and give full consideration to, every constructive suggestion that any member of the fellowship has to offer. This is the sincere and friendly intent of this conference.

. . .

"Here is a statement of our proposed procedure.

. . .

"1.   That the General Council, speaking for itself, authorize the calling of the first meeting of the General Synod of the United Church of Christ.
"2.   That the General Council join with the General Synod of the Evangelical and Reformed Church in naming the city of Cleveland as the place, and the dates June 25 to 27, 1957 as the time for the holding of the first meeting of the General Synod of the United Church of Christ.
"3.   That the General Council elect 355 members of the 1956 General Council with authorization to represent it in the first meeting of the General Synod of the United Church of Christ.

". . (A)t the time of the Union for administrative purposes, such as the subsequent elections of delegates to the General Synod, every member of either communion will be assumed to be a member of the United Church of Christ.

. . .

"An *assumption* is not necessarily a fact. Absence of authority is inherent in the word. Only subsequent events can establish its verity. The Basis of Union with Interpretations is an interim instrument—to serve until a constitution is drafted and ratified. During that time we assume all members of both communions are and will continue to be members of the United Church of Christ.

". . . (A)ny member, any church, any association can by its own action deny the assumption. . . .

"... (T)he new joint organizational forms of the present Boards, Council, Commissions, Conferences, Synods and Associations will be determined freely and voluntarily by the several parties themselves, as provided in the Basis of Union with Interpretation.

. . .

"When the new organizational forms have been thus appropriately decided upon, and the Constitution as previously described has been written, ratified by the churches voting, and adopted by the General Synod, nothing in said constitution shall in any way abridge the freedoms and rights now (1956) enjoyed by the churches or congregations such as the calling of miniters, (sic) the writing of a statement of faith or covenant, owning and controlling its own properties, determining its own name, and ordering its own worship.

"As far as Congregational Christian churches and the church members are concerned, their relationship with the new General Synod, the reorganized Conferences and Associations, and the reorganized Boards, Councils and Commissions of the larger fellowship (The United Church of Christ) will be the same free and voluntary relationship which now exists between these churches and their members on the one hand and our present fellowship organizations on the other hand.

"At the time the Constitution of the United Church of Christ is properly adopted, any Congregational Christian Churches (or ministers) desiring more time in which to decide what their relationship with the larger fellowship will be, or desiring not to be identified with this larger fellowship (the identity of which is to be found in the present Associations, or Conferences when acting as Associations). They shall have continuing Association standing with undiminished access to the services of the Congregational Christian fellowship. Such churches or ministers may join in the larger fellowship of the associations or conferences participating within the United Church of Christ at their own pleasure and in the same manner that such relationships are now (1956) established between churches and Congregational Christian Associations or Conferences."

Unanswered Challenges

During the morning of the April 4, 1956 consultation there was a series of challenges to the *Statement* and the assumptions upon which it was based. I protested omission of the 1952 and 1954 General Council actions, "which supercede previous votes. *Every* Council has the authority to rescind or modify decisions of earlier Councils. The *only* nearly unanimous action of the Council is flouted in favor of a 1948 action favored by less than 2/3 of the

Churches." Bladen and Trexler took me to task, but Anderson, Kennedy, Butman, Meek and Conn joined with Gray.

Rev. Howard Conn then introduced the crucial issue, asking, "How can you *assume* everybody is a member of the United Church of Christ?" This provoked vigorous debate in which Buschmeyer asserted the "assumption is just for the purpose of ascertaining a basis for franchise," that is, a basis for the selection of delegates to the proposed Uniting Synod in 1957. Bradshaw immediately challenged, "Is the Executive Committee prepared to sacrifice basic principle for the sake of getting a proper portion of delegates?" Mrs. Fiebiger replied, "The CC Churches are members of the CC fellowship; of couse they will be members of the UCC." To which Conn replied, "You can't *assume* a thing for anybody." Clinchy added rather tartly, "You people seem to forget that 2595 Churches, 48% of the total either voted *no* or *didn't vote*. You *can't* assume them to be in." Buschmeyer was a bit up-tight, "Don't *you* forget that we have the majority, and the majority *rule*."

Gray pressed for an answer to Conn's question, "Are the CC Executive Committee and the ER General Council willing to say that no Church joins the United Church except by its own vote?" Trexler countered, "No! But, they don't have to come in if they don't want to. They can vote to stay out." Gray replied, "You say two different things in one sentence. No CC Church can be required to vote by the CC Executive Committee. *Every* CC Church *is* and *will remain* a CC Church without any vote whatsoever. YOU are the ones who propose to change your denomination." This precipitated somewhat heated exchanges among Butman, Trexler, Gray, Walker, Heaney, Buschmeyer, Beach, Bradshaw, and Graves. The denouement was Whittaker's question, "Will the 1957 union be a union of those present, or, of the Churches?" to which Bladen replied, "The only members of the UCC will be the 600 or 700 members of the Uniting Synod. I *hope* there will be more."

Conn brought the tense discussion to a terminus, "Since the UCC is a great and holy cause, why don't you just start a Church of 600 or 700? What are you afraid of that makes you avoid another ballot?" Walker invited any member of the Executive Committee to answer Conn. Nobody did.

In Search of Substance

Mr. Doane presided at two o'clock and suggested we adopt "a positive approach." Rev. Albert B. Coe delivered what amounted to a speech, the substance of which was, "It is remarkable that as many Churches voted as did. There are many 'lonely little Churches' that want a parent in the United Church. As I travel as moderator I do not see the dark picture painted by some. Great tides are running for the union. Young people, laymen and women are all for it. Everything I see points to union as a great good. Why can we not find a way to fulfill our destiny with happiness and peace?"

Revs. Howard Conn and H. D. Davies responded simultaneously. Davies said, "Let the Churches vote." Conn commented, "A plebiscite is the way to peace *if* both sides can frame the question to be asked!"

Butman, Bladen and Trexler got into an argument concerning *who* would be *in* the UCC at the Uniting Synod. Bladen stuck with the delegates, "There will be 710 identifiable members." Trexler disagreed, "I don't want to say Mr. Bladen is wrong, but the whole Omaha General Council will have joined, all 1500 members of it."

Walker, Mrs. Fiebiger, Bradshaw, Greenawalt, Gray, Dollar, Buschmeyer, Calvert, Burton disputed the question, "When will the union take place legally."

Before the mid-afternoon recess, Rev. Raymond B. Walker attempted a summary of the CC Executive Committee view. (1) The United Church of Christ is established when the Uniting Synod votes to unite. (2) "As an entity with members and Churches, the UCC emerges only when the constitution is written." (3) "CC Churches are members of Associations *and* of the UCC. There will be dual standing. As long as there are Churches which don't want to belong to the UCC the Association remains as a home for them. The critical point is when an Association joins the UCC, . . . the historic continuity is unbroken."

My reply to Walker's statement was, "You have added *your new* set of Interpretations to the Basis of Union. On page 15 the BU states, 'the Basis of Union' will be 'the interim constitution.' Are you, or are you not, going to follow the BU? Bluntly, let's recognize (1) We *know* what Congregationalism is; the Polity and Unity Report is the norm. (2) We *know* what E/R polity is, the ER Constitution says what it is. (3) The bottom line problem is the obscure, contradictory, debatable nature of the Basis of Union, Interpretations and all the assumptions you keep adding. If this merger is 'made in heaven' it should be possible to say *what it is* and *when it takes place*, who is *in*, and who is *out* in plain language."

Mr. Doane recessed the meeting.

Rev. Everett C. Parker asked approval of a press release from the day's meetings. Anderson objected to the inclusion of the *size* of the new denomination, "That's something we don't know." The innocuous release which was approved is before me. Its vacuity speaks volumes.

At Mr. Doane's suggestion we again attempted the positive approach. I suggested that a joint CC/ER constitutional committee be appointed, with representatives of differing viewpoints, that the committee prepare a constitution, and that the constitution be submitted to the Churches for vote.

Mrs. Fiebiger objected strongly. "The Basis of Union is our document . . . and we intended to live by it." she asserted. Mr. Trexler concurred, "We want to unite *now*. We've waited long enough for you people to catch up. We know it will take years to make real what we do at the Uniting Synod. But that doesn't bother us."

Messers Bailey and Burton rebutted Trexler saying, "Let the E & R join in writing a constitution which can be ratified before the 1957 Synod meets."

The Rev. Truman Douglass entered the room during the discussion, just after the recess. He commented, "Most of us believe the Churches are ready to unite. Once the Uniting Synod is held the 710 members will be joined by thousands upon thousands. Your people will simply be left out." Mr. Gibbons expanded, "You all must be aware that a new commission of *any* kind would imperil the time schedule for union," to which Mr. Anderson replied, "If we can get closer to each other as a Congregational family, a postponement beyond 1957 would be a trivial price to pay."

"If we make these proposals to the E & R we'll jeopardize the merger." countered Mr. Gibbons. Mr. Bladen continued, "*Any* change could only be made after consultation with the E/R. This Executive Committee must honor our obligations to the ER. We can give no commitment . . ." I think it was Mr. Scott who interrupted. After the interruption Mr. Bladen said abruptly, "I have nothing to say for the record."

I returned to the appointment of a committee on the constitution. There was disagreement as to the value thereof. My notes are not clear at this point. There were too many persons present and the time available was much too short to permit thorough discussion. Rev. Truman Douglass saw that, and was one of those who suggested a follow-up, small, informal meeting.

In retrospect the proponents of the CC/ER merger entered the meeting NOT to reconsider the Basis of Union and Interpretations BUT to satisfy critics that the Mediators had been heard. Similarly, the CC/ER Merger opponents were interested ONLY in stopping the merger.

As early as the 1950 Cleveland General Council (or before) the stance of the proponents had been stated—and maintained. Rev. Albert J. Penner of Broadway Tabernacle Church put the point clearly:[27]

"In your letter of May 4, you expressed the desire that some of us could sit down to discuss the merger situation, in the hope that a sensible solution might be found for our present impasse. . . . As I see it, Pros and Antis can only get together if both are willing to compromise, but to compromise within an overall understanding that we want this union to occur. . . . I do not say that any compromise is possible or any conversation is helpful with those who are uncompromisingly against the whole union idea and who are only out to kill it. . . . If in what I have here stated you feel any possible area of agreement or fruitful conversation, Let me know."

Appeal to the Churches

Rev. Wallace W. Anderson, member of the Executive Committee, informed me of the Committee's April 5, 1956 action.[28]

"I do want to express my appreciation for all that you contributed to the meeting that we had in New York last Wednesday. The keenness of your reasoning and the graciousness of your Christian spirit meant a great deal to me. I was so hopeful that it might be one of several meetings. I would like to sit down and talk with you some time about the next step. The next day we did share with the General Council of the E & R church every one of the suggestions presented to us. Needless to say, nothing happened! Some of the suggestions gave them the impression that we were back in October '54. I personally felt that in a very real sense we had gone back there as a result of our meeting the day before. After meeting with them for several hours, they met as a group and we met as a group. When we met as a group a motion was made that we re-affirm the actions of October '54 and each succeeding step and proceed to go ahead adhering strictly to the Basis of Union with Interpretations. This was the same thing that we voted on back in October '54 and as a result, Mr. Doane and Mrs. Kennedy and I registered negative votes. I also added that in the light of this action I felt that I could not conscientiously serve as a member of the Planning Committee. So the next day I resigned from that Committee. I would only have served until June '56 anyway when my term expires as a member of the Executive Committee. However, I felt that by resigning I might be freer to speak some of my sincere convictions at Omaha this June.

"I feel so strongly that the purpose and intent of the Claremont Resolution was disregarded by action of our Executive Committee. I also agree with you that only through such a resolution could we have hoped to preserve unity within our fellowship. I am distressed and heartsick as I look ahead to the future.

"I don't think anything can be done about some of these matters, but I just wanted to share with you some of the things that are on my heart as I returned from those sessions last week in New York."

On April 19 I addressed the Hartford Congregational Ministers as follows:[29]

"Throughout the decade during which the proposed union has been under discussion, I have held it to be my duty to do everything possible to draw together those of differing viewpoints in our fellowship. I will continue to work for reconciliation and I will make every possible effort to avert a break in our fellowship. This has been and is my policy because I believe in brotherliness, kindliness, and cooperation.

"I have not been and am not in favor of the proposed 'Basis of Union.' It is an ambiguous instrument. It proposes an over-all national constitution, and a 'standard procedure' for church-pastor relations which calls for over-head approval. It changes membership status from the local church to a denominational body. It proposes a highly centralized General Synod with tremendous power over foreign missions, home missions, education, publication, the ministry and ministerial relief, evangelism, stewardship, social action, and institutional benevolence. It places in the constitution of the General Synod matters like ministerial standing, which are presently reserved to the Association only. It establishes a judicial procedure with the right of appeal to successively more distant bodies. It gives no indication whatsoever as to *how* General Synod members are to be elected (after the first meeting) or whether they are (or are not) to be responsible to the churches. For all these reasons the 'Basis of Union' is not an adequate or proper document for the uniting of the Congregational Christian Churches and the Evangelical and Reformed Church.

"I am opposed to the almost fantastic procedure by which the proposed union has been prompted. First, we were assured in print, in the same pamphlet in which the 'Basis' was contained, that a 75% vote would be required. Approximately 64% of the churches voted 'yes.' 1165 churches voted 'no.' Instead of accepting the vote, the time for voting was extended and much money was spent in an effort to reach 75%. The 75% was never reached. Instead, by an amazing parlimentary move, the Cleveland, 1949 special meeting voted to deem 72.8% acceptable. At this point, Union was held up by court action. Then, the 1950 Cleveland Council appointed a 21 member (representing all points of view) 'Committee on Polity and Unity.' That committee reported at New Haven in 1954 and had its careful, thoroughly documented study attacked by General Council lawyers *before the chairman had even presented the report to the Council.* Meantime, the 1952 Claremont Council instructed the Executive Committee to move toward a constitution for the proposed General Synod alone, with the co-operation of representatives of all points of view, and in consultation with the Polity and Unity Committee. The New Haven Council of 1954 *re-affirmed* the Claremont resolution. Then, in October 1954, hardly *four months* after that re-affirmation, the Executive Committee repudiated the Claremont resolution and declared itself free to enter the union exactly as set forth in the Basis of Union, with the Interpretations. Next, on April 4, 1956, the Executive Committee, meeting at long last with 16 representatives of points of view other than its own, agreed to give consideration to the preparation of a constitution, along the lines indicated in the Claremont Resolution. But on April 5, 1956, the Committee (with 3 negative votes) laid aside all but the Basis of Union with Interpretations, because the Evangelical and Reformed General Council (ex. com.) refused to consider any other alternative. The procedures followed in this matter have not been, and are not now, the sort of honorable, godly, gracious and patient procedures which should characterize negotiations looking toward church union.

"Church union is a spiritual matter. I believe in all church cooperation or church union which helps men to be better Christians, or which helps them to be better witnesses for Christ. I will gladly cooperate with others to these ends. I do not believe there is any gain whatsoever in church union which is just bigness, enlarged 'lobby' power or the like. The power of Christ is moral and spiritual power. I do not believe in centralized bureaucracy, either in a country or in a church. Christ is the *sole* Head of the Church. Under Christ conscience outweighs ecclesiastical decrees. This is 'the liberty wherewith Christ has set us free.' Any form of church union which trades in that liberty for the so-called securities of size is a step back toward medievalism.

"Therefore, I shall continue to do all I can to uphold, increase, and make effective the work and witness of the free church. I shall strive unceasingly to work for a union that shall give not a *less* but a *more* effective free church witness. If, in the end, my work shall prove to be in vain, and there shall be insistence upon an over-all national constitution with provision for disciplinary reference and other associated bureaucratic powers, then, whether I stand alone or with many, I shall hold fast to the liberty of Christ as the free pastor of a free people."

Rev. William A. Keith edited this statement, added to it, and counselled "send your document to Church Trustees. If it is so addressed it may get past ministers who would throw it in the waste basket."[30] Students at Yale Divinity School expressed their fear of official displeasure should they pass along to Church members pro-Congregational writings. So did ministers serving many small Churches who felt themselves dependent on the State Superintendent for recommendation to a larger Church, for committee membership in the Conference, and for leadership at youth conferences, Church workshops and the like.

Many Associations acted on the CC/ER Merger at the spring 1956 meeting. In Hartford Congregational ministers met at Asylam Hill Congregational Church on March 22 and March 29. From those meetings the Revs. Keith M. Jones and Lawrence M. Upton, both ardent proponents of the CC/ER merger sent to the General Council Executive Committee Chairman a plea for the preservation of the Congregational fellowship.[31]

"To: Dr. Raymond Walker, Chairman of the Executive Committee

"Dear Dr. Walker,

"You were gracious to discuss some of our concerns over the telephone last Thursday. At your invitation, we are writing you and the Executive Committee, delineating some of the issues which we think merit your attention.

"Our Hartford Association of Ministers has discussed these matters, and we have been involved in these conversations; but this message should be considered simply as an open letter from two ministers who have consistently favored the Union and whose bias in its favor may have, until recently, obscured the relevance of certain arguments against the Union made by people who honestly favor an effective unity with the E & R Church.

"In the first place, it would seem to us highly important that the Executive Committee recommend to the General Council at its Omaha meeting a resolution so carefully formulated that only those who are 'categorically' opposed to Union would have to vote negatively on it. In other words, while it is probably impossible to secure the consent and cooperation of everyone in the proposed

Union, we feel that the Executive Committee should make every reasonable effort to formulate a resolution which will not alienate churches or persons who genuinely desire this Union.

"We feel that most of the confusion and growing uncertainty centers in the issue of the nature and inclusiveness of the proposed Constitution. We seem to find in our area, at least, that more and more questions are asked about this problem. There is almost no question regarding the Constitution for the General Synod. We also find that there is almost uniformly a desire for an effective Union with the E & R church and there is none among us whose hopes for the Union are limited to 'top-level tinkering' with ecclesiastical machinery. However, more and more, questions of this kind are being asked:

"Is it appropriate to our polity and practice to have a Constitution for the whole church, regulatory for the General Synod (which it must be) and even though it only acknowledges and describes the inherent freedoms, duties and relationships of the local churches and other church bodies?

"We fully acknowledge that the intent of a Constitution for the United Church is not to regulate nor define the local churches and smaller church bodies; but in our culture and language the word 'Constitution' tends to connote a government document. There are those who are insisting that even the acknowledgment of the rights of the local churches and smaller bodies in an over-all constitution tends to imply that the rights derive from the Constitution. We believe that this objection merits further study.

"Whether one agrees or not with this position, we would like to raise this question:

"Is it possible for the United Church to acknowledge and describe the rights of the local churches and smaller bodies in a document other than the constitution without violating the Basis of Union and Interpretations or demand its amendment?

"If this were possible, we believe that much of the confusion and opposition would be 'by-passed' for those who basically desire Union. The validity of this belief is supported, we feel, by the following considerations:

"1/ The resolutions at Claremont and New Haven, which received the highest proportion of affirmative votes of any resolutions on the Union, contemplated the formation of a Constitution limited to the General Synod. We understand why (on the basis of timing) the preparation of the Constitution before the Union is consummated would be out of harmony with the Basis of Union and Interpretations; and we understand the possible E & R opposition to a Union which, they fear, is only for the head, and not for the hand and heart, but we are not convinced that the *Constitution must* acknowledge and describe the rights and relationships of the churches and smaller bodies.

"2/ We believe that part of the importance of this Union is that it can provide the framework for further unity with other Christian bodies. We like the category 'umbrella' here. We think that organic union at the level of the General Synod and non-constitutional manual of relationships of churches and smaller bodies would provide a structure or 'umbrella' under which other church groups could unite without having either to accept a Congregational or Presbyterial pattern, however modified, or to change their beliefs and practices. They could retain their local and regional relationships and still unite at the national level. This is no plea for loose confederation, but for a vital union with all bodies which can cooperate organically at the national level while retaining their cherished relationships at the local and regional level.

"3/ Perhaps a non-constitutional manual of relationships might be more appealing to the E & R people too, for in this document many more features of the presbyterial polity could be retained than the Congregational Christian Churches would likely accept in a Constitution.

"4/ We believe that a manual of relationships would be more flexible, useful and dynamic if it were not in the Constitution in which more formal and elaborate steps for amendment must be followed. There would be less inclination to worry over 'jots and tittles' in a non-constitutional document.

"5/ In the minds of many, the Basis of Union and Interpretations contemplates a polity which varies in a greater or lesser degree from our present Congregational Christian polity. Most of us would say that, however minute, some change of polity is to come in the United Church, particularly if the Constitution includes non-regulatory features pertaining to the local churches and smaller bodies. If this is true, then if the General Council votes to consummate the Union as planned, it thereby declares itself qualified to change the polity of the Congregational Christian Churches.

"But is the General Council qualified thus to change our polity? In our understanding, this has not been claimed by the General Council.

"One of the ways to sharpen this point is to ask: If we want to change our polity, is the General Council the instrument for doing it? (We leave out any consideration of church union for the moment). We believe that since the General Council is not a body strictly representative of the churches, its members coming from units of membership in an association, conference, institutions, etc., therefore, it is not the proper body to change the polity of the Congregational Christian Churches without authority from the churches or regional bodies. There is no question that the General Council can regulate itself as it pleases, but the only way for us properly to change our polity (formally) is to have the votes of the churches and other bodies or their representatives on specific changes.

"This line of argument leads us to the tentative conclusion that to make the acknowledgement and description of relationships a part of the Constitution is to change the polity in a manner which the General Council cannot properly vote. That the General Council can vote to unite with the General Synod and regulate its own affairs is assumed, but we increasingly feel that this is all it can properly do in a Constitution.

"We would urge that the wisdom of the Executive Committee be applied to this search for a resolution to be submitted to the Omaha meeting which would call for a constitutional regulation of the General Synod and non-constitutional description of the rights, duties and relationships of the churches and smaller bodies.

"Very sincerely yours,

"Keith M. Jones, Minister	Lawrence M. Upton, Director
The Church of Christ in	Christian Activities Council
Wethersfield	Hartford"

Among other documents submitted to the CC Executive Committee or to the Moderator were "A Resolution Aimed at Safeguarding the Integrity of Ecclesiastical Procedures . . . and at Protecting the Public Reputation of the Ministerial Calling."[32] This was signed by 36 students enrolled in 5 Theological Schools, Andver-Newton, Bangor, Chicago, Oberlin and Yankton (31 at Bangor alone). The gist of the student concern is in the following excerpts of the Resolution.[33]

"WHEREAS Vote 18 of the 1942 General Council actually authorized its Commission on Interchurch Relations and Christian Unity 'to explore the possibilities of organic union between the Evangelical and Reformed Church and the *General Council of* Congregational Christian Churches,' but did NOT authorize that commission or any other commission or committee to explore the possibilities of organic union 'between the Evangelical and Reformed Church and the Congregational Christian Churches,' and

"WHEREAS the Executive Committee, in its *Letter Missive* of October 18, 1954, page 2, omitted the words *General Council* of from its quotation of said Vote 18 . . .

"WHEREAS the same Executive Committee, through its Information Committee, sent to the Congregational Christian Churches a similarly altered quotation of Vote G28 of the 1952 General Council, substituting 'a constitution for the United Church' for a constitution 'for the General Synod of the United fellowship,' thereby misrepresenting it . . .

"WHEREAS these altered quotations of the General Council's own votes were offered by the Executive Committee in support of action attributed by it to the 'guidance of the Holy Spirit,' thereby raising ethical and theological questions of the utmost gravity, and

. . . .

"WHEREAS the *Letter Missive* of October 18, 1954, wherein the incorrect quotation of Vote 18, 1942 was transmitted to the churches, bore the signatures of the Chairman of the Executive Committee, and of its Secretary, and

. . .

"BE IT HEREBY RESOLVED . . . that we call upon Dr. Albert Buckner Coe, the highest official of our fellowship of Congregational Christian Churches, to ascertain and to make known to the churches who is responsible for the Executive Committee's sending to the churches these misquotations whereby Vote 18 of the 1942 Council and Vote G28 of the 1952 Council were distorted into agreement with the expressed wishes and votes of the Evangelical and Reformed Church, and we authorize the publication of this Resolution with our signatures attached."

Typical of Conference and Association Resolutions are the following sentiments: From Illinois[34] "it is still our hope and prayer that the Congregational Christian fellowship may not be broken." From Hampshire Assoc. MA[35] "regardless of any action at Omaha, this Association recognizes the right of every Church to withhold its approval of the proposed United Church until its constitution has been drafted and studied."

From Central-West Association, IL[36] "the Central-West Association by and through its member churches, on its behalf and on behalf of its member churches will not be presumed to be a member of the 'United Church of Christ,' unless or until said member churches of this Association and this Association itself, shall have

530

taken definitive action themselves or its self to become members of said 'United Church of Christ'. . ."

Resolutions, proposed resolutions, and letters proclaimed the positions cited to members of the CC Executive Committee, to State Conference officers, and to delegates to the Omaha General Council. One of the major hurdles of effective conference and General Council meetings was election of persons available to attend. Officers of a national state and cognate bodies attended 'expenses paid;' so did delegates who held certain official positions. Wealthy Churches could choose to finance delegates chosen from their membership, but, in actual practice it was impossible to elect delegates solely on merit, since few could take a vacation "at will," or, finance attendance with ease. By necessity Conference Superintendents and Association nominating committees had to suggest "persons who might be able to attend." In years when CC/ER Merger and/or Social Action matters were being decided those with strong opinions (for or against!) *sought* to be elected as delegates. This meant that most state and national meetings were not as representative as a Church Meeting, and it is hard to imagine circumstances which would cause them to be fully representative of the membership of the Churches. The wisdom of the Congregational Way is expressed when *the Churches* are present by delegates in the wider bodies, and when all actions of the wider bodies are limited to "advice, counsel and such common action as is requested by the Churches."

At the Moderator's Invitation

The Rev. Albert B. Coe was concerned at the prospect of presiding over a racous General Council Meeting. At his invitation[37] a group of 18 assembled at Hotel Cleveland in Cleveland Wednesday June 6th. Revs. Meek, Keith, Whittaker, Spinka and Gray came from the Mediators; Revs. Coe, Penner, Douglass, Alden, Babcock, and Messers Bladen, Neff, Schellenger, Smith and Thayer were merger proponents. Mr. D. Howard Doane was a CC/ER merger opponent, President James F. Findlay of Drury College favored the merger but had questions about possible General Synod control over theological schools.

Mr. Coe's call to the meeting had four names in addition to his own.[38] His proposed agenda letter carried three names besides his own.[39] The agenda stated the meeting's purpose.[40]

"Congregational Christian people who cherish common purposes in connection with the union . . . share a desire to contribute to visible unity . . . are devoted to our heritage of freedom and to the encouragement of a kind of fellowship which makes ample room for diversity of belief and practice . . . in disagreement not over ultimate objectives or basic principles but over questions of ways and means . . . meeting for the purpose of finding closer understanding."

The exchange at this meeting was vigorous and to the point, as is indicated in my 30 note cards, my 8-page typed record, and Superintendent Everett A. Babcock's 2-page typed record.

Positions Pesented

The morning session on June 6th began with a clear and forceful presentation by the Rev. Truman Douglass who concluded "The Basis of Union must be accepted. This is fundamental."[41] Attorney Thayer followed with a 10-15 minute explication of the view that the provisions of the BU represented "no change for our Churches."[42] Mr. Bladen modified the protagonist position somewhat, "There may be some parts of the BU which are a bit confusing, but it is well within the acceptable range. There is nothing to worry about."[43]

The Douglass/Thayer/Bladen positions were immediately challenged by Mr. Doane who pressed the idea that, "If we cannot agree on the BU *as is*, the only right thing to do is go back to the E/R Church." This brought a storm of protest.

Revs. Meek, Whittaker, Keith and Gray cited the Oberlin 1948 parlimentary device used to extend voting, the Cleveland 1949 acceptance of 72.8%, as if it were 75%, the "charter" of the Claremont '52 Resolution. President Whittaker stated, "The Report of the Committee on Free Church Polity and Unity merited serious consideration, which it was not accorded. That Report has in it wise procedures for achieving church union which should be followed."

At this point many spoke simultaneously so that I recorded phrases. One of these sparked rather violent objection. I had described the contrast between Congregational polity and the structure proposed by the BU with Interpretations as "vertical versus horizontal." Mr. Douglass objected, "Do you descend to using epithets?" I replied, "Let's not hide behind shibboleths. Congregational is essentially *horizontal*, emphasizing the quality of Churches, the democratic character of decision making, and the total absence of wider bodies with power over the Churches. It is no secret that the BU & I provides an essentially *vertical* structure with the national body at the top and all other bodies, including the Churches, related to *it*."

Revs. Keith and Meek added their support, and Mr. Douglass finally said, "There is some truth in the distinction of *vertical* and *horizontal*, but I still contend these are not proper words to - describe polities. They have an element of charicature in them."[44]

Mr. Doane made a plea for *some* agreement, "These issues concerning the BU&I will be settled here today or there is no hope. What is the price of union in our own fellowship? Is it worth division. You (proponents of CC/ER Merger) have told us the opposition was insignificant. Now you have called us together and those who are here are *not* insignificant. Have you changed your viewpoint? What *are* you willing to change?"[45]

Mr. Bladen answered, "The E/R feel that *they* have given up, little by little, things they consider essential. They want a union from top to bottom and that's what we have promised."[46] As the morning session ended Mr. Douglass stated, "One important reason for the retention of the BU is to facilitate the merging of the Boards. Certainly, according to its charter, the Board of Home Missions could become the agent of *any* body. All that needs to be done to operate jointly is to keep the funds properly segregated."[47] Mr. Bladen added, "After all, the BU provides for union of the General Synod of the E/R Church and the General Council of the CC Churches. All other bodies, including the Board of Home Missions, unite by their own votes."[48]

An Afternoon of Argument

Rev. Truman Douglass led off in the afternoon, speaking to Mr. Doane "Do you recognize certain *levels* of adjustment in the process of uniting? For example, do you accept the right of the CC Executive Committee and the ER General Council to agree on certain points within the framework of the Basis of Union?"[49]

Mr. Doane's reply caught the chairman by surprise. He moved, "That the CC Executive Committee express its willingness to sit down with the opposition to consider a revision of the Basis of Union (BU)."[50]

Before the motion could be seconded Mr. Douglass demanded, "*What* revisions do you intend to discuss?"[51] Mr. Doane countered, "Come open-handed, wanting to know from the opposition what *the opposition* is willing to give and take."[52] To which Mr. Douglass replied, "Everything's open that can be done unilaterally."[53]

It had appeared to Meek, Keith, Whittaker and Gray that the morning yielded no progress, and so proposals were discussed at lunch. When Mr. Douglass used the words, "Everything's open" (even though restricted) the time seemed right to introduce a six-point program aimed at union of the CC/ER without splitting the CC Churches.

I stated the need for an alternative to the proponent/opponent impasse over the CC/ER merger, "Let us begin by agreeing that all of us welcome the united witness of as many Churches as will unite. *If* we agree that united witness is good then the question is *how* to unite. Here is a six-fold program:

"1. Write a constitution in accord with the Claremont Resolution, *now*.

"2. *Divide* into two documents those elements that are *regulatory* and those that are *descriptive*.

"3. Review the relationships between Churches, Associations and Conferences.

"4. Have all viewpoints represented on all committees that have to do with the union.

"5. Define and put into proper context the powerful 'Mid-Winter Meeting.'

"6. Add a preamble to the proposed statement of faith defining the statement as a testimony and not a test."[54]

The Rev. Frederick M. Meek asked, "Is that a motion?" I said, "Yes." He responded, "I second the motion. The time is ripe for a fresh approach to church union, especially the presently proposed union of the CC/ER which has brought too much anguish to be properly designated as 'of God.' I hope we can here devise an acceptable answer to the all too obvious spiritual needs of our Churches and of these perilous times in which we live."[55]

Mr. Thayer reported, "A group of CC/ER lawyers has considered the writing of a constitution. They doubt that one could be adopted before the United Church was formed."[56]

Rev. William A. Keith immediately retorted, "Does that mean a constitution cannot be *written*, or does it mean one cannot be *adopted*? I'm in favor of writing a constitution, now. It's the only way to get straightened out what authority is claimed by the Council—or *any* body beyond the Church. Right now, I'd say the Michigan Conference is almost 40% in favor of the *middle*. If we can head off a vote to unite *now* at Omaha, we can buy time to write a constitution."[57]

President James F. Findlay supported Mr. Keith, "People in the pews are confused. The right climate for consideration of the

534

issues must be created so they can vote intelligently. I'm in favor of any move that will release adequate information to the people."[58]

Mr. P. J. Neff of First Congregational Church, St. Louis now spoke at some length. "If you take a vote to push this CC/ER merger through at Omaha, you'll drive our Church into the opposition camp. As President Findlay says, the big problem is lack of understanding without which there can be no confidence. I favor Mr. Doane's suggestion of talking frankly to the opposition NOW."[59]

Rev. Truman Douglass faced Mr. Neff, "Why *don't* you have confidence? We're honorable people."[60] The immediate response was an outpouring by every single one of the Mediators. The substance of their rather blunt remarks was in the words of Rev. William A. Keith, "When reasonable people read what the CC Executive Committee did on October 13, 1954 they question the whole merger procedure—*the whole of it.*"[61]

That caused the matter of confidence to be dropped.

We returned to what I shall call "the 2-document" concept, that there should be written a regulatory constitution for the national-level bodies *only* and, alongside it, there should be a memorandum of agreement on everything else. Mr. Bladen asserted, "It's my considered opinion that the E/R Church would not agree to two different documents."[62] Then followed an extended statement by Mr. Bladen, whose main points were as follows. "The E/R cannot bear any more delay. Further, we must consider the effect of our union on all other churches. We cannot act for ourselves. We do not live in a vacuum. This union has an importance far beyond us. If we fail we will have done Protestantism a great disservice. What's needed is confidence. I would have confidence that a constitution *and* a manual of procedure would be prepared after union has taken place."[63]

Rev. Albert Penner put the position of the CC/ER Merger proponents forthrightly, "I have no objection to the writing of a constitution. But if the price of it is that the union will be killed, then I cannot vote for it. In my view there is nothing we can do at Omaha which touches, changes, or amends the Basis of Union with Interpretations. This group may *request* that a constitutional commission be appointed at Omaha, *asking* that the Evangelical and Reformed Church do the same. It would even be proper to request such a constitutional commission to 'spell out' the regulatory and the descriptive features of the constitution. But that must not delay the merger."[64]

To all this the Rev. Frederick M. Meek spoke with quiet intensity. "Procedural flaws have plagued this proposed CC/ER union from the beginning. Among these none has been more unfortunate than the tyranny of time. The way of the Congregational Churches has been hammered out on the anvil of time. Great decisions have not been made to meet unimportant deadlines. It should be our aim to transcend the tyranny of time that we may serve the purposes of eternity."[65]

The reflective mood of the meeting was shattered by Rev. Truman Douglass, "It is of the utmost importance that we stand by the Basis of Union. This is our charter under which we carry out the interim plan for coordinating the work of the Boards. I would remind you again that it is the Basis of Union which enables us to plan a united program without mingling funds or merging organizations."[66]

To this contention Mr. Doane made an extended reply. "It is apparent that we must decide that we *are* or we *are not* willing to consider modifying the Basis of Union. Our conference has yet to reach *some* recommendations. I suggest these:

"1.   The committee representing all points of view be appointed *now* to prepare a memorandum of understanding for further action.

"2.   One committee assignment would be the constitution and by-laws of the proposed General Synod, the other would draw up a Statement of Faith.

"3.   Another committee is needed to consider proposals for uniting Boards and agencies.

"4.   Over *all* committees there must be a steering committee to integrate sub-committee reports, approve or modify these reports and submit the revised documents to the CC Churches and the E/R Church.

"5.   Dates should be set, the method of voting, and the percent approval required. These should all be approved by *both* CC and ER bodies.

"6.   Finally, let *all parties* 'stand by' till the Churches have voted on the constitution."[67]

Mr. Penner spoke rather bruskly, "I can't see how tampering with the Basis of Union can be done without endangering the union."[68]

Superintendent Frederick Alden asked tartly, "If it is not possible to modify the Basis of Union then why do we meet here?"[69] Mr. Douglass smoothed over the problem, "Oh, within bounds changes can be made. We can change anything which does not require

536

formal alteration of the Basis of Union."[70] "Wait a moment," said Mr. Penner, "it is out of the realm of the possible to add more 'interpretations' at Omaha."[71]

At this point we appeared to be right back where we started. I suggested that, rather than debating our differences, we try to state our agreements. Rather quickly it was unanimously agreed upon motion by Mr. Thayer seconded by Mr. Smith, "That we recommend that the Executive Committee Minutes be divided in their presentation for vote by the General Council so that those minutes having to do with the proposed union could be presented separately from all other parts of the minutes, and at a special session announced for that purpose."[72]

Considerable discussion swirled around my request that the CC Executive Committee be asked to "take back" the statement that all Churches are considered members of the United Church of Christ at the time of union in June 1957. In the end there was general agreement that the statement should not have been made.[73]

Mr. Doane returned to the issue of constitution writing and moved to lay the CC/ER Merger issue "on the table" at Omaha. This sparked an outburst by Mr. Bladen, "If this is how you feel, line up your forces. Go to Omaha and ask the Executive Committee to resign. That's the parliamentary way to deal with Mr. Doane's motion. You will have a bigger fight with the protagonists of union with this motion than we have ever had with the anti's on the Basis of Union."

Rev. Albert B. Coe pleaded, "Gentlemen, I have to preside at Omaha. I hoped today's meeting would ease tensions, not increase them. Can't we find more items on which we agree?"[74]

At this point I reintroduced the five points made early in the afternoon and moved their adoption. Rev. Frederick M. Meek seconded the motion. Vigorous debate ensued and some modifications were made. Then the following was voted, 11 for and 4 opposed.

"That the following resolution be sent to the Executive Committee:

"That this General Council hereby instructs its delegates to the Constituting General Synod of the United Church of Christ:

"1. That they shall vote for the preparation of a Constitution for the General Synod, which constitution shall be submitted to the first regular meeting of the General Synod and within the succeeding biennium to the churches and synods for their vote.

"2. That they shall vote for a constitution for the General Synod only.

"3. That they shall vote for a memorandum describing the free and voluntary relations which the churches and church bodies shall sustain to each other, which memorandum shall not be an integral part of the constitution.

"4. That they shall see to it that the chief viewpoints among us are represented on the constitution committee and on all other important committees dealing with the Union.

"5. That they shall vote for a statement of faith in which the preamble shall affirm that it is not a test, but a testimony."[75]

Then on motion by Mr. Thayer, seconded by Mr. Penner it was voted:

"That we request the Executive Committee to present for vote to the General Council the resolution approved by the joint committee of lawyers and sent to the joint Executive Committees, namely, as follows:

"Be it RESOLVED that the delegates of the General Council to the Constituting Meeting of the General Synod be instructed to vote for the following amendment to the Basis of Union.

"(1) That the present polity of the Congregational Christian Churches and the present polity of the Evangelical and Reformed Church be continued until such time as the Constitution and By-laws of the proposed United Church of Christ have been duly submitted and approved as provided for in said Basis of Union, and

"(2) That the term polity as used herein shall be interpreted to include the General Synod of the Evangelical and Reformed Church, the General Council of the Congregational Christian Churches, and all of their related boards, agencies, commissions, procedures and judicatories, who shall be so advised.

"This resolution shall not be construed in any sense as to interfere, restrict, or restrain cooperative action of the merging groups as authoritatively determined.

"Voted: 14 for and 3 opposed."[76]

Next on motion by Mr. Keith, seconded by Professor Spinka it was voted:

"That two committees shall be formed, one in the eastern part of the country and one in the western part of the country; these groups to communicate with the opposition concerning the actions taken by this group and that the committee of five who called this meeting shall arrange to meet with the opposition groups at Omaha.

"Carried—with Mr. Bladen not voting and 3 opposed."[77]

Finally it was generally agreed that all of those present who were in attendance at the Omaha General Council Meeting would meet to act as a steering committee to see that the adopted resolutions were favorably presented and supported. It was agreed that notes of the Cleveland Meeting would be sent to all participants.

Afterthoughts From Cleveland

The Rev. William A. Keith wrote the following report, in which I concurred.

"Dear Friends of the Cleveland Meeting:

"We came away from the Cleveland meeting of June 6 enthused with the real possibility that our discussion had resulted in enough common agreement to unite all viewpoints and would appeal to the General Council when it met in Omaha.

"W. A. Keith spent 2½ hours with Howell Davies in Chicago the next morning and had a half-hour telephone conversation with Malcolm Burton the next Sunday afternoon presenting the proposals and giving assurance that by vote of the group a meeting would be held with opposition groups as soon as possible at Omaha. Henry David Gray gave his stenographic report of the meeting to Mr. Harold Bailey of the League to Uphold Congregational Principles. We found these individuals receptive.

"We both went to Omaha early for the purpose of furthering the Cleveland spirit and hoped the action taken might be the means of finding a way into union with unity."[78]

In addition I wrote to delegates to the Omaha General Council as follows:

"Dear fellow-delegate:

"I have just returned from a meeting in Cleveland called by Moderator Albert Coe to search for a means of reconciliation between opposing groups at Omaha. It was a good meeting, frank, friendly, kindly. It was also a meeting which made quite clear the wide gulf which separates those who are determined to unite with the E & R at almost any cost and those who are determined not to unite with the E & R on the present Basis of Union with Interpretations.

"Certain very useful recommendations were voted by the 16 persons who had met 'on call.'

"1. It was unanimously voted to request the Executive Committee to offer its Minutes for approval in two parts (1) those parts not dealing with the proposed union, with the time of presentation of part (b) (concerning the proposed union) to be announced in advance.

"2. It was voted unanimously to request the Executive Committee to withdraw the statement that all churches would be assumed to be members of the United Church.

"3. It was voted almost unanimously to submit to the Executive Committee and to the Council a resolution drawn up by a joint CC-ER lawyers committee which would instruct delegates to the constituting meeting (scheduled by June 1957 in Cleveland) to vote (1) for continuance side by side of CC and ER polity until a constitution is prepared, (2) for the preparation of a constitution for the national level bodies only and (3) for the development of nothing but cooperative work in the interim period.

"4. It was voted 11-4, with 1 abstaining, to submit to the Executive Committee and to the General Council, a resolution which would instruct the delegates to the constituting meeting of the United Church (a) to vote for preparation of a constitution in time for submission to the first regular session of the National Synod (1959), (b) to vote for a constitution limited to the national level bodies only, (c) to vote for a 'memorandum' describing the free and voluntary relationships of the Churches and church-bodies, NOT to be an integral part of the constitution, (d) to vote for committee personnel which insures the representation of all major viewpoints among us on the constitutional committee, and on all other important committees dealing with the union, (e) to vote for a statement of faith with a preamble stating that it is 'a testimony and not a test.'

"These recommendations offer some measure of hope to those of us who believe church union to be valuable when, as and if it contributes to the advance of goodwill, of freedom-in-fellowship, and of glad witness to the gospel of reconciliation.

"Omaha will be well nigh tragic if either extreme dominates the meeting; for it is sure to produce illwill, and either two groups claiming to be Congregational, or a frustrated protagonist party. *Any one* of these alternatives will weaken our fellowship.

"It is my hope and prayer that the Council shall not be limited to these alternatives; but that the great 'center' of our fellowship will express itself by both voice and vote, to the end that we shall have union on a free and voluntary basis such as seems to be envisaged in the resolutions."[79]

The Rev. Howard Conn conceived the idea of a direct mail Appeal to the Delegates to the General Council meeting at Omaha. In early May, 1956 he drafted a five-page typed document and circulated this to the Revs. Meek, Gray and President Whittaker. President Whittaker indicated the reaction of the Mediators to Mr. Conn's *Appeal.*[80]

The Exchanges which took place during May and early June were indicative of both the hope and despair of the Mediators as they anticipated the 1956 Omaha General Council. Here, in all relevant sentences are the chief items of the exchange.

Conn to Gray, Meek, Whittaker[81]

"Replies have come from both Fred Whittaker and Henry David Gray. I agree that my statement was too long, and that a briefer one should be prepared. Through these letters I learn that the three of you are going to a meeting with Truman Douglass on June 6th. Therefore any united action should be left in your hands. I have not been invited, for I suspect that I am regarded as a rather intransigent opponent. I recall that in early June two years ago before New Haven I chaired a meeting in Chicago by which we tried to work out a compromise on the CSA controversy. That effort ended in triumph for the organizational point of view, and I suspect that the only good that can come out of the meeting to which you are going is to smooth the path for the pro-union agitators.

"By the time your meeting is over I shall be on my way to Europe. It is too late now to do anything in which I would be included, so I will have to leave the battle in your hands.

"I will only conclude by saying what I think you already know, that I would welcome rather than deplore a schism in our fellowship. It is perfectly clear that Truman Douglass has his heart set on a United Church for Protestantism, and has persuaded many to his viewpoint. On the other hand, I am basically opposed to any form of Protestant union that involves organic merging of denominations. I am secretary of the Minneapolis Study Section of the North American Conference on Faith and Order. We have the major theological and ecclesiastical viewpoints represented in our group. As we have been discussing together it is increasingly clear that there cannot be any kind of organic unity. Attempt at such will only create further dissension and destroy the spiritual unity we seek.

"Your saner counsel will have some effect on this Omaha deliberation, I hope and pray. My best to you."

Whittaker to Conn, Meek, Gray[82]

541

"I have Henry's letter of May 5th and Howard's letter of May 13th. I have now taken my turn at cutting down and revising the original statement which Howard prepared. Since we seem to agree that the statement should be as short as possible, I have been quite drastic in making deletions.

"In view of Howard's proposed plan to leave the country may I suggest that Henry, if he is willing, carry on from this point. Between now and June 5th I simply must concentrate on Seminary affairs."

Gray to Whittaker, Meek, Conn[83]

"Dear Friends:

"I have Howard Conn's letter of May 13th, and Fred Whittaker's of May 18th.

"Enclosed is a re-draft of 'An Appeal To The Delegates At Omaha' as I have tried to cut it down still further.

"The most important change is in the latter part where I have endeavored to make out of the various suggestions simply three proposed votes. This is in the interest of clarity and definiteness.

"While I was working on the manuscript Howard called from Minneapolis and I checked these three with him. He suggesed that you send to me, forthwith, the names of as many people as possible who might be signers of this appeal, and suggested that I send to them a copy of the appeal at once. If we are to get it into the hands of the delegates we shall need lists of delegates from all of you as you have them from your own states. We will also need to get them from other states and I would welcome your help in doing this. It is quite a task, and an especially difficult one for me to undertake at this point when I am preparing to take 21 young people to the Holy Land! Nevertheless, the matter is of critical importance and we must proceed as rapidly as we possibly can.

"So, may I ask that you return this revision of the appeal to me with your further editorial comments and corrections and authorize me to send it out, and send me the list of persons to whom it is to be sent.

"Howard suggested that his Church would be willing to split the cost of this, and I hope that you, Fred Meek, would be willing to join with him and me in doing this. I doubt that the Seminary has any fund to which such a thing might be charged so I'm not including Fred Whittaker. Hope you don't mind Fred W.!

"I shall look forward to hearing from all of you at your very earliest convenience. Time is of the essence. I think the three of us who are going to Cleveland (providing that meeting is finally called) ought to have this in our hands to take with us.

"My assumption is that it would be printed very attractively and would be got out very speedily.

"We owe our thanks to Howard and to Fred Whittaker for doing so much work on this appeal. I think that it has a lot to it and will be very valuable."

Conn to Whittaker, Meek, Gray[84]

"This morning I have taken new heart. Fred Whittaker's letter arrived with its excellent abridgement of my original statement. This revision was drastically needed, and it seems to me that he has done it well.

"By phone I have contacted Henry in Hartford. He is of a similar opinion, and is preparing copies to send out for the approval to a large number of our friends. I am sending to him the list of some names of fellows who I think would be sympathetic. We trust that all of us will do this. In this way it should be possible to gather in a short time an impressive list of signers, to get the document printed, and to have it distributed at Omaha.

"Henry suggests that we attempt to get the names of delegates from as many states as possible. All of this material we shall forward to him. He has graciously consented to carry on our mutual interests.

"As the time approaches I regret increasingly that I shall not be at Omaha. You may be sure that my prayers and interests will be with you."

Conn to Gray[85]

"I have read through your revision in comparison with Fred Whittaker's. You have shortened it even more, but on the whole strengthened it. I endorse your final revision and urge that it be sent out for signers."

Conn to Gray[86]

"I am finishing up my correspondence before my departure early Monday morning. I have not heard anything from you recently, but trust that plans for the printing of the appeal to the delegates at Omaha has gone forward. I am sure there is a real desire for such. A couple of days ago I received a letter from Bill Jacobs at Aurora, Illinois expressing the hope that some of us will take a strong middle position.

"I also have a fine letter from Harry Johnston at Boise in which he says that he hopes the anti-Merger group will remain quiet if there is assurance that a middle group will make its voice heard. This would of course be the proper strategy. As your plans develop I hope you will drop a line to Harry and suggest to him that he try to restrain some of the people in his camp.

"Our family spent the Memorial Day with the Bill Halfakers up north. Bill feels that an effective floor strategy must be planned in advance. He feels that a motion to lay on the table the actions of the Executive Committee would be a mistake because the issue would not be clear. The delegates would not be clear as to whether this was a definite postponment or simply a removal of the discussion until a specific date. The first vote taken will be of supreme importance because it will seem to set the drift of the Council. Bill's suggestion is that the first vote for which the Moderates seek approval be a positive one which clearly puts the whole question before the delegates, so that they are not confused by any secondary issue. I think we'll pass this suggestion along for whatever it may be worth. I surely hope that the Moderates will recognize you as the floor leader for this viewpoint.

"As the time approaches, I wish more and more that I were going to be present at Omaha."

Encouragement came from Rev. Edward W. Day of Iowa,[87] Mr. William Randall of Massachusetts,[88] Rev. Wallace W. Anderson of Connecticut.[89] These are typical of the many letters and phone calls. Distribution of the *Appeal* was made by mail to a lengthy list of known delegates to the Omaha General Council, and to known Mediators in accord with the suggestions of Revs. Conn and Whittaker. (Rev. Frederick M. Meek participated via telephone. He was physically unable to do more.) President Whittaker's final note on the *Appeal* read:

"This is a hurried reply to yours of May 22nd. I have made a few additional changes in the proposed draft. Please send me a copy of the final draft, which I understand you will circulate among other 'moderates.' May I suggest that we need *quality* rather than quantity so far as additional signatures are concerned. I believe the printed document should be distributed at Omaha rather than mailed now; this would save time and money and be just as effective.[90]

Here is the document as distributed:

"'AN APPEAL TO THE DELEGATES AT OMAHA'

"You are a delegate to one of the most important meetings of the General Council. A group of us who call ourselves 'moderates' (because we do not belong to any of the organized groups which have been flooding our churches with literature, either 'pro' or 'anti') are deeply concerned with the proposed plan of union with

544

the Evangelical and Reformed Church. We have the traditional Congregational interest in inter-church cooperation but we believe that uncritical acceptance of the proposed plan will endanger our larger interests in the ecumenical Christian movement, and will divide our own fellowship.

"We urge that you support (we want support of *all three*) the alternative proposals suggested at the end of this document.

"We present the following reasons for our plea:

"1. *We Congregationalists are not spiritually ready for this union.* We have been bickering over the proposed union for a decade. Basic differences of viewpoint are apparent. Some of us thought that the 'Claremont Resolution' (calling for a national-level constitution) was a bridge-building rapprochment between two extremes, but this attempt at reconciliation was set aside by Executive Committee action, thus leaving us further apart than ever before. We are more torn by dissension today than at any time in fifty years or more. The unity or agreement of spirit to carry us forward into Church union does not exist.

"2. *The 'Claremont Resolution'* acknowledged that most of us looked forward to eventual union with the E & R's; and it intended to remove previous tensions by authorizing the preparation of a national-level constitution prior to union. Even though the Executive Committee may have been within legal rights by its October '54 decision to proceed with the proposed union on the *Basis of Union* and *Interpretations* such action violated the spirit of reconciliation which prompted the Claremont formula, a formula re-affirmed at New Haven just four months prior to the Executive Committee action. Restoration of harmony is possible if we begin with the only near-unanimous vote yet given, that is, the vote on the 'Claremont Resolution.'

"3. *We have been puzzled and distressed by the fact that the statements of the General Council witnesses and lawyers*, because of which the Cadman case was dismissed from the courts, contradict many of the recent pronouncements of the Executive Committee. The General Council lawyers claimed, and the courts decided, *that the General Council can act only for itself* and cannot bring any churches or individuals into the United Church 'except as such churches by their own independent action after the consummation of the proposals in the said *Basis of Union* and *Interpretations* choose to associate themselves with such proposed fellowship.' We cannot but contrast this statement with the Executive Committee 'Letter Missive' sent out December 16, 1955, which stated: (a) 'At the time of Union every member of every congregation would be assumed to be a member of the United Church;' (b) 'If any congrega-

545

tion votes to withdraw from the United Church, nothing will prevent such withdrawal.'

"4. *We Congregationalists are asked to approve* a proposed union with *the assumption* that every member of every congregation will automatically become a member of the new United Church! Will this involve churches which have not wanted to vote on the proposed union until the details of a constitution have been presented? Are churches, which because of indifference or ignorance have taken no action, to be involved without their consent? Is our Congregational tradition of local initiative and autonomy to be so altered as to require a defensive action by the local group in order to protect itself against assumptions of national organizations? If so, Congregationalism will be drastically changed, and those who protest against such procedures will be upholding ancient and honorable Congregational principles, which offer the most promising hope for wider church union which leaves ample room for diversity.

"5. No one knows how much support the churches would now give to the *Basis of Union* and *Interpretations.* No vote has been taken among the churches for seven years, during which time a quarter to a third of the members of every church are new. By the time of the 1948 General Council only 63.3% of the then-voting churches had responded favorably to the proposal of union. By aid of an intensive campaign and with an extension of time this percentage was changed by January 1, 1949, to 72.8%. Even this was short of the 75% vote originally suggested as the goal.

"Today, after years of controversy, we believe the number supporting union (on the present Basis of Union and Interpretations) would be substantially less. This cannot be proven unless a vote is taken. The matter is of sufficient importance that it should be resubmitted to the churches. Only by the churches can the decision be made. No delegate or Council has authority to commit the local churches. Yet without local church participation any talk of a united church is travesty.

"WE URGE THE DELEGATES AT OMAHA TO THE FOLLOWING MINIMUM ACTION:

"FIRST

"*Vote not to ratify* the actions of the Executive Committee during the past biennium which relate to the proposed union, especially its vote to consummate the union in June, 1957.

"SECOND

"*Vote to make a fresh approach* to the E & R Church; and to elect a committee representing all points of view among us, with power to write a national-level constitution as the basis for union, and with instruction to submit that constitution to the churches and synods for their vote prior to any act intended to consummate the proposed union; and authorize this same committee to negotiate with the Disciples of Christ and/or the American Baptist Convention with a view to union of our respective felllowships.

"THIRD

"*Vote to re-submit to our churches* the question as to whether or not they wish to unite with the E & R Church on the *Basis of Union* and *Interpretations*, in the event that our E & R brethren do not desire to proceed with a fresh approach.

"The General Council has the power to act for itself. If we cherish the welfare of the larger fellowship we will re-submit the whole question of union to the local churches. The basis of Congregationalism is the will of the churches as they strive to fulfill the will of Christ."[91]

Omaha Council Anticipations

There were at least four different expectations for the Omaha Council. Protagonists of the CC/ER Merger felt they had waited long enough. Opponents were determined to use every device possible to stop the merger. An unnumbered host shared sentiments expressed by Superintendent James F. English of Connecticut.

"Let us hope that this will be a profitable meeting and that we will find a satisfactory solution to the matters that concern us. I am sure that if we manifest a spirit of charity and patience, much can be accomplished. I will look forward to seeing you at Omaha and if there is anything I can do to be of help to you while there, please call on me.

"Faithfully yours,

"James F. English, Superintendent"[92]

The Mediators found hope in the promise of Moderator Coe to support the resolutions hammered out at Cleveland, June 5th.

The situation was exacerbated by publication of "They Are Planning To Take Your Church" by the League to Uphold Congregational Principles and The Continuation Committee of the CC Churches. I received (6-21-56) a copy of the CC Executive Committee rebuttal. Both documents were intemperate at a time when patience, firmness and hope were in short supply.

Setting For Struggle

The convention center at Omaha broiled in the fierce summer heat, with high humidity adding to discomfort. The exhibition space contained too many biased exhibits seeking to influence delegates for or against the CC/ER Merger, or certain social issues.

Separate hotels were the gathering places of proponents and opponents of the CC/ER merger, and of social action advocates. Tension filled the air-cooled Music Hall when Moderator Albert B. Coe convened the General Council at 2 p.m. on Wednesday, June 20, 1956. By happy choice Rev. Arthur H. Bradford clearly, graciously, and without "propoganda" presented the history of the CC/ER merger negotiations. And in keeping with the June 5th Cleveland recommendation the Executive Committee asked approval of routine business minutes only. Wednesday evening scheduled a communion service and the chief business of Thursday morning, the Constitutional Commission Report, is chronicled in Chapter Nine.

Of Persons and Procedures

Proponents of merger like Revs. Jerry W. Trexler, Judson E. Fiebiger, Douglas Horton, Albert J. Penner, Arthur S. Wheelock, Joseph F. King, Lawrence L. Durgin were determined to consumate the CC/ER Merger; for them it was the "wave of the future." They conferred with each other, met in strategy sessions, and kept constant liaison with the protagonist majority of the CC Executive Committee. The seventeen ER Ecumenical Delegates were consulted each time proposals were made for modification of the program set forth by the October 13, 1954 joint meeting of the CC Executive Committee and the ER General Council.

Opponents of the CC/ER Merger gathered in one hotel and met daily—often more than once, and late into the night. Ministerial leaders were Revs. Malcolm K. Burton, Neil Swanson, Jr., Leslie Deinstadt, Arthur A. Rouner, Sr., Erwin A. Britton, Marion J. Bradshaw and John H. Alexander. Prominent among the opponents were distinguished Church members, Attorneys Joseph D.-Fackenthal, Kenneth W. Greenawalt, Robert Heany; Professors Palmer D. Edmunds and George V. Bohman; Messers. Henry W. Valentine and Walter D. Arnold, Misses Evelyn Baumgartner, and Hilda M. Camp, and Mesdames George J. Mead and Paul Quaintance.

A broad representation of the Mediators was present including Revs. C. Victor Brown, Arthur A. Rouner, Jr., Alan Jenkins, William A. Keith, Perry D. Avery, Charles Gerlinger, David Julius, Henry David Gray and President Frederick W. Whittaker.

The written report authored jointly by Revs. William A. Keith and Henry David Gray records the predicament of the Mediators with regard to the compromise voted at the June 5, 1956 consultation in Cleveland.

> "W. A. Keith and H. D. Gray arrived at Omaha on Tuesday, June 19, expecting to meet with the Cleveland group and do what we could to help implement its action. We discovered members of the Committee and the Executive Committee had not received copies of the minutes. We made inquiry of Everett Babcock who dictated this statement: 'I wrote up the minutes and mailed original copy to Coe on June 7 with the understanding he would have them duplicated and sent to members of the Committee. I received a letter from Coe stating Mr. L. Thayer had found an error in my reading of his written insertion into his lawyer's resolution and asking me to rewrite this resolution and send it with his correction and accompanying letter to those present. I sent this to the ministers for whom I had addresses and sent enough copies of the corrected resolution and accompanying letter to Coe for him to mail to lay members whose addresses I did not have.'
>
> "Keith and Gray approached Coe at the close of the afternoon session on Wednesday and asked if a meeting was being arranged with Opposition Groups or with the Cleveland group who were present at Omaha. He asked if we would undertake to get any of Cleveland group who were in Omaha together and agreed to meet at our suggestion on Thursday morning at 7:30. We then discovered the Ex. Comm. was meeting at that time and left a note in Coe's box saying this. So far as we are aware no additional attempt was made to gather the group and no attempt was made to contact the opposition groups.
>
> "The Ex. Comm. met Tuesday afternoon. It was reported to us by members present that Coe, Doane and Bladen made oral reports. We were disturbed, however, that afterwards some said there were conflicts in these reports as to the findings of the Cleveland meeting."[93]

More indicative of the character of the Omaha 1956 General Council than the marshalling of opposing forces was the mood of the meeting, and the powerful influnce of non-delegates or ex officio members like Revs. Bedros Baharian, Archie A. Hook, Fred S. Buschmeyer, Charles C. Merrill and John R. Scotford. The atmosphere was that of a tumultous political convention rather than a meeting of Church members for counsel. Key decisions such as the Order of Business were made in private by the CC Executive Committee or even by individuals on the platform. Executive Committee members controlled presentation of the

CC/ER meger and usurped access of speakers to the microphones so that *they* could speak whenever they chose at length, *others* were often ruled "out of order" on flimsy pretexts and were limited in time permitted so seriously as to preclude meaningful debate. The result was a *staged* performance whose results were assured by whipping up fanatic feelings till Rev. Ned B. McKenney demanded an immediate vote on the "enabling resolution of the CC/ER Merger saying belligerently "We've listened to these people (i.e. all not in favor of merger) for years. They have obstructed the work of this Council. Mr. Moderator, we've reached the limits of patience and endurance. We demand a vote *now*."[94] The exasperation was understandable, even if unbecoming. One prime irritant was the bruhaha over the 1954-1956 Minutes of the CC Executive Committee.

On the 1954-1956 Executive Committee Minutes

One of the three crises of the 1956 Omaha General Council meeting concerned the constitutional requirement that the 1954-1956 Minutes of the CC Executive Committee be reported in full, to be approved or otherwise by the meeting. This issue has been reported in full elsewhere.[95] The Mediators were appalled at the actions and words of CC/ER merger proponents and opponents. *Legal issues* dominated the discussion and led to the all night reading of the 1954-1956 Executive Committee Minutes in a carnival atmosphere, Friday-Saturday night June 22, 23, 1956. Whatever possibility of rational/spiritual search-sanity existed had evaporated by 9:10 a.m. when the morning session was called to order. The Minutes hassel virtually doomed the efforts of the Mediators to win favorable action on the proposals of the June 5, 1956 Cleveland consultation.

Mediators In Action

While the *Minutes* wrangle was in progress, the Mediators were busy, beginning Tuesday afternoon June 19. Here is the exact record.[96]

"Keith and Gray . . . undertook to personally do everything possible to see that the Cleveland resolutions had consideration. We secured the only copy of the minutes at Omaha from Coe and had them mimeographed. . . . Late that night we gave copies to some members of the Ex. Comm. and placed in boxes of others copies with this notation, 'For your information: H. D. Gray, W. A. Keith.'

"Thursday morning we concluded no further consideration was to be given to the proposals of the Cleveland Meeting. We then asked the Ex. Comm.

"1. If the Ex. Comm. would present them to the Council.
"2. Or give Keith and Gray the privilege of presenting them from the platform.
"3. Or we would notify them as to a point in the proceedings at which we would introduce them as an amendment to business on the floor.

"Before the Thursday morning session started the Ex. Comm. gave us assurance we could present the report but reserved decision as to timing. No presentation was made that morning as the Council was on business of approval of minutes.

"Keith and Gray then had a notice read from the platform asking all who shared a 'moderate' position and particularly any who desired to see a constitution written first, to meet with them at the close of the Thursday morning session in front of the auditorium. Despite the fact that many delegations were holding meetings, including some from the mid-west, more than 100 people gathered with us. After an hour's presentation and discussion most of those who still remained, 70, voted:

"1. They would like to have this material presented to the Council.
"2. Appoint a Committee to plan procedures.
"3. Committe as follows: Gray and Keith, Donald J. Simpson of Ill., Neil Swanson of Wis., Robert M. Bowen (alternate Alan R. Anderson), Minn., Alfred Grant Walton of N.Y. This group met at noon and decided to mimeograph the essential resolutions from the Cleveland meeting and Keith and Gray were to contact Ex. Comm. and inform them of the desire of this group to place them before the Council. We were told by the Ex. Comm. opportunity would be given and that night Mr. Bladen as a representative of the Ex. Comm. gave us copies of the proposed substitute for the 'Lawyer's Resolution' portion.

"At the Friday morning sessions when the Ex. Comm. introduced their 'Official Report on Approval of the Basis of Union with Interpretations by the General Council of the Congregational Christian Churches,' Gray moved and Keith seconded and Whittaker (having arrived) also added a seconding speech on a motion to amend by adding the Cleveland resolutions as point 8 (see below) with this heading added: 'With these actions of the previous General Councils we associate the following resolutions of the 1956 G.C.' and with the word 'instruct' as on the mimeographed copies distributed to the assembly, changed to 'pledged.' Truman Douglass spoke in support of considering the substance of the motion with the exception of that part relating to the Boards.

"After debate the proposal was laid on the table as germane but not strictly in order since all other items in the motion were of historical character.

"Keith, Gray and Whittaker then conferred at lunch and discussed at great length the substitute 'Lawyer's Resolution' to be introduced by the Ex. Comm. and concluded it changed the basic intent especially by substituting the merging of the boards for the cooperation of the boards in the period prior to the adoption of a constitution. Keith and Gray had lengthy discussions with T. Douglass previous to this point and late that night. Keith, Gray and Whittaker then decided that Saturday morning when the Ex. Comm's substitute for the Lawyer's Resolution was presented, we would then reintroduce the Cleveland resolutions as a substitute motion. Gray moved and Keith seconded the revised Cleveland resolutions as a substitute motion. We had by conference between Gray, Keith and Whittaker decided to change the word pledged to request and added the phrase 'subject to the approval of the Evangelical and Reformed Church.' T. Douglass and Wm. Frazier were immediately recognized by the chair and told the assembly:

"1. The Lawyer's Resolution would make impossible the carrying through of plans already made by the Board of Home Missions.
"2. They were contrary to the Basis of Union.
"3. The passing of these resolutions would endanger the present agreements on such matters as Annuity Fund.

"Some discussion followed until the 'previous question' was moved and our substitute motion was overwhelmingly defeated."

A Last Minute Effort

Friday June 22, 1956 I met with Rev. Truman B. Douglass for almost eight hours. He had been designated somehow by the proponents to meet with the Mediators. Mr. Ashby Bladen was present for a few minutes. Rev. William A. Keith was present much of the morning and for the concluding half-hour in the evening.

I welcomed this meeting. Mr. Douglass seemed to me the intellectual giant among CC/ER Merger proponents. I had (and have) great respect for his vigorous mind, grasp of issues, and forthrightness of speech. He was the ideal person with whom to negotiate.

Little time was now wasted on past history, procedures, and legalities. The issues were faced unapologetically. At noon, Revs. Keith and Gray met at lunch to consider the Council's afternoon session, Rev. Truman B. Douglass' stance, and possible Mediator action. We concluded that no progress could be made on the committment of the proponents of the CC/ER Merger to the Basis of Union and Interpretations *unless* the Douglass/Gray discussions could propose a compromise which side-stepped the BU & I, or, which accepted but moved beyond the BU & I. "Somehow, Henry, we're not reaching Truman. There's no *give*. I'll go to the afternoon meeting. I don't see much use talking any more, but keep on if you think it might help. It's our last chance."

With Mr. Keith's reservations fresh in my mind, I approached the afternoon on a different level, a theological level. Mr. Douglass and I had spent several days discussing Frederich Schleiermacher's *The Christian Faith*.[97] Discussion had centered on the concept of the Church as the community of believers in which and through which God speaks and acts.

"Will the proposed CC/ER merger increase God-consciousness, and implement God's way in the Churches and in society?" I asked. There followed an intense exploration of alternative theories as to *how* God spoke to "The Great Church" with an eloquent and erudite defense of "prophetic religion" in contrast to "private piosity." Mr. Douglass viewed merger opponents as champions of "private religion" who wished Churches to be "quiet, comforting clubs," and who were "out of date by half a dozen generations."

By late afternoon the question of *power* was addressed. My advocacy of the power of the Spirit was seen as "very attractive, but impractical." In the end I asked, "Do you really think prophetic leadership requires political power?" He replied, "That is central to meeting the massive, entrenched evils of our time. Power must speak to power. Big government and big conglomerate corporations will not listen to weak whispers. Henry, power must speak to power if the Great Church is to influence the Great Society. We *have to have* this merger and others until the prophetic voice of the Great Church can no longer be ignored. Otherwise we are divided, weak, and easily discarded. Henry, truth has *social dimensions*. You can't find truth in a private religious club."

Late Friday night, with Rev. William A. Keith present *this* was the denouement. At bottom, the issue of the CC/ER Merger was theological and political. It concerned the nature of power. The lodging of "leadership" in the "prophet," and the activity of God in the world through "power speaking to power." It was about 2 a.m. when I fell on my knees at my bedside.

The Enabling Resolution

At the Saturday morning session of the Omaha Council on June 23, 1956 the Chairman of the Executive Committee introduced the enabling resolution.[98] After rehearsing the "official version" of CC actions from January 22, 1947 through 1954, Mr. Raymond Walker moved acceptance of the report with power to implement as follows; that, "The General Council instruct its Executive Committee to . . . authorize . . . delegates . . . to represent the General Council at a joint meeting . . . which meeting shall constitute the first meeting of the General Synod of the United Church . . ." Mr. Walker added, "On behalf of the Executive Committee, I now move the adoption of the official report to be made at the first meeting of the General Synod of the United Church of Christ."[99] The motion was seconded. The Moderator ruled that speeches be limited to five minutes, and, on behalf of the Mediators, I was the first speaker.

The Cleveland Proposals Presented

The *Minutes*[100] read:

"The Rev. Henry David Gray of Connecticut, moved to amend the enabling resolution by the addition of the following sections to be known as paragraphs 8A and 8B as follows:

"'With these actions of previous General Councils concerning the Basis of Union with the interpretations, we associate the following resolutions of the 1956 General Council:

"8A BE IT RESOLVED THAT the delegates of the General Council to the Constituting Meeting of the General Synod, if such be chosen, be requested to vote for the following amendment to the Basis of Union, subject to the approval of the Evangelical and Reformed Church.

"(1) That the present polity of the Congregational Christian Churches and the present polity of the Evangelical and Reformed Church be continued until such time as the Constitution and By-Laws of the proposed United Church of Christ have been duly submitted and approved in accordance with said Basis of Union, and

"(2) That the term polity as used herein shall be interpreted to include the General Synod of the Evangelical and Reformed Church, the General Council of the Congregational Christian Churches, and all of their related boards, agencies, commissions, procedures and judicatories, who shall be so advised.

"(3) This resolution shall not be construed in any sense as to interfere, restrict or restrain cooperative action of the merging groups as authoritatively determined.

"8B BE IT FURTHER RESOLVED THAT this General Council hereby requests its delegates to the Constituting General Synod of the United Church of Christ, if such be chosen:

"(1) To vote for the preparation of a Constitution for the General Synod, which constitution shall be submitted to the first regular meeting of the General Synod and within the succeeding biennium to the churches and synods for their vote.

"(2) To vote for a *constitution* for the General Synod only.

"(3) To vote for a *memorandum* describing the free and voluntary relations which the churches and church bodies shall sustain to each other, which memorandum shall not be an integral part of the constitution.

"It would be our expectation that the chief viewpoints among us would be represented on the constitution committee and on all other important committees dealing with the Union.'"

I have before me six note cards detailing my presentation of the Cleveland Resolution. After listing those who called the meeting, and those who were present, I said, "We came away from the Cleveland meeting feeling there was a great new possibility of *union with unity*, which many of us have longed for and prayed for. We have moved from a focus on the *legal* to concern for the *religious and moral*."

Second, I emphasized, "Many Churches and some Associations, feeling that the situation NOW is quite different from 1948-49, wish to see a constitution written at this point in our proceedings."

Third, "Here at Omaha, Dr. William A. Keith and I, representing the Mediators, called a caucus (6-21-56) attended by about 100. It was the desire of 70 members of this caucus that the 'Cleveland Resolutions' be presented to this Council."

Fourth, "Resolution 8a was unanimously adopted by CC/ER Joint Lawyers Committee in June 1955, which committee was appointed jointly by the CC Executive Committee and the ER General Council."

Fifth, The heart of the question of church union is addressed in Resolution 8b, "designed to express the concern of the Churches as to the nature of the proposed constitution." This Resolution "seeks to allay the fear that the writing of a constitution will be put off indefinitely." It "says clearly that the constitution is for the General Synod only." It "offers a new suggestion concerning all matters in the Basis of Union which describe the free and voluntary relations of Churches and church bodies in a manual of procedure.

Sixth, "Although not stated in these Resolutions it is our feeling that a great deal of confusion and misunderstanding would be eliminated if all major viewpoints among us were represented on the constitutional committee and on any other major committees planning for the proposed union."

Seventh, "Those on whose behalf I introduce these resolutions are deeply concerned with religion. We want and will *support a union with unity*. Let us so act that all may see how Christians *can* work out their differences. Let us not create division in the cause of union. Let there be an upsurge of spiritual vitality from this council by the healing of hurts and the bridging of gaps with FAIRNESS AND VISION."

At that point I introduced the Cleveland Resolutions.

After making the motion I addressed the issue, "The Central Issues may be set forth quickly:

"*The Religious and Theological Issue* concerns the entire character of our faith. We believe in and are committed to a living Christian fellowship as opposed to any national structure which replaces conscience with creed, or conviction with a code of conduct."

"*The Constitutional Issue* is purely derivitative from religious and theological roots. Our plea is for separation of administrative from ecclesiastic, for responsible freedom of association rather than centralized authority, and for separation of the regulatory from the descriptive, the former in a constitution and the latter in a manual."

"*The Procedural Issue* is a matter of accuracy in the historical record. The 'official report' *omits* the key points of the 1953 Claremont Resolution, e.g., as to the representation of all points of view, *overlooks* the report of the Polity and Unity Committee, and *glosses over* the 1954 General Council mandate. We really should be accurate in our reports. It is quite unnecessary to be inaccurate; the vast majority here present will not be swayed against the Merger by a right reading of the record."

"*The Pragmatic Test* in the Christian Churches is the ultimate test. Does what we vote yield the fruits of the Spirit? Will it persuade the Churches to vote for a constitution with joy, gladness, peace and love?

"Union WITH unity is our central plea, whether or not this means modification of the Basis of Union. The great—and valid— aim of any enabling resolution is to further the Kingdom of God, to persuade the world that Churches have a message as to *how* differences can be resolved, and to bear witness that our union, or any union of Churches is not exclusive but inclusive, not based on legalities but founded on the love of God made known in Jesus Christ our Lord."

The Rev. William A. Keith seconded the motion, and in so doing stressed the serious attempt made at Cleveland to avoid denominational division. "I favor this union but I want to see it accomplished in the best way so that it will yield the best results." President Frederick Whittaker also seconded the motion, emphasizing his long standing committment to the CC/ER merger. Mr. Whittaker's remarks were specifically directed to the pursuit of the CC/ER union without splitting the CC fellowhsip.

THOSE WHO AGREED TO SUPPORT THE RESOLUTIONS AT CLEVELAND KEPT SILENT.

Rev. Alden Mosshamer, on a point of order "asked if the amendment was part of the historical review, . . . and was informed by the Moderator that it was not."[101]

"On a point of order, the Moderator ruled that the Gray Amendment was not germane to the historical review."[102] On appeal to the Council, the Moderator's ruling was sustained.

Thus Rev. Albert B. Coe at whose invitation the Cleveland June 5, 1956 meeting was held, who had endorsed the Cleveland Resolutions, and who had (with the Executive Committee) arranged to have the Cleveland Resolution introduced at that specific point, ruled the motion out of order.

Late Saturday afternoon I re-introduced the Cleveland Resolutions. Rev. Truman Douglass informed the Council that the Resolutions would imperil agreements reached with great difficulty concerning ministerial annuities and the uniting of the Boards. Rev. William Frazier, treasurer of the Board of Home Missions, told the Council that the financial and legal aspects of the merger were far too fragile and complicated to be subjected to further debate and possible modification. The Rev. Ralph Hyslop advised the Council that ER officers who were present were dismayed by any tampering with the Basis of Union and Interpretations. Rev. Clayton Gill made a plea for moderation. Rev. John

Alexander and Mr. George Gullen, supported the Cleveland Resolutions.

The hour being late, "the Moderator limited debate to one minute for each speaker."

The finale' is recorded as follows:[103]

> "Mr. Bladen of New Jersey moved the previous question. This motion was seconded and it was
>
> "56G57. VOTED: To return to the previous question.
>
> "The previous question being before the Council, the Moderator put the Rev. Mr. Gray's Resolution to a vote. It was lost."

This terminated the Mediators attempt to achieve union with unity.

"Rights Are Dangerous"

The third major CC/ER union item at Omaha in 1956 concerned a "Declaration on Rights of Churches and Ministers."

I had first drawn up a declaration of rights in 1947 when I was Moderator of the Los Angeles Association, in connection with open meetings held by the Association prior to a vote on the Basis of Union at the 1948 annual meeting in Pasadena. I was, therefore, predisposed to favor a well stated "Bill of Rights."

Unfortunately the *nature* of the "rights" was submerged by concern for the *legal* interpretation of "rights."

The 1956 Omaha situation may be stated succinctly.

At Omaha *two* "Declarations on Rights of Churches and Ministers" were submitted. One set containing nine points was submitted by Rev. Malcolm K. Burton on behalf of the "Continuation Committee of the CC Churches" and the "League to Uphold Congregational Principles." The second set consisting of twelve points was submitted by the Executive Committee. Both declarations were defeated.

The Burton rights declaration was introduced Thursday morning, June 21, 1956, with an accompanying Executive Committee letter. Much back-stage discussion took place both in committees and elsewhere among delegates. At the Saturday morning session an attempt by Professor George A. Bowman to attach the Burton "rights" to the "Enabling resolution" for the CC/ER merger was ruled out of order.[104]

Late Saturday afternoon "the Council voted to remain in session until a vote had been taken upon the Declaration on the Rights of Churches and Ministers."[105] The official record continues.

558

"At this juncture, Mr. Horton addressed the Council with the following words: 'We are in a very dangerous position indeed. A great many of us have memories extending back a few years and will realize that the situation is almost precisely that of Oberlin. We were certain that the Interpretations decently described the Basis of Union. Today we are almost certain that these rights interpret perfectly the Basis of Union and Interpretations. Therefore, I move you to thank both Mr. Burton and the Executive Committee for setting forth Declarations on the Rights of Churches and Ministers in our fellowship for adoption by this General Council, and to approve the letter of the Executive Committee to Mr. Burton dated June 20, 1956, with the omission of the last paragraph beginning "Although it is as a sufficient description of those rights in respect of the proposed Union with the Evangelical and Reformed Church." That will mean that we adopt no rights. These are very dangerous.' The motion was seconded.

"A point of order was called for; in reply to which the Moderator commented that this was a motion offered by Mr. Horton. The point of order being renewed, the Moderator requested that he might clear up one question by asking Mr. Horton about the motion and what it involved.

"Mr. Horton repeated his motion as follows: 'I move you to thank both Mr. Burton and the Executive Committee for setting forth Declarations on the Rights of Churches and Ministers in our fellowship for adoption by this General Council, and to approve the letter of the Executive Committee to Mr. Burton dated June 20, 1956, with the omission of the last paragraph beginning "Although it is a sufficient description of those rights in respect of the proposed union with the Evangelical and Reformed Church".'

"Mr. Horton's motion was again seconded.

"Mr. Robert Heaney of Michigan moved, as a substitute motion, the Declaration on Rights that the Executive Committee had distributed earlier and which the Executive Committee was itself going to present.

"Mr. Horton requested an opinion of the Executive Committee on this question to which Mr. Bladen replied, 'We believe we have discharged our duty in presenting those Resolutions to you, and the Executive Committee supports it.'

"Subsequent to further discussion, which did not resolve the issue, the Moderator announced that the Parliamentarian would make a statement.

"Mr. Bridges, as Parliamentarian, suggested that the time which had been allotted for the discussion had expired; that the question before the house was such a very important question that neither party would care to have it settled hastily. Unless a further extension of time were voted, it would seem that a motion to recess would be in order.

"It was moved, seconded and

"56G60.   VOTED: (By standing vote) That the Council be recessed until 7:30 P.M. this day.

"The Moderator declared the Council in recess until 7:30 P.M."

Nearly 27 years later, reading this record raises interesting questions as to the circumventing of the Council's vote "to remain in session until a vote had been taken" by Mr. Bridges, as Parliamentarian, especially as the parliamentary ruling immediately followed Mr. Ashby Bladen's revelation that the Executive Committee no longer supported *its own* statement of rights. As a matter of fact the Executive Committee was deeply divided on the subject, voting 10 to 5 to present a lengthy explanation of its actions.[106] By late Monday afternoon the Council majority handily defeated *both* statements of rights. Why?

Quite simply, protagonists of the CC/ER Merger had had all the delays they would tolerate, felt the proposals to be unnecessary, and were persuaded the ER people were distressed at the whole Omaha bruhaha. Patience was exhausted.

What Were the Rights?

The Executive Committee version of the Rights of Ministers and Churches was as follows:

"1.   There is no power or authority, and none is claimed, by which the General Council of the Congregational Christian Churches can make any Congregational Christian church a part of the fellowship of the United Church of Christ. Fellowship with the United Church of Christ depends upon the voluntary and free *assent* of such church.

"2.   No action taken by the General Council of the Congregational Christian Churches, or by delegates representing it, leading to a consummation of, or in consummating, the union will in any way obligate any individual Congregational Christian church to be in fellowship with the United Church of Christ.

"3.   No Congregational Christian church can be brought into the fellowship of the United Church of Christ or into any organizational relationship therewith, by reason of any act or declaration of the General Council of the Congregational Christian Churches. It is the General Council's position that no Congregational Christian

Church can be brought, without the assent of such church, into the fellowship of the United Church of Christ, or into any organizational relationship therewith, by reason of any act or declaration of any Congregational Christian Conference or Association in which such church presently holds membership.

"4. It is the position of the General Council that no Congregational Christian church should be regarded as being a member of, or as having an organizational relationship with, the fellowship of the United Church of Christ if such church does not wish to be so regarded.

"5. Any act heretofore taken by a Congregational Christian church in voting for or against proposals contained in the Basis of Union, either with or without the Interpretations, will not commit it as a member, or to become a member of the fellowship called the United Church of Christ or other organization contemplated by the proposals in said Basis of Union, and failure of any individual Congregational Christian church to vote for or against the consummation of the proposals contained in said Basis of Union will not commit it as a member, or to become a member of the fellowship called the United Church of Christ or other organization provided for in the provisions of the Basis of Union with Interpretations.

"6. It is the position of the General Council that no member of a Congregational Christian church should be assumed to be in fellowship with the United Church of Christ if such member does not wish to be so regarded.

"In order to insure proper numerical Congregational Christian representation in the General Synod of the United Church of Christ, and in the belief that most churches will wish to be in fellowship with the United Church of Christ, the General Council will request the Conferences to count each member of a Congregational Christian church within its territory as a 'communicant' for the purpose of determining its quota of delegates to the General Synod of the United Church of Christ as provided in Section E of Article X of the Basis of Union, but this action of the Conference will not affect the rights of the churches as set forth herein.

"7. It is the position of the General Council that no minister of a Congregational Christian church should be enrolled as a minister of the United Church of Christ if such minister does not wish to be so enrolled.

"8. It is the position of the General Council that any Congregational Christian church that wishes not to be in fellowship with the United Church of Christ shall in no wise lose its Congregational Christian standing. No action need be taken by such a church to retain its Congregational Christian standing.

"9.   It is the position of the General Council that any Congregational Christian minister who wishes not to be a minister of the United Church of Christ shall be (sic) no wise lose his Congregational Christian standing. No action need be taken by such a minister to retain his Congregational Christian standing.

"10.   Each Congregational Christian church which is in fellowship with the United Church of Christ will continue to possess the same freedom of faith and manner of worship as heretofore enjoyed, and there will be no intrusion in or abridgment of traditional Congregational polity and usage through fellowship of independent autonomous congregations free of authoritative control.

"11.   It is the position of the General Council that participation by any Congregational Christian church or member or minister thereof in the fellowship called the United Church of Christ, or in any of its activities, or in any of the organizations that may be formed pursuant to the Basis of Union with Interpretations, will not affect its, his or her status with respect to the Congregational Christian fellowship, churches, Conferences or Associations, and the related Boards and Societies; and the General Council will, insofar as it has the power, protect such status.

"12.   It is the position of the General Council that no action of a Conference or Association in participating in the fellowship called the United Church of Christ will bind a Congregational Christian church or minister to be in such fellowship, without its or his assent, or will affect its or his standing as a Congregational Christian church or minister."[107]

A Personal Point of Decision

As I emerged from the air-conditioned comfort of the assembly hall at noon on Saturday, June 23, 1956 there was a sudden tug at my arm. It was the Rev. Bedros Baharian, "I've got to talk to you, Henry." he said urgently. "O.K. go ahead." "No," he replied, "I mean *really* talk. Come inside." I stepped back inside and away from the doors. "O.K. let's hear it. What can I do for you?"

"Look," he said, "you're not dumb. You know the merger is going to be voted through. Your influence can help make the transition smooth. I've talked off the record with members of the Executive Committee, and with members of my own committee." "Your committee?" I queried. "Yes, I'm chairman of the nominating committee. Here's the deal. You vote for the enabling resolution and you'll be assured a place on the Committee to write the Constitution. You are well qualified. It's a logical appointment. You can get your points across in the committee. You can influence the whole setup. It's a big opportunity. There will be *only nine* on that Committee. I was asked to get your O.K. before the afternoon session." I said nothing—speechless. Mr. Baharian took my arm again, "Come on. You've got nothing to lose and everything to gain. There are dozens of men who'd give a lot to have that Constitution Committee place. It's an opportunity, man."

I looked at him, dumbfounded, "I vote for the resolution and I will be on the Constitutional Committee. Is that it?"

"Yes," he said eagerly, "you've got it!"

I shook my head sadly. "Bedros," I replied, "my vote is not for sale." and turned quickly so he wouldn't see the tears in my eyes. I knew he did not represent all the protagonists, but, somehow, he *had* support to "make a deal" on an issue of spiritual values and personal integrity. From that moment onward I found it very difficult to contemplate ANY CC/ER union at all.

What Was Accomplished?

In spite of the rancor, bickering and bargaining at Omaha, neither I nor the other Mediators ceased to hope, pray and work for a more sensible CC/ER union, though our hopes were dim, our prayers ardent and our labors unflagging.

Nevertheless we had questions. Rev. William A. Keith posed the key one, "Did we really accomplish *anything* at Cleveland, or at the meeting with the Executive Committee in New York?" Patently we had *not* changed the course of events at Omaha. "Why did Coe call the meeting if there was to be no compromise?", Rev. Wallace Anderson asked. "I think Dr. Coe's great aim was to smooth the way so that he could preside over a relatively harmonious General Council Meeting at Omaha." I replied. "Then," retorted Wally, "he didn't get what he hoped for. But that doesn't explain why men like Truman Douglass and Al Penner met with us." "They wanted to get us 'in'," replied Bill. "That's been the big thing for these fellows. Prevent a split. Get people like Henry and you and me to 'cooperate'—or keep quiet. Well, they didn't succeed in *that*. But the bottom line is, they got the vote."[108] On that we all had to agree.

Interim

Wednesday June 27, 1956 the General Council Meeting in Omaha closed. Friday June 29 the 1956 Old South Odyssey began in New York. Lecturing, guiding, counselling twenty-one teenagers in England, Scotland, Ireland, France, Switzerland, Italy, Egypt, Lebanon, Syria, Jordan, Israel, Turkey, and Greece occupied me day and night until Sunday evening September 2.

Interest in the CC/ER merger extended beyond U.S. borders. Dr. N. J. McLellan in London, Mr. E. Cunningham in Cambridge, Rev. Basil Cozens in Coventry, Rev. W.B.J. Martin in Edinburgh, Rev. Alex Jackson in Ireland, Mr. Renard and World Council of Churches leaders in Geneva, the brilliant Waldensian pastors throughout Italy, especially Moderator Achille Deodato, the Baptist minister in Cairo, Mr. Haddad in Lebanon, Pastor D. Mitri in Damascus, American Board representatives in Istanbul, Patriarch Athenogoras at Phanos/Istanbul, Dr. Kyriakakis and Pastor Philotheos Zikas in Greece all questioned us closely about the CC/ER Merger. I wrote a "log" at the close of each day recording our activities including conferences with all those mentioned.[109]

Ministers in the British Isles were divided in reaction to the CC/ER Merger. None were enthusiastic. Mostly they wished to hear a first-person report from Omaha. At Geneva the WCC viewed the CC/ER Merger as a pioneer "inter-confessional" venture but the Swiss Reformed Church pastors did not seem to have their minds made up. The Waldesians, Greeks, and Eastern Orthodox were interested but skeptical. Patriarch Athenogoras suggested, "The *spiritual* ties of all the Orthodox Churches to the Ecumenical Patriarchate hold more promise for union of Churches than is possible in what you call 'mergers.' I do not need, and *I do not want* ANY authority over the Churches except what is freely given to me on a spiritual level." "What about Rome?" Tom Richardson asked. A beneficent smile suffused his face. "We are prepared to recognize the Pope . . . immediately . . . as the first among equals, provided, of course, that the Pope recongizes us . . . as equals."

The cardinal question raised by the summer's experiences was, "Will the merging of denominational organizations advance the unity of Christ's Churches?" The answer was equivocal in Britain, tentative in Switzerland, and a resounding "No" throughout Southern and Eastern Europe and the Levant.

As soon as the pressing program of South Church permitted, I answered the accumulated correspondence of the summer and charted one more Mediatorial attempt.

Congregational Christians—After Omaha

It is not my purpose to report in detail further attempts of the Mediators to amiliorate the harsh opposition of those determined to "push the merger through" and those resolved to "avoid merger at any cost." My files bulge with correspondence and publications related to both sides.

My purpose is to indicate the major actions and attitudes of the Mediators up to, and including, the debacle on the streets of Cleveland in June 1957.

In mid September 1956 I replied to the accumulated correspondence as follows:[110]

"September, 1956"

"CONGREGATIONAL CHRISTIANS—AFTER OMAHA

"Dear Friends:

"Many of you have written to me asking two questions: (1) *What happened* to produce the overwhelming vote at Omaha? and (2) *What comes next*?

"*What happened* was that no compromise of any sort was permitted by a council under control of the unionists. The council has not reflected, proportionately, the views of the churches for many years, as was pointed out by many prior to Omaha. The unionist vote simply underscores this known fact.

"*What comes next*? Constituting Synod, June 1957 in Cleveland, with (according to a last week's press release from the ER Synod) no merger of boards, etc., until a constitution is written and adopted by vote of the churches (CC) and synods (ER).

"Many have asked for my personal position. Here it is. I have not altered my fundamental convictions that the local church must acknowledge no authority above that of Christ, and that all churches of Christ should work together in fellowship. In our present situation,

"1. We should state our convictions *positively and powerfully* that they may be given full consideration by those who are chosen to prepare a constitution for 'The United Church.'
"2. We should keep the fellowship with our associations, conferences, and the General Council.
"3. We should band together in the National Association of Congregational Christian Churches to take counsel together for effective witness to those things in which we believe. A meeting is called for October 25th and 26th in Wauwatosa, Wisconsin.
"4. We should be certain that no act of the local church, (whether by vote or by election of delegate) commits the church to be part of 'The United Church' until a constitution has been

drawn up and has been presented to our churches for vote.
(See any of the many 'protective resolutions.')

"5. We should be certain to counteract the means of propoganda
used by unionists ('Advance,' Conference, Association,
Churchmen—Women, and Pilgrim Fellowship meetings,
etc.)

"6. We should *immediately* create organs for *regular* communication so that no one who holds free Church convictions
shall feel isolated or alone. This means regional gatherings, a
national weekly or monthly periodical, a quarterly devoted to
basic studies, seminars for ministers and ministerial students.

"7. We should *immediately* explore the many alternative possibilities open to us if an authoritarian, centralized constitution
is written and is approved by 2/3 of our churches.

"I feel that the urge toward union is often a flight from the real
struggles of the soul which alone can re-make the world. What is
needed most is not new top-heavy organizations but new heart-
ready persons. The re-making of our world does not wait for the
emergence of a monolithic church; it waits for the appearance of
single-minded persons deeply dedicated to Christ. We have the
Gospel to proclaim as it has been given by God in Christ. This is our
central task. If we can persuade others to follow the free way in a
constitution for the national-level bodies alone; then, let us do so,
and let it never be said that we left any possible means of persuasion
un-used. But if the constitution is written as one more fateful human
authority interposed betwixt the church and its Lord, then, as I see
it, we shall have no choice but to stand for what we believe—alone if
need be!"

An Incredible Letter Missive

In the accumulated correspondence was the July 31, 1956
Letter Missive,[111] the report from Omaha of the CC Executive
Committee. The report of *actions taken* was accurate, but the
assertion of wisdom, courage, patience and earnestness belies the
harsh, racous, inflexible words and actions. The sheen of glib
religiosity must have shocked all who were present, regardless
of viewpoint.

The Letter Missive stirred deep resentment and led directly to
the next move of the Mediators.

The Revs. Otis A. Maxfield, and William A. Keith took the
initiative.

The Rev. Otis A. Maxfield wrote:[112]

"It was a real privilege to meet you in Omaha and to have brief opportunities to talk with you. I found your movements and strategy on the floor of the General Council stimulating to say the least.

"I hope in the fall time and circumstance will make it possible for us to see more of each other."

I replied:[113]

"Dear Otis:

"It was a delight to have your letter waiting for me when I got home from the Odyssey. That experience was as high and lofty as Omaha was otherwise.

"Now, it seems to me that there is a lot to be done, namely, setting forth in some positive form the fundamental Congregational principles for which a lot of us stand, and will continue to stand.

"I am going to the meetings of the National Association very reluctantly, for the reason that it seems to me that they are a continuation of the continuation committee. So far as I can see that means nothing but squabbles and no positive action anywhere. Nevertheless, they have done a service, and I feel obligated to go, if for no other reason than to sound a more moderate and more positive note than is likely to be sounded.

"But, the real line of progress seems to me to lie in getting together some people like Meek, Maxfield, Keith, Conn, Avery of Oregon, Anderson of Bridgeport, Whittaker of Bangor, etc. What do you think? I shall be most interested to have your reaction."

The Rev. William A. Keith wrote:[114]

"Dear Henry:

"I have just returned from Boston for P.C. (American Board Prudential Committee) meetings and on to New York for a joint policy committee with Home Boards. There is evidence that work of the various groups to more definitely define the merger issues is not all lost. Truman Douglas (sic) expressed concern that E. and R. at their Lancaster Synod had passed the 'Lawyer's Resolution' as Thayer told us in June he understood they intended so to do. Now Douglass and others are arranging a meeting with them to ask what it means and take out its obvious meaning. The Home Boards are, under his leadership, determined to press ahead immediately. The American board at present is going slowly. There is a Mr. Buck, a lawyer, from A. G. Walton's church on the Policy Committee of the Home Board who is our ally. Unless you see objections I will send him our packet of documents, as he was not at Omaha, and have some correspondence with him on this issue as he is in a position of influence in their affairs.

567

"I have agreed to go to Des Moines next Friday and speak to a group being gathered from all concerned churches on the merger issue. I have given as a topic, 'The Search for a Middle Position' as I want to stand there. I also had lunch with Fred Meek in Boston. He is fully recovered. He had a letter and a proposition from Howard Conn which I have not seen. It occurs to me that it might be well for you to bring Howard up to date on the Cleveland and Omaha meetings. Meek would seem to be in agreement with my present purpose, still to get as many churches as possible, to pass our resolution as a protective measure and give all parties a reason to pause in their headlong rush. The general sentiment here in Michigan, headed by Skidmore, is that nothing need be done. I shall counter that by saying something is being done and we should not sit by idly.

"I wrote Vere Loper after Omaha saying I regretted he did not get a chance to speak. He indicated he intended to say we should pass the 'Rights' and let the chips fall where they may.

"Hope you are home after a fine summer. When you get time please bring me up to date on these affairs as you see them. Greetings to your fine wife."

I replied:[115]

"Dear Bill:

"Thanks for your good letter of September 29.

"Yes, I have a copy of Conn's statement. It is a bit too individualistic. Our biggest problem at the moment is that we are disorganized— or rather unorganized.

"I feel a kinship with you and Meek and Conn and Walton, and all others who are like-minded. I also feel that we need to make as soon as possible a definite declaration of a Congregational platform.

"Yes, I had noted in the press the report of E & R action, and was puzzled by it. I have written to Douglass asking him what he thinks it means.

"I'm glad you are going to Des Moines, and I hope you get a chance to go to Park Street Grand Rapids as well.

"I'm going to Wauwatosa, with very mingled feelings, for it seems to me that it represents at the present time only a continuation of the continuation. That is by no means what is needed just now. Nevertheless, I feel that I should go, for without their work we would never be even as far along as we are now, and we owe them something or other.

"My chief concern would be that we should exchange some correspondence relative to a positive position, and that we should enlarge our circle of correspondence for these purposes to include people like Avery in Oregon; Maxwell in Springfield, Massachusetts; Anderson in Bridgeport; Victor Brown, Dean of Elmira College; and probably some others whom we would agree upon together. If you think well of this idea, why not start by simply sending a letter from your desk to all of us suggesting this, and I shall certainly do all I can to follow it up.

"We had a wonderful summer, and the kids did a magnificent job overseas. It was the best yet. Helen and I send our very best to you."

Following exchanges of letters and phone calls, I wrote to the chief Moderators.[116]

"Howard Conn, Frederick W. Whittaker, Frederick M. Meek, Wallace W. Anderson, William Keith, Raymond A. Waser, Alfred G. Walton, Lawrence Upton, Joseph F. King, Matthew Spinka, Philip M. Sarles, Charles M. Houser, Allen S. Lehman, Elden H. Mills, John Webster, Victor Brown, Harold J. Ockenga, James Henry Hutchins, Fred W. Niedringhaus, Charles F. Parker, Emerald L. Olson, Richard A. Dawson, John J. Barbour, Otis Maxfield, Perry Avery, Clement F. Hahn.

"Dear Friends:

"All of us whose names appear on this letterhead are among those who have been concerned about the merger. We are, I think, all of a single mind in agreeing that co-operation among Christians is desirable, and that some sort of closer association of the free churches is a good thing. I believe we are also all agreed that this co-operation is best when it is *free*. I think we are also agreed that the action of the General Council at Omaha does not seem to promise a free church union unless considerable change of heart takes place, and a constitution for the national-level-bodies alone eventuates from the discussions. I think we are also agreed that there needs to be an emphasis on the positive principles for which those of us who believe in the free church stand. I think most, if not all of us, do not wish to be 'agin'ers.' While recognizing the fact that anti-movements have played an important part as a delaying action, we are more positively-minded than anti-minded.

"If the mind of the group of us is somewhat as pictured above, it seems to me that we have a very important role to play in church life in America at this juncture. That role, it seems to me, is to set forth with clarity and vigor exactly what are the positive principles in which we believe. To that end I would propose that, at our own or at our churches' expense, we meet and take several days together to draw up a set of principles, stated in clear and kindly language. I would suggest that this be circulated throughout our churches, and that we proceed to plan ways in which the viewpoint we represent can be given thorough representation on any constitution writing committee; and that we plan what action we shall take in the event a vertical constitution is prepared for presentation to the churches.

"It would be my suggestion that, if all of us are so minded, we do the preliminary work by correspondence, and then with the results of our study in hand, circulated to all of us, come together for at least three days in order to be sure that we fully share in the whole process of thinking and arrive at a conclusion or set of conclusions which we can jointly and fully support.

"I shall look forward eagerly to hearing from you with your thoughts on this matter."

The Mind of the Mediators

Replies to my October 12, 1956 letter provide an excellent picture of the attitude of the Mediators after Omaha.

1. O. A. Maxfield[117]

"I agree with the point of your letter of October 3rd, that any real progress will not come through the informal getting together of some of us who are concerned not with the moderate position in the sense of compromise, but with a moderate position in the sense of trying to conserve the values in all the approaches being made to this proposed union.

"I shall be glad to participate in any kind of session you feel fit to call."

2. W. A. Anderson[118]

"I have your communication of October 12th and thank you for including my name. I find myself in hearty agreement with what you said. I'm sure that this church would welcome the opportunity of having their minister sit in a meeting where we can take several days to draw up a set of principles stated in clear and kindly language. I feel sure that the Executive Committee would welcome a representation from this group on any constitution-writing committee appointed in 1957 at the first General Synod meeting.

"At the request of our Board of Deacons, I am going out to Wauwatosa, Wisconsin next week as an official observer of the National Association. It is distinctly understood that in no way am I going as a delegate from this church, but many of our laymen wanted a first-hand report from that meeting as to the material covered and the spirit that pervades the meeting. I saw a copy of the program and note with interest that you are to take part. It will be good to see you there. In the meantime, please count on me as one who wants to join the group which you are working to bring together."

3. L. Upton[119]

"It was a pleasure to receive your letter this morning and to sense again the tone of your thinking about the Union.

"At this time, and on the basis of my reflection about what happened and about the mood which was apparent at the Omaha meeting, I have largely given up the hope that the descriptive element concerning the state and local bodies of the church can be in a document separate from the constitution. My emphasis shall be more in the direction of encouraging everyone involved in the Convening Synod to strive for a constitution which will be acceptable to the vast majority of our Congregational churches. I think I believe that the Basis of Union demands a vertical constitution and that there is little indication that the General Council or its Executive Committee will respond favorably to any suggestion that the relationships of the smaller church bodies should not be in a constitution. In other words, I think I have given up on that struggle. I shall not, however, give up on the hope that this vertical constitution will be as permissive as possible or that it will spell out the principles of a truly free church polity. It seems to me that the constitution must reflect much more of the Congregational spirit or it will never be accepted by even a sufficient majority of the churches to put into effect.

"I think that the gathering of such a group of men as you have listed at the top of your letter for the purpose of discussion and possibly for arriving at a set of principles might be very profitable. I feel, however, that we are stuck with a vertical constitution and that we should work as hard as we can to guarantee that within this verticle constitution there shall be a maximum of freedom and Congregationalism.

"I look forward to the report you will probably give us of the thinking of these men as is reflected in the letters which you will receive.

"Thank you for all you are doing in all the relationships in which you invest your efforts."

4. A. G. Walton[120]

"I have your letter regarding a possible meeting of a group of ministers in our fellowship to consider the issues which have been raised by the merger.

"It would be very desirable to have such a meeting if it can be carried out successfully and I would make every possible effort to attend. I doubt if it would be necessary to take three days for such a gathering, but it would be valuable to have the group mentioned, get together.

"There seems to be a genuine opposition to the merger on the part of many of our outstanding ministers, but in some instances, the opposition has not been vigorously expressed. A group of the type that you mentioned would carry weight in any pronouncement that they might make.

"I will be much interested to see how this thing develops."

5. A. S. Lehman[121]

"Thank you for your letter of the 12th including me in that group. I believe you have stated the position with which many of our people agree; at least I think I do.

"There are certain points in my own thinking which I would like to emphasize.

"One, I believe in closer unity with Protestantism. It is coming sooner or later anyway and I would like to see our denomination take the lead in this movement.

"Two, I want to see our churches remain united in this movement, otherwise any move in this direction of denominational unity would lack any real force.

"Three, I believe our churches and our ministers should remain free. It is the best contribution we can make to any united denominational body.

"Four, any constitution that is formulated ought to be for the General Synod and the national bodies only and not for conferences, associations or churches.

"Is this a restatement of what you already mentioned in your letter? Some of the above, I believe, is already implied in the Basis of Union, but not all. On this point I believe the 'agin'ers' are way out in left field.

"I would be very much interested in the replys (sic) to your letter and any further steps which might be considered.

"Thanks!"

6. R. A. Waser[122]

"I was interested in your Columbus Day letter concerning your concern and that of others about the merger. I don't know exactly what I could contribute, but I wish at this point to record my interest.

"I hope you were able to attend the Wauwatosa meeting. Pilgrim Church could only send one delegate and it seemed to me that our layman was the logical candidate. I hope you will have a chance to visit with him. His name is Mr. Ellson Smith."

7. R. A. Dawson[123]

"I greatly appreciate the interest you have in preserving some elements that have made Congregational Churches strong during the centuries of democratic growth. Sometimes I am puzzled not knowing if our precious heritage is an essential element for the Church of the 21st century. I do appreciate that church organization, like the technique of prayer, is very important for the most effective presentation of the gospel, but it is the spirit that counts most.

"The church in Palos Verdes which you helped to bring into the Congregational fold, is undoubtedly strong as a community church— I doubt if it will every brook the imposition of authority outside itself. The Council of the church has declared itself unwilling to be considered a part of any denominational group to be formed in the future until it has thoroughly examined the proposed constitution of such a national body.

"I would take it, however, that your letter has a concern apart from the local churches which we individually serve. We have a responsibility to preserve the best in the merging churches, through strong representation in the constitutional committee, perhaps. We do believe, regardless of what happens, that the Congregational way has commended itself and should commend itself. I am, therefore, vitally interested in contributing to any thought in the matter before us as a concerned group of Congregationalists. I cannot promise at this time to attend a meeting but there is a possibility that I might be able to do so. Whether I do or not you may be sure I follow all your efforts with both interest and prayers."

8. J. P. Webster[124]

"Thank you for your letter of October 12 concerning your proposition for a positive approach to the problems involved in the merger at this present stage. I am wholeheartedly in favor of this attitude and approach . . .

"I . I hope I will be kept informed so that I can share in any way possible."

From these replies, NOT written by those of us vigorously supporting a Mediatorial position, it is clear that a kindly, constructive attitude prevailed, and that desire to advance free churchmanship was well-nigh universal.

The Revs. Conn, Keith, Whittaker, Meek and Gray, in November and December 1956 sought to assemble "a sizeable group of concerned men to prepare a statement prior to the mid-winter meeting."[125] This proved impossible. We met with the new Secretary of the General Council, Rev. Fred Hoskins, in Boston at the beginning of Lent. As a statement of positive principles we circulated a slightly revised version of my Theological Bases of Congregationalism.[126]

Failure to form a large, active, organization meant failure to influence CC/ER merger proceedings. Many were resigned, like Rev. Lawrence Upton, to acceptance of the leadership of the CC Executive Committee. They retained the hope that they might influence the *content* of the constitution for the new denomination.

Invitation to the UCC Uniting Synod

When I agreed to accept nomination as a delegate to the Uniting Synod, at Omaha, Rev. Fred Hoskins, Minister and Secretary of the CC General Council, assured me that the Congregational Christian delegates represented only the General Council, and were not, personally, opting to become members of the projected United Church of Christ. The Rev. Fred S. Buschmeyer, acting minister of the CC General Council acknowledged the problem posed by the announcement of the Uniting Synod.[127]

"Just a note to give personal acknowledgement to your letter of January 4 addressed to the Executive Committee of the General Council through me.

"Needless to say I can recognize the difficulties raised by the 'assumed to be members' phrase in the December 16, 1955 Letter Missive. I can assure you that the intent of the phrase was not to sweep any person or church willy nilly into a legal or structural relationship which would have authoritative implications concerning any of the present rights and freedoms enjoyed by either the church or the individual.

"The intent, at least as far as I understand it, was to indicate that the right of participation in any and all consultations or programs of the United Church was guaranteed to all of our people regardless of personal views as to the advisability of the union in any particular form.

"Of course, your letter will have to be responded to or acknowledged in some way by the Executive Committee itself, but I did want to make this personal response. Please know that I am ready at any time to do whatever I may be able to do to hold our fellowship together both in understanding and in action.

"Best personal wishes to you as you start this new period of service."

Dated March 10, 1957 the official notice of the convening of the Uniting Synod in Cleveland, June 15-27, 1957 arrived. The notice read:[128]

"Notice is hereby given that the delegates of the Evangelical and Reformed Church elected by the 1956 Lancaster General Synod, and the delegates of the General Council of the Congregational Christian Churches elected by the 1956 Omaha Council, are called to convene in Cleveland, Ohio, June 25, 1957 for the purpose of adopting appropriate resolutions declaring the Basis of Union with Interpretations in effect and the formation of the United Church of Christ, to engage in public worship and the celebration of the Holy Communion, to proceed to implement the provisions of the Basis of Union with Interpretations, to attend to addresses by Bishop Leslie Newbigin and others, and to engage in such other activities and business as may be appropriate to the Uniting General Synod of the United Church of Christ."

I wrote to Rev. Fred Hoskins for clarification.[129]

"I'm finding myself puzzled about the Cleveland meeting. What is it that we are doing there? Are we forming the General Synod of the United Church of Christ as the successor to the General Council and its opposite number body in the Evangelical and Reformed Church? Are we meeting in a 'Uniting Synod' simply in order to declare our purpose to unite and to choose members for a constitution-writing body?

"I interpret my election at Omaha as being in line with the idea that the meeting in Cleveland is simply a gathering of those officially representing the CC General Council and the Evangelical and Reformed Church in accordance with its own laws and usages. Under this interpretation I shall be happy to be a delegate."

The reply puzzled me so I submitted it to Attorney Barclay Robinson, a trusted advisor, eminent lawyer, and devoted member of South Church. Here is the reply.[130]

"It was good to have your letter of March 6 and I am, of course, perfectly delighted that you are to be one of the delegates to the Cleveland meeting.

"As a delegate to the General Synod in Cleveland you are legally representing the General Council and it alone, and you will be meeting with those who represent the Evangelical and Reformed Church in accordance with its own laws and usages.

"The delegates will be forming a General Synod of the United Church of Christ, which will be the successor of the General Council of the Congregational Christian Churches and the General Synod of the Evangelical and Reformed Church (B. of U. X B.) The General Council however will remain in existence in order to fulfill necessary legal functions. The rate at which functions will be transferred to the General Synod will depend, I suppose, upon future developments.

"I understand the foregoing to be the legal situation, but after our recent conversation in Boston I am sure that you and I are in agreement that it would be erroneous to describe the events to take place at Cleveland only in technical legal terms. The great opportunity before us in Cleveland will be to undertake to create a more effective instrument to be used by our churches in the fulfillment of their mission to the whole world. That you are going to share in this will be a source of encouragement to large numbers of people."

After conferring with Mr. Robinson I felt an urgent need for the advice and counsel of the South Church's Prudential Committee. This was partially a personal need to share a most distressful situation with devoted members of the Church for whose wisdom I had great respect. Then, too, it was because I felt that the stand already voted by the Church needed to be officially reaffirmed.

Tuesday, March 12, 1957 the Prudential Committee heard the invitation to the Uniting Synod and requested a meeting with the Rev. Fred Hoskins. Thursday, April 4, 1956 Dr. Hoskins was the Lenten preacher at the South Church. The Prudential Committee, of which Mr. Robinson was a member discussed at length the exact nature of the Uniting Synod. Extensive notes of this consultation were kept by Mrs. Warren S. Archibald, and are before me as I write.

Action was taken at the monthly meeting, April 9, 1957[131]

"The following motion regarding the new denomination to be known as the 'United Church of Christ' was passed unanimously: 'Inasmuch as we feel that Dr. Gray's status as a delegate to the meeting of the General Synod in Cleveland, Ohio, June 1957, is not clear, and inasmuch as his presence there could be misinterpreted by our own and by other congregations, and inasmuch as our legal counsel has recommended nonattendance, and inasmuch as the past history and present status of union negotiations is unsatisfactory to this Church, it is therefore the respectful request of the Prudential Committee, acting on behalf of the congregation of South Church, that Dr. Gray not attend the meeting of the General Synod at Cleveland, Ohio, June, 1957, as a delegate from General Council.'"

A committee was appointed to draw up a statement of the Church's position. I thereupon wrote to Rev. Fred Hoskins the following two letters.

"Dear Fred:

"I regret the necessity of sending you the enclosed letter.

"In a close examination of the Omaha vote, it became clear

"1.   That I personally, as a delegate, become a part of the United Church of Christ if I attend as a delegate.
"2.   That the delegates are 'empowered' only to act within the bounds of the BASIS OF UNION and its INTERPRETATIONS.

"As you know, I have no objection to union as such. It is precisely the BASIS OF UNION to which I object. That this dubious document should have remained unchanged since 1947 in the face of all objections, suggestions, votes of General Councils, etc., is well-nigh unbelieveable. The reason is, of course, that change required bilateral actions. But that would have been possible. It may, in fact, still be possible by the instruction to delegates.

"As you know, my interest is in the union of free churches with the largest possible cooperative work. It would be extremely difficult if even possible—for me to accept the idea of an over-all constitution of any kind. I believe in a 'Christonomous' Church—to coin a word, since 'autonomous' does not rightly describe my convictions—and therefore it is hard to see how any other authority can be permitted to take the place which belong (sic) to Christ alone. I believe it is possible to devise a polity for free church union on a Christonomous basis. This indeed is the most urgent need of the ecumenical movement. It seems to me a tragedy that this is not being attempted. I have given gladly of my time and energy in that cause, and will always be glad to do so. I'm sure you know that."[132]

"Dear Dr. Hoskins:

"This is to request that my name be taken off the list of delegates from the General Council of The Congregational Christian Churches to the first synod of The United Church of Christ to be held in Cleveland in June, 1957. The Prudential Committee of South Congregational Church, one of the oldest churches of our fellowship, voted unanimously to recommend this action for the following reasons.

"First. A recent publication issued by the General Council office indicates that delegates to the Cleveland meeting *will be members of the General Synod of the new denomination*. I do not wish to become a member of a new denomination without knowledge of its statement of faith or its constitution.

"Second. Another recent publication issued from the General Council office affirms that the new denomination will have a constitution which describes the relationship of churches, associations, conferences, ministers and churches, and thereby presumes to govern our free fellowship which has never had and does not now have any over-all constitution. In view of these intentions the Prudential Committee of South Church feels that no useful purpose could be served by the pastor's delegate status at Cleveland.

"Third. All recent publications of the General Council indicate that the BASIS OF UNION, with the INTERPRETATIONS of it added in 1948, is to be the governing document for the new denomination from the time of the uniting synod in June, 1957, until a new constitution has been written, presented to a future synod, approved by 2/3 of the churches voting, and declared to be in effect. This process will take years. Meantime, the new denomination will operate under the BASIS OF UNION. The provisions of that BASIS have been *the* stumbling block toward union. The BASIS OF UNION has been oppositely interpreted by thoughtful and reverent men like the late President James A. Blaisdell of Pomona College and the late President Albert Palmer of Chicago Theological Seminary. In spite of the fact that more than 1,100 churches voted against it, the BASIS has remained unchanged due to the unwillingness of its proponents to alter it in any way, even though the General Councils of 1952 and 1954 and the findings of the Polity and Unity Committee indicated the need for revision. There appears to be no real desire to include South Church, and other like-minded churches, in a free church union. Since we are denied that opportunity, it seems pointless to be present at the Cleveland meeting.

"Fourth. A 'new denomination' is to be begun in Cleveland, according to a recent publication of the General Council. The South Church has voted twice *not* to join a new denomination founded on the present BASIS OF UNION. The Prudential Committee has the responsibility to carry out the will of the Church, and unanimously agrees with the votes of the Church. It is our belief that the pastor's presence at Cleveland might be interpreted as representing a change in the viewpoint of South Church. We wish to make it clear that we recognize fully the right of any Congregationalist to depart from our fellowship in order to enter a new denominaton with the BASIS OF UNION as the interim governing document. But we also wish to make it clear that we propose to continue our voluntary association with all other churches which choose to remain part of the Congregational Christian fellowship.

"Fifth. It is with heavy hearts and great reluctance that we view the impending departure of some of our churches and ministers to found a new denomination, thus creating one more Protestant denomination, ironically named "The United Church of Christ." We shall continue, as heretofore, to work and pray for the kind of church unity which calls no group 'a small, reactionary and schismatic company;' but which rather includes within its scope all who share sincerity, conscience under Christ, voluntary cooperation, and Christian concern. We believe that God has called us into a faith which gladly joins in a free fellowship, and we are greatly saddened at the departure of some to found a new denomination."[133]

The Rev. Fred Hoskins replied.[134]

"I am heart sick that you will not be a delegate of the Cleveland meeting. I have so much hoped that we might have the benefit of your leadership and wisdom at the session there.

"I do know your fine spirit toward this whole matter and I am going to continue to rely upon it to provide us guidance at many needed points.

"I will, of course, honor your request to remove your name from the list of delegates from the General Council to the Uniting Synod of the United Church of Christ. I am sure that the whole Executive Committee will share my regret."

At the request of the Prudential Committee, my letter to Dr. Hoskins incorporating the statement of the South Church position was mailed to every Congregational Christian delegate to the Uniting Synod.

It provoked a storm of protest and paeans of praise. Many delegates, especially Mediators, shared our viewpoint.

May 1957 I wrote a final plea to the delegates and to the Churches.[135]

"964 to 55

"Friday night, June 20, 1952, ninety-five per cent of the delegates to the General Council of the Congregational Christian Churches meeting at Claremont, California voted in favor of a resolution concerning the proposed union with the Evangelical and Reformed Church.

"This is the only nearly unanimous action ever taken, either by our churches or by a General Council meeting.

"In 1948 the churches initially voted for the union by less than sixty-five per cent. When these churches voted in 1948 more than one in three voted 'No.' In 1949 efforts made during the extension-of-voting period had raised that to 72.8 per cent of the churches voting. Over 1,100 churches voted against THE BASIS OF UNION! At Omaha in 1956 one in eight of the General Council delegates voted against union.

"At Claremont in 1952 only one in nineteen voted against union!

"In June 1952 we were virtually a united fellowship and the General Council vote expressed 'the substantial unity' of the churches, as it is required to do by its constitution.

"'The Claremont Resolution' gained a nearly unanimous vote because it expressed the basic position of our churches. It still does.

"THE CLAREMONT RESOLUTION

"'The Claremont Resolution' looked forward to a united fellow-ship with the Evangelical and Reformed Church and asked the joint executive committees to draft a proposed constitution for the General Synod of the united fellowship. It provided for 'representatives of the different points of view among us on all important committees dealing with the union . . .' and required that 'every effort be made to preserve all the spiritual and temporal freedoms and rights now possessed by the Churches' and other bodies. This was sound churchmanship, representative of the great spirit of the Claremont meeting under the gracious, firm, and fair leadership of Moderator Vere Loper. When fairness prevailed and the spirit of the Master was given sway, the result was a resolution upon which 95 per cent could agree. Here is a real basis upon which our churches can unite with the Evangelical and Reformed Church.

"Here is a basis for union rather than a basis for division.

"Here is a bridge between the opposing viewpoints in our fellow-ship by which those who regard church union as a modern mandate and those who regard free churchmanship as a sacred trust can be brought together.

"A NATIONAL-LEVEL CONSTITUTION ONLY

"There is not now, and there never has been, any valid reason for unwillingness to follow 'The Claremont Resolution.' Even within the terms of that difficult-to-interpret document known as THE BASIS OF UNION, it is possible to instruct delegates to vote for a constitution limited to the national-level bodies, a constitution for the General Synod only.

"In 1955 a joint lawyers' committee, appointed by the national executive committees of the two church bodies, unanimously recommended the use of the procedure of instructing the delegates.

"The executive committee of the General Council could remind the delegates even now of the will of the Council expressed in 'The Claremont Resolution' (1952), and reaffirmed at the 1954 New Haven Council meeting. Furthermore, a constitution could be written now. A commission has been appointed to draw up a statement of faith, as provided in THE BASIS OF UNION. There is absolutely no reason why a similar commission could not now prepare a constitution for presentation in June, 1957. The commission could and should represent the different points of view among us. The General Synod would have to confirm the appointments, but we would all know now whether the document is to be 'an over-all constitution' describing the voluntary relationships of free churches, their associations and conferences, (and subject to amendment in the future), or 'a General Synod constitution only' similar to the present constitution of the General Council. A plain declaration of purpose at this point is essential. If agreement on this matter has not yet been reached with the Evangelical and Reformed Church, it should be reached at once. If there is agreement, the Congregational Christian Churches ought to have the information from the joint executive committees at once. Uncertainty at this crucial point means needless confusion, heartaches and controversy; it also means that churches and ministers that intend to remain free can no longer hope to bridge the foolish gap between opposite extremes which do not rightly represent the clearly expressed vote of the churches in 1948, or the equally plain intent of 'The Claremont Resolution.' We are compelled to conclude that no middle ground exists and that there is no desire for real church unity on the part of either of those who refuse to alter one word of THE BASIS OF UNION or of those who refuse to consider any kind of basis for union. What both parties seem to want is their own way, regardless of the consequences. The present situation is a disgraceful commentary on lack of spiritual unity, without which any type of church union is valueless.

"THE MOTIVE FOR UNION

"Many of us are eager for spiritual union. We are also eager to avoid the extremes of authoritarianism and libertarianism. To us, the fundamental motive for church union is to increase devotion and service to God according to the kindly, righteous, judicious, free spirit of Jesus Christ. To us, the Church is Christ's Church and its task is to bear witness to God's grace made known to us in Him. Church union is of worth insofar as it serves spiritual purposes. Unity of the spirit is an aim devoutly to be sought, but that goal *may* or *may not* be brought closer by organizational unification. We find it strange to read about organizational 're-union' of a Church of Christ which has never been organizationally united! In today's world those lands in which one Church dominates are examples of what we do not want to become (e.g., Spain, Eire, Italy, Greece, etc.) We believe free churchmanship offers the best way into spiritual oneness, into union without unification, into the largest possible usefulness for Christ! We believe the great present need of the ecumenical movement is a new, broad, creative free polity. We believe it is tragic that no attempt is being made to find and follow divine guidance toward such a polity. We believe the outmoded notions of centralization now being urged upon us will make necessary a new reformation in days to come. We believe the Church of Christ Universal is best served by vigorous, dedicated, free churches in the closest possible voluntary fellowship.

. . . . .

"FREE FELLOWSHIP IN THE FUTURE

"At the present, we Congregational Christians are a fellowship. A fellowship is a voluntary association of equals. We are drawn together because we are like-minded and because we share a common spirit. Those of us who believe in Christ as the sole Head of the Church will continue to be a free fellowship, either (1) in company with all with whom we seek to serve our Lord at present, or (2) as a small fellowship of Congregational churches in fellowship with another free church group such as the Disciples of Christ. These are a few of the possible alternatives to absorption in a 'National Church' governed by an over-all constitution.

"As a fellowship of Congregational churches our best contribution to the Universal Church of Christ is to bear witness to the power of God in Christ as He speaks and acts through His local churches and their cooperative agencies, according to the word and example of the New Testament, dedicated to the liberty wherewith Christ has set us free and accepting Him as our sole Lord.

"'The Claremont Resolution' is the surest guide we have toward this goal at present. 964 to 55 reflects the desire of the churches for the kind of union which recognizes the Church's allegiance to Christ and to Him alone, the kind of union which draws together the cooperative work of the churches under a national-level-only constitution, the kind of union which is possible on the unambiguous basis of a national-level-only constitution written NOW.

"In the name of unity under God let us act on the sure foundation of THE ONLY VOTE on the proposed union which has expressed 'the substantial unity' of the Congregational Christian Churches."

The date was Tuesday, June 25, 1957. The place was Cleveland. The event was "The Procession (Delegates, Associate Delegates and Fraternal Delegates) moving from the Hotel Cleveland."[136] The time was 7:30 p.m. Some of the Mediators, in pulpit gowns with academic hoods, gathered to declare that they would not march in the procession unless they were assured that by so doing they did NOT become members of the United Church of Christ. The Rev. Frederick Meek, with others, refused to move. A flurry of discussions were held on the street. At the last minute Rev. Fred Hoskins said he would see that the Mediators conscientious objections were respected. *But it proved impossible to secure confirmation* from Rev. James E. Wagner or any ER leaders. Rev. Frederick Meek said he would accept the unilateral assurance. Several agreed with him. The others joined the Rev. William A. Keith and viewed the proceedings from the gallery.

To the last instant, the nature of CC/ER merger was unclear.

To the last moment, the Mediators sought clarification. Their quest for Spirit and Truth was unending—and unanswered.

CHAPTER 10 NOTES

1. Oneonta Messenger, Calif. Jan. 9, 1955
2. Burton, M. K., *Committee for Continuation of the Congregational Christian Churches*, Chicago, Jan. 15, 1955 report.
3. Ibid, p. 1, 2, 3
4. Continuation Committee, Pontiac, MI, 9-14-55, communication signed by Malcolm K. Burton
5. Meek to Gray, June 21, 1955
6. Rev. Perry D. Avery to Gray, 7-15-55
7. *Advance*, NY, Sept. 21, 1955, p. 7
8. Douglass, op.cit., p. 7
9. Ibid.
10. Douglass, op.cit., 7-8
11a. H. D. Gray, Central Convictions . . . Daring Deeds, Twin Cities Assoc., MN 10-19-55
11b. L. Wendell Fifield to Gray, May 1, 1956
11c. R. A. Waser to Gray, April 30, 1956
12. M. K. Burton to Gray, 12-1-55, from Pontiac, MI
13. Illinois, Central West Association, Wataga, 10-15-55
14. NYC Congregational Church Assoc., 11-3-55
15. H. D. Gray, "Central Convictions—Daring Deeds," Hartford, Old South Church, 1-5-56
16. F. L. Fagley to Gray, 5-8-56
17. D. Howard Doane to Gray, 1-10-56
18. F. W. Whittaker to Gray, 1-10-56

19. F. Groetsema to Gray, 1-20-56
20. Rev. Raymond B. Walker to Gray, 2-28-56
21. Gray to Walker, 3-3-56
22. F. W. Whittaker to Walker, 3-8-56
23. Walker To Gray, 3-17-56
24. Rev. Howard Conn to Meek, Whittaker, Gray, 3-31-56
25. Rev. Keith M. Jones, sec. Hartford Association
26. Chairman's *Statement*, NY, 4-4-56
27. Penner to Gray, June 13, 1950
28. Anderson to Gray, April 11, 1956
29. Hartford Congregational Ministers, Asylum Hill Congregational Church, April 19, 1956
30. Rev. William A. Keith to Gray, April 13, 1957 and 1956
31. Revs. K. M. Jones and L. M. Upton, to Rev. R. Walker, 4-2-56
32. Rev. M. J. Bradshaw *An Open Letter*, etc.; Bangor, ME, 1-25-56
33. Op.Cit. 3, 4
34. Congregational and Christian Conference of Illinois, Annual Meeting, May 1956 Resolution
35. Executive Committee Hampshire Association, Florence, MA, 4-16-56
36. Central West Assoc. IL, Galva, IL, 4-18-56
37. Rev. Albert Buckner Coe to Gray, Whittaker, Meek, May 3, 1956
38. Coe to Gray, et al., May 23, 1956 (Ronald Bridges, D. Howard Doane, Truman B. Douglass, Frederick M. Meek)
39. Coe to Gray, et al., May 31, 1956 (Doane, Douglass, Meek)
40. Ibid
41. Ibid
42. H. D. Gray, notes 1
43. Gray, op.cit.
44. H. D. Gray Report of June 6-56 meeting, Cleveland, 2
45. hdg notes, op.cit, 4
46. Ibid, 4
47. Ibid, 7
48. Ibid, 5
49. Ibid, 7
50. Ibid, 8
51. hdg notes, op. cit, 8
52. Ibid, 8
53. Ibid, 8
54. Ibid, 9, also hdg Report, op.cit, 2
55. hdg notes, op.cit, 9, hdg Report, op.cit, 2
56. Ibid, 10
57. hdg notes, 11
58. Ibid, 12
59. Ibid, 13
60. hdg Report, 3
61. hdg Report, op.cit, 4
62. hdg notes, op.cit, 14
63. A. Bladen, hdg notes, Ibid, 16
64. Rev. Albert J. Penner, hdg notes, Ibid, 17 a&b
65. Rev. F. M. Meek, hdg Report, Ibid, 5
66. Rev. Truman Douglass, hdg notes, 19

67. D. H. Doane, hdg, Ibid, 20, 21
68. Rev. A. Penner, Ibid, 22
69. Rev. F. Alden, Ibid, 23
70. Rev. T. Douglass, hdg notes, op.cit., 22
71. Rev. A. Penner, Ibid, 24
72. hdg Report, op.cit, 6, also E. A. Babcock, *Action Voted*, June 6, 1956, 1
73. hdg notes, Ibid, 25, Also Report, Ibid 6
74. Rev. A. B. Coe, hdg notes, Ibid, 26, 27
75. hdg Report, op.cit, 7, also E. A. Babcock, *Action Voted*, op.cit.2
76. hdg Report, op.cit., 6, Also Babcock, *Action Voted*, op.cit. 1
77. Babcock, op.cit, 2
78. William A. Keith/Henry David Gray, n.d., post June 6, 1956
79. Gray to Omaha General Council Delegates, 5-23-56
80. F. W. Whittaker to H. Conn, May 7, 1956
81. H. Conn to H. D. Gray, F. M. Meek, F. W. Whittaker, May 13, 1956
82. F. W. Whittaker to Conn, Meek, Gray, May 18, 1956
83. Gray to Whittaker, Meek, Conn, May 22, 1956
84. Conn to Whittaker, Meek, Gray, May 22, 1956
85. Conn to Gray, May 23, 1956
86. Conn to Gray, June 7, 1956
87. E. W. Day to H. Conn, May 24, 1956
88. W. Randall to H. D. Gray, May 24, 1956
89. W. W. Anderson to H. D. Gray, May 25, 1956
90. F. W. Whittaker to H. D. Gray, n.d. by pen, rec'd. May 29, 1956
91. H. Conn, F. W. Whittaker, H. D. Gray, *Appeal, etc.* 5-29-56
92. Rev. J. F. English to Connecticut Delegates, June 7, 1956
93. Gray/Keith *A Report of the Cleveland Meeting*, written jointly Sunday June 24, 1956
94. hdg notes. See *Minutes* of General Council, 1956 NY, 28-29
95. *Minutes* 1956 General Council, 17-25, Rev. Malcolm K. Burton, *The Story of Merger Action at Omaha*, July 10, 1956, Chicago 6 printed report
96. Gray/Keith, *A Report of the Cleveland Meeting*, written jointly Sunday, June 24, 1956
97. Discussions on skipboard, Oct.-Nov. 1945 en route to and from War Damage Survey in Britain, recorded in detail in hdg notebook Oct.-Nov. 1945
98. *Minutes*, 1956 General Council, NY, 26-27
99. Ibid, 27
100. Ibid., 27-28
101. Minutes op.cit. 28
102. Ibid, 28
103. Minutes, op.cit. 36
104. Minutes, op.cit, 29-30
105. Ibid, 36
106. *Minutes*, op.cit, 38-40
107. Mimeographed sheet distributed at Omaha Council, 1956
108. hdg notes, June 1956, Omaha
109. H. D. Gray, *The Flying Pilgrims* Vol. IV, 1956 pub. by The South Congregational Church, Hartford.
110. H. D. Gray, *Congregational Christians—After Omaha*, Sept. 1956, South Church, Hartford.

111. A. E. Bladen & Ex. Com., *Letter Missive,* July 31, 1956, General Council NY

112. O. A. Maxfield to Gray, July 6, 1956

113. Gray to Maxfield, Oct. 3, 1956

114. W. A. Keith to Gray, Sept. 29, 1956

115. Gray to Keith, Oct. 3, 1956

116. Gray to Mediators, Oct. 12, 1956

117. O. A. Maxfield to Gray, Oct. 11, 1956

118. W. A. Anderson to Gray, Oct. 16, 1956

119. L. Upton to Gray, 10-16-56

120. A. G. Walton to Gray, 10-17-56

121. A. S. Lehman to Gray, 10-20-56

122. R. A. Waser to Gray, 10-22-56

123. R. A. Dawson to Gray, 10-24-56

124. J. P. Webster to Gray, 10-31-56

125. H. Conn to Meek, Gray, Keith, 11-15-56

126. See ante Polity and Unity Committee Report.

127. F. S. Buschmeyer to Gray, 1-24-56

128. J. E. Wagner, F. Hoskins, *The Uniting General Synod*, March 10, 1957, NY and Phila.

129. Gray to Hoskins, March 6, 1975

130. Hoskins to Gray, March 12, 1957

131. *South Church Courier*, April 28, 1957

132. Gray to Hoskins, April 12, 1957

133. Gray to Hoskins, April 12, 1957

134. Hoskins to Gray, April 21, 1957

135. H. D. Gray, *Better Than 1310 to 179/964 to 55*, May 1957 South Church, Hartford

136. Program for the Uniting Synod

CHAPTER ELEVEN

Power Without Glory

The experience of the Mediators in the merger of the Congregational Christian Churches and the Evangelical Reformed Church parallels that of devout and learned men like Professor Ian Henderson of the University of Glasgow in the move to unite the Church of Scotland and the Church of England.

The Modern Ecumenical Movement

Why? The answer is to be found in the character and in the history of the modern ecumenical movement. This history begins at the 1910 Edinburgh Missionary Conference. The 1,355 delegates represented Protestant missionary societies. Within four months after the Edinburgh Conference the US Episcopal Church resolved "That a joint commission be appointed to bring about a Conference for the consideration of questions touching Faith and Order, and that all Christian Communions throughout the world which confess our Lord Jesus Christ as God and Saviour be asked to unite with us in arranging for and conducting such a Conference."

World War I intervened but in 1920, at Geneva, representatives of about seventy Churches arranged an agenda for a Conference at Lausanne in 1927. Out of great differences[1] there was issued a Call to Unity. The "Call" begins "God wills unity. Our presence in this Conference bears testimony to our desire to bend our wills to His. However we may justify the beginnings of disunion, we lament its continuance and henceforth must labour, in penitence and faith, to build up our broken walls."[2]

One of the motions passed at Lausanne read "In view of (1) the place which the Episcopate, the Councils of Presbyters, and the Congregation of the faithful, respectively, had in the constitution of the early Church, and (2) the fact that the espiscopal, presbyterial, and congregational systems of government are each to-day, and have been for centuries, accepted by great communions in Christendom and (3) the fact that episcopal, presbyterial, and congregational systems are each believed by many to be essential to the good order of the Church, we therefore recognize that these several elements must all, under conditions which require further study, have an appropriate place in the order of life of a reunited Church, and that each separate communion, recalling the abundant blessing of God vouchsafed to its ministry in the past, should gladly bring to the common life of the united Church its own spiritual treasures."[3]

Ecumenical Claims

These two Lausanne statements have been repeated often; their language is one of the keys to understanding modern ecumenicals. The statement says "God wills unity" but this bland declaration is given no support in the New Testament, and there is no indication of what *kind* of unity God wills. It is quite impossible to discuss the statement intelligently, as the Mediators discovered; there is much emotional, but no intellectual or spiritual content. The phrase has power to generate response but it has none of the glory of the doxologies Paul appended to his dedicated reasoning.

Even more revealing is the claim that delegates at Lausanne were gathered to bend their wills to the will of God. In point of fact the delegates were present because of the shrewd and determined ecclesiastical politics of the US Episcopal Church. But Lausanne set a pattern; thence forward, each move toward One Big Church quickly claimed that it was being taken "according to God's will." The Mediators heard this claim made by the Secretary of the General Council, and by many others. But the only *will* evident in the carefully staged General Council meetings at Grinnell (1946), Oberlin (1948), Cleveland (1949), Cleveland (1950) and New Haven (1954) was that of the officials of the General Council and a cohort of determined individuals like Rev. Albert Penner, Rev. Shirley Greene, Rev. Joseph King, Miss Ruth Isabel Seabury, and Rev. Ray Gibbons. *Ecumenical lanugage* is fraught with difficulties since it honors its *own* definitions.

Ecumenical Language

It is important to recognize the double meaning of words like "communion" applied to a denomination. The word communion means the Lord's Supper to most Protestants. Episcopalians, who use the word to mean "denomination" are exactly those who *restrict* participation in the Lord's Supper to those who follow *their* rules. Thus, in ecumenical language, "communion" *means* those who refuse to commune. Which is just a bit difficult to comprehend!

Equally incomprehensible is the use of "communion" to avoid recognition of the fact that there are "Episcopal Church*es*" by referring to the Anglican "communion." This becomes arcane when an attempt is made to elide the wonderful variety of Congregational Churches in a fictitious Congregational Communion; the capital "C" compounds the Canterbury Tale.

The Lausanne words about episcopal, presbyterial and congregational all bringing their treasures to a united church have been a veritable banner for ecumenicals. The Mediators met it most violently at New Haven. The phrase seems engagingly inclusive; it is devastatingly exclusive. The Church of South India illustrates the point. After thirty years all ordination is episcopal. In other words, death is the agent of the ecumenicals to kill presbyterial and congregational polities. There are faint traces of nascent episcopacy in a few very late New Testament writings, but the dominant New Testament polity is congregational, and there are stirring passages which vehemently deny any ministerial Call other than God's Call and the testimony of a people of God to that Call.

Lambeth Quadrilateral 1888

The four point proposal adopted by the Anglican (Episcopal) Churches in 1888 has been quoted almost as much as Lausanne. The four points were adopted first by the Episcopal Church in the USA in 1886, then modified and adopted by the Anglican Lambeth Conference Committee on Home Reunion. The four points are reproduced in Rouse and Neill, *A History of the Ecumenical Movement, 1517-1948*[4] as follows: (1) "The Holy Scriptures of the Old and New Testaments as the revealed Word of God; (2) The Nicene Creed as the sufficient statement of the Christian Faith (and the Apostles Creed) as the Baptismal Symbol; (3) The two Sacraments—Baptism and the Supper of the Lord—ministered with unfailing use of Christ's words of institution; (4) The Historic

Episcopate, locally adapted in the method of its administration to the varying needs of the nations and peoples called of God into the unity of His Church."

Superficially the four points have much to commend them, and were regarded by the Mediators as an interesting start toward church unity. This was especially true because of a number of great Congregationalists like Rev. Edward Thompson, Rev. Raymond McConnell and Rev. Warren Seymour Archibald used much of the Episcopal *Book of Common Prayer* in sacraments, holy rites, prayer for the sick, and public prayer. Congregational historians like Rev. Arthur C. McGiffert and Rev. Frederick Whittaker tended to interpret modern Congregationalism as a direct descendent from the Church of England of King Henry VIII and of Queen Elizabeth I. And even advocates of extreme independence like Rev. James Fifield, Jr., donned cassock and surplice, and genuflected facing the cross.

The four points are not a satisfactory basis for unity, because they constitute a legal framework rather than a spiritual foundation. Each point has its own shortcomings.

Concerning the first point, the Holy Scriptures, the razor keen thinking of Origen, Tertullian, Jerome, Calvin, John Robinson, Thomas Hooker, P. T. Forsyth, and Raymond C. Brooks calls for unfettered adventures of the mind and heart to discover ever more truth in both Old and New Testaments. The Mediators agreed that the Word of God is revealed in the Old and New Testaments but they did not worship the Bible! The Lord of the Bible was more important than the Bible as touchstone of faith. It still is.

Creeds and Convictions

The second point sets the Nicene Creed as the sufficient statement of Christian Faith. Congregational thinkers were aware that the Council of Nicea was a hassel, that the Nicene Creed was a compromise, and that another Council had to be called at Chalcedon to rectify Nicea. The basic problem for the Mediators is the setting up of *any* Creed as "the sufficient statement of Christian Faith." God is so great, good and glorious that no words can define or describe Him. The mediators thought in the great tradition of Schleiermacher, Ritschl, Troeltsch, Harnack, Oman, H. R. Macintosh, Principal Selbie, Gladden and Gordon. They were (and are) quite unprepared to squeeze the Christian Faith down into the queer shaped jugs of Nicea, which cannot hold it all. As for the "Apostles Creed;" nobody has ever proved that it had anything to do with the Apostles. Some of the Mediators accepted it as an historical testimony of great interest and import, but certainly not as "the Baptismal Symbol." It is no substitute for belief in the God and Father of our Lord Jesus Christ on the part of new Christians, or parents of a child in a Christian family.

Baptism and the Lord's Supper

It might seem that number three could be universally accepted, but that, too, is because of the unique ecumenical language in which it is couched. Congregational scholars have wrestled with the evidence for Baptism and the Lord's Supper in the New Testament, and have reached varied conclusions, but have agreed that both sacraments have profound religious and historical meaning. Jesus did not baptize anyone. His own baptism was in accord with the custom of His time. And it is open to question whether or not the words of the "great commission" were uttered by the Master; if they were, they were in no sense a "command" to baptize as a requirement of salvation, which would contradict His life and teaching.

The most quoted account of the Lord's Supper is the single reference of the Apostle Paul who was not present. Zwingli was close to the view of many Congregational scholars when he advocated communion as a "remembrance of me," in which, by faith, Christ is spiritually present. As Rev. Albert Peel has demonstrated,[5] there really isn't any scholarly basis for the assertion that the beautiful, tender, loving words of Christ to those at Table in the Upper Room beneath the shadow of the cross were "words of institution" to be repeated, like a magic spell, each time a Church gathered round the Table made Holy by its association with Him. Nowhere in the New Testament does Jesus attach importance to ritual of any kind. In varying degrees all the Mediators were uneasy, puzzled, and dismayed by the Episcopal demand for *form* and by *any* demand which unchurched noble souls like John Woolman, Rufus Jones, Dwight L. Moody, Charles G. Finney, Thomas Kelly, and Elton Trueblood. That doesn't make sense.

Castes or Christians

The fourth point sets the "Historic Episcopate" as a requirement for union with Episcopalians. Congregationalists historically (and presently) are a plain folk, more given to hard thinking than pomp. In New England John Cotton, John Wise, Horace Bushnell, Jonathan Edwards, Edward Tyler, and Nathanael Emmons resisted bishops who claimed to be the sole custodians of "orders" or "grace." The Mediators were their spiritual children. Men like Rev. John M. Phillips, Professor Benjamin D. Scott, Presidents James A. Blaisdell and Donald Cowling were far too well read to be gullible. They knew that there is no "unbroken line" of episcopal succession, that the Greek word *episcopos* means minister of a church, and that it was political rather than spiritual power which sought to establish authoritative bishops in each Roman province after the Council of Nicea in 325.

The whole concept of "castes" in Christ's Churches was, and is, repugnant to the Mediators; and "orders" with explicit titles, garb, prerequisites, and grace—conveying powers are simply "castes" under another name.

Yet deeper, fine Congregational scholars recognized the blasphemy in the claim to convey "grace." Dr. William Ames was as clear on this as was Rev. John Robinson. None dealt with this theme in greater detail than the distinguished Vice Chancellor of Oxford University, Rev. John Owen. I can remember no distinguished Congregational scholar who thought "grace" was conveyed only by a bishop. Certainly not one of the Mediators subscribed to such a dogma: they knew the grace of God as God's gracious personal presence, and nothing else.

Is Union Possible?

If it were desireable, which is doubtful, is Church Union possible?

So long as the Lambeth quadrilateral stands, Presbyterians and Congregationalists can unite with Episcopalians only by becoming Episcopalians, as was done in South India.

But that's not all. Rome will welcome Canterbury *only if* Canterbury recognizes papal primacy, and possibly also papal infallibility. Phanos/Constantinople will welcome Rome *only if* Rome accepts the first five General Councils, *and* the parity of the Eastern Orthodox patriarch and bishops with the Pope. Copts, Mar Tomans, Abyssinians, and Jacobites want no union without "Mary the Mother of God" (Theotokos), icons, and a biblical literalism which puts American fundamentalists to shame.

The Mediators were open-eyed. Notable East European experts like Professor Matthew Spinka groaned at the childishness of talk about the Coming Great Church, understanding clearly that the vast majority of the world's Christians could not be included. At this point ecumenical language pained some of the noblest Congregational thinkers.

I must not leave the impression that Canterbury, Rome, Cairo/ Alexandria, Addis Abbaba, or Phanos/Istanbul are harsh, unbending, uninterested bystanders in the ecumenical current. Not at all. Patriarch Athenogoras was a most gracious and loving person. *His* patriarchate was benign and beautiful; but who could guarantee the stance of his successor? And who could gainsay the deep devotion he had to the Theotokos, to his most precious icon, and to his conviction that all Christians must accept only the five early councils? What needs to be clear is that unity among Churches cannot be achieved without intellectual and spiritual wrestling with "the sufficient statement of Christian Faith." Goodwill and compassion alone cannot bridge the doctrinal gaps; though they may create a climate favorable to the study of them.

Where Congregationalists Came In

Congregationalists were caught up in the Church union movement in at least two ways.

First, locally, Congregationalists like Rev. Rockwell Harmon Potter were leaders in forming co-operative Councils of Churches, then later the Federal Council of Churches, the International Council of Religious Education, the Missionary Council, the YM and YWCA's. For the first third of the twentieth century Congregationalists were active in gathering "Community Churches" in which separate membership rolls were kept, but in most ways the entire body functioned as a single Church. I suppose the fact that New England Congregational Churches were in actuality *community* Churches encouraged this, as did the frequent New England name "Second Church of Christ in Hartford"—or Boston . . . In both Councils of Churches and Community Churches differences in doctrine were accepted and no creeds were used. Not until the National Council of Churches adopted the statement of Jesus as God and Savior was there a significant split. For example, the Hartford Council, one of the first in America, had both Unitarians and Universalists among its founders. But when the Lutheran Churches joined the National Council, the Hartford Lutheran Church refused to join the Hartford Council unless the National (and World) Council statement was accepted. After much debate the Hartford Council Executive Committee voted to accept the creed by one or two votes, and so ruled out some of the most devout Christians in our midst—Quakers, Unitarians and Universalists.

Congregationalists came into the modern ecumenical movement in a second way. Congregational leaders like Principal Nathaniel Michlem, Rev. John Marsh, Rev. Daniel Jenkins, Professor C. H. Dodd, Professor Walter M. Horton, Rev. Henry Smith Leiper, and Rev. Douglas Horton shared in the series of Conferences which followed Lausanne and harked back to the Lambeth Quadrilateral.

The more important gatherings were the Stockholm Conference on Life and Work, 1925, Life and Work Conference at Oxford, and the Faith and Order Conference at Edinburgh, both in 1937— a week apart. At the Oxford and Edinburgh gatherings a motion to merge the Life and Work and Faith and Order movements garnered an overwhelming vote of approval. A provisional body meeting at Utrecht in 1938 wrote a Constitution for the World Council of Churches. At Amsterdam, 1948, this Constitution was accepted. Lund, 1952, followed . . . and Madras, Toronto . . . and others. In all of these meetings Prof. Walter Horton, Rev. Douglas Horton, and Rev. Henry Smith Leiper and other US Congregationalists were deeply involved. Their personal involvement became a commitment to "the Coming Great Church."

WHAT Theological Synthesis?

One of the really bothersome questions about *all* types of ecumenical enterprise is its theological basis.

The World Council of Churches accepted (1948) the dogma "Jesus Christ as God and Savior," not exactly as a creed, but nevertheless, as a requirement for membership in the WCC. Manifestly, the statement is theologically suspect. Does it not imply a rejection of the trinity? If Jesus is God and Savior, who is God? Who is the Holy Spirit? Indeed, who is Jesus? There are difficulties aplenty in the doctrine of the trinity, but, at least, it asserts the reality of a Creator—Father, a Savior—Son, and an ever present, sustaining Holy Spirit. The theological meaning of the phrase "Jesus Christ as God and Savior," (whatever it is!) needs explication. It is surely unwise and disconcerting to set as a test of membership in the WCC a phrase of uncertain theological meaning.

The creeds of "the first five councils" are ALL that the Orthodox Churches are willing to accept. But there are no other Churches under the sun which fully agree; so, how *can* there be an inclusive, that is, an ecumenical church? In fact, at the Toronto Central Committee meeting of the WCC the principle was adopted that "the member churches of the World Council of Churches do not necessarily recognize each other as true, healthy or complete churches,"[6] which is mind boggling; a Council of *Churches* which does not recognize each other as *Churches!*? Mary as Mother of God, icons, liturgy, creeds, lack of social concern, persecution of other Christians, and collusion with state governments make a mockery of all pretense that most Orthodox Churches are, will be, or can easily be equal partners with Protestants in One Great Church. The assumption is arrogant and preposterous.

Roman Catholic Theology

Reconciliation of Protestantism with the approved version of Roman Catholic theology is equally far-fetched.

Acceptance of the pope as the head of the church, instead of Christ, is quite impossible to New Testament Christians, even to Roman Catholic Professor Hans Küng[7] of Tübingen. But that's just the beginning! Veneration of Mary originated in the tenth century, was backed by Monte Cassino Monastery, and became THE central worship of the high middle ages: it continues to be of prime importance to Roman Catholics. God and Christ may be distant. Mary is close at hand. Novenas to Mary are an intimate aspect of contemporary Roman devotion; Pope John Paul II is reported in the press as saying a daily "novena"—wherever he travels. In 1870 the *dogma* of the Immaculate Conception was promolgated. Since then, Mary has been addressed as *co-redemptress.* Is any New Testament Christian prepared to accept this non-scriptural concept? And if not, exactly how are *justification by faith in Jesus Christ,* and *salvation by intervention of Mary and the saints* to be reconciled?

Will the magical notion of *grace* as a conveyed "essence" (like a surgeon's medical injection) be easily reconciled with the biblical concept of grace as God's personal relation to us in holy love? This question of *grace* lies at the root of the "seven sacraments" (listed by Peter Lombard about 1150), the fictitious "apostolic succession," and the Roman Church as "the ark of salvation" outside of which no person can be saved.

I submit the ecumenicals gloss over or totally ignore these, and many other theological dogmas and doctrines of the Roman Catholic Church. *The idea that One Great Church can be achieved is an illusion based on failure to take seriously the real, substantial, separation of the two thirds of all Christendom represented* by the Eastern Orthodox and Roman Catholic (and perhaps even Anglican) Churches.

Sheer Numbers

One wonders if Congregational, and other Free Church leaders ever wrestled with the obvious fact that *any* Great Church would be *both* committed to unscriptural dogmas, *and* exclusive of the millions of Southern Baptists, Quakers, Assemblies of God, Churches of Christ, and dozens of other evangelical Protestants?

The dogma of "baptismal regeneration" is not going to be laid aside by Orthodox, Roman Catholic or high Anglican in favor of the Baptists; neither is infant baptism going to be gainsaid in favor of the Baptist believer's baptism.

The "apostolically ordained" "clergy" of Orthodox, Roman Catholic and Anglican are not about to be unfrocked in favor of Spirit-inspired, Church called Ministers of Christ.

The liturgies of Basil and Chrysostom, the Roman Missal, and the Anglican "prayer book" are mutually exclusive! And not any one of them can or will satisfy seeking souls in Meeting Houses of Quaker, Baptist, Congregational, Assembly of God—or dozens of other devout Churches.

Unless one is prepared to give *unification* a higher priority than *salvation by faith*, it is quite impossible to overlook the real and valid differences between denominations.

The Ministry

The Church of South India solved the question of ordination by accepting the idea that Congregational ministers ought to die! Thirty years after the promolgation of union *all* ordinations became episcopal, which is another way of saying that *only* episcopal ordination is valid.

There is not a shred of evidence in the New Testament for the *sole* validity of ordination by bishops. Bishops in the New Testament were local ministers in any case. The "hints" in the pastoral epistles concerning ordination are sketchy and scant. The cardinal requirements are not ecclesiastical but spiritual. A person *called of God* is primary. When that personal, spiritual call is attested by the election of a people of God who see in a person that which causes them to seek him as their minister the requirements of Scripture are fulfilled.

What then of conveyed grace? Can a *non* episcopally ordained minister impart grace in baptism, the Lord's Supper, confirmation,

596

marriage, ordination, or at death? Let me reverse the question, *Can an episcopally ordained clergyman or priest convey the grace of God?* The answer is a resounding NO. Grace is a gracious personal relation of the all-loving, all-holy Person to unloving and unholy persons and peoples. The New Testament gives no credence to the false notion of "infused grace," grace which can be administered as if it were a substance kept and doled out by "licensed practitioners!"

Furthermore there are no separate "orders" for members of the New Testament Churches. All who sincerely seek to follow Christ, and who love Him and serve Him are "saints." As Hans Küng[8] has so clearly demonstrated, the priesthood of believers is at the center of the scripture. Ecumenical theology has yet to square itself with the New Testament concept of the ministry.

Polity and Theology

Christian Church polity is theologically based. That's why it *is* Christian, and not Greek, Roman, Gupta or Han.

To speak of "taking episcopacy into our system" of polity is nonsensical. It is, specifically, *non*sense. Waiting for the leading of the Lord in Church Meeting is poles apart from compromises of power in a cantankerous council of bishops. Episcopacy means government from above, by "superiors," by "those who know best," by "the experts," by "those with wider experience" through legislative, executive and judicial decrees. Episcopacy and Congregationalism are irreconsilable opposites. One cannot, at the same time, accept the validity of government by bishops and synods AND government by the people of God met to humbly seek His way and His will.

It is not only that the *process* is wrong! Beyond that! delegation of personal responsibility to seek and follow God's direction IS NOT POSSIBLE. Conscience cannot be delegated to a bishop— or a presbytery. Each Christian and each Christian Church is, by the gospel, inescapably required to seek the way, the truth and the light, and, to follow the leading of the Father of truth, light, and love, *because the Father's Word convinces* AND NOT because of any exterior authority whatsoever.

The Way of Love

Is there, then, any possibility of Church unity? There is; it is the way of loving forbearance, the way of accepting each other's sincerity and dedication, the way of mutual recognition of the validity of all ministries which own Jesus as Lord and sincerely seek to worship the God and Father of our Lord Jesus Christ in spirit and in truth.

In practical terms this means that organizational unification in a "United Church of Christ" is impossible; and the asumption of the title is arrogance or ignorance. *The impossible must be laid aside in favor of the possible; in favor of a warmhearted, cordial, loving fellowship . . . a co-operative Federation of all who will; all who will accept each other as fellow Christians without drawing exclusive circles which shut out sincere lovers of our Lord.*

We should abandon the terms "ecumenical" and "ecumenicity;" for there is not now ANY organized body on earth inclusive of all Christians, and there never has been.

We should expand our co-operative efforts in missions, in publishing, in human service, in study and, above all, in prayer and worship.

We should kindle the spiritual fires of faith by united Bible study, visitations, testimonies, and every possible compassionate interchange.

We should accept the co-existence of all Churches of Christ as equals, so that one Church in Greece or Erie does not persecute, or lay civil disabilities upon, any other Church.

We should welcome each others' ministers, with no distinction of preeminence or "order."

We should gladly accept the validity of each others' sacraments and holy rites. This is true in civil law almost universally. Marriages are valid regardless of denomination. What a condemnation that acceptance is *not* general among the Churches!! Our acceptance of each other is *less* than that of civil authorities. Shame!

The prayer of our Lord in John 17 should be affirmed by all of us in its true meaning, "that we all may be one, that the world may believe . . . as you Father are in me, and I in you." Spiritual oneness need wait for no ecclesiastical majesty, no pomp, no pectoral cross, no authorized ministry, no massive organization, no august ceremonial. It can be and will be established wherever and whenever the Spirit of God in Christ reconciles us to each other.

The Power and the Glory

One Great Church is a practical, theological, and ecclesiastical impossibility—even supposing it were desirable.

598

Why then, has there been a twentieth century yen for it on the part of many liberal Protestant Churches?

The sociological roots are two world wars, secular centralization, political "bigness," loss of evangelistic zeal, diminution of Church membership, and loss of secular influence.

It is especially true that certain leaders came to believe that they must "unite or perish."

Perhaps the more basic reason is a hope of glory. I mean glory in the New Testament sense, *doxa* in Greek, a hope of doing something great to save the peoples of the world from destruction. On very careful and lengthy consideration, this seems to me to have been the cardinal motivation of the Rev. Douglas Horton in his life long campaign for world church unification, and Congregational leadership therein. The goal to be sought was the healing of societies, the transmutation of hatreds and antagonisms into peaceful co-existence. Over against huge multinational corporations, extensive mass media of communication, big labor unions and the "military-industrial complex" there was envisioned the power of One Big Church. This One Big Church was seen as the antidote to almost everything wrong with persons or peoples. "Evangelical" came to be spelled "ecumenical;" "inspiration" was replaced by "organization." Power was the lever needed to release the energies of goodness so that the children of light might overcome the children of darkness.

So, in the end, the failure was theological. Power in an organized One Big Church takes the place of Trust in One God and Father of us all. It is the ancient confusion of power and glory in modern garb.

But the only power which brings glory is the power of love in redeemed persons and peoples. And the sole glory is not of persons or their institutions; it is the glory of God in the face of Jesus Christ reflected in lives made holy and loving by His Spirit, manifest in a loving fellowship at work with all God's peoples, in the whole of God's world.

That alone is the power and the glory sought by the Mediators.

CHAPTER 11 NOTES

1. Lausanne, art. *Oxford Dictionary of the Christian Church*, 1957, Oxford University Press, N.Y.
2. Bell *Documents on Christian Unity*, 1st and 2nd Series, 1948, Oxford, London, p. 159
3. Ibid, 159 f.

4. 1954, Westminster Press, Philadelphia
5. Christian Freedom, 1938, Independent Press, London, 67-84
6. Albert C. Outler. *The Christian Tradition and the Unity We Seek*, 1957, Oxford, NY, pp. 98, 99 (quote)
7. Hans Küng. See *Structures of the Church* and *The Church*, Eng. trans., *passim*
8. Hans Küng, *The Church* (see fulsome index)

INDEX

605

606

609

Monte Cassino Monastery 595
Monterey, CA 358
Moody, D. 591
Mosshamer, A. 557
Mother of Carmel 142
Mount Holyoke College 133
Mount Sinai 486
Munger, T. 112
Music 75, 76
Myld 431

National Assn. of Congregational
Christian Churches 434, 488, 510,
513, 534, 565, 567
National Committee of our Christian
World Mission 212
National Council By-Laws of 1913-
1930 115
National Council of Congregational
Churches 21, 29, 80, 104, 113 ff.,
126 f., 189, 210, 267, 292, 314,
320, 351, 359
National Council of Churches 29, 104,
126, 127, 244, 593
National Council Digest, The 115,
313, 314, 320
National Missionary Society 205
National Societies 82, 205
National Synod (1959) 540
Naugatuck Assn., CT 308, 310
Naugatuck Valley, CT 308
Nebraska 355, 357
Needham, MA 323
Neff, P. J. 531, 534
Neill, S. 589
Netherlands 244, 268
New England 17, 106, 108, 110, 132,
254, 297, 306, 310, 330, 337, 379,
398, 425, 591
New England Churches 71
New England Panel 62, 167, 381
Report 167
New Hampshire 168, 193, 284, 285,
321, 322, 328, 334, 337, 355, 397
New Hampshire Assn. 328
New Hampshire Conference Charter
355
New Haven 164, 225, 231, 237, 238,
244, 247, 250, 251, 253 ff., 263,
264, 265 ff., 270, 339, 343, 361 ff.,
396, 402, 404, 405, 474, 475, 476,

514, 525, 526, 541, 545, 580,
589, 590
New Haven Church 453
New Haven Council 214
New Haven County 112
New Jersey 282, 337, 367, 464, 558
New London 52
New York 29, 30, 35, 36, 52, 56, 67,
71, 85, 128, 164, 173, 210, 218,
242, 243, 264, 274, 285, 291, 330,
343, 347, 354, 355, 379, 422, 423,
424, 476, 487, 506, 511, 513, 515,
516, 523, 524, 551, 563, 564, 567
New York City Assn. (CC) 487, 508
f.
New York Conference Charter 354
New York Congregational Christian
Conference 61, 345, 393, 414
New York Courts 384
New York State Conference 250
New York Superior Court 204
New Zealand 244, 262, 383
Newbury, VT 381
Newton Highlands 512
Nicea 590 ff.
Nicene Creed 589 ff.
Niebuhr, R. 140
Niedringhaus, F. 568
Niemoller, M. 140
Niles, D. 139
Nominating Committee (CC Gen.
Council) 26, 374, 377, 562
Nominating Committee (WCC) 243
Nordstrom, N. 159, 331
Norenberg, J. 329
North, S. 123 ff., 128, 184
North Congregational Church 112
North Dakota 153, 274, 334, 352
North Dakota Congregational
Conference By-Laws 352
North Wilamette Assn., OR 153
Northcott, C. 139, 140, 141, 142
Northern California 86, 284, 300,
334, 349
Nye, P. 105

Oakes, U. 109
Oberlin 3, 80, 237, 344, 532, 559, 589
Oberlin Theological School 38, 530
Ockenga, H. 568
Odyssey 67

AN ACKNOWLEDGMENT

The author pays grateful tribute to Terry Riggs who patiently and skillfully typed and re-typed the manuscript of this book, proof-read the galleys, and compiled the Index.

624